Historical Dictionary of
War Journalism

HISTORICAL DICTIONARY
OF WAR JOURNALISM

Mitchel P. Roth

JAMES S. OLSON, ADVISORY EDITOR

Greenwood Press
Westport, Connecticut • London

Library of Congress Cataloging-in-Publication Data

Roth, Mitchel P., 1953–
 Historical dictionary of war journalism / Mitchel P. Roth.
   p. cm.
 Includes bibliographical references and index.
 ISBN 0–313–29171–3 (alk. paper)
 1. War in the press—Dictionaries. 2. War correspondents—
Biography—Dictionaries. I. Title.
PN4784.W37R68   1997
070.4'333'03—DC20   96–35024

British Library Cataloguing in Publication Data is available.

Library of Congress Catalog Card Number: 96–35024
ISBN: 0–313–29171–3

First published in 1997

Greenwood Press, 88 Post Road West, Westport, CT 06881
An imprint of Greenwood Publishing Group, Inc.

Printed in the United States of America

The paper used in this book complies with the
Permanent Paper Standard issued by the National
Information Standards Organization (Z39.48–1984).

10 9 8 7 6 5 4 3 2 1

This book is dedicated to Rosanne and Leila, the two women in my life.

Contents

Preface

In 1981 a rare book dealer contacted the Amon Carter Museum in Fort Worth, Texas, concerning some old daguerreotype photographs from the Mexican War. At that time the Beinecke Rare Book Room at Yale University possessed twelve daguerreotypes from the conflict, the only photographs taken of the war in Mexico known to still survive. Cognizant of the Amon Carter's interest in Mexican War images, the dealer notified the institution that these daguerreotypes were being offered for sale to a military museum at that very moment. After clandestine negotiations worthy of some Cold War thriller the Amon Carter purchased thirty-eight more Mexican War photographs. Examination of these images revealed not only portraits of recognizable military figures, but also rare scenes of Mexico, some of which were actual variations of the Yale photographs. However, to this day the identity of the world's first war photographer remains a mystery.

The first war correspondent, like the first war photographer, remains a somewhat shadowy and elusive figure. Although this person was probably male, and from New Orleans, the evidence remains sketchy due to the exigencies of newspaper reporting in the 1840s. Until recently the history of newspaper reporting has been neglected, in part due to the impersonal nature of this journalistic enterprise. Until the twentieth century, bylines were seldom used as reporters labored in anonymity. Occasionally journalists were identifiable through clever pseudonyms or initials. The Mexican War produced the first identifiable war correspondents.

Sketch artists had long recorded the glories and horrors of the battlefield. However, with technological advances in printmaking and the advent of photography in 1839, news took on a greater immediacy, especially with the clarity provided by the photographic image. Eyewitness reports ranged from on-the-spot coverage to accounts collected secondhand days or weeks later. Sketches from field artists were later translated by lithographers far from the battlefield, sometimes losing accuracy in the process.

War with Mexico was declared barely two years after the advent of the telegraph, in an era that coincided with the rise of the penny press and a dramatic increase in literacy. By September 1846 over 1,200 miles of telegraph lines connected the great cities of America, compared to only 175 miles in England. The demand for national news stimulated by the Mexican War continued unabated, demonstrating the value of war news in increasing circulation, establishing a pattern that continues to this day.

The larger history of the war correspondent has not been thoroughly explored. A historical dictionary covering war correspondents has probably not been previously attempted due to the difficulties in identifying anonymous or pseudonymous journalists. The *Historical Dictionary of War Journalism* is designed to fill this existing gap in the history of not only war journalism, but military affairs, literature, imperialism, and the Victorian era as well. The war correspondent is a comparatively new phenomenon. Prior to the Mexican War, military commanders preferred to report their own victories and resented the presence of any civilian correspondents. But, with the introduction of the telegraph in the 1840s, a new urgency was given to news gathering.

Several guidelines have been followed in selecting the various entries for this work. In the course of my research for this book I found reference to literally thousands of war correspondents. Over five hundred reported the Civil War, while over sixteen hundred covered the Korean War, and as many as five thousand were in Vietnam. It was necessary to be selective and choose reporters who covered significant events and left behind more than a trace of their presence at the frontlines, or this project would never end. Other than a few exceptions, in order to be classified as a war reporter, photographer, or artist, an individual must represent a newspaper, a magazine, radio, television, or some other news source. Restricting entries with this criterion excludes army officers, many freelancers, and other eyewitnesses. It is necessary to be selective rather than all-inclusive, since literally hundreds of correspondents covered such conflicts as the American Civil War and the Spanish-American War, with thousands eventually reporting World War II. Other entries include significant events, persons, or terms relevant to the history of war reporting from 1846 to the recent Gulf War and Yugoslavian conflict. Each entry concludes with a reference for further information on the subject, and cross-references within the text are designated by an asterisk. I have used several reference works which are cited by their better-known acronyms. *DAB* refers to the *Dictionary of American Biography, DNB* is the *Dictionary of National Biography*, and *DLB* refers to the *Dictionary of Literary Biography*.

War reporting remains the most dangerous profession. According to the Overseas Press Club of America, Inc., and the Public Affairs Office of the Department of Defense, between 1935 and 1994, 244 American journalists and photographers representing both the print and electronic media have been killed in war-related assignments. This book is in part a tribute to the noble craft of the war correspondent.

I would like to acknowledge the aid and assistance of the Newton Gresham Library staff at Sam Houston State University, who were especially gracious in extending renewal times for reference books and other sources. Cutty Gilbert provided stalwart typing assistance at various stages of the book and Alan Chep gave me sincere encouragement whenever I needed it. A special thanks is due my friend and animal Svengali Kay Pence, who provided counseling and friendship to Dillon, Cody, Zoie, and Tommy while I was searching the stacks for Boer War correspondents. I am grateful for the friendship and guidance of Jim Olson, who proposed the project to me three years ago. Finally, the book is dedicated to my wife and best friend, Rosanne Barker, who was forced to listen to an entry each time she transgressed into my office while I was writing this book, and my mother, Leila Holstein, who has always encouraged me to write.

A

ABEND, HALLETT EDWARD (1882–1955). Born in Portland, Oregon, and educated at Stanford University, Abend was the Far Eastern correspondent for the *New York Times* from 1926 to 1940 and was bureau chief in Shanghai when the Japanese attacked in 1937. He was one of the earliest casualties among Western correspondents in China and one of the first of World War II* when he was injured during an aerial bombardment of the city. Abend developed his own intelligence service using sources in both the Chinese and Japanese armies prior to American entry into the war. Any information he received was passed directly to either the State Department or the armed forces. In September 1940, he delivered one of his greatest news scoops four days before the official announcement which revealed that Japan was about to conclude a military alliance with Germany and Italy.

He joined the Washington bureau of the *Times* in April 1941, but left in August to cover New Zealand, Australia, and the Dutch East Indies for *Reader's Digest*. When the war in Asia came to a close in 1945, Abend was among the journalists reporting the story of the Air Transport Command and how it accomplished its task flying weapons and soldiers over the Himalayas between India and China when the Burma Road was closed. Among his many books on Asia are *Ramparts of the Pacific* (1942), *Pacific Charter* (1943), *Japan Unmasked* (1941), and *My Life in China* (1943).
REFERENCES: Robert W. Desmond. *Tides of War*. 1984; Eric Downton. *Wars Without End*. 1987.

ABRAMS, ALEXANDER ST. CLAIR (?). The Louisiana native had served in the Confederate army and as a reporter for the *Vicksburg Whig* during the siege of Vicksburg before turning full-time to journalism with the *Atlanta In-*

telligencer after the campaign. His account of the siege of Vicksburg was carried in both the *Whig* and the *Mobile Advertiser and Register*. Fellow war correspondent John H. Linebaugh* ranked Abrams' report as the most complete account of the siege. Later that year his dispatches were collected and published as *The Siege of Vicksburg*. In 1864 he covered the Atlanta campaign and produced the best account of the Battle of Oostanaula for the *Intelligencer*. Abrams' dispatches appeared above his sobriquet "St. Clair" until he left wartime journalism in July 1864. A champion of the foot soldier, he wrote several articles detailing the mistreatment of soldiers by officers.
REFERENCE: J. Cutler Andrews. *The South Reports the Civil War*. 1970.

ABYSSINIAN WAR. *See* ETHIOPIAN WAR.

ACTIVE SERVICE. Stephen Crane's* 1899 novel revolves around fictional *New York Eclipse* war correspondent Rufus Coleman and the 1897 Greco-Turkish War.* The novel is based in part on some of Crane's observations as a war correspondent during the conflict. In this romantic potboiler Coleman follows his fiancée to Greece after her classics-professor father drags her away in an attempt to keep her from marrying too far down the evolutionary ladder. However, after the intrepid correspondent on "active service" rescues the professor, his students, and family from the vile Turks, Coleman wins the consent of the professor to marry his daughter.
REFERENCES: Stephen Crane. *Active Service*. 1899; Howard Good. *The Image of War Correspondents in Anglo-American Fiction*. 1985.

ADAMS, EDWARD "EDDIE" T. (b. 1933). Born on February 20, 1933, in Kensington, Pennsylvania, Adams joined the *Philadelphia Bulletin* as a photographer in 1959. In 1962 he moved to the Associated Press and later to *Time* magazine in 1972. From 1976 to 1980 he worked as a special correspondent for the Associated Press.

In 1969, he was on his third tour of Vietnam for the AP when he took probably one of the most famous photos of the Vietnam War.* During the Tet offensive he recorded Brigadier General Nguyen Ngoc Loan, commander of the Vietnam National Police, executing a prisoner with a pistol shot to the head at point-blank range. Adams won a Pulitzer Prize and a place in photographic history. Following the war the police commander moved to America and opened a restaurant in Virginia. Since 1980 Adams has worked as a freelance photojournalist.
REFERENCE: Clarence R. Wyatt. *Paper Soldiers: The American Press and the Vietnam War*. 1993.

ADIE, KATE (b. 1945). Educated at Newcastle University, where she specialized in Scandinavian studies, Adie worked in southern Lapland before entering broadcast journalism with a local Durham radio station. She came to prominence in 1980 covering the Iranian embassy siege in London. She delivered a dramatic on-the-scene account of the Strategic Air Services (SAS) rescue of the hostages. According to one source she was the first woman on British television to broadcast live from such a potentially dangerous situation. In 1986 she covered the U.S. bombing of Tripoli, Libya, for the BBC. Adie received the International News Story of 1986 Award for her coverage.

Over the next three years she continued to report from the world's hot spots, including Armenia, Afghanistan, Africa, and Libya once more. In 1989 she covered the student revolt in China's Tiananmen Square and witnessed the massacre of Chinese students. For her courage under fire the BBC created a special position for her as chief news correspondent. Adie reported the attempted coup in Trinidad in 1990, the Palestine refugee problem, and the 1991 Gulf War.* She noted that her most dangerous assignment was the Yugoslavian conflict.
REFERENCE: Anne Sebba. *Battling for News*. 1994.

ALDRICH, THOMAS BAILEY (1836–1907). Better known today as a poet, editor, and writer of children's books, Bailey was born in Portsmouth, New Hampshire. Rejected in his attempts to secure a military appointment at the outbreak of the American Civil War,* he joined the *New York Tribune* as a war correspondent in late 1861. He accompanied General Louis Blenker's German division, part of the Army of the Potomac in Virginia. He left his assignment early the following year. He went on to a long, distinguished literary career.
REFERENCE: Ferris Greenslet. *The Life of Thomas Bailey Aldrich*. 1908.

ALEXANDER, PETER WELLINGTON (c. 1820–1866). Described as the "Prince of Correspondents" by one Southern newspaper, the Georgian-born Alexander practiced both law and journalism before becoming one of the most important reporters for the South during the American Civil War.* His accounts appeared in the *Savannah Republican*, the *Atlanta Confederacy*, the *Columbus Sun*, the *London Times*, and many others. He covered the 1861 Manassas campaign, during which he criticized the performance of Brigadier General Richard Ewell. He also covered the Battle of Shiloh, and the Maryland and Virginia campaigns in 1862. His report on the Battle of Fredericksburg was based on secondhand accounts due to problems of military censorship. He later reported the Battles of Chancellorsville, Antietam, Gettysburg, Chickamauga, Chattanooga, the Wilderness, Spotsylvania, and Petersburg, as well as the fall of Atlanta. His accounts of the poor conditions confronting the common soldier enhanced his popularity among the ranks. After the war he returned to his law practice in Georgia.
REFERENCES: J. Cutler Andrews. *The South Reports the Civil War*. 1970; Stewart Sifakis. *Who Was Who in the Civil War*. 1988.

ALLEN, LAURENCE EDMUND (1908–1975). Born in Mt. Savage, Maryland, he gained early experience on papers in Ohio, West Virginia, and Washington, D.C. He worked for the Associated Press beginning in the 1930s, when he was stationed in Prague. With the outbreak of World War II* Allen worked out of the Rome bureau. In 1942 he was awarded the Pulitzer Prize for his coverage of the British fleet in the Mediterranean. He was aboard the *Illustrious* in January 1941 when it weathered a seven-hour attack by German planes before being put out of action at Malta. Later that year he was on a British cruiser when it was torpedoed while protecting Crete from a German sea attack. Allen spent almost an hour in the water before being rescued and would spend several months recovering from a bout with pneumonia.

He returned to the Mediterranean in mid-1942 and took part in a British commando raid on Tobruk. He was aboard the destroyer *Sikh* when it was sunk in Tobruk harbor. Allen was captured by Italian forces and began a twenty-month internment. While being transferred to German custody he escaped but was eventually recaptured after being severely wounded. He was released in an exchange of wounded prisoners in May 1944. The next year he was the recipient of the Bronze Star, for defending freedom of the press as a prisoner of war.

Following the war he served as foreign correspondent in Poland, Moscow, Tel Aviv, and the Caribbean. Allen served as war correspondent in Southeast Asia during the 1950s French war in Indochina and was awarded the Croix de Guerre from the French High Command for his frontline reporting in 1952.
REFERENCE: Robert W. Desmond. *Tides of War.* 1984.

ALPERT, MAX (1899–1980). A pioneer in the field of Soviet photojournalism, Alpert published his first photographs in 1924. As a war photographer* and correspondent for TASS during World War II* he covered the battles of the Fourth Ukrainian Front in Czechoslovakia and the siege of Stalingrad. In addition he reported and photographed Maxim Gorky's return from Italy, the rescue of General Nobile's expedition, and construction of the first Five-Year Plans. Following the war he worked for the Soviet Information Bureau, *Novosti*, and *Pravda*.
REFERENCE: Daniela Mrazkova and Vladimir Remes, eds. *The Russian War: 1941–1945.* 1975.

AMERICAN CIVIL WAR. The Civil War was the most thoroughly documented war of its era. While the Northern press gave it the most attention, there were contingents of correspondents representing the Confederate states as well as members of the European press, more significantly from Great Britain.

The British press generally favored the Confederacy. On various occasions British journalists reportedly accepted bribes to write and publish Southern propaganda. While the *London Daily News* gave the most evenhanded account of the war, the first British paper to send a correspondent was the *Times*, when William Howard Russell* arrived in New York in March 1861 prior to the actual outbreak of hostilities. Russell, the preeminent war reporter of his time, did not endear himself to the American military when he criticized the Union Army in a dispatch to the *Times* after the debacle at Bull Run in July. After copies of his reports were circulated in Washington, D.C., he was derided as ''Bull Run Russell.'' In March 1862 his permission to accompany the Union armies was revoked and he returned to England.

Other British correspondents of note spent stints in America covering the war, including Antonio Gallenga* and Charles MacKay* for the *Times*, Edwin Godkin* for the *London Daily News*, and Frank Vizetelly* of the *Daily News*. Additional coverage was supplied by George Augustus Sala* and Edward James Dicey* of the *Daily Telegraph*, and Samuel P. Day* of the *Morning Herald*.

The Reuters* News Agency is credited with providing the most consistent coverage for the British press. Both the *Times* and Reuters chartered dispatch boats to insure that war news reached a public clamoring for information in a timely fashion. These boats intercepted incoming ships which had arranged to relay special dispatches by tossing them overboard in watertight cylinders attached to floating devices. At night these canisters were made visible with flares. They would then be picked up in nets and brought to shore to be telegraphed to London. By means of private telegraph lines secretly extended to the most western reaches of the Irish coast, Reuters received telegraph transmissions eight hours before its competition.

Despite the presence of pools of European correspondents, most of the news of the war reported in Europe was based on Union press coverage. Close to three hundred special correspondents represented the Northern press at some point during the war. The Union press representation became so unwieldy that the War Department required that all war reports be accompanied by a byline. The tradition of reportorial anonymity was broken with the Civil War. Dispatches appeared above either a correspondent's initials, pen name, or birth names.

Of the more than three hundred reporters covering Union armies during the Civil War, the average age was in the early twenties, with at least six still in their teens. Several had prior experience reporting foreign wars. Many were well educated, with degrees from Harvard, Yale, Columbia, and Amherst. Several were killed by enemy gunfire and at least six perished from camp diseases.

The best coverage in the North was provided by the *New York Herald*. Publisher James Gordon Bennett* was well prepared for this conflict, having dispatched correspondents to Southern cities before the war broke out. Close to forty reporters would eventually accompany the Union Army for the *Herald*. As publisher of the best-represented newspaper at the front, Bennett paid his writers the highest wages and could afford the best correspondents, ever cognizant that he could easily recoup his investment with enough news scoops. Leading *Herald* reporters included Charles Henry Farrell, Bradley Osbon,* Henry Villard,* George Hosmer, George Alfred Townsend,* William Young, and William F. G. Shanks.*

The *New York Tribune* claimed up to twenty reporters in the field, with Albert Deane Richardson,* Junius Henri Browne,* George W. Smalley,* Henry E.

Wing,* Homer Byington,* Samuel Wilkeson,* and James Wilkeson the most recognizable names. The *New York Times* offered excellent coverage, having up to three dozen reporters with the Union Army. Among the more notable representatives were William Conant Church,* Henry J. Raymond,* Franc B. Wilkie,* Major Benjamin Truman,* William Swinton,* and Lorenzo Crounse.* Other important war correspondents for the North included Sylvanus Cadwallader* for the *Chicago Times*, Charles Carleton Coffin* of the *Boston Journal*, Murat Halstead* and James R. McCullagh for the *Cincinnati Commercial*, and Uriah Painter* for the *Philadelphia Inquirer*.

More than one hundred Southern reporters covered the war at various times. They ranged from the paid "specials" to volunteers, officers, and enlisted men who regularly sent letters and telegrams from the different theaters of operation. Among the best-known Southern correspondents were Peter Alexander* of the *Mobile Advertiser* and the *Richmond Dispatch*, Felix Gregory de Fontaine* of the *Courier*, Dr. William Shepardson* and James Sener of the *Richmond Dispatch*, and John H. Linebaugh* for the *Memphis Appeal*. The *Mobile Register* was well represented, with an aggressive staff that included Henry Watterson, Albert Street,* Israel Gibbons,* and Samuel Reid Shepardson. In addition, the Confederate Press Association* provided war reports for newspapers that could not afford their own special correspondents.

Compared to their Union counterparts, Southern reporters were allowed to operate with an unusual degree of freedom, although Southern authorities made various ineffective attempts at censorship. During President Jefferson Davis' inauguration ceremony he promised freedom of the press, and never closed down a newspaper during the conflict, unlike his Union counterpart. Initially, reporters were allowed to view camp conditions as long as no dispatches were filed detailing troop strengths, movements, or other logistical information. However, in January 1862 the Army of the Potomac banned all correspondents, and any security breach by the press would be a viewed as a criminal act. Following this new policy, reporters had to filter telegraphic dispatches through military censors.

The federal government prosecuted newspapers that published information that could be construed as helpful to the enemy. Several papers were closed temporarily for printing false rumors harmful to the Union war effort, and the *Chicago Times* was ordered to cease publication simply for attacking the Lincoln administration.

War correspondents came under vitriolic attacks on both sides of the Mason-Dixon Line. Confederate general Braxton Bragg had several reporters arrested for jeopardizing security and often instituted censorship of telegraph dispatches. Other Southern generals who expressed outward hostility to the press included Earl Van Dorn, Joseph E. Johnston, P.G.T. Beauregard, John Bell Hood, Thomas "Stonewall" Jackson, and Robert E. Lee.

Union reporters fared little better. General William Tecumseh Sherman loathed correspondents and barred them from his encampments. He was hostile to all "specials" and once suggested hanging *New York Herald* correspondent Thomas W. Knox.* On one occasion General George G. Meade took umbrage with reporter Edward Crapsey and had him placed backward on a horse with the sign "Libeler of the Press" tied around his neck and had him escorted out of camp to the tune of the "Rogue's March." Crapsey's colleagues rallied to his defense by eliminating Meade's name from any future dispatches, and in the process probably thwarted his political career. General Henry W. Halleck expelled several dozen journalists from the western theater in 1862 and General Burnside would have shot William Swinton* of the *New York Times* had not General Ulysses Grant intervened.

By 1864, Secretary of War Edwin Stanton was so concerned over public morale as the war dragged on and casualties continued to mount that he began reporting the war himself. He altered casualty figures and issued his own reports. REFERENCES: J. Cutler Andrews. *The North Reports the Civil War.* 1955; J. Cutler Andrews. *The South Reports the Civil War.* 1970; Ian F. W. Beckett. *The War Correspondents: The American Civil War.* 1993; Hodding Carter. *Their Words Were Bullets: The Southern Press in War, Reconstruction and Peace.* 1969; Emmet Crozier. *Yankee Reporters, 1861–65.* 1956; Robert Neil Mathis. "Freedom of the Press in the Confederacy: A Reality," *Historian.* 1975; Louis M. Starr. *The Bohemian Brigade.* 1954; Bernard A. Weisberger. *Reporters for the Union.* 1953.

AMERICAN INDIAN WARS. War reporting during the western Indian Wars between 1860 and 1890 offered correspondents many more challenges than the American Civil War.* As opposed to the Civil War, where reporters had access to towns, railroads, and telegraph lines, Indian War correspondents were rarely afforded such luxuries. Journalists were required not only to share the hardships of the various campaigns but also to participate in the fighting when required. Press coverage of various Indian campaigns began following the Civil War.

In 1867 and 1868 several correspondents accompanied the campaigns of Generals Philip Sheridan and Winfield Scott Hancock in Kansas and Oklahoma. Correspondents with Sheridan included Henry Stanley* of the *St. Louis Democrat*, artist Theodore R. Davis* of *Harper's Weekly*, and Randolph Debenneville Keim* for the *New York Herald*. They filed their stories by military mail couriers and regular mail. The most newsworthy story to come out of Sheridan's campaign was the Battle of the Washita River between General George Armstrong Custer's Seventh Cavalry and the Cheyennes in 1868.

In 1872–1873 the Modoc War broke out in southern Oregon and California when 160 Modoc Indians went on the warpath, terrorizing and killing local settlers. Among the contingent of correspondents covering this campaign were Robert D. Bogart* and H. Wallace Atwell* of the *San Francisco Chronicle*, Alex McKay* of the *Yreka Union*, and Edward Fox* of the *New York Herald*. This was the first Indian War covered by a foreign correspondent, with William Simpson* of the *Illustrated London News* serving a short stint in the field.

The most significant era and most active phase of warfare for Indian War correspondents was from 1875 to 1881. The biggest battle of the wars was the Battle of the Rosebud in southern Montana in June 1876. Five correspondents reported this epic battle, including John F. Finerty* of the *Chicago Times*, Reuben Briggs Davenport* of the *New York Herald*, Robert Strahorn* of the Denver-based *Rocky Mountain News*, Thomas C. MacMillan* representing the *Chicago Inter-Ocean*, and Joe Wasson* of the *Alta California, Philadelphia Press*, and the *New York Tribune*. Most of these correspondents plus Jerome B. Stillson* of the *New York Herald* were present with Generals George C. Crook and Alfred Terry at the Battle of the Little Big Horn. Only the ill-fated Mark Kellogg* of the *Bismarck Tribune* accompanied General Custer's command to his death, the lone correspondent to perish in the Indian Wars.

Following the Battle of the Little Big Horn other correspondents were drawn to the battlefield. Among the most notable were Charles Sanford Diehl* of the *Chicago Times*, Barbour Lathrop* of the *San Francisco Evening Bulletin*, James J. O'Kelly* of the *New York Tribune*, and representing the *Chicago Tribune*, James William Howard.* Diehl, Stillson, Lathrop, O'Kelly, Howard, and Finerty reported the Nez Perce War from 1877 to 1879.

In 1890 a new field of operations seemed to be developing in South Dakota, drawing a new group of correspondents. Of the almost two dozen journalists, less than a handful would witness any action. Among the best-known were Charles W. Allen of the *New York Herald*, William F. Kelley of the *Lincoln State Journal*, Charles (Will) Cressey of the *Omaha Bee*, Teresa Dean* of the *Chicago Herald*, and Frederic Remington* for *Harper's Weekly*. The Sioux Indian disturbances, as they came to be known, had certain trappings of a war story, but could hardly be called a war. From 1890 to 1891 the Sioux were attempting to hold on to their lands and retain their cultural identity as the reservation system became more pervasive and restrictive. The massacre of over two hundred men, women, and children at Wounded Knee on the Pine Ridge Reservation signaled an end to the Indian Wars. Most sources indicate that only three correspondents witnessed this tragedy, including Charles W. Allen, Charles H. Cressey, and William F. Kelley.

REFERENCES: Robert W. Desmond. *The Information Process*. 1978; Oliver Knight. *Following the Indian Wars*. 1960; George R. Kolbenschlag. *A Whirlwind Passes: Newspaper Correspondents and the Sioux Indian Disturbances of 1890–91*. 1990; Roger L. Nichols. "Printer's Ink and Red Skins: Western Newspapermen and the Indians," *Kansas Quarterly*. 1971; Elmo Scott Watson. "The Indian Wars and the Press, 1866–67," *Journalism Quarterly*. December 1940; Elmo Scott Watson. "A Checklist of Indian War Correspondents, 1866–1891," *Journalism Quarterly*. December 1940; Elmo Watson. "The Last Indian War, 1890–91—A Study of Newspaper Jingoism," *Journalism Quarterly*. September 1943.

AMERY, LEOPOLD CHARLES MAURICE STENNETT (1873–1955). Born in India, he obtained his first newspaper job with the *Manchester Guardian*, which gave him a free hand covering events in the Near East. Soon after, the Oxford-educated journalist and future politician became assistant to the foreign editor of the *Times* in 1899, where he organized its correspondents for the Boer War.* A schoolmate of Winston Churchill's* at Harrow, he became the chief war correspondent for the *Times*.

Amery was authorized to accompany Boer forces until being expelled by Boer general Petrus Joubert. He was not unsympathetic to the Boers, having taken time to learn the Afrikaner language. He shared a tent with Churchill prior to his capture by the Boers; however, as luck would have it, Amery elected to stay in the tent as his ex-schoolmate went out to board the armored train that was later waylaid by Boer forces. Following the war he edited the seven-volume *Times History of the War in South Africa*. In 1902 he was called to the bar before embarking on a long political career. A Conservative M.P., he represented South Birmingham from 1911 to 1945.

During World War I* he organized some of the first recruiting campaigns and worked as an intelligence officer in the Balkans. Amery was on the *Caledonian* when it was torpedoed in the Mediterranean. He escaped the submarine attack by hiding in the masts of a small boat that was later rescued by a hospital ship. Of his two sons, his eldest, John, was executed for treason during World War II.*

REFERENCES: Dennis Griffiths, ed. *The Encyclopedia of the British Press.* 1992; *DNB,* 1951–1960; Phillip Knightley. *The First Casualty.* 1975.

ANANNIN, MIKHAIL (b. 1912). Born in Minsk, he joined the staff of *Pravda* in 1931. With the outbreak of World War II* he covered the front as a photographer-correspondent and fought with partisan forces. He suffered permanent injuries from several wounds he received in the fighting. After his injuries his wife Alexandra assisted him, as they worked as a correspondent team for *Soviet Union* magazine. Together they recorded the discovery of the mass grave at Katyn and the Polish campaign.

REFERENCE: Daniela Mrazkova and Vladimir Remes, eds. *The Russian War: 1941–1945.* 1975.

ANDERSON, FINLEY (?). He covered the American Civil War* for the *New York Herald*. Anderson cultivated an especially close relationship with General Winfield Scott. During the siege of Vicksburg Admiral Porter attempted to run gunboats through Confederate batteries. In February 1863, Anderson was among the three reporters aboard the gunboat-ram *Queen of the West* when it came under heavy fire. Despite taking at least a dozen hits, it made it through one battery and continued downstream, where it was put out of commission by another Confederate battery when it ran aground. The indecisive Anderson was captured while waiting for the captain to return to destroy the ship and spent a year in a Confederate prison in Texas, while his compatriots Joseph Burbridge McCullagh* of the *Cincinnati Commercial* and Albert Bodman* of the *Chicago Tribune* managed to escape with the rest of the crew.

Anderson would return to the battlefront in 1864, where on May 9, three months after his release from prison, he was wounded in the arm at the Battle of Spotsylvania Court House following the Wilderness campaign. Faced with increasing censorship, in order to have his account of the Battle of Petersburg published, he acceded to Stanton's demand that he reduce the number of Union casualties in his report by two thousand, or one third of the actual figure.

Following the Civil War Anderson was made the *Herald*'s London correspondent and reported the Austro-Prussian War* of 1866. He cabled the full speech of the king of Prussia announcing the end of the war to the *Herald* at a cost of $6,500 gold. This was reportedly the first newspaper story carried by the Atlantic cable.

REFERENCES: J. Cutler Andrews. *The North Reports the Civil War.* 1955; Louis M. Starr. *Bohemian Brigade.* 1954.

ANDERSON, JOHN R. L. (?). Anderson was dismissed from the British Indian Army prior to World War II* after he contracted a case of amoebic dysentery. Soon after he found employment as a reporter for the *Manchester Guardian.* Within a month the energetic ex-soldier was promoted to military correspondent,* beginning a twenty-five-year relationship with the paper. During the last year of the war in Europe he was the paper's chief correspondent in Germany.

REFERENCE: David Ayerst. *The Manchester Guardian: Biography of a Newspaper.* 1971.

ANGLO-SAXON PRESS. During the Mexican War* numerous correspondents and printers founded newspapers in Mexico's occupied cities rather than simply sending the news back to their home offices in the States. These fledgling enterprises became known collectively as the ''Anglo-Saxon'' press. Beginning with the *Corpus Christi Gazette*, they would eventually number twenty-five in fourteen cities. Most were ephemeral in nature, although some lasted until the end of the conflict. The first English-language newspaper to be published in Mexico City was the *American Star*, founded during the occupation of the Mexican capital by two enterprising journalists from New Orleans, John H. Peoples* and John R. Barnard. Having already established the *Vera Cruz Eagle* and other papers, they set to work in Mexico City publishing proclamations, military orders from American officers, and sundry news items. The real significance of these newspapers to the American public was that they offered more reliable news than releases coming through official and military channels.

REFERENCES: Robert W. Johanssen. *To the Halls of the Montezumas: The Mexican War in the American Imagination.* 1985; Lota M. Spell, ''The Anglo-Saxon Press in Mexico, 1846–1848,'' *American Historical Review.* October 1932.

ANGLY, EDWARD (1898–1950). Angly was born in Palestine, Texas, and attended the University of Texas before beginning a ten-year affiliation with the Associated Press as foreign correspondent in 1920. He joined the *New York*

Herald Tribune as chief correspondent and chief of the London bureau in 1930. In 1940 he covered the French front, the British Expeditionary Force in retreat from Flanders, and then the Russian war before moving to the *Chicago Sun* in 1941 as its Far East correspondent. He was one the first three war correspondents to reach Pearl Harbor from the United States following the surprise attack and beginning in March 1942 was the first correspondent to report the arrival of U.S. troops in Australia. Later that year he covered action in New Guinea and the Southwest Pacific theater.

Angly later reported developments in the Soviet Union and the Baltic states and was one of only two journalists to cover the Teheran Conference in 1943. He then covered the war on the western front against Germany and headed the Paris bureau for the *Sun* in 1944. Following the war he turned to freelance writing.
REFERENCE: Robert W. Desmond. *Tides of War.* 1984.

ARCHIBALD, JAMES FRANCIS JEWELL (b. 1871). Archibald was born in New York and educated at Ohio Wesleyan University. He served in the Sino-Japanese War, was with General Nelson Miles in the Sioux and Apache campaigns and was with the Fifth Army Corps through the Spanish-American War.* Representing the *San Francisco Post* during the Spanish-American War, he was the first American wounded, albeit superficially, in the first encounter with Spanish troops.

Archibald was among the seven war correspondents permitted to accompany General Shafter aboard the flagship *Seguranca* during the initial American invasion. During the El Caney operation he was an aide-de-camp on the general's staff with the First Division. He was responsible for leading soldiers into El Caney in the search for hidden Spanish soldiers. In the process they were to destroy or confiscate weapons and arrest ambulatory civilians. *Leslie's* published a series of articles by Archibald and illustrated by Howard Chandler Christy* detailing this action. He also witnessed the surrender of Spanish troops after the fall of Santiago.

Following the war he continued to report from the battlefront. He covered the Chippewa campaign on Leach Lake, was with the army of occupation in Cuba, and in 1899 was with British forces in the Sudan on the staff of General Ludlow. During the Boer War* he covered the Boer army and later reported on Castro's army during the Barcelona campaign in Venezuela. He was with the Philippine constabulary in its campaign against the Ladrones and covered the Russian army during the Russo-Japanese War* for *Collier's Weekly*.

In 1910 Archibald was with the French army in Morocco and then with the Turkish army during the revolution in Albania. The following year saw him in Lisbon during the Portuguese revolution, and two years later he was with Chinese troops during the revolution in China. He accompanied Austrian and German armies at the outset of World War I,* but was arrested and then released

by British authorities for violating war censorship. He wrote *Blue Shirt and Khaki* and *Tales from the Trenches.*
REFERENCES: Charles H. Brown. *The Correspondents' War.* 1967; *Who's Who in America.* 1910–1911.

ARMIT, R. H. (?). During the Franco-Prussian War* the *Manchester Guardian* hired naval officer Armit to cover German forces throughout the hostilities. When not with military expeditions he was in the company of a British volunteer ambulance. His routine exemplified the freedom afforded correspondents prior to the twentieth century. Often he traveled alone across the battlefields at night with only a compass and the light of a cigar to guide him. His dispatches took up to two weeks to reach his paper and were characterized by detailed but precise descriptions of each battle of the war.
REFERENCE: David Ayerst. *The Manchester Guardian: Biography of a Newspaper.* 1971.

ARNETT, PETER (b. 1934). Born in Riverton, New Zealand, on November 13, 1934, Arnett entered the American consciousness, vilified as "Baghdad Pete" by Senator Alan Simpson during Operation Desert Storm, for broadcasting for CNN from the Iraqi capital of Baghdad. In reality Arnett has been one of the most dependable war correspondents for the last thirty-five years.

He worked for various Australian newspapers and the *Bangkok World* while still in his twenties before becoming a stringer* for the Associated Press (AP) in Laos. Arnett continued to work for the AP in the Far East throughout the early 1960s. He began his coverage of South Vietnam in June 1962 and was one of the few correspondents to cover the conflict through the fall of Saigon thirteen years later. The often controversial Arnett probably saw more action than any other reporter during the Vietnam debacle. In 1966 he won the Pulitzer Prize for his coverage.

After Vietnam he made the shift from print reporter to what he described as "a video version of the Associated Press" working for the fledgling CNN in 1980. The first war he covered outside Southeast Asia was Cyprus in 1974 after the Turkish army invaded. In the early 1980s he reported the carnage in El Salvador and Nicaragua, as well as the Israeli invasion of Lebanon in 1982. That same year Arnett made his first trip into Afghanistan to cover the resistance of the mujahideen to the Soviet invasion.

He covered the aftermath of the Panama invasion in 1989 and the subsequent capture of strongman Manuel Noriega, which he described as "the first war as media event." Perhaps his greatest scoop took place during the Gulf War,* when a U.S. military raid destroyed a shelter, killing more than three hundred civilians. The United States claimed it was a legitimate military target despite Arnett's firsthand account, which found no evidence of an Iraqi military presence. Arnett became a controversial figure during the Gulf War, denounced in Congress as the "Joseph Goebbels of Saddam Hussein's Hitler-like regime," labeled a turncoat, a "video Benedict Arnold," and a traitor by a conservative spokesman. CNN, to its credit, resisted attempts to have him fired. Besides the Pulitzer Arnett has won numerous other awards such as the George Polk Memorial Award, an Emmy, and three ACE awards from the National Cable Television Association. In his autobiography, *Live from the Battlefield* (1994), Arnett counters charges that his reporting was manipulated by Saddam Hussein.

REFERENCES: Peter Arnett. *Live from the Battlefield*. 1994; Phillip Knightley. *The First Casualty*. 1975.

ARNOT, CHARLES P. (?). Arnot worked as a frontline correspondent in various capacities over a forty-eight-year career. He covered World War II,* the 1967 Arab-Israeli War, the Indo-Chinese War of 1962, Vietnam,* and other conflicts. He was affiliated with the Associated Press for more than a quarter century. Following his retirement he wrote several books, including *Don't Kill the Messenger* (1994), which recounts his life as a war correspondent and the deaths of numerous foreign correspondents since 1935.

REFERENCES: Charles P. Arnot. *Don't Kill the Messenger: The Tragic Story of Welles Hangen and Other Journalistic Combat Victims*. 1994; Robert W. Desmond. *Tides of War*. 1984.

ARTIST-CORRESPONDENTS. The birth of the artist-correspondent coincided with the rise of pictorial journalism. By 1842 print technology made it possible for woodblocks of pictures to be printed next to type for long runs. Illustrated papers like the *Illustrated London News* were instantly popular with an increasingly literate public clamoring for information. The popularity of British illustrated papers was in part connected with the colonial wars of the Victorian era.

There have always been war artists, but artist-correspondents variously known as war artists or "specials" working for the pictorial press served a different purpose. They had to serve a dual function as artist and journalist. Artist-correspondents were expected to supplement their sketches with a written report. Engravers employed by the paper would then take the sketch and redraw it on a block, often embellishing the original product.

Besides the professionally trained artists and the "specials" of the illustrated journals, there were artists hired by publishers to produce paintings of frontline action that could be reproduced as lithographic prints. This method was particularly fashionable in the 1850s and 1860s. While there was no inherent news value in these images, they were produced by eyewitnesses and were considered colorful war souvenirs. Sets of lithographic prints were sold in sets complemented by detailed captions. Currier and Ives in America and Day and Son in Great Britain were the preeminent lithographic printers of this era. One of the most outstanding practitioners of this method was William Simpson,* who covered the Crimean War* for a London print seller. The Crimean War produced several outstanding war artists, such as Joseph A. Crowe,* Edward A. Goodall,* Robert T. Landells,* and the aforementioned Simpson.

Until the founding of the *Graphic* in 1869 the *Illustrated London News* was unchallenged by major competition in Great Britain. But soon after the publication of the *Illustrated London News* imitators cropped up in America and throughout Europe, creating new markets for the growing pool of artist-correspondents. The two best-known American pictorials were *Frank Leslie's Illustrated Newspaper*, founded in 1855, and *Harper's Weekly*, founded by Fletcher Harper* two years later. Both publications made remarkable contributions to the visual record of the American Civil War.* Among the most outstanding artist-correspondents of the Civil War were Edwin Forbes* and Henri Lovie,* who were two of more than eighty artists representing *Leslie's*, while *Harper's* could boast the talents of Alfred and William Waud,* Thomas Nast,* Winslow Homer,* and Theodore R. Davis.*

Most Civil War artists covered only one theater of operations. Alfred Waud, for example, spent the whole war in Virginia, and Alex Simplot* covered the western river war. There were of course exceptions, such as Lovie, who covered both the East and the West; William Waud, who reported from the West and the Deep South; and the peripatetic Theodore R. Davis, who covered more ground than any of his colleagues.

Civil War artists carried a minimum of accoutrements. Although Alf Waud wore a holstered pistol, most did not carry weapons, unlike their British counterparts, who often took part in the colonial wars. Battle sketches were usually done in pencil, while crayon and charcoal was the medium of choice for camp scenes. Other essential equipment included powerful field glasses, drawing supplies, a horse, rations, and a rolled blanket. The most skilled artists developed a kind of shorthand with sweeping lines filling in for the horizon or distant trees, a wavering circle in place of shells exploding in the air, and short lines representing troop formations. Notes were then written in the margins for the engravers, in order to avoid consuming time with minute details. In this way veteran war artists could produce sketches in minutes. Once the special artists completed their work, the sketches were rushed by mail or courier to the offices of the illustrated weeklies in New York. It generally took from three to four weeks for sketches to reach the newspaper page from the sketch pad.

The main obstacles faced by Civil War artists were lack of time and limited visibility. While the shorthand method was best for saving time, they worked on horseback as often as possible in order to cover the entire field of operations. They would avoid getting too close to the front lines, which were usually obscured by battle smoke, instead opting for vantage points such as elevated ridges, rooftops, and even balloons.

Artist-correspondents relied on engravers to reproduce their field sketches. Good engravers could improve the quality of poor sketches, while careless engravers ruined many fine examples of battle art. The best lithographers could be found at *Leslie's*. Frank Leslie,* himself a skilled engraver, supervised the preparation of each illustration. Prior to the 1860s war illustrators were often uncredited. At the outset of the Civil War, artists who produced the sketches for engraving were seldom acknowledged, quite often because they neglected to sign their sketches.

The siege of Paris in 1870–1871 during the Franco-Prussian War* was a watershed for war correspondents and artists. The *Graphic* editorialized that the war artist had come of age during the Franco-Prussian War. The golden years for war illustrators ended in the late nineteenth century. Some of the most recognized war artists plied their trade at this time, including the preeminent war illustrator of the era, Melton Prior,* the legendary Frederic Villiers,* W. T. Maud,* Charlie Fripp,* Frederic Remington,* Howard Chandler Christy,* and Charles Sheldon.* By the 1880s photographic methods began to replace the block drawings of the engravers and never again would the artist correspondent have such fame and influence.

REFERENCES: Pat Hodgson. *The War Illustrators.* 1977; The Library of Congress. *An Album of American Battle Art.* 1947; Frederic E. Ray. *"Our Special Artist," Alfred R. Waud's Civil War.* 1994; Philip Van Doren Stern. *They Were There: The Civil War in Action As Seen by Its Combat Correspondents.* 1959; W. Fletcher Thompson, Jr. *The Image of War: The Pictorial Reporting of the American Civil War.* 1959.

ASHMEAD-BARTLETT, ELLIS (1881–1931). He witnessed his first war as special correspondent during the 1897 Greco-Turkish War.* Unfortunately, while in the company of Turkish forces he was captured by Greek troops. Following the war he enlisted in the Second Bedfordshire Regiment at the outset of the Boer War.* In 1904 he represented the *Daily Telegraph* during the Russo-Japanese War,* reporting the conflict from the Japanese side. In 1907 he covered the French campaign in Morocco and two years later was with the Spanish army in Morocco during the war against the Riffs.

Ashmead-Bartlett was again at the front for the *Telegraph* in 1911, when he accompanied the Italian army on its advance toward Tripoli, and the next year was stationed at Turkish headquarters in the First Balkan War. The following year he reported the conflict from the Serbian side. With the outbreak of World War I* he hurried from London for the Continent, the first London correspondent to do so. He was present during the German bombardment of Rheims, but soon after was arrested by French forces for ignoring censorship restrictions. Because of the obstacles presented by the censors of the War Office, many reporters gave up covering the war in the winter of 1914–1915. Ashmead-Ellis joined the Red Cross in order to follow the action, while acting as ambulance attendant and hospital orderly.

In 1915, he was chosen by the National Press Association to cover the Dardanelles expedition for the London press. The campaign was a disaster, but due to harsh censorship restrictions he was barred from reporting the debacle. Any attempt to publish realistic accounts or casualty figures was intercepted by War Office censors. After he circumvented the censor, William Maxwell, and at-

tempted to smuggle reports of the bungled Gallipoli campaign to Prime Minister
Asquith, he was expelled and deprived of his accreditation. Ashmead-Bartlett
returned to London and testified in front of the Dardanelles Committee, providing information which ultimately led to the dismissal of the commanding officer
at Gallipoli, Sir Ian Hamilton. Except for a short stint at the French front in
1916, his career as a war correspondent was cut short when his name appeared
on the War Office blacklist. Following the war he published his account of the
Gallipoli campaign in *Despatches from the Dardanelles* (1918) and *Some of My
Experiences in the Great War* (1918).
REFERENCES: Emmet Crozier. *American Reporters on the Western Front 1914–1918*.
1959; Phillip Knightley. *The First Casualty*. 1975.

ATKINS, JOHN BLACK (1871–1954). Educated at Cambridge, he joined the
Manchester Guardian as its first special correspondent in 1897, when he covered
the thirty-day Greco-Turkish War.* The next year he reported the Spanish-
American War* from Cuba. Following this short-lived conflict Atkins was sent
to cover the Boer War* from 1899 to 1900. During the war, correspondents
were instructed to send only very short news telegrams, these to be followed
up by more detailed accounts by mail several weeks later. He was promoted to
London editor in 1901. In 1907 he left this position to assume the assistant
editor position with the *Spectator*. Besides his war dispatches Atkins also wrote
The Relief of Mafeking and the two-volume *The Life of Sir William Howard
Russell, the First Special Correspondent* (1911).
REFERENCE: David Ayerst. *The Manchester Guardian: Biography of a Newspaper*.
1971.

ATKINSON, GEORGE (1822–1859). Atkinson served as artist with the Bengal Engineers in India between 1840 and 1859. He published several collections
of lithographs based on his experiences in the British army during the Indian
Mutiny (1857–1859), including *Pictures from the North* (1848), *The Campaign
in India* (1859), and *Curry and Rice* (1860). The *Illustrated London News* published lithographs of several of his Indian sketches.
REFERENCE: Pat Hodgson. *The War Illustrators*. 1979.

ATWELL, H. WALLACE (c. 1832–1888). Writing under the pen name "Bill
Dadd the Scribe" for the *Sacramento Record*, he covered the Modoc War
(1872–1873). Born in Windsor, Vermont, he moved to California and had a
peripatetic twenty-two-year newspaper career before covering the Modoc War.
Atwell would eventually replace Robert D. Bogart* as the correspondent for the
San Francisco Chronicle when Bogart was arrested and court-martialed for an
old embezzlement charge. While covering the Three Days' Fight at the Lava
Beds, Atwell and the other two correspondents, Edward Fox* and Alex Mc-
Kay,* figured out a way to pool their reports, presaging an arrangement which

would become more refined during World War II.* During this battle Atwell narrowly missed getting killed in an ambush.

Ultimately, Atwell would serve as war correspondent during the Modoc War for not only the *Sacramento Record* and the *Chronicle*, but the *New York Herald* and the *Chicago Inter-Ocean* as well. He was the only reporter to cover the entire conflict from February to October. Following the end of the uprising and the capture of the Modoc leader Captain Jack, Atwell unsuccessfully sought justice for the prisoners. The Modoc War was the first American Indian War* to be so extensively covered, with correspondents competing to get their news into print. On his way home at the conclusion of the conflict Atwell had the misfortune to be riding a stagecoach that was waylaid by highwaymen near Yreka. When queried as to his valuables Atwell responded "two bits," whereupon they let him keep it. Upon his return to California he remained in journalism, doing stints with the *Visalia Delta* and the *Sunset Route*.
REFERENCES: Oliver Knight. *Following the Indian Wars.* 1960; Keith A. Murray. *The Modocs and Their War.* 1959.

AULTMAN, OTIS A. (1874–1943). Born in Holden, Missouri, he was a pioneer in motion picture work. He was employed with the International News Service and then Pathé News during the Mexican Revolution. Between 1916 and 1917 he was under contract with Pancho Villa. He covered the major events of the Mexican Revolution as a commercial photographer and news cameraman, including Villa's raid on Columbus, New Mexico. He died in El Paso, Texas.
REFERENCES: Turner Browne and Elaine Partnow. *Photographic Artists and Innovators.* 1983; Raymond Fieldong. *The American Newsreel 1911–1967.* 1972.

AUSTIN, ALEXANDER BERRY (1903–1943). With the outbreak of World War II* Austin joined the RAF and became a member of the press section of the Fighter Command until the Battle of Britain, which he covered as an air correspondent and accredited war correspondent for *The Daily Herald*. Austin received high praise when he accompanied and trained with the commandos who made the ill-fated raid on Dieppe in 1942. He was the only representative of the British press to witness this action.

Austin covered the First Army throughout the Tunisian campaign before joining the Fifth Army for the landing at Salerno. He was killed on the road to Camarelle in Italy. Besides his war dispatches he wrote three books on his battle exploits, including *Fighter Command*, about the Battle of Britain; *The Birth of an Army*, about the Tunisian campaign; and his account of the Dieppe raid, *We Landed at Dawn*.
REFERENCES: Robert W. Desmond. *Tides of War.* 1978; Dennis Griffiths, ed. *The Encyclopedia of the British Press.* 1992.

AUSTRO-ITALIAN WAR. The Austro-Italian war, also known as the Austro-Piedmont War, lasted from April to July 1859. It began when Austrian military forces invaded Piedmont on the Italian peninsula. French intervention led to the formation of the kingdom of Italy in 1861 and ultimately to the unification of Italy in 1870. Besides the invasion and the July armistice the main actions of the war took place at the Battles of Magenta and Solferino.

Few correspondents were on hand to cover the war. The Piedmont military commander had threatened to hang any that he caught in his camp. The only French press representative on hand was the artist-correspondent Charles Emile Yriarte of the *Monde Illustré*. The best reportage was produced by British correspondents led by Joseph A. Crowe* and Ferdinand Eber of the *Times*, both reporting the war from the Piedmont side. Other correspondents reporting from the Piedmont side included Henry Wreford and Antonio Gallenga,* also for the *Times*. Coverage from the Italian side was provided by the stringer* Mrs. Jessie White Mario for the *Daily News*, Frank Vizetelly* of the *London Illustrated Times*, and with the *New York Times* Henry J. Raymond* and Dr. W. E. Johnstone, whose reports appeared under the name "Malakoff."
REFERENCE: Robert W. Desmond. *The Information Process*. 1978.

AUSTRO-PRUSSIAN WAR. The seven-week Austro-Prussian War began on June 16, 1866. The war was triggered by the Prussian seizure of the duchy of Holstein. The Germanic states of Hanover, Bavaria, and Saxony sided with Austria against Prussia, which was supported by Italy. Since the military controlled the press in the countries involved in the war, the best coverage was provided by the British press, which was represented by five London papers. William Howard Russell* and C. B. Brackenbury* were there for the *Times* and George Alfred Henty* for the *Standard*. Other prominent war correspondents included Frank Vizetelly* and Hilary Skinner* of the *Daily News* and Edward Dicey* of the *Daily Telegraph*. American correspondents included Finley Anderson* of the *New York Herald*, and George W. Smalley* and Henry Villard* for the *New York Tribune*.
REFERENCE: Robert W. Desmond. *The Information Process*. 1978.

AXELSSON, GEORGE (1899–1966). Born in Sweden, he moved to the United States in his teens and began his newspaper career in California. He returned to Europe in 1926 to work for the Paris edition of the *Chicago Tribune*. During the Spanish Civil War* he accompanied General Francisco Franco's forces as correspondent for the *New York Times*. Following the outbreak of World War II* and the fall of France in 1940 he witnessed the French surrender ceremony in the Compiègne Forest and Hitler's famous jig of triumph, captured for posterity by photographers. Prior to American entry into the war he worked at the *Times* Berlin bureau, before moving to the Stockholm bureau.
REFERENCE: Robert W. Desmond. *Tides of War*. 1984.

B

BAGBY, GEORGE W. (1828–1883). Prior to the American Civil War* Bagby was a Lynchburg physician. He hesitantly entered the field of journalism with several articles for the *Lynchburg Virginian* and as Washington correspondent for the *Richmond Whig* and the *Charleston Mercury*. He served as editor of the *Southern Literary Messenger* in Richmond for most of the war. Bagby had joined the Confederate Army at one point but was found unfit for the field. He returned to journalism as occasional correspondent for almost twenty Southern publications. Among his sobriquets during the war were "Hermes" for the *Charleston Mercury*, "Gamma" for the *Mobile Register*, and "Pan" for the *Columbus Sun* of Georgia. In the words of at least one Southern editor, he was "literally the best newspaper writer in the Confederate States."

Bagby was one of the first journalists to call attention to Stonewall Jackson. In 1862 he reported from the perimeter of the Battle of Seven Pines and in 1864 from Petersburg, the closest he would come to witnessing live combat. After the war he continued in the newspaper business in New York but was forced to retire when his eyesight deteriorated. He returned to Virginia and went on a highly successful lecture circuit. Toward the end of his career he worked as state librarian and wrote several short works.

REFERENCES: J. Cutler Andrews. *The South Reports the Civil War*. 1970; Joseph Leonard King. *Dr. William Bagby, a Study of Virginian Literature, 1850–1880*. 1927; Stewart Sifakis. *Who Was Who in the Civil War*. 1988.

BAILLIE, HUGH (1890–1966). Born into a newspaper family in Brooklyn, New York, Baillie got his start in the business with the *Los Angeles Record* as a police reporter. In 1912 he began a lifelong affiliation with the United Press. By the outbreak of World War II* he had risen to president of the United Press;

however, this did not deter him from traveling to the combat zones, reporting from the Sicilian campaign in 1943 and the following year from France. In 1945 Baillie was injured in a jeep accident near the city of Aachen. After visiting First Army units near the German city, Baillie was thrown through the windshield of the jeep and was saved only by his steel helmet. He later reported the occupation of Japan. Baillie chronicled some of his wartime exploits in *High Tension* (1959). In addition to his coverage of World War II, Baillie interviewed both Hitler and Mussolini, and reported from the Spanish Civil War* and the Korean War.*

REFERENCE: Robert W. Desmond. *Tides of War*. 1984.

BAKER, GEORGE (1915–1975). Born in Lowell, Massachusetts, at the outbreak of World War II* Baker was a cartoonist for Disney Studios. After enlisting in the army in 1941 he found an outlet for his talent on the staff of *Yank* magazine. His most enduring contribution to the war was his creation of the cartoon character "Sad Sack," which became a weekly strip in the magazine. Baker traveled the world as unofficial ambassador for *Yank*, promoting the magazine wherever it was distributed. Following the war "Sad Sack" went into world syndication and was reproduced in newspapers, books, and even a Paramount movie starring Jerry Lewis in the title role. However, as the war era faded from memory, the comic strip lost its appeal.

REFERENCE: Art Weithas. *Close to Glory*. 1991.

BALDWIN, HANSON W. (1903–1991). Born in Maryland and educated at the U.S. Naval Academy, he began his newspaper career as a police reporter for the *Baltimore Sun*. He joined the *New York Times* in 1929 and eight years later became its military and naval correspondent. In 1943 he received the Pulitzer Prize for a series of articles on his tour of the Solomon Islands and South Pacific war area. Although he was not an official war correspondent he visited many battle areas in his capacity as military correspondent.* In 1943 he visited the North African battlefront and the next year was with the invasion fleet during the Normandy invasion, joining Allied forces in the advance to Paris in July.

REFERENCE: Robert W. Desmond. *Tides of War*. 1984.

BALDWIN, HERBERT (?). He was assigned by the Central News Agency to report the 1912 Balkan War. He started out following Turkish forces. His account was published as *A War Photographer in Thrace—An Account of Personal Experience During the Turco-Balkan War, 1912* in 1913. He apparently chafed under the restrictions imposed on press photographers by the Ottoman armies, which forbade photographing Turkish women and prevented any real action pictures. In one instance he was afforded the opportunity to take battle images during the Turkish retreat following Lula-Burgas but his camera malfunctioned. Baldwin noted that the best way to secure good combat photos was to be on the losing side because the retreat process presented more opportunities

for action shots than an offensive attack, which most often left the photographer stranded behind the front lines.
REFERENCE: Jorge Lewinski. *The Camera at War.* 1978.

BALTERMANS, DMITRI (b. 1912). He was born in Moscow and studied mathematics at the University of Moscow. A self-taught photographer, Baltermans took up the profession of photography while still teaching mathematics in Moscow in 1936. During World War II* he was a photo-reporter for the Red Army and *Izvestia* and *Na Razgrom Varaga* (*To Destroy the Enemy*) newspapers. He covered most of the important battlefronts during the war, including the defense of Moscow and Sebastopol, the Battle of Stalingrad, the occupation of Poland, the liberation of the southern Soviet Union, and the climactic battles for Berlin. Following the war he spent three decades as chief press photographer for *Ogonjok* magazine.
REFERENCES: *Contemporary Photographers.* 1982; Jorge Lewinski. *The Camera at War.* 1978; Daniela Mrazkova and Vladimir Remes, eds. *The Russian War: 1941–1945.* 1975.

BARBER, NOEL (1909–1988). Author and foreign correspondent Noel Barber reported for the *Yorkshire Post* and the *Manchester Daily Express.* He left journalism during World War II* to serve in the RAF. Following the war he worked eight years for the *Continental Daily Mail* before joining the *Daily Mail* in 1953. He was wounded twice while covering combat stories. In 1954 he was wounded in Morocco while covering the North African War, and in 1956 he was again injured while reporting the Hungarian uprising. He went on to a prolific career writing both fiction and nonfiction works.
REFERENCE: Noel Barber. *The Natives Were Friendly.* 1985.

BARBER, WILFRED C. (d. 1935). Will Barber was a sportswriter for the Associated Press and a member of the Paris staff of the *New York Herald* before going to Addis Ababa to report the Ethiopian War.* Shortly after he arrived in Ethiopia he was stricken with malaria and died, the only correspondent to perish in the campaign. In 1936 he was awarded posthumously a Pulitzer Prize for "distinguished service."
REFERENCES: Robert W. Desmond. *Tides of War.* 1984; John Hohenberg. *The Pulitzer Prizes.* 1974.

BARING, MAURICE (1874–1945). Baring was born Mayfair, London. He left Cambridge early to enter the diplomatic service in 1898. After serving at various European postings he joined the *Morning Post* as a war correspondent in 1904 to cover the Russo-Japanese War,* which he reported from the Russian side. He was present at the Battle of Liaoyang. His exploits during the war are chronicled in *With the Russians in Manchuria.* His detailed scholarly dispatches from Manchuria led his editor to call him back to London, where he was promoted to drama critic. However, in 1905 he was again reporting under hostile conditions from Russia, where he remained until 1909.

In 1912 he was hired as the Balkan correspondent by the *Times*, and he was stationed in the Balkans until the outbreak of World War I.* He chronicled his early exploits as a war correspondent in *The Puppet Show of Memory* (1922). During World War I he joined the Intelligence Corps, rising to the rank of major. After demobilization from the military in 1918 he continued his career in journalism and wrote numerous volumes of poetry and articles on Russia.
REFERENCES: *DNB*; Dennis Griffiths, ed. *The Encyclopedia of the British Press.* 1992; Phillip Knightley. *The First Casualty.* 1975.

BARNARD, GEORGE N. (1819–1902). Barnard was a skilled photographer at the outbreak of the American Civil War,* when he became an army photographer under Captain Poe, chief engineer of the Military Division of the Mississippi. Due to the nature of the photographic process, photographers were forced to remain content recording the aftermath of battles rather than the action as it occurred. The complexities of the collodion wet-plate process remained a barrier to actual battle coverage until the twentieth century. In his capacity as the Union's official photographer, Barnard was typically called on to take plates of bridges, railways, and military structures. However, he was responsible for some of the most enduring and earliest images of the conflict. Barnard accompanied William Tecumseh Sherman on his "March to the Sea," and his series of photographs are considered classics. Following the war he remained active in photojournalism.
REFERENCE: Pat Hodgson. *Early War Photographs.* 1974.

BARNES, RALPH W. (1899–1940). He was born in Salem, Oregon, and garnered his first newspaper assignment with the *Brooklyn Daily Eagle* in 1924. Later that year he joined the staff of the *New York Herald Tribune.* He served in the Paris and Rome bureaus before becoming Moscow correspondent in 1931. He went on to report from Berlin (1935–1939) and then London (1939). He was killed when the British bomber on which he was flying was shot down over Yugoslavia in November 1940 while he was covering the Italo-Greek campaign. He was the first American correspondent killed in World War II,* a year before the United States entered the conflict.
REFERENCE: Richard Kluger. *The Paper.* 1986.

BARTHOLOMEW, FRANK HARMON (1898–1985). The Oregon-born Bartholomew began his fifty-year affiliation with the United Press in 1921. Prior to entering the field of journalism he attended the University of Oregon and joined the Student Army Training Corps during World War I.* Already a veteran of several local newspapers, in 1921 he was made Portland bureau manager for the United Press.

Following the Japanese attack on Pearl Harbor in 1941, Bartholomew headed war news coverage for the San Francisco division of the UP before assuming the role of war correspondent accredited to the Pacific theater of operations. In 1943 he covered the New Guinea campaign and then the Aleutian campaign from 1943 to 1944. In 1945 he was with the Tenth Army in Luzon, Philippines, and then with the Thirty-eighth Division. While covering the Okinawa campaign he became the first correspondent to enter Naha, the capital of the island. His last story of World War II* covered the Japanese surrender aboard the USS *Missouri* in Tokyo Bay in 1945.

Bartholomew reported the Bikini atomic bomb tests in 1946 and the Korean War* four years later. In 1954 he covered the last year of the French war in Indochina. One of his greatest scoops occurred when he reported the story of the U.S. Strategic Air Command's "fail safe" strategy for national defense during the Cold War. He retired from journalism in 1972.

REFERENCES: Robert W. Desmond. *Tides of War.* 1984; *New York Times*, March 28, 1985.

BARZINI, LUIGI (1874–1947). The Italian journalist and caricaturist worked for the *Fanfulla* from 1898 to 1900, before joining Italy's largest newspaper, *Corriere della Sera*, for the next quarter century. His name became so linked to the paper that newsboys touted issues by announcing, "Article by Barzini." He also sporadically contributed to the *London Daily Telegraph*. He took his first photographs in China while reporting the Boxer Rebellion* in 1900. He was by most accounts equally adept with both pen and the camera.

In 1904 Barzini traveled to the Far East to cover the Russo-Japanese War.* Most reporters tired quickly of Japanese censorship restrictions and departed, leaving Barzini and two other correspondents to cover the war. As the only correspondent to witness the pivotal Battle of Mukden, he amassed several hundred photos and hundreds of pages of notes and diagrams. His chronicle of the battle is reportedly still studied in Japanese military schools. According to one authority he was the only correspondent to comprehend the significance of the first war in which Asian forces defeated a Western nation. Following the Russo-Japanese War, Barzini covered two Balkan conflicts, the Mexican Revolution, and then World War I.* His son, the writer Luigi Barzini, Jr., stated that Barzini took his last war photograph during the Italo-Turkish War of 1911, capturing the Italian cavalry in action at Tripoli.

Although Barzini covered eight wars as a reporter and became one of the most famous European journalists of his time, he was the rare breed in a time of wars in that he did not glorify the slaughter. He eschewed military decorations from foreign governments, ever cognizant these could be construed as some type of payment for services rendered. He directed several papers, wrote books and articles, and in 1934 was elected to the Italian senate.

REFERENCES: Phillip Knightley. *The First Casualty.* 1975; Nicolas Monti. *Africa Then.* 1987.

BASS, JOHN FOSTER (1866–1931). The largest contingent of war correspondents covering the 1897 Greco-Turkish War* for any one paper was from
the *New York Journal* led by John Foster Bass from Chicago. He had prior
experience on the front lines as the only American press representative covering
the Egyptian-Sudan campaign in 1894 for the *Chicago Record*. Bass later covered the Spanish-American War* for the *New York Evening Post* and then the
subsequent Philippines campaign for the *Journal*.

He left the Philippines in 1901 for a posting in St. Petersburg for the *Chicago
Daily News*. During the Russo-Japanese War* he headed the *Daily News* war
coverage and witnessed the final engagements of the war, including the surrender
at Port Arthur. Following the war he returned to St. Petersburg, remaining until
1915. During World War I* he reported the German capture of Warsaw and
was wounded while covering the Russian front in 1916. After recovering from
his wounds he covered campaigns in France, Italy, and the Balkans. He also
took part in various government missions and covered the 1919 Peace Conference.

REFERENCES: Robert W. Desmond. *The Information Process*. 1978; Robert W. Desmond. *Windows on the World*. 1980.

"BATTLE FOG" POLICY. Prussian military theorist Carl von Clausewitz
described the chaos of swiftly moving events as "the fog of war." One recent
attempt to control press access to the battlefield has been referred to as "battle
fog" policy. This involved blocking foreign correspondents from covering combat zones during the first crucial days of the conflict. This policy was employed
by the Israelis during the invasion of Lebanon. The policy has been heavily
criticized for heightening the suspicion among the foreign press concerning Israel's true goals in the region. Journalists resorted to deception in an attempt to
find unauthorized routes to the war zone. Most sources have concluded that the
"battle fog" policy was counterproductive during the 1982 campaign.

REFERENCE: Derrik Mercer, Geoff Mungham, Kevin Williams. *The Fog of War: The
Media on the Battlefield*. 1987.

BEAN, CHARLES EDWIN WOODROW (1879–1968). Born in Bathurst,
New South Wales, Australia, Bean attended Oxford on scholarship, graduating
with honors in 1902. He was called to the bar the following year. For several
years he practiced law in Australia while writing articles sporadically for several
Sydney newspapers. In 1908 he left law for journalism when he joined the staff
of the *Sydney Morning Herald*. When World War I* broke out he began writing
a "War Notes" column for the *Herald*. In 1915 Bean became the official press
correspondent with the Australian Imperial Force (AIP) beginning with the disastrous 1915 Gallipoli campaign. As a member of the expeditionary force Bean
would remain a citizen but wear an officer's uniform without badges or identifying emblems. The army equipped him with a horse and rations, and he was
made an honorary captain of the mess.

Bean was one of three correspondents to witness the Gallipoli landings on April 25, 1915. Rather than watching the battles from the safety of the warships, Bean shared the danger and rigors of the frontline soldiers. He began keeping a diary with the notion of writing the official history of Australian participation in World War I. Over the next four and a half years Bean filled 120 handwritten diaries. Following Gallipoli, Bean reported the western front in France and began compiling a photographic record of the campaign. In 1942 he completed the last of his six volumes in the series *The Official History of Australia in the War of 1914–1918*.

REFERENCE: Kevin Fewster, ed. *Gallipoli Correspondent: The Frontline Diary of C.E.W. Bean*. 1983.

BEATO, FELICE A. (d. 1903). Born in Venice, Italy, he became a naturalized British citizen during the heyday of the British Empire. He has been described as the first photographer to convincingly record the true face of war. The photographic technology of his time precluded reproducing actual combat scenes. Although identified with his graphic war photographs, Beato was primarily interested in landscape photography. From 1852 to 1865 he was a partner of James Robertson's.* They arrived in the Crimea at about the time Roger Fenton* departed. Their photographic business was known as Robertson, Beato and Company and was active in the Middle and Far East. Their most lasting images document the Crimean War* and the Indian Mutiny.

Beato was also active outside the partnership, taking pictures on his own at the siege of Lucknow and the Opium War. With an interest in architectural photography, Beato was commissioned by the War Office to photograph the destruction of the buildings at Lucknow. In 1860, following the assault on the Taku forts during the Second China War, Beato took pictures of the interior of the forts littered with corpses, some of the most memorable and graphic images of nineteenth-century warfare. According to one witness he asked the soldiers burning the dead not to move them until he had finished his work.

He was one of the first European photographers to work in Japan, where in 1864 he took perhaps his earliest action photographs, capturing the French landing force debarking at Akama Fort. He photographed the Korean War of 1871 and the Wolseley Nile expedition of 1884–1885. Beginning in the late 1880s he worked as a trader and photographer in Burma.

REFERENCES: Christopher Hibbert. *The Dragon Awakes*. 1970; Pat Hodgson. *Early War Photographs*. 1974; Lawrence James. *Crimea, 1854–56*. 1981.

BEATTIE, EDWARD W., JR. (b. 1909). A graduate of Phillips Exeter Academy and Yale University, Beattie was on holiday in Germany in 1931 when he joined the staff of the United Press in Berlin. He covered most of the major events of the developing world war, including the Ethiopian War,* the "China Incident," Dunkirk, and the fall of France in 1940, at which time he was accredited to the British Expeditionary Forces (BEF) in France. He returned to

London in 1940, where he reported the Battle of Britain. He reported the D-Day landings for the U.S. media from London in 1944 and returned to France in September, where he was captured along with two other correspondents and held by the Germans as a prisoner of war. Beattie was held at the Moorsburg prison camp for transfer to a camp at Luckenwalde. He was released when Red Army forces liberated it in April 1945.

REFERENCES: Richard Collier. *Fighting Words: The War Correspondents of World War II.* 1989; Robert W. Desmond. *Tides of War.* 1984.

BEECH, KEYES (1913–1990). Prior to covering the Korean War* for the *Chicago Daily News*, Beech had been a Marine combat correspondent at the Battle of Iwo Jima. He was in his third year covering the Asian scene when Communist forces broke South Korean lines and advanced on Seoul. Beech narrowly escaped to Japan, where he filed his account of the Communist breakthrough. He returned to Korea in July 1950, representing the *London Evening Standard* as well as the *Daily News*. Reporting the Communist victory at Taejon, Beech described it as "the Americans' worst defeat." The ex–Marine sergeant remained throughout the conflict a critic of American war preparedness. In 1951 he was awarded the Pulitzer Prize for his informed dispatches from the Korean war front.

Following the Korean War, Beech reported the American buildup of the Vietnam War* to its conclusion in 1975. Beech, like other members of the war correspondent contingent from World War II and Korea, chided the reporting of the younger journalists in Vietnam as "lopsided" in their criticism of the Saigon regime and the U.S. war effort. Beech worked for the *Chicago Daily News* until its demise in 1978. He worked briefly for the *Los Angeles Times* in Asia before retiring in 1983.

REFERENCES: Michael Emery. *On the Front Lines.* 1995; William Prochnau. *Once upon a Distant War.* 1995; John Toland. *In Mortal Combat: Korea, 1950–1953.* 1991.

BELDEN, JACK (1910–1989). Belden was born in Brooklyn, New York, and educated at Colgate University. Following graduation he traveled to China, where he spent a decade before turning to reporting first with United Press International News Service and then *Time* magazine. He worked as an independent war correspondent in China between 1937 and 1942. During World War II* he accompanied General Joseph Stilwell's forces on the Burma Road, which he chronicled in his book *Retreat with Stilwell*.

In 1943 he covered the British Eighth Army in North Africa and then Italy, where he was wounded. During the 1943 Sicilian campaign he took part in the amphibious landings at Gela and later at Salerno. In 1945 he covered the German breakthrough in the Ardennes.

Belden wrote *Still Time to Die* (1975) and *China Shakes the World* (1949), which was one of the few books published after the war about Communist guerrillas in the civil war era (1946–1949). Following the rise of Mao in China and the concomitant rise of McCarthyism in America few books saw the light of day that portrayed the Communists in a favorable manner. Belden felt that his book *China Shakes the World*, a classic in war reporting from the Communist side of the conflict, was poorly reviewed due to McCarthyism and turned away from writing books. He spent the last twenty years of his life in Paris, where he supported himself driving a taxi. He made one last visit to China in the early 1970s, where journalists with the Nixon entourage reported him in such dire straits that he did not even possess a winter coat. He was apparently ill and was researching a book on Lin Piao.

REFERENCES: Robert Desmond. *Tides of War*. 1984; Peter Rand. *China Hands*. 1995.

BENJAMIN, ANNA NORTHEND (1874–1902). Born in Salem, Massachusetts, Benjamin set new standards for female reporters in an era when men dominated the medium. She represented *Leslie's* during the Spanish-American War,* covering American preparations for the conflict in Tampa and Key West. Although the army attempted to block her access to the hostilities in Cuba, she was one of only two women correspondents to reach the front lines at Santiago, where the combined might of the army and navy defeated Spanish forces.

Benjamin was one of the first reporters to break the mold of the woman correspondent. Prior to the Cuban conflict, female reporters were expected to report from the ''women's angle,'' emphasizing stories concerning their own gender, chance meetings, health problems, and care of the wounded in the hospitals. Her dispatches were devoid of the usual sentimental renderings of the military camp life. She investigated the bad food, unsanitary conditions, and unsuitable uniforms issued to soldiers. Her reports deglamorized the conflict, depicting Theodore Roosevelt's Rough Riders as ''Teddy's Terrors,'' as they stole pigs and chickens and generally terrorized the civilians of Tampa. Following the war she became a popular figure on the lecture circuit, delivering her accounts of adventure as a war correspondent.

Following the Spanish-American War she reported the Philippine insurrection for the *New York Tribune* and *San Francisco Chronicle*. Her reports were usually filed behind her male counterparts' but were deeper and more detailed. Eschewing the telegraph, she usually would mail in her reports. She was in Manila when it came under attack by rebel fire. Benjamin was in Peking for the *Tribune*, where she narrowly escaped the Boxer Rebellion.* August of 1900 found Benjamin reporting the construction of the Trans-Siberian Railroad; she compared the primitive conditions she encountered to the nineteenth-century American West. Besides the *Tribune*, Benjamin's articles appeared in the *Atlantic Monthly* and *Outlook*. She died in France from a brain tumor at the age of twenty-seven.

REFERENCES: Charles B. Brown. ''A Woman's Odyssey: The War Correspondence of Anna Benjamin,'' *Journalism Quarterly*. Fall 1969, pp. 522–530; Charles H. Brown. *The Correspondents' War*. 1967.

BENNETT, JAMES GORDON (1795–1872). Born in Scotland, Bennett emigrated to the United States in 1819. After working as a proofreader and book salesman in Boston, Bennett discovered his bailiwick when he became Washington correspondent for the *New York Enquirer* in 1827. Within eight years he had saved enough to establish his own penny daily, the *New York Herald*. He is credited with many innovations related to war journalism. During the Mexican War* he inaugurated an overland express service to facilitate delivering war news to New York City. In order to accelerate the delivery of news from Europe, he began using fast dispatch boats to intercept New York–bound ships fifty to a hundred miles away from landfall. In the course of the American Civil War* Bennett employed sixty-three different correspondents to report war news. He was the first editor to employ European correspondents, the first to use illustrations for news stories, and the first to hawk papers through newsboys. His son was James Gordon Bennett, Jr.,* the so-called father of yellow journalism.*
REFERENCE: John Hohenberg. *Foreign Correspondence: The Great Reporters and Their Times.* 1964.

BENNETT, JAMES GORDON, JR. (1841–1918). The son of James Gordon Bennett,* founder of the *New York Herald* and the so-called father of yellow journalism,* was born on May 10, 1841. Educated in Europe, he returned to the United States and served in the Union Navy during the American Civil War.* Following the war, after a training stint in each department, he assumed the post of editor in 1866. On his father's retirement the following year, he assumed the directorship of the *Herald*, presiding over it for more than fifty years. His interest in news of the exotic variety led to his sponsorship of various foreign expeditions, most notably Henry Stanley's* search for David Livingstone in Africa. While on assignment Stanley covered the British invasion of Abyssinia. With the rise of competing papers in the 1880s the *Herald* suffered a loss of prestige and circulation. Bennett died of heart disease in France.
REFERENCE: Richard O'Connor. *The Scandalous Mr. Bennett.* 1962.

BENNETT, LOWELL (?). Well suited to the life of a foreign correspondent, by the time Bennett was twenty-one he had already experienced a lifetime of adventures. He had worked his way across the American continent and voyaged to Australia in 1939, where he joined the Royal Australian Air Force. He had to resign when it was revealed he was an American citizen. Next, he went to England and joined an international brigade organized by Kermit Roosevelt to fight for Finland in the Russo-Finnish War. However, by the time the young sergeant reached the front the fighting had ceased.

Prior to the capitulation of France he joined the French Foreign Legion but again resigned when he learned that Americans, as neutrals, were prohibited from serving in combat units. He next joined the American Volunteer Ambulance Corps and was captured by the Germans shortly before the French surrendered. He was imprisoned in a concentration camp for five months. Following his release he made his way to England, where he joined the Free French Army. In 1940 he served in an ambulance corps during the London blitz and parachuted with the French resistance until once again U.S. citizenship hastened his departure.

In July 1941 he joined the International News Service as correspondent in London. In 1943 he reported the entire Tunisian campaign and was one of three correspondents who flew with paratroopers who captured an airfield near the Algerian-Tunisian border. While accompanying a U.S. Air Force bombing run over Berlin in December 1943, his aircraft was disabled by a German interceptor plane and he was forced to bail out at a four-mile altitude. He was taken prisoner again but eventually escaped when he was being transferred between vehicles. However, it was not long before he was recaptured and held in Stalag Luft No. 1 in Pomerania. In the spring of 1945 he was freed by the advancing Allied armies. Bennett returned to the United States following the end of the war in Europe.
REFERENCE: Robert W. Desmond. *Tides of War.* 1984.

BENSON, EUGENE (1839–1908). Benson made the switch from struggling art student to war artist at the outbreak of the American Civil War.* His renderings of the attack on Fort Sumter were published in *Frank Leslie's Illustrated Newspaper*. He continued to work for the paper until leaving journalism to continue his art studies in Europe.
REFERENCE: Stewart Sifakis. *Who Was Who in the Civil War.* 1988.

BENTLEY, HENRY (?). Bentley covered Union forces in the American Civil War* for the *Philadelphia Inquirer*. He witnessed the Battle of Shiloh, where he was captured. He escaped and returned to Philadelphia with his eyewitness account of the battle from behind Confederate lines. He accompanied Burnside's Roanoke Island expedition (1862), and his account was the first published of the Battle of Roanoke Island.
REFERENCE: J. Cutler Andrews. *The North Reports the Civil War.* 1955.

BERNSTEIN, WALTER (b. 1919). Born in Brooklyn, New York, he graduated from Dartmouth College, where he edited the college newspaper and contributed articles to the *New Yorker*. With the outbreak of World War II* he joined the army, transferring to *Yank* magazine from the Eighth Infantry in 1942. Bernstein reported from army training camps and later covered the Italian campaign. In 1944 he interviewed Yugoslavian leader Tito. Following the war he became a successful screenwriter and director of such films as *Fail Safe, The Molly Maguires, Yanks*, and many others. He chronicled his experiences as a blacklisted writer during the 1950s in the movie *The Front*.
REFERENCE: Art Weithas. *Close to Glory.* 1991.

BERRY, IAN (b. 1934). Born in Preston, Lancashire, England, he entered the ranks of photojournalism as press photographer for the *Daily Mail* and later for *Drum* magazine, both based in Johannesburg, South Africa. He covered his first conflict in 1960 when he photographed the massacre of protestors in Sharpeville for *Drum*; however, because of political censorship these pictures were never published. Between 1960 and 1964 Berry made at least six trips to the Congo to cover the conflict there. He covered skirmishes between the Katangan insurgents and mercenaries at Leopoldville, Elizabethville, and the most spectacular fight of the war when Belgian paratroopers stormed the rebel stronghold at Stanleyville. He left war photojournalism after his years in Africa, shifting to more tranquil settings for his subject material as a freelancer and photographer for Magnum Photos.
REFERENCES: *Contemporary Photographers.* 1982; Jorge Lewinski. *The Camera at War.* 1978.

BEWLEY, CYRIL (1904–1944). Born in Rotherham, England, he covered World War II* for the *Sheffield Telegraph and Star.* Reporting preparations on the British Isles for a German invasion in 1939, he was one of the first reporters from a provincial paper to be accorded accreditation with the Northern Command. He covered the campaign in Africa (1943) before being transferred to Italy to follow the Fifth and Eighth Armies. In May 1944, Bewley was on his way to cover the capture of Cassino with correspondent Roderick MacDonald when one of them stepped on a land mine, killing both men.
REFERENCES: Robert W. Desmond. *Tides of War.* 1984; Dennis Griffiths, ed. *The Encyclopedia of the British Press.* 1992.

BICKHAM, WILLIAM DENISON (1827–1894). He reported the Union side of the American Civil War* for the *Cincinnati Commercial.* Almost immediately upon his arrival in the camp of the newly renamed Army of the Cumberland he became the favorite of fellow Ohioan Major General William S. Rosecrans. Partisan politics came into play when the staunchly Republican Rosecrans designated Bickham his volunteer aide-de-camp with the rank of captain and the reporter wrote complimentary articles about the general. Bickham, sometimes referred to as "Rosecrans' Boswell," came under criticism from rank-and-file soldiers in the field for what seemed inflated accounts of Rosecrans' successes.

Bickham covered the Battle of Rich Mountain (July 1861) and the Seven Days' Battles. He witnessed the Battle of Murfreesboro (1862) and in 1863 published his account of it in *Rosecrans Campaign.* In 1863 he cut short his career as a war reporter to begin his new paper, the *Dayton Journal.*
REFERENCES: J. Cutler Andrews. *The North Reports the Civil War.* 1955; Stewart Sifakis. *Who Was Who in the Civil War.* 1988.

BICYCLES. Bicycles were sometimes used by correspondents on campaign during the Victorian era. Frederic Villiers* was one of the most notable boosters

of this vehicle and used one in the Sudan. A prototype of a bike for correspondents was developed which one report described as being sturdy and noted that "upon the handlebar is to be attached a typewriter," which the rider could use to record impressions of the battlefront in his path. There are no reports of anyone having put this contraption to use. During the 1912 Balkan War photographer-correspondent Herbert Baldwin* of the Central News Agency suggested that the bicycle was a better mode of transportation than the horse.
REFERENCE: Pat Hodgson. *The War Illustrators.* 1977.

BIDDLE, GEORGE (1885–1973). During World War II,* at the age of fifty-eight, he was recruited as an artist-correspondent by *Life* magazine from the army's short-lived art unit. He was born into a socially well-connected Philadelphia family and knew President Roosevelt by his first name from their days together at Harvard. During the Depression he collaborated with Roosevelt on the establishment of the Federal Art Project under the Works Progress Administration. He covered the North African and Italian campaigns from 1943 to 1944. His sketches and paintings strove to capture the horrors of war rather than upbeat and life-affirming imagery.
REFERENCE: Frederick Voss. *Reporting the War.* 1994.

BIGART, HOMER (1907–1991). Though he was handicapped by a slow writing style and a bad stutter, his career as a newspaper reporter spanned forty years. For half of this period (1943–1963) he acted predominantly as a war correspondent, first for the *Herald Tribune* (1927–1955), where he won two Pulitzer Prizes, and then the *New York Times* (1955–1972).

Born in Hawley, Pennsylvania, he enrolled in the New York University School of Journalism before dropping out in 1929 to work at the *Herald Tribune* full-time. Promoted to war correspondent in 1942, he covered the London blitz, the bombing of Germany, and campaigns in North Africa, Italy, and southern France. Following V-E Day he covered the final months of the Pacific theater in the Philippines, Guam, and Japan, for which he won his first Pulitzer. He was one of the earliest Americans to enter Hiroshima after the nuclear bomb was dropped.

With the end of the war Bigart spent the remainder of the 1940s reporting from Prague and Warsaw (1946), Palestine (1946–1947), and in 1948 Greece, Yugoslavia, and Hungary. In 1951 he won his second Pulitzer while covering the Korean War,* leading *Newsweek* to laud him as "the best war correspondent of an embattled generation." In the years to come his controversial reportage would see him summarily evicted from a host of countries, including Hungary, Egypt, Syria, Lebanon, Jordan, Saudi Arabia, Oman, and Vietnam.

Recognizing that the *Herald Tribune* was on the decline and only a few years from expiration, he jumped ship to the *New York Times*, but not without regrets. Known for his memorable prose style, he covered World War II, the Greek

Civil War, the Korean War,* and finally the Vietnam War* as a member of the Saigon press corps.
REFERENCES: Richard Kluger. *The Paper: The Life and Death of the New York Herald Tribune.* 1986; Betsy Wade, ed. *Forward Positions: The War Correspondence of Homer Bigart.* 1992.

BIGELOW, POULTNEY (1856–1954). The son of diplomat John Bigelow, Poultney Bigelow was educated in Europe and was a classmate of Kaiser Wilhelm of Germany. He was hired by the *New York Herald* and the *London Times* to cover the Spanish-American War,* but lost his credentials to travel with the army to Cuba when he criticized the quality of American officers and the efficiency of the army organization in an article in the May 28 *Harper's Weekly*. Richard Harding Davis* joined the chorus of outrage directed at the Englishman, although in private he shared Bigelow's opinions concerning the preparedness of the army.
REFERENCE: Charles H. Brown. *The Correspondents' War.* 1967.

BILLMAN, HOWBERT (?). Billman reported the Spanish-American War* for the *Chicago Record*. Unlike many of his colleagues he witnessed much of the conflict firsthand. He was present at the five-hour battle for Cusco Hill, which gave American forces the control of Guantanamo Bay. Billman also covered the El Caney operation, one of the most difficult engagements of the war, and the Spanish surrender following the capitulation of Santiago.
REFERENCE: Charles H. Brown. *The Correspondents' War.* 1967.

BLAIR, ERIC ARTHUR (1903–1950). Better known as the author George Orwell, Blair was born at Motihari, Bengal. Following his education he departed from tradition by turning away from the university to join the Imperial Police in Burma for a five-year stint. Following this experience he traveled around Europe on a shoestring budget, as chronicled in his book *Down and Out in Paris and London* (1933).

His work was already leaning toward an anticapitalist philosophy when he volunteered for the Republican army in the Spanish Civil War.* Orwell went to Spain as a freelance reporter but ended up fighting in Barcelona. Early on he noted that totalitarianism was present on both sides of the battlefield, but the *New Statesman* refused to print his reports. He enlisted in the Twenty-ninth POUM, also known as the Rovira Division. Six months later he was severely wounded when shot through the neck by a sniper's bullet. Orwell was told he would never get his voice back, but several months later his voice suddenly returned. Returning to writing in the following months, he produced work characterized by anti-Stalinist rhetoric. His book *Homage to Catalonia* recounts his six months at war and was seen as a tough sell by his publisher because of its then unpopular political stance. When he died in 1950, less than a thousand copies had been sold. Orwell is best remembered for his apocalyptic vision of

the future in *Nineteen Eighty Four* (1949). He also wrote *The Road to Wigan Pier* (1937), *The Lion and the Unicorn* (1941), and *Animal Farm* (1945).
REFERENCES: *DNB*, 1941–1950; Phillip Knightley. *The First Casualty*. 1975; Peter Wyden. *The Passionate War*. 1983.

BLUNDEY, DAVID (1945–1989). Born in London, England, he began his newspaper career with the *Burnley Star* in 1967, and then later the *Evening Post*, before beginning a sixteen-year stint with the *Sunday Times* in 1970. He served as the paper's Middle East correspondent from 1981 to 1986, when he reported the carnage in Beirut, the massacres in the Palestinian refugee camps, and the American retaliatory raids on Libya. He joined the recently created *Sunday Correspondent* in 1989 as its Washington correspondent and found his next assignment in Central America. On November 17, 1989, Blundey was mortally wounded while covering warfare in San Salvador.
REFERENCE: Dennis Griffiths, ed. *The Encyclopedia of the British Press*. 1992.

BODMAN, ALBERT (?). Bodman covered the 1863 Vicksburg campaign for the *Chicago Tribune* and was aboard the Union gunboat-ram *Queen of the West* when it was scuttled after an encounter with a Confederate battery. Of the three correspondents on board the vessel only Finley Anderson* was captured. Bodman was one of the first on the Union side to enter Vicksburg following its capitulation on July 3. He also covered the Chattanooga campaign.
REFERENCE: J. Cutler Andrews. *The North Reports the Civil War*. 1955.

BOER WAR. The Boer War, variously referred to as the Second Boer War or South African War, was the most widely reported British war up to the twentieth century, with as many as three hundred correspondents spending time in the field. The two Boer republics of South Africa declared war on Great Britain on October 11, 1899, inaugurating the longest and bloodiest conflict fought by British forces between 1815 and World War I. The war began when Boers laid siege to the cities of Mafeking,* Kimberly, and Ladysmith.*

The best-represented British press organizations were the *Times* and Reuters.* Well prepared, with correspondents already in South Africa, Reuters would supply close to one hundred stringers* and staff during the two-and-a-half-year conflict, with two fatalities. Among the best-known correspondents for the news agency were H. A. Gwynne,* J. de Villiers Roos,* William Hay Mackay, and Roderick Jones.* Reuters had a reputation for fairness that contributed to its accessibility to both sides of the war.

Correspondents for the *Times* included Lionel James,* Angus Hamilton, Percival Landon,* and Bron Herbert. While few journalists from outside Great Britain reported the war, other British papers sent reporters soon after the outbreak of hostilities. The *Daily Mail* organized a special war service pool which included George Warrington Steevens,* Charles E. Hands,* Frederick Slater Collett, Edgar Wallace,* and Americans Richard Harding Davis* and Julian

Ralph.* Bennet Burleigh* and Percy S. Bullen represented the *Daily Telegraph*, and the *Morning Post* sent Winston Churchill* and Edward Frederick Knight,* who would lose his right arm to a dumdum bullet during the Modder River campaign.

Other British war veterans of the press included Melton Prior* for the *Illustrated London News*, Frederic Villiers* and Harry H. S. Pearse* for the *Daily News*, Henry W. Nevinson* and George Lynch* for the *Daily Chronicle*, John Black Atkins* for the *Manchester Guardian*, and William T. Maud* of the *Graphic*. In addition to the British press corps noted authors Rudyard Kipling* and Arthur Conan Doyle* spent stints covering the brutal war. In addition to the print journalists numerous photographers were on hand to report the conflict. The London illustrated papers reportedly existed almost solely on Boer War photographs. One of the distinguishing features of this war was the prevalence of photographers led by the teams from the *Daily Mail* and the *Black and White*. The *Black and White* sent fifteen artists, correspondents, and cameramen, resulting in increased circulation of more than a half million, while the *Mail* published illustrated supplements to the paper bound up and sold as *With the Flag in Pretoria*. Also present were the first cameramen to record moving pictures of a war for the British public. Early newsreels* from the Biograph Company depict General Redvers Buller's troops leaving Southhampton for war, as well as British Red Cross crews coming under fire on the South African veldt, although this was discovered to have been fabricated on a studio back lot safe in Great Britain.

Fifteen correspondents were killed during the war and are commemorated by a plaque in the crypt of St. Paul's Cathedral in London. An additional thirty-seven were wounded and several taken prisoner. The only non-British correspondent to perish in the conflict was Colonel De Villebois-Mareuil of the Paris-based *Liberté*.
REFERENCES: Byron Farwell. *The Great Anglo-Boer War*. 1976; Thomas Pakenham. *The Boer War*. 1979; Raymond Sibbald. *The War Correspondents: The Boer War*. 1993; Frederic William Unger.* *With Bobs and Kruger: Experiences and Observations of an American War Correspondent in the Field with Both Armies*. 1901.

BOER WAR SIEGE NEWSPAPERS. During the siege of Ladysmith,* Natal, in December 1899 several newspapers were published by journalists attempting to relieve the monotony of the siege. These included the *Ladysmith Bombshell* and *Ladysmith Lyre*. The *Mafeking Mail* was supervised by Baden-Powell during the siege of Mafeking,* Cape Province, from November 1, 1899 to June 15, 1900. As the siege wore on newsprint ran out, and the remaining issues were printed on ledger paper.
REFERENCE: Byron Farwell. *The Great Anglo-Boer War*. 1976.

BOGART, ROBERT D. (b. 1842?). He reported the Modoc War for the *San Francisco Chronicle* after a stint in the U.S. Navy and working on the staff of the *New York Sun*. Of the four correspondents who reported the conflict, he reportedly produced the least accurate work, usually basing his accounts on secondhand information.

The New Jersey–born Bogart had been in California for less than a year when the Modoc War broke out. He had edited a newspaper in Hoboken, New Jersey, and had been a paymaster in the navy before his western exploits. On March 5, 1873, he was replaced in the field by his paper for making irresponsible charges in an attempt to stir up controversy over the peace negotiations. Soon after, he was arrested by the navy and court-martialed for allegedly embezzling while he was employed as paymaster in 1869. Sentenced to two years' imprisonment, he escaped from a navy ship. It is unknown what transpired afterward. His only paper trail consists of several articles he wrote in 1878 for the *San Francisco Daily Stock* and the *Boston Commercial Bulletin*.
REFERENCE: Oliver Knight. *Following the Indian Wars*. 1960.

BOHEMIAN BRIGADE. The term "Bohemian Brigade" was invoked half seriously by members of the Northern press to describe themselves during the American Civil War.* Many of them reveled in a "nomadic, careless, half-literary" lifestyle. In the late 1850s and early 1860s the Bohemian movement was transported to America from Paris. So-called Bohemians met in coffeehouses to discuss art and politics and drink wine. Many of the era's newspaper reporters and artists of the illustrated weeklies were drawn to spots such as Pfaff's Café in New York where they could rub shoulders with prominent literary figures like Walt Whitman and William Dean Howells. By the time of the Civil War the term was used in reference to the Northern war reporters, particularly from New York City. Correspondent Junius Browne* defined a Bohemian as a person "of aesthetic and luxurious tastes, born out of place, and in opposition to his circumstances."
REFERENCES: Joseph J. Mathews. *Reporting the Wars*. 1957; Louis M. Starr. *Bohemian Brigade*. 1954.

BOHROD, AARON (1907–1992). He was invited to join the army's art unit in 1943. At that time he was artist in residence at Southern Illinois University. Bohrod was trained at the Art Institute of Chicago and the Art Students League in New York City. Assigned to the Pacific theater, he accompanied the first wave of American forces during the amphibious assault at Rendova. While in the field he made rough sketches and took photographs which ultimately would be used to produce a series of paintings chronicling the Rendova campaign.

Soon after, Congress disbanded the army art unit, but in late 1943 he was a war artist for *Life* magazine. Bohrod was transferred to the European war in May 1944. He landed at Normandy's Omaha Beach shortly after the initial beachhead was gained. Too late to sketch any fighting, he captured massive movement of arms and equipment onto the French shores. He followed American forces into Germany and sketched the last days of the war. His portrait,

with a backdrop of rubble and debris, appeared on the cover of *Life* on April 30, 1945.
REFERENCE: Frederick S. Voss. *Reporting the War*. 1994.

BONSAL, STEPHEN (1865–1951). Born in Baltimore, Maryland, he was a student in Germany before entering journalism in 1885, when he accompanied the Bulgarian army during the Bulgarian-Serbian War. Following the war he returned to the United States to continue his journalism career. He returned to Europe in 1887 as a representative of the *World* and then the *New York Herald*. In 1890 he established his reputation with several articles repudiating accusations of Turkish atrocities in Macedonia. The next year he reported social upheaval in Africa, which is chronicled in his book *Morocco As It Is*. He served in the Foreign Service from 1893 to 1897 in a variety of Asian postings and also reported the Sino-Japanese War of 1894–1895.

In 1897, prior to American involvement in Cuba, Bonsal took a fact-finding tour of the island, where he found hundreds of thousands of Cubans forced from their homes by Weyler's "depopulation by proclamation program" and on the brink of mass starvation. The looming tragedy was chronicled the following year in his book *The Real Condition of Cuba Today*.

With the outbreak of hostilities, Bonsal headed for the action as a member of *McClure's Magazine*. He witnessed the Battle of El Caney and the appalling treatment of the wounded at Siboney. In August 1898 Bonsal transferred to the Philippines to cover the outbreak of the insurrection and subsequent political developments for the *New York Herald*.

In 1900 Bonsal remained in the Far East, where he covered the Boxer Rebellion* and four years later the Russo-Japanese War* from the Japanese side. Prior to World War I* he reported the Balkan Wars and was in Mexico City when President Diaz was forced out of office. Later he served as interpreter for President Woodrow Wilson during the 1919 Versailles Peace Conference. Among his books are *The Real Condition of Cuba* (1897), *The Fight for Santiago* (1899), *Heyday in a Vanished World* (1937), and *Unfinished Business, Paris-Versailles, 1919* which garnered him a Pulitzer Prize for history in 1945.
REFERENCES: Charles H. Brown. *The Correspondent's War*. 1967; Gerald W. Johnson, Frank R. Kent, H. L. Mencken, and Hamilton Owens. *The Sunpapers of Baltimore, 1837–1937*. 1937.

BOURCHIER, JAMES DAVID (1850–1920). Born in Limerick County, Ireland, he was educated at Trinity College, Dublin, and King's College, Cambridge. After ten years as a teacher at Eton and afflicted with increasing deafness he joined the staff of the *Times* in 1892. He had been in Sofia, Bulgaria, since 1888 seeking medical treatment for his hearing loss before being assigned to head up the Sofia bureau for the *Times*, a post he would hold until World War I.* With a reputation as an authority on Balkan affairs he was often called on to serve as an intermediary between Cretan freedom fighters and Greek authorities.

In 1903 he was present when Bulgarian peasants in Macedonia attempted to overthrow the Ottoman rulers. Bourchier, sympathetic to the patriots, publicized Turkish atrocities. In 1915, he was unprepared for news that Bulgaria had chosen to align itself with Austria-Hungary and Germany. Since he was supposedly an expert on the region, his reports lost much of their credibility after this unforeseen turn of events. His paper lost faith in his reporting and Bourchier moved to neighboring Rumania, where he remained until 1917. When the country was overrun by the Central Powers Bourchier relocated first to Odessa and then to Petrograd. While in Russia he covered the October Revolution and was granted rare interviews with Lenin and Trotsky. He returned to England in 1918 and spent the remainder of his life as an unofficial spokesman for Bulgaria and other Balkan states. His affinity for the region led to his 1920 appointment as Bulgaria's consul general in London. Before assuming this position he made a final visit to Bulgaria. He died in Sofia shortly after his arrival and was buried with high honors.

REFERENCES: Robert W. Desmond. *Windows on the World.* 1980; DNB. 1912–1921.

BOURKE-WHITE, MARGARET (1906–1971). One of the greatest photojournalists of the twentieth century, Bourke-White joined the staff of *Life* at its inception in 1935. She gained early prominence for photo stories on daily life in quintessentially American small towns. Her first wartime assignment became her first scoop, or so it seemed, when she found herself the only photojournalist in Russia on June 22, 1941, when Nazi troops invaded the Soviet Union. Unfortunately, Russian authorities had issued an edict forbidding any photos of the invasion under penalty of death. Instead, Bourke-White opted for the safety of her suite as the world plunged further into chaos.

However, only days after the invasion she was in position atop the American embassy to record raids by the Luftwaffe. Among her memorable pictures in 1941 was a spread of Joseph Stalin, the first American photographer to be granted such access. Her tenure in Russia resulted in many classic war photos.

Margaret often had to overcome discrimination by the military brass in order to gain permission to accompany the troops into battle. She covered the North African campaign and was on board a ship torpedoed by a U-boat; this yielded her another photo scoop, on the hazards of the war at sea. On January 22, 1943, she became the first woman to fly on an American combat mission. Among the most lasting images of World War II* are her photographs of the liberation of the German concentration camps.

While covering the Korean War* she noticed the first symptoms of Parkinson's disease, which effectively ended her career as a war correspondent. In addition to her other work she went on to write six books.

REFERENCES: Julia Edwards. *Women of the World.* 1988; Frederick Voss. *Reporting the War.* 1994.

BOXER REBELLION. Following the Japanese victory over China in the Sino-Japanese War of 1894–1895, secret societies began forming in China in response to a mounting antiforeigner sentiment. Some of these societies banded together into a league whose name, translated into English, meant "Fists of Righteous Harmony," or "Boxers," and whose main goal was to drive out foreigners. After several riots and violent attacks on foreign residents the Chinese government was called on to suppress the Boxers. When it failed to adequately respond a coalition of eight governments sent forces into China between June and August 1900.

As eighteen thousand British, French, U.S., Japanese, Russian, and German troops assisted various besieged foreign legations, war correspondents began flocking to China. Among them were numerous correspondents who had been following the Philippine insurrection, including Frederick Palmer,* Stephen Bonsal,* Oscar King Davis,* Robert M. Collins,* David Morris, and Martin Egan,* in addition to Ralph D. Paine* and Charles E. Kloeber. Other correspondents, including Dr. Robert Coltman,* Thomas F. Millard,* and Wilmott Harsant Lewis,* had prior China experience. Joseph Medill Patterson,* George Lynch,* Dr. Emile Joseph Dillon,* and Dr. George Morrison* also contributed outstanding firsthand accounts of the conflict.

Foreign correspondents were in abundance as well during this multinational operation. Gaston Chadbourne and Louis Marie Julien Viaud,* better known as the novelist Pierre Loti,* represented French papers, and Luigi Barzini* was in China for the Milan-based *Corriere della Sera*.

Those reporting the Boxer campaign faced more than their share of logistical hardships. Transportation and communication activities were impeded by the tremendous distances and cost of sending dispatches from China to Europe by way of Siberia. Rates varied between $1.62 and $1.72 per word for dispatches bound for London or New York.
REFERENCES: Robert W. Desmond. *The Information Process*. 1978; Peter Fleming. *The Siege at Peking*. 1959; Henry Keown-Boyd. *Boxer Rebellion*. 1995; Richard O'Connor. *The Spirit Soldiers*. 1973.

BOYLE, FREDERICK (b. 1841). Boyle covered the 1868 Abyssinian War and the 1873 Ashanti campaign for the *Daily Telegraph*. He witnessed the victorious British entry into the fortress at Essaman. Four years later he reported the Russo-Turkish War* for the *Standard*, but was expelled for violating military security in one of his dispatches, as he chronicled in his 1877 book, *Narrative of an Expelled Correspondent*. He also wrote *Through Fanteeland to Commmassie: A Diary of the Ashantee Campaigns in Africa* (1874).
REFERENCE: Robert Wilkinson-Latham. *From Our Special Correspondent*. 1979.

BRACKENBURY, CHARLES BOOTH (1831–1900). London born, he graduated from the Royal Military Academy at Woolwich in 1847 and was commissioned as a lieutenant in the royal artillery. After service in the Crimean

War* he was promoted to captain and became an instructor at his alma mater. In 1866 he was hired as a war correspondent by the *Times*. While accompanying the Austrian army during the Austro-Prussian War* he witnessed the Battle of Königgrätz. He also reported the Franco-Prussian War* and was with Prince Frederick Charles during the Le Mans campaign. He covered the Russo-Turkish War* in 1877, crossing into the Balkans with General Gourko's forces.

Following his years as a war reporter he resumed his military career, eventually rising to colonel in the army and later to director of the artillery college at Woolwich in 1899. He died of a heart attack in June 1900. He published a variety of works on warfare and tactics.
REFERENCE: *DNB*, 245–246.

BRADY, MATHEW B. (1823–1896). The son of Irish immigrants, Brady was born in Warren County, New York. He was named after Matthew in the Bible and added the B. to his name merely to lengthen it—it meant nothing. He came to photography after a short stint as a itinerant portrait painter. In 1841, his art teacher introduced him to Samuel Morse, inventor of the telegraph and an early practitioner of daguerreotype* photography. In 1844 Brady opened his first studio, Brady's Daguerrian Miniature Gallery, embarking on his photographic career. An innovator, entrepreneur, and tireless self-promoter, he created daguerreotype portraits of the most celebrated Americans of the mid-nineteenth century that led to fame and medals and were widely exhibited.

In 1854 he shifted from daguerreotypes to the wet-plate process. Alexander Gardner* joined him two years later as the manager of his Washington studio, and Brady began to specialize in life-size portraits when Gardner introduced him to enlarging techniques. Photographs from the Brady studio were widely used for engravings by illustrated publications such as *Harper's Weekly* and *Frank Leslie's Illustrated Newspaper*. In 1860 he took the first of eventually thirty-five photographs of Lincoln. Lincoln, in part, attributed his election to that first picture, noting that "Brady and the Cooper Union speech made me President."

With the outbreak of the American Civil War* Brady turned from social portraiture to war photography* when he obtained official permission to follow the campaigns. Brady's motivations for recording the war were both commercial and historical. Maintaining his staff of from ten to twenty photographers would ultimately lead to his financial ruin. During the war he supported four field units which covered thirty-five bases of operation in three states. He was able to outfit his traveling darkrooms with large-format cameras and a profusion of equipment and supplies on an open expense account. In addition he maintained the practice of purchasing the work of other battlefield photographers. Since he was a man of business rather than action, there persists much controversy as to whether Brady himself spent much time at the front lines. His collection of war photographs, however, offers the most complete documentation of any nineteenth-century war. In the early months of the conflict all photographs taken by his employees carried the attribution "from a photograph of Brady."

Only a portion of the photographs attributed to Brady were actually his work, since he spent time in Washington overseeing his extensive network. Following the war his associate Gardner finally received credit for his contributions. But, it is clear that Brady was on hand for the initial Union debacle at Bull Run, Chancellorsville, and the aftermath of Gettysburg and Antietam. With eyesight failing he took great risks to cover the Battles of Fredericksburg and Petersburg.

Following Gardner's exit in 1862 and the financial burdens of his wartime project, Brady slowly inched toward financial ruin. When his Washington studio went out of business he attempted to sell his photographic collection to Congress for $100,000. By this time the value of his prints had plummeted as the public interest in the war declined. Faced with public and congressional indifference and his failing eyesight, he put his work into storage, but when he was unable to pay his storage bill the priceless images were sold at auction to clear his debt. The War Department purchased the collection for $2,840, the price of the debt, and Brady remained uncompensated.

Brady's great achievement was completing a comprehensive visual record of the war. Ultimately he was forced into bankruptcy in both New York and Washington between 1868 and 1873. However, in 1874 he received $25,000 from the War Department, as his collection began to deteriorate in storage. In the 1880s he suffered from a cornucopia of maladies including rheumatism, blindness, and injuries from a carriage accident. His health crisis was augmented by depression and alcoholism. He died in the paupers' ward of a New York hospital from kidney disease and assorted ailments on January 15, 1896. While much of his priceless work is catalogued in the National Archives and the Library of Congress, many prints are still missing.

REFERENCES: James D. Horan. *Mathew Brady: Historian with a Camera*. 1955; Jorge Lewinski. *The Camera at War*. 1978; Roy Meredith. *Mathew Brady's Portrait of an Era*. 1982.

BRIGHAM, CHARLES D. (b. 1819). Born and raised in upper New York State, Brigham had been the editor of the *Troy Whig* prior to the American Civil War.* He was the Charleston correspondent for the *New York Tribune* during parts of 1860 and 1861 reporting the opening salvos of the Civil War. Northern reporters were subject to tar and feathering or worse if caught by local vigilance committees. In February 1861 he was arrested by the Charleston police and given an ultimatum to leave town. Following his departure, the *Tribune* replaced him with pairs of correspondents, which the paper rotated periodically. Southern newspaper coverage was considered so dangerous for Northern reporters that the *Tribune* usually held one man in reserve in case his colleague was arrested. Brigham was assigned to edit their dispatches to make their letters appear the work of one individual. Most Southern newspapers and Northern competitors refused to believe the newspaper had correspondents in Charleston and accused the *Tribune* of publishing synthetic correspondence fabricated at the home desk.

Following his prewar experiences in the South he covered the western theater of operations. In 1862 Brigham reported one of the major stories of the war in a twenty-two-page telegram to the *Tribune* recounting the battle of the ironclads *Monitor* and *Merrimac* at Hampton Roads. Brigham later reported the 1863 Chattanooga campaign and was rebuked by General Hooker for his criticism of his actions during the operation; Hooker went as far as requesting Secretary Edwin Stanton to expel Brigham from the field. In 1864 Brigham left the *Tribune* to join the *Pittsburgh Commercial* as managing editor.

REFERENCES: J. Cutler Andrews. *The North Reports the Civil War.* 1955; Louis M. Starr. *Bohemian Brigade.* 1954.

BRODIE, HOWARD (b. 1915). Born in Oakland, California, and educated at various art schools, Brodie was formerly a staff artist for the *San Francisco Chronicle* before becoming the best-known artist for *Yank** magazine. In addition to *Yank*, Brodie served as staff artist for *Life, Collier's*, the Associated Press, and CBS News. As sketch artist for *Yank* magazine during World War II* Brodie was teamed with writer Mack Morriss.* Together they covered the war in New Georgia and Guadalcanal in the Pacific theater, and in the European theater of operations they covered the Huertgen Forest Battle and the Ardennes breakthrough during the Battle of the Bulge. He was awarded the Bronze Star for his coverage of the war. As sketch artist he went on to cover the Korean* and Vietnam Wars.* His war drawings were collected in *Howard Brodie's War Drawings* in 1963. The dean of CBS courtroom artists, Brodie sketched some of the most notorious trials of the twentieth century, including those of Jack Ruby, James Earl Ray, Sirhan Sirhan, My Lai murderer William Calley, Charles Manson, and the Chicago Seven; he also sketched the Watergate hearings.

REFERENCE: Art Weithas. *Close to Glory.* 1991.

BROUN, HEYWOOD (1888–1939). The seemingly perpetually disheveled Broun, at six foot four and 250 pounds, was regarded as one of the most respected journalists of his era. He was originally a drama critic, but his claustrophobia forced him to give up the theater for the outdoors. Born in Brooklyn, New York, he was educated in private schools and then Harvard. He left college after his second year to work for the *New York Morning Telegraph*, covering sporting events. In 1911 he left the penurious *Telegraph* over a rejected pay raise and joined the *Tribune* for even less money.

With the outbreak of war in Europe, in 1917 Broun accompanied General Pershing's Allied Expeditionary Forces to France. On October 19, Frederick Palmer* chided him for being absent without leave, having left the monotony of the front lines for Paris along with other correspondents. Broun breached military censorship on several occasions and often expressed contempt for the news reporting restrictions set by the military. His credentials were revoked over his critical pieces on the army and Pershing, of whom he wrote that American soldiers would never call the imperious general "Papa." But his short stint in Europe as a war correspondent resulted in two books the following year, *The A.E.F.: With General Pershing and the American Forces* and *Our Army at the Front.* He went on to work for a succession of newspapers and wrote eleven more books, but never covered another war.

REFERENCES: Emmet Crozier. *American Reporters on the Western Front, 1914–18.* 1959. Richard O'Connor. *Heywood Broun: A Biography.* 1975.

BROWN, CECIL (1907–1987). Brown was born in New Brighton, Pennsylvania, and educated at Western Reserve University and Ohio State University. After a short life at sea and stints with various newspapers he became a freelance writer in Europe. On the strength of his freelance articles he was hired by the International News Service to cover Paris and Rome in 1931.

In 1940 CBS hired Brown to report German and Italian developments that could draw the United States into the rapidly developing conflict. The following year he was expelled from Italy by Fascist officials. Brown next reported the war from Belgrade, Yugoslavia, where he reported the advance of Nazi forces, barely escaping himself. He went on to report the war from Turkey, Syria, and Cairo and transmitted news of the German invasion of Crete for CBS. He was awarded the Distinguished Service Award for his coverage of the escape of Greece's King George from German forces. He continued to report from North Africa before being transferred to Singapore at the end of 1941. He was aboard the British battleship *Repulse* when it was torpedoed during a Japanese bomber attack on December 10, 1941. He was among the two thousand survivors plucked from the water several hours later. Brown received a National Headliners' Club award for his CBS broadcast of the sinking.

Shortly after, Brown was banned from broadcasting news stories from Singapore by British authorities for painting a bleak picture of the worsening situation in Singapore and Malaya. Continuing his broadcasts from the Far East, he was next stationed in Australia where he reported that the British were unready for a Japanese invasion.

After the war he continued his association with CBS, before jumping to ABC in 1957 and then NBC the following year. He left journalism and broadcasting in 1967 to assume a teaching post in communications and international affairs at California State Polytechnic University. He wrote *Suez to Singapore* (1942).

REFERENCE: Robert W. Desmond. *Tides of War.* 1984.

BROWN, STEPHEN R. (b. 1947). He was initially assigned to cover the landing of the U.S. Marines in Beirut in 1982. Originally scheduled to cover the Lebanese conflict for a few days, he stayed for two months. According to Brown he will not partake of war coverage again.

REFERENCE: Frances Fralin. *The Indelible Image.* 1985.

BROWNE, JUNIUS HENRI (1833–1902). He was born in Seneca Falls, New York, and educated at St. Xavier College in Cincinnati. He entered the newspaper trade at the age of eighteen. After working for several Cincinnati papers he joined the *New York Tribune* as a war correspondent when the American Civil War* broke out. He covered the campaigns in the Southwest and along the Mississippi River, including the Battle of Vicksburg in 1863. He was among a group of journalists captured by Confederate forces when their ship was sunk by batteries on the cliffs protecting Vicksburg. Browne and his *Tribune* colleague Albert D. Richardson* were not immediately released with some of the others due to their connections with the *Tribune*, which was associated with the abolition movement. For over a year he was incarcerated in various Confederate prisons, including the notorious Libby Prison. Browne, Richardson, and several other prisoners finally escaped from Salisbury Prison, after which they endured a four-hundred-mile trek through enemy country before reaching the Union lines at Knoxville. His book *Four Years in Secessia* (1865) was an account of his experiences following the Battle of Vicksburg. He covered Fremont's Missouri campaign and the Battle of Fort Donelson, where he actually took up arms himself.

Following the Civil War Browne worked for various newspapers and contributed articles to several popular magazines. He wrote *The Great Metropolis* (1869) and *Sights and Sensations in Europe* (1871), as well as a series of books on the French Revolution.

REFERENCES: J. Cutler Andrews. *The North Reports the Civil War.* 1955; Stewart Sifakis. *Who Was Who in the Civil War.* 1988.

BROWNE, MALCOLM W. (b. 1931). Born in New York City and educated at Swarthmore College, Browne worked as a chemist following college until he was drafted during the Korean War.* In Korea he drove a tank before landing a position on the staff of *Stars and Stripes.*

He reported his next war in Vietnam,* beginning a five-year stint in 1961 as bureau chief for the Associated Press. Browne's greatest scoop of the war came when he photographed the self-immolation of a monk in Saigon. His 1964 Pulitzer Prize–winning photograph was only the first of hundreds that would chronicle the Buddhists' revolt against President Ngo Dinh Diem in South Vietnam. Browne's pictures reportedly led president Kennedy to withdraw his support of the Diem regime, and on November 1, 1963, Diem was overthrown and assassinated. Browne resigned from the AP in 1965, disillusioned by the war, but stayed in Saigon with ABC television and then the *New York Times*. Browne spent a total of ten years in Indochina, only exiting when Saigon fell in 1975. According to Browne, he was the oldest journalist to cover the Gulf War.* He is currently a senior writer for the *New York Times*.

REFERENCES: Malcolm W. Browne. *Muddy Boots and Red Socks: A War Reporter's Life.* 1993; William Prochnau. *Once upon a Distant War.* 1995.

BRYSON, GEORGE EUGENE (?). An old Cuban hand at the time of the Spanish-American War,* Bryson initially covered Cuban affairs for the *New York Herald* and the *New York World* before moving to the *New York Journal* in early 1897. Bryson made a name for himself prior to the outbreak of the war with a series of sensational stories which inflamed American public opinion against Spain. His story of the machete executions of hospital patients and the arrest and subsequent imprisonment of several nuns by the Spanish made front-page news in the *Journal* in early 1897. Not long after, Bryson reported the imprisonment by Spanish officials of a beautiful young woman who became better known in the press as the "Cuban Girl Martyr." Known simply as Evangelina, she was apparently related to the former president of the Cuban Republic. His story created another *cause célèbre*, and when he attempted to secure her release Bryson was expelled from the country. Evangelina eventually bought her way out of prison.

The following year he smuggled his account of the sinking of the *Maine* out of Cuba. Based on slim evidence, his early report that the *Maine* was destroyed by a torpedo provided impetus for the increasing anti-Spanish fervor gripping America. The *Journal*, ever vigilant for a news scoop, ran Bryson's dispatch under the headline "WAR! SURE!" accompanied by Bryson's intelligence: "*Maine* DESTROYED BY SPANISH . . . THIS PROVED ABSOLUTELY BY DISCOVERY OF THE TORPEDO HOLE." Bryson's scoop led to one of the most hysterical newspaper campaigns in American history. It is almost ironic that the reporter who contributed so much to the outbreak of the war left once the actual bloodletting began. Following the war Bryson went into business in Havana, where he owned and operated an independent news bureau.
REFERENCES: Charles H. Brown. *The Correspondents' War*. 1967; Joyce Milton. *The Yellow Kids*. 1989.

BUCKLEY, CHRISTOPHER (d. 1950). Buckley was a veteran war correspondent for the *Daily Telegraph* when he was killed reporting the Korean War.* During World War II* he covered the North African desert war, including the pivotal battle of El Alamain on October 25, 1942. The following year he reported the Sicilian operation before moving across the Strait of Messina to cover the Italian campaign. In 1944 he landed with the first wave during the invasion of Normandy before accompanying the British Second Army pushing into Belgium and Holland later that year. He was covering the Burma theater when the war ended. Buckley died in August 1950 when the jeep he shared with the *Times'* Ian Morrison* struck a land mine, killing both correspondents
REFERENCES: Richard Collier. *Fighting Words*. 1989; Robert W. Desmond. *Tides of War*. 1984.

BULGARIAN ATROCITIES. Beginning in May 1876, word leaked out of Bulgaria that demonstrators against Turkish rule had fallen victim to harsh retaliation. Rumors emanated from Constantinople that thousands of Christians had been massacred and many villages destroyed. The British government, which had been allied with Turkey since the Crimean War,* attempted to suppress the rumors, worried that Russia, as defender of the Christian faith, might intrude. When correspondent Januarius MacGahan* offered to investigate these rumors for his paper the *New York Herald* he was rebuffed. His offer was accepted by the *London Daily News* and he set off for Bulgaria. In a series of articles in the summer of 1876, MacGahan substantiated the rumors of Turkish atrocities. These dispatches were collected and published as a booklet. The accuracy of his reports were indeed confirmed by an investigation the following year, when it was found that over twelve thousand men, women, and children had been murdered. Russia responded to the confirmation by declaring war on Turkey in April 1877, inaugurating the Russo-Turkish War* of 1877–1878. MacGahan, who died of typhus soon after war broke out, is viewed as a national hero by Bulgarians; his actions were commemorated at an annual mass for years after his death.

REFERENCES: Robert W. Desmond. *The Information Process.* 1978; Phillip Knightley. *The First Casualty.* 1975.

BULL, RENÉ (d. 1942). Born in Ireland, Bull was one of the first war correspondents employed by the newly established *Black and White* in 1890. He served as writer, artist, and photographer for the new journal, which attempted to use photographs rather than sketches whenever possible. Stationed as special artist in Constantinople, he reported the Armenian massacres before leaving for India to cover the plague in Bombay.

In 1897 he reported the Greco-Turkish War* along with Bennet Burleigh* of the *Daily Telegraph.* He was captured by the Greeks after attempting to recover some personal items he left behind when the Turks took Volo. Firmly established as a member of the war correspondent establishment, he next ventured to India and the North West Frontier, where Pathan tribesmen were wreaking havoc. He was with the British advance into the Maidan Valley and the Tirah Valley Expedition. Bull and Melton Prior* of the *Illustrated London News* were with a Sikh column when they were attacked by Aridis warriors. In one episode the correspondents were cut off with several Sikhs from the main party when they were ambushed and pressed into battle, where they reportedly acquitted themselves quite well.

In 1896 Bull reported Kitchener's expedition to reconquer the Sudan. In 1898 he witnessed the Battle of Omdurman and afterward toured the battlefield littered with thousands of dead Mahdist warriors. The following year found Bull reporting the Boer War.* He narrowly escaped the siege of Ladysmith* along with Bennet Burleigh at the outset of the conflict. Bull accompanied the Ladysmith relief column under General Buller in December 1899. On December 15, 1899, he reported the British advance on Colenso, where Buller's army marched into a deadly trap and was decimated.

On February 24, 1900, the *Black and White* published Bull's account of the

Battle of Spion Kop, the last battle of 1899 and a terrible defeat for the British, who lost over 1,700 men taking a hill that they withdrew from the following day. Following the defeats of Colenso and Spion Kop, Ladysmith was not relieved until March. In 1901 he was severely wounded and returned to England for recuperation. Bull's career as a war artist and reporter ended with the Boer War, after which he turned to book illustrating. He served in the Royal Navy Volunteer Reserve and the RAF during World War I.*
REFERENCES: Pat Hodgson. *The War Illustrators.* 1977; Robert Wilkinson-Latham. *From Our Special Correspondent.* 1979.

BUNKER, WILLIAM MITCHELL (b. 1850). Born in Nantucket, Massachusetts, he reported the Modoc War of 1872–1873. A third-generation newspaperman, he was one of the top reporters for the *San Francisco Evening Bulletin* when the conflict broke out in the Lava Beds. Most of the stories at the end of the campaign came from the pen of Bunker, including the capture of Captain Jack, the Modoc leader. Following the war he continued his journalism career in San Francisco. Having risen to city and news editor of his newspaper, he acquired his own two years after the war when he purchased the *Daily Evening Report*.
REFERENCE: Oliver Knight. *Following the Indian Wars.* 1960.

BURCHETT, WILFRED (1911–1983). Born in Melbourne, Australia, in 1911, he became one of the most controversial journalists of the Cold War era. His radical bent was acquired in his youth when he was exploited along with other unskilled workers in the cane fields of Queensland during the 1930s Depression. Consistently accused of being a KGB agent and a Communist sympathizer, for seventeen years he and his family were denied passports by the Australian government for reporting the Communist side.

Burchett acquired his first posting as a war correspondent with the Australian-based *Digest*, and then the *Sunday Telegraph*. Shortly after arriving in China, he joined the staff of the *Daily Express* as he covered the Pacific theater of World War II* from 1941 to 1943. In January 1942 he was sent to cover the Japanese invasion of Burma. He reported the invasions of the Marianas, Guam, and Peleliu. Burchett was the first Western reporter to reach Hiroshima after the dropping of the atom bomb in August 1945. His story debunked the American claims that there could be no atomic sickness because the bomb had been detonated at a height that avoided any "residual radiation."

He covered the Chinese Revolution in the 1950s as well as the Korean War.* As a champion of radical causes he became embroiled in the Korean and Vietnam Wars,* and he counted Premier Chou En-Lai and Ho Chi Minh among his intimate acquaintances.

At the age of seventy he survived ambush by Khmer Rouge in Cambodia. He completed the last of thirty-five books, *Shadows of Hiroshima*, shortly before his death in 1983.

REFERENCES: Wilfred Burchett. *At the Barricades*. 1981; Ben Kiernan, ed. *Burchett Reporting the Other Side of the World*. 1986.

BURKE, JOHN (?). Burke was a professional British photographer in the Punjab of India. He was hired by the Indian government as a civilian to take pictures during the Second Afghan War in 1878–1880. Burke was one of a number of professional photographers in India who earned their living taking portraits of British soldiers. Most sources note that India was better served photographically because there were so many experienced photographers on the scene. Many, like Burke, were hired to accompany various punitive expeditions. Terms of payment usually included a fee, honorary rank, and free transportation and food for himself and his servants. Burke accompanied the First Division of the Peshawar Valley Field Force in 1879 and spent the winter in Kabul. He captured the signing of the peace treaty, which was soon after broken by the murder of Major Sir Louis Cavagnari, head of the peace mission. Sketches of Burke by a war artist appeared in the *Graphic*. With the murder of Cavagnari in September 1879, Burke's photograph of the peace mission provided him with a real scoop when an engraving made from his picture appeared in the *Graphic*.
REFERENCE: Pat Hodgson. *Early War Photographs*. 1974.

BURLEIGH, BENNET (c. 1840–1914). Born in Glasgow, Scotland, as a young man he fought for the Confederate Army during the American Civil War* and twice escaped death sentences by firing squads. After the war he entered journalism as an editor for the *Houston Telegraph*, but left for England shortly after. He turned to war reporting in 1882, covering the Arabi Revolt for the Central News Agency before transferring to the *Daily Telegraph* later that year. As the newspaper's preeminent special war correspondent he covered numerous campaigns between 1882 and 1911.

Burleigh was the premier special during the 1882 Sudan expedition for the *Daily Telegraph*. He covered the Sudan campaign of 1884–1885, reporting and witnessing the Battles of El Teb and Tamai in March 1884. After Gatling guns jammed, rifles malfunctioned, and bayonets and swords bent like ''hoop-iron'' at the Battle of Abu Klea, Burleigh wrote a critical dispatch on the quality and inefficiency of British weapons.

During the Battle of Abu Kru several noted war correspondents were killed by friendly fire, and Burleigh narrowly escaped death when he was hit in the throat by a ricocheting bullet. However, it did not penetrate, only raising an egg-size lump under his ear. Virtually all of the war correspondents covering this action were wounded by the haphazard shooting and subsequent ricocheting of bullets.

Burleigh's major scoop of the campaign came when he courageously rode through hostile territory to Dongola, where he telegraphed his paper and the world the stunning news of General Gordon's martyrdom at Khartoum.

He covered the Greco-Turkish War* from the Turkish side and reported from the 1895 Ashanti campaign. During the Sudan campaign of the late 1890s against the Mahdist forces he reported and took part in the Battle of Atbara and in 1898 the Battle of Omdurman. The *Times* also printed his account of the battle when it lost both of its correspondents to battle wounds at Omdurman. His book on Atbara, *Sirdir and Khalifa*, was published in July 1898, barely three months after the battle. The following year he was in South Africa covering the Boer War* for the *Daily Telegraph*. He escaped from Ladysmith* shortly before the siege began. Apparently, due to excessive censorship his main coups during the war were interviewing Boer General Joubert and carrying news of peace past the military censors. In 1903 he reported the minor punitive expedition to Somaliland and the following year covered the Russo-Japanese War.*

In his seventies he witnessed his last war while reporting the 1912 Balkan conflict. Burleigh has often been compared to William Howard Russell* for the quality of his work and the value of his criticism in leading to the improved efficiency of the British military system. He died in June 1914, shortly before the outbreak of World War I.*

REFERENCES: F. Lauriston Bullard. *Famous War Correspondents*. 1914; Robert Wilkinson-Latham. *From Our Special Correspondent*. 1979.

BURNS, GEORGE (1902–1964). Born in Albany, New York, he wrote for the *Albany Times Union* before enlisting in the army and joining the staff of *Yank** magazine during World War II.* Burns served in the Pacific theater of operations, where he covered the landings in the Marianas, Leyte, Iwo Jima, and Okinawa. He reported one of *Yank*'s greatest scoops when he witnessed and reported in both print and photographs the attempted suicide of Japanese prime minister Tojo in Tokyo at the conclusion of the war.

He narrowly missed another classic scoop at the flag raising on Iwo Jima. He photographed the event with Joe Rosenthal* of the Associated Press. However, Rosenthal's negatives went directly through to the AP, while Burns' was held up by the Signal Corps labs. Following the war Burns continued his career as a photojournalist with *Life, Look*, and the *Saturday Evening Post*. He won numerous awards, including Photographer of the Year in 1964.

REFERENCE: Art Weithas. *Close to Glory*. 1991.

BURROWS, LARRY (1926–1971). Born in London, he began his career in photojournalism as a laboratory technician in London's *Life* office in the early 1940s. In 1944, during the Normandy invasion, he was the unlucky darkroom assistant who destroyed most of Robert Capa's* D-Day photos by applying too much heat to the negatives.

Burrows covered the Vietnam War* for nine years as well as conflicts in Africa and the Middle East. He was killed along with three other photographers on February 10, 1971, when the Vietnamese helicopter shuttling them over Laos was shot down by antiaircraft fire. The last pictures he took were of the accidental bombing of South Vietnamese soldiers by U.S. naval planes. He received

the Overseas Press Club's Robert Capa Award twice and in 1966 was named Magazine Photographer of the Year. His book *Larry Burrows—Compassionate Photographer* was posthumously published in 1972.
REFERENCE: Frances Fralin, ed. *The Indelible Image*. 1985.

BURTON, JAMES (b. 1871). Born in London, he came to the United States in 1894. Burton worked as an illustrator for the *New York Herald, Harper's, Leslie's*, and other New York and London papers. He covered the Spanish-American War* as a photographer for *Harper's Weekly*. He recorded the Battles of San Juan Hill* and El Caney, and the advance on Santiago. Burton noted the impossibility of taking action shots when he came under fire on the front lines while accompanying the Seventh Infantry Regiment at San Juan Hill. He commented that shooting actual battle scenes was out of the question because of the distance at which the fighting was conducted and the long grass and thickly wooded topography. Following the Battle of El Caney, Burton took one of the few pictures of American dead to be published during the conflict. It appeared in *Harper's* on July 30, 1898, under the caption "Killed on the Field of Battle."
REFERENCES: Susan D. Moeller. *Shooting War*. 1989; *Who's Who in America*. 1910–1911.

BUSCHEMI, JOHN (d. 1944). Prior to World War II* he was a news photographer for the *Gary Post Tribune*. Following his induction into the army in 1941 he joined the staff of *Yank** the next year. Between 1942 and 1944 he covered the fighting in New Georgia, Guadalcanal, Munda, Tarawa, and Kwajalein. He was killed at the battle on Eniwetok Island.
REFERENCE: Art Weithas. *Close to Glory*. 1991.

BYINGTON, AARON HOMER (?). A newspaper reporter since the age of fourteen, Byington was the editor and owner of the Norwalk, Connecticut, *Gazette* at the start of the American Civil War* and a part-time correspondent for the *New York Tribune*. He scored one of the biggest news scoops of the war when he organized a crew to repair telegraph lines in Hanover, Pennsylvania, following the Union victory at Gettysburg. For his services Byington was given a monopoly on the wire for two days. Once this agreement had been concluded he returned to the battlefield only sixteen miles away, where he interviewed witnesses to the first two days of the pivotal battle. His dispatch was the first complete account of the first two days of Gettysburg to hit the newsstands on July 4, 1863. The *Tribune* sold sixty-five thousand copies of this extra before noon. By August 1863, Byington had been made chief of the *Tribune* war correspondents with the Army of the Potomac. He later reported the Mine Run campaign and the Battles of the Wilderness.
REFERENCES: J. Cutler Andrews. *The North Reports the Civil War*. 1955; Louis M. Starr. *Bohemian Brigade*. 1954.

C

CADWALLADER, SYLVANUS (b. 1826). Born in Ohio in 1826, he served as city editor of the *Milwaukee Daily News*. During the American Civil War* he was persuaded by the *Chicago Times* to replace its star reporter, who was languishing in a military prison for ignoring journalistic protocol. The owners of the *Times* begged the thirty-six-year-old Cadwallader to obtain a personal interview with Grant and to report on the movements of the western army. Described as distant and unsociable, he somehow gained a reputation for successfully obtaining news that had eluded his fellow war correspondents. However, this success was not the result of some uncanny resourcefulness. It was later revealed Cadwallader had helped Grant escape rebuke for a drinking binge on board the *Diligent* during the Vicksburg campaign and had been rewarded with a pass that allowed him unprecedented access to Grant's forces. He was the only newspaperman on board the steamer *Magnolia*, which was Grant's headquarters during the siege of Vicksburg. On the battlefield his tent was usually located next to Grant's, and he was permitted to use the general's official mail pouch to send off his dispatches.

Much of the credit for Cadwallader's success as a war reporter was due to his ability to respect the confidentiality of much that he was privy to. He followed Grant through his western campaign in Tennessee and Mississippi, including the Battles of Vicksburg and Chattanooga, and was at the general's side in 1865 during the peace signing at Appomattox, Virginia. He was captured by Confederate forces twice, and both times escaped by means of chicanery. The *Herald* promoted him to the supervisory position of correspondent-in-chief in charge of more than a dozen reporters after his second escape. Shadowing Grant from 1862 through 1865, he had an unrivaled position to observe the Union command.

After the war he became head of the *Herald*'s Washington news bureau. In 1896, at the age of seventy, he finished a manuscript chronicling his wartime career. It was not published at the time, languishing in a library before being edited and published in 1955. Recent scholarship suggests that Cadwallader might not have witnessed firsthand much of what he reported, instead gleaning information from camp gossip.

REFERENCES: J. Cutler Andrews. *The North Reports the Civil War.* 1955; Sylvanus Cadwallader. *Three Years with Grant,* edited by Benjamin P. Thomas. 1955; Stewart Sifakis. *Who Was Who in the Civil War.* 1988.

CAGNONI, ROMANO (b. 1935). Born in Pietrasanta, Italy, he was self-taught in photography. Cagnoni is predominately a freelance photographer whose pictures have appeared in the *Observer, Paris-Match, Life, Stern, L'Espresso, Newsweek*, and many other magazines. He was the only photographer to cover the entire war in Biafra and in 1965 was the first independent photographer admitted into North Vietnam after the fall of Dien Bien Phu eleven years earlier. He appeared in Afghanistan shortly after the Soviet invasion and secretly photographed the conflict through his partly unbuttoned coat.

Cagnoni is recognized as one of the first photojournalists to become deeply attached to the people he covered, often living among them during conflicts. During the Biafran conflict he would often blacken his face; otherwise Nigerians would have taken him for one of the hated white mercenaries. He was present as the Biafran resistance in Nigeria crumbled and General Ojukwu made his final escape. His scoop was featured in *Life* magazine.

While in North Vietnam, Cagnoni was denied access to combat missions but witnessed several American bombing raids. He also covered the war in Cambodia in 1974. His work has been collected in *Presenting Romano Cagnoni.*

REFERENCES: *Contemporary Photographers.* 1982; Jorge Lewinski. *The Camera at War.* 1978.

CALDWELL, ERSKINE (1903–1987). Born in Moreland, Georgia, Caldwell is best remembered as a writer of realistic novels such as *Tobacco Road* and short stories portraying poor southerners. He collaborated with his wife and *Life* photographer Margaret Bourke-White* on a series of articles on wartime Moscow. In 1941 he represented *PM*, the New York daily, in Russia. His account of his wartime exploits in Russia is chronicled in *All Out on the Road to Smolensk.* In late 1941 he visited Chungking, China, in the aftermath of the recent Japanese invasion.

REFERENCE: Robert W. Desmond. *Tides of War.* 1984.

CAMERON, JAMES (1911–1985). Born in London, he entered journalism with several newspapers in Manchester and Dundee. He was rejected for wartime service in the 1940s and spent ten years with the *Sunday Post*. A committed pacifist, he became a lifelong opponent of nuclear weapons.

Representing the *Picture Post*, he arrived with the rest of the British press corps at the beginning of the Korean War,* in time to report the Pusan breakout. Cameron was accompanied by veteran photographer Bert Hardy,* who had covered World War II* and had been Mountbatten's personal photographer in the Far East. From the start, the pacifist Cameron felt the war was futile and was skeptical of America's true war goals.

Cameron demonstrated he was capable of covering a large-scale military operation when he reported the successful landing of United Nations forces at Inchon on September 15, 1950. He witnessed the bombardment and took part in the landing operation. Cameron started a furor when he described atrocities perpetrated by South Korean soldiers on political opponents of the Syngman Rhee regime. After a slew of similar stories by other British correspondents, Douglas MacArthur, the commanding general, imposed full military censorship on the press. Cameron departed shortly after the restrictions went into effect.

In 1952 Cameron left the *Picture Post* for the *News Chronicle*, with which he remained until 1960, shortly before its demise. In the 1960s he visited Hanoi as both a print and television journalist and reported the Vietnam* conflict from the North Vietnamese perspective. His experiences with Communist forces is chronicled in the book *Witness* (1966) by Romano Cagnoni* and Malcolm Aird. REFERENCE: Trevor Royle. *War Report*. 1987.

CAMERON, JOHN ALEXANDER (d. 1885). Born in Inverness, Scotland, he left his position as a bank clerk for India, where he quickly rose through the ranks of the *Bombay Gazette* to acting editor by 1878. In 1879 he reported the Afghan War for the *Standard* while accompanying the relief column to Kandahar under General Phayrer. He reached a telegraph with news of General Roberts' victory, a day and a half before his competitors. His dispatch from the battlefield of Maiwand (1880) elevated him to the top ranks of war reporters of his day.

With the outbreak of the First Boer War in December 1880, he traveled from Bombay to Natal, again beating his competitors to the news. In January 1881 he witnessed the Battles of Laing's Nek and Ingogo before being captured after the debacle at Majuba Hill in February. His account of the defeat of British forces at Majuba Hill (1881), later published by the *Illustrated London News* with illustrations by Melton Prior,* is considered a classic. In June 1882, following the denouement of the Boer insurrection, Cameron reported the combined bombardment of Alexandria by French and British forces in retaliation for the massacre of Christians in the vicinity. He witnessed the British bombardment of the city on board the flagship *Invincible*. He covered the subsequent Egyptian campaign and later reported from Madagascar.

Cameron next accompanied French forces to Indochina and was in Tonkin when the French were beaten back by the Black Flags. Thereafter English correspondents were barred from covering the conflict, and on his way back to Britain he stopped at Suez to cover the advance of Osman Digma on Suakin.

Cameron barely escaped alive from the defeat of Baker Pasha's forces by the Arabs.

He returned to North Africa in 1884 with the British expeditionary force and covered the battles of Trinkiat, El Teb, and Tamanieb. After a brief return to England he joined the 1884 Nile expedition and was with General Gordon at the siege of Khartoum. On January 19, 1885, Cameron was killed at the Battle of Abu Kru, where he was reporting Wolseley's unsuccessful attempt to move south to rescue Pasha Gordon. A tablet in the crypt at St. Paul's Cathedral commemorates the deaths of Cameron and six other correspondents who sacrificed their lives covering the 1883–1885 Sudan campaigns.

REFERENCES: *DNB*; Robert Wilkinson-Latham. *From Our Special Correspondent.* 1979.

CAMPBELL, ARCHIBALD DOON (b. 1920). Born in Annan, Dumfriesshire, he worked for several newspapers in Scotland between 1938 and 1941 before joining Reuters* in 1941 as the youngest war correspondent accredited to Allied headquarters in Algiers. While covering the Royal Marine Commandos at Sword Beach during the D-Day landing he was reportedly the first correspondent to come ashore. In 1945 he crossed the Rhine inside a glider with the Seventeenth American Airborne Division. He was awarded the American Glider Wings and the Combat Star for his wartime reporting. He continued with Reuters until 1973. In 1984 he received the Order of the British Empire.

REFERENCE: Robert W. Desmond. *Tides of War.* 1984.

CAMPBELL, GERALD FITZGERALD (1872–1933). Following short stints with *Punch* and the *World* he joined the *Times* in 1908. He was one of the first reporters to witness the action at the western front with the French. Returning to France in 1915 after a fact-finding mission in Switzerland, he was arrested for espionage. However, his paper, with the help of the British legation in Berne, interceded and he was released. The following two years he covered French headquarters before returning to the western front. He wrote *Verdun to the Vosges* (1916).

REFERENCE: Robert W. Desmond. *Windows on the World.* 1980.

CAPA, CORNELL (b. 1918). Born in Budapest, Hungary, as Kornel Friedmann on April 10, 1918, he graduated from Madach Imre Gymnasium in 1936. A photojournalist like his more famous brother Robert, he served as staff photographer for *Life* from 1946 to 1954. He covered the Israeli Six Day War in 1967, the Argentine Revolution, and the Somoza assassination.

REFERENCE: Richard Whelan. *Robert Capa: A Biography.* 1985.

CAPA, ROBERT (1913–1954). Born Andrei Friedmann in Budapest, Hungary, he studied journalism in Berlin. In 1932 he began his career as a freelancer for *Life, Time*, and other magazines. In 1935 he changed his name to Robert Capa, under the impression he would make more money if he was thought to be an American photographer. He was also associated with Magnum Photos, which he cofounded in 1947.

Capa covered the Spanish Civil War* with his lover and photography partner Gerda Taro*; she was crushed to death under a Loyalist tank in the confusion of retreat. In 1938, he was watching raw soldiers attacking a well-guarded machine gun nest when he caught in a series of photographs his most famous image, a soldier frozen in his moment of death. This shot of the ''Falling Soldier,'' also known as the ''Death of a Loyalist Soldier,''* identified the name ''Capa'' with war photojournalism for posterity. In years to come he would justify his success by noting that ''if your pictures aren't good, you aren't close enough.''

Following the Spanish Civil War, he reported the Japanese invasion of China in 1938. Capa was initially prevented from covering World War II* due to his classification as an enemy alien because of his Hungarian citizenship. In 1942 he was informed that in the interest of national security he had to turn in his photographic equipment and not stray more than ten miles from New York City. However, in March 1943 he received the elusive accreditation and travel permits that would allow him to cover another war.

He covered the European theater of the war for *Life* from 1943 to 1945. His greatest scoop of the war was covering the D-Day invasion in 1944. One of only four news photographers allowed to accompany the invasion forces, Capa was among the first soldiers to land on the Normandy beach as he took pictures of men desperately trying to stay alive. His six hours of photos were sent to the processing lab aboard the USS *Chase*. However, a week later he learned his shots, which were the best of the invasion, were ruined by an overzealous darkroom assistant who in his excitement used too much heat on the negatives. Only 11 of 106 pictures survived this calamity. Later in the war he jumped with parachutists into Germany, covered the Anzio invasion, and was almost killed by friendly fire in Belgium when American soldiers mistook him for a German soldier. A week after the German surrender, *Life* featured on its cover another famous Capa photo, an American corporal offering a mock Nazi salute in front of the huge swastika on Nuremberg's sports stadium.

Following the war Capa and other unemployed war photographers formed the Magnum Picture Agency. He served as its first president and anchor until his death in 1954. He covered the birth of Israel from 1948 to 1950. In 1954 *Life* asked him to cover the French war in Indochina. On May 25, bored with waiting at a Viet Minh roadblock, Capa headed up the road in search of action when he triggered a land mine. He was found with a hole in his chest and one foot blown off.

REFERENCES: Robert E. Hood. *12 at War*. 1967; Frederick S. Voss. *Reporting the War*. 1994; Richard Whelan. *Robert Capa: A Biography*. 1985.

CAPUTO, PHILIP (b. 1943). Caputo served in the marines from 1960 to 1967, including sixteen months in Vietnam. His experiences in Vietnam are chronicled in the highly acclaimed 1977 book *A Rumor of War*. In 1972 Caputo joined the staff of the *Chicago Tribune* and shared the Pulitzer Prize for investigative reporting. Following a stint as Rome correspondent he was assigned to cover the Middle East, where he was captured by Palestinian guerrillas. He was a recipient of the Overseas Club's George K. Polk* Award for his account of his captivity. He returned to Vietnam in 1975 and covered the final stages of the Vietnam conflict. Later that year he was shot in both legs while reporting the Lebanese civil war in Beirut. After recuperating he was reassigned to Moscow. His 1983 novel *DelCorso's Gallery* tells the story of combat photographer Nick DelCorso, who rushes from war to war attempting to exorcise the demons that still haunt him from pictures taken in the Vietnam War during a village burning by American paratroopers ten years earlier.

REFERENCES: Philip Caputo. *A Rumor of War*. 1977; Philip Caputo. *DelCorso's Gallery*. 1983; Howard Good. *The Image of War Correspondents in Anglo-American Fiction*. 1985.

CARPENTER, IRIS (b. 1906). Born in England, after a short stint as a film critic for the *London Daily Express* Carpenter opted for staying home to raise a family before returning to the *Daily Express* and then the *London Daily Herald* to cover the London blitz and bombings in 1940. It was a common conceit in the early war years that women were acceptable for covering the home front but should not be allowed to accompany the armed forces to the Continent. When Carpenter applied for accreditation with the British Expeditionary Force in 1942 she was rebuffed. Not easily dissuaded, she circumvented the process by becoming an American reporter for the *Boston Globe*, and accompanied the American First Army instead. Carpenter noted that the American War Department was much more tolerant than the British War Office when it came to allowing women to report the war. While General Montgomery flatly vowed that "we will not tolerate them," American officials were of the notion that there were certain aspects of the war better covered by women.

After the Normandy invasion Carpenter followed the army through Caen, across the River Orne around Falaise. However, women were prevented by the Supreme Headquarters Allied European Forces (SHAEF) from witnessing the jubilation of the liberation of Paris. When she finally made it to Paris Carpenter accompanied French liberation troops as they hunted down the remaining Germans left in the city. She suffered a shattered eardrum from the bombing at St. Lô, which became infected and led to a case of mastoiditis. Rather than leaving the front lines she moved with the hospital, staying close to the action, compiling stories about how Americans cared for their wounded.

Carpenter went on to cover the Battle of Arnhem and followed American troops through Antwerp and Aachen and ultimately to the Rhine. She was accredited to the First Army, with whom she witnessed the Battle of Huertgen Forest. From there she retreated from the developing Battle of the Bulge, but accompanied troops toward the Rhine and the Remagen bridge. She reported the breakup of Nazi Germany and the liberation of the concentration camps as

well as the meeting of the Allied and Russian armies. After the war Carpenter continued to write and worked for the Voice of America. In 1946 she published *No Woman's World*, about her exploits as a woman war correspondent.
REFERENCE: Lilya Wagner. *Women War Correspondents of World War II*. 1989.

CARRIER PIGEONS. Pigeons have been trained to carry messages as far back as the fourth century B.C. in Egypt. Other accounts report that they were used by the ancient Romans and in the Middle East by the twelfth century at the latest. As late as the present century Japan used pigeons to return film from a news event to the home office. By the late 1830s the *Times* of London was using carrier pigeons to send news from the European continent across the English Channel. Beginning in 1840, the *Boston Daily Mail* introduced what became known as the "pigeon express." Thirty years later carrier pigeons were used to get news out of besieged Paris during the Franco-Prussian War.*
REFERENCE: Robert W. Desmond. *The Information Process*. 1978.

CARTIER-BRESSON, HENRI (b. 1909). Born near the French village of Chanteloup, he first studied painting before turning to photography in 1931. Cartier-Bresson rose to the top of his profession with a minimum of equipment, most often resorting to his Leicas. In 1937 he made a documentary film with Jean Renoir about the Loyalists during the Spanish Civil War* entitled *Return to Life*. He was a corporal in the French army in 1940 when the Germans invaded France. He was captured and spent almost three years in a prison camp. He escaped in 1943 on his third attempt and joined the French resistance. Soon after he joined a resistance group and helped other prisoners and escapees.

Following World War II* he cofounded the international distribution agency Magnum along with Robert Capa* and David Seymour.* He covered the 1947 war in Kashmir from both sides. The following year he arrived in China shortly before Mao Tse-tung's forces took control of Peking. After spending five weeks covering the Communist forces he was in Nanking when Chiang Kai-shek and his followers departed. In September 1948 he left China for India and the police action against the Hyderabad state.

His photographs have been widely reprinted and published in collections such as *The Decisive Moment* (1952), *People of Moscow* (1955), *China in Transition* (1956), and *the World of Henri Cartier-Bresson* (1968). He was the first photographer to have his works exhibited at the Louvre.
REFERENCE: Robert E. Hood. *12 at War*. 1967.

CASEY, ROBERT JOSEPH (1890–1962). Born in Beresford, South Dakota, Casey earned a reputation for his adventurous exploits. He served as correspondent for the *Chicago Daily News* from 1920 to 1947. Prior to joining the paper he had served as a captain in World War I* and had reported for the *Des Moines Register and Leader*. He covered World War II* action in the company of British, American, and French forces in campaigns from the Middle East to the

Mediterranean, and in the South Pacific. He covered the British army in Egypt and Libya in 1941, and the following year was with the U.S. fleet in the South Pacific during the Battles of Wake Island, Coral Sea, Midway, and the Marshall Islands. Casey was with the British navy in the Adriatic, the Mediterranean, and the Middle East before reporting the invasion of Normandy in 1944. He accompanied the U.S. First Army through France, Belgium, Luxembourg, and then Germany. He wrote over two dozen books based on his exploits including *I Can't Forget*, the story of the German invasion of Holland and France, and *Torpedo Junction*, which chronicles his experiences as a foreign correspondent on a U.S. warship in the South Pacific.
REFERENCE: Jack Stenbuck, ed. *Typewriter Battalion*. 1995.

CASSIDY, HENRY C. (b. 1910). Cassidy became European correspondent for the Associated Press in 1936 and began his career as a war correspondent two years later when he covered the Battle of the Ebro from the Spanish Republican side of the Spanish Civil War.* With the outbreak of World War II,* he was accredited to the French armies in 1939, before covering the British army and air force in France. He remained in Paris until German forces entered the city following the defeat of France in 1940. Soon after, he went to Berlin and then to Moscow as chief of the AP bureau. His experiences in Russia are recounted in *Moscow Dateline*.
REFERENCE: Robert W. Desmond. *Crisis and Conflict: World News Reporting Between Two Wars, 1920–1940*. 1982.

CHANDLER, EDMUND (1874–1926). Born in Norfolk, England, and educated at Cambridge, he was hired as special correspondent for the *Daily Mail* to cover the British expedition to Tibet in 1904. At the Battle of Hot Springs Chandler was wounded in twelve places when attacked by four Tibetans.

With the outbreak of World War I* he was assigned by the *Times* and the *Daily Mail* to cover the western front. He covered the Mesopotamia campaign between 1915 and 1918, the same year he became the *Times* correspondent in the Middle East. He wrote several books, including *A Vagabond in Asia* (1899), *The Unveiling of Lhasa* (1905), and *Youth and the East* (1924). He died on January 4, 1926.
REFERENCE: Robert Wilkinson-Latham. *From Our Special Correspondent*. 1979.

CHAPELLE, GEORGETTE "DICKEY" (1918–1965). It is somewhat ironic that Dickey Chapelle, the daughter of pacifist parents, grew up to become the first American woman war correspondent killed in action and the first woman photographer accredited to the war in the Pacific. Chapelle left the Massachusetts Institute of Technology early to pursue a career in aviation. After her nearsightedness contributed to her crash landing a plane she was forced to abandon her first ambition. She stayed in the aviation field as a publicist for several airlines and took a course in photography, eventually marrying her instructor, TWA publicity photographer Tony Chapelle, in 1940. After her husband enlisted in the navy following Pearl Harbor, she applied for photography jobs with various news services. In 1944 Chapelle was assigned to a hospital ship bound for Iwo Jima.

Photographer-correspondent Chapelle was a latecomer to World War II* reportage when she took one of the most famous photos of the war. On board the hospital ship *Samaritan*, which was steaming toward the Battle of Iwo Jima, she snapped a photo of a seriously wounded marine being lifted on board the ship. The picture, "The Dying Marine," would be used in countless blood drives for the remainder of the war. She was thereafter assigned by the navy to photograph casualties for possible use in future blood drives for the mounting numbers of wounded in the Pacific campaign. She survived the Battles of Iwo Jima and Okinawa, as well as some of the most deadly kamikaze attacks of the war.

In 1956 Chapelle covered the revolt in Hungary for *Life* magazine and was jailed in Budapest for three months by the Soviets for helping the freedom fighters. This experience would lead to a lifelong disdain for Communism, reflected in much of her coverage of the Cuban Revolution and the Vietnam War.* In 1958 she was sent to document the Algeria war for independence. Her investigation revealed that the French were using NATO weapons in their campaign to protect their African possessions. Her photos became poignant reminders of the brutality and inhumanity of colonialism. Later that year Chapelle covered the landing of the marines in Lebanon and Castro's revolt against the Batista regime in Cuba. During the Cuban campaign she witnessed four engagements in Oriente Province and was injured when her jeep overturned during a mortar attack. The next year she was on hand at Quemoy Island, off the coast of China, when it was bombarded by Communist forces.

Beginning in 1961 Chapelle witnessed the Vietnam conflict as a freelancer, which required the endorsement of two news agencies, in this case the *National Observer* and the *Wall Street Journal*. Already an accomplished pilot, Chapelle gained the respect of troops by parachuting with them in full combat gear. She would eventually repeat this exercise over thirty times during five different tours of duty. In 1962 Chapelle took the first photographs of combat-ready American advisors in Vietnam, which were featured in her picture-story "Helicopter War in South Viet Nam" in *National Geographic* magazine. She received the 1962 George Polk* Award "for the best reporting, any medium, requiring exceptional courage and enterprise abroad." In 1965 Chapelle accompanied U.S. Marines when they landed in the Dominican Republic. On November 4, 1965, she was with a marine patrol during Operation Black Ferret in Vietnam when someone triggered a booby trap made of a grenade wired to an 81mm mortar round. Hit in the throat by shrapnel, Chapelle died almost instantly.

REFERENCES: Dickey Chapelle. *What's a Woman Doing Here?* 1961; Julia Edwards. *Women of the World: The Great Foreign Correspondents.* 1988; Roberta Ostroff. *Fire in the Wind: The Life of Dickey Chapelle.* 1992.

CHAPMAN, FRANK C. (?). Chapman is credited with one of the greatest news scoops of the American Civil War.* However, the *New York Herald* correspondent was accused of lacking scruples for the way he delivered it. Following the Battle of Shiloh, Chapman was granted access to the army telegraph facility on the pretense that he was on General Ulysses S. Grant's staff. Chapman's controversial account soon came under fire for its inaccuracies as well as its exaggeration of Grant's role in the battle.

After General Halleck expelled all reporters from the western army Chapman transferred to the East, where he was rewarded for his Shiloh scoop with the position of chief correspondent with General John Pope's army. The intrepid reporter resorted to subterfuge once more after the first day of the Battle of Gettysburg. Reaching Baltimore ahead of his competition, Chapman telegraphed his account using the services of the only two telegraphers on duty to speed up his transmissions. As they quickly relayed his account a correspondent from the *Tribune* breathlessly arrived to send his dispatch. In order to stall the telegraphers Chapman handed them a copy of the Bible and told them to add it to his transmission until he returned. Since protocol insured that telegraph messages should be sent in order of arrival, Chapman was able to control the wires throughout the day as his competitors waited powerlessly in line.

Throughout the war, the *Herald* spared no expense in the pursuit of war news. On one occasion, following the insignificant Battle of Mine Run, Chapman offered five hundred dollars to a sutler's clerk to smuggle newspaper reports through enemy territory to Washington.

REFERENCES: J. Cutler Andrews. *The North Reports the Civil War.* 1955; Louis M. Starr. *Bohemian Brigade.* 1954.

CHENERY, THOMAS (1826–1884). Born in Barbados, he was educated at Eton and Cambridge. While serving in Constantinople as officer of the East India Company's army, in 1854 he joined the *Times* as its Constantinople correspondent during the Crimean War.* Prior to the war Chenery had been a barrister in London. His descriptive reports of the primitive conditions at the hospital of Scutari and the inadequate medical care afforded the wounded aroused public indignation back in England. His dispatches, along with W. H. Russell's,* are credited with bringing Florence Nightingale's nurses to the Crimea.

The eclectic and eccentric Chenery was an ex-professor of Arabic and a linguist fluent in French, German, Greek, and Turkish. In the 1860s and 1870s he produced several works of Arabic scholarship as well as the publication *Suggestions for a Railroad Route to India.* In 1878 he began a seven-year stint as editor of the *Times.*

REFERENCES: *DNB*; Robert Wilkinson-Latham. *From Our Special Correspondent.* 1979; Oliver Woods and James Bishop. *The Story of THE TIMES.* 1983.

CHESTER, THOMAS MORRIS (1834–1892). He was born in Harrisburg, Pennsylvania, the son of a former slave. At the age of eighteen he sailed to Liberia, where he opened a school and founded a newspaper. He returned to the United States in early 1863, shortly after the government authorized the creation of a black volunteer regiment. Chester was appointed captain of the regiment and shortly after was hired by former war correspondent John Russell Young* of the *Philadelphia Press* to report the American Civil War.*

His coverage of the war lasted from August 1864 to June 1865. Chester's dispatches describe camp life, the reaction and responses of Confederates and civilians to black troops, various military engagements, and the initial stages of Reconstruction. He participated in and reported action during the expedition against Fort Fisher, North Carolina, and the battles leading up to the fall of Petersburg and Richmond. He was one of the first reporters to enter Richmond, and was with the black troops of the Twenty-fifth Army Corps, which were symbolically the first to enter the Confederate capital.

Following the war Chester became the European agent for a freedman's aid society and traveled widely through the continent. He earned a law degree in Great Britain and was the first black American to join the English bar. He came back to the States in 1871, settling in New Orleans, where he remained active in politics and practiced law.

REFERENCES: R.J.M. Blackett, ed. *Thomas Morris Chester: Black Civil War Correspondent.* 1989.

CHETWYD-TALBOT, JOHN (1910–1991). Born in Sidmouth, Devon, and educated at Eton, he entered journalism with Reuters* in 1929. At the outbreak of World War II* he reported from the Ministry of Information before transferring to the battlefront in June 1941, when he covered Admiral Vian's assault on Spitzbergen. He reported Russian naval operations before switching to the Mediterranean theater, where he accompanied the Malta convoys.

He narrowly missed death at sea on several occasions. Fate intervened for the first time when he left the battleship *Hood* shortly before it was sunk by the *Bismarck*, and he just missed a posting on the Far Eastern voyage of the *Prince of Wales*, which was sunk several months later along with the *Repulse* by Japanese bombers off the coast of Malaya.

Using the sobriquet of John Talbot he covered the Operation Torch invasion of North Africa in 1942, following which he became the first reporter to cover Marshal Tito's guerrillas in Yugoslavia. Early on he was captured by German forces and prepared for execution, but was saved at the last moment by the intervention of an American news photographer. He spent the next several months as a prisoner of war. Following the war he continued to work for Reuters in Europe and Africa before retirement in 1975.

REFERENCES: Robert W. Desmond. *Tides of War.* 1984; Dennis Griffiths, ed. *The Encyclopedia of the British Press.* 1992.

CHINA HANDS. ''China Hands'' refers to a small corps of eccentric Western writers and journalists who lived and reported from China between 1900 and the formation of the People's Republic of China in 1949.
REFERENCE: Peter Rand. *China Hands.* 1995.

CHRISTY, HOWARD CHANDLER (1873–1952). Born in Morgan City, Ohio, he began working for the illustrated periodicals in the early 1890s. He achieved prominence as a war artist for *Leslie's Weekly* during the Spanish-American War.* He witnessed the landing of American troops in Cuba on June 22, 1898. Following the first land battle of the war at Las Guasimas on June 24 Christy sketched the wounded returning to camp. His articles and sketches appeared in both *Leslie's* and *Harper's* during the war, and he was one of the illustrators for Wright's history of the war. Following the war he became well known as a poster and portrait artist.
REFERENCE: Pat Hodgson. *The War Illustrators.* 1977.

CHURCH, WILLIAM CONANT ''PIERREPONT'' (1836–1917). Church was born in Rochester, New York. He entered journalism as co-owner of the *New York Chronicle*, a religious daily newspaper, with his father, a Baptist clergyman. Prior to the American Civil War,* Church was publisher of the *New York Sun*. At the outbreak of war he headed the *New York Times* war correspondence staff and was a member of the Bohemian Brigade.* He was considered one of the most outstanding of the 150 accredited war correspondents during the war. Under the pseudonym ''Pierrepont,'' he reported the 1861 Port Royal operation and was wounded in the leg by a bullet during the Battle of Fair Oaks. His wound did not keep him from producing an account of the battle that filled the entire front page of the *Times* on June 3, 1862. Church took a six-month respite from the Civil War to serve as a roving reporter in Europe in 1862 and later served as a captain in the Union Army for nine months.

In 1863 he cofounded the *Army and Navy Journal* with his brother, fellow *Times* war correspondent Francis P. Church. Church became perhaps the greatest military expert within the ranks of American journalism as he presided over the military journal until his death in 1917. He also cofounded *Galaxy* magazine, which would eventually merge with the *Atlantic Monthly*.
REFERENCES: J. Cutler Andrews. *The North Reports the Civil War.* 1955; George H. Phillips. ''The *Army and Navy Journal* Before Two Wars,'' *Journalism Quarterly.* Fall 1961. Louis M. Starr. *Bohemian Brigade.* 1954.

CHURCHILL, SIR WINSTON LEONARD SPENCER (1874–1965). One of the greatest statesmen of the twentieth century, he was one of its preeminent men of letters as well. Born at Blenheim Palace on November 30, 1874, he was educated at Sandhurst. In 1895 he was commissioned in the Fourth Queen's Own Hussars. In October of that same year he journeyed to Cuba in order to observe the insurrection against the Spanish. Reporting for the *Daily Graphic*, he witnessed action for the first time on his twenty-first birthday. His coverage appeared in the paper in a five-part series entitled "The Insurrection in Cuba." For his service he was awarded the Spanish Order of the Red Cross.

Following his excursion to Cuba he took a respite in London before setting with his regiment for India. While on leave in the summer of 1897 he contracted with two papers to cover the conflict with the Pathans on the North West Frontier. Writing for the *Daily Telegraph*, Churchill was criticized for overstepping the scope of typical war reporting by commenting on political issues in order to further his own career. The result of his reportage was *The Story of the Malakand Field Force* (1898). Thanks to his American-born mother's connections he was next assigned to the Twenty-first Lancers as they advanced on Khartoum in September 1898, where he took part in the last British cavalry charge during the Battle of Omdurman. The following year Churchill completed *The River War*, his highly praised account of the Sudan expedition.

In October 1899 he arranged to cover the Boer War* for the *Morning Post*. After his arrival in Durban, South Africa, he was caught in a Boer ambuscade while aboard an armored freight train and taken prisoner. Shortly after, he escaped from Pretoria. With a bounty on his head, after a perilous journey he made it back to Durban, where he joined the South Africa Light Horse. It is worth noting here that his dual service as correspondent-officer during the previous 1898 Nile campaign led to a prohibition against such an arrangement. However, Churchill was able to circumvent this rule to perform the same role during the Boer War, one of only several soldiers to do so. During the Sudan campaign he disguised his reports as private letters addressed to a fictitious "my dear" who in reality was the editor Oliver Borthwick of the *Morning Post*. In June 1900 he returned to England to write several books based on his South African exploits. His books *London to Ladysmith, via Pretoria* (1900) and *Ian Hamilton's March* (1900) were based on his reports for the *Morning Post*. His career as a war correspondent was short and amazingly successful, with four profitable books to his credit by the time he was twenty-six. However, his career as writer and statesman was just beginning. He died on January 24, 1965.

REFERENCES: Keith Alldritt. *Churchill, the Writer*. 1992; Winston Churchill. *The Boer War*. 1990; *DNB*, 1961–1970; Robert Wilkinson-Latham. *From Our Special Correspondent*. 1979.

CIVIL WAR. *See* AMERICAN CIVIL WAR.

CLAPPER, RAYMOND LEWIS (1892–1944). Clapper was born in La Cygne, Kansas, and educated at the University of Kansas. He began writing for the *Kansas City Star* while still in college. He joined the staff of United Press International in 1917, serving in the nation's capital for the next sixteen years. Disgusted by the nepotism, graft, and political patronage of the city, he wrote *Racketeering in Washington* (1933). The next year he joined the *Washington*

Post and became a popular syndicated columnist with his daily column "Between You and Me."

During World War II* he became a traveling war correspondent, reporting the invasion of Sicily and the bombing of Rome, before transferring to the Pacific theater in late 1943 to cover action from New Britain, New Guinea, and Guadalcanal. He was reporting the invasion of the Marshall Islands in 1944 when the plane that was carrying him over the devastated airfield at Eniwetok hit another American bomber, killing all on board. Following his death colleagues established the Raymond Clapper Memorial Association, which annually rewarded a Washington correspondent. Its first recipient was war correspondent Ernie Pyle.* Clapper's collected work was published as *Watching the World* in 1944.
REFERENCES: Robert W. Desmond. *Tides of War.* 1984; *DAB* 3.

CLARK, WILLIS GAYLORD (1827–1898). Born in New York, he served as both coeditor and frontline reporter for the Confederate newspaper the *Mobile Register.* Clark studied law in Illinois before moving to Mobile to practice. He first entered journalism as editor for the Democratic *Southern Magazine* before moving over to the *Mobile Daily Advertiser*, which merged with the *Register* at the outbreak of the war. He left war reporting for a career in manufacturing and railroading.
REFERENCE: Stewart Sifakis. *Who Was Who in the Civil War.* 1988.

CLARKE, SIR BASIL (1879–1947). Born in Cheshire, England, he was educated at Oxford before entering the banking profession. In 1904 he joined the *Manchester Guardian* as a special correspondent. He assumed the same position in 1910 with the *Daily Mail.* When World War I* broke out he covered the German invasion of Belgium in 1914. In 1915 he reported the Balkan campaign and the following year witnessed warfare in Holland and Scandinavia as well as the naval blockade of Germany. Joining Reuters* that same year, he was with the British army at the Battle of the Somme. Following the war he left journalism for the Special Intelligence Branch of the Ministry of Reconstruction, with which he remained for the next twelve years. He continued his career with the Ministry of Health and was knighted in 1923.
REFERENCE: Dennis Griffiths, ed. *The Encyclopedia of the British Press.* 1992.

CLARKE, THOMAS (1884–1957). Clarke was born in Bolton, England, and entered journalism while still in his teens. In 1903 he was hired by the *South China Morning Post* in Hong Kong. Soon after, he was covering events in French Indochina for the *Daily Mail* and the *Chicago Tribune.* He reported the Russo-Japanese War* and returned to England shortly after the conflict.

In 1911 Clarke joined the staff of the *Daily Mail* on a full-time basis. He went on to hold a variety of posts with several other papers as well as serve in World War I.* During World War II* he worked as a news broadcaster for the

BBC Latin American service. He wrote several books, including two about the power of the press, *Northcliffe in History* (1950) and *My Northcliffe Diary* (1931).
REFERENCE: *DNB*. 1951–1960.

CLIFFORD, ALEXANDER GRAEME (?). Prior to becoming Berlin correspondent for Reuters* in 1939 he had covered the Spanish Civil War* for the news agency. With the outbreak of World War II* Clifford went to the British headquarters in France as an "eyewitness"* for the entire British press establishment. By 1940 he was with the *Daily Mail* reporting the conflict in Greece and Yugoslavia before accompanying the British Expeditionary Force to North Africa during the Egyptian-Libyan desert campaign the following year. During the winter of 1943–1944 Clifford was on the Italian front, where he was cited for the second time for "gallant and distinguished services." In 1944 he returned to France after five years to cover the post–D-Day campaign. Following the liberation of Paris Clifford accompanied the British Second Army on its push into Belgium, Holland, and finally Germany.
REFERENCES: Richard Collier. *Fighting Words*. 1989; Robert W. Desmond. *Tides of War*. 1984.

COBB, IRVIN SHREWSBURY (1876–1944). Cobb was born in Paducah, Kentucky, and got his start in journalism working for his hometown newspaper. Primarily remembered as a humorist, Cobb worked for a variety of papers, often doubling as a political reporter and humor columnist. While employed by the *Saturday Evening Post* he was twice sent to Europe to cover World War I.* He reported the battles at Chateau-Thierry, Louvain, Mons, and the occupation of Brussels. He was bedridden in a London hotel when the city was bombed by German zeppelins in 1918. During the war he viewed combat from an observation balloon above the Aisne River and was nearly shot as a spy by a Prussian officer. Following each of his European stints he went on the lecture circuit once back home.

In 1922 he left the *Post* for Hearst's *Cosmopolitan* magazine. Cobb continued to write books and articles, met seven presidents, and wrote for vaudeville and silent films.
REFERENCES: Emmet Crozier. *American Reporters on the Western Front 1914–18*. 1959; Fred Gus Neuman. *Irvin S. Cobb: His Life and Achievements*. 1934.

COCKBURN, CLAUD (1904–1981). Born in Peking, Cockburn was one of the most eccentric and controversial reporters to cover the Spanish Civil War.* He was educated at Oxford and was a cousin of the writer Evelyn Waugh.* Following graduation he entered journalism with the *Times* and by 1929 was a full-time journalist and foreign correspondent. However, within four years he had drifted toward radical politics and resigned. He established the *Week*, which published stories not typically handled by the establishment press. The London-based paper reported the developing conflict in Spain well ahead of its competition.

By the summer of 1936 Cockburn was in Spain himself, joining the ranks of the Fifth Regiment. He would be just one of many journalists who took up arms during the Spanish Civil War. After several weeks in the field he was persuaded to return to journalism, where his talent for propaganda could be better put to use. Upon his return to London he turned his efforts to overturning England's policy of nonintervention in the conflict. The publication of his polemic, *Reporter in Spain*, and his pro-Communist sympathies led the British government to deny him a visa due to his participation in the Republican militia. Despite efforts to bar his return, several weeks later Cockburn was sending dispatches to the *Week* and the *Daily Worker* from Spain.

One of his best pieces on the war involved an event which never occurred. From August 1936, the border between Spain and France had been closed to arms traffic, which the Republic forces drastically had need of. Cockburn convinced the French prime minister, Leon Blum, to reopen the border in March 1938 by concocting a story of a major Nationalist setback in Morocco. He was heavily criticized for distorting the truth and using the press to achieve his political goals.

In 1941 Cockburn's paper the *Week* was banned along with the *Daily Worker* because of their antiwar stance. Except for a brief stint in the field at the onset of the war Cockburn functioned more as propagandist than war correspondent. His request for accreditation as a war correspondent was denied on account of his Communist leanings and his potential for impairing morale within the armed forces. Following the war he lived in Ireland and kept his hand in journalism as a regular contributor to the *Irish Times*, the *New Statesman*, and other periodicals.

REFERENCES: Phillip Knightley. *The First Casualty.* 1975; Trevor Royle. *War Report.* 1987; Peter Wyden. *The Passionate War.* 1983.

COFFIN, CHARLES CARLETON (1823–1896). Born in Boscawen, New Hampshire, Coffin was, according to some sources, the only reporter to cover all four years of the American Civil War.* He worked for several Boston newspapers, including the *Boston Journal*, which released him soon before the outbreak of the Civil War. Coffin covered the Battle of Bull Run at his own expense, figuring at worst he could sell his story to another paper. The *Journal* was so impressed by his reporting of the battle that he was rehired as a "special" to cover the war. During the conflict his letters appeared regularly in the Boston papers under the pen name "Carleton."

Coffin became a familiar fixture along the front lines with his notebooks and topographical maps on hand to ensure accuracy. His reputation for precision was enhanced by the fact that he was one of the few reporters to include diagrams with his dispatches. His simultaneous coverage of both the western and eastern battle fronts was also a rarity. Among his feature scoops were Grant's victory at Fort Donelson, Tennessee, and the Union recapture of Charleston. He reported on the Battles of Antietam, Gettysburg, and the Wilderness, as well as Lincoln's Gettysburg Address and the capture of Richmond. In the process he gained national prominence as one of the foremost reporters of the war. After the war he embarked on a lecture tour around the world recounting his wartime exploits. He wrote thirteen books ranging from travel and children's stories to novels. Among his works recounting his career as a war reporter were *My Days and Nights on the Battlefield* (1864), *Following the Flag* (1865), *Four Years of Fighting* (1866), and *Marching to Victory* (1888). Coffin entered the political arena in 1884, serving a term in the Massachusetts state assembly before entering the state senate in 1890. He died of apoplexy in Boston on March 2, 1896, hard at work on a speech concerning his life as a war correspondent.

REFERENCES: J. Cutler Andrews. *The North Reports the Civil War.* 1955; Patricia Faust, ed. *Historical Times Illustrated Encyclopedia of the Civil War.* 1986; William Elliot Griffis. *Charles Carleton Coffin.* 1898; Louis M. Starr. *Bohemian Brigade.* 1954.

COLBURN, ROBERT T. (?). Colburn covered the western theater of the American Civil War* for the *New York World*. He was one of the first reporters to arrive at Cairo, Illinois, in early 1862 as the Western Army of Tennessee prepared to move up the Tennessee River to strike at the heart of the Confederacy. He was captured along with correspondents Junius Browne* and Albert Deane Richardson* while attempting to run the batteries at Vicksburg and reach Grant's command. Colburn was released within a month, while his colleagues endured almost two years in seven different Confederate prisons. Confederate authorities explained that the disparity in the sentences was due to the other reporters' affiliation with the *New York Tribune*, which they blamed for inaugurating the war.

REFERENCES: J. Cutler Andrews. *The North Reports the Civil War.* 1955; Louis M. Starr. *Bohemian Brigade.* 1954.

COLLINGWOOD, CHARLES CUMMINGS (1917–1985). Born in Three Rivers, Michigan, the future Rhodes scholar was hired by Edward R. Murrow as a network correspondent for CBS radio during World War II.* Following graduation from Cornell University he attended Oxford on a scholarship, intending to pursue a law career. In 1940 he went to work for the United Press.

Joining the likes of William L. Shirer,* Howard K. Smith,* and Eric Sevareid,* all recruited by Murrow to make up the CBS broadcast team during the war, Collingwood was first assigned to North Africa, where he would be awarded the rank of captain as war correspondent with the British army. In 1943 he won the Peabody Award for best foreign reporting and was sent stateside. He went on to a successful career in television newscasting, winning another Peabody Award in 1963. In the 1960s he began covering American involvement in Vietnam* and in 1968 was one of the first American news reporters permitted broadcast access to North Vietnam. He received Emmy awards for his coverage of the Vietnam War in 1968 and 1969.

REFERENCES: Dennis Griffiths, ed. *The Encyclopedia of the British Press.* 1992; *New York Times.* October 4, 1985.

COLLINS, ROBERT MOORE (1868–1937). As Reuters* correspondent he covered the Boxer Rebellion,* the Philippine insurrection, and the Russo-Japanese War* as the chief Reuters correspondent in China. He returned to England soon after the Portsmouth Treaty was signed and worked for the Associated Press until 1925.

REFERENCE: Dennis Griffiths, ed. *The Encyclopedia of the British Press.* 1992.

COLTMAN, ROBERT (b. 1862). Coltman was born in Washington, D.C., and graduated from Jefferson Medical College in Philadelphia. He was practicing medicine in Peking as well as reporting for the *Chicago Record* from 1895. When the Boxer Rebellion* broke out in 1900, Coltman chronicled the siege from inside the city. He was able to smuggle the news scoop of the Boxer siege through the Boxer pickets with the assistance of a local beggar, and was thereby responsible for alerting the outside world to the siege of Peking. He wrote *The Chinese: Medical, Political and Social* (1891) and *Yellow Crime, or Beleaguered in Peking* (1901).

REFERENCE: M. L. Stein. *Under Fire: The Story of American War Correspondents.* 1968.

CONFEDERATE PRESS ASSOCIATION. During the American Civil War* many Southern newspapers could not afford special war correspondents and relied on the members of the Confederate Press Association, also known as the Press Association of the Confederate States. Established on March 1, 1863, the new organization encompassed all Confederate dailies east of the Mississippi River. Once Dr. Robert W. Gibbes, the editor of the *Columbia South Carolinian,* was elected president and headquarters was established in Atlanta, correspondents were recruited and telegraph facilities were arranged with both the military and Southern telegraph companies. Each newspaper that subscribed to the association paid twelve dollars a week for a news report that could not exceed 3,500 words. In order to control access to the service the association copyrighted its reports.

Correspondents were instructed to eliminate opinion from their dispatches and to stress factual reporting. They achieved a creditable record for objective reporting, eschewing rumor and unsubstantiated information. Leading journalists for the association included Bartholomew Riordan, John Hatcher, Jonathan Albertson, A. J. Wagner, and W. O. Woodson.

REFERENCES: J. Cutler Andrews. *The South Reports the Civil War.* 1970; Hodding Carter. *Their Words Were Bullets: The Southern Press in War, Reconstruction and Peace.* 1969.

CONNIFF, FRANK (1914–1971). Born in Danbury, Connecticut, and educated at the University of Virginia, Conniff joined the Hearst newspaper chain following graduation. Beginning in 1944 he covered most theaters of conflict during World War II,* including Africa, Italy, and Germany. He was with Allied forces after the capture of Rome and was part of the International News Service French invasion team. After World War II he reported the Korean War.* Following his interview of Soviet premier Khrushchev in 1955 he received the Pulitzer Prize along with fellow correspondents Howard Kingsbury Smith and W. R. Hearst, Jr. He retired from journalism in 1967.
REFERENCE: Jack Stenbuck, ed. *Typewriter Battalion.* 1995.

COOKE, JOHN ESTEN (1830–1886). Cooke was the leading war correspondent for the *Southern Illustrated News* during the American Civil War.* He served as staff officer on different occasions for Generals J.E.B. Stuart and Thomas J. "Stonewall" Jackson. In addition to the *Illustrated News* he filed dispatches with other Richmond papers. His coverage of the Battle of Fredericksburg while with Stuart was one of the best accounts of the engagement and appeared in the *Richmond Whig* under his pen name "J.E.C."
REFERENCE: J. Cutler Andrews. *The South Reports the Civil War.* 1970.

COOPER, JAMES LEES (1907–1980). Born in Darwen, Lancashire, he joined the *Darwen News* before leaving for the *Daily Express.* In 1941 he became its war correspondent, covering the Malta Convoys, the Eighth Army campaign in North Africa, and action in Sicily, Italy, and Madagascar. Following the war he returned to Fleet Street before becoming the first staff reporter for the paper in Canada. He left the *Daily Express* in 1958 to return to London and join the *Globe and Mail.* The next year he returned to Toronto, where he was promoted to editor and publisher. He retired in 1974.
REFERENCE: Dennis Griffiths, ed. *The Encyclopedia of the British Press.* 1992.

COOPER, ROBERT WRIGHT "BOB" (1904–1992). Born in Toronto, he joined the *Times* in 1924 and became its sports reporter. In 1939 he became a war correspondent covering French forces. After the debacle at Dunkirk, Cooper fled back to England before reporting from India, Orde Wingate's Burmese campaign, the Normandy invasion on D-Day, the liberation of Paris and Belgium, and finally the surrender of German forces. He received accolades for his coverage of the Nuremberg trials, following which he became the chief *Times* correspondent in Germany.
REFERENCES: Robert W. Desmond. *Tides of War.* 1984; Dennis Griffiths, ed. *The Encyclopedia of the British Press.* 1992.

COWAN, RUTH (b. 1902). Born in Salt Lake City, she graduated from the University of Texas before joining the staff of the *San Antonio Evening News* in 1928. Her first assignment as a war correspondent was in Algiers in 1942.

She was reassigned to London, where she would stay until the Normandy invasion. Her coverage of the evacuation and treatment of the wounded contributed to her being permanently assigned to follow the U.S. armies for the duration of the war. During her two and a half years as a war correspondent Cowan interviewed Generals Eisenhower, Bradley, and Patton and covered major battles such as the Battle of the Bulge. Shortly before V-E Day she returned to the United States and a posting with the Washington Bureau of the Associated Press. In 1956 she married Bradley D. Nash, the undersecretary of commerce, and retired from the AP.
REFERENCE: Lilya Wagner. *Women War Correspondents of World War Two*. 1989.

COWLES, VIRGINIA (1910–1983). Born in Brattleboro, Vermont, Cowles entered journalism in the early 1930s with the *Boston Breeze*. She covered the Spanish Civil War* for the *Daily Telegraph*, the *Sunday Times*, and the Hearst newspapers. With the outbreak of World War II* she reported the Russo-Finnish War and the fall of France for the *Sunday Times*, before returning to England. In 1941 she published *Looking for Trouble*, and from 1942 to 1943 she was special assistant to the American ambassador to London.

Cowles reported the North African campaign for the *Chicago Sun* and the London *Sunday Times*. She eventually covered the conflict from Germany, Russia, and Czechoslovakia. Following the war she remained in London, marrying future British cabinet official and member of Parliament Aidan Crawley in 1945. Cowles died in an automobile accident near Biarritz while revisiting sites from her Spanish Civil War days. She published numerous biographies and works of nonfiction including *Winston Churchill: The Era and the Man* (1953), *The Phantom Major: The Story of David Stirling and His Desert Command* (1958), and *The Russian Dagger: Cold War in the Days of the Czars* (1969).
REFERENCES: Robert W. Desmond. *Tides of War*. 1984; Library of America. *Reporting World War II*. 1995; Anne Sebba. *Battling for News: The Rise of the Woman Reporter*. 1994.

CRANE, STEPHEN (1871–1900). Born in Newark, New Jersey, he broke into journalism with his brother's local newspaper covering the New Jersey coastal resorts. He moved to New York City, publishing occasional articles in local newspapers and working on his novel *Maggie: A Girl of the Streets*, which he self-published under the pseudonym Johnston Smith in 1893. He wrote for several periodicals while completing *The Red Badge of Courage*. Sent to Cuba to cover the insurrection in 1896, he was in a ship that went down off the coast of Florida just after the new year. His thirty-hour fight for life on a small raft was the grist for his *Scribner's* story "The Open Boat."

In 1897 Crane covered the Greco-Turkish War* for the *New York Journal* and the following year the Spanish-American War* for the *New York World*. He witnessed the landing of the marines at Guantanamo as well as most of the battles of the short war. His health began to decline, resulting in his evacuation.

After a dispute over finances he left the *World* for the *Journal*, and returned to cover the action on Puerto Rico. His novel *Active Service** (1899) tells the story of war correspondents in action. Richard Harding Davis,* the preeminent war correspondent of his era, called Crane the best correspondent of the war. Crane died from tuberculosis at the age of twenty-eight.

REFERENCES: James B. Colvert. *Stephen Crane.* 1984; *DAB* 2.

CRAWFORD, KENNETH GALE (1902–1983). Crawford was born in Sparta, Wisconsin, and educated at Beloit College. He joined the United Press in 1924 and five years later became its Washington correspondent. In 1943 he was hired by *Newsweek* as a war correspondent. He covered action in North Africa, the Middle East, France, and Italy. He was reportedly the first American reporter to hit the beaches at Normandy during the D-Day invasion. His wartime reporting led to various awards, including the European Theater Ribbon, the Navy Commendation, and the French Liberation Medal.

In 1945 he returned to Washington as editor of the local *Newsweek* bureau. After a long career at the magazine he retired from journalism in 1970. He died of lung cancer on January 13, 1983. He wrote *The Pressure Boys* (1939) and *Report on North Africa* (1943).

REFERENCES: Robert W. Desmond. *Tides of War.* 1984; *New York Times.* January 14, 1983.

CRAWFURD-PRICE, WALTER (1881–1967). Born in London and educated at the University of Wales, Crawfurd-Price covered the Turkish counterrevolution for the *Daily Mail* in 1909. In 1911 he joined the *Times* as special correspondent for Greece and Macedonia. He covered the Turkish army during the First Balkan War (1912) and was with the Greek army the following year. During World War I* he accompanied the Serbian army. He covered the signing of the 1919 Peace Treaty for the *Sunday Times* and stayed with the paper until 1925. Among his numerous travel books was *A Tangier Visit* (1935).

REFERENCE: Dennis Giffiths, ed. *The Encyclopedia of the British Press.* 1992.

CREELMAN, JAMES (1859–1915). Born in Montreal, Canada, Creelman moved to New York at the age of twelve. Six years later, he found work as a cub reporter for the *New York Herald.* Presaging his future fame, he received plaudits for his coverage of the Hatfield-McCoy feud while under gunfire as well as for interviewing Sitting Bull and surviving a crash in a gas airship. In 1889 he became editor of the London branch of the *Herald.* In 1893, after several stints with other papers, he was hired by Joseph Pulitzer's *New York World* to cover events in Asia, including the Sino-Japanese War.

Creelman followed the Japanese armies and covered the Battles of Pyongyang and Port Arthur and the naval engagement of Yalu. He received the first of several combat-related wounds while accompanying the army in Manchuria when the explosion of an artillery shell threw him off his horse, causing several injuries. In December 1894 he was involved in perhaps his most controversial story when his account of a massacre of Chinese civilians at Port Arthur hit the newsstands.

In 1896 Creelman covered the insurrection in Cuba, again publicizing atrocities, before being expelled by Spanish authorities for his investigative proclivities. He was responsible for giving Captain-General Weyler, the Spanish commander in Cuba, his moniker "The Butcher."

Successfully lured away from the *World* by Hearst's *New York Journal*, he was assigned to Europe, where he covered the Greco-Turkish War.* He would claim to be the first correspondent to cross the frontier to the Turkish lines. In June 1898 he was sent to Cuba to cover the Spanish-American War.* He ended up leading the charge against fortifications at El Caney when it turned out he was the only American who knew the back way up the hill. He was wounded while explaining surrender terms to a Spanish officer. Later that same year Creelman was wounded twice more while covering the American conflict with the insurgents in the Philippines.

Creelman returned to the *New York World* in 1900, and then spent short stints with several other papers over the next decade. In 1915 he was sent to cover what would be his last battle in Europe; he died of Bright's disease in Berlin shortly after his arrival. He published several books, with *On the Great Highway: The Wanderings and Adventures of a Special Correspondent* (1901) being the most notable.

REFERENCES: Willis J. Abbott. *Watching the World Go By*. 1933; *DAB* 2. 533; Jeffrey M. Dowart. "James Creelman, the *New York World* and the Port Arthur Massacre," *Journalism Quarterly*. 1973, pp. 697–701.

CRIMEAN WAR. The Crimean War broke out in October 1853 when Turkey declared war on Russia. This conflict was an outgrowth of an ongoing territorial dispute between Russia and Turkey which resulted in Russian forces occupying the Danubian Principalities to coerce Turkey into accepting certain concessions. Great Britain joined France in a declaration of war on Russia in March 1854. In September a combined Anglo-French force landed in the Crimea and advanced against the Russians at Sebastopol. Subsequent battles occurred at the Alma River, Balaklava, and Inkerman. The war ended in December 1856 when the Austrians threatened to join the alliance. Both Turkey and Russia made concessions, but more significantly, Turkey was drawn closer into the sphere of Western nations.

Compared to the Mexican War,* which was covered more by solitary correspondents, the Crimean War attracted groups of correspondents on foreign assignment, in numbers not seen before. The majority of reporters were members of the London press, with the *Times* the best represented. In addition artist-correspondents* covered their first war, and pioneer war photographers* such as Roger Fenton,* James Robertson,* and Karl Baptist von Szathmari* provided considerably more photographic coverage than in any previous wars.

The Crimean War introduced the legendary William Howard Russell* to the annals of wartime journalism. Over the next two decades he became the pre-eminent war correspondent of the nineteenth century. Russell is best remembered for contributing the phrase "the thin red line" in his description of the British infantry at Balaklava. His report of "the charge of the Light Brigade" reportedly inspired Alfred Lord Tennyson's poem of the same title.

This war also introduced a prejudicial attitude among the high command toward war correspondents. The commander of the Crimean expedition, Lord Raglan, and General Sir Arthur Wellesley, later better known as Lord Wellington, expressed objections to their presence and would have nothing to do with them. General Sir William Simpson perhaps more eloquently christened war reporters as "the curse of modern armies."

With war reportage still in its infancy, the rules of this craft were still being written. Correspondents were expected to be self-supporting, providing their own shelter, food, transportation, and communication channels. Other correspondents besides Russell represented the *Times*, including Dr. Humphrey Sandwith, John Barkley, Thomas Chenery,* Ferdinand Eber, Frederick Hardman,* Andrew Archibald Paton, and T. M. O'Bird. Several of their group perished, some of the first casualties of this profession. Henry Stowe died of enteric fever and Charles Naysmith was killed in battle.

Other reporters reporting the war included Edwin L. Godkin* of the *Daily News*, George Alfred Henty* of the *Morning Post*, and Nicholas A. Wood for the *Morning Chronicle*. There were many others as well. Some spent only short stints in the Crimea and others stayed for over a year. Among the more notable artist-correspondents were William Simpson* of the *Illustrated London News* and Joseph A. Crowe* of the *Daily News*. The more strictly controlled Russian press provided little press coverage, relying on official reports instead. An important innovation stimulated by the war effort was the extension from Vienna to the Black Sea coast of Bulgaria of telegraph services, which the British extended to Sebastopol and Balaklava.

REFERENCES: Nicholas Bentley, ed. *Russell's Despatches from the Crimea, 1854–1856.* 1967; Lawrence James. *Crimea, 1854–1856: The War with Russia from Contemporary Photographs.* 1981; Andrew Lambert and Stephen Badsey. *The War Correspondents: The Crimean War.* 1994.

CRONKITE, WALTER LELAND, JR. (b. 1916). Born in St. Joseph, Missouri, Cronkite became the elder statesman of American newscasting. He gravitated toward a career in journalism while still in high school. In the 1930s he left the University of Texas before graduating to work for the *Houston Post*. After several other jobs in newscasting and public relations he was hired by the United Press in 1940. With the outbreak of the war in Europe Cronkite rose to prominence as one of the first American journalists accredited to cover the conflict. Posted to London in 1942, he participated in many bombing raids and witnessed the North African campaign, the invasion of Normandy, and the Battle of the Bulge. He continued to report from Europe after the war, including the Nuremberg trials.

He returned to the States in 1948 and continued to make a name in radio and television broadcasting. In 1962 he became the CBS anchorman. He made several visits to Southeast Asia and Vietnam in the 1960s, but his career as a war correspondent ended with World War II.*

REFERENCES: Les Brown. *The New York Times Encyclopedia of Television.* 1977; Gary Gates. *Air Time: The Inside Story of CBS News.* 1978.

CROSBY, CHARLES E. (d. 1897). Born in Great Britain, Crosby had been a soldier and a civil engineer in Latin America when the conflict in Cuba began to develop in the late 1890s. He covered the Cuban insurrection prior to the Spanish-American War* for the *Chicago Record*. Landing at Havana in January 1897, Crosby headed for the insurgent stronghold of General Maximo Gomez. After sending back several dispatches under his pen name ''Don Carlos,'' he was killed in March during an engagement between the rebels and Spanish forces. Although his pseudonym was an attempt to evade Spanish authorities, some of his work had fallen into enemy hands. The Spanish had apparently posted a description of Crosby and were actively searching for him when he was killed.

REFERENCE: Charles H. Brown. *The Correspondents' War.* 1967.

CROSS, HENRY (1855–1898). Born in Bedfordshire and educated at Oxford, Cross covered the Sudan campaign for the *Manchester Guardian*. Cross had agreed to pay his own expenses like many of his colleagues, and had arranged to be paid for each article or ''letter'' he sent back to the paper. He witnessed the defeat of the Mahdist forces at the Battle of Omdurman on September 2, 1898. Shortly after the battle he was stricken with enteric fever and died. However, his account of the pivotal battle was published three days after his death. In good faith the newspaper paid Cross' estate twenty-five percent more than the agreed upon rate for the story.

REFERENCES: David Ayerst. *The Manchester Guardian: Biography of a Newspaper.* 1971; E. N. Bennett. *The Downfall of the Dervishes.* 1899.

CROST, LYN (?). Crost began her newspaper career writing for the *Providence Star-Tribune* while still a student at Brown University. After graduation she moved to Hawaii and in 1944 was hired by the *Honolulu Star-Bulletin* to cover the American-born Japanese soldiers, known as the Nisei, who were fighting in Europe. She covered their actions in Italy, Germany, and France, concentrating on the human side of the war rather on combat stories. Crost wrote the first story about the Nisei hero and future senator, Lieutenant Daniel Inouye, who won the Distinguished Service Cross during the Po Valley campaign. She was one of the first American correspondents to arrive at Buchenwald. After the war

she worked as the Washington correspondent for the *Star-Bulletin* and as a special assistant in the White House during Eisenhower's first term.
REFERENCE: Lilya Wagner. *Women War Correspondents of World War Two*. 1989.

CROUNSE, LORENZO L. (1834–1909). Born in Sharon, New York, Crounse demonstrated an affinity for the newspaper profession by the age of twelve, when he traveled thirty miles in a wagon in response to an advertisement for a printer's apprentice. Initially rebuffed because of his youth, two years later he landed a job on the *Milwaukee Free Democrat*. Less than eight years later he had risen to editor and co-owner of the paper. With the outbreak of the American Civil War* Crounse took to the field for various western newspapers before joining the staff of the *New York World* and then the *New York Times*.

Crounse and William Swinton* would become the preeminent correspondents for the *New York Times* covering the Army of the Potomac. During the war he had two horses shot from under him and in 1862 lost the use of his arm when struck by a shell fragment. On another occasion he was captured by Mosby's raiders, who confiscated his notebooks and turned the news over to Richmond newspapers. For much of the conflict Crounse was accompanied by his brother Silas, who served as his dispatch courier. In 1863 he traded the front lines for the night editor position with the *Times*.

Crounse lost his first horse while reporting the Peninsular campaign for the *New York World* following the Battle of Gaines Mill. In addition to the *World* he represented the *Cincinnati Commercial* and the *Chicago Tribune* during the expedition against Roanoke Island in 1862.

He delivered one of his greatest scoops with his account of the Battle of Chancellorsville for the *New York Times*. In June 1863 Crounse reported the cavalry battle at Beverly's Ford and Brandy Station. By the time of the Gettysburg campaign Crounse was chief correspondent for the *Times* with the Army of the Potomac. He narrowly escaped capture on his way to Gettysburg when he stumbled upon Confederate troops. Crounse claimed that his reconnaissance report to Major General John Reynolds of Confederate troop movements toward Gettysburg precipitated the battle. During the battle he had another horse shot from under him and witnessed the annihilation of General Pickett's division during its attack on Cemetery Ridge.

Crounse later covered the Battle of Wauhatchie, the capture of Lookout Mountain, the fall of Richmond, and the surrender of General Robert E. Lee. Following the war he became a top Washington correspondent for the *Times*.
REFERENCES: J. Cutler Andrews. *The North Reports the Civil War*. 1955; Louis M. Starr. *Bohemian Brigade*. 1954.

CROWE, SIR JOSEPH ARCHER (1825–1896). Best known for his histories of painting, Crowe was born in London. Son of a newspaper correspondent, he went to work for the *Morning News* and then the *Daily News*. One of the first of the "special artists," Crowe, a watercolorist, was the artist for the *Illustrated*

London News in the Crimean War* and a correspondent for the *Daily News* (1846–1852) and the *Times* during the Indian Mutiny. Crowe arrived at Balaklava in September 1854, where he witnessed the Russian attack on the heights of Balaklava and later reported that he had had a good view of the charge of the Light Brigade. He was with the Ninety-fifth Regiment at the Battle of Inkerman in November 1854. Following the battle Crowe was stricken with a serious case of frostbite and was forced to return to England. While home he lectured on the war and was well enough to return to the Crimea in June 1855. In September he witnessed the fall of Sebastopol.

Following the Crimean War he became the superintendent of an art college in India. In the late 1850s he pursued the craft of art history and acted as correspondent during the Indian Mutiny. He left India in 1859 due to poor health before reporting the Austro-Italian War* that same year for the *Times*, during which he reported the Battle of Solferino. He entered the Foreign Office in 1860 when he was appointed consul general for Saxony, in which capacity he represented French interests at Leipzig during the Franco-Prussian War* of 1870. In 1872 he was appointed consul general for Westphalia and the Rhenish provinces and in 1880 was made commercial attaché to the embassies at Vienna and Berlin. After leaving journalism Crowe embarked on a career as a diplomat and art critic. He died shortly after retiring as commercial attaché in Paris.

REFERENCES: *DNB*; Pat Hodgson. *The War Illustrators*. 1977.

CROZIER, EMMET (1893–1982). Crozier was a correspondent and founding member of the American Newspaper Guild. He began his newspaper career with the *Kansas City Star* in 1912; following that he worked for the *New York Herald Evening World* and then the *New York Tribune*, for which he worked as a war correspondent during World War II* covering the Pacific theater of operations. He was the author of several books on war journalism history, *Yankee Reporters: 1861–65* (1956) and *American Reporters on the Western Front: 1916–18* (1959).

REFERENCE: M. L. Stein. *Under Fire*. 1968.

CUNNINGHAM, ALFRED (1870–1918). Born in London, Cunningham became one of the preeminent and best-traveled war correspondents of his day. He first became a special correspondent in 1894 when he covered the Sino-Japanese War* for the Central News Agency. Two years later he was in the Philippines with Spanish forces while covering the Spanish-American War* for the *New York Journal*. In 1900 he reported the Boxer Rebellion* and the relief expedition into Peking for the *Daily Mail* and the *New York Sun*. Five years later he represented the same two papers during the Russo-Japanese War* and was awarded the Imperial Japanese Order of the Rising Sun. He wrote many books, including *The French in Tonkin and South China, The Chinese Soldier and Other Sketches*, and *Today in Egypt*.

REFERENCES: Dennis Griffiths, ed. *The Encyclopedia of the British Press*. 1992; Robert Wilkinson-Latham. *From Our Special Correspondent*. 1979.

CUNNINGHAM, ED (1913–1984). He was the first *Yank** correspondent sent overseas at the start of World War II.* On his way overseas his plane was forced off course in a storm, crashing in the Brazilian jungle, where he was rescued ten days later. During the war he served in the China-Burma-India theater under General Joseph Stilwell. He landed several exclusive interviews with the general by charting his privy schedule so he could join him in privacy. Once they were sitting together the general confided his concerns about combat-related problems. Cunningham also covered the fighting in the Middle East, North Africa, and the last advance of the German army during the Ardennes breakthrough.

REFERENCE: Art Weithas. *Close to Glory*. 1991.

D

DAGUERREOTYPE. Commercially popular between 1841 and 1860, this photographic technique was developed by the French physicist and artist Louis Jacques Mandé Daguerre in 1839. This process does not require a negative image, so each daguerreotype is a one-of-a-kind positive image that cannot be reproduced. In the daguerreotype process an illuminated image is exposed to a polished surface coated with an iodine vapor, and later separately treated with mercury and a sodium solution. This process was phenomenally popular in mid-nineteenth-century America, where more daguerreotypes were produced than anywhere else in the world.

The first examples of war photography were daguerreotypes taken during the 1846–1848 Mexican War,* but technical limitations made it impossible to photograph actual combat scenes. Only twelve images from this conflict were known to exist until 1981, when an additional thirty-eight daguerreotype portraits were discovered in a Connecticut barn. By the time of the American Civil War* wet-plate photography had replaced the daguerreotype, although it remained an occasional alternative.
REFERENCES: Pat Hodgson. *Early War Photographs*. 1974; Martha A. Sandweiss, Rick Stewart, and Ben W. Huseman. *Eyewitness to War*. 1989.

DANIEL, JOHN MONCURE (1825–1865). Born in Stafford County, Virginia, Daniel briefly studied law and worked as a superintendent in a library before entering the newspaper business in the 1840s. After a short stint as editor of the *Southern Planter* he moved over to the *Richmond Examiner* in the same capacity in 1847 and soon became the sole proprietor of the paper. He left journalism for several years when President Pierce appointed him to a diplomatic post in

Sardinia. He returned to the States and the editorial desk at the *Examiner* in late 1860.

During the American Civil War* Daniel sporadically left his desk to report the progress of the Confederate armies on the battlefields. He traveled with General A. P. Hill's army as his aide and was present at the Battle of Gaines' Mill in June 1862. He soon returned to his paper and was wounded in a duel with the Confederate treasurer in 1864. He became ill the following year and died shortly before his plant was torched after the capture of Richmond.
REFERENCE: J. Cutler Andrews. *The South Reports the Civil War.* 1970.

DA PONTE, DURANT (?). Da Ponte moved to New Orleans from Illinois when he was twelve years old. The grandson of the composer of the libretto for the opera *Don Giovanni* began working for the *New Orleans Crescent* as a reporter in his early teens. In 1861 he covered the Virginia campaign beginning with the Battle of Manassas for the *New Orleans Delta*. Following the battle he returned to New Orleans before joining General Johnston's army as a reporter and captain on the staff of Major General Earl Van Dorn. By 1862 Da Ponte had risen to editor of the *Delta* and left the field of battle temporarily. When federal troops took New Orleans later that year he moved to Richmond, Virginia.
REFERENCE: J. Cutler Andrews. *The South Reports the Civil War.* 1970.

DAVENPORT, REUBEN BRIGGS (1852?–1932). Born in New York City, Davenport graduated from the College of the City of New York in 1871 before joining the *New York Herald* the following year. He covered the American Indian Wars* from 1875 to 1881. After covering the Jenny-Newton expedition into the Black Hills in 1875 he rode alone through hostile country to report negotiations with the Sioux over the purchase of the Black Hills. He was reportedly unpopular with military commanders because of his penchant for criticism.

In 1876 Davenport joined the Crook expedition into the Black Hills for the *New York Herald*. At the Battle of the Rosebud he took part in the fighting and later covered the Battle of Slim Buttes, in which he corrected the total number of soldiers killed in the battle. He was with General George Crook during the advance to the Little Big Horn. A constant critic of General Crook, he labeled Crook incompetent, and one of his articles even cast doubt on the general's supposed spartan lifestyle, suggesting that each night he was brought an excess of supplies by a mule packer. However, one of Crook's staunchest supporters challenged this. Charles King, in his *Campaigning with Crook* (1880), labeled Davenport a coward as well. Davenport threatened a libel suit, forcing King to retract his charge.

Following the Crook expeditions Davenport remained with the *Herald* until 1882. He went on to a career with several other top-flight papers including the *Morning News* and the *New York Times*. Davenport later established the *New Haven Morning News* in Connecticut and covered the Spanish-American War*

for the Associated Press. He worked as a foreign correspondent for the *New York Times* and as chief editorial writer for the *Herald*'s Paris edition from 1920 until his death in 1932.
REFERENCES: Robert W. Desmond. *The Information Process.* 1978; Oliver Knight. *Following the Indian Wars.* 1960.

DAVIES, CHARLES MAURICE (1828–1910). Born in Wales, he attended Durham University and University College. He left his position as headmaster of the West London Collegiate School for a journalism career in 1868. He covered his only war when he reported the Franco-Prussian War* from the French side for the *Daily Telegraph*. In one incident he was arrested as a spy while searching for fellow correspondent George Augustus Sala.*
REFERENCE: *DNB*, 1901–1911.

DAVIS, OSCAR KING (1866–1932). Born in Baldwinsville, New York, Davis reported his first foreign assignment when he covered the Spanish-American War* in the Philippines for the *New York Sun, Harper's Weekly*, and the Laffan News Bureau. In 1900 he joined the exodus of correspondents from the Philippines to China to report the Boxer Rebellion* and four years later was in Tokyo following the developments of the Russo-Japanese War.* Following his stint as a war correspondent in the Far East, Davis settled down to a long career spent mainly in Washington, D.C.
REFERENCE: Robert W. Desmond. *The Information Process.* 1978.

DAVIS, RICHARD HARDING (1864–1916). The preeminent journalist and war correspondent of his time was born in Philadelphia. An indifferent student, Davis attended Lehigh and Johns Hopkins Universities before embarking on a journalism career with the *Philadelphia Record* and the *Philadelphia Press* beginning in 1886.

In 1892 he headed out west to write a series of articles for *Harper's Weekly*. During his trip he got his first taste of war reporting when he accompanied the U.S. Cavalry in its pursuit of Mexican revolutionaries near Laredo. This assignment apparently led to his fascination with the military.

As one of the best-known reporters in New York while still in his twenties, Davis was sent by Hearst to cover the Cuban rebellion in 1896 with Frederic Remington* for the *New York Journal*. However, he resigned when Hearst altered one of his dispatches. Following his resignation he left for England, where he was hired by the *Times*. Following his coverage of Queen Victoria's Diamond Jubilee he was sent to report the Greco-Turkish War* in April 1897. While covering his first engagement at the Battle of Velestino, his rivalry with Stephen Crane* turned into genuine animosity, with Davis criticizing Crane for reporting the battle by using secondhand information.

In 1898 Davis returned to Cuba to cover the Spanish-American War.* He accompanied General Schafter and his troops aboard the *Seguranca*. However,

Schafter would not allow anyone but soldiers to disembark with the first landing party. Following this incident Davis would never write a positive comment about the general. Davis linked up with the Rough Riders and followed them through several actions, taking part in the fighting at Las Guasimas and San Juan Hill.* A critic of American strategy during the war, he witnessed the fall of Santiago and the occupation of Puerto Rico.

He next covered the Boer War* from 1899 to 1900 for the *New York Herald.* Although he was sympathetic to the Boers, he joined the British so that he could watch a more modern and newsworthy army in action. Davis found British censorship and protocol vexing, to say the least. He accompanied the British troops into Ladysmith* after the lifting of the 118-day siege. He next decided to view the war from the Boer side. Davis compared them to the minutemen during the American Revolution. Recently married, he brought his wife with him, nearly getting trapped between the two armies. His coverage from the Boer side resulted in a public backlash in England, leading to a decline in his popularity. Davis ultimately found the Boer War unjust and wasteful.

In 1904 he reported the Russo-Japanese War,* and then the Matos Revolution in Venezuela, the border conflict between Mexico and America, and the American occupation of Veracruz. He covered his last war, World War I,* for the *Daily Chronicle.* Among his most vivid accounts are his descriptions of the German advance into Brussels and the burning of Louvain. Davis was with a group of correspondents following the German army in 1914 and was arrested three times. The Germans suspected him of spying and being a British officer because of a passport photo in which he was wearing a West African Field Force uniform that he had found comfortable eight years earlier. While it did not look like a military uniform then, by the time war had broken out English soldiers had adopted the look in a variety of divisions. He recounts these exploits and his brush with a firing squad in *With the Allies* (1914). He left the front for good in 1916 and was at work on what would be his last book, *With the French in France and Salonika* (1916), when he died of a heart attack at Mount Kisco, New York. He was a prolific writer with seven novels, twelve volumes of short stories, and several plays to his credit. His most memorable works based on his war reportage were *Cuba in War Time* (1897), *A Year in a Correspondent's Notebook* (1898), *The Cuban–Porto Rico Campaign* (1899), *With Both Armies in South Africa* (1900), and *Notes of a War Correspondent* (1910).

REFERENCE: Arthur Lubow. *The Reporter Who Would Be King.* 1992.

DAVIS, THEODORE RUSSELL (1840–1894). Born in Boston and educated at Rittenhouse Academy in Washington, he joined *Harper's Weekly* in March 1861 as a traveling artist, covering the South before the war. Although he had many close calls covering the American Civil War,* he described this trip as the most harrowing of his journeys. Along with Al Waud,* he was one of the magazine's most important artists during the Civil War. One of the most widely traveled and prolific artists of the war, he recorded the capture of Port Royal, the battle between the *Monitor* and the *Merrimac*, the Battle of Shiloh, the capture of Corinth, the Battle of Antietam, the surrender of Vicksburg, the Battle of Chattanooga, and Sherman's march to the sea. He was the only artist with Sherman during the Atlanta campaign in 1864.

Subscribing to the notion that artists must see the actual carnage of battle, Davis often dangerously compromised his health by exposing himself to the dangers of the front lines. He was wounded twice in battle, and one report described him threatening at the point of a gun doctors who attempted to amputate his leg. His technique in recording frontline action was to make sketch notes and later complete the details.

Following the war he was on assignment to the western states when his stagecoach was attacked at Smokey Hill Spring by hostile Indians. Davis was the first reporter to accompany an Indian campaign. Along with Henry Stanley,* he was attached to the command of General Winfield S. Hancock and Lieutenant Colonel George A. Custer in the 1867 expedition to Nebraska and Kansas. Davis secured firsthand knowledge of western warfare. He witnessed several Indian skirmishes with the Sioux and was present when the remains of Lieutenant L. S. Kidder and ten of his men were found in Kansas.

He returned to New York after his 3,000-mile western trip and turned to freelancing in 1884. Few of his original sketches still exist; however, we still have his published illustrations, which were redrawn or traced on woodblocks before the engraving process. He died from Bright's disease.

REFERENCES: Pat Hodgson. *The War Illustrators*. 1977; Edgar M. Howell. ''A Special Artist in the Indian Wars,'' *Montana, the Magazine of Western History*. Spring 1965; Robert Taft. *Artists and Illustrators of the Old West, 1850–1900*. 1953.

DAY, SAMUEL PHILLIPS (?). Samuel P. Day was one of a score of British correspondents who covered parts of the American Civil War.* He covered the opening salvos of the war while with the Confederate Army. After being granted a pass by General Beaureguard he reported the First Battle of Bull Run. He was affiliated with the London publications the *Spectator* and *Macmillan's Magazine*.

REFERENCE: Joseph Mathews. *Reporting the Wars*. 1957.

DEAN, TERESA HOWARD (d. 1935). Born in New York, she moved to Wisconsin in 1855, while still a young girl. She was educated at Lawrence College, where she gravitated from painting toward journalism. On the strength of several essays she was hired by the *Chicago Herald*. Dean covered church activities and then the Ghost Dance troubles among the Dakota Sioux on the Pine Ridge Reservation in 1891 following Wounded Knee. There were numerous other reporters on the scene by the time Dean arrived, and plans had been made to have a group picture taken. However, the consensus was that Dean should be excluded because of the emasculating effect a fashionably dressed woman would have on the death-defying image the reporters had been conveying in their newspaper reports. The closest she came to experiencing action was when she accompanied fifty soldiers and assorted Sioux scouts and Indian policemen investigating the killing of a Sioux woman and her three children. She was present when one of the Sioux policemen identified the slain woman as his sister.

Dean later reported for the *Chicago Inter-Ocean* and then *Town Topics*. She went on to cover the Pennsylvania coal strikes in 1896, the Spanish-American War* from Cuba, the Philippine insurrection, the 1900 Boxer Rebellion,* the Army of Cuba pacification in 1906, and the Mexican Revolution of 1913–1914. One source described Dean as the first woman war correspondent.

REFERENCES: Douglas C. Jones. "Teresa Dean: Lady Correspondent Among the Sioux Indians," *Journalism Quarterly*. Winter 1972; George R. Kolbenschlag. *A Whirlwind Passes*. 1990.

"DEATH OF A LOYALIST SOLDIER." In 1936, during the Spanish Civil War,* Robert Capa* took one of the most memorable and controversial war photographs ever taken. According to many photojournalists who were veterans of the conflict, the forging of pictures was a relatively common occurrence. Capa had arrived in Spain in early 1936 devoted to the Loyalist cause. His photograph of a Loyalist soldier in his moment of death made Capa an international celebrity.

However, in the 1970s veteran correspondent O. D. Gallegher* became the first to question the authenticity of the image as well as to candidly state that the picture was a planned fake. Gallegher and Capa shared a room in Spain and Capa had recounted how Franco's troops often dressed in uniforms for simulated combat replete with smoke bombs and defensive stratagems. Capa explained that he had taken some photographs of attacking troops being repulsed; Gallegher later noted that these were reprinted in newspapers and identified as authentic, although the locality and identification of the military units were unknown. Gallegher is convinced that it was during these re-creations that Capa took his immortalized picture.

Gallegher further claimed that Capa had explained to him how to get "lifelike action shots" by keeping the camera slightly out of focus and slowly moving the camera when taking the shot. Gallegher insists that no shot better exemplifies this technique than the "Death of the Loyalist Soldier."

However, author John Hersey* refuted this claim, noting that Capa had told him a different story. According to his account Capa was covering heavy fighting in Andalusia and had sought refuge in a trench with Republican soldiers. These soldiers were untrained and so zealous in their support of the Republican cause they charged Nationalist machine-gun placements on several occasions only to be mowed down. The way Capa told it was that as they attacked once more he raised his camera over the top of the trench without looking and snapped the button at the sound of the first machine-gun fire. Two months after sending his film to Paris to be developed he found out he was famous, since

the picture had been reprinted throughout the world. Many fellow war correspondents, including Martha Gellhorn,* believe this was Capa's way of joking.
However, both Gellhorn and Herbert Matthews* are convinced of the picture's
authenticity. There are still many questions surrounding the photograph, although it has been generally accepted as authentic.

   Recent evidence suggests that Capa's photograph was indeed real. Capa had
originally reported that the photograph was taken on September 5, 1936. An
amateur historian decided to plumb the military archives in Madrid and Sala-
manca and found that only one man died that day at Cerro Muriano, a mill
worker by the name of Federico Borrell. With the help of another intrepid investigator, the amateur historians located his widow who confirmed the picture
was of her husband and in the process has rehabilitated Capa's Spanish Civil
War reputation.
REFERENCES: Phillip Knightley. *The First Casualty*. 1975; Jorge Lewinski. *The Camera at War*. 1978.

DE BLOWITZ, HENRI STEFAN OPPER (1825–1903). Prior to joining the
Times, de Blowitz had emigrated from Bohemia to France, where he taught
German and foreign literature for many years. He was in Marseille in 1870,
when he was reportedly hired to travel to the besieged city of Paris, then in the
grip of the revolutionary Commune. Arriving in Paris in January 1871, he met
Laurence Oliphant,* chief correspondent for the *Times*. He invited the intrepid
de Blowitz to become his assistant. De Blowitz reported the preliminary peace
negotiations in Versailles while Oliphant reported from Paris. In February 1875,
he was promoted to Paris correspondent, a position he would hold until 1902.
His greatest news scoop was his coverage of the Berlin Congress of 1878.
REFERENCES: Robert W. Desmond. *The Information Process*. 1978; Oliver Woods and
James Bishop. *The Story of THE TIMES*. 1983.

DEEPE, BEVERLY (b. 1936). Following graduation from the University of
Nebraska and the Columbia School of Journalism Deepe traveled around the
world before settling in Saigon in 1961. She remained in Saigon until 1969
covering the Vietnam* conflict as a stringer* for the *London Daily Express*, the
Christian Science Monitor, and *Newsweek*. In 1963 she reported the overthrow
of President Diem and the Buddhist protests. Her reports to *Newsweek* describing
the killing of dozens of Buddhists by the Diem government turned American
public opinion against the government. However, a United Nations investigation
three months later concluded that there was no evidence of any monks being
killed.

   By 1964 Deepe was also reporting for the *New York Herald Tribune* prior to
its demise the next year. Consistently challenged for inaccuracies in her dispatches, she became increasingly unpopular with American authorities. By the
following year she was the only American reporter regularly excluded from
official briefings. Deepe reported the Tet offensive from Saigon in a three-part

series for the *Christian Science Monitor*. She left Vietnam in 1969 and after a brief stint in 1970 at the Pentagon left journalism to start a family.
REFERENCE: Virginia Elwood-Akers. *Women War Correspondents in the Vietnam War, 1961–1975*. 1988.

DE FONTAINE, FELIX GREGORY (1834–1896). He was born in Boston, the son of a French nobleman who had accompanied Charles X into exile in Edinburgh. He entered the newspaper world as a Washington congressional reporter before moving to Charleston, South Carolina, on the eve of the American Civil War.* In 1860 he founded the *Daily South Carolinian*, in which he published many articles regarding the worsening sectional crisis. In 1861 the *New York Herald* began publishing accounts of Southern conditions. His friendship with the Confederate Beauregard allowed him to witness the attack on Fort Sumter, his first major news scoop. His account was the first to appear in the Northern press.

He accompanied a South Carolina regiment throughout the Civil War as a correspondent and was accorded the rank of major. In 1861 De Fontaine reported the Manassas campaign and the following year the Battle of Shiloh, the Corinth campaign, the Seven Days' Battles, and the Virginia campaign. His dispatches on the Battle of Antietam are considered his outstanding achievement of the war and the best account of it in the Southern press.

In 1863 he covered the Union assaults on Charleston and Battery Wagner, the Chattanooga campaign, the Battle of Lookout Mountain, and the Knoxville campaign. Absent from the field for most of 1864, he was active again in 1865 reporting the Atlanta campaign and the Federal occupation of Columbia.

His reportage appeared under the pen name "Personne" in the *Charleston Courier* until the end of 1863, when he became co-owner and editor of the *Columbia Daily South Carolinian*. When Sherman entered Columbia he destroyed De Fontaine's press. After the Civil War De Fontaine moved to New York, where he continued his writing career with the *Telegram* and the *Herald*. A Southern sympathizer to the end, at his death he was writing a book on the missing records of the Confederate cabinet from documents he had gathered in 1865.
REFERENCES: J. Cutler Andrews. *The South Reports the Civil War*. 1970; *DAB*; Stewart Sifakis. *Who Was Who in the Civil War*, 1988.

DE LUCE, DANIEL (b. 1911). De Luce was born in Yuma, Arizona, and educated at the University of California. He began his newspaper career with the *Los Angeles Examiner* and in 1939 went to London for the Associated Press. Later that year, while stationed in Eastern Europe, he reported German preparations in Czechoslovakia for the invasion of Poland. He went on to witness the Italian conquest of Albania and the fall of Greece. De Luce was the only correspondent in Iran covering British-Soviet operations there in October 1941. The intrepid foreign correspondent's penchant for globe-trotting for news led fellow AP reporters to say of him while he was in the field that "De Luce is on da loose."

In 1942 he was sent to Burma, where he reported the fighting before fleeing to India just ahead of Japanese forces. The next year found him covering Allied operations from North Africa to Sicily and the subsequent Italian campaign. His greatest scoop came in 1943 when he became the first war correspondent to enter the war zone controlled by Marshal Tito's partisan forces along the coast of Yugoslavia, although he stayed for only several days. His series of five articles on the Yugoslav partisans led to a Pulitzer Prize in 1944. In 1944 he was among the first correspondents to enter Rome, and his dispatch datelined from the city was the first by an American correspondent since December 1941.
REFERENCE: Frederick S. Voss. *Reporting the War.* 1994.

DE MONFRIED, HENRI (1879–1974). Born in La Franqui, France, he left his uneventful life as a businessman to travel to the Red Sea coast in 1911. Six years later he was selling weapons and diving for pearls near Djibouti. After being expelled from Ethiopia for his political views he returned in 1936 as a photographic war correspondent during the Ethiopian War.* In 1940 he was arrested by the British army and exiled to Kenya, where he stayed until returning to France in 1948. He continued to travel and photograph Africa, and disappeared at sea for several weeks near Mauritius while in his late seventies.
REFERENCE: Turner Browne and Elaine Partnow. *Photographic Artists and Innovators.* 1983.

DENNY, HAROLD NORMAN (1899–1945). Born in Des Moines, Iowa, and educated at Drake University, he worked on newspapers in Des Moines, St. Paul, and Minneapolis between 1913 and 1922, when he joined the *New York Times.* He reported the Moroccan War in 1922, the 1927–1928 Nicaraguan crisis, and the Cuban crisis of 1930–1931. In 1934 he began a five-year stint in Moscow. This assignment was interrupted when he covered the beginning of the Ethiopian War* in 1935 and then again two years later when he reported further developments in the conflict. He covered the Moscow treason trials of 1936–1938, the 1938 German invasion of Czechoslovakia, and the Russo-Finnish War the following year.

With the outbreak of the war in Europe he was accredited with the British Expeditionary Force in France and later covered the Libyan campaign. In 1941 he was captured by Rommel's forces in North Africa. Denny was a neutral correspondent when he was initially held in Italy, but his status was changed to enemy correspondent when Pearl Harbor was attacked and he was moved to a Berlin prison. His subsequent account of his imprisonment was published as *Behind Both Lines.* Following a prisoner exchange in June 1942 he returned to the States and became the *Times* correspondent in Spain. In 1944 he covered the invasion of France, and he was slightly wounded covering the fighting in the Ardennes during the Battle of the Bulge.

REFERENCES: Robert W. Desmond. *Crisis and Conflict*. 1982; Robert W. Desmond. *Tides of War*. 1984.

DEPARDON, RAYMOND (b. 1942). The French photographer served as a war reporter in Algeria while in the French army during the 1960s. Following Algerian independence he covered wars in Chile, Chad, Lebanon, and Afghanistan. He has produced numerous documentaries and is a member of Magnum, originally founded by Robert Capa.*
REFERENCE: Frances Fralin, ed. *The Indelible Image*. 1985.

"DERELICT, THE." Richard Harding Davis' 1902 short story is based on his impressions of the horde of correspondents who were drawn to the Spanish-American War.* It was suggested when the story was first published that the title character was based on Stephen Crane.*
REFERENCE: Howard Good. *The Image of the War Correspondent in Anglo-American Fiction*. 1985.

DE ST. JORRE, JOHN (b. 1936). Born in London, he graduated from Oxford and entered the diplomatic service. He served as an officer in Malaya during the 1950s insurgency. He was stationed at the British embassy in the Congo during the turbulent postindependence years in 1960–1961. He later was posted to other African assignments. He turned to journalism in 1963, resigning from the foreign service to write for the *Observer* and other papers. He covered the conflict surrounding Rhodesian independence in 1963–1965 and from 1966 to 1967 he reported conflicts in Zambia, Congo, Uganda, Aden, and Nigeria. De St. Jorre reported from both sides during the Nigerian civil war and was with the first correspondents allowed access to the war zones following the capitulation of Biafra. He became Paris correspondent for the *Observer* beginning in 1969.
REFERENCE: John de St. Jorre. *The Brothers' War*, 1971.

DIAMENT, RAFAIL (b. 1907). Diament began publishing his photographs in the 1920s. In 1937 he moved to Moscow and became a professional photojournalist. During World War II* he served as a correspondent with the Russian navy in the North Sea.
REFERENCE: Daniela Mrazkova and Vladimir Remes, eds. *The Russian War: 1941–1945*. 1975.

DICEY, EDWARD JAMES STEPHEN (1832–1911). Born near Lutterworth, Leicestershire, England, he attended King's and Trinity Colleges before receiving his degree from Cambridge in 1854. Following college he traveled and dabbled in business and foreign politics. In 1861 he published *Rome in 1860* and *Cavour—A Memoir*. That same year he began his affiliation with the *Daily Telegraph*. In 1862 he reported the American Civil War* for *Macmillan's Mag-*

azine and the *Spectator*, and in 1863 his Civil War experiences resulted in the poorly received *Six Months in the Federal States*.

His acumen on foreign issues led to a full-time position on the staff of the *Telegraph* by 1862. Dicey covered the Schleswig-Holstein War in 1864 and the Austro-Prussian War* of 1866. His accounts of these wars are collected in *The Schleswig-Holstein War* (1864) and *The Battlefields of 1866* (1866). In the late 1860s his travels in Egypt, Russia, and Turkey resulted in several travel books, and in 1869 he accepted the post of editor for the *Daily News*, which he held for three months. Shortly after, Dicey filled a similar post with the *Observer*, which he held for almost two decades.

REFERENCES: *DNB*, 1901–1911; Joseph J. Mathews. *Reporting the Wars*. 1957.

DIEHL, CHARLES SANFORD (1854–1946). Born in Flintstone, Maryland, and raised in Illinois, he was hired to replace special correspondent Mark Kellogg,* who was the only reporter to die with Custer at the Battle of Little Big Horn. Diehl made his reputation covering the American Indian Wars* on the Plains in the 1870s and early 1880s. He had been with the *Chicago Times* for three years when he was assigned to cover General Alfred Terry's command following the Custer debacle. According to Diehl, Terry showed him a copy of the directive issued Custer prior to his last expedition. Terry added that Custer would have been court-martialed had he survived. Diehl interviewed Terry, attempting to get the "real" story of the Custer defeat.

In 1877, on his second assignment to Indian country he was given the opportunity to interview Sitting Bull when he accompanied Terry's peace mission to Canada, where the Sioux chief had taken sanctuary. When Sitting Bull agreed to turn himself over to the American government in 1880, Diehl was sent to cover the surrender at Fort Buford. In the thick of winter Diehl traveled 175 miles by army sleigh and bobsled through blizzard conditions to reach his destination. When the Sioux balked at coming into the fort, Diehl joined the skirmish line that attacked the Indian camp, which they found empty. An artillery barrage brought the Indians out of their hiding places in the woods and after a brief action many of the Sioux surrendered; however, Sitting Bull was not among them. After the Poplar River fight Diehl returned to his paper, albeit without his story of the legendary chief's surrender.

After his career with the *Chicago Times*, Diehl became the assistant general manager for the Associated Press. He was in charge of the Associated Press' coverage of the Spanish-American War.* Following his tenure with the AP he purchased the *San Antonio Light*, with which he was still affiliated at his death. Diehl chronicled his exploits as a correspondent in *The Staff Correspondent* in 1931.

REFERENCES: Charles H. Brown. *The Correspondents' War*. 1967; Oliver Knight. *Following the Indian Wars*. 1960.

DILLON, EMILE JOSEPH (1854–1932). Born in Dublin, Ireland, and educated at several European universities, Dillon could reportedly speak twenty-six different languages and write newspaper leaders in five. One of the greatest philologists of his day, Dillon was reputed to possess a "cloak and dagger complex." He taught comparative philology at the University of Kharkov in Russia, where he entered journalism first with *Le Musson* and then the *Odessa Messenger*. In 1887 he began a twenty-seven-year affiliation with the *Daily Telegraph*. In 1894, he circumvented the Sultan's edict prohibiting journalists from Armenia, when he covered the conflict disguised as a Russian officer, Kurdish chief, and Turkish woman. He again donned disguise in 1897 as a rebellious monk when he covered the Greco-Turkish War.*

During the Spanish-American War* he covered the Spanish side of the conflict, and in 1900 he was in China during the Boxer Rebellion.* While employed by the *Daily Telegraph*, Dillon was stationed in St. Petersburg from 1886 until the beginning of World War I.* He accompanied Russian troops to Peking via the Trans-Siberian Railroad and later covered the second Dreyfus trial, the Portsmouth Peace Conference at the end of the Russo-Japanese War,* and the Paris Peace Conference (1919). He retired from the newspaper in 1919 and lived in Mexico and Spain until his death. He wrote numerous books, including *Leaves from My Life* (1932).

REFERENCES: Robert W. Desmond. *Windows on the World.* 1980; *DNB*, 1912–1921; Dennis Griffiths, ed. *The Encyclopedia of the British Press.* 1992.

DIMBLEBY, RICHARD (1913–1965). Born into a newspaper family, he began his career in journalism with the family-owned *Richmond and Twickenham Times*, in Surrey, England. By the age of twenty-one he was news editor for *Advertiser's Weekly*. In 1936 he joined the BBC, where he came to prominence with his radio commentaries on the Spanish Civil War.*

Dimbleby was an innovator for the BBC, introducing the first mobile recording van, essential for on-the-spot interviews and providing a sense of participation that most newspaper reporting lacked. At the outset of World War II* Dimbleby was with the British Expeditionary Force headquarters in France. In 1941 he was one of the earliest arrivals at the Greek front before covering action in Iraq, Syria, Lebanon, and Iran later that year. In 1942 he reported the resumption of the desert campaign in North Africa.

In 1943 he was one of seven observers flying in RAF Liberator bombers in a night attack on Berlin. More significantly, this was the first major action outside Britain in which correspondents were allowed to participate. The following year he covered the D-Day landings for the BBC. During the crossing of the Rhine into Germany, he was injured when his glider crash-landed. He witnessed the liberation of the Belsen concentration camp and the taking of Berlin. Following the war he became a well-known television personality while continuing to publish in newspapers and magazines.

REFERENCES: Richard Collier. *Fighting Words.* 1989; Robert W. Desmond. *Tides of War.* 1984.

DINWIDDIE, WILLIAM (1867–1934). Born in Charlottesville, Virginia, Din-widdie was a war photographer* and journalist for *Harper's Weekly* during the Spanish-American War.* He covered both the Cuban and the Puerto Rican campaigns in 1898. Following the war he became the magazine's chief correspondent on Cuban affairs. One of his most memorable photographs was of American troops at Daiquiri in June 1898. He also took one of the few action photographs of the war when he captured Captain Capron's artillery firing on the Spanish during the Battle of El Caney.

He later covered the Philippine insurrection for the *New York Herald*, where he became an islands administrator during the first year of American occupation. Soon after he left for South Africa to report the Boer War* and then later the Russo-Japanese War* in 1904 for the *Herald*. He wrote *War Sketches, in Truth, Puerto Rico and Its Possibilities* (1899), *The War in the Philippines*, and *The War in South Africa*.

REFERENCES: Robert W. Desmond. *The Information Process*. 1978; Susan D. Moeller. *Shooting War: Photography and the American Experience of Combat*. 1989.

DISHER, LEO S. (1912–1969). Educated at Duke University, Disher was a war correspondent for the United Press beginning in 1939. In November 1942 he was badly wounded by Vichy troops while accompanying the British navy near Oran, Algeria. He became the first civilian to be awarded a Purple Heart during the war. Disher coauthored *Springboard to Berlin*, based on the Battle of Oran. He returned to the war in 1943, accredited to the British Home Fleet. Disher covered the North Africa landings and the Normandy invasion.

Following the war he headed the United Press bureaus in Czechoslovakia, Bulgaria, and Rumania. In 1948 he left Eastern Europe and joined the United Information Service.

REFERENCE: Robert W. Desmond. *Tides of War*. 1984.

DIXIE, LADY FLORENCE CAROLINE (1857–1905). Better known as a travel writer, she was born Florence Douglas in London and educated primarily at home. In 1875 she married Sir Alexander Churchill Dixie and in 1878–1879 traveled through Patagonia, describing her experiences in *Across Patagonia* (1880). Dixie represented the *Morning Post* in South Africa during the 1879 Zulu War. Competitors ridiculed the *Post* when it sent out probably the first woman war correspondent. Dixie shared with her two brothers a predilection for eccentricity. One of her brothers was killed while climbing the Matterhorn and another had the dubious distinction of being the ninth marquis of Queensberry, who established the rules for the sport of pugilism.

By the time she arrived in South Africa the hostilities had ceased and the peace conference was under way. Dixie supported the release of Zulu chief Cetewayo and the restoration of Zululand following the British intrusion. Ultimately her efforts were rewarded when the king was freed and returned home to Zululand. She chronicled her exploits and views on the Zulu conflict in *A*

Defence of Zululand and Its King (1882) and *In the Land of Misfortune* (1882). She later became involved in the women's movement in Great Britain and became an advocate for the prevention of animal cruelty with her books *Horrors of Sport* (1891) and *The Mercilessness of Sport* (1901).
REFERENCES: *DNB*, 1901–1911; Robert Wilkinson-Latham. *From Our Special Correspondent.* 1979.

DOBSON, GEORGE (1850–1938). Fluent in Russian, he was the *Times* correspondent in Russia for over a quarter century. He covered the Czar's army during the Russo-Turkish War* and witnessed the siege of Plevna. His book *Russia's Railway Advance into Central Asia* was based on his adventures as the first Englishman to travel Russia's newly built military railway to Samarkand.

Upon leaving the *Times* he joined Reuters* and wrote for various English papers. He resumed his relationship with the *Times* to cover the Russian Revolution. He was working in the British embassy when Soviet troops attacked it, killing a captain and imprisoning Dobson and several associates for five weeks. Following a stint with the War Office Intelligence Section Dobson continued to play an important role in evacuating British civilians and Russian colleagues from the beleaguered country. He wrote *Russian Under the Red Terror and Harmsworth's History of the Great War* (1919).
REFERENCE: Robert W. Desmond. *Windows on the World: World News Reporting, 1900–1920.* 1980.

DONOHOE, MARTIN (1869–1927). Born in Galway, Ireland, in the early 1890s he emigrated to Australia, where he entered journalism in 1892 with the *Sydney Courier Australian.* After stints with several other papers he joined the *London Daily Chronicle* and reported the Boer War* in South Africa beginning in 1899. He covered the advance of Methuen's forces from the Orange River to Magersfontein and witnessed Hector "Fighting Mac" MacDonald's engagement at Koodoesberg Drift, after which he reported Lord Roberts' forces near Enslin. Captured after the battle of Paardeberg, he was released following the fall of Pretoria.

In 1905 Donohoe covered the Russo-Japanese War* while with the Japanese forces. He accompanied the Japanese First Army during the Battles of Yalu, Motien Pass, Towan, Liaoyang, and the Shaho. Throughout the war he was continuously hampered by restrictions and press censorship. Following the war he shifted his attention to conflict in the Balkans. He reported the Turkish revolution (1909) and the capture of Constantinople by the Young Turks, and was the first reporter to be granted an interview by the newly installed Sultan.

In the years leading up to World War I* he covered the Portuguese revolution (1910), the Italo-Turkish War, and the Balkan War (1912–1913). During World War I Donohoe was in demand by the British intelligence corps due to his experience in foreign affairs and proficiency in linguistics. He served in the Balkans, Russia, and the Middle East.
REFERENCE: Robert W. Desmond. *Windows on the World.* 1980.

DORR, RHETA CHILDE (1873–1948). Dorr was born in Omaha, Nebraska, and attended the University of Nebraska for two years. She entered journalism with the *New York Evening Post* in 1902, editing the women's pages. During her four years in this position Dorr gathered notes for what would become her first book, *What Eight Million Women Want* (1910). She became active in the suffragette movement and edited the *Suffragist*. In the years leading up to World War I* she remained active as a freelance journalist, writing for *Collier's, Cosmopolitan*, and other magazines.

Dorr had already covered several European assignments prior to the war. In 1906 she reported the coronation of King Haakon of Norway, before traveling at her own expense to St. Petersburg, Russia, where she covered the Duma as it attempted to defuse the developing revolutionary conflict. An activist for women's rights, she visited Great Britain in 1912 and 1913, reporting the suffrage movement there.

In her forties, she began her second career as war correspondent and foreign correspondent in 1917, returning to Russia following the February revolution. She covered women soldiers at the Russian front, noting in one dispatch that half had been killed or wounded. She reported World War I for the *New York Evening Mail* and a syndicate representing over twenty newspapers. Following the war she was a foreign correspondent in Prague and wrote *A Woman of Fifty* in 1924.

REFERENCE: Julia Edwards. *Women of the World: The Great Foreign Correspondents.* 1989.

DOS PASSOS, JOHN RODERIGO (1896–1970). Best known as author and playwright, he was born in Chicago, the illegitimate son of a corporate lawyer. As a child he was known as John Madison, adopting his father's surname upon entering Harvard University in 1912. With a predilection for socialist politics and a wish to serve in World War I* in some volunteer capacity, upon graduation in 1916 he followed his father's wishes instead and studied architecture in neutral Spain.

After his father's death the following year he returned to New York City and socialized with well-known radicals Emma Goldman and Max Eastman. Soon after he joined an ambulance corps and returned to France, where he later witnessed his first war during the Battle of Verdun. By November 1917 he was with a Red Cross unit in Italy, but the following spring was discharged for writing letters critical of American intervention. He then joined the Army Medical Corps and served in Europe until the 1918 armistice.

Although he was never affiliated with a newspaper he went to Spain during the Spanish Civil War* to observe the activities of Loyalist forces, whose cause he had great sympathy for. Some of his best work on the war was published in *Esquire* magazine. Among his most prominent books are *Three Soldiers, Manhattan Transfer, Nineteen Nineteen*, and *Adventures of a Young Man*.

REFERENCE: Virginia Spencer Carr. *Dos Passos: A Life.* 1984.

DOWLING, JAMES GRAHAM (d. 1955). Born in Philadelphia and educated at the University of Notre Dame, Dowling worked for the *Chicago Times* and the *Newark Star-Ledger* before joining the *Chicago Sun* in 1941. During World War II* he reported from the Pacific war fronts, including the Battle of Guadalcanal, where he landed with the second wave of the amphibious assault. In 1943 he was with U.S. naval forces involved in the Solomon Islands campaign, and the following year he injured both ankles while parachuting with the Eleventh Airborne Division on the island of Luzon in the Philippines and was awarded paratrooper wings. He saw his last action in Burma in the waning months of the war. Following World War II he joined *Time* magazine as Singapore bureau chief. Dowling died tragically in a plane crash with twenty-four others on June 16, 1955 in Paraguay.
REFERENCES: Robert W. Desmond. *Tides of War*. 1984; Jack Stenbuck, ed. *Typewriter Battalion*. 1995.

DOWNING, JOHN (b. 1940). Born in Wales, he became a skilled photographic printer before joining the *Daily Express* as a freelance photographer in 1962. During his twenty-eight-year career with the paper he has covered major conflicts in Vietnam,* Beirut, the Falkland Islands* and the Persian Gulf. He accompanied guerrilla forces in Sudan, Nicaragua, and Afghanistan. His imprisonment by Idi Amin in Uganda led to a widely published photo from inside the prison. He was also present when the IRA bombed the Grand Hotel in Brighton. He has received many awards for his photojournalism, including the Member of British Empire in 1992.
REFERENCE: Dennis Griffiths, ed. *The Encyclopedia of the British Press*. 1992.

DOWNTON, ERIC (b. 1917). Downton covered his first war as a young journalist for the *Daily Worker* during the Spanish Civil War.* By the late 1930s Downton was night editor of the English-language *Singapore Free Press*. In 1939 he arrived in Shanghai, China, and the following year became chief editor for Reuters'* Far Eastern organization. After a three-year term in the Royal Canadian Navy he rejoined Reuters, covering the war in Europe beginning in 1944. As war correspondent with the Third Army Downton reported the execution of prisoners, the Battle of the Bulge, and bombing raids over Germany; he also learned to parachute.

Following the war he covered the Greek Civil War and the first Arab-Israeli War in 1948 before taking over the New Delhi bureau for the *Daily Telegraph*. In the 1950s he reported the Korean War,* witnessed the French Foreign Legion in action during the war in Indochina, and during the 1953–1955 Mau Mau uprising in Kenya claimed to wear a firearm for the first and last time. Downton would return to Africa in 1960 to report the troubles in the Congo for the *Daily Telegraph*. Throughout the postwar era he reported coups in Nigeria, Ghana, Sudan, Somalia, the Congo, Zaire, and Rwanda. Downton went on to report the revolt in Yemen, the Greek-Turkish conflict on Cyprus, the Vietnam War,* and the civil war in Lebanon.

REFERENCE: Eric Downton. *Wars Without End.* 1987.

DOYLE, SIR ARTHUR CONAN (1859–1930). The creator of Sherlock Holmes was born in Edinburgh, Scotland. The son and grandson of artists and men of letters, Doyle was educated at Stonyhurst and Edinburgh University. He practiced medicine at Southsea from 1882 to 1890. His first novel, *A Study in Scarlet* (1887), introduced the world to one of its most enduring fictional characters, Sherlock Holmes.

During the Boer War* he acted as senior physician to a field hospital and wrote an early account of the war in *The Great Boer War* (1900). He accompanied Lord Roberts on his advance against Johannesburg and Pretoria, and his account appeared under "Days with the Army" in the *Strand.* Doyle was knighted following the war and became an important voice for army reform. Besides his Holmes novels he wrote several Napoleonic War stories, and several works on World War I.* The latter included *A History of the British Campaign in France and Flanders* (six vols., 1916–1920) and *A Visit to Three Fronts* (1916), a series of sketches based on his visits to France and Italy, where he narrowly missed being killed by an Austrian shell while at the front lines. He died on July 7, 1930.

REFERENCES: John Dickson Carr. *The Life of Sir Arthur Conan Doyle.* 1949; *DNB*, 1922–1930.

DUELL, PEGGY HULL. *See* HULL, PEGGY.

DUNCAN, DAVID DOUGLAS (b. 1916). Born in Kansas City, Missouri, sometime during his college years at the University of Miami and the University of Arizona he took up photography as a hobby. He began freelancing for newspapers in 1938. Two years later he was assigned to accompany the Chile-Peru expedition of the American Museum of Natural History as its photographer.

In 1943 he joined the U.S. Marine Corps and was soon photographing military operations for the South Pacific Air Transport Command, covering guerrilla fighting in the Fiji Islands, marine combat aviation on Okinawa, and the official Japanese surrender aboard the USS *Missouri* in 1945.

Following the war he joined *Life* magazine. Duncan covered the Korean War* in 1950 and was present at the retreat of the marines from Chosin Reservoir in North Korea after Chinese Communist forces crossed the Yalu River, which he chronicles in his book *This Is War!* Before leaving *Life* in 1956 he reported from South Africa, French Guinea, Morocco, and Egypt.

In 1967 he began covering the Vietnam War* for *Life* and ABC news and then became a special correspondent for *Collier's.* In 1968 his collected photographs of the war were published as *I Protest.* He received the Overseas Press Club Award twice and was awarded the *U.S. Camera* Gold Medal for his book

This Is War! Royalties from this book are contributed to a fund for the families of marines killed in action. Duncan also was the recipient of a Legion of Merit, a Purple Heart, two Distinguished Flying Crosses, and other medals testifying to his bravery under fire. In 1970 he published *War Without Heroes.*
REFERENCES: Davis Douglas Duncan. *Yankee Nomad: A Pictorial Odyssey.* 1966; Robert E. Hood. *12 at War.* 1967.

DUNNING, JOHN P. (?). Dunning was a foreign correspondent for the Western Associated Press beginning in the late nineteenth century. In 1889 he was sent to the Samoan Islands to report a disagreement between the United States, Germany, and Great Britain over who controlled the islands. While on this assignment he witnessed one of the most catastrophic hurricanes to ever strike the South Seas. In 1891 Dunning was the only American correspondent reporting the civil war raging in Chile. Beginning in 1898 he reported the Spanish-American War* in Cuba and then the Philippines. He was one of six correspondents to witness the battle of Las Guasimas on the advance to Santiago, Cuba. He was also credited with telegraphing the scoop of the Battle of Santiago.
REFERENCES: Charles H. Brown. *The Correspondents' War.* 1967; Robert W. Desmond. *The Information Process.* 1978.

DURANTY, WALTER (1884–1957). Born in Liverpool, England, he was an only child and lost his parents in a train accident when he was ten. After graduating with honors from Cambridge, he traveled widely through the United States and Europe, intermittently writing articles for Frank Munsey's *Argosy* magazine.
He gained his first full-time position in journalism when he joined the staff of the *New York Times* in Paris in 1913. He served as war correspondent for the paper at French army headquarters and on the western front during World War I.* He cowrote with fellow *Times* correspondent Wythe Williams* one of the best accounts of the Battle of Verdun in 1916. After covering the Paris Peace Conference in 1919 he traveled to the Soviet Union, where he reported political unrest and famine in the Baltic states following the Russian Revolution. In Finland he received his first glimpse of the repercussions of the revolution, noting in a dispatch the bitter fighting and executions.
Duranty served as Moscow correspondent for the *Times* from 1922 to 1934. In 1932 he was awarded the Pulitzer Prize for his economic reporting in Russia. During this era he became recognized as an expert on Soviet affairs and was one of the most controversial analysts of the Stalinist period. He interviewed Stalin twice and reported Lenin's death in 1924, the same year he lost his left foot in a train wreck in France. After resigning from the Moscow post in 1934 he was a roving reporter, spending parts of each year in the Soviet Union. He later covered the Spanish Civil War* in 1936 and the early years of World War II.* He wrote *I Write As I Please* in 1935.
REFERENCE: Michael Emery. *On the Front Lines: Following America's Foreign Correspondents Across the Twentieth Century.* 1995.

E

EDWARDS, HENRY SUTHERLAND (1828–1906). Born in Hendon, England, he was educated in France. After a brief interlude as a staff writer for *Punch* he wrote several light farces for the London stage. Fluent in French, he covered the 1852 coup d'état in Paris and four years later represented the *Illustrated Times* in Russia at the coronation of Czar Alexander II.

Edwards reported the Polish insurrection for the *Times* in 1862 and 1863 before being expelled by Russian authorities for his favorable coverage of the Polish rebels. From these experiences he wrote *Polish Captivity, an Account of the Present Position of the Poles in Austria, Prussia and Russia*, (two vols., 1863) and *The Private History of a Polish Insurrection* (two vols., 1865). In 1871 he reported the Franco-Prussian War* while attached to the Prussian army for the *Times*. His observations were collectively published as *The Germans in France, Notes on the Method and Conduct of the Invasion*. Besides his work as a war correspondent Edwards became the first editor of the *Graphic* in 1869, and wrote books on foreign affairs and musical history, as well as several novels. REFERENCE: *DNB*, 1901–1911.

EGAN, MARTIN (1872–1938). Egan covered the Philippine insurrection during the Spanish-American War* for the *San Francisco Chronicle* in 1899. The following year he represented the Associated Press in China during the Boxer Rebellion.* By the outbreak of the Russo-Japanese War* Egan was chief of the AP bureau in Tokyo. He reported from the Japanese side during the conflict. Egan left the AP in 1907 to become editor of the *Manila Times*. He continued in this role for seven years, then moved to New York as public relations advisor to J. P. Morgan and Company, a position he held until his death in 1938.

REFERENCES: Robert W. Desmond. *Windows on the World.* 1980; David Shavit. *The United States in Asia.* 1990.

EHRENBURG, ILYA (d. 1967). The well-known Russian writer served as correspondent with the Red Army during World War II.* He reported the Russo-German war for *Red Star* magazine and Moscow-based *Izvestia* and chronicled the Battle of Stalingrad. His propagandizing dispatches with their vehemently anti-German slant were widely reprinted in the West prior to American entry into World War II. His accounts of the German death camps in August 1944 were some of the earliest descriptions of the German final solution. These accounts were reprinted in many American newspapers.
REFERENCES: Robert W. Desmond. *Tides of War.* 1984; Phillip Knightley. *The First Casualty.* 1975.

EMENY, STUART (1904–1944). He reported the Italian invasion of Ethiopia for the *Daily Chronicle* in 1935. His battle reportage while accompanying Haile Selassie's forces was widely distributed. Following the war he returned to England before covering conflict in Palestine, where he barely survived an ambush.

During World War II* he reported the Bengal famine in 1942, as well as a disastrous tidal wave. He rode on U.S. air bomber missions before being assigned to cover General Orde Wingate's Chindit guerrillas behind enemy lines in Burma. He was killed on March 24, 1944, along with colleague Stanley Wills* when Wingate's aircraft crashed, killing all aboard.
REFERENCE: Robert W. Desmond. *Tides of War.* 1984.

EMERSON, GLORIA (b. 1929). Emerson left her position as reporter for the women's section of the *New York Journal American* in 1956 and bought a one-way ticket to Saigon to visit a boyfriend in the marines. Returning to the States the following year, she joined the *New York Times.* By 1960 she was with the Paris bureau. Over the next ten years she covered stories in the Middle East, Africa, Eastern Europe, and London. She also reported the Nigerian civil war in 1968 and the conflict in Northern Ireland the following year.

Arriving in Saigon for the *New York Times* in 1970, she became an outspoken critic of the war, concentrating on the effect of the war on the Vietnamese people. In 1971 she was the recipient of the George Polk* Memorial Award for excellence in foreign reporting from Vietnam.* Her freelance work has appeared in *New York, Harper's, Saturday Review,* and many other magazines. Her book *Winners and Losers: Battles, Retreats, Gains, Losses and Ruins from the Vietnam War* (1976) is a scathing portrait of American military intervention in Southeast Asia.
REFERENCE: Virginia Elwood-Akers. *Women War Correspondents in the Vietnam War, 1961–1975.* 1988.

ETHIOPIAN WAR. The Ethiopian War of October 1935–May 1936 between Ethiopia and Fascist Italy is also known as the Italo-Ethiopian War or the Abyssinian War. In December 1934 Italian troops clashed with Ethiopian forces on the Italian Somaliland frontier. Fascist Italy, intent on creating its own African empire, signed an agreement with France in January 1935 which recognized Italian claims in Africa and was thought a form of reassurance for France against Nazi aggression. In October 1935 Italian troops crossed into Ethiopia from Italian Eritrea and the Somaliland. The war was protested by the League of Nations, Great Britain, and other countries. However, France, Germany, and Japan raised no objections. After the war ended in an Italian victory in May 1936, Italy withdrew from the League of Nations and formally annexed Ethiopia.

War correspondents descended on Rome following the outbreak of hostilities in Ethiopia. Among the 120 Anglo-American correspondents who reported the conflict were O. D. Gallegher,* Evelyn Waugh,* newsreel* cameraman Laurence Stallings, photographer Alfred Eisenstaedt, and George Steer* of the *Times.* Sympathy was overwhelmingly in favor of the embattled African country and its emperor Haile Selassie. Italian dictator Mussolini launched a juggernaut of 250,000 troops against the ancient kingdom defended by barefoot troops armed with swords and daggers.

Almost two hundred Italian reporters and writers were accredited to cover the war. Following the war, most produced books of poetry or history, or plays chronicling the war. Italian authorities would eventually invite forty foreign correspondents and various film units to record the war. The only two American or British correspondents with the Italian forces at the outset were Webb Miller* of the UP and Floyd Gibbons* representing the *Chicago Tribune.* Other correspondents reporting the onslaught of the Italian army included Will Barber* of the *Chicago Tribune,* Robinson Maclean for the *Toronto Telegram,* John T. Whitaker* of the *New York Herald Tribune,* and William W. Chaplin of Universal Service. Jim Mills of the AP was among the correspondents covering the Ethiopian side of the conflict.

Sometime after December 6, 1935, Haile Selassie ordered all journalists to return to his capital of Addis Adaba, where they would remain until the end of the war. On one hand Selassie was afraid tribesmen were unable to tell the difference between Italians and friendly Europeans, and he could not guarantee their safety outside the city. On the other hand he suspected some of the reporters of being spies. By the beginning of the new year only three correspondents from America and one from Great Britain were still with Italian forces, including Reynolds Packard* of the UP, Eddie Neil of the AP, Christopher Holme* of Reuters,* and Herbert Matthews* of the *New York Times.* Correspondents found it virtually impossible to get anywhere near the main front in the north, and many out of sheer boredom left the country before the conclusion of the war.

Each correspondent had to go through the accreditation process with the Abyssinian Foreign Office, which required each newspaper's guarantee that a certain sum of money would be made available to the Foreign Office in the event a reporter was "required to leave the country by reason of a misdemeanor." Communication lines out of the country were primitive if they existed at all. Cables often arrived at various newspapers so unintelligible that they needed a team of cryptographers to decipher them. This was in part due to the fact the Ethiopian cable operators did not understand the cacophony of languages they were faced with transmitting, although they still managed to send dispatches totaling 30,000 words per day.

REFERENCES: Angelo Del Boca. *The Ethiopian War, 1935–1941*. 1969; Robert W. Desmond. *Crisis and Conflict*. 1982; James Dugan and Laurence Lafore. *Days of Emperor and Clown*. 1973; John Hohenberg. *Foreign Correspondence*. 1964; Phillip Knightley. *The First Casualty*. 1975.

"EYE-WITNESS." Beginning with World War I* the British military imposed censorship restrictions on the wartime press. Lord Kitchener and the War Office were unusually suspicious of reporters and refused to allow any newspapermen near the western front. Their solution was to appoint an official "eyewitness" to relay the army's official daily reports to the journalists. Each report was scrutinized by Kitchener and other generals before being released to the public under the byline "Eye-witness."

The Allied general staffs adapted the World War I "eyewitness" system for World War II as well. However, rather than employing an army officer to fill the role of "eyewitness," the journalist Alexander Clifford* was appointed instead.

REFERENCE: Phillip Knightley. *The First Casualty*. 1975.

F

FAAS, HORST (b. 1933). Born in Berlin, he began his career in photojournalism in 1951 with Keystone, a British newsphoto agency in Munich. Five years later he joined the Associated Press. From 1956 to 1960 he covered West German politics. In 1961 he covered the conflict in the Congo, where he was beaten by Katangan rebels and forced to eat his United Nations pass. He next covered the Algerian independence movement before establishing his name as a war correspondent in Vietnam* beginning in 1962. His pictures from the bloody battle of Dong Xoai in 1965 appeared in *Life* magazine. In 1965 he became the first cameraman to win the Pulitzer Prize and the Robert Capa* Award in the same year.
REFERENCE: Robert E. Hood. *12 at War*. 1967.

FALKLANDS WAR. The 1982 Falkland War between Great Britain and Argentina was triggered by Argentinean attempts to reclaim the British possessions of South Georgia and the Falkland Islands through the use of armed force. From the start the British military attempted to exclude war correspondents from the campaign. A compromise was worked out with the Ministry of Defence, with the task force agreeing to allow six correspondents to accompany the expedition. This was eventually increased to twelve, including a camera team and representatives from the British Broadcasting Corporation (BBC) and the Independent Television News (ITN). Further pressure was exerted by a consortium of Fleet Street newspaper editors and proprietors to add more press representation. The military authorities relented and allowed fifteen correspondents and photographers to travel with the task force. They would be joined by thirteen more members of the press who would follow in the converted civilian liner *Canberra*.

British authorities controlled not only how many correspondents would cover the war but which organizations would be represented. No foreign correspondents were included, and the only international news agency represented was London-based Reuters.* The accreditation system for determining the selection process was severely flawed. There was no agreement concerning censorship guidelines, and some journalists formally agreed to the Officials Secrets Act, while others did not. Many of the journalists were inadequately briefed, clothed, and equipped for the military action.

The most recognized correspondent to come out of this abbreviated war was Max Hastings* of the *London Standard*. His fame was ensured when he made the front pages as "the First Man into Stanley." The Falklands War presented reporters with problems akin to those endured by their Victorian-era counterparts. Separated by eight thousand miles from England, they found communications difficult. Reporters relied on the navy communications systems to relay dispatches back to London. Since no provisions had been made for live television coverage and the Ministry of Defence was lukewarm to facilitating any live transmissions, film had to be returned to London by plane or ship. At the heart of the controversy over live coverage was the lingering American experience of the Vietnam War* and how it had impacted morale at home. Military censors demanded that pictures of body bags be deleted from film footage.

The Ministry of Defence initiated a set of rules for newspaper editors called "D" notices. Each day briefings were conducted by Ian McDonald, a member of the ministry's public relations department. His job was not unlike the "Five O'Clock Follies"* briefings of the Vietnam War. His task was to provide the official spin on the day's activities.

War correspondents were assigned to various units and were dependent on their relationship with the commanding officer. Besides Hastings, Brian Harahan and Michael Nicholson provided excellent coverage considering the media environment, reporting engagements at Goose Green and at San Carlos. Other journalists regularly broadcasting from the conflict included Robert Fox of the BBC, Kim Sabido for the Independent Radio News, and John Shirley and John Witherow of the *Sunday Times*. The Falklands War demonstrated that 130 years after the Crimean War,* war still sold news.

REFERENCES: Derrik Mercer, Geoff Mungham, and Kevin Williams. *The Fog of War: The Media on the Battlefield.* 1987; Trevor Royle. *War Report: The War Correspondent's View of Battle from the Crimea to the Falklands.* 1987; *Sunday Times* of London Insight Team. *War in the Falklands.* 1982.

FALL, BERNARD (1926–1967). He was born in Vienna, Austria, and grew up in France. His parents were killed by the Nazis, and he fought with the French resistance and then the French army during the liberation of France. Following the war he worked as an investigator for the Nuremberg War Crimes Tribunal and then began his college education at the University of Paris in 1948. He went on to receive his M.A. and Ph.D. from Syracuse before taking an academic position in international relations at Howard University in 1956.

After completion of his doctoral research on the Viet Minh insurgency in 1953, Fall became a recognized authority on the former French colony. His exploits with French troops in the field during the First Indochina War are chronicled in his *Street Without Joy* (1961). He continued to visit Southeast Asia throughout the early 1960s and subsequently wrote numerous articles and essays which were collected in *Viet-Nam Witness* (1966). His book *Hell in a Very Small Place*, published that same year, is a classic study of the French debacle at the Battle of Dien Bien Phu.

As the foremost authority of his generation on Vietnam, Fall warned that the capacity of the Vietnamese people to endure great hardships would thwart American efforts to defeat Vietnamese nationalism. Fall demonstrated great affection for Vietnam and its people and was an implacable critic of both colonialism and the Communist Viet Minh. Fall was diagnosed with an incurable disease shortly before he was killed by a Viet Minh land mine while accompanying a marine unit in the field.

REFERENCES: *DAB* 8; Bernard Fall. *Last Reflections on a War.* 1967; *New York Times.* February 22, 1967.

FALLACI, ORIANA (b. 1930). The renowned Italian foreign correspondent arrived in South Vietnam in 1967, and reported her first battle of the war at Dak To that November. No stranger to war, Fallaci grew up in Fascist Italy, where her father fought with the partisans. Oriana participated as a child in the war against the Axis by assisting downed fliers and escaped prisoners of war along underground escape routes.

Fallaci spent only several months in Vietnam* on her first stint in 1967. She returned the following year intending to report the Tet Offensive, but did not arrive on the battlefront until the after the final Battle of Hue. In May 1968 she was under fire once again during a mortar attack at Dak To. That October Fallaci covered the student protests in Mexico City against the Olympic Games. She was with the students when Mexican soldiers fired into them. Fallaci was seriously wounded, lying alone for hours before being taken to a hospital.

She returned to Vietnam for the last time in 1972 to interview President Nguyen Van Thieu. Following the war in Vietnam Fallaci remained an active and controversial journalist, interviewing and antagonizing world figures from the Ayatollah Khomeini to Libya's Muammar Khadafy. In 1981 she was the subject of a *Playboy* interview. Fallaci wrote the critically acclaimed novel *A Man* in 1980 and several works chronicling her career in journalism, including *Interview with History* (1976) and *Nothing, and So Be It* (1972).

REFERENCE: Virginia Elwood-Akers. *Women War Correspondents in the Vietnam War, 1961–1975.* 1988.

FAUST, FREDERICK (d. 1944). Better known for his fiction under the pen name Max Brand, Faust was the author of the scripts for the highly successful

Dr. Kildare series of motion pictures. He was killed by German mortar fire while covering the 1944 Italian campaign for *Harper's* magazine.
REFERENCE: Robert W. Desmond. *Tides of War.* 1984.

FENTON, ROGER (1819–1869). Fenton had been a leader in British photography prior to the Crimean War.* Educated at University College, London, following graduation he studied painting before turning to law in 1844. But, it was during his study of painting that photography first piqued his interest, and in 1847 he helped founded a photographic club. Six years later he was a founding member of the Photographic Society, later to become better known as the Royal Photographic Society.

With the intense interest in the Crimean War at home in England, Fenton was hired and financed by Thomas Agnew, a Manchester publisher, to take photographs which Agnew would sell for a profit. Although Fenton has often been referred to as the first war photographer, he was preceded by others who covered the 1846–1848 Mexican War* and the 1848–1849 Second Sikh War in the Punjab.

By 1854 Fenton had an impressive portfolio as a landscape and portrait photographer. He could count the royal family as one of his clients, and thanks to their support and patronage he was able to document the Crimean War. In addition, letters of introduction to British commanders from Lord Raglan on down made his stay in the Crimea comfortable and relatively free from restrictions. It was hoped Fenton would photograph scenes that would counter negative accounts concerning the hardships faced by British forces in the Crimea. Although his over three hundred images of the conflict are devoid of graphic war scenes, his work has been described as the first extensive photodocumentation of a war. Wood engravings made from several of his images were published in the *Illustrated London News.*

Fenton was sick for much of his stay in the Crimea, which only lasted from March through June 1855. He took 360 photographs during these three months. Upon his return to England, the French emperor was so impressed by the quality of the war images that he sent several French photographers to capture the rest of the conflict.

A full account of Fenton's Crimean venture can be found in the January 1856 *Journal of the Photographic Society.* He reportedly used the wet collodion process, which was first made public in 1851. The wet-plate process utilized a glass plate which had to be wet through the entire process. This process entailed first submerging the glass plate in a sensitizing solution, which was then exposed in the camera, then taken out and developed. The process necessitated the constant availability of a portable darkroom. Fenton's photographic van replete with photographic equipment was a frequent target of enemy artillery. Although his images of military encampments, forts, and harbors are priceless documents for this era, they are little more than posed sets, which when compared to Mathew Brady's* war images compromise the true horror of war. This was in part due to the technology of the day, which required exposures of three to twenty seconds. Any movement within this time span would result in blurring: therefore the necessity of posing each shot. Since part of his mission was to reassure the British public, Fenton knew that portraits of the dead would be unacceptable.

In October 1855 an exhibition of most of his photographs was held in London. The exhibition toured throughout England, eliciting much excitement and public interest. Several large folios of Fenton's prints were published, but interest in the conflict was declining. Following the end of the fighting and the fall of Sebastopol in September 1855 and the subsequent peace negotiations Fenton auctioned off his remaining stock of war photos.

In 1859 he recorded the horrors of war for the last time when he accompanied troops to the Piedmont in several battles with Austrian forces during the Austro-Italian War.* It was said the carnage distressed him to such an extent that he never covered the front lines again. In 1862, at the zenith of his fame he retired from photography to practice law.

REFERENCES: Helmut and Alison Gernsheim. *Roger Fenton: Photographer of the Crimean War.* 1973; Pat Hodgson. *Early War Photographs.* 1974; Lawrence James. *Crimea, 1854–56.* 1981; Jorge Lewinski. *The Camera at War.* 1978.

FINCASTLE, VISCOUNT ALEXANDER EDWARD MURRAY (1881–1962).

Born in London, he joined the army in 1891 following his graduation from Eton. He served as an assistant to the viceroy of India from 1895 to 1897 and during the Frontier War he fought in the Battle of Landaki while serving as a special for the *Times.* He received the Victoria Cross for his attempt to save the life of Lieutenant Greaves, a reporter for the *Times of India.* Fellow correspondent Winston Churchill* attempted to quickly publish his collected dispatches of the campaign but was beaten to the publisher by Fincastle. Fincastle rose to captain and served in the Boer War* and World War I.* Better known as Lord Dunmore beginning in 1907, he won the Distinguished Service Order during the Somme campaign. He is the only journalist to have been awarded the Victoria Cross.

REFERENCE: Dennis Griffiths, ed. *The Encyclopedia of the British Press.* 1992.

FINERTY, JOHN F. (1846–1908).

He is best known for his coverage of the American Indian Wars* from 1876 to 1881 for the *Chicago Times.* Born in County Galway, Ireland, he was the son of a newspaper editor. In 1864, he fled Ireland and a possible jail sentence after a brief flirtation with the Irish freedom movement. Upon his arrival in America he enlisted in the Union Army to serve in the American Civil War.*

Following the war, the classically educated Finerty moved to Chicago, where he found employment with the *Chicago Republican* in 1868. In 1871 he switched his allegiance to the *Chicago Tribune,* where he would remain until 1875 when he moved to the *Chicago Times.* His first assignment was to cover General George Crook's 1876 expedition against the Sioux and the Northern

Cheyennes. Finerty was not content to play the passive reporter and often took part in the fighting. He participated in the skirmish on the Tongue River, the Battle of the Rosebud, and the Sibley Scout, all resulting in citations for bravery.

In 1879 he covered Nelson Miles' expedition against the Sioux along the Canadian border. That same year he covered the suppression of the Ute uprising. In 1881 he went into the field during the Apache uprising. However, in the last two campaigns he saw no action. Tall and lanky, he was sometimes referred to as "Long John." After his career as an Indian War correspondent he served as a Washington correspondent and was active in various Irish societies.
REFERENCES: John Finerty. *War-Path and Bivouac*. 1961; Oliver Knight. *Following the Indian Wars*. 1960.

FIORILLO, LUIGI (?). The Italian photographer specialized in portraits from the Middle East before covering the Egyptian army rebellion led by Arabi Pasha in 1881. He witnessed the naval bombardment of Alexandria on July 11, 1882. His images of this incident are collected in *Album Souvenir d'Alexandrie: Ruines*. In 1887 he documented the Italian campaign in Abyssinia as a guest of an artillery officer.
REFERENCE: Nicolas Monti. *Africa Then*. 1987.

FIRST CASUALTY, THE. The 1975 book *The First Casualty, from the Crimea to Vietnam: The War Correspondent as Hero, Propagandist, and Myth Maker*, by Phillip Knightley, takes a controversial and updated look at the history of war reporting. The title refers to California senator Hiram Johnson's warning about American intervention during World War I,* that "the first casualty when war comes is truth."
REFERENCE: Phillip Knightley. *The First Casualty*. 1975.

FISHER, PHILIP D. (?). Originally from Ohio, Fisher went west as a civil engineer for the Union Pacific Railroad following his service in the Union Army during the American Civil War.* He was in Kansas during the 1867 Indian troubles and shortly before the arrival of *Harper's* sketch artist Theodore R. Davis.* Several of Fisher's sketches of the American Indian War* were published by *Harper's* that year. Among them was a drawing of the Hancock expedition at Fort Harker.
REFERENCE: Peggy and Harold Samuels. *Samuels' Encyclopedia of Artists of the American West*. 1985.

FISKE, STEPHEN RYDER (1840–1916). Born in New Brunswick, New Jersey, Fiske demonstrated an early interest in the newspaper business. By the time he was fourteen he had published several articles and edited a small newspaper. After being expelled from Rutgers University for writing a novel satirizing one of his professors he was hired by the *New York Herald*. During the American Civil War* he served briefly as a war correspondent and then as the paper's

drama critic. He left for Europe in 1866 and was with Giuseppe Garibaldi in Rome during the revolution. Fiske returned to the States in 1879 and founded the *New York Dramatic Mirror*. He remained active in the theater as a critic and playwright up to his death.
REFERENCE: Robert B. Downs and Jane B. Downs. *Journalists of the United States.* 1991.

FITZGERALD, FRANCES (b. 1940). The well-connected Fitzgerald was the daughter of a former deputy director of the CIA. She went to Vietnam* as a freelance journalist in 1966. Intending to stay only a month she remained for a year. She returned to Vietnam five years later to cover the 1971 elections. When her highly acclaimed book *Fire in the Lake* was released in 1972 she was praised for her deep insights into Vietnamese culture, and it went on to become a best-seller and Pulitzer Prize winner. The next year she was honored with the George Polk* Memorial Award for her Vietnam coverage. In 1973 Fitzgerald covered the Vietnam cease-fire. Over the next year she reported form Cuba, Syria, and Lebanon, and in late 1974 was in Hanoi for a nineteen-day fact-finding trip.
REFERENCE: Virginia Elwood-Akers. *Women War Correspondents in the Vietnam War, 1961–1975.* 1988.

"FIVE O'CLOCK FOLLIES." "Five O'Clock Follies" was the derisive term used by reporters to describe daily briefings given by the Joint United States Public Affairs Office (JUSPAO) in Saigon each day at five o'clock during the Vietnam War.* The briefings were controlled by the Military Assistance Command—Vietnam (MACV), which compiled data related to current military operations. It came under criticism for its penchant to inflate enemy casualty counts and underestimate enemy successes. It did just the opposite with American gains and losses.
REFERENCES: Daniel C. Hallin. *The "Uncensored War": The Media and Vietnam.* 1986; Clarence R. Wyatt. *Paper Soldiers: The American Press and the Vietnam War.* 1993.

FLEESON, DORIS (1901–1970). Fleeson was born in Sterling, Kansas, and entered journalism with the *Pittsburg Star* in Kansas. In 1934 she joined the *New York Daily News* and in 1943 became war correspondent for the *Woman's Home Companion*, covering the Sicilian campaign and the D-Day landing at Omaha Beach. Following the war she became the first woman political columnist to be syndicated.
REFERENCE: Robert B. Downs and Jane B. Downs. *Journalists of the United States.* 1991.

FLEISCHER, JACK (1903–1966). Born in Luxembourg and educated at the University of Missouri, Fleischer joined the International News Service in 1929. Five years later he headed up its Berlin bureau. He covered German military affairs until the fall of France in 1940. Prior to American entry into World War II* he was allowed to cover German forces up to the Soviet frontier. However, beginning in October 1941 the Nazi government introduced censorship restrictions that barred foreign journalists from covering the developing war with the Soviet Union. In December 1941 he was among the American journalists arrested in Berlin. He eventually joined the U.S. Army after the bombing of Pearl Harbor but did not see any combat. Following the war he returned to journalism with the INS and the Hearst Headline Service as a columnist, reporter, and United Nations correspondent.

REFERENCES: Robert W. Desmond. *Tides of War*. 1984; Jack Stenbuck, ed. *Typewriter Battalion*. 1995.

FLYNN, SEAN (1941–1970). The son of movie legend Errol Flynn was freelancing and on assignment for *Time* magazine in Cambodia when he was captured by Vietnamese Communists and reportedly executed. Flynn and Dana Stone* of CBS news were riding motorcycles along Route 1 near Chi Pou, close to the South Vietnamese border, when they were seized. Flynn and Stone were just two of eleven journalists, photographers, and members of television camera teams seized at a Vietnamese roadblock during the first week of April 1970. Their bodies have never been recovered. Contrary to accounts that he was simply an adventure seeker with a death wish, Flynn was an accomplished professional photographer and cameraman who had published work in *Time* and had had news footage broadcast on the CBS television network.

REFERENCES: Charles C. Arnot. *Don't Kill the Messenger*. 1994; Perry Deane Young. *Two of the Missing*. 1975.

"FOG OF WAR, THE." *See* "BATTLE FOG" POLICY.

FORBES, ARCHIBALD (1838–1900). Born in Morayshire and educated at Aberdeen and Edinburgh, it was after a course taught by the preeminent war correspondent of his day, William Howard Russell,* that Forbes enlisted in the Royal Dragoons in 1857. He published his first war pieces with the *Morning Star* and *Cornhill Magazine* while still in the military.

He left the army and published a weekly journal called the *London Scotsman* from 1867 to 1871. In 1870 his career as a war correspondent was given a boost when he was assigned by the *Morning Advertiser* and then the *Daily News* to cover the siege of Metz during the Franco-Prussian War.* At the Battle of Metz he suffered a minor leg wound which became gangrenous, nearly necessitating amputation. Forbes recovered and went on to cover the siege of Paris and was the first correspondent to enter the city after its fall in January 1871.

Formerly, most correspondents had made only occasional use of the war telegram. However, as competition among the newspapers for coverage intensified, one of Forbes' contributions to his craft was his making full use of the telegraph to effectively relay his eyewitness accounts.

Forbes made his reputation as one of the foremost war correspondents of his era while engaged by the *Daily News*. Entering Paris with the victorious Prussian army he was nearly drowned by French citizens who suspected him of being a German spy. After covering the Franco-Prussian War and the subsequent carnage of the Paris Commune (1871), he witnessed the Carlist fighting in Spain and the Russo-Turkish War,* and accompanied the Khyber Pass force to Jalabad (1878–1879). During the Russo-Turkish War Forbes accompanied the Russian army and witnessed the key Battles of Plevna and Schipka Pass. When the Czar was informed of the Russian victory at Schipka Pass through Forbes' dispatch he was so elated that he awarded the war correspondent the highest Russian award for valor.

In 1880 Forbes reported the Zulu War and rode 110 miles following the Battle of Ulundi to Landman's Drift in less than a day. Two days later he appeared 170 miles away with news of the British victory and was able to wire his dispatch to England before official sources. His death-defying journey of 300 miles in fifty hours, better known as the "Ride of Death" was a journalistic coup, widely hailed but little rewarded. While some members of parliament thought a Victoria Cross was in order, he did not receive so much as a campaign medal. Coincidentally, it was also his last war.

Although he was just into his forties, Forbes' health began to decline after all the years of hardships on the battlefield, and he retired to England, where he lectured and continued to write over the last two decades of his life. Besides his voluminous war reportage Forbes published numerous books related to distinguished soldiers and his military exploits, including *My Reminiscences: 1870– 71* (1871), *War Correspondence of the Daily News* (1878), *Glimpses Through Cannon Smoke* (1880), *The Afghan Wars of 1839 and 1879* (1892), *The Soldiers I Have Known, Memories and Studies of War and Peace* (1895), and the Men of Action series.

REFERENCES: Robert W. Desmond. *The Information Process*. 1978; *DNB*; Robert Wilkinson-Latham. *From Our Special Correspondent*. 1979.

FORBES, EDWIN (1839–1895). Forbes, an American Civil War* illustrator, devoted much of his career to rendering his sketches into paintings and an elaborate book of illustrations, which was published as *Life Studies of the Great Army*.

In 1861, he was hired by *Frank Leslie's Illustrated Newspaper* to follow the Army of the Potomac under General George McClellan. He performed the dual functions of artist and reporter while covering the Union troops from 1862 to 1864. In 1862 he sketched most of Stonewall Jackson's campaigns in the Shenandoah as well as the Second Battle of Bull Run. He went on to witness the Battles of Gettysburg (1863), the Wilderness (1864), Cold Harbor and the Spotsylvania Courthouse, and many others. After the war Forbes recollected that the Battle of Antietam was the most "picturesque" battle that he had covered. Like most other sketch artists employed by the press he made quick drawings on the battlefield and completed them later in the studio. Some of his techniques in covering the field of battle contradict the popular image of the war correspondent. At one battle he sat on his stoic mount Kitty on an elevated ridge almost half a mile from the action sketching the battle through his binoculars. He wrote and illustrated his memoirs of the war in the two-volume *Thirty Years After, An Artist's Story of the Great War* (1891). An artist to the end, he became paralyzed on his right side shortly before his death. Assisted by his wife, he taught himself successfully to draw with his left hand up until his death in 1895.

REFERENCES: Pat Hodgson. *The War Illustrators*. 1977; W. Fletcher Thompson, Jr. *The Image of War*. 1960; Philip Van Doren. *They Were There*. 1959.

FORSYTH, FREDRICK (b. 1938). He worked for Reuters* from 1961 to 1965. The future best-selling novelist of *The Day of the Jackal* and *Dogs of War* was criticized by his superiors for injecting "imagination and language" into his journalism. He wrote *The Biafra Story* after spending many months in Biafra, but according to Nigerian civil war historian John de St. Jorre,* Forsyth's book is disappointing not only for its partisanship but for its failure to give an accurate portrait of life in Biafra.

REFERENCES: John de St. Jorre. *The Brothers' War*. 1972; Donald Read. *The Power of News*. 1992.

FORTESCUE, GRANVILLE (1875–1912). Fortescue dropped out of the University of Pennsylvania to serve in the Spanish-American War,* where he caught the attention of Colonel Theodore Roosevelt, who later selected him as a White House military aide. In 1907 he accompanied an expedition exploring the Orinoco River in South America.

Fortescue served as a military observer during the Russo-Japanese War,* where he began a long friendship with correspondent Ellis Ashmead-Bartlett.* In 1909 Fortescue covered the Riff War in Morocco, his first assignment as a war correspondent, at the behest of Ashmead-Bartlett for the *London Standard*. Fortescue happened to be on vacation with his family on the North Sea coast when Germany invaded Belgium in 1914. Ashmead-Ellis arranged to have him cover the story for the *Daily Telegraph*, resulting in a first-rate eyewitness account from the fighting near Liège for the paper and future assignments with the *New York Tribune*. He later covered fronts in Russia and France.

REFERENCES: Emmet Crozier. *American Reporters on the Western Front, 1914–18*. 1959; Robert W. Desmond. *Windows on the World*. 1980.

FOX, EDWARD (d. 1895). Fox covered the Modoc War of 1872–1873 for the *New York Herald*. An Englishman who had served in the British army, he was often compared to Henry Stanley* for his courage under fire. Fox had been the yachting editor back in New York when the war broke out, and he journeyed overland to San Francisco and by stage to the mining town of Yreka on the outskirts of the conflict. He covered the first meeting of the peace commission and got his first scoop when he rode alone into hostile country to successfully interview the Modoc leader Captain Jack. The *Herald* headlined one of his stories about the Modoc chief with the fanciful "Rob Roy Mac-Modoc." Fox's interview has been described as perhaps the most outstanding individual feat of the war.

He later covered the Three Days' Fight after peace negotiations failed and some officers were ambushed. He narrowly escaped being killed in an ambush. He left for New York shortly before the end of the war. Following his battle exploits he was nicknamed "Modoc" Fox by New York newspapermen. Fox returned to California to cover the execution of Captain Jack in October 1873.

In 1874 he exposed management corruption at the Red Cloud Agency and testified before a congressional committee the following year. He continued with the paper, then tried Wall Street before moving back to England. He fought in several duels and was instrumental in establishing the Anglo-colonial paper the *British Australian*. In 1894 he moved to Australia to enter the mining business and died in a yachting accident near Perth.

REFERENCE: Oliver Knight. *Following the Indian Wars*. 1960.

FRANCO-PRUSSIAN WAR. The Franco-Prussian War began on July 19, 1870, and ended with a Prussian victory on May 10, 1871. The ten-month war witnessed one of the great battles in history at Sedan and several long sieges. The siege of Paris from September 19 to January 28 saw revolution break out in Paris as well as the creation of a temporary government. The outbreak of the Franco-Prussian War in 1870 signaled a new era in European war reporting. Two records for press coverage emerged from the conflict. Not only was it the most expensive war to cover up to that time, but it also marked the first use of wireless for transmitting news from the scene of battle. It was the most thoroughly covered European conflict up to that time. While the Crimean War* and subsequent campaigns were reported by mostly British correspondents, the Franco-Prussian War was covered by the press of at least six countries.

Initially the French government prohibited foreign war correspondents from the field, while the Prussians were more accommodating to the press. The best coverage of the war was provided by the French daily *Le Gaulois*, with twenty-six correspondents. Eventually neutral journalists could be found with both armies. *Daily Telegraph* correspondents included John Merry Lesage,* George Augustus Sala,* and Frank Lawley.* Reporting for the *Times* were Frederick Hardman,* Laurence Oliphant,* and William Howard Russell* with Prussian forces reporting his last war. Reporting for the *Daily News* were Archibald Forbes,* Hilary Skinner,* Henry Labouchere,* and four members of the Vizetelly* family. Only a handful of American correspondents appear in the annals of war literature on the conflict, with Januarius MacGahan,* beginning a short but eventful career as a war reporter, being the most recognizable.

The Franco-Prussian War marked a new era in war reporting. With the departure of William Howard Russell from the battlefield, his place was taken by a new breed of war reporter that would depend on the telegraph and cable facilities to speed news reports to the public regardless of the cost. Accurate, succinct, but precise accounts replaced the florid, subjective descriptions which had formerly been the norm prior to the American Civil War.* During the four-month siege of Paris, carrier pigeons* and balloons were used to facilitate the transmission of news through Prussian forces. However, no outcome of the war was more significant than the emergence of the German Empire, the unification of Italy, and the establishment of the French Republic.

REFERENCES: Robert Desmond. *The Information Process*. 1978; Michael Howard. *The Franco-Prussian War*. 1961.

FRASER, DAVID (1869–1953). The Scottish-born correspondent left a banking career in 1900 for military service in Lumsden's Horse during the Boer War.* Following the war he was initially rebuffed in his attempts to land a position as foreign correspondent for the *Times*, but another interview resulted in a posting as an assistant to the Far East correspondent. During the Russo-Japanese War* he followed the Japanese land forces while his supervisor covered the naval campaign. Fraser's account of General Kuroki's victory at the Battle of the Yalu River was widely printed. After the Battle of Shako he ceased to cover the land war and he returned to London to join the staff of the *Times*. Over the next few years he reported from the Indian subcontinent, Turkey, and China. He retired as Far East correspondent in 1940.

REFERENCE: Robert W. Desmond. *Windows on the World*. 1980.

FREANER, JAMES L. (?). Freaner was one of the outstanding war correspondents of the Mexican War* and George Wilkins Kendall's* strongest competitor during the conflict. Representing the *New Orleans Delta*, he wrote articles appearing under his nickname "Mustang," a sobriquet bestowed on the reporter following the Battle of Monterrey, where Freaner killed a Mexican lancer officer and took his steed. During the Battle of Monterrey and other actions in the Valley of Mexico campaign he served with McCulloch's Texas Rangers. He was with the American army as it made its way from Veracruz to Mexico City.

Prior to entering the newspaper profession Freaner wandered through Texas and Louisiana before accompanying a New Orleans regiment to the Rio Grande at the outset of the war. He later joined a Texas Ranger company led by Captain Jack "Coffee" Hays. Freaner copied Kendall's method of sending stories by special courier as news competition became intense toward the close of the war.

Freaner was involved in the controversial publication of the "Leonidas letter," a hoax which overstated the importance and accomplishments of General Pillow during the Mexican War. On separate occasions Freaner personally transported important official documents. In November 1847 he carried dispatches to Washington on behalf of General Winfield Scott, and in February 1848 he conveyed the Peace Treaty of Guadalupe Hidalgo from peace emissary Nicholas

Trist to President Polk. Following the war Freaner was hired to cover the story of the California gold rush.
REFERENCES: F. Lauriston Bullard. *Famous War Correspondents*. 1914; Fayette Copeland. *Kendall of the Picayune*. 1943.

FREDENTHAL, DAVID (1914–1958). The Detroit artist-correspondent was one of the members of the army art unit who joined *Life* after the dissolution of the unit in 1943. Assigned to the Pacific in late 1943, he covered military operations under General Douglas MacArthur, including three island invasions. His most memorable work came during the American assault on Arawe in New Britain. In September 1944 he was transferred to Europe to cover partisan activities against the Germans in Yugoslavia. He witnessed the liberation of Belgrade by partisan and Russian forces.
REFERENCE: Frederick Voss. *Reporting the War*. 1994.

FRIEND, THE. Before the Boer War* an English-language newspaper called *The Friend of the Sovereignty and Bloemfontein Gazette* was published in Bloemfontein. The chief press censor of the British army asked a group of correspondents to transform it into the first army newspaper, called the *Friend* starting on March 16, 1900. During its one-month run, it published articles by most of the Boer War correspondents, including Bennet Burleigh,* Lionel James,* and even Rudyard Kipling.*
REFERENCE: Byron Farwell. *The Great Anglo-Boer War*. 1976.

FRIPP, CHARLES EDWIN (1854–1906). Born in Hampstead, London, the son of a successful landscape painter, Fripp received his art training at the Royal Academy in Munich. He covered his first conflicts as a special artist for the *Graphic* during the Kaffir War (1878) and the Zulu War of 1879. His eccentric manner made him the subject of endless anecdotes among his colleagues. On one occasion during the Zulu War Fripp, an avid swimmer, insisted on swimming despite intermittent sniper fire. He refused an officer's order to leave the water and had to be removed by force. In another incident the reportedly mild-mannered artist had to be restrained from slugging General Buller, "who annoyed him."

In 1881 he covered conflict in South Africa and in 1885 he reported the Sudan campaign. During the Sino-Japanese War* he was with the Chinese forces. Beginning in 1890 his sketches appeared in the new *Daily Graphic* as well as the *Graphic*. He covered the Sino-Japanese War from 1894 to 1895, and then the Second Matabele War in 1896–1897. In the late 1890s he traveled throughout the American West before accompanying American forces in the Philippine campaign during the Spanish-American War* in 1899. The year 1900 found Fripp covering the Boer War.* Some of his sketches were drawn from notes provided by soldiers in the field. Following the war he relocated to Canada, where he recorded the Klondike story.

REFERENCES: Pat Hodgson. *The War Illustrators*. 1977; Robert Wilkinson-Latham. *From Our Special Correspondent*. 1979.

FULLER, SARAH MARGARET (1810–1850). Fuller was born in Cambridge, Massachusetts, and is considered by some authorities to be the first woman war correspondent. Better known for her feminist and transcendentalist writings, her book *Woman in the Nineteenth Century* (1845) was an important influence on the 1848 Seneca Falls convention on woman's rights.

In 1844 she joined the staff of Horace Greeley's *New York Tribune* as literary critic. Two years later she was made a foreign correspondent and sent to Europe, where she reported on social conditions in Great Britain, interviewed notable political and artistic figures, and became embroiled in the Roman revolution. From Italy she reported the French bombardment and capture of Rome. While in Rome she married Angelo Ossoli and had a son. She served as both nurse and reporter on the battlefield, which saw her husband fighting on the Italian side. Following the capitulation of Rome, Fuller and family fled the country by sea. They perished when their ship was lost off the coast of Fire Island in July 1850, shortly before her fortieth birthday.

REFERENCES: John Hohenberg. *Foreign Correspondence*. 1964; Ishbel Ross. *Ladies of the Press*. 1936.

FYFE, HENRY HAMILTON (1869–1951). Born in London, he followed his father onto the staff of the *Times*. In 1902 he transferred to the *Morning Advertiser* before moving to the *Daily Mirror* the following year. In 1907 he began an eleven-year affiliation with the *Daily Mail*. He covered the developing revolution in Russia in 1911 and two years later was in Mexico covering Carranza's revolution on special assignment for the *Times*. Fyfe returned briefly in 1916, the only foreign news correspondent during this period of the conflict. Shortly afterward the Irish troubles in Ulster became a major story and Fyfe was called back to Europe.

With the outbreak of World War I* in 1914 he was soon reporting from France and Belgium. His reputation soared after his telegram to the *Daily Mail* reporting the retreat from Mons was reprinted in the *Times*. His coverage portrayed the true horrors of war and dissuaded anyone of the notion that the war would be of short duration. In 1915–1916 he reported the war in Russia and the killing of the court mystic, Rasputin. The following year he was sent on diplomatic missions to the United States. Besides his journalistic activities, Fyfe wrote numerous works of fiction and nonfiction, plays, and biographies.

REFERENCES: Robert W. Desmond. *Windows on the World*. 1980; *DNB*, 1951–1960.

G

GALLEGHER, JAMES WESLEY "WES" (b. 1911). Born in Santa Cruz, California, Gallegher was educated at various California schools and the University of San Francisco before joining the *Register Pajaronian* in Watsonville as a sportswriter in late 1929. He gradually moved into other areas of news reporting and received a master's degree in journalism from Louisiana State University in 1935. He just missed witnessing the assassination of Huey Long, but was on the scene soon enough to make one of the earliest accurate reports of the incident.

After being hired by the Associated Press in 1938, he was assigned to its Buffalo bureau, and later was transferred to New York, where he was promoted to foreign correspondent. He was on his way to cover the Russo-Finnish War, but the conflict ended before he got there. He was in Copenhagen when the German army invaded in April 1940, and he covered the final stages of the Norwegian campaign.

He was in Yugoslavia when Italy invaded Greece, and he covered the Albanian front until he was hospitalized with jaundice. By 1942 he was back in action covering the invasion of North Africa as head of the AP news crew. The following year he suffered back and face injuries when his jeep overturned. In 1944 Gallegher was placed in charge of the AP field crew covering the Normandy invasion and later directing postwar European coverage. From his wartime experiences came *Free Men Are Fighting* (1944).

Following the war he continued his career with the AP, rising to general manager in 1962. The AP continued to develop under his tenure and in 1976 he was made director of the Gannett Company. He also wrote *Back Door to Berlin: The Full Story of the American Coup in North Africa* (1943).

REFERENCES: *DLB*, 254–255; Library of America. *Reporting World War II*. 1995.

GALLEGHER, O'DOWD "O. D." (b. 1913). South African–born Odie Gallegher represented the *London Daily Express* during the Ethiopian War.* According to one source, the inexperienced reporter was selected merely for being an African native. He left Ethiopia prior to the end of the war when he was assigned to interview Emperor Haile Selassie, who was in exile in Jerusalem. The resulting interview was carried in the *Express* under the headline "Gallegher Sees Emperor," and was a minor sensation.

Gallegher covered the Spanish Civil War,* first with the Nationalists and then with the Republicans. He was one of the few journalists to report virtually the entire war, although he was twice expelled from the country by Falangist insurgents. According to Phillip Knightley, Gallegher claimed that Robert Capa* insinuated to him that his famous photograph "Death of a Loyalist Soldier"* had been faked. When Madrid fell in March 1939 Gallegher was the only full-time war correspondent on hand to observe the entry into the city of the victorious Nationalist troops. While hiding in the Ritz Hotel the intrepid journalist was able to smuggle several short dispatches to the telegraph office before he was captured by Nationalist authorities and narrowly escaped being shot.

In 1939 he covered the war in France, before transferring to the Pacific theater. He was aboard the ill-fated battle cruiser *Repulse* only days after Pearl Harbor when he witnessed the worst British naval disaster of the war. On December 10, 1941, Japanese torpedo bombers sank the *Repulse* and the battleship *Prince of Wales* in the Gulf of Siam, with a heavy loss of life. Gallegher and his notes survived a plunge into the oily sea; and after he was rescued with the only other two correspondents to witness the engagement, he was taken back to Singapore, where he filed his scoop, much to the chagrin of the slow-footed censors. He later reported the 1942 Burma campaign for the *Daily Express*.

REFERENCES: Robert W. Desmond. *Crisis and Conflict.* 1982; Robert W. Desmond. *Tides of War.* 1984; Phillip Knightley. *The First Casualty.* 1975.

GALLENGA, ANTONIO (1810–1895). Born in Italy, he became a naturalized British citizen in 1846. Gallenga was a professor of foreign languages in Nova Scotia and of Italian literature at University College before returning to Italy in 1859. Even though he was a British subject he was allowed to hold a seat in the Piedmontese parliament. It was during this time that he began his affiliation with the *London Daily News* and the *Times*.

In 1863 he was assigned to report the American Civil War.* He reported from the western theater of the war, and among his first stories was an account of the internecine bloodshed on the Kansas-Missouri border. He chronicled the advance of the Union Army of the Cumberland under Rosecrans and the Battle of Chickamauga. Gallenga returned to England in December 1863, claiming ill health. However, most sources indicate he had tired of restrictions imposed by Federal authorities which prohibited any member of the *Times* from accompanying armies in the field.

REFERENCE: Ian F. W. Beckett. *The War Correspondents: The American Civil War.* 1993.

GARANIN, ANATOLI (b. 1912). Born and educated in Moscow, Garanin was self-taught in photography. Prior to World War II* he worked as a photojournalist for several publications. He was not limited to covering the front lines, having carved a career in both scenic and theater photography. During the conflict he was a reporter for *Frontovaya Illustracia.* Following the war he worked as special correspondent for *Soviet Union* magazine and for the Moscow Theater.
REFERENCES: *Contemporary Photographers.* 1982; Daniela Mrazkova and Vladimir Remes, eds. *The Russian War: 1941–1945.* 1975.

GARDNER, ALEXANDER (1821–1882). Born in Paisley, Scotland, Gardner worked as a jeweler's apprentice from 1835 to 1843. At the same time he pursued interests in chemistry and optics. Prior to moving to America in 1856 and working as Mathew Brady's* assistant, Gardner worked as a reporter for the *Glasgow Sentinel.* Gardner, self-taught in wet-plate photography, introduced Brady to the techniques of enlargement. In 1858 he operated Brady's Washington studio, but within five years he resigned to strike out on his own. As one of Brady's most important photographers, he felt he had not been given enough credit or payment for his work.

Gardner opened his own portrait establishment, where he advertised a set of "Photographic Incidents of the War." Soon after, he was named official photographer for the Army of the Potomac, although he continued to photograph the progress of the war by deploying teams much in the tradition of Brady. In 1866 Gardner published *Sketch Book of the War,* which was comprised of one hundred original photographs by various photographers. In 1867 he became the official photographer for the Union Pacific Railroad and went west to photograph the frontier. While Gardner is most often identified with the American Civil War,* he also documented some remarkable events such as execution of the Lincoln conspirators, Lincoln's funeral procession, the trial and execution of Andersonville commandant Wirz, and the life of the Great Plains Indians.
REFERENCES: Alexander Gardner. *Gardner's Photographic Sketch Book of the Civil War.* 1959; D. Mark Katz. *Witness to an Era: The Life and Photographs of Alexander Gardner.* 1991.

GELLHORN, MARTHA (1908–1983). Born in St. Louis, she dropped out of Bryn Mawr College a year before graduation to pursue her goal of becoming a foreign correspondent. Her first steps in journalism were taken with the *New Republic* and the *Albany Times Union.* In the early 1930s she traveled in Europe and wrote her first novel, *What Mad Pursuit,* published in 1934. In 1936 she met Ernest Hemingway,* who would eventually become her husband. In 1937 Gellhorn joined Hemingway in Spain, where she was persuaded by *Collier's* to become its special correspondent. She returned to the States to drum up support for the Loyalist side in the Spanish Civil War.* In late 1937 she was back in Spain writing from the battlefront. During the conflict she worked in field hospitals and visited the Loyalist fronts.

In 1939 she covered the Russian invasion of Finland and then the developing Asian theater of the war, reporting from Singapore, the Dutch East Indies, and the Burma Road. By the time Pearl Harbor was bombed she was already a seasoned war reporter and the wife of Hemingway. She became aware that some had attributed her literary success to her relationship with the best-known writer in the world and took steps to keep her name from being forever linked with his.

Sent to London in 1943 by *Collier's*, she became its official war correspondent. After she requested that Hemingway join her in London, he took out his displeasure at having been left behind in the States by offering his services to *Collier's*. The U.S. press corps protocol allowed for only one frontline correspondent per magazine and Gellhorn lost her position to her husband. She left Hemingway after this and covered the war on her own, having lost her accreditation. However, while Hemingway was with the official war correspondents preparing for the Normandy invasion, Gellhorn secretly boarded a hospital ship that preceded the landing craft with the correspondents, infuriating Hemingway in the process. Scooping Hemingway on this story should have been her best revenge, but her story was accorded secondary status by *Collier's* as Hemingway's eyewitness account was the front-page story.

Gellhorn went on to cover the British Eighth Army and the Battle of the Bulge. She collaborated with Virginia Cowles* on the play *Love Goes to War* (1946), a comedy about war correspondents. She also reported the Indonesian rebellion against the Dutch and the Nuremberg war crime trials. After the war she returned to novel and travel writing before reporting the Vietnam War* in 1966 as correspondent for the *Guardian*, the 1967 Six Day War, and the 1980s wars in Central America. Her best-known work is probably *The Face of War*, a collection of her war reportage (1986).

REFERENCES: Bernice Kert. *The Hemingway Women*. 1983; Lilya Wagner. *Women War Correspondents of World War II*. 1989.

GEYER, GEORGIE ANNE (b. 1935). The Chicago-born Geyer entered the journalism profession in 1960 with the *Chicago Daily News*. A graduate of Northwestern University, prior to joining the *News* Geyer studied overseas on a Fulbright scholarship and reported for the *Southwest Economist*. In 1965 she covered her first foreign assignment when she was dispatched to the Dominican Republic to cover the revolution there. Over the next several years she developed a reputation as a specialist in Latin American affairs.

By most accounts Geyer began covering the Vietnam War* in 1967 after falling in love with correspondent Keyes Beech,* who was stationed in Saigon for the *Chicago Daily News*. Their relationship ended abruptly but led Geyer to one of her greatest scoops when she obtained an interview with Prince Sihanouk

of Cambodia after all other journalists had been expelled from the country. Apparently Geyer hid the fact that she was actually a journalist, although the Cambodian leader later sent her a cable noting how pleased he was with the objectivity of her final report. She left Vietnam in early 1969, but not before writing a series of articles noting the disillusionment among American servicemen. Following the war she continued as a foreign correspondent, specializing in Latin America, and became a columnist for the Universal Press Syndicate.
REFERENCE: Virginia Elwood-Akers. *Women War Correspondents in the Vietnam War, 1961–1975.* 1988.

GIBBONS, FLOYD (1887–1939). Born in Washington, D.C., Gibbons was educated at Georgetown University before being expelled for pranksterism. After trying his hand at police reporting with the *Minneapolis Daily News* and then the *Milwaukee Free Press* he joined the *Minneapolis Tribune*. In 1912 he landed a job with the *Chicago Tribune*. Two years later he was sent by the paper to cover the American mobilization along the Mexican border during the Mexican Revolution. Among his much-publicized exploits was his warm relationship with Pancho Villa, who outfitted a special railroad car for the intrepid reporter despite his threat to hang the first American reporter to fall into his hands. He also reported the Battle of Ciudad Juarez from El Paso. In 1916 Gibbons accompanied General John J. Pershing's expedition to punish Villa for his raid on New Mexico.

In 1917 he was assigned to cover World War I* in Europe for the *Tribune*. Gibbons almost made a fatal mistake when he ignored instructions to cross the Atlantic on the *Frederick VIII*, which carried a German ambassador, and instead opted for the SS *Laconia*, which was torpedoed by U-boats two hundred miles off the coast of Ireland. His account of the sinking was widely printed and was probably his greatest scoop.

While covering the war in France, Gibbons left the carefully controlled press column and on his own initiative left for training with the Sixth Field Artillery for six weeks, resulting in several news scoops. Gibbons was almost killed while accompanying a marine assault in the Belleau Wood. He was attempting to aid a gravely wounded major who was trapped by machine-gun fire when he was hit in the arm, shoulder, and head. One bullet ricocheted off a rock and tore out his left eye. He returned to the States and the lecture circuit wearing what would become his trademark eye patch.

He returned to Europe following the war unsatisfied by his new management position. In 1919 he covered the Sinn Fein rebellion and the next year was the only reporter at the front during the Polish-Russian conflict. In 1921 he scored one of his greatest scoops as the first reporter to cover the Russian famine. In 1925 he covered the French and Spanish war with the Riffs in Morocco.

He ended his fifteen-year relationship with the *Tribune* in 1926 and wrote the biography of the German war ace Baron von Richthofen, which was serialized for twenty-six weeks in *Liberty* magazine. His attempts at fiction writing were, however, unsuccessful. He moved into radio broadcasting with NBC in 1929 and was an immediate success with his rapid-fire delivery. His radio contract contained a provision that if a war broke out he could break his contract and head to the front. In 1931 he covered the Sino-Japanese conflict for Hearst's International News Service. In the meantime he still broadcast reports for NBC. His interview in Mukden with the commander of Japanese forces was the first radio broadcast from the headquarters of an army in the field and the first to bridge the Pacific Ocean from the Asian continent. Gibbons went on to cover Italy's 1935 invasion of Ethiopia* and the Spanish Civil War* in 1936, which he described as the most brutal and inhumane of the nine wars he covered. He became one of the most recognized personalities of his day. He died of a heart attack on September 24, 1939. He wrote several books, including *How the Laconia Sank*, and *The Militia Mobilization on the Mexican Border: Two Masterpieces of Reporting* (1917).

REFERENCES: *DAB* 22, Supp. 2, 230–231; Edward Gibbons. *Floyd Gibbons, Your Headline Hunter*. 1953; Douglas Gilbert. *Floyd Gibbons, Knight of the Air*. 1930.

GIBBONS, ISRAEL (?). The Northern-born Gibbons reported the American Civil War* from the Southern side. Prior to the war he worked as a compositor and local reporter for the *New Orleans Crescent*. He described Confederate camp life in his trademark folksy style at the outset of the conflict. He was one of the few Confederate war correspondents to cover the opening of the 1862 campaign in the West, reporting the fall of Nashville and the siege and bombardment of Island Number 10. After a furlough in Mobile he rejoined General Braxton Bragg's army in September 1863. Following the federal takeover of New Orleans in 1862, Gibbons reported for the *Mobile Register*.

REFERENCE: J. Cutler Andrews. *The South Reports the Civil War*. 1970.

GIBBS, SIR PHILIP ARMAND HAMILTON (1877–1962). Born in Kensington, England, he joined the publishing house of Cassell, where he wrote *Founders of the Empire* (1899). After a short spell as literary editor he joined the *Daily Mail* and then Pearson's *Daily Express* before moving to the *Daily Chronicle*. He continued to flit from one paper to another before rejoining the *Daily Chronicle* in 1908, when he reported the siege at Sydney Street and helped expose as a hoax Dr. Cook's claim to have reached the North Pole first. In 1912 he covered the Balkan War for the *Daily Graphic*.

In Paris at the outbreak of World War I,* Gibbs was appointed correspondent to the British Expeditionary Force. He was one of only five reporters allowed to wear the green brassard which distinguished the expedition correspondents. His dispatches were widely printed and syndicated in the United States as he became one of the preeminent British war correspondents of World War I. He was knighted in 1920 and made a chevalier of the Legion of Honor. Among his books on the war were *The Soul of War* (1915), *The Battles of the Somme* (1917), *From Bapaume to Passchendale* (1918), and *Realities of War* (1920).

Following the war he turned to freelance journalism and writing fiction, producing almost fifty books. During World War II* he reported from France for the *Daily Sketch*. He narrowly averted blindness in the 1940s when improvements in eye surgery were made available. Gibbs wrote several volumes chronicling his years on Fleet Street. He died on March 10, 1962.
REFERENCES: Robert W. Desmond. *Windows on the World*. 1980; *DNB*, 1961–1970.

GILES, GEOFFREY DOUGLAS (1857–?). An accomplished painter of the sporting life with exhibitions at prestigious galleries, Giles represented the *Graphic* during the Boer War,* accompanying the Kimberley Relief Column. He had prior military experience, having retired as an officer in the Indian army in 1884.
REFERENCE: Pat Hodgson. *The War Illustrators*. 1977.

GLOVER, RIDGEWAY (d. 1866). He was a freelance photographer covering Fort Phil Kearny in Wyoming at the outbreak of the 1866 American Indian War.* Before leaving Philadelphia he made arrangements to send back news reports and photographs to the Philadelphia *Photographer* and *Frank Leslie's Illustrated Newspaper*. Although Glover was aware of hostile Indian activity around the fort, he persisted in venturing out alone, armed only with his photographic equipment and a butcher knife. He was killed by Arapahos on September 17, 1866, during one of his solitary excursions. Glover was apparently attempting to photograph Red Cloud's Sioux warriors near the fort. *Leslie's* published letters from the post chaplain and an officer detailing the demise of Glover on October 27 in an article entitled ''The Fate of a Frank Leslie Special.'' He was reportedly the first photographer killed while attempting to take news photos in America.
REFERENCES: Michael L. Carlebach. *The Origins of Photojournalism in America*. 1992; Oliver Knight. *Following the Indian Wars*. 1960.

GODKIN, EDWIN LAWRENCE (1831–1902). Godkin was born in Moyne County, Wicklow, and educated at Queen's College, Belfast. He left his law studies for journalism and a writing career shortly after his graduation in 1851. His early interest in military affairs is exemplified by the publication of his first book, *The History of Hungary and the Magyars from the Earliest Period to the Close of the Late War* (1853). In 1853 he was hired as special correspondent by the *London Daily News* to cover the outbreak of the Crimean War* in Turkey and was one of the first correspondents on the scene. With the outbreak of the conflict he accompanied Omar Pasha's army and remained in the Crimea until the cessation of hostilities in September 1855. His experiences during the conflict led to a lifelong disdain for warfare. He noted in his autobiography that the most significant outcome of the Crimean War was the creation of the profession of war journalism.

Shortly after moving to the United States in 1856 he toured the South, conducting a study of the slavery system, and in 1860 he became a member of the New York State bar. He was touring Europe in 1861 when the American Civil War* broke out. Unlike many of his countrymen he was a fervent supporter of the Union. Upon his return to the States in 1862 he covered the conflict for the *London Daily News* and also for American papers such as the *New York Times* and the *North American Review*, although not from the front lines.

In 1865 he established the *Nation*, a weekly magazine of opinion, which he edited and wrote for until selling it to the *Evening Post* in 1881. A confirmed advocate of peace, later in life he opposed the Spanish-American War,* the Boer War,* and America's annexation of Hawaii and the Philippines.

REFERENCES: Robert W. Desmond. *The Information Process*. 1978; Edwin Godkin. *Reflections and Comments*. 1895; Rollo Ogden. *Life and Letters of E. L. Godkin*. 1907.

GOODALL, EDWARD ANGELO (1819–1908). Goodall was a landscape artist with exhibitions at the Royal Academy and the Old Watercolour Society to his credit when he turned to war journalism in 1855. He served as war artist for his only campaign when he represented the *Illustrated London News* during the Crimean War.* However, the pioneer war photographer* Roger Fenton* criticized his sketches for ''their total want of likeness to the reality.'' Following the war he returned to landscape painting.

REFERENCES: Helmut and Alison Gernsheim. *Roger Fenton, Photographer of the Crimean War*. 1973; Pat Hodgson. *The War Illustrators*. 1977.

GOODE, SIR WILLIAM ATHELSTANE MEREDITH (1875–1944). Born in Newfoundland to missionary parents, after attending Foyle College in Londonderry, Ireland, Goode went to sea and in 1892 enlisted in the U.S. cavalry. He entered journalism in 1898, when he represented the Associated Press of America during the Spanish-American War.* He accompanied Admiral Sampson on board his flagship for most of the war. His exploits at sea are recorded in *Sampson Through the War* (1899). Following Lieutenant Hobson's courageous sinking of the *Merrimac* at the entrance to Havana harbor under an intense shelling, Goode scooped the competition by getting Hobson's only interview immediately after the action.

Goode was assigned to London as special correspondent from 1898 until 1904, when he joined the *Standard*. In 1911 he became joint news editor of the *Daily Mail*. During World War I* he organized various relief committees and was a member of the British delegation at the Peace Conference. In the postwar years he was best known for his reports on economic conditions and relief missions to Central Europe. He was knighted in 1918.

REFERENCES: Charles H. Brown. *The Correspondents' War*. 1967; *DNB*, 1941–1950; Oliver Gramling. *AP: The Story of News*. 1969.

GORE, WILLIAM W. ''BILLY'' (1871?–1935). Born in Norfolk, England, he went to sea as a young man and then lived in Canada. In the 1890s he returned to England and became one of the first photographers with the London News Agency. He covered his first war from Tripoli during the Italian invasion before moving to the *Daily Sketch* and covering the 1912 Balkan War. While with the Bulgarian army he finagled permission to fly in one of the earliest air reconaissance missions over a battlefield and in the process took the first aerial war photographs.

With the outbreak of World War I* in 1914 he took the first photographs of the war while with the *Daily Sketch* in Belgium. In 1920 he covered the conflict in Ireland for the *News Chronicle* and narrowly escaped being executed in a firing squad. For the next fifteen years he continued to work for the same paper, landing one of his greatest coups when he took aerial photos of the Dartmoor mutiny.

REFERENCE: Dennis Griffiths, ed. *The Encyclopedia of the British Press.* 1992.

GORRELL, HENRY T. (1911–1958). Born to American parents in Florence, Italy, Gorrell entered the newspaper business with the United Press in Kansas City in 1930. Three years later he was assigned to the Buenos Aires bureau. With the outbreak of the Ethiopian War,* Gorrell was dispatched to Rome as assistant UP manager. He went on to cover the Spanish Civil War* and World War II* as war correspondent for the *United Press.*

In 1936 he was captured first by Republican soldiers and two weeks later was arrested by Spanish rebel forces. At the outset of World War II he was attached to the British fleet. In early 1941 he was with British and Greek troops under attack by German forces in Athens before moving on to Egypt, where he was accredited to the British Middle East Command.

In 1943 he received the Air Medal for saving the life of an injured bomber crewman while under heavy German fire during the raid on Navarino Bay on the Greek coast. He was also recognized by the Headliners' Club for his coverage of the war in Greece. Following his excursion with the British Eighth Army in Libya, Gorrell moved on to Algiers, where he flew with a U.S. bomber group on raids over Italian naval forces in Naples. He went on to report the landing at Salerno during the Italian campaign and the 1943 Cairo Conference.

In 1944 Gorrell covered the D-Day landings and the capture of the port of Cherbourg. He covered the French campaign into 1945, before accompanying Allied forces into Germany for the final phase of the war in Europe. He was the first correspondent to cross into Germany, as a passenger in the lead vehicle as it entered Roetgen on September 11, 1945. After retiring from the UP later that year he joined *Veteran's Report* as its editor and publisher.

REFERENCES: Robert W. Desmond. *Tides of War.* 1984; Jack Stenbuck, ed. *Typewriter Battalion.* 1995.

GOTTO, BASIL (?). Basil Gotto was a professional sculptor who turned to war journalism to cover the Boer War.* He combined his two avocations to

sculpt the Army and Navy Club war memorial and the Newfoundland battle memorial. Following the war he served as a staff officer during World War I.*
REFERENCE: Robert Wilkinson-Latham. *From Our Special Correspondent.* 1979.

GOVIN, CHARLES (1873–1896). Govin was a young correspondent for the Key West *Equator-Democrat* when he was assigned to cover the Cuban insurrection in 1896. Three days after landing he was killed rather ignominiously by a Cuban officer. He was apparently captured while in the company of insurgent forces. When the Cuban army officer found out he was an American, Govin was tied to a tree and hacked to death with machetes. Because he was a member of a prominent Key West family, his death caused a minor sensation in the United States.
REFERENCE: Charles H. Brown. *The Correspondents' War.* 1967.

GOWRAN, CLAY (?). Following graduation from Northwestern University he worked for the *Evansville Review* before joining the *Chicago Tribune* as a reporter, beginning a thirty-four-year relationship with the paper. He began covering World War II* in 1942. The first major operation he covered was the Allied counteroffensive against Japanese forces in the South Pacific during an amphibious landing at New Georgia Island in the Solomons. In 1943 he received the Edward Scott Beck Award for excellence for his account of a Japanese surprise attack that was repulsed by marines after they had slogged through water up to their necks in a counterattack during the Solomon Islands campaign. In 1944 he accompanied the Allied advance into Greece. Gowran was among the nine correspondents who flew on Superfortress bombing runs, the first American B-29 bombing attacks over Japan in June 1944.

Following the war he was engaged as foreign correspondent in the Middle East. He went on to cover conflicts and revolutions in Italy, Yugoslavia, Greece, Lebanon, and Palestine. During the campaign to create the state of Israel, Gowran joined the Jewish underground in Jerusalem to write a first-person account of the Stern gang, one of the terrorist groups vying to establish the Jewish homeland.
REFERENCES: Jack Stenbuck, ed. *Typewriter Battalion.* 1995; Lloyd Wendt. *Chicago Tribune: The Rise of a Great American Newspaper.* 1979.

GRAHAM, GEORGE EDWARD (b. 1866). Born in Albany, New York, Graham covered the Spanish-American War* for the Associated Press. He was with Admiral Schley aboard the flagship *Brooklyn* when the Spanish fleet attempted to escape from Santiago Harbor. He witnessed the subsequent naval battle which secured Santiago and virtually ended the war. He was the only noncombatant to witness the destruction of Cervera's fleet. He chronicled his wartime exploits in the 1902 book *Schley and Santiago.*
REFERENCES: Charles H. Brown. *The Correspondents' War.* 1967; Oliver Gramling. *AP: The Story of News.* 1940.

GREBNEV, VIKTOR (b. 1907). Grebnev began his career in photojournalism in the 1930s. With the outbreak of World War II* he began reporting for the army newspaper *Krasnaya Zvezda* or *Red Star*. He later transferred to the *Frontovik* or *Frontline Fighter* to get closer to the battlefield. He accompanied several other photographers raising the Soviet Banner of Victory over the Reichstag after the fall of Berlin. Following the war he worked as a journalist in Soviet-occupied Germany and then turned to sportswriting upon his return to the Soviet Union.

REFERENCE: Daniela Mrazkova and Vladimir Remes, eds. *The Russian War: 1941–1945.* 1975.

GRECO-TURKISH WAR. In 1897 revolutionaries on Crete attempted to overthrow Turkish rule. The Greek government supported the movement by declaring war on Turkey. The conflict lasted five weeks and ended with a Turkish victory on May 21, 1897. The war drew a large contingent of war correspondents. While the majority came from Great Britain, the best-represented newspaper was the *New York Journal.*

American correspondents included *Journal* correspondents John Foster Bass,* Richard Harding Davis,* Stephen Crane,* James Creelman,* and Julian Ralph.* Other Americans on the scene of note were Sylvester Scovel* for the *New York World*, Frederick Palmer* for the *New York Press*, and Percival Phillips* for the *Pittsburgh Press.*

Among the formidable British war correspondents were Dr. Emile Joseph Dillon* and Bennet Burleigh* of the *Daily Telegraph*, Melton Prior* of the *Illustrated London News*, Francis Scudamore* of the *Daily News*, Frederic Villiers* for the *Standard*, and W. T. Maud* of the *Graphic*. Representing the *Times* were James David Bourchier,* Clive Bingham, and Edward Frederick Knight.* Other war reporters included George Warrington Steevens* of the *Daily Mail*, Henry W. Nevinson* for the *Daily Chronicle*, and John B. Atkins* of the *Manchester Guardian*, and for Reuters* W. Kinnaird Rose, H. A. Gwynne,* and Fergus Ferguson. Journalists accompanied armies on both sides of the conflict.

There is no evidence that any Greek or Turkish reporters were in the field. The only major continental power to have provided identifiable correspondents was France, with German, Russian, Austrian, and Italian representatives noticeably absent.

REFERENCES: Robert W. Desmond. *The Information Process.* 1978; Robert Wilkinson-Latham. *From Our Special Correspondent.* 1979.

GRENADA INVASION. On October 25, 1983, the United States launched a massive invasion of the Communist-governed island nation of Grenada. Noticeably absent were any members of the press. This was the first American military campaign from which the Defense Department successfully excluded all journalists. With no independent reportage the media were forced to improvise. The

Washington Post attempted to monitor developments through ham operator transmissions which gave conflicting accounts of the military operation. Networks resorted to three-dimensional maps, models, and file footage. Two days later the first reporters were permitted to visit Grenada. On the first day fifteen journalists and photographers were flown in for several hours, accompanied by a military escort. On the next day twenty-four were given permits and fifty more the following day. These military-directed pooling arrangements came under intense criticism. A commentary on how unwieldy the presence of the news media has become on the battlefield is the fact that two days following the invasion there were 369 journalists waiting for accreditation in Barbados to report a war against approximately six hundred Cuban soldiers.

REFERENCES: Derrik Mercer, Geoff Mungham, and Kevin Williams. *The Fog of War: The Media on the Battlefield.* 1987; Donald Atwell Zoll. "The Press and the Military: Some Thoughts After Grenada," *Parameters, Journal of the U.S. War College.* 1984.

GRIFFITHS, PHILIP JONES (b. 1936). The self-taught photojournalist was born in Rhuddlan, Wales. He left the pharmacy business to become a freelance photojournalist in 1961. Since then he has covered the Vietnam War,* the Algerian War, the Yom Kippur War, and conflict in Cambodia and Thailand. He has served as president of Magnum.

His three years covering the Vietnam conflict are chronicled in his collection of images entitled *Vietnam, Inc.*, which took four years to produce. With its emphasis on the horrors of war and its effects on civilians, it has often been described as one of the finest documents of war photography.* After its publication in the United States, the South Vietnamese government banned his return to Saigon.

In 1973 Griffiths returned to Cambodia for his third visit to the conflict, narrowly escaping death at the hands of the Khmer Rouge during an artillery attack. He was one of the first photojournalists to arrive in Israel at the outbreak of the Yom Kippur War in October 1973. With new censorship restrictions implemented since the Six Day War, Griffiths was forced to rely on his own resourcefulness to get to frontline action. He hired private drivers to help him evade Israeli roadblocks. During his three-week stay in Israel he would end up losing three cars, one of which took a direct hit by a shell. Due to prohibitive laboratory fees and military censorship he smuggled his pictures out of the country. One photograph would grace the cover of *Newsweek* magazine.

REFERENCES: *Contemporary Photographers.* 1982; Jorge Lewinski. *The Camera at War.* 1978.

GROSS, GAD SCHUSTER (d. 1991). Born in Rumania and educated at Harvard, Gross, representing *Newsweek* on a freelance basis, was the only journalist killed during the Gulf War.* He was killed on March 21, 1991, while traveling with several colleagues in the Kurdish region of northern Iraq.

REFERENCE: Michael Emery. *On the Front Lines.* 1995.

GRUNEISON, CHARLES LEWIS (1806–1879). Born in Bloomsbury, England, he became one of the earliest war correspondents after joining the *Morning Post* as a special and covering the Carlist army during the Spanish Civil War of 1834–1839. His dispatches were so accurate that he was arrested by the conservative Carlist supporters of Don Carlos, the pretender to the throne of Spain. Tried as a spy, he escaped with his life thanks to the intervention of the British government. Following his deportation one Spanish officer commented that the reporter had done more damage with his pen than the Carlist generals had done with their swords and that he would have no compunction about shooting all Carlist correspondents. In 1839, following his Spanish exploits he was made the *Morning Post* correspondent in Paris for the next five years. He returned to London, where he became well known as the music critic for the *Athenaeum*. He wrote *The Opera and the Press* (1869).
REFERENCE: Robert Wilkinson-Latham. *From Our Special Correspondent*. 1979.

GUERNICA. One of the best-known and most controversial incidents of the Spanish Civil War* was the bombing of Guernica, a small town near the Basque capital of Bilbao, in northern Spain. The Basques of Guernica supported the Republican government in its war against the Nationalists. In March 1937 Nationalist general Emilio Mola proclaimed that unless the Basques submitted to his forces he would destroy parts of their homeland. After they failed to do so Mola ordered his air force, composed of German planes and pilots, to level Guernica. Although it is uncertain how many died on April 26, 1937, estimates vary between one and two thousand.

One of the first correspondents to enter the city was George Steer* of the *Times*. His account of the bombing was featured on the front pages of the *New York Times* and the *Times* of London. What is most significant about his report is the claim that the town did not represent a military objective. When Franco's forces took control of the town several days later, the Nationalists countered with claims that the Basques destroyed the town themselves to gain sympathy for the Loyalist cause. What added to the controversy was a feature article run by the aforementioned papers which gave credence to the Nationalist contention that the destruction of the town was due to Basque incendiaries rather than strategic bombing. Recent evidence contradicts the claim that the town was not a military objective and that the bombing was meant to demoralize the population. According to historian Hugh Thomas, Guernica could have been used as a destination for Basque and Republican forces to regroup and was thus a military objective.

This incident was but a harbinger of the age of indiscriminate bombing of civilian targets and total warfare that would characterize World War II.* Most analysts of World War II are convinced that the mass destruction and haphazard bombing of civilian targets which characterized the war had its genesis during the Spanish Civil War, in which the German Luftwaffe went through practice runs in preparation for the looming conflict.

REFERENCES: Phillip Knightley. *The First Casualty*. 1975; Phillip Knightley. *The Master Spy*. 1989.

GULF WAR. In August 1990 Iraqi troops invaded Kuwait, inaugurating a new era in war journalism in which print reporters were consistently scooped by television newscasts from CNN that delivered the news instantaneously, while it took up to several weeks for print coverage to reach the public. According to media historian Johanna Neuman, the Gulf War was the "first showdown between military hardware and satellite communication, pitting global media saturation against military needs for security." The Gulf War was the beginning of an era in which television viewers did not necessarily watch warfare, but the collecting of news in a war zone. For the first time in U.S. military history Western television journalists covered war from enemy capitals and reported the damage caused by American firepower.

Perhaps no news service was impacted as strongly as was CNN, which saw its viewership reach more than one million. By the time allied troops were advancing toward Baghdad, CNN was drawing a nightly audience of almost seven million, just two million shy of the major networks. The main difference between the cable network and the big three was that CNN's audience was worldwide. The advent of rooftop journalism* made stars of correspondents Peter Arnett,* John Holliman, Bernard Shaw, and others, as they described aerial assaults and missile attacks in "real time" to viewers around the world. The introduction of satellite journalism was unprecedented. But, technology stopped at the edge of the battlefield as reporters labored to send their dispatches back to New York. Some reports took as long as two weeks to reach Dharan from the battlefield, while one photographer waited six weeks for his film to arrive. However, despite the proximity to the war zone, the American public was not bombarded at the dinner table by images of dead and wounded GIs, as it was during the "uncensored" Vietnam War.* What the public did see and hear was a potpourri of high-tech weapons, military officers and defense experts conducting interviews, enemy soldiers surrendering to American reporters, and careful censorship.

The war consisted of two phases, consisting of a five-month buildup and then a 100-hour desert war. By the time the ground war began in February 1991, more than 1,400 journalists had arrived in Saudi Arabia to report the war. The correspondents averaged forty-seven stories during an average tour of seven weeks. Journalists were reliant on military briefings, interviews with military officials, or pool activity for updated information. The war in the Persian Gulf was one of the most restricted battlefields of the modern era. Photographers were often prevented from getting anywhere near the front lines. Correspondents noted the similarities between the Gulf War and the 1982 Falklands War,* in which the media were skillfully manipulated. There were precedents in recent American military campaigns for the Gulf censorship. During the 1983 Grenada* invasion reporters were kept three hundred miles away from the action, and during the 1989 Panama incursion the press pool was kept on a U.S. air base until the fighting was over. During the Gulf War, of the initial 150 journalists chosen for the pool system, only half were allowed to accompany troops at any one time. However, by the time the brief desert campaign got under way 159 correspondents were with American combat units, more than twice the coverage of any previous modern war.

At times there were as few as sixteen reporters covering over a half million troops. There were numerous anomalies in the press coverage. It took the vaunted *New York Times* three weeks to place a correspondent in the press pool, and only three pool positions were available for some three hundred foreign journalists. Correspondents for the radical magazine *Mother Jones* were refused coverage, while a fashion magazine was selected for a pool spot. Any infraction by the media was swiftly dealt with. After one correspondent wrote an article about Iraqi soldiers being torn apart by Apache helicopters his position was revoked, and when another reported numerous U.S. military vehicles missing he was ejected from the press pool.

Numerous reports were censored or held up. One reporter claimed that only one third of his twenty-seven stories escaped the censor's pen. While public opinion surveys demonstrated that Americans found press coverage adequate and favored military censorship, a correspondent noted that "if World War II had been covered by pools there would never have been a national treasure named Ernie Pyle."* Coverage of the war became more difficult for reporters as the campaign pushed out into the desert. Army field phones and tactical fax machines were not adaptable to Saudi Arabia's commercial telecommunications system and most were kept off limits to the press corps. While the army had designed a pony-express-style courier system, it was understaffed and poorly trained, resulting in news copy, film, and videotape getting lost in the desert wastes.

As the ground war proceeded in February 1991, journalists left their military escorts to accompany the myriad forces advancing on Kuwait. American correspondents entered the war zone with Egyptian, Saudi, and Kuwaiti forces and arrived in Kuwait City a day before the official pool reporters. Because of press censorship and the pool system the coverage of the Gulf War was relatively superficial. Among the thousands of photographs taken by forty photographers on the battlefield there are no shots of American tanks firing during massive tank engagements and there are few pictures of dead soldiers. One correspondent designated the conflict "the Unseen War" because of the number of reports and photographs that have not been released.

REFERENCES: Michael Emery. *On the Front Lines.* 1995; John J. Fialka. *Hotel Warriors: Covering the Gulf War.* 1991; Johanna Neuman. *Lights, Camera, War: Is Media Technology Driving International Politics?* 1996.

GWYNNE, HOWELL ARTHUR (1865–1950). Born in the district of Kilvey, near Swansea, he was educated on the Continent. His chance meeting with the king of Rumania while on holiday, and their ensuing friendship, led to his career in journalism. He served as Balkan correspondent for the *Times* and in 1893 became the Reuters* correspondent in Rumania, beginning a ten-year relationship as a war reporter for the news agency.

He covered the Ashanti War in 1895 and the following year was with Kitchener at Dongola. Over the next several years he reported from the Turkish side during the 1897 Greco-Turkish War* and then from Peking the following year. In 1898 Gwynne was the only civilian correspondent allowed up the Nile with Kitchener's punitive Sudan expedition after the death of Gordon, and for a short time he covered the Spanish-American War* in Cuba. With the outbreak of war in South Africa in 1899, he organized Reuters' war service there. Gwynne was in charge of almost one hundred Reuters reporters and stringers* during the Boer War.* He gave Edgar Wallace* his first position in journalism. Gwynne was present during Methuen's campaign, and the Battle of Magersfontein, and later began a long friendship with Lord Roberts, accompanying his forces into the field.

He returned to England for a short time in 1902, but soon after was with Joseph Chamberlain on a political tour of South Africa. After the murder of the Serbian king and queen in 1904 he went to Belgrade as Reuters' foreign director and later that year became editor of the *Standard*. In 1911 he began a long tenure as editor of the *Morning Post*.

REFERENCES: *DNB*, 1941–1950; Donald Read. *The Power of News*. 1992.

H

HAILE, CHRISTOPHER MASON (?). Born in Rhode Island, Haile received a West Point appointment in 1836. He left the academy early and moved to Louisiana, where he joined the *Planter's Gazette* as editor. He later quit the paper for the *New Orleans Picayune* and gained a following with his satirical letters under the byline "Pardon Jones." During the Mexican War* he represented the paper as a war correspondent under the direction of George Wilkins Kendall.*

Kendall, Haile, and another correspondent were escorted by Texas Rangers as far as Matamoras, on the Rio Grande border, where they reported the progress of the army under General Zachary Taylor. Haile accompanied General Worth's column as it advanced from the west at the Battle of Monterrey. Kendall joined Haile in the western part of the city, and their account of the battle filled nine columns of the *Picayune*. Their coverage was criticized for having only witnessed the fighting in the western part of the city, where casualties were much less, and not reporting the more bloody and spectacular struggle on the eastern side.

Following the victory Kendall left for New Orleans, while Haile remained with Taylor's troops. Haile compiled a list of the dead and wounded at Monterrey and wrote an informative account of the aftermath, listing captured arms and munitions as well as the names, ranks, places, and dates of the dead and wounded.

After Monterrey, Haile turned to less serious fare, writing light sketches in the form of reports from the quixotic "Pardon Jones" to General Taylor and President Polk. Haile was not long behind Kendall in returning to the Crescent City. However, as the war dragged on, Haile was assigned to follow the Veracruz campaign along the coast. The army made use of Haile's military training when during the siege of Veracruz he was commissioned a lieutenant, leaving Kendall the only war correspondent for the *Picayune*.

REFERENCES: Fayette Copeland. *Kendall of the Picayune*. 1943; Robert W. Johannsen. *To the Halls of the Montezumas*. 1985; Martha A. Sandweiss, Rick Stewart, and Ben W. Huseman. *Eyewitness to War*. 1989.

HALBERSTAM, DAVID (b. 1934). Born in New York and educated at Harvard, he entered journalism in 1956 with the *Nashville Tennessean*. Four years later he was hired by the *New York Times*. In 1960 Halberstam covered his first conflict when he reported the Katanga uprising in the Congo. During the Vietnam War* he quickly developed a reputation for his controversial reporting, coming under fire from the Pentagon and the White House. As a Vietnam correspondent for the *New York Times* during the 1960s, he was one of the first reporters to question the veracity of official death counts and defeats represented as victories. He shared the Pulitzer Prize with Malcolm W. Browne* in 1964.

He left the *Times* in 1967 for *Harper's* magazine. After leaving that magazine he embarked on a highly successful career writing nonfiction, including the bestsellers *The Best and the Brightest* (1972), *The Powers That Be* (1979), *The Making of a Quagmire* (1963), and most recently *The Fifties*.

REFERENCES: Michael Emery. *On the Front Lines*. 1995; William Prochnau. *Once upon a Distant War*. 1995.

HALL, SYDNEY PRIOR (1842–1922). The Cambridge-educated war artist was hired by the *Graphic* to cover his only war, the Franco-Prussian War* in 1870. The son of a prominent painter of the sporting life, Hall had achieved a reputation as an artist in his own right before taking employment as an illustrator for the newly established *Graphic*.

Following his arrival in France he came under suspicion with his sketch book, a risk assumed by all war artists. He was arrested three times by the French in August alone. In September he was arrested by the Germans. One of his colleagues described Hall as the best artist among the specials of the period; however, it is difficult to judge the quality of his work since the engravings made from his sketches for his paper were somewhat mediocre. But his book, *Sketches from an Artists's Portfolio* (1875), supports the contention of his aforementioned colleague. One of the preeminent war reporters of his era, Archibald Forbes,* opined that Hall's sketches of the Franco-Prussian War were so remarkable that they "can never cease to be remembered by anyone who saw them."

In October 1870 Hall arrived with the Prussian army in Paris, where he bought a horse and named it "Graphy" after his employer. He continued with the *Graphic* following the war and received recognition for his illustrations of royal tours and court functions. Later he journeyed through the American West for the *Graphic*.

REFERENCE: Pat Hodgson. *The War Illustrators*. 1977.

HALSTEAD, MURAT (1829–1908). After graduation from college in 1851 Halstead worked for several Cincinnati newspapers before going to the *Cincinnati Commercial* in 1853, where he would be employed for the next half century. His first national assignment as a congressional reporter allowed him the opportunity to stop at Harpers Ferry en route to Washington, where he witnessed the hanging of the abolitionist John Brown.

His early criticism of the Union war effort during the American Civil War* led his competitors to give him the sobriquet "Field Marshal." He covered the Battle of Fredericksburg (1862), which he described as a "blunder and disaster" after witnessing the decimation of his home state Ohio regiments. After being told by Henry Villard* that Brigadier General Sherman had requested two hundred thousand men Halstead became convinced that Sherman was "unhinged," resulting in the headline "General Sherman Insane" in the *Cincinnati Commercial*. This misleading story was widely reprinted in other newspapers.

While he was on vacation in Paris in 1870 the Franco-Prussian War* broke out and he immediately applied for authorization to cover it. Reporting for Cincinnati, Ohio, a city and a state with a large German population, he recognized that reporting this conflict would enlarge the *Commercial*'s readership. Ordinarily the *Commercial* would not be able to afford to cover the war and would rely on newsletters from English correspondents, so that Halstead's presence in Paris was quite a coup for the newspaper.

In France he was constantly harassed by military censors and endless reporting restrictions. After his application for war correspondent credentials was denied he headed to Germany, where he witnessed firsthand his only battle of the war, the Prussian victory at the Battle of Gravelotte. Also present from his vantage point were the American general Philip Sheridan, Chancellor Bismarck, and von Moltke. He wrote numerous books of history, biography, and public affairs, including his most successful book, a biography of McKinley which sold over 700,000 copies after his assassination in 1901.

REFERENCES: *DLB* 23, 155–160; Donald Walter Curl. "An American Reporter and the Franco-Prussian War," *Journalism Quarterly* 49. Fall 1972, 480–88.

HANDS, CHARLES E. (1860–1937). Hands entered journalism with the *Birmingham Daily Mail* while in his twenties, before moving to the *Pall Mall Gazette* and the *Star*, where as "Starman" he became well known for his descriptive writing style. In 1896 he joined the *Daily Mail* and began his career as one of the best-known war correspondents of his era.

In 1898 he covered the Spanish-American War* from Cuba and in 1900 was in South Africa reporting the Boer War* when he was wounded while attached to the Mafeking* relief force on May 12. He covered the Russo-Japanese War* in 1904, although restricted by the extraordinary Japanese press censorship.

REFERENCE: Robert Wilkinson-Latham. *From Our Special Correspondent*. 1979.

HANGEN, WELLES (1930–1970). After graduation from Brown University and a stint as a foreign correspondent for the *New York Times*, news correspondent Welles Hangen, after a twelve-year career with NBC, disappeared with three television newsmen south of the Cambodian capital of Phnom Penh in May 1970. He was one of eleven correspondents to disappear along a dangerous stretch of highway controlled by the Khmer Rouge shortly before the Cambodian holocaust, which claimed over one million victims. Local villagers recounted that the missing journalists were held for three days, then killed and buried. Twenty-two years later a U.S. Department of Defense team unearthed the remains of Hangen and several of his colleagues from their graves along a riverbed thirty-four miles from Phnom Penh.

REFERENCE: Charles P. Arnot. *Don't Kill the Messenger.* 1994.

HARDEN, EDWIN W. (1868–1903). Harden reported the Spanish-American War* from the Philippines for the *New York World*. Harden was abroad the *McCulloch* as the Asiatic Squadron approached the Spanish fleet in Manila Harbor. Harden was one of only three correspondents to witness the Battle of Manila Bay on May 1, 1898. Commodore George Dewey's squadron sank eleven Spanish ships without the loss of any American seamen or ships. Harden's account of the battle scooped the competition.

REFERENCES: Charles H. Brown. *The Correspondents' War.* 1967; Robert W. Desmond. *The Information Process.* 1978.

HARDMAN, FREDERICK (1814–1874). Son of a London merchant, he rebelled against the placid life of the countinghouse by joining the lancers of the British Legion in Spain in 1834. He returned to England after being severely wounded in one of the final actions against the Carlists. Back home he became a regular contributor to *Blackwood* magazine. In 1850 he became a foreign correspondent for the *Times*. He covered the Russo-Turkish War,* in which he exposed the problems of drunkenness in the British army. Hardman witnessed the campaigns in Lombardy, Morocco, and Schleswig as well as the military actions at Tours and Bordeaux in 1870–1871 during the Franco-Prussian War.* He later became the chief correspondent for the *Times* in Paris.

REFERENCES: Robert W. Desmond. *The Information Process.* 1978; *DNB*; Joseph J. Mathews. *Reporting the Wars.* 1957.

HARDY, ALBERT "BERT" (b. 1913). The self-taught photographer was born in London. He began his career using a small plate camera that he bought for ten shillings. Later he would become one of the first photojournalists to use the early Leicas. He served as a photographer in the British army in France and Germany from 1942 to 1946. Early in the war he began his affiliation with the *Picture Post*. His pictures of the London blitz were among the best and closest to the action of any cameraman. His overseas coverage began in 1944 with the D-Day invasion and the Dieppe raid. Perhaps his best work came during the liberation of Paris and the preparation and crossing of the Rhine River into

Germany. He also photographed the Greek Civil War, the Burmese war against the Karens, and the Malayan insurrection.

Hardy was once again at the frontlines with the outbreak of the Korean War.* Representing the *Picture Post*, he was teamed with writer James Cameron.* Hardy and Cameron accompanied amphibious forces during the Inchon landing in 1950 and later reported the mistreatment of North Korean prisoners by South Korean troops. Although Hardy spent less than two months in Korea, his pictures are among the most memorable of the conflict. His last story of the war, on the Inchon landing, was awarded the *Encyclopedia Britannica* Award for the best picture series of the year. His war photography* is chronicled in *Bert Hardy, Photojournalist* (1975).

REFERENCE: Jorge Lewinski. *The Camera at War.* 1978.

HARE, JAMES H. "JIMMY" (1856–1946). Born in London, the son of a successful camera manufacturer, Hare left college early to enter his father's trade. By the early 1880s he had become a freelance photographer before taking employment with the *Illustrated American* in 1895. He showed an early interest in naval photography. In 1898 he put it to use following the mysterious sinking of the battleship *Maine* in Havana Harbor. Hare offered his services to *Collier's Weekly*, or as one contemporary remarked, "The *Maine* BLEW UP and JIMMY BLEW IN." He was promoted to special correspondent by the weekly on the strength of his pictures of the aftermath of the ship explosion.

After his arrival in Cuba his pictures of the damaged battleship and conditions in the internment camps led to his elevation in status to "special photographer" for the *Weekly*. After a respite in the States, Hare returned to Cuba after war was declared. He was encouraged along with other correspondents by Sylvester Scovel* of the *New York World* to gather information that might be helpful to the military. Hare's photographs verified the position of various Spanish coastal fortifications.

On Hare's next expedition he was assigned to relay the news of American intervention in the Cuban conflict to the Cuban rebel leader General Maximo Gomez. On April 25, 1898, Hare and *Chicago Tribune* reporter Henry James Whigham and several others landed on the Cuban coast. Assisted by Cuban rebels they delivered their message personally to Gomez three days later. Following this adventure Hare covered the periphery of the conflict over the next six weeks before joining the American army near Santiago on June 29.

On July 1, Hare joined the correspondent corps, which included Stephen Crane* and Richard Harding Davis,* as they prepared to cover the American advance. He witnessed the battle at the "Bloody Bend" of the Aguadores River, when Crane came upon a friend from college mortally wounded. Hare recorded the scene for posterity, with the classmate in the center of the frame. During his first combat assignment he accompanied the charge of the Rough Riders on Kettle Hill on July 1. His coverage of the Spanish-American War* elevated him to the top ranks of the photojournalists of his day.

Following the Spanish-American War,* Hare spent the next five years covering shipwrecks, political rallies, Latin American affairs, and the travels of President McKinley. He reputably took the last photograph of McKinley, minutes before he was assassinated on September 6, 1901.

In 1904 he was in San Francisco preparing for the anticipated hostilities between Russia and Japan. *Collier's* would ultimately send fourteen correspondents to cover the war, including Frederick Palmer*, Richard Harding Davis, and Henry James Whigham. Upon arrival in Japan, the more celebrated journalists were viewed with suspicion, with Jack London* being placed under arrest for taking unauthorized pictures. After a month of waiting, a select group of reporters including Hare was allowed to proceed to Manchuria to cover the Russo-Japanese War,* but press coverage would be controlled and severely limited.

Hare accompanied Major General Kuroki's First Army along with most of the other members of the press. He witnessed the Japanese victory at the Battle of the Yalu, which Hare reported established Japan as a serious player in international affairs. Hampered by restrictions, Hare took what pictures he was allowed, such as the crude field hospitals, and was one of the first members of the press corps to cross the Yalu. After the Japanese took Hung-Sha Pass, Hare became the first newsman to enter Liaoyang, recording the entrance of Japanese troops into the fallen city. On October 17, he covered the Russian offensive at Sha-ho, where the Russians suffered 41,000 casualties.

Hare returned to the States in late 1904. The following year *Collier's* released *A Photographic Record of the Russo-Japanese War*, edited by Hare. However, due to Japanese censorship, photographers were not allowed into the trenches at the height of battles, but were required to take pictures prior to the fighting or at its conclusion. So the most of the photographic record for the Russo-Japanese War, aside from several of Hare's photos of shrapnel exploding, conformed to the restrictions set by the armed forces. The Japanese were so successful in their control of the media and their limitation on news regarding its troop movements that they set a precedent for future military censorship. In 1907 Hare was awarded a medal for his service by the emperor of Japan. Thirty-five years later, when he offered the medal to the first pilot to bomb the Imperial Palace in Tokyo he found out that it was a "phony" brass medal.

Bored with his domestic assignments, in 1912 the conflict in the Balkans drew Hare to Eastern Europe. Unfortunately, the Bulgarians modeled their system of news access after the Germans', which meant keeping correspondents away from the front. Rather than risk the divulging of military secrets, the specials were provided the news that military officials wanted them to print. He returned to America after three months of photographing supervised incidents.

The Mexican Revolution would offer a freer environment for war correspondents. In 1911 Hare had covered the battle at Ciudad Juarez from the front lines and was warned by *Collier's* that he would be no use to them "if dead or wounded." In 1914 he reported the American occupation of Veracruz and marines subduing Mexican resistance. In June and July 1914 he witnessed the Battle of Zacatecas.

In 1914, with the outbreak of war in Europe seeming imminent, Hare expected to receive his new assignment momentarily. He was astonished when *Collier's* declined to send him. Perhaps it was his age of fifty-eight or the new management, with its emphasis on fiction at the expense of news and photojournalism. After receiving this news, Hare wasted little time in offering his services to *Leslie's Weekly*, and on August 20, 1914, he was on a ship bound for England and his next war.

Reaching London a week later, Hare found such tight censorship that it was necessary to obtain a special permit for each individual photographic assignment in Great Britain. He found this out firsthand when arrested by a detective for taking pictures of cheering crowds without the requisite permit. News restrictions were no less tight in Paris, so he left for Belgium. He was able to take pictures of the German siege of Antwerp before retreating back to England. Throughout 1915, press restrictions continued to handicap photographic war correspondents, with the threat of arrest omnipresent. While it was not a substitute for covering the front lines, on May 7, 1915, Hare rushed to the Irish coast in time to record the arrival of the survivors of the *Lusitania*.

In October 1915, after facing the same restrictions in Italy, Hare gravitated to the Balkan front and the Greek city of Salonika. In August 1916 he photographed trench warfare on the Somme. As America prepared to enter the war the following year he was called home to capture the domestic phase of the war effort. He covered the training camps, but was barred from taking pictures of soldiers leaving for Europe. On December 6, 1917, he covered the massive explosion that devastated Halifax, Nova Scotia.

Hare returned to Europe in 1918, covering the Italian army following its defeat at Caporetto. On June 23 he witnessed the Austrian advance and the Italian counteroffensive near Nervesa, locally known as the "Hog's Back." Hare followed the Italian forces in October when they beat the Austrians, effectively removing them from the war. He returned to New York at the end of the year.

He continued to work for *Leslie's* following the war and in 1920 covered the Polish war with the Russians. It would be his last conflict. At last weary of censors, and with the folding of his sponsor, *Leslie's*, he could rest on his laurels and make the lecture circuit. He died in Teaneck, New Jersey, shortly after his ninetieth birthday.

REFERENCES: Lewis L. Gould and Richard Greffe. *Photojournalist: The Career of Jimmy Hare.* 1977; Jimmy Hare and Cecil Carnes. *Jimmy Hare, News Photographer: Half a Century with a Camera.* 1940.

HARMON, DUDLEY ANNE (?). As a special contributor to the *Christian Science Monitor* in 1942 and 1943, Harmon was one of the few women war correspondents accredited to the Allied forces during World War II.* In 1942 she joined the information service of the Free French at Brazzaville in French

Equatorial Africa. Harmon was considered somewhat of an authority on the French underground, having been introduced to its major figures in London and Africa at the outset of the war. During the Italian campaign she covered the air war for the United Press agency and following the Normandy invasion was among the wave of correspondents descending on France. Harmon entered Paris with the liberation forces in August 1944.
REFERENCE: Robert W. Desmond. *Tides of War.* 1984.

HARPER, FLETCHER (1806–1877). Born in Newtown, Long Island, Harper entered the world of publishing with J. and J. Harper, the firm started by his two older brothers in 1817. The youngest and last of four brothers to join the family firm, Fletcher had the most impact on American Civil War* journalism. He managed his brothers' *Harper's New Monthly Magazine* in the 1850s before founding *Harper's Weekly* in 1857. This illustrated journal battled *Frank Leslie's Illustrated Newspaper* for dominance in the field of illustrated journalism during the Civil War. Both provided markets for the sketch artists covering both sides of the conflict. Following the war he founded *Harper's Bazaar.*
REFERENCES: *DAB*; Stewart Sifakis. *Who Was Who in the Civil War.* 1988.

HARSCH, JOSEPH C. (b. 1905). Born in Toledo, Ohio, and educated at Williams College in Massachusetts and Cambridge University in England, he joined the *Christian Science Monitor* after college. While he also worked occasionally as a radio commentator for the BBC and CBS, he was affiliated with the *Monitor* until his retirement.

Harsch reported from most theaters of action during World War II* either by radio or through print. While reporting from Berlin prior to American entry into the war, he was prevented from covering frontline action in the Low Countries and France in May 1940 as punishment by German authorities for his reporting conditions in Denmark following the German invasion in April. Harsch described this punishment as "a badge of honor in the craft." He returned to the States in February 1941. Harsch was in Honolulu when the Japanese attacked Pearl Harbor and would later cover stories from New Zealand, Australia, and Java. His exploits are chronicled in *Pattern of Conquest* (1941) and *The Curtain Isn't Iron* (1951).
REFERENCES: Robert W. Desmond. *Tides of War.* 1984; Jack Stenbuck, ed. *Typewriter Battalion.* 1995.

HASTINGS, MACDONALD (1909–1982). Educated at Stonyhurst, the son of noted playwright and journalist Basil Macdonald, Hastings joined the *Picture Post* in 1938. He became well known for his reporting form northwest Europe during World War II.* Following the war, he became the editor of the *Strand* and reported on big game hunting from India and Africa. In 1951 he cofounded

Country Fair and in the 1950s became somewhat of a television personality while reporting for the BBC. He wrote over thirty books.
REFERENCE: Dennis Griffiths, ed. *The Encyclopedia of the British Press*. 1992.

HASTINGS, MAX (b. 1945). The son of Macdonald Hastings* was born in London and educated at University College. In the 1960s he was a researcher for the BBC before joining the *Evening Standard* in 1965. Despite intermittent stints with the BBC throughout the 1960s he continued his relationship with the *Standard* on a more permanent basis beginning in 1973. As the paper's roving correspondent for the next twelve years he reported from hot spots in more than sixty countries. He covered wars in the Middle East, Indochina, Angola, India-Pakistan, Cyprus, and Rhodesia.

He received his highest recognition while covering the Falklands War.* He accompanied British troops into Port Stanley and was designated Journalist of the Year as well as Grenada TV Reporter of the Year in 1982. In the 1980s he continued his distinguished journalism career with several other papers and was named Editor of the Year in 1988. In addition Hastings has become a formidable military historian. His books include *Ulster, 1969: The Struggle for Civil Rights in Northern Ireland* (1970), *Yoni: Hero of Entebbe* (1979), *Bomber Command* (1979), *Battle of Britain*, coauthored with Len Deighton (1980), *Das Reich* (1981), *The Battle for the Falklands* (1983), *Overlord: D-Day and the Battle of Normandy* (1984), *Victory in Europe* (1985), *The Korean War* (1987), and many others.
REFERENCES: Dennis Griffiths, ed. *The Encyclopedia of the British Press*. 1992; *Sunday Times* of London Insight Team. *War in the Falklands*. 1982.

HEARST, WILLIAM RANDOLPH (1863–1951). One of the true titans in the field of journalism, Hearst was born in San Francisco. He was expelled from Harvard prior to graduation for juvenile pranks. Hearst served a brief apprenticeship on the *New York World* before convincing his father to give him the *San Francisco Examiner*, which he had recently purchased. Following the death of his father in 1891 he invested family money in the acquisition of the *New York Morning Journal* in 1895. Not long after, Hearst became interested in the Cuban insurrection against the Spanish. After the mysterious explosion on board the *Maine* in Havana Harbor, Hearst, without a shred of evidence, attributed its sinking to a Spanish torpedo and urged an American declaration of war, in part because it was good for business. Prior to the outbreak of hostilities Hearst sent artist Frederic Remington* to illustrate the dispatches of correspondent Richard Harding Davis.* Remington telegraphed the home office, "Everything is quiet. There is no trouble here. There will be no war. I wish to return." Legend has it that Hearst responded, "Please remain. You furnish pictures. I will furnish war."
REFERENCE: Phillip Knightley. *The First Casualty*. 1975.

HEMINGWAY, ERNEST (1899–1961). Born in Oak Park, Illinois, he entered journalism with the *Kansas City Star* while still in his teens. With the outbreak of World War I* six months later, Hemingway resigned from the *Star* and joined the American Red Cross ambulance service. Assigned to the Italian campaign, he was seriously wounded and spent several months recuperating. His experiences during the war are chronicled, albeit embellished, in several short stories and his first novel, *A Farewell to Arms* (1929).

Upon his return to the States he continued in journalism as a part-time writer for the *Toronto Star* from 1919 to 1920 as he pursued his literary goals as well. Based in Paris, he served as its roving correspondent in Europe from 1921 to 1923, and on an intermittent basis until 1926. He interviewed the French wartime premier Georges Clemenceau in 1922, and from Istanbul he reported the last stages of the Greco-Turkish War of 1922–1923, including the Greek evacuation from Thrace.

With the publication of *The Sun Also Rises* (1926), Hemingway was on his way to establishing his credentials as one of the greatest writers of his era. In the 1930s he contributed articles to *Esquire* magazine on a variety of outdoors themes, war, and politics. In 1937 he returned to war correspondence when he covered the Spanish Civil War* for the North American Newspaper Alliance (NANA). This experience provided the inspiration for his books *Spanish Earth* (1938) and *For Whom the Bell Tolls* (1940). While in Spain he met the journalist Martha Gellhorn,* a war correspondent and literary talent in her own right. They married in 1940.

Hemingway's Spanish Civil War dispatches have been criticized for being meager, rambling, and self-centered, and Phillip Knightley even describes them as "abysmally bad." A literary writer, he often resorted to heavy-handed similes and contrived imagery to bring the war home to his readership. Although sympathetic to the Loyalist cause, his coverage of the conflict remained politically neutral. One of his best pieces was "The Fall of Tereul."

He returned to war journalism to report the Sino-Japanese theater of World War II* for *PM*. Following this assignment he returned home and patrolled the Caribbean looking for submarines. In 1944 he was hired by *Collier's* as a feature writer in the European theater of operations. Having a preoccupation with proving his personal courage which bordered on obsession, Hemingway was not possessed with the best instincts for the journalism profession. During his World War II service his penchant for personal derring-do continually compromised his objectivity as a war reporter.

No incident exemplifies his wartime exploits better than his behavior during the Allied advance on Paris following the Normandy invasion. Having narrowly missed participation in the greatest amphibious landing in history, Hemingway was accompanying Allied forces twenty-five miles southwest of Paris when he met up with a band of French resistance fighters and used his influence to procure them weapons. In a short time, Hemingway was leading his compatriots on reconnaissance sorties, looking for hidden German troops. He was one of the first Americans to enter liberated Paris. His fellow correspondents protested to army authorities that Hemingway had seriously breached wartime press protocol. His celebrity and official connections insulated him from the chorus demanding that he surrender his accreditation.

Joining American troops in the German Huertgen Forest in November 1944, Hemingway was attired with a Thompson submachine gun draped over his shoulder, once again oblivious to press protocol. During the subsequent heavy fighting, he unslung his weapon and helped repulse a German offensive, in the process putting out of commission a German mortar. He was awarded the Bronze Star in 1947. Following the war, Hemingway continued his literary career with very few journalistic interludes. He was awarded the Nobel Prize for literature in 1954, several years after the publication of *The Old Man and the Sea*. But, he had reported his last war, and in the late 1950s his health deteriorated, leading him to commit suicide with a shotgun in July 1961.

REFERENCES: Robert W. Desmond. *Tides of War*. 1984; Sarah R. Shaber. "Hemingway's Literary Journalism: The Spanish Civil War Dispatches," *Journalism Quarterly*. Autumn 1980; Frederick S. Voss. *Reporting the War*. 1994; William White, ed. *By-Line, Ernest Hemingway*. 1967.

HEMMENT, JOHN C. (?). As one of the leading war photographers* of the Spanish-American War,* Hemment represented the *New York Journal* and *Harper's Weekly*. He was the first newsreel* motion picture photographer to capture a battlefront. At the outset he had been hired by the federal government to take photographs of the wreckage of the *Maine* for the congressional investigation. William Randolph Hearst* had seen to it that Hemment would be the best equipped of all the photographers covering the conflict, even allowing him to use his large steam yacht, the *Silvia*, as a floating darkroom. There was apparently so much space on the yacht that besides his darkroom, he could bring duplicates of every type of equipment he needed, including cameras of several different sizes. Hemment photographed the battleground at Las Guasimas, the graves of the Rough Riders killed there, and the encampment at Sevilla. He later covered World War I* for the Hearst papers. He wrote *Cannon and Camera* (1898).

REFERENCES: Charles H. Brown. *The Correspondents' War*. 1967; Pat Hodgson. *Early War Photographs*. 1974; Joyce Milton. *The Yellow Kids*. 1989; Susan D. Moeller. *Shooting War*. 1989.

HENTY, GEORGE ALFRED (1832–1902). Best known as a writer of adventure stories for children, Henty was born at Trumpington near Cambridge. Bedridden for much of his youth with rheumatic fever, he turned to writing poetry. To fend off youthful critics of such a dandified pastime he became proficient in pugilism as well. He cut short his academic studies at Cambridge to enlist with his brother in the Crimea*-bound British army. His brother died of cholera shortly after. The *Morning Advertiser* published his letters describing the siege of Sebastopol, which led to his being hired in 1859 by the *Standard* as a correspondent. In 1866, accompanying Giuseppe Garibaldi's Italian forces in the Tyrolese campaign, he was aboard an Italian ship when he witnessed the naval battle of Lissa on July 20.

Over the next decade he would cover Lord Napier's expedition to Abyssinia (1867–1868), the opening of the Suez Canal (1869), the Franco-Prussian War,* the Paris Commune (1871), the Russian conquest of Khiva (1873), Lord Wolseley's Ashanti expedition (1873–1874), and the Carlist insurrection in Spain (1874). His coverage of the Napier expedition was collected in the book *The March to Magdala* (1868).

While Henty was covering the Ashanti War, fellow correspondent Henry Stanley,* to break the monotony between battles, proposed a trip to the mouth of the Volta River in a boat owned by the *New York Herald*. His intention was that they would watch the British expedition, whose mission was to put down the tribes of the Volta and who were about to launch an attack on Kumasi. Their mission resulted in informative news dispatches and the near drowning of Henty.

His last assignment as a special correspondent was to follow the Turkish army during the Turko-Serbian War of 1876. Although he continued his affiliation with the *Standard* he devoted most of his remaining years to writing juvenile fiction, due to the fact that success had eluded him as a writer for adults. Regarded as the most imperialist of the imperialists for his Victorian attitudes, he published more than eighty titles over the next quarter century.

REFERENCES: *DNB*; Robert Wilkinson-Latham. *From Our Special Correspondent.* 1979.

HERBERT, ST. LEGER ALGERNON (1850–1885). Born in Kingston, Canada, and educated at Oxford, he toiled in the Canadian Civil Service before his appointment as secretary to Sir Garnet Wolseley in 1878. He accompanied Wolseley in his campaigns in Cyprus (1878) and South Africa (1879) and was awarded the Companion of the Most Distinguished Order of St. Michael and St. George in 1880 after taking part in the storming of Sekokoeni's Mountain.

Herbert had begun his journalism career in 1878 with the *Times*. In 1883 he joined the *Morning Post* as its special in Egypt and in the Sudan campaign, and was present at the battles of El Teb and Tamai, where he was shot through the leg. On January 19, 1885, he was killed with fellow correspondent John Alexander Cameron* of the *Standard* at the Battle of Abu Kru. Conspicuously dressed in his red jacket, Herbert was found dead among the camels following the battle. He is one of seven war correspondents killed in the Sudan campaign commemorated by a plaque in St. Paul's Cathedral.

REFERENCES: *DNB*; Frederic Villiers,* *Pictures of Many Wars.* 1920; Robert Wilkinson-Latham. *From Our Special Correspondent.* 1979.

HERBST, JOSEPHINE FREY (1892–1969). Born in Sioux City, Iowa, Herbst attended the University of Iowa, where she gravitated toward a literary career.

During World War I* she drifted toward radical politics and moved to Berkeley, California. Over the ensuing two decades she performed social work, hobnobbed with the literati, and published her first novel in 1928.

Increasingly drawn into the orbit of radicalism, she began writing for the *New Masses* during the Depression. By the 1930s she had published several more novels. Her star began to rise when she turned to journalism in the turbulent years before World War II.* Prior to American intervention she covered the underground movement in Cuba, the rise of Hitler in Germany, and the Spanish Civil War,* where she developed a reputation for courage under fire. Her wartime experiences are chronicled in her 1941 novel *Satan's Sergeants* and in the play *The Spanish Road*, written to raise funds for Loyalist Spain in 1938.
REFERENCES: *DAB*; Peter Wyden. *The Passionate War: The Narrative History of the Spanish Civil War.* 1983.

HERSEY, JOHN (1914–1993). Born in Tientsin, China, to missionary parents, he spent the first decade of his life there. He attended college at Yale and Cambridge. After serving as secretary for Sinclair Lewis he was employed by *Time* in 1937. In 1939 he covered events in Asia. After 1942 he covered the Pacific and European theaters of World War II* for *Life* and *Time* and published three books on the war: *Men on Bataan* (1942), *Into the Valley* (1943), based on an incident during the Battle of Guadalcanal, and *Hiroshima* (1946), which originally began as a story for the *New Yorker* on the effects of the atomic bomb on the inhabitants of the city. In 1944 he won the Pulitzer Prize for his novel about the American occupation of Sicily, *A Bell for Adano*. Following the war he had a successful career as a novelist and wrote several books of nonfiction.
REFERENCE: Frederick S. Voss. *Reporting the War.* 1994.

HERSH, SEYMOUR (b. 1937). Born in Chicago and educated at the University of Chicago, Hersh was a former Pentagon correspondent for the Associated Press when he heard about the My Lai incident from former members of William L. Calley's army unit. Hersh received a grant to travel as a freelance reporter to interview the participants in the tragedy. After he pieced together the story of what actually happened on March 16, 1968, when hundreds of Vietnamese civilians were murdered by American troops, it was published by the Dispatch News Service, a fledgling news syndicate. Prior to his taking the story to the Dispatch News Service, no major news organization would touch it, including *Look* and *Life*. His first My Lai article was carried in three dozen papers, including the *St. Louis Post-Dispatch*, on November 13, 1969. The following year Hersh was unanimously awarded the Pulitzer Prize.
REFERENCE: Phillip Knightley. *The First Casualty.* 1975.

HIETT, HELEN (1913–1961). Born in Chenoa, Illinois, after graduating from the University of Chicago in 1934 she headed for Europe on a scholarship. In 1939 she left graduate school at the London School of Economics and moved to France. The following year she became one of the first female correspondents to report for NBC. Among her radio news scoops was the fall of France in 1940. Fleeing France just ahead of the Nazi advance, she made it to Madrid, where Spanish news censorship prevented her from sending out news dispatches. She won the National Headliners Award for her scoop of the bombing of British Gibraltar. She returned to America the following year.

In 1944 Hiett returned to Europe for the Religious News Service. She was in Milan days before the arrival of Allied forces and was present when Mussolini's body was still hanging from the lamppost. After the war she transferred to the *New York Herald Tribune*. She died on August 22, 1961, from injuries sustained in a mountain climbing accident in France.

REFERENCE: David H. Hosley. *As Good As Any*. 1984.

HIGGINS, MARGUERITE (1920–1966). Higgins was born in the crown colony of Hong Kong. She was stricken with malaria during infancy and sent to recuperate in Vietnam. Her family moved to Oakland, California, in 1923 and Marguerite attended the University of California at Berkeley, where she wrote for the campus newspaper. After graduating with a degree in journalism in 1942 she joined the *New York Herald Tribune*.

Higgins entered the ranks of professional journalism at an opportune time, with many male reporters joining the armed forces in the 1940s. By 1943 she was one of the few *Herald Tribune* staffers to receive a byline. Rebuffed in her attempts to secure a position as a foreign correspondent, Higgins violated protocol by going over the heads of her superiors to the owner's wife, Helen Rogers Reid. Besides taking an active role in the management of the paper, Reid was known for her support of feminist issues, and in 1944 Higgins was on the *Queen Mary* bound for England with seven other war correspondents.

Confined to the London bureau, Higgins was determined to report from the battlefront. In 1945, during the closing days of the war, she finally got her opportunity when she was assigned to the Berlin bureau. In March 1945 she received her first taste of conflict when the Eighth Army Air Force offered to allow journalists to view the aftermath of German bombing raids. Although she served as war correspondent for only six weeks she managed to witness the liberation of the concentration camps at Buchenwald and Dachau as well as the capture of Munich. She was awarded the Army Campaign Ribbon for outstanding service under difficult conditions and the New York Newspaper Women's Club Award as best foreign correspondent of 1945 for her coverage of the events surrounding the liberation of Dachau. She went on to report the Nuremberg trials, the treason trial of Pétain, the Berlin Blockade, and the developing Cold War.

With her reputation as a war correspondent firmly established by 1947, Higgins was elevated to Berlin bureau chief for the *Herald Tribune*, but prone to pettiness and competitive to a fault, she was ill suited for a supervisory position. In May 1950 Higgins was transferred to Tokyo, which, according to fellow correspondent Keyes Beech,* she found "about as exciting as a duck pond." She could little have known that her new position as Far East bureau chief would lead to her greatest story when North Korea crossed the thirty-eighth parallel on June 25, 1950, inaugurating the Korean War.*

Higgins covered the fall of Seoul for the *Herald Tribune*, barely eluding Communist forces. Shortly after, she was joined by a more seasoned war reporter, Homer Bigart,* with whom she would have a legendary rivalry. Management wanted Higgins to return to her post in Tokyo, and when she refused was given the ultimatum to either return or lose her job. She stayed and reported the first actions of the war. However, she was forced to leave when the commander of American forces in Korea issued an edict banning all women. Higgins again beseeched Helen Rogers Reid to aid her in circumventing protocol. Appealing the decision directly to General Douglas MacArthur won Higgins permission to return to the battlefront.

Higgins covered many of the major campaigns of the conflict, including landing with the U.S. Marines under fire at Inchon. She gained the respect of her male counterparts as well as the foot soldiers for sharing in their hardships. Her reports continued to appear in the *Herald Tribune*, occasionally on the same page as her competitor Bigart's. In October 1950 *Life* magazine ran a feature on Higgins with an array of photographs of her in battle fatigues, further adding to her legend as a war reporter. In 1951 she published *War in Korea*, which became a best-seller. That same year, along with five other correspondents, she was awarded the Pulitzer Prize in the international-reporting category, the first woman to be so honored. Over the next several years she received dozens of awards, including the Overseas Press Club's George Polk Award and the 1951 Woman of the Year Award from the Associated Press.

In 1953 she was in Vietnam covering the siege at Dien Bien Phu when her friend and colleague Robert Capa* was killed by a land mine nearby. Shortly after, Higgins received word that she had been granted a visa to visit the Soviet Union, the first American granted such access since the death of Stalin. Her book *Red Plush and Black Bread*, published in 1955, chronicled her 13,500-mile excursion through Russia. With the publication of *News Is a Singular Thing* that same year she became recognized as an expert on Russian affairs.

Her journalistic instincts led her again to a hot spot when she covered the Congo crisis in 1961, the first *Herald Tribune* journalist to report on that region since Henry Stanley* came in search of David Livingstone in 1877. Higgins returned to Vietnam* in 1963. In the prescient *Our Vietnam Nightmare* (1965), she described the dangers of American intervention. She left the *Herald Tribune* in late 1963 but kept her hand in journalism by writing weekly columns for *Newsday* and continuing to travel abroad. Her tenth trip to Vietnam proved her undoing when she contracted the tropical disease leishmaniasis. She was hospitalized at Walter Reed Hospital and died two months later. Higgins was buried at Arlington National Cemetery.

REFERENCES: Julia Edwards. *Women of the World*. 1989; Richard Kluger. *The Paper:*

The Life and Death of the New York Herald Tribune. 1986; Antoinette May. *Witness to War: A Biography of Marguerite Higgins.* 1983.

HILL, RUSSELL (b. 1919). Following graduation from Columbia University in 1939, he turned down a scholarship to Cambridge to pursue a career in journalism. That year he traveled to Berlin, where he was hired by the *New York Herald Tribune.* He became an assistant to Ralph Barnes of the *Tribune* and then to William L. Shirer* of CBS. During the German invasion of Holland, Belgium, and Luxembourg in May 1940, Hill accompanied the German *Wehrmacht.* On the day before the signing of the French surrender in the Compiègne Forest in June 1940, both Hill and Barnes were expelled from Germany for critical pieces they had written.

Following his expulsion, Hill went to the Balkans and covered the Yugoslav and Greek campaigns, making a daring escape from the Germans in a small fishing boat with fellow correspondents Leigh White* of CBS and Robert St. John* of the AP. Their boat was strafed by enemy aircraft on several occasions, with White and St. John sustaining serious injuries.

As one of the youngest correspondents of the war, Hill next relocated to Cairo and would cover events and military affairs in Syria and Iran. During the North African campaign he covered the British Eighth Army's action against Rommel's Afrika Corps. His exploits in North Africa were chronicled in two well-received books, *Desert War* and *Conquest of Africa.* In 1944 he reported the Italian campaign and the Allied advance on Rome. Hill's closest brush with death occurred in October 1944 near the German city of Aachen on the Belgian border. While he was covering mopping-up operations around the recently captured city, his jeep triggered an antivehicular Teller mine. Hill suffered a broken arm, cuts, and bruises, but the army driver and passenger David Lardner* of the *New Yorker* magazine were killed. Hill continued to report the Allied advance into Germany and was one of the first Western correspondents permitted to tour the Soviet zone of Germany following V-E Day.

REFERENCES: Richard Collier. *Fighting Words.* 1989; Robert W. Desmond. *Tides of War.* 1984.

HINDUS, MAURICE GERSCHON (1891–1969). Born in Bolshoye Bikovo, Russia, he immigrated with his family to New York City in 1905. After graduating from Colgate University and attending Harvard University's graduate school for one year he turned to freelance writing. In 1920 he published his first book, *The Russian Peasant and the Revolution.* His observations of a Russian émigré community in Canada resulted in a series of articles published by *Century* magazine. Impressed by his work, the magazine assigned him to return to Russia and observe the collective farming system. He chronicled this experience in *Humanity Uprooted* (1929) and *Red Bread* (1931).

Although his work focused on Russian peasant life, he served three years as a war correspondent during World War II,* covering the Russo-German war.

Employed by the *New York Herald Tribune*, he wrote the book *Mother Russia* (1943), which captures wartime conditions in the Soviet Union. Hindus was present when the first flight of U.S. bombers from African bases reached the Soviet airfields in June 1943. During the Cold War he became a recognized authority on Soviet affairs. He played an important role in establishing sympathy for the Soviet Union during the war, but became increasingly critical of Soviet policy during the postwar years. Ever critical of the Soviet hierarchy, he always maintained an affinity with the Russian people. A prolific writer of twenty books and numerous articles, Hindus traveled widely throughout the 1940s. His books include *Russia and Germany, We Shall Live Again*, and *Russia and Japan*.
REFERENCES: *DAB* 8; Robert W. Desmond. *Tides of War*. 1984; *New York Times*. July 9, 1969.

HOLLINGWORTH, CLAIRE (b. 1911). Educated at the University of London, she entered journalism with *The Daily Telegraph* at the outset of World War II,* as the only British reporter present to inform the world that the invasion of Poland had begun on September 3, 1939. She also reported the conflict from the Balkans and the Western Desert. Following the war she covered the Greek Civil War and the Palestine conflict.
     Although stationed in Paris for the *Manchester Guardian* until 1963, she covered the Algerian War, Egypt, Aden, and Vietnam.* From 1967 to 1973 she was a roving correspondent for the *Daily Telegraph*, and reported the Vietnam War. After the Vietnam conflict she served as defense and China correspondent for her paper. Among her books are *Poland's Three Weeks War* (1940), *There's a German Just Behind Me* (1945), and *Front Line* (1990).
REFERENCE: Anne Sebba. *Battling For News*. 1994.

HOLME, CHRISTOPHER (?). Holme covered the Ethiopian War* for Reuters* and then the Spanish Civil War.* In 1937 he covered one of the most controversial episodes of the war when he accompanied George L. Steer* of the *Times* to the town of Guernica* in the Basque region of Spain. They were in the village of Ambacegui, several miles from their destination, when German planes attacked them from the direction of Guernica. The planes strafed the village and attempted to kill the two correspondents before continuing on. Holme and Steer responded to a rumor that Guernica had been leveled and decided to check it out, by now joined by Noel Monks* of the *Daily Express*. The destruction of Guernica, a city that was not a military objective, became a major news sensation and heralded a decade of total war.
REFERENCE: Phillip Knightley. *The First Casualty*. 1975.

HOMER, WINSLOW (1836–1910). Born in Boston, the best-known artist of the American Civil War* was apprenticed to a local lithographer at the age of nineteen. During his two years he learned to draw directly on wood for engraving. He opened his own studio at the age of twenty-one and began sending engravings to the pictorial press. In October 1861 *Harper's* sent him to sketch the first Lincoln inauguration and then the siege at Yorktown, Virginia, at the start of McClellan's Peninsular campaign. The sketches he sent back were then translated into engravings for the journal's pages. More interested in art than reporting, after covering the action at Yorktown and Fair Oaks in May 1862 he returned to the studio, where he used his wartime sketches and engravings as models for more serious paintings. He subsequently made occasional visits to the battlefront as a freelance artist up to the siege of Petersburg, Virginia, toward the end of the war.

Homer had not risen to prominence at the time of the Civil War. He was always more comfortable illustrating the more mundane activities of camp and civilian life than the carnage on the battlefield, and his wartime experiences were limited to operations against the Confederate Army of Northern Virginia. Unlike many of his colleagues, Homer did not draw a complete battle scene. His technique is exemplified by his sketch ''The Sharpshooter'' of 1863, in which he shows only a solitary soldier, hiding in a tree, demonstrating the new kind of impersonal warfare. Besides his work published in *Harper's* he produced a book of lithographs entitled *Campaign Sketches* in 1863.

REFERENCES: Pat Hodgson. *The War Illustrators*. 1977; Philip Van Doren Stern. *They Were There*. 1959.

HOOPER, JIM (?). Formerly a television documentary writer and professional skydiver, Hooper turned to war reporting in 1984. Since then he has covered wars exclusively in Africa, covering conflicts in Chad, Sudan, Uganda, South Africa, Namibia, and Angola. He was one of the first Western journalists to be given almost unrestricted access to the bush war in Southwest Africa/Namibia, when he accompanied the Koevoet, the deadly counterinsurgency unit, against the revolutionary South West Africa People's Organization (SWAPO). A freelance defense photojournalist, he has written articles for the *Economist, International Defense Review, Jane's Defense Weekly*, and *Armed Forces*. His book *Beneath the Visiting Moon: Images of Combat in Southern Africa* is a chronicle of his career as a modern war correspondent.

REFERENCE: Jim Hooper. *Beneath the Visiting Moon*. 1990.

HOPKINSON, TOM (b. 1905). Best known as the editor of *Picture Post* in England, the Oxford-educated Hopkinson worked as a freelance journalist and in advertising and publicity before moving into editorial work. He resigned from the *Picture Post* during the Korean War* when the owner suppressed a story by Bert Hardy* and James Cameron* which reported the mistreatment of North Korean prisoners by the South Koreans.

Hopkinson traveled extensively in Africa beginning in 1958, when he edited the magazine *Drum* in South Africa. He covered the Congo conflict and the fighting in Katanga when Moise Tshombe set up his separate state. Between

1963 and 1966 he trained African journalists on behalf of the International Press Institute.
REFERENCES: Tom Hopkinson, ed. *Picture Post 1938–50*. 1970; Jorge Lewinski. *The Camera at War*. 1978.

HORNE, WALTER H. (1883–1921). Horne was born in Hallowell, Maine. He worked in his family tanning business as a young boy before leaving for New York City shortly after the turn of the century. After contracting tuberculosis he moved to El Paso, Texas, in 1905, hoping to improve his health. He found an outlet for his entrepreneurial skills when he entered the picture postcard* business in 1911 after the outbreak of the Mexican Revolution just across the border. He traveled widely, visiting military encampments and taking photographs. He eventually took thousands of pictures of American troops along the border, who would then buy the images to send to family back home. By 1914, his picture postcard business was booming, at one point making five thousand postcards a day. He claimed to have taken the best photographs of the Second Battle of Ciudad Juarez in November 1913. His best-selling card was reportedly of a triple execution of three Mexicans in Ciudad Juarez in 1916.
REFERENCE: Paul J. Vanderwood and Frank N. Samponara. *Border Fury*. 1988.

HOUSE, EDWARD HOWARD (1836–1901). Born in Boston, Massachusetts, he studied music composition before joining the *Boston Courier* as its music and drama critic in 1854. He transferred to the *New York Tribune* in 1858 and covered John Brown's raid on Harpers Ferry the following year. With the outbreak of the American Civil War,* he was made special correspondent with Union forces in the Virginia campaign. He was present when Colonel Elmer E. Ellsworth, commander of a New York regiment, was shot and killed by a secessionist business proprietor in Alexandria, Virginia, while at the head of his troops. Although hostilities had not yet officially erupted, Ellsworth was the first Union death of the war. House also witnessed the First Battle of Bull Run.

Following the war he became involved in theater management before returning to the *Tribune* in 1868. He joined the *New York Times* two years later, and in 1871 he obtained a university teaching position in Tokyo. He developed an instant affinity for Japan, where he spent the next several years as journalist and teacher. In 1873 he accompanied a punitive expedition to Formosa as war correspondent for the *New York Herald*. He returned to America in 1880 and then moved to London, where he worked on Edwin Booth's British tour. He suffered a stroke in 1883 but continued to write articles and work toward popularizing Western music in Japan. House eventually returned to Japan, dying in Tokyo in 1901.
REFERENCES: J. Cutler Andrews. *The North Reports the Civil War*. 1955; *DAB*; David Shavit. *The United States in Asia*. 1990.

HOVEY, GRAHAM (?). Following graduation from the University of Minnesota, Hovey worked for two years as a war correspondent for the International

News Service (INS). Beginning in 1943 he covered the Allied landings in North
Africa at Casablanca, Oran, and Algiers, covered the 1944 Italian campaign,
and was with the forces entering Rome in June 1944. He also reported the
invasion of France and the advancing Allied forces at the Rhine River. Hovey
later worked for the Associated Press, the *New Republic*, and the *New York
Times* before returning to academia as director of the Michigan Journalism Fel-
lows Program.
REFERENCES: Robert W. Desmond. *Tides of War*. 1984; Jack Stenbuck, ed. *Typewriter
Battalion*. 1995.

HOWARD, HUBERT (d. 1898). A lawyer by trade, Howard was war correspondent for the *Times* and the *New York Herald* during the conflict in the Sudan
in the 1890s. He began his career covering the front lines in 1894 when he
accompanied Cuban insurgents in their rebellion against the Spanish. He next
covered the Matabele War in South Africa and in 1896 was present at the attack
on Sekombo's Kraal, in which he acted as adjutant and took part in the fighting.
He returned to South Africa in 1897 when conflict again erupted in Matabeleland
and Mashonaland. The following year he was with Lord Kitchener's forces as
they moved against the dervish army near Khartoum. During the battle of Omdurman Howard rode with Winston Churchill* in the charge of the Twenty-first
Lancers. Following the charge, Howard was inspecting the Khalifa's palace
when it was hit by several artillery shells. He was killed instantly when a shell
fragment struck the back of his head.
REFERENCE: Robert Wilkinson-Latham. *From Our Special Correspondent*. 1979.

HOWARD, JAMES WILLIAM "PHOCION" (1833–1893). Howard was a
member of the so-called Bohemian Brigade,* which covered the American Civil
War,* and was apparently the only one to cover the American Indian Wars* as
well. Born in Rising Sun, Indiana, on Independence Day, he left his studies at
the seminary to work as an apprentice in a newspaper shop, which led to his
affinity for reporting. He worked for several papers in Kentucky and Illinois
before serving in the Civil War.

Following the war he moved to Chicago and a job with the *Chicago Tribune*.
He reportedly had covered at least one army expedition into Sioux country prior
to General Alfred Terry's 1876 mission against the Sioux after the Custer defeat.
Howard joined infantry reinforcements in Bismarck before embarking on a thou-
sand-mile steamboat trip to Terry's camp near the Rosebud River in 1876.

Howard's reports from Indian territory, which appeared under his pen name
"Phocion," were written more for entertainment value than news. In one column, he noted that Sitting Bull had learned French from the legendary Father
DeSmet and was able to read the history of the Napoleonic Wars in French and
therefore borrow Napoleon's tactics. Howard soon tired of Terry's uneventful
campaign and returned to Chicago, where he continued his journalism career,
specializing in political writing.
REFERENCE: Oliver Knight. *Following the Indian Wars*. 1960.

HOWLAND, JOHN DARE (1843–1914). Born in Zanesville, Ohio, he ran away at the age of fourteen. He joined the American Fur Company at St. Louis and traveled up the Missouri River. By the time he was fifteen he had hunted buffalo, traded with the Sioux, and tried his luck at the Pike's Peak gold mines. With the outbreak of the American Civil War* he joined the Colorado Volunteers and fought in New Mexico. He soon took up the brush and quill, becoming a sketch artist and correspondent for *Harper's Weekly*. He saved enough to study art in Paris for two years following the war.

Returning to America in 1867 he served as secretary of the Indian Peace Commission for two years while continuing his affiliation with *Harper's* covering the American Indian Wars.* Howland was one of the earliest artists to reside in the Rockies. He designed the Civil War monument near the Colorado state capitol.

REFERENCE: Peggy and Harold Samuels. *Samuels' Encyclopedia of Artists of the American West*. 1985.

HUDSON, FREDERIC (1819–1875). Born in Quincy, Massachusetts, he entered journalism with the New York–based Hudson's News Rooms, a news-gathering agency founded by his older brother. Assigned to scour the waterfronts for news from abroad for the agency, he made the acquaintance of James Gordon Bennett,* who hired him for the *New York Herald* in 1837. In 1845, Bennett was approached by the editor of the *New York Journal of Commerce* with a proposition to establish together a news-gathering agency. With the outbreak of the Mexican War* the following year, this proposal seemed most timely. While Bennett was in Europe for much of the war, Hudson set up lines of communication extending to New Orleans, the major news center for the war. War news was transmitted from the battlefront to New Orleans and then the East Coast by means of a series of relays using horse express, railroad, and telegraph.

Hudson eventually was promoted to managing editor and played an important role in refining methods of collecting news and developing newsroom organization by coordinating copy and directing reporters in the field. As the outstanding managing editor of his day, he was responsible for choosing all of the war correspondents for his paper during the American Civil War.* He stayed with the *Herald* until he retired in 1866. He died in 1875 in a railroad accident. Hudson wrote *Journalism in the United States from 1690 to 1872* (1873), the first comprehensive history of American journalism.

REFERENCE: J. Cutler Andrews. *The North Reports the Civil War*. 1955.

HULL, PEGGY (1889–1967). Born Henrietta Eleanor Goodnough in Bennington, Kansas, she began her journalism career as a typesetter with the *Junction City* (Kansas) *Sentinel*. Following her marriage to George Hull they moved to Hawaii, where she worked as a reporter for the *Honolulu Star*. Four years later she divorced Hull, after his drinking led him to climb a flagpole in the nude.

After returning to the States, she was with the *Cleveland Plain Dealer* in

1916 when the Ohio National Guard was sent to Texas to join Pershing's punitive expedition to capture Pancho Villa. When her request to cover the guardsmen was rebuffed she quit and went to Texas on her own. In El Paso she worked for several papers, and although she never actually made it to the front, Hull did accompany the troops on a ninety-mile, two-week training march into the desert. In one incident she became separated from the troops in a sandstorm and was rescued by an Indian family.

In February 1917, her story of the return of the Pershing expedition appeared on the front page of the *El Paso Morning Times*. She almost stole the thunder from Pershing when newsreel* cameramen convinced her to mount a horse and pull alongside the general's. The image of the female reporter and Pershing leading troops out of Mexico appeared in newspapers around the world under the caption "American girl correspondent leads troops out of Mexico with General Pershing."

With America's entrance into World War I,* Hull headed for France at her own expense, with her paper agreeing to publish her articles if she was able to get to the front. She was able to connive her way to Paris in time to witness the first appearance of the Allied Expeditionary Forces (AEF) on July 4, 1917. Newspapers were required to post a $10,000 bond to ensure the good behavior of accredited correspondents. Peggy first needed sponsorship by a newspaper. After rejection by fifty newspapers she was finally endorsed by the Newspaper Enterprise Association, affiliated with the Scripps-Howard press service.

Army accreditation officers continued to deny her requests to cover combat. However, in September 1918 Hull became the first woman correspondent accredited by the U.S. War Department to cover a war zone. After obtaining accreditation, she became the only American reporter to cover the American expedition to guard supplies for the White Army in Siberia, which was still in a civil war with Bolshevik forces. She was in Russia when the armistice was signed ending the war in Europe. Hull spent nine months covering the atrocities and horror along the Siberian railroad, one of the few reporters to do so, but saw no warfare.

She was in Shanghai in 1932 when Japanese troops invaded, and she reported the fighting for the *New York Daily News*. Hull received accreditation to cover the Pacific conflict in November 1943 and covered most of the major campaigns, including Guam, Saipan, Guadalcanal, and the New Hebrides. Although her stories chronicled GI life much like Ernie Pyle's,* she witnessed her share of violence, including the deaths of Japanese soldiers outside her tent on Guam and baskets of amputated feet on Saipan. She died in Carmel, California, at the age of seventy-seven.

REFERENCE: Emmet Crozier. *American Reporters on the Western Front, 1914–1918.* 1959; Julia Edwards. *Women of the World: The Great Foreign Correspondents.* 1989.

HUNT, FRAZIER "SPIKE" (1885–1967). Born at Rock Island, Illinois, in 1885, Hunt filed dispatches from south of the border during the Mexican Rev-

olution, before reporting World War I* and the Russian Revolution. In early 1918 he went to France as war correspondent for *American Red Cross Magazine* before transferring to the *Chicago Tribune* later that year. He reported naval operations, troop convoy movements, and fighting at the front before being sent to cover the American expeditionary force in northern Russia. His dispatches from the Russian Civil War were influential in bringing about the withdrawal of American troops from this theater of operations. As the first reporter to enter Petrograd in six months, he continued to cover the conflict, reporting pogroms, famine, and various atrocities. His reports were unique for this era in predicting victory for the Bolsheviks. He wrote several books, including *Blown in by the Draft* (1918) and *The Rising Temper of the East* (1922).
REFERENCES: Eugene Lyons. *We Cover the World*. 1937; Lloyd Wendt. *Chicago Tribune*. 1979.

HURLEY, JAMES FRANCIS "FRANK" (c. 1885–1962). Born in Sydney, Australia, he covered his first major story in 1911 when he was the official photographer on the Australian Antarctic expedition. In 1914 he performed the same function with Sir Ernest Shackleton's ill-fated expedition, which was trapped by ice for a year. During World War I* he was made official Australian war photographer* in 1917, recording the Battles of Ypres, Menin Road, and Passhenduck. Following the war he traveled widely before making the transition to motion picture photography. During World War II* he headed the Australian Imperial Photographic Unit and the was director of British Army Features and Propaganda. Never without his camera equipment, he made dozens of films and documentaries, including *With Allenby in Palestine* (1917), *Siege at Tobruk* (1941), and one depicting the Battle of Jericho in 1922. Hurley also wrote numerous books.
REFERENCE: Turner Browne and Elaine Partnow. *Photographic Artists and Innovators*. 1983.

HUYNH, UT CONG (b. 1951). Born in Saigon, Vietnam, he was affiliated with the Associated Press as a war photographer beginning in 1966. His older brother was killed while covering the Vietnam War* for the Associated Press in 1965. Huynh won the Pulitzer Prize in 1973 for one of the most memorable images from the war, when he captured several small children, one naked, all crying, as they ran from their napalmed village twenty-five miles away from Saigon. That same year he was also awarded the George Polk Memorial Award, the Overseas Press Club Award, and the National Press Club Award.
REFERENCE: Turner Browne and Elaine Partnow. *Macmillan Biographical Encyclopedia of Photographic Artists and Innovators*. 1983.

HUYSHE, WENTWORTH (1846–1934). At his death on December 2, 1934, he was reputedly the oldest war correspondent in England. He served on the staff of the *New York Herald* during the Russo-Turkish War* and the *Times* during the Sudan campaign, where he witnessed the bloody Battle of Suakin on March 22, 1885. Following the war he worked for various papers, including the *Graphic* and the *Daily Graphic*.

REFERENCES: Dennis Griffiths. *Encyclopedia of the British Press.* 1992; Robert Wilkinson-Latham. *From Our Special Correspondent.* 1979.

I

IRWIN, VIRGINIA (1908–1980). Born in Quincy, Illinois, and educated at Lindenwood College and Gem City Business College, Irwin entered journalism with the *St. Louis Dispatch* in 1932. With the onset of World War II* she covered the home front, and after she was rebuffed in her attempts to gain accreditation as a war correspondent she went to Europe to work for the Red Cross. She finally managed to get her credentials from the War Department shortly before the Normandy invasion in 1944.

Irwin arrived in France the following month and covered the conflict in Belgium, Holland, Luxembourg, and Germany. In April 1945 she bypassed official channels and went to Berlin, where she witnessed the final bloodletting of the war in Europe. Irwin was also present when U.S. patrols linked up with the Red Army on the Elbe River on April 25. Her unauthorized trip to Berlin with Andrew Tully of the *Boston Traveler* resulted in the first eyewitness account by any Western correspondent of the devastated capital and seemed a sure scoop for the intrepid reporters. However, for acting without official permission, their credentials were revoked and the publication of their stories was delayed. She continued with the *Post-Dispatch* at its New York bureau until 1960.
REFERENCE: Robert W. Desmond. *Tides of War. 1984.*

IRWIN, WILLIAM HENRY (1873–1948). Irwin was born in Oneida, New York, and educated at Stanford University. In 1900 he joined the *San Francisco Chronicle*, and after stints with the *New York Sun* and *McClure's Magazine* he took a respite from journalism to write fiction. While employed by *McClure's*, he wrote one of his best-known stories when he covered the San Francisco earthquake and fire. Although he was not given a byline, the story was quickly credited to him and he was forever linked to the city by the bay.

With the outbreak of World War I* he returned to reporting with the *New York Tribune, London Times,* and the *Daily Mail.* In 1915 he reported but did not witness the entire First Battle of Ypres in Belgium, including a German poison gas attack in which he was himself injured by gas residue following the battle. He discovered that due to censorship the British public was unaware of the heroic victory by the British soldiers three months previously at Ypres. Irwin defied the British War Office and, using confidential government sources, described a battle costing 50,000 British soldiers out of 120,000 engaged, a proportional loss unequaled in any previous war. His article ''The Splendid Story of the Battle of Ypres'' was written with the power of observation that a three-month perspective would offer and had an incredible impact when it ran in British papers. Its publication elevated Irwin to the top ranks of the war's correspondents; however, he would be forever resented by his colleagues in the British press, who had been curtailed by censorship. In addition Irwin lost his credentials and was blacklisted by both the French and British.

After marrying for the second time in 1916 he returned to the battlefront after a two-year hiatus, this time for the *Saturday Evening Post,* and was promptly injured by a shell explosion in Italy, resulting ultimately in deafness in his right ear.

After the war he crusaded for international peace and the League of Nations. A prolific writer, he continued to produce journalistic and fiction pieces. During World War II* he wrote for the North American Newspaper Alliance and other syndicates. He died following a series of strokes in 1948.

REFERENCES: Emmet Crozier. *American Reporters on the Western Front, 1914–18.* 1959; *DLB* 25.

ITALO-ETHIOPIAN WAR. *See* ETHIOPIAN WAR.

J

JACOB, ALARIC (b. 1909). Formerly a Reuters* correspondent in the Middle East, Jacob arrived in Tobruk to cover the North African desert campaign in August 1941. He had earlier spent six years as Washington correspondent and tended toward Marxist views. He covered the crucial Battle of El Alamein in 1942. Jacob left Reuters for the *London Daily Express* in 1942 and the following year covered the Burma front. In January 1944 he reported the war in Russia. REFERENCE: Richard Collier. *Fighting Words*. 1989.

JACOBY, MELVILLE (1916–1942). Jacoby began his career in journalism with the *Stanford Daily* and then the *San Francisco Chronicle* following graduation from Stanford University. When war broke out in the Far East, Jacoby was studying at Lignan University in Canton, China. He joined the staff of *Time* and *Life* in 1940 and left China for the Philippines, where he covered the Japanese siege of the islands. His dispatches to *Time* magazine were some of the most vivid accounts of the fighting around the Philippines. On a more controversial note, Jacoby's reports formed the basis for John Hersey's* 1940s bestseller *Men of Bataan*. Jacoby had been under the impression that the magazine would use his dispatches in the magazine, but instead *Time* allowed Hersey to use the cables for his book. In compensation they offered Jacoby and his wife $450 for his research.

With the fall of Manila, Jacoby and his wife, *Time* correspondent Annalee Whitmore, and reporter Clark Lee* fled by boat to the island fortress of Corregidor and then to the Bataan Peninsula. Several weeks later they fled by boat to Australia, where Jacoby perished in a freak airplane accident in early 1942, only weeks after their arrival. Jacoby was waiting with others, including Brigadier General H. H. George, to board a plane when the propeller detached from

an out-of-control fighter plane and crashed into the bystanders, killing all of them. Jacoby was the first American correspondent to die in a combat theater in World War II.* His short career as a war correspondent is commemorated by his alma mater in the form of the annual Melville Jacoby Fellowship at Stanford University for a graduate student in journalism specializing in Far Eastern affairs.
REFERENCES: Robert W. Desmond. *Tides of War.* 1984; Peter Rand. *China Hands.* 1995.

JAMES, EDWIN "JIMMY" L. (1890–1951). Prior to World War I* he was on the staff of the *New York Times*, covering the state capital scene in Albany. James was a principal correspondent with the American Expeditionary Force in 1918 during World War I* for the *New York Times*. He had been sent as a replacement for the recently expelled Wythe Williams.* James was present when French and American forces stopped the Germans at Chateau-Thierry on the Marne River, but when he returned to press headquarters at Neufchateau to file his story he found that headquarters had been moved back to Paris, almost two hundred miles away. Having not been apprised of the change he missed perhaps his greatest scoop, as he was forced to wait several hours before sending his cable. He later was with occupation forces in Germany and in 1919 became Paris bureau chief and director of its European service. In 1930 he returned to New York and two years later became managing editor of the *Times*. After one of his correspondents was killed flying as an observer on a World War II* bombing mission he advised his reporters not to take unwarranted risks.
REFERENCES: Emmet Crozier. *American Reporters on the Western Front 1914–18.* 1959; Robert W. Desmond. *Windows on the World.* 1980.

JAMES, LIONEL (1871–1955). James left his indigo plantation in India to join Reuters* at the age of twenty-four. In 1895 he accompanied the relief expedition to Chitral on India's North West Frontier. He reported the campaign for the *Bombay Times of India* and for the *Calcutta Englishman*, as well as taking part in the fighting. In 1898 Reuters assigned him to cover the warfare in the Sudan. Shortly afterward he moved over to the *Times*. During the Boer War* he was among the contingent of correspondents holed up during the siege of Ladysmith.*

The *Times* was the first news organization to make use of the wireless as a means of transmitting war reports; James pioneered the new technology during the Russo-Japanese War.* Following his exploits in South Africa, James had gone to South America and then the Balkans when war broke out in the Far East. He rushed to the front lines of the Russo-Japanese War in a chartered steamer outfitted with a mobile radio station. He had persuaded the *Times* to charter the *Haimun*, a 311-ton steamer in Hong Kong, and had a radio transmitter installed. However, the ever vigilant Japanese officials agreed to let him operate only if he allowed an intelligence officer of the Japanese navy to accompany the vessel. James planned to send his messages to a shore station in neutral China; they would in turn be relayed back to London without being tainted by Japanese press censorship. James was able to assemble important data on naval actions, most significantly the sinking of the Russian flagship by a mine off Port Arthur, with eight hundred deaths, including that of Admiral Stepan Osipovich Makarov. James is credited with sending the first telegraphic report of a naval engagement directly from the scene of operations to the office of a news agency. He also reported the Japanese naval blockade at Port Arthur. After three months this operation was ended by pressure from the Japanese military. Later James would report the Balkans conflict of 1912 and warfare between Russia and Turkey.

REFERENCES: Robert W. Desmond. *The Information Process.* 1978; Robert W. Desmond. *Windows on the World.* 1980; Dennis and Peggy Warner. *The Tide at Sunrise: A History of the Russo-Japanese War.* 1974.

JEFFRIES, JOSEPH M. N. (?). Jeffries was one of the outlaw* correspondents who bypassed official channels and went directly from England to France to cover World War I* for the *Daily Mail.* He served as Paris bureau chief and reportedly set a record by reporting the conflict from at least seventeen countries prior to 1918. Among the countries he visited were Egypt, Albania, Greece, Italy, Austria, Belgium, and France. In August 1918 he covered the landing of British and French forces in the Black Sea area of Russia. Jeffries continued his affiliation with the *Mail* until 1933.

REFERENCE: Robert W. Desmond. *Windows on the World.* 1980.

JENKS, PAUL (1965–1992). Primarily a freelance photographer, he was killed by a sniper near the city of Osijek while covering the Yugoslavian conflict. As a correspondent for the European Picture Agency, he was on his third tour covering the civil war when he became the first British victim in the conflict. Jenks was the twenty-third combat journalist to die in Yugoslavia.

REFERENCE: Dennis Griffiths, ed. *The Encyclopedia of the British Press.* 1992.

"JOAN" (?). The *Charleston Courier* was apparently the first Confederate newspaper to employ a woman war correspondent, beginning in 1861. Her real name is lost to posterity, since her dispatches appeared under the pseudonym "Joan." She initially offered her services as a Virginia correspondent so she could be near her son, who was in Johnston's army. Her first letter appeared shortly after the First Battle of Bull Run. Over the next four months she wrote several dispatches in the form of letters describing the war in Virginia from a woman's perspective. She spent two months in Richmond reporting from the home front before securing permission to see her son at the front. Reporting from Richmond in August, "Joan" noted the prevalence of disease and overall poor medical conditions among the Confederate troops.

REFERENCE: J. Cutler Andrews. *The South Reports the Civil War.* 1970.

JOHNSON, EDD (d. 1954). Johnson worked as a war correspondent for the *Chicago Sun* during World War II.* He covered the 1944 Italian campaign and later that year followed Allied forces on the advance through France to the Rhone River Valley. Johnson was the recipient of a special citation for aiding wounded soldiers while under fire during the advance of the Seventh Army. In another incident he rode into Grenoble in a tram with another correspondent and was greeted by the inhabitants as the liberators of the town. Johnson was among the twenty-five victims of a plane crash in Mexico in 1954.
REFERENCES: Robert W. Desmond. *Tides of War*. 1984; Jack Stenbuck, ed. *Typewriter Battalion*. 1995.

JOHNSON, THOMAS M. (?). The veteran *New York Sun* correspondent and military historian began covering World War I* in October 1917, when he was accredited to the American Expeditionary Force. He arrived at Neufchateau in time to report his first war story when he covered General Pétain's visit to American headquarters. In May 1918 he covered the advance at Cantigny and the fighting at Chateau-Thierry, where American forces stopped the German drive on the Marne and saved Paris. Johnson reported but did not witness the Battle of Belleau Wood. He attended the 1919 Paris Peace Conference and following the war wrote *Without Censor* (1928).
REFERENCE: Emmet Crozier. *American Reporters on the Western Frontier 1914–18*. 1959.

JOHNSTON, STANLEY (1900–1962). Born in Australia, he joined an artillery unit during World War I* at the age of seventeen. Following the war he returned home and attended the University of Sydney. Later, he fled France when it fell to the Nazis in 1940 and joined the London office of the *Chicago Tribune*. He reported the Battle of Britain and in 1942 was assigned to the South Pacific theater. His coverage of the Battle of the Coral Sea is considered a classic example of war reportage. Johnston's book *Queen of the Flat-Tops* chronicles his experiences on the aircraft carrier *Lexington*. He was aboard the ship when it was sunk during the Battle of the Coral Sea. Johnston was recommended for a citation for bravery for risking his life attempting to save others.
REFERENCE: Robert W. Desmond. *Tides of War*. 1984.

JONES, RODERICK (1877–1962). Born in England, Jones moved in his youth to South Africa, where he entered the newspaper business with the *Pretoria Press* and the *Pretoria News* while still in his teens. In 1896 he scored his first scoop when Paul Kruger granted him the first interview with Dr. Jameson after the latter's capture during his unsuccessful raid on Johannesburg. Jones later joined the Reuters* bureau in Cape Town and reported for the *Cape Times*. In 1900 he accompanied British forces under Field Marshal Roberts in the Boer War* and two years later served a brief stint at Reuters headquarters in London. He returned to Cape Town in 1905 and for the next ten years supervised the news bureau offices in South and Central Africa. In 1915 he returned to London as general manager of Reuters and the following year became its principal owner. He was knighted in 1918.

REFERENCE: Donald Read, *The Power of News*. 1992.

K

KAHN, ELY JACQUES "E. J." (1917–1994). Born in Manhattan, after graduation from Harvard in 1937 he began a fifty-seven-year association with the *New Yorker*. Serving in the army from 1941 to 1945, he wrote accounts of his life as a chief warrant officer in the South Pacific, which were published in the *New Yorker*. He also served as war correspondent for the magazine during the Korean War,* an experience which resulted in the book *The Peculiar War: Impressions of a Reporter in Korea* (1952). Kahn wrote twenty-seven books, including *The Stragglers* (1962), which chronicles the stories of Japanese soldiers who hid in the jungles for decades following World War II.*
REFERENCE: *New York Times*. May 29, 1994.

KALISCHER, PETER (1915–1991). Kalischer arrived in Korea with the first American troops in 1950 as war correspondent for the UP. Along with Tom Lambert* of the AP, he was later prohibited from covering the combat zone for giving "aid and comfort to the enemy" by using the term "lost battalion" to describe a unit in turmoil with high casualties. General Douglas MacArthur would later reinstate them. Kalischer covered the Vietnam War* sporadically for CBS. In 1975 he delivered the first bulletin announcing the fall of Saigon.
REFERENCE: Michael Emery. *On the Front Lines*. 1995.

KALTENBORN, HANS V. (1879–1965). Born in Milwaukee, Wisconsin, and educated at Harvard, Kaltenborn was the son of a former Hessian officer. He is best known as the dean of radio commentators and is considered one of the creators of "electronic journalism." He served in the Spanish-American War* before beginning a twenty-five-year affiliation with the *Brooklyn Eagle* in 1902. In 1914 he reported German war preparations, but returned to the States prior to the outbreak of hostilities. In 1927 he resigned to devote himself to radio. He joined CBS as a full-time commentator in 1930 and rose to prominence with his broadcasts from the French-Spanish frontier in August and September 1936, the first radio broadcasts of battle in history.

Kaltenborn broadcast virtually every aspect of the diplomatic crisis emerging in Germany before, after, and during the Munich conference. However, by 1939 press censorship was imposed on foreign correspondents, and when Kaltenborn flew to Berlin intending to broadcast for CBS, he was forced to return to London on the next flight. The following year he moved to NBC and continued his work from New York.

REFERENCE: Michael Emery. *On the Front Lines*. 1995.

KAPLAN, DAVID (1947–1992). Kaplan was in the first day of a special assignment for ABC news when he was killed by a sniper's bullet in the war-torn Bosnian capital city of Sarajevo. Kaplan had two decades of experience as a television news producer, including the Gulf War,* when he arrived in Yugoslavia to interview Prime Minister Milan Panic. It is unknown which side of the conflict was responsible for the bullet fired at Kaplan's motor vehicle, clearly marked with a large "TV" sign. He was the first American journalist killed while on assignment in the former Yugoslavia and the fortieth journalist killed since the conflict had begun the previous year.

REFERENCE: Charles P. Arnot. *Don't Kill the Messenger*. 1994.

KAPUSCINSKI, RYSZARD (b. 1932). Born in Pinsk, Poland, he began his career in journalism in 1958, after studying Polish history at Warsaw University. While employed by the Polish Press Agency between 1958 and 1980, often as its only foreign correspondent, Kapuscinski covered twenty-seven revolutions and coups, primarily in Third World nations. In 1960 he was stationed in the Congo, when Patrice Lumumba was assassinated. Escaping to neighboring Burundi, he was sentenced to death in absentia. On several other occasions he was sentenced to death. He covered the hundred-hour "Soccer War" following the World Cup between Honduras and El Salvador in 1969.

In the 1970s he was in Cyprus when violence broke out between Turkey and Greece (1974), between Ethiopia and Somalia (1976), in Algeria (1965), in Nigeria (1966), and in Angola (1973). He recounts most of these incidents in his book *The Soccer War* (1991). His other books include *The Emperor: Downfall of an Autocrat* (1978), which chronicles the fall of Ethiopia's Haile Selassie, and *Shah of Shahs*.

REFERENCES: *International Who's Who*. 1976; *Who's Who in the World*. 1978, 1979.

KAZICKAS, JURATE (?). Born in Soviet Lithuania after World War II,* she escaped with her family to the free world and finally America. Kazickas was a freelance photojournalist who covered the Vietnam War* beginning in February 1967. Prior to the war she worked for *Look* magazine. Rebuffed in her attempts to secure accreditation as a war correspondent, she won enough money on a television game show to buy herself a one-way ticket to Saigon. She published her first article in *Mademoiselle* magazine several months later. After several requests to report the war in the field she was allowed to accompany a marine unit on a five-day patrol into the jungle looking for a North Vietnamese regiment.

She was tested under fire for the first time at Pleiku in June 1967. Kazickas continued to report from the front lines, leading marines to believe she was a jinx since each time she appeared an artillery attack would soon follow. In November 1967 she reported the battles at Dak To and the following year was in the besieged camp of Khe Sanh interviewing one of the officers when it came under a rocket attack. Kazickas suffered shrapnel wounds to her cheek, legs, forearm, and buttocks. She left Vietnam for good in May 1968 after a failed love affair and sudden fears for her own mortality.

REFERENCE: Virginia Elwood-Akers. *Women War Correspondents in the Vietnam War, 1961–1975.* 1988.

KEIM, RANDOLPH DEBENNEVILLE (1841–1914). Born in Reading, Pennsylvania, he attended Beloit College in Wisconsin for a short time. After organizing the City Zouaves of Harrisburg, Pennsylvania, in the heady days following the attack on Fort Sumter, Keim joined the *New York Herald* as a correspondent. He covered twenty-six battles of the American Civil War* prior to the surrender at Appomattox. Some sources claim that his flattering coverage of Grant's command led to the latter's promotion to commander of the Union Army. In the course of war reporting he developed lasting relationships with several officers who would play important roles in the post–Civil War American Indian Wars.*

Following the war Keim became the premier Washington correspondent. In 1868 he was assigned to cover General Phil Sheridan's successful winter campaign on the southern Plains. Keim missed perhaps his greatest story and a place in the pantheon of great journalists while out of the country on a visit to Ceylon. He just missed a letter from his editor offering him the assignment to find the explorer and missionary David Livingstone, who had been missing in Africa for three years. When Keim failed to respond to editor James Gordon Bennett's* offer, the assignment was given to correspondent Henry Stanley.*

Keim acted as a defender of Sheridan's strategy of total war against the Cheyennes and their allies during the five-month winter expedition. Keim's dispatches appearing in the *Herald* under the heading "Indian War" provide a fairly comprehensive account of military conditions on the plains of western Kansas. Most of his reports were mailed to his paper rather than telegraphed. Keim is credited with giving the name to the "Battle of the Washita" in his report of Custer's engagement along the Washita River, because neither Custer nor Sheridan referred to the action using this term. In 1870 he published what is considered one of the three best memoirs of the Indian Wars by a correspondent, *Sheridan's Troopers on the Borders: A Winter Campaign on the Plains.*

Following the war in the West he returned to his position as Washington correspondent and was said to be the only reporter granted access to the White House during the Grant years. Keim wrote numerous books, including a series of tourist handbooks for various Washington area sites. He died from complications of diabetes.

REFERENCES: Randolph DeBenneville Keim. *Sheridan's Troopers on the Border*, with foreword by Paul A. Hutton. Reprint 1985; Oliver Knight. *Following the Indian Wars.* 1960.

KELLOGG, MARCUS HENRY (1833–1876). Kellogg was the only reporter to accompany Lieutenant Colonel George Custer's fatal expedition to the Little Big Horn. Born in Vermont, by the 1850s he was training to be a telegraph operator in Wisconsin. He entered journalism after meeting the editor of the *La Crosse Democrat* while he was still working as a telegrapher. After an unsuccessful run for political office in 1867 and a short stint as editor for the Council Bluffs *Daily Democrat* he returned to La Crosse in 1870, where he returned to telegraphy. In the early 1870s his articles under the pen name "Frontier" appeared in the *St. Paul Pioneer.* He worked as a stringer* for various newspapers as he followed construction of the Northern pacific Railroad from Minnesota to North Dakota.

In 1873 he was employed by the *Bismarck Tribune* as a staff writer and stringer. While working for the Dakota Territory paper he met George Armstrong Custer. Custer violated an order against bringing journalists with him on his expeditions when he invited Clement A. Lounsberry,* the *Tribune*'s publisher, to accompany his expedition to the Little Big Horn. Unfortunately for Kellogg, Lounsberry sent him in his place when his wife fell ill.

When Kellogg perished with Custer's command, no less than five papers claimed him as their own, including the *New York Herald* and the *Chicago Tribune.* In reality, besides the *Bismarck Tribune*, he did contribute to several St. Paul papers and probably the Western Associated Press. Kellogg wrote in his most quoted and last dispatch, "We leave the Rosebud tomorrow and by the time this reaches you we will have met and fought the red devils, and what result remains to be seen. I will go with Custer and will be at [sic] the death."

Kellogg had little to write about prior to his last battle. His dispatches portrayed Custer with sycophantic zeal—brave, dashing, and fearless. When Kellogg's horse expired he shifted to a mule. No special favors would be granted him as they continued on to the Little Big Horn. Editor Lounsberry forwarded Kellogg's last dispatches to the *New York Herald*, which published the most complete account of the Custer debacle.

REFERENCES: Oliver Knight. *Following the Indian Wars.* 1960; Lewis O. Saum. "Colonel Custer's Copperhead: The Mysterious Mark Kellogg," *Montana, the Magazine of Western History.* October 1978.

KENDALL, GEORGE WILKINS (1809–1867). Kendall was the most celebrated war correspondent of the Mexican War.* Born in Mount Vernon, New Hampshire, he worked as a printer and for Horace Greeley's *New Yorker* before relocating to New Orleans, where he cofounded the *Picayune* in 1837.

He joined General Zachary Taylor's command soon after the Mexican War broke out in 1846. At the Battle of Chapultepec he was wounded in the leg. During the Battle of Monterrey he captured a Mexican flag and sent it home as a war souvenir to his newspaper. Kendall is credited with inventing General Zachary Taylor's famous order "A little more grape [shot], Captain Bragg."

There was intense competition among members of the press during the conflict. Kendall organized his own pony express service in Mexico to scoop his adversaries. This courier service, better known as "Mr. Kendall's Express," also carried official dispatches. He went on to witness the capture of the San Patricio flag at the Battle of Churubusco, the carnage at Cerro Gordo, and the peace negotiations following the fall of Mexico City. As the lone witness from the press corps at the Battle of Churubusco he reported the desertion trial of the San Patricio battalion.

After the war, Kendall covered revolutions in Europe before returning to Texas and a ranching career. Besides his newspaper reports he wrote *Narrative of the Texas Santa Fe Expedition* (1844) and collaborated with Carl Nebel on *War Between the United States and Mexico* (1851).

REFERENCES: Fayette Copeland. *Kendall of the Picayune*. 1943; Martha Sandweis, Rick Stewart, and Ben Huseman. *Eyewitness to War: Prints and Daguerreotypes of the Mexican War, 1846–1848*. 1989.

KENICHI, KIMURA (1905–1973). Born in Hiroshima, he was an army photographer when he was assigned to document the aftermath of the atomic bombing of his hometown. The Tokyo Medical Army Museum requested that he photograph the wounded of the city. His wife perished in the attack. His work has been published in the *Chugoku* newspaper.

REFERENCE: Frances Fralin, ed. *The Indelible Image*. 1985.

KENNAN, GEORGE (1845–1924). Kennan was born in Norwalk, Ohio. His father was a lawyer, enamored of the technology of the electric telegraph. He passed his preoccupation with telegraphy to his son, who demonstrated an early proficiency in its use. Rebuffed in his attempts to enlist in the American Civil War,* Kennan worked as a military telegrapher in Cincinnati. His expertise brought him to the attention of the Western Union Telegraph Company, which selected the twenty-year-old Kennan as a member of its Siberian expedition team, whose purpose was to survey a possible telegraph route from the United States to Siberia by way of Alaska and the Bering Strait. The expedition concluded two years later when word arrived that the Atlantic cable had successfully been introduced. Kennan's exploits are chronicled in *Tent Life in Siberia* (1870), published to wide acclaim.

He returned to Russia in 1870 to study the culture and traditions of the Caucasus region. He became an acknowledged authority on Russia and was a highly sought-out lecturer. He wrote *Siberia and the Exile System* (1891), which detailed the abuses of the Romanov government. Its publication had great ramifications for the future Russian Revolution.

Kennan turned to war reporting during the 1898 Spanish-American War.* He covered the Cuban campaign for *Outlook* magazine and volunteered for the Red Cross. His exploits are recounted in *Campaigning in Cuba* (1899). During the Russo-Japanese War* he reported from the Japanese side. Although he never attended college, Kennan became fluent in Russian and a world-respected scholar and journalist. He also wrote *The Tragedy of Pelée* (1902), the story of the devastating Martinique eruption; *Folk-Tales of Napoleon* (1902), which is based on folk tales surrounding the march on Moscow; and a biography of E. H. Harriman.
REFERENCES: Charles H. Brown. *The Correspondents' War*. 1967; *DAB*.

KENNEDY, EDWARD (1905–1963). Born in Brooklyn, New York, and educated at Carnegie Tech, in 1931 he joined the Paris bureau of the *Herald Ledger* after stints with several other papers. The following year he joined the Associated Press. Kennedy covered the Spanish Civil War* and the developing conflict in the Balkans and the Middle East. In 1940 he was with General Archibald Wavell's British Expeditionary Force sent to help the Greek resistance when German parachutists captured Crete. He was the only American reporter to witness the British capture of Tobruk. He later reported the Italian campaign and the landing at Anzio. In 1945 he promised to delay reporting the capitulation of the Germans for twenty-four hours, but he broke his pledge and was fired by the AP and stripped of his press credentials. Following the war he worked for newspapers in Santa Barbara and Monterey, California.
REFERENCE: John Hohenberg. *Foreign Correspondence*. 1964.

KERTESZ, ANDRE (b. 1894). Born in Budapest, Hungary, Kertesz graduated from the Academy of Commerce in 1912 and entered business. He showed an early proclivity for photography and in 1914 was drafted into the Hungarian army. He barely escaped death in 1915 during World War I* when shot near the heart on the Polish front, resulting in paralysis of his left hand for a year. Following experimental surgery he regained its full use. He took his first war photographs during the war, few of which have survived.

In the 1930s he became a serious freelance photographer while covering the Spanish Civil War* and in 1936 moved to the United States and began his relationship with Condé Nast publications. He went on to photograph World War II* and the Korean War.*
REFERENCE: Robert E. Hood. *12 at War*. 1967.

KESSEL, DMITRI (b. 1902). The Russian-born war photographer* was serving in the Ukraine army when one of his superiors smashed his camera over his

head, outraged at Kessel's photographing of the massacre of a Polish army unit. In 1923 he moved to the United States and joined the staff of *Life*. He covered the Greek Civil War, the German retreat during World War II,* and conflicts in the Middle East and the Congo.
REFERENCE: Frances Fralin, ed. *The Indelible Image*. 1985.

KHALDEI, YEVGENI (b. 1916). Khaldei covered the greatest battles of the Russian theater of World War II.* Reporting for TASS News Agency and *Pravda*, he covered the conflict in Rumania, Bulgaria, Yugoslavia, Austria, and finally Berlin. He was present at the Potsdam Conference and the Nuremberg trials. Following the war he joined the magazine *Soviet Culture*, or *Sovyetskaya Kultura*.
REFERENCE: Daniela Mrazkova and Vladimir Remes, eds. *The Russian War: 1941–1945*. 1975.

KILGALLIN, JAMES LAWRENCE (1888–1982). Born in Pittston, Pennsylvania, he attended college in Chicago, where he entered journalism with the *Chicago Tribune*. After stints with several smaller papers he joined the International News Service in 1921. Following the attack on Pearl Harbor he went to Honolulu and later covered the Pacific theater with the navy. Kilgallin would see action in almost every theater of operations, including Africa, Italy, France, Germany, and the Pacific. In 1944 he reported the Italian campaign and was made INS chief in Naples. He accompanied Allied forces during the capture of Rome. He was among the twenty-one media representatives selected to witness the German unconditional surrender to the Allies in May 1945.
REFERENCE: Robert W. Desmond. *Tides of War*. 1984.

KILGORE, MARGARET (?). Following graduation from Syracuse University, Kilgore spent fifteen years with the UPI, covering the congressional and White House beat for half the time. Interested more in the politics of war than in actual warfare, she arrived in South Vietnam for UPI in 1970. She had the misfortune of arriving at the same time that America was reducing its presence in Vietnam, making it difficult to gain access to air transportation that was formerly accessible to war correspondents. As the war crossed the borders into neighboring countries reporters were faced with strict censorship in Laos and a dearth of communication facilities in Cambodia, where correspondents had to make it to Phnom Penh to transmit dispatches.

Although she considered herself more an observer and political commentator than an actual war reporter, this did not save her from confronting firsthand the horrors of war. During her tenure in the supposedly safe confines of South Vietnam she survived a midnight rocket attack and a near miss by enemy fire while aloft in a helicopter. By 1971 an alarming trend was developing as correspondents were being killed and captured on a regular basis. She returned to

the States after covering the 1971 South Vietnamese elections and left foreign reporting for public relations work.
REFERENCE: Virginia Elwood-Akers. *Women War Correspondents in the Vietnam War, 1961–1975.* 1988.

KILLING FIELDS, THE. The 1984 motion picture *The Killing Fields* was based on the wartime experiences of *New York Times* reporter Sydney Schanberg.* Schanberg was the recipient of the Pulitzer Prize for his coverage of the war in Cambodia. In the film, war reporter Schanberg returns to the United States after the conflict and is faced with the reality that his journalistic aspirations might have been responsible for the death of his interpreter and friend Dith Pran. Schanberg embarks on a Conradian odyssey of repentance in an attempt to find his loyal assistant.
REFERENCE: Howard Good. *The Image of War Correspondents in Anglo-American Fiction.* 1986.

KINGSLEY, MARY (1862–1900). Known primarily for her exploits as an explorer in West Africa, she covered the Boer War* for the *Morning Post* in 1900. In addition to her duties as a special correspondent, Kingsley volunteered to minister to sick Boer soldiers. She became ill with enteric fever and died on Whitmonday, 1900, at the age of thirty-eight. She was buried at sea at her request. She is best known for her works *West African Studies* (1899) and *Travels in West Africa* (1897).
REFERENCE: Robert Wilkinson-Latham. *From Our Special Correspondent.* 1979.

KINGSTON, WILLIAM BEATTY (1837–1900). Kingston became the Berlin correspondent for the *Daily Telegraph* in the 1860s. He would spend a decade reporting from Central Europe, including Vienna, and in 1870 he covered the Prussian army during the Franco-Prussian War.* Accompanying the Prussian army, he was with the headquarters staff in Versailles when the siege of Paris began. There he managed his greatest coup, scooping his British competitors with news of the fall of Paris. In 1877 he covered the Russian side during the Russo-Turkish War.*
REFERENCE: Robert W. Desmond. *The Information Process.* 1978.

KINNEAR, ALFRED (d. 1912). One of the most widely traveled war correspondents of the Victorian era, when not attached to the Central News Agency he reported for such papers as the *Pall Mall Gazette* and *Chambers' Journal.* His career spanned conflicts in North and South America, India, China, Russia, Japan, and West Africa. As the veteran reporter for the Central News Agency he reported the Boer War* from Magersfontein to the capture of Bloemfontein, covering most of the battles of the war, including Belmont, Graspian, and the Modder River. He wrote *To Modder River* (1900) and *Across Many Seas* (1902).
REFERENCE: Robert Wilkinson-Latham. *From Our Special Correspondent.* 1979.

KINROSS, ALBERT (1870–1929). The London-based Kinross covered the Russo-Japanese War* for the *Morning Post.* Following the war he left journalism to become a novelist. He returned to journalism during World War I,* serving as a captain in France and the Middle East, where he set up the *Balkan News* and the *Palestine News* for the armed forces.
REFERENCE: Dennis Griffiths, ed. *The Encyclopedia of the British Press.* 1992.

KIPLING, JOSEPH RUDYARD (1865–1936). Kipling's name is synonymous with the literature of the British Empire. He worked as a reporter for the Lahore-based *Civil and Military Gazette* in 1882, and in the following years the imperialist-minded reporter attained literary acclaim with such works as *Soldiers Three* (1890) and *Plain Tales from the Hill* (1886). His articles continued to appear in the leading British periodicals. While he was stationed in South Africa in 1900 the Boer War* started. Offered a huge sum by the *Daily Mail* to act as its war correspondent, Kipling joined the staff of the *Bloemfontein Friend,* the official army newspaper. He continued his prodigious literary output after the war, receiving many accolades, many of which he refused. He became the first English writer to be awarded the Nobel Prize in 1907. Following his death on January 18, 1936, he was laid to rest in Westminster Abbey.
REFERENCES: *DNB*; Joseph J. Mathews. *Reporting the Wars.* 1957.

KIRKPATRICK, HELEN (b. 1909). Born in Rochester, New York, Kirkpatrick was educated at Smith College and the University of Geneva. Following graduation she worked for the Geneva-based *Research Bulletin.* A hub for international news, Kirkpatrick made contacts with various newspapers. Soon after, she quit the *Bulletin* to work as a stringer* for the *Manchester Guardian,* the *London Daily Telegraph,* and the *New York Herald Tribune.* During World War II* she served as foreign correspondent for the *Chicago Daily News* in London from 1939 to 1944. Through her well-placed connections she scooped her competitors with her prediction that Hitler was preparing to invade neutral Belgium. Well informed on international issues, she wrote *This Terrible Peace* (1938) and *Under the British Umbrella* (1939).

In London she witnessed the blitz and quickly achieved a reputation as one of the best journalists in Europe. However, when Edward R. Murrow* attempted to hire her, he was overruled by CBS, which opted for a younger, inexperienced, and more important, male correspondent named Charles Collingwood,* who would go on to a stellar career in this field. Kirkpatrick was disappointed, but continued to cover the war.

In 1942 Kirkpatrick and Mary Welsh* became the first women to be accredited to accompany the Allied forces. She accompanied the Free French forces, covering the Normandy invasion and the liberation of Paris. In the later stages of the war she reported Allied operations from North Africa to Italy, in France, and at the end of the war, in Germany. After the war Kirkpatrick joined the *New York Daily Post* and continued her journalism career.

REFERENCES: Julia Edwards. *Women of the World.* 1989; Frederick S. Voss. *Reporting the War.* 1994.

KLUCKHOLN, FRANK (1907–1970). Born in St. Paul, Minnesota, and educated at the University of Minnesota and in Spain, he joined the *St. Paul Dispatch* in 1926 and then the *Boston Globe* in 1929. Later that year he moved to the *New York Times.* Kluckholn covered the Spanish Civil War* in 1936 from the insurgent side. He was the first to get the news out that Italian and German planes manned by pilots from those countries had reached Spain. When Franco found out about this news scoop, Kluckholn was stripped of his accreditation by the insurgents and narrowly escaped with his life. He was a presidential correspondent in the years leading up to World War II.* He reported the war beginning in 1942, when he landed with Allied forces in North Africa. At the conclusion of the campaign he was assigned to the Pacific theater in New Guinea, where he witnessed the marine landing at New Britain.

In 1943 he returned to North Africa to cover the Allied landings at Casablanca, Oran, and Algiers. He reported the clashes with Vichy forces and flew with paratroopers who captured an airfield near the Algerian-Tunisian border. Kluckholn arrived in Casablanca shortly before the conference met, but became embroiled in a controversy over censorship and was disciplined by being barred from the front for ten days. He was with the U.S. First Army as it ended German and Italian resistance in Tunisia. Following the Japanese surrender he interviewed Emperor Hirohito.

REFERENCE: Robert W. Desmond. *Tides of War.* 1984.

KNICKERBOCKER, HUBERT RENFRE (1898–1949). Born in Texas and educated at Columbia University and in Europe, Knickerbocker began his newspaper career in 1920 on the staff of the *Newark Morning Ledger.* In 1924 he went to Germany as a foreign correspondent for the *New York Evening Sun Post* and the *Philadelphia Public Ledger.* He was awarded the Pulitzer Prize in 1931 for correspondence and in 1935 began covering the Ethiopian War* for the International News Service (INS) in Addis Ababa. Knickerbocker moved on to the Spain next, where he covered the outbreak of the Spanish Civil War.* At one point he was among several correspondents abducted by rebels and declared missing for several days.

In 1941 he joined the *Chicago Sun* as director of foreign service and the following year was covering the war in the Far East from Java and Sumatra. Knickerbocker fled to San Francisco as the Japanese seized the East Indies. He next covered the developing Pacific war from Honolulu, Batavia, and then Australia. In 1942 he covered the Allied landings in North Africa. Two years later he was accredited to Allied Force Headquarters (US–UK) during the Italian campaign and in June of that year covered the invasion of France. He witnessed the capture of the port of Cherbourg from bluffs overlooking the city. Knickerbocker wrote seven books dealing with the repercussions of the war.

REFERENCE: Robert W. Desmond. *Tides of War.* 1984.

KNIGHT, EDWARD FREDERICK (1852–1925). The Cambridge-educated Knight was a successful barrister, soldier, and journalist. Joining the *Morning Post*, he reported conflicts from many parts of the world beginning in the early 1870s before answering the call of the bar. In 1891, he returned to journalism, covering the Hunza-Nagar campaign for the *Times*. Throughout the 1890s he was in constant action, covering the conflict in Matabeleland (1893–1895), the French seizure of Madagascar (1895), the Sudan campaigns of 1896–1898, the Greco-Turkish War,* and the Spanish-American War.*

He was reporting the Boer War* for the *Morning Post* when he was severely wounded in the right arm while covering Lord Methuen's forces at an engagement near Belmont. Shortly after, the arm was amputated at the shoulder on November 23, 1900. After his recovery, his final battlefield reports came from the Russo-Japanese War* in 1904 and the conflict in Turkey in 1908. His experiences as a war correspondent are chronicled in *Letters from the Sudan* (1897) and *Reminiscences: the Wanderings of a Yachtsman and War Correspondent* (1923).

REFERENCES: F. Lauriston Bullard. *Famous War Correspondents*. 1914; Robert Wilkinson-Latham. *From Our Special Correspondent*. 1979.

KNOX, THOMAS WALLACE (1835–1896). Born in Pembroke, New Hampshire, Knox followed his father into the shoe-making trade before becoming a teacher and establishing his own academy in Kingston, New Hampshire. He followed a gold strike to Colorado in 1860 and became a reporter for the *Denver Daily News*. With the outbreak of the American Civil War,* he enlisted in the Union Army and served in the southwestern theater. Knox covered the 1861 Missouri campaign for the *New York Herald*. He was present at the Battle of Wilson's Creek, and in 1862 he witnessed a gunboat battle near Memphis. He was wounded and after returning to active duty served on the staff of the California National Guard.

Like many reporters during the war, Knox earned the wrath of General Sherman for his reporting and was actually court-martialed for disobeying orders. Following the edict known as General Order No. 8, all civilians were excluded from army encampments, and anyone who reported the western campaign on the Mississippi River near Vicksburg would be arrested and treated as a spy. For violating this proclamation Knox lost his accreditation and returned to civilian life in New York. A sample of his wartime dispatches is collected in *Camp-fire and Cotton-field* (1865).

In 1866 he was again in the employ of the *Herald* when he accompanied a Western Union expedition on its attempt to survey a telegraph route from America to Siberia. His main accomplishment during this adventure was gaining a patent for transmitting battlefield plans by telegraph. His account of this survey was published as *Overland Through Asia* (1870). An inveterate tinkerer, he invented an instrument for telegraphing by Morse code the exact location of each bullet's impact on a target. In the late 1870s he explored parts of the Far

East and continued to produce a couple of books a year. He wrote numerous travel books for young boys.
REFERENCES: J. Cutler Andrews. *The North Reports the Civil War.* 1955; *DAB.*

KOESTLER, ARTHUR (1905–1983). Born in Budapest, Hungary, and educated at the University of Vienna, Koestler spent stints as a foreign correspondent in the Middle East and Europe. In 1932 he became a member of the Communist Party and after visiting the Soviet Union covered the Spanish Civil War* for the *News Chronicle* in 1937. He was among the correspondents who reported the conflict from both sides. After reporting from the Republican side he was captured by the Fascist insurgents following the fall of Málaga, and sentenced to be executed for spying. After a hundred days on death row he was exchanged for another prisoner. His experiences in Spain are chronicled in *Spanish Gladiators* (1937), which was published five years later in America as *Dialogue with Death*, and *The Gladiators* (1939). He had resigned from the Communist Party by the time the second book was published.

During World War II* Koestler served in the French and British armies. Although he wrote exclusively in German until his mid-thirties, he became a leading English-language writer after moving to England in 1940. He wrote several novels and works of nonfiction. He was granted permanent residence in the United States by a special act of Congress in 1951. During the 1960s he wrote for the *Observer*.
REFERENCE: Robert W. Desmond. *Tides of War.* 1984.

KOREAN WAR. On June 25, 1950, Communist North Korean troops crossed the thirty-eighth parallel and invaded South Korea, inaugurating the Korean War. Almost simultaneously, journalists began to arrive from the United States and from the Tokyo bureaus. Prior to the war there were only twenty-seven correspondents accredited with the Far East Command. Over the first few months of the war about 280 correspondents from nineteen different countries came to Korea. However, it is estimated that less than a quarter of that number were at the front at the same time. Several hundred more would join their ranks by the end of the war three years later.

The only regular journalist in Korea when the invasion began was *Chicago Tribune* correspondent Walter Simmons.* Simmons had arrived in Seoul to cover the South Korean national assembly and had decided to stay over a couple of extra days. His scoop was the first by someone other than a wire service reporter. Among the first to respond was veteran correspondent Keyes Beech,* who reported the fighting at the Changjin reservoir. Other American correspondents included Hal Boyle, Don Whitehead,* Stan Swinton, Bill Shinn, Relman Morin,* and Tom Lambert* for the Associated Press; Homer Bigart* and Marguerite Higgins* for the *New York Herald Tribune*; Jim Lucas* for Scripps-Howard; Phillip Potter for the *Baltimore Sun*; Carl Mydans* for *Life* magazine; Bob Considine for Hearst newspapers; Edward R. Murrow* for CBS; Hal

Levine for *Newsweek*; and Peter Kalischer,* Peter Webb, and Rutherford Poats for the UP. In 1951 Higgins, Beech, Bigart, Morin, Fred Sparks of the *Chicago Daily News*, and Whitehead received Pulitzer Prizes for their reporting of the Korean War. Three other Pulitzers would be awarded over the final two years of the conflict.

Numerous British correspondents could be found among the foreign press corps, including Christopher Buckley* of the *Daily Telegraph*, Ward Price* of the *Daily Mail*, James Cameron* of *Picture Post*, René Cutforth of the BBC, Ian Morrison* of the *Times*, and Jack Percival of *News Chronicle*. Cameron was assisted by veteran photographer Bert Hardy.* Among the more critical journalists concerning American war aims were Cameron and Reginald Thompson of the *Daily Telegraph* and author of the 1951 book *Cry Korea*, a vitriolic account of the war and his fellow journalists.

Correspondents faced myriad problems including censorship and poor communications. At one command post seventy reporters had to share one military telephone to Japan. Soon after the outbreak of hostilities General MacArthur instituted a policy of self-censorship, which he explained as the only recourse because of the dearth of qualified censors. Correspondents were never completely sure what information would be construed as giving aid and comfort to the enemy. This system was arbitrary, resulting in several unjust prosecutions for violating censorship restrictions. MacArthur was later forced to set up a more conventional system. According to a Reuters* journalist, "Ninety percent of the correspondents in Korea have indicated they would prefer open censorship" to MacArthur's capricious system.

Unlike previous wars, correspondents felt there was no place to hide, which meant that if you were in the field you were consistently under attack. According to one reporter, "It was not like other wars. In other wars you had a pretty good idea of where the enemy was and where you were. In Korea you didn't."

Journalists were assisted by the Army Signal Corps, which operated two radio-teletype machines enabling dispatches to reach Tokyo from Korea in less than two hours; this compared with twelve to twenty-four hours at the outset. The best coverage of the war was provided by the *New York Herald Tribune* team of Bigart and Higgins, who received as much publicity for their much-publicized feud as they did for their Pulitzer Prize–winning reportage.

The Korean War was considered one of the more hazardous frontline assignments, with six American correspondents losing their lives in July 1950 alone. On July 10, Ray Richards of the INS and Ernie Peeler of *Stars and Stripes** were the first two correspondents to die when their position was overrun by North Korean troops. When Albert Hinton of the *Norfolk Journal and Guide* was killed in a plane crash on July 27, he became the first black war correspondent killed during the three major wars of the first half of the twentieth century. By the time the conflict ended in 1953, of the total of 350 correspondents accredited to the United Nations headquarters in Korea a total of eighteen correspondents and photographers had perished, including ten Americans.

REFERENCES: Michael Emery. *On the Front Lines*. 1995; John Hohenberg. *Foreign Correspondence: The Great Reporters and Their Times*. 1964; Phillip Knightley. *The First Casualty*. 1975; Trevor Royle. *War Report: The War Correspondent's View of Battle from the Crimea to the Falklands*. 1987; M. L. Stein. *Under Fire*. 1968.

KUDOYAROV, BORIS (1903–1973). Kudoyarov was one of the pioneers of Soviet photojournalism. He became a platoon deputy commander in the Red Army during the Civil War while still in his teens. Prior to the outbreak of World War II* he wrote for several news magazines. During the war he was a foreign correspondent for the Moscow-based *Pravda*. As the only photographer to survive and record the entire 900-day siege of Leningrad, he produced an incredible photographic account of a battle in which one thousand Russians died each day. Ironically, he died in a peacetime motor vehicle accident while working in Tashkent.

REFERENCES: Jorge Lewinski. *The Camera at War*. 1978; Daniela Mrazkova and Vladimir Remes, eds. *The Russian War: 1941–1945*. 1975.

L

LABOUCHERE, HENRY "LABBY" DU PRE (1831–1912). After graduating from Cambridge in the early 1850s Labouchere traveled widely throughout the United States. Upon his return to Europe he entered the British diplomatic service, and after stints in Russia, Sweden, Prussia, Italy, and Turkey, he returned to England, where he became a member of Parliament and in 1868 part owner of the *London Daily News*. Labouchere covered the Franco-Prussian War* for his newspaper after he found himself trapped in Paris when the siege broke out in 1870, and remained in the city for four months. His reports were smuggled through the Prussian siege forces by means of a not so dependable balloon service. His dispatches appeared in his paper and the *New York Tribune* under his initials "H. L." Following the war his letters were collected and published in *Diary of a Besieged Resident*. In 1877 he began publishing a weekly magazine called the *Truth*.

REFERENCES: Robert W. Desmond. *The Information Process*. 1978; *DNB*, 1912–1922.

LADYSMITH, SIEGE OF. From November 2, 1899, to February 28, 1900, the city of Ladysmith, Natal, was besieged by a force of five thousand Boer farmers. Close to twelve thousand British soldiers were reduced to slaughtering their horses for food during the two-month-long siege. Also inside were eight British war correspondents, including Henry W. Nevinson* and George Lynch* of the *Daily Mail*, William T. Maud* of the *Graphic*, John Stuart of the *Morning Post*, Harry Pearse* and Ernest Smith* of the *Daily News*, William Maxwell* of the *Standard*, Melton Prior* of the *Illustrated London News*, and Lionel James* of the *Times*. In addition George W. Steevens* of the *Daily Mail* perished from enteric disease. Lynch managed to escape, while Winston Churchill* was captured near Ladysmith shortly after the siege was under way.

Correspondents resorted to every type of innovation to get their dispatches out of the besieged town. Some used a British heliograph service, a form of code system, but newspapers were restricted to only thirty words per day. Others hired Kaffir couriers to attempt to break through Boer siege lines. Steevens and Prior reportedly paid a runner more than $400 at one point.

REFERENCES: Robert W. Desmond. *The Information Process.* 1978; Kenneth Griffith. *Thank God We Kept the Flag Flying: The Siege and Relief of Ladysmith.* 1974.

LAMBERT, TOM (?). Lambert covered the Korean War* for the Associated Press. He found himself trapped along with reporters Marguerite Higgins,* Keyes Beech,* and Gordon Walker at the tiny airport of Suwon, as North Korean troops advanced toward it. Lambert and Beech attained a measure of heroism when they rescued a jet fighter pilot who had crashed his plane near the airport. The correspondents made it to safety three days ahead of the invading forces. At one point Lambert was barred along with Peter Kalischer* from covering the front when he characterized an army battalion as the "lost battalion" because of its high death counts and confusion surrounding its status. He was later reinstated. His assignment was not without its risks, as demonstrated when he broke his foot. He later reported the Israeli Six Day War from Lebanon.

REFERENCE: Michael Emery. *On the Front Lines.* 1995.

LANDELLS, ROBERT THOMAS (1833–1877). Trained as an engraver, the London-born war artist-correspondent* covered his first action for the *Illustrated London News* when he was sent to report the end of the Crimean War* in 1856. In 1863 he reported the war between Denmark and Prussia over Schleswig-Holstein and received decorations from both armies.

In 1866 he was attached to the staff of the Prussian crown prince during the Austro-Prussian War.* Landells put his knowledge of Prussian affairs to good use when he covered the Franco-Prussian War* in 1870–1871. Fluent in German, Landells joined the Prussian staff at Versailles and was with Prussian forces throughout the siege of Paris. He was rewarded for his services as an artist and ambulance driver with the Prussian Cross and Bavarian Cross for valor. Following the conflict he gave up war reporting and returned to his painting career.

REFERENCES: Dennis Griffiths, ed. *The Encyclopedia of the British Press.* 1992; Pat Hodgson. *The War Illustrators.* 1977.

LANDON, PERCIVAL (1869–1927). As special correspondent for the *Times*, the Oxford-educated Landon first saw action covering the Boer War* in 1900. In between practicing law and a short-lived position as assistant to the governor of New South Wales, he covered the British expedition to Tibet for the *Times*. Joining the *Daily Telegraph* in 1905, over the next twenty years he rose to become one of its most respected staff writers. Prior to World War I* he covered conflicts in Russia, Egypt, Sudan, and Mesopotamia. During World War I he was assigned to the western front (1914–1915) and the Italian campaigns. Following the war he covered the Peace Conference and continued to report from the Middle and Far East. Among his books are *Lhasa* (1905) and *The Story of the Indian Mutiny* (1907).

REFERENCES: Robert W. Desmond. *The Information Process.* 1978; Dennis Griffiths, ed. *The Encyclopedia of the British Press.* 1992.

LANGHAM, SAMUEL F. (1866–1898). One of the most popular and experienced war correspondents of the Press Club, he covered the Ashanti War in 1873. He went on to report the Sudan campaign for the *Morning Post* and *Black and White* and the Abyssinian campaign for the *Daily Mail* (1898). Shortly after Abyssinia, he returned to England in ill health and committed suicide by taking poison and lying down on a busy railway track.

REFERENCE: Dennis Griffiths, ed. *The Encyclopedia of the British Press.* 1992.

LARDNER, DAVID (d. 1945). A son of noted writer Ring Lardner, he was killed while covering his first war assignment for the *New Yorker* magazine on October 19, 1945. He was riding in a jeep, returning from the captured city of Aachen on the Belgian border, when it struck an antivehicle Teller land mine.

REFERENCE: Robert W. Desmond. *Tides of War.* 1984.

LARDNER, JOHN ABBOTT (1912–1960). A son of the writer Ring Lardner, he was born in Chicago, Illinois. He attended private schools and showed an early proclivity for journalistic writing; a family friend published a column of the ten-year-old Lardner's work. After graduation from Harvard in 1929 he studied at the Sorbonne and worked for the *New York Herald Tribune* for a few months. Upon his return to the States in 1931 he joined the *Herald Tribune* full-time. Less than three years later he quit the paper and was hired by the North American Newspaper Alliance (NANA), an affiliation he would hold until 1948.

He reported World War II* as a war correspondent for *Newsweek*, beginning two months after Pearl Harbor. His coverage appeared throughout the war years under the caption "Lardner Goes to the Wars." He reported from the European and Pacific theaters, the North African and Italian campaigns, and the last major battles at Iwo Jima and Okinawa. During the war years he continued to publish in NANA papers, as well as in major magazines such as the *Saturday Evening Post* and the *New Yorker.* Many of these pieces are collected in *Southwest Passage: The Yanks in the Pacific* (1943).

Lardner lost two brothers during the European conflicts. His brother James was killed fighting for the Loyalists in the Spanish Civil War* and David,* a war correspondent for the *New Yorker*, was killed while covering World War II. Following the war Lardner wrote a variety of articles for the top periodicals. A man of diverse interests, he was best known for his sportswriting. By 1958 his health was in decline due to multiple sclerosis. He fulfilled his prediction that he would die young when he passed away before his forty-eighth birthday.

REFERENCES: *DAB* 6; Ring Lardner, Jr. *The Lardners: My Family Remembered.* 1976; *New York Times.* March 25, 1960.

LARRABEE, CONSTANCE STUART (b. 1914). Born in England, she has been an American citizen since 1953. Larrabee became South Africa's first woman war correspondent in World War II.* She was accredited to the South African magazine *Libertas* as a war photographer.* Larrabee covered the European theater during the last two years of the war. Her illustrated war diary, *Jeep Trek*, was published in 1946. She has developed an international reputation for her coverage of World War II and tribal documentary photography.
REFERENCE: Frances Fralin, ed. *The Indelible Image: Photographs of War—1846 to the Present.* 1985.

LATHROP, BARBOUR (1846–1927). Born in Virginia and educated at Harvard, Lathrop was the only war correspondent of the American Indian Wars* to come from a background of wealth. In July 1876, several years after moving to San Francisco, he went out to the frontier to report the aftermath of the Custer story. He joined General George Crook's Sioux campaign as a representative of the *San Francisco Evening Bulletin.* However, the spartan conditions and poor management of Crook's command led Lathrop to transfer to Alfred Terry's for the remainder of the campaign. Most of Lathrop's reports emphasize the grumbling of the soldiers rather than any actual combat. By September Lathrop was on his way back to San Francisco as the expedition grounded to a halt.

    After inheriting a fortune later in life he became a philanthropist and supporter of the plant importations of horticulturist David G. Fairchild. Lathrop took the entomologist and plant explorer on a trip around the world and continued to finance his travels after Fairchild created the Section of Seed and Plant Introduction for the Department of Agriculture. As a result, seedless raisin grapes from Italy, Chilean avocados, nectarines, new varieties of okra, onions, red peppers, cucumbers, and peanuts became staples of the American kitchen.
REFERENCE: Oliver Knight. *Following the Indian Wars.* 1960.

LAURENT, MICHEL (1945–1975). Born in France, Laurent was employed as a war photographer* for the Associated Press and then the Paris-based Gamma Photo Agency. He covered conflict in Africa, the Middle East, and Asia, including the Nigerian civil war and the 1973 Arab-Israeli War. In 1972 he shared the Pulitzer Prize with Horst Faas* of the Associated Press for photo coverage of soldiers bayonetting traitors during the 1971 India-Pakistan War. Their widely published photo essay was entitled ''Death in Dacca.'' Laurent covered his last war in 1975 when he became the last journalist killed during the Vietnam War.*
REFERENCE: Turner Browne and Elaine Partnow. *Macmillan's Encyclopedia of Photographic Artists and Innovators.* 1983.

LAWLESS, PETER (1890–1945). The former professional rugby player was killed in action while reporting the war in Europe for the *Daily Telegraph*. Formerly a sports reporter for the *Morning Post*, he joined the *Daily Telegraph* in 1937. Between September 1939 and May 1940 he accompanied the Royal Air Force in France. He joined the Army Intelligence Corps after the fall of France in 1940. In 1944 he returned to the *Telegraph* as a special correspondent with the American First Army after the Normandy Invasion. He was killed by shell fire in March 1945, while covering the taking of the Remagen bridge, one of the last intact bridges over the Rhine River. As one of the last journalistic casualties in the war, his death brought the number of Allied newspapermen killed in action to forty-six—sixteen British and thirty American.
REFERENCE: Dennis Griffiths, ed. *The Encyclopedia of the British Press*. 1992.

LAWLEY, FRANCIS CHARLES (1825–1901). Born in Yorkshire, England, and educated at Oxford, the wellborn Lawley joined the *London Times* in 1862 after a brief political career which included a stint in Parliament and a position as private secretary to Chancellor of the Exchequer and future prime minister Gladstone. He was assigned to replace W. H. Russell* as ''special correspondent'' covering the Southern side of the American Civil War* after Russell was recalled for angering federal authorities with his unflattering portrayal of the Confederate rout of Union troops at the First Battle of Bull Run.

Lawley became a sympathetic admirer of the Southern war effort. As ''special correspondent'' he wrote approximately one hundred letters for the *Times*, which appeared under the heading of ''The Southern Confederacy'' or the ''Confederate States.'' His coverage of the Battles of Fredericksburg (1862), Chancellorsville (1863), and Gettysburg (1863) are considered classics. His close relationships with Generals Lee, Stuart, and Longstreet accorded him the rare opportunity to observe these battles with the Confederate leaders from the best vantage spots. One source claimed that he was the only correspondent to witness the wounding of Jackson at Chancellorsville, the surrender at Appomattox, and the final meeting between Lee and Longstreet. Lawley had his detractors as well, who labeled him a propagandist for the Confederacy. After the Civil War he returned to England to accept a better-paying position with the *Daily Telegraph*. In 1870, he covered the Franco-Prussian War.*
REFERENCE: William Stanley Hoole. *Lawley Covers the Confederacy*. 1964.

LAWRENCE, WILLIAM H. (1916–1972). Lawrence was born in Lincoln, Nebraska, and entered journalism after dropping out of the University of Nebraska. After stints with several papers he joined the United Press in 1936 and five years later moved over to the *New York Times*. After reassignment to Moscow in 1943 he visited the site of the Babi Yar massacre in Kiev and the Majdanek concentration camp near Lublin, Poland. He subsequently covered the war in the Pacific in Guam and Okinawa and was an observer on bombing raids over Japan. He landed in Japan with the occupation forces in 1945.

Lawrence was known as "Political Bill" at his paper to differentiate him from fellow reporter William H. Laurence, whose moniker was "Atomic Bill." Following World War II* he reported from Eastern Europe and South America and covered the Korean War* for the *Times*. Later he served as Washington correspondent for the *Times* and as White House correspondent for ABC beginning in 1961.
REFERENCES: Robert W. Desmond. *Tides of War*. 1984; Library of America. *Reporting World War II*. 1995.

LEA, TOM (b. 1907). The El Paso muralist was already a well-known artist when he was hired as artist-correspondent* by *Life* magazine to cover World War II.* He accompanied Allied troops to North Africa, the Pacific, and China. His battlefield sketches were turned into grim oil paintings of war once he was back in the studio. One of his most graphic paintings depicts the assault on the Pacific island of Peleliu in September 1944. When his controversial painting *The Price* appeared in *Life* magazine an avalanche of letters protested the publication of an injured marine covered in blood. His combat experiences are recounted in *A Grizzly from the Coral Sea* (1944) and *Peleliu Landing* (1945). Besides his paintings, Lea also wrote several highly praised books, including *The King Ranch* (1957) and *The Brave Bulls* (1949).
REFERENCE: Anne Dingus. "War Paint," *Texas Monthly*. August 1994.

LEDERER, EDITH M. (b. 1943). Educated at Cornell and Stanford, Edie Lederer joined the Associated Press in 1966. Six years later she was assigned to Saigon and in 1973 covered the Arab-Israeli War from Egypt and Syria, reporting some of the major tank battles of the conflict. In 1975 she became the first woman to head a foreign bureau for the AP when she was assigned the Peru office. However, five months later she was expelled by the military government there for writing an unflattering piece about a military training exercise. From 1978 to 1981 she was based in Hong Kong. In June 1980 she covered the Soviet invasion of Afghanistan briefly and later reported the Falklands War.* In 1990 she completed compulsory physical training in order to qualify for field coverage during the Gulf War.* The only woman correspondent during the conflict who had covered the Vietnam War,* Lederer ended up spending over five months reporting the Gulf War. She was named AP bureau chief in Dharan during the war, marking twenty-five years of service with the news agency.
REFERENCES: Julia Edwards. *Women of the World*. 1989; Anne Sebba. *Battling for News*. 1994.

LEDRU, FILIPPO (?). Ledru was one of the earliest photographer correspondents. He recorded natural disasters such as the 1883 Casamicciola earthquake and the 1887 Etna eruption and covered man-made carnage while documenting the Italian colonial experience of the late nineteenth century. He was with Italian

troops in the advance on Massawa in 1885 and in 1896 during the Battle of Adwa, where he lost all of his photographic equipment.
REFERENCE: Nicolas Monti, ed. *Africa Then*. 1987.

LEE, CLARK (1907–1953). The son of the founder of the United Press was born in Oakland, California. After attending Rutgers University he joined the Newark bureau of the Associated Press and in 1933 he took over the Mexico City bureau. From 1939 until 1941 he covered the Japanese side during the invasion of China. He was warned to leave Shanghai by Japanese officers three weeks before Pearl Harbor. He had barely reached Manila when it fell to Japanese forces. Lee was able to escape to Corregidor. His notes and dispatches from the siege of Corregidor were collected and published as *Bataan Bylines* in 1942. Lee was able to escape to Australia before Corregidor fell. Out of the five hundred correspondents in England hoping to cover the Normandy invasion, Lee was one of the twenty-eight allowed to accompany the landing. He served as a roving correspondent for the International News Service covering the occupation of Japan following the war. He died of a heart attack in California at the age of forty-six. He recounted his exploits in the Philippines in his book *They Call It Pacific*.
REFERENCE: John Hohenberg. *Foreign Correspondence*. 1964.

LE HIR, GEORGES (?). Le Hir wrote perhaps the best account of the 1916 Battle of Verdun during World War I.* A French journalist, he had joined the staff of Paris bureau of the *New York Times* in 1915.
REFERENCE: Robert W. Desmond. *Windows on the World*. 1980.

LEROY, CATHERINE (b. 1945). The French war photographer* first rose to prominence with her coverage of the Vietnam War* from 1966 to 1968 and subsequent capture by North Vietnamese forces. While held in North Vietnam Leroy was allowed to record daily life behind enemy lines. Arriving in Vietnam with a one-way ticket, intent on becoming a photojournalist, she was hired as a stringer* by Horst Faas,* picture editor for the Associated Press in Vietnam. According to one source, Leroy covered more combat than any other woman correspondent. She garnered attention for her parachute drop with the 173rd Airborne during a battle called "Operation Junction City." Subsequently she was awarded paratroop wings with a gold star making her combat jump. Her coverage of the marine assault on Hill 881 near Khe Sanh was reprinted throughout the world and merited a six-page spread in *Life* magazine.

In May 1967 she was hospitalized after being wounded by shrapnel while with marines near the DMZ. After a month of convalescence she was back in the field and won several awards including the Capa. During the Tet offensive she was trapped in the Communist-controlled part of Hue as it came under fire from South Vietnamese troops. She narrowly averted capture by posing as a neutral French reporter as she made her way to the U.S. military compound.

In 1974 she covered Cyprus and spent the following two years in Lebanon reporting the civil war mainly from the Progressivist side. She has also recorded conflicts in Afghanistan, Africa, and Iran.

REFERENCES: Virginia Elwood-Akers. *Women War Correspondents in the Vietnam War. 1961–1975.* 1988; Frances Fralin, ed. *The Indelible Image.* 1985; Jorge Lewinski. *The Camera at War.* 1978.

LESAGE, SIR JOHN MERRY (1837–1926). Born in Clifton, England, and educated in Bristol, the future editor of the *Daily Telegraph* worked for several small papers before joining the *Telegraph* in 1863. He served as a special correspondent covering the Franco-Prussian War,* while accompanying the Prussian army. His first news scoop was his coverage of the Prussian army entering a defeated Paris in 1871. Shortly after, he reported the Paris Commune. In 1882 he accompanied Sir Garnet Wolseley's expedition against Arabi Pasha. He went on to a forty-year career as managing editor of the *Telegraph.* In 1918 he was awarded a knighthood for his long career in journalism.

REFERENCES: *DNB,* 1922–1930; Dennis Griffiths, ed. *The Encyclopedia of the British Press.* 1992; Robert Wilkinson-Latham. *From Our Special Correspondent.* 1979.

LESEUER, LAURENCE EDWARD (?). The son of a *New York Herald Tribune* correspondent, Leseuer joined the United Press in 1931 following his graduation from New York University. Six years later he went to Europe as a radio commentator for the Columbia Broadcasting System (CBS). During the early years of World War II* he reported the activities of the RAF and the British army in France. Following the French surrender in 1940 he was hired as an assistant to Edward R. Murrow* in the London office of CBS. In the fall of 1941 he was assigned to Russia, where he covered the Russian war from the siege of Moscow, which he referred to as "a correspondent's purgatory," to the relief of Stalingrad. Leseuer was the first radio correspondent to broadcast from Moscow. He recounted these events in *Twelve Months That Changed the World.* In 1944 he reported the Normandy invasion and the liberation of Paris, broadcasting from the city prior to the arrival of French troops. Following the war he continued his foreign correspondence from the Middle East and Africa.

REFERENCE: Robert W. Desmond. *Tides of War.* 1984.

LESLIE, FRANK (1821–1880). Founder of *Leslie's Illustrated Newspaper* and American innovator in pictorial journalism, he was born Henry Carter in Ipswich, England, on March 29, 1821. Artistically inclined, he had several drawings published in the *Illustrated London News* under his pen name "Frank Leslie" in the late 1830s. Immigrating to the United States in 1848, he went to work for several early picture magazines as a wood engraver before launching *Frank Leslie's Ladies' Gazette of Fashion* and the *New York Journal of Romance* in 1854.

In 1855 he established the first successful illustrated news weekly, *Leslie's*

Illustrated Newspaper, which became the most successful of its kind in America. Its rise paralleled and was helped by the opening of the American West and the coverage of the American Civil War.* With the outbreak of the Civil War, Leslie's newspaper was in the position to dominate pictorial news coverage as the most experienced and largest staff of artists and engravers. However, by the end of the war it had lost ground to its competitor *Harper's Weekly*.

During the Civil War *Leslie's Illustrated Newspaper* assumed a strong neutral stance, offering to buy sketches from both Union and Confederate soldiers. The objectivity of Leslie's paper stands in contrast to *Harper's*, which took an increasingly Northern stance, castigating the Southerners as rebels and barbarians. Leslie's newspaper suffered some misfortune when one artist lost months of work while covering the Red River campaign; and after the Battle of Shiloh Henri Lovie,* one of Leslie's most experienced artists, quit the campaign due to exhaustion. At the Battle of Shiloh Lovie produced perhaps his best work, resulting in a sixteen-page spread of his battle sketches. On the other hand *Harper's* was without an artist-correspondent at the battle and was forced to create sketches from newspaper reports. However, Lovie's withdrawal from his post was a severe setback for Leslie. One historian noted that Lovie, Leslie, and Leslie's engravers formed "the outstanding artist-publisher partnership of the war." With Lovie gone Leslie was without an experienced artist in the western theater of the war.

During the Civil War, *Leslie's* would have up to a dozen correspondents in the field at one time. In addition eighty artists produced more than three thousand sketches of battles and military life. Gradually, Leslie's star began to wane. He lost artists such as Thomas Nast* to his competitors, his personal and business life became increasingly complicated, and his policy of nonpartisan coverage of the war lost him many readers.

In 1875 Leslie's enterprises had expanded to twelve different publications. Although his free-spending lifestyle led to bankruptcy in 1877, he continued to manage his journals until his death in 1880.

REFERENCES: *DLB* 43; Budd Leslie Gambee, Jr. *Frank Leslie and His Illustrated Newspaper, 1855–1860.* 1964.

LEWIS, SIR WILMOTT HARSANT (1877–1950). Lewis was born in Cardiff, Wales, and educated at Heidelberg and the Sorbonne. He first entered journalism while traveling in the Far East, reporting the Boxer Rebellion* in 1900 and then the Russo-Japanese War* for the *New York Herald* before moving to the Philippines in 1911, where he began a six-year stint with the *Manila Times*. His international expertise came to the attention of General John Pershing in 1919, when he requested that Lewis come to France to cover the Paris Peace Conference for the American information and propaganda services. From 1920 to 1948 Lewis represented the *Times* as its Washington correspondent. He was knighted in 1931 and died in Washington on January 4, 1950, two years after retirement.

REFERENCES: Robert W. Desmond. *The Information Process.* 1978; *DNB,* 1941–1950.

LIEBLING, ABBOTT JOSEPH "A. J." (1904–1963). Born in New York City, Liebling graduated from Columbia University's Pulitzer School of Journalism in 1925. After jobs with several newspapers he was hired by the *New Yorker* in 1935. During World War II,* beginning in 1939, he covered the London blitz and the invasions of North Africa and Normandy, and in 1944 he witnessed the liberation of Paris. His war reports were published in several collections, *The Road Back to Paris* (1944) and *The Republic of Silence* (1947). In 1952 France awarded him its Legion of Honor medal for his war service. A prolific writer, his wartime articles were collected posthumously in *Mollie and Other War Pieces* in 1964. The overweight gourmand suffered from a variety of maladies, including gout. In 1963 a bout of pneumonia led to heart failure and renal collapse on December 28.

REFERENCES: Library of America. *Reporting World War II: Part Two.* 1995; A. J. Liebling. *Liebling Abroad.* 1981.

LIEFDE, JACOB B. de (1847–1878). Educated in Holland, Liefde was war correspondent for the *Daily News* during the Franco-Prussian War.* Posted to the Prussian army, along with most of the English-based reporters, he worked closely with Archibald Forbes.* He was in Paris for the fall of the Paris Commune. He wrote *Great Dutch Admirals* (1873).

REFERENCE: Dennis Griffiths, ed. *The Encyclopedia of the British Press.* 1992.

THE LIGHT THAT FAILED. Rudyard Kipling's* 1899 novel was published during the so-called golden age of war correspondents. Its protagonist is a young artist-correspondent* named Dick Heldar who is accompanying a British column in the relief of General Charles Gordon at Khartoum. As a result of a head wound suffered while he was engaged in hand-to-hand fighting with the dervishes he loses his sight several months after returning to England. Unable to accompany his friends back to the Sudan in a new campaign against the Mahdi, Heldar catches up to the expedition at the moment the dervishes attack. He asks his friends to be put in the forward defense and he is dropped almost immediately with a bullet through the head.

REFERENCES: Howard Good. *The Image of War Correspondents in Anglo-American Fiction.* 1985; Rudyard Kipling. *The Light That Failed.* 1899.

LINEBAUGH, JOHN H. (d. 1864). Linebaugh was a leading Southern war correspondent during the American Civil War,* whose dispatches were filed under the pen name "Shadow." Prior to the war Linebaugh was an Epsicopal clergyman. The *Memphis Appeal* special correspondent was attending church

services in Chattanooga when Union forces began bombarding the city. He fled the city shortly before the Battle of Chickamauga and in September 1863 his arrest was ordered by General Braxton Bragg, about whom he had written several critical pieces. In late 1864 Linebaugh was on his way to Hood's army to represent the Associated Press Association when he drowned. He was one of only two Southern war reporters to perish in the conflict. Linebaugh was on a steamboat, five days out of Richmond, when it ran aground along the Alabama River. He attempted to swim to shore with other passengers but was lost in the swift current.
REFERENCE: J. Cutler Andrews. *The South Reports the Civil War.* 1970.

LIPSKEROV, GEORGEI (b. 1896). A seasoned photographer at the outset of World War II,* Lipskerov became the oldest Russian photojournalist to record the war. As a member of the staff of a Russian army newspaper he covered the entire war from the battlefront. Unlike other war photographers unencumbered with military affiliation, Lispkerov did not have the opportunity to roam freely; instead he spent the war with his unit. His unit defeated the Sixth Army Corps of Field Marshal Paulus near Stalingrad, affording Lispkerov the chance to take the first pictures of one of the greatest victories of the Russian theater of the war. Following the war he remained active in the field of photography.
REFERENCE: Daniela Mrazkova and Vladimir Remes, eds. *The Russian War: 1941– 1945.* 1975.

LLOYD, JAMES (c. 1828–1913). The British painter and photographer moved to Natal, South Africa, in the early 1850s. He was one of the first two press photographers in Natal. His sketches were reproduced in the *Illustrated London News.* He came to public attention with his photographs from the 1879 Zulu War.
REFERENCE: Frances Fralin, ed *The Indelible Image.* 1985.

LOCHNER, LOUIS PAUL (1897–1975). Born in Springfield, Illinois, and educated at the University of Wisconsin, Lochner joined the Associated Press in 1921 and was AP correspondent in Berlin from the years 1924 to 1941, the last fourteen of which he was bureau chief. In 1939 he was the recipient of the Pulitzer Prize for distinguished correspondence as foreign correspondent and became the first foreign correspondent to follow the German army into Poland. He then covered action on the German western front in Holland, Belgium, and France, where he witnessed the Channel coast action as the Germans advanced on the British at Dunkirk. In 1941 he was with the German army in Yugoslavia, Greece, Finland, and Russia. When Germany declared war on the United States that December, he was interned in Bad Nauheim along with other American correspondents. The following year he was repatriated to America. Shortly after he returned to France. He recounted his life in Germany in the book *What About*

Germany? In March 1945 he accompanied the Allied advance into Germany, but in June was seriously injured in a jeep accident when a Red Army vehicle plowed into it and left without stopping. It took Lochner several weeks to recuperate from a concussion and other injuries.
REFERENCE: Robert W. Desmond. *Tides of War.* 1984.

LONDON, JOHN "JACK" (1876–1916). Born in San Francisco, after a youth filled with poverty and adventure at sea he turned to writing in 1893. After winning an essay-writing contest that year he began to submit stories to various publications with little success. In 1900 his career was jump-started by the publication of the collection of short stories entitled *The Son of the Wolf.*

In 1902 he was hired by the American Press Association to travel to South Africa to report on the Boer War* and its repercussions on British colonies. But he abruptly changed his plans and went to London instead. After several weeks observing life in the crowded slums he wrote *The People of the Abyss.*

Well established as a novelist, London covered his first war in 1904 when he reported the Russo-Japanese War* from Korea for the *New York Journal.* Among the other war correspondents that sailed on the SS *Siberia* with London were Lionel James,* Frederick Palmer,* and James Hare.* The day before he debarked he put the finishing touches on *The Sea Wolf.* Like most correspondents during the war, London was faced with endless restrictions imposed by Japanese authorities. He had several encounters with the Japanese military command, leading to his arrest on two occasions. In one incident he was held for court-martial after he assaulted a Japanese officer. However, he was soon released and headed back to the United States. While he did not witness actual combat, his reports give a vivid description of behind-the-lines activity during the Russo-Japanese War.

In May 1914 London was hired by *Collier's Weekly* magazine to cover the United States marine landing at Veracruz, Mexico. On May 30 he was stricken with dysentery and was forced to return to the United States nine days later. London died just two years later.
REFERENCE: King Hendricks and Irving Shepard, eds. *Jack London Reports.* 1970.

LOTI, PIERRE. *See* VIAUD, LOUIS MARIE.

LOUNSBERRY, CLEMENT A. (?). Lounsberry was the owner of the *Bismarck Tribune* and had planned to accompany General Alfred Terry's Yellowstone expedition as war correspondent, when his wife became sick. Changing his plans at that fateful moment, he assigned in his place Mark Kellogg,* a part-time telegrapher and writer, who would be the only reporter to perish with Custer at the Little Big Horn. Lounsberry and Custer were both from Michigan and had begun their friendship during the American Civil War.* When Custer arrived at Fort Abraham Lincoln in 1873 they renewed their relationship. In 1874 Custer's official dispatch rider brought Lounsberry the scoop that gold had been discovered in the Black Hills. Custer's leaks to various newspapers led to his testifying in front of a congressional committee and to his losing the command of not only the 1876 Sioux expedition, but his own regiment as well.

Lounsberry had to write General Terry for permission to send another reporter in his place. After he obtained it, the ill-fated Kellogg rode with Terry's forces, riding the horse meant for Lounsberry, and wearing his supervisor's Civil War belt. Before leaving for the Rosebud and his death Kellogg wrote to Lounsberry, "I go with Custer and will be at [sic] the death."

From notes made by Kellogg and interviews with various survivors of the Terry expedition, Lounsberry wrote a comprehensive, eighteen-thousand-word account of the Custer battle and forwarded it to the *New York Herald* at a cost of almost $3,000. It took more than two hours for the telegraph transmission to be completed. Controversy developed for Lounsberry, who attempted to capitalize on having the only accredited correspondent with the Custer expedition, when both the *New York Herald* and the *Chicago Tribune* claimed Kellogg represented their papers.

REFERENCE: Oliver Knight. *Following the Indian Wars.* 1960.

LOVIE, HENRI (d. 1866?). Although not much is known about his personal life, Lovie was the senior artist-correspondent* for *Frank Leslie's Illustrated Weekly* during the American Civil War.* Besides working as a sketch artist for the newspaper, he supported his family with a lithograph business in Cincinnati. He was first assigned to follow Lincoln from Springfield to Washington in 1861. Following the inauguration he accompanied McClellan's army. At the beginning of the campaign he covered the Battle of Philippi. His work method is aptly demonstrated by his coverage of this battle. At Philippi he moved out of harm's way to a vantage point above the carnage on a hillside, providing himself a panoramic view. Following the fighting he would walk the field sketching the detritus and debris of battle. He would then tour the encampments interviewing the exhausted soldiers. His methods were not without risks—several times he was questioned for spying and he became a target for more than one sentry.

Lovie sketched the Battle of Rich Mountain, Fremont's Missouri campaign, and the western naval war, including the capture of Forts Henry and Donelson. He had his greatest scoop with his dramatic sketches of the Battle of Shiloh in April 1862. As the only artist to record the entire two days of the epic battle, he received great acclaim for his work. According to one historian, no other artist in the war illustrated a battle as well as Lovie covered Shiloh. In 1863, tired of covering the war, he invested in cotton and retired from *Leslie's*. Lovie died soon after Appomattox.

REFERENCES: Pat Hodgson. *The War Illustrators.* 1977; W. Fletcher Thompson, Jr. *The Image of War.* 1959.

LUCAS, JAMES GRIFFING (1914–1970). Lucas was born in Checotah, Oklahoma, and attended the University of Missouri before joiniing the *Muskogee*

Daily Phoenix in 1934. He tried his hand at broadcasting and then worked for the *Tulsa Tribune* before joining the marines as a combat correspondent during World War II.* Technical Sergeant Jim Lucas began his affiliation with the Scripps-Howard newspapers toward the end of World War II and used his prior newspaper experience to his advantage as a marine combat correspondent, covering the Battles of Guadalcanal, Iwo Jima, and Tarawa, where he was listed killed in action for three days. He received the 1943 National Headliners Award for his coverage of the Battle of Tarawa, which has been described as the most vivid eyewitness account of the landings there. In 1944 he was promoted to second lieutenant when he covered the Marianas campaign.

During the Korean War* he won the Pulitzer Prize in the field of international reporting and the Ernie Pyle* Memorial Award, which he would win again during the Vietnam War* in 1964. Lucas had been on hand when the French were defeated in Indochina in 1954. As the only correspondent for an American daily newspaper assigned to troops in the field he covered the buildup in Vietnam from the Mekong Delta for five months in 1964. Lucas recounted this experience in *Dateline: Vietnam* in 1966. He shared with David Halberstam* the opinion that the press had done a poor job covering the war zone, exemplified by the fact that in the middle of 1964 there were only two dozen correspondents in all covering the developing conflict. He was the recipient of numerous other awards as well as eight battle stars, the Bronze Star, and the Presidential Unit Citation as combat correspondent with the U.S. Marines in World War II.

REFERENCE: Michael Emery. *On the Front Lines*. 1995.

LUMLEY, ARTHUR (1837–1912). Born in Dublin, Ireland, Lumley immigrated to the United States in the 1850s. For several years he supported his art school education by selling illustrations to *Leslie's Illustrated Weekly*. With the outbreak of the American Civil War* he was assigned by the magazine to cover army encampments on the perimeter of Washington, D.C., and cover the Army of the Potomac. He covered the First Battle of Bull Run, where he sketched the bayonet charge of the New York City Fire Zouaves, one of the most heroic images of the war. Frustrated with endless sketching of camp life, Lumley left *Leslie's* for the *New York Illustrated News*. That year (1862) he covered McClellan's Yorktown campaign, the Battle of Fair Oaks near Richmond, and the Seven Days' Battles. During the seven days of incessant battles, he produced as many sketches as his four competitors combined. Lumley was so exhausted following this series of battles he needed to return to New York to recuperate and oversee the engraving of his sketches. On several occasions Lumley made sketches from the vantage point of a balloon. He also illustrated several executions and sketched scenes from the Battles of Chancellorsville and Fredericksburg. Lumley retired from the battlefront toward the end of 1863 and continued his career as an illustrator. He never returned to the battlefield.

REFERENCES: Philip Van Doren Stern. *They Were There*. 1959; W. Fletcher Thompson, Jr. *The Image of War*. 1959.

LUMSDEN, FRANCIS ASBURY (d. 1860). Born in North Carolina, Lumsden cofounded the *New Orleans Picayune* with George Wilkins Kendall* in 1837. This would be the first cheap paper in the South, joining perhaps a dozen other papers in the Crescent City in the heady days of the penny press. In the late 1830s he made a trip to the Republic of Texas to check on circulation possibilities. In 1842, after Kendall was imprisoned following the ill-fated Santa Fe expedition, Lumsden traveled to Mexico in an attempt to have his partner and friend released. But it would be months later before Kendall was freed.

With the outbreak of the Mexican War* in 1846, Lumsden began organizing volunteers into the Orleans Regiment. However, when a better-equipped company from Georgia known as the Gaines Rangers elected Lumsden as its captain, he ended his recruitment drive and left for the border with the Rangers. Perhaps he should have kept to his original plan, for after reaching the Mexican border word came that the ship carrying their supplies and ammunition had gone down in a storm. So they disbanded in Matamoros shortly after their enlistment period ended.

Lumsden stayed in Mexico and was among the *Picayune* staff strategically placed throughout Mexico to record war news for their paper. He covered General Scott's Veracruz campaign in early 1847 as an aide to the staff of General Shields. In September 1860, Lumsden and his family were among the three hundred passengers who drowned when the steamer *Lady Elgin* sank in a storm on Lake Michigan following a collision with another boat.
REFERENCE: Fayette Copeland. *Kendall of the Picayune*. 1943.

LYNCH, ARTHUR ALFRED (1861–1934). Born in Smythesdale, Victoria, Australia, Lynch graduated from the University of Melbourne. He later attended graduate school at the University of Berlin and practiced medicine in Paris before turning to journalism in 1889. He covered the 1896 Ashanti campaign for the *Evening News* and joined the staff of the *Daily Mail* later that year. With the outbreak of the Boer War* in 1899 he went to Pretoria for the Paris-based *Le Journal*. However, upon his arrival in January 1900 he joined the conflict on the Boer side, and was appointed colonel of a group composed of seventy men from virtually every country in Europe. After six months he returned to Paris.

His participation in the Boer conflict led to a parliamentary seat representing Galway, but when he left Ireland to take his seat in England he was arrested for treason and sentenced to death. His sentence was commuted to life imprisonment, but he was released within the year. In 1908 he returned to the practice of medicine. He was elected to Parliament again in 1909, and his vigorous support of the war efforts against the Germans prior to 1918 led to his vindication for supporting the Boers.
REFERENCE: *DNB*, 1931–1940.

LYNCH, GEORGE (?). Lynch covered the Spanish-American War* from Cuba for the *Daily Chronicle*. He was accredited as war correspondent by the *Morning Herald*, the *Echo*, and the *Illustrated London News* during the Boer War* and was bottled up with twelve thousand British soldiers during the siege of Ladysmith.* He was the only correspondent to get out of Ladysmith during the siege, although he was captured by Boer forces not far from the siege lines. Lynch was imprisoned at Pretoria and released following the capitulation of the town.

When the siege of Peking and the Boxer Rebellion* broke out in 1900 he hurried to the scene, representing the *Daily Express* and the *Sphere*. He next reported the Russo-Japanese War* for the *Daily Chronicle*. Later he reported World War I* for the *London Illustrated News*. One of his greatest contributions to the conflict was his invention of a special pair of gloves for handling the ubiquitous barbed wire.

REFERENCES: Robert W. Desmond. *The Information Process*. 1978; Kenneth Griffith. *Thank God We Kept the Flag Flying: The Siege and Relief of Ladysmith*. 1974; Robert Wilkinson-Latham. *From Our Special Correspondent*. 1979.

M

MACCOSH, JOHN (?). Soldier and pioneer photographer John MacCosh was one of the earliest war photographers. He was a surgeon during the Second Sikh War of 1848–1849, when he took pictures of his fellow officers, and in 1852–1853 he had perfected his techniques enough to allow him to photograph troops and the captured cities of Rangoon and Prome during the Second Burma War. REFERENCES: Pat Hodgson. *Early War Photographs*. 1974; Jorge Lewinski. *The Camera at War*. 1978.

MACDONALD, RODERICK (1914?–1944). MacDonald worked for various Australian newspapers and on Fleet Street in the 1930s before becoming a war correspondent for the *News Chronicle* and the *Sydney Morning Herald* during World War II.* In 1941 he was sent by the *Sydney Morning Herald* to Chungking to cover the Japanese invasion of China. He was assigned to the Burma theater following the bombing of Pearl Harbor and later was posted to North Africa. During the Sicilian campaign he was the only journalist to land with the glider-borne troops. He was captured, but quickly freed by British troops. In May 1944 he was killed along with Cyril Bewley* by a land mine near Cassino. REFERENCE: Robert W. Desmond. *Tides of War*. 1984.

MACGAHAN, JANUARIUS ALOYSIUS (1844–1878). The preeminent American war correspondent of his day was born in rural Ohio. At the age of twenty-four he traveled to Europe with the intention of improving his general education. He was in Brussels when France declared war on Prussia. In 1871 Macgahan offered his services to the *New York Herald*, and his amazing seven-year career as a journalist had begun. During the Franco-Prussian War* he covered the defeat of the Algerian Boubaki before heading to Paris to witness the Paris Commune. Suspected of spying, he was arrested and narrowly averted hanging thanks to the intervention of an American diplomat.

Following the siege of the Paris Commune he traveled widely for the *Herald*. In his most celebrated exploit for his paper he made a one-thousand-mile horseback trek in 1873 across the unknown stretches of the Kyzil Kum desert of Central Asia to join the advance of the Russian army against the khanate of the ancient city of Kiva. On his treacherous journey he eluded Cossack and Turkoman forces who were responsible for enforcing the Russian prohibition against news correspondents.

Before returning from Asia he rode with Cossacks in their subjugation of Turkoman tribesmen. Macgahan next covered the Carlist War in Spain in 1874. While accompanying the forces of Don Carlos, the pretender to the throne, he witnessed the major battle of the war at Abarzuza-Estella. The following year he was assigned to cover an Arctic expedition searching for the fabled Northwest Passage aboard the ship *Pandora*.

The year 1876 found the intrepid Macgahan investigating reports of Turkish atrocities in Bulgaria.* After a disagreement with James Gordon Bennett* of the *Herald* he left the paper for the *London Daily News*. His dispatches to the *Daily News* were credited with instigating the Russo-Turkish War* of 1877–1878 and were published as *The Turkish Atrocities in Bulgaria* in 1876. Today he is remembered in Bulgaria as the "champion of Bulgarian freedom," with streets and statues commemorating his investigative reporting.

He covered the war from the crossing of the Danube through the signing of the peace treaty, including the Battle of Plevna. His dispatches from the major battlefields are considered classics of the genre. Shortly before his thirty-fourth birthday he died of typhus in Constantinople. Five years later he became the first war correspondent to be conveyed to the United States after death by a warship, when the cruiser *Powhatan* brought his body back to lie in state at New York city hall before interment near his birthplace in Ohio.

REFERENCES: F. Lauriston Bullard. *Famous War Correspondents*. 1914; Dale L. Walker. *Januarius MacGahan*. 1988.

MACGOWAN, GAULT (1894–1970). After service in France and the Middle East during World War I,* MacGowan covered the North West Frontier of India in 1923 as a correspondent for the Associated Press. The following year he was hired as editor of the *Times of Mesopotamia*, but resigned in 1925 and returned to London and the *Times*. In 1926 he became Paris correspondent for the *Daily Press*.

After stints with the *Evening Express* and *Londoner's Diary* he was the managing editor for the *Trinidad Guardian* from 1929 to 1934. He traveled widely as foreign correspondent for the *New York Times* and reported the Spanish Civil War* for the *New York Sun* prior to World War II.*

During the world war he reported the Battle of Britain and the Battle of the Atlantic, and accompanied commandos on a mission. In June 1944, after cov-

ering the landings at Normandy beach, he was captured by Germans while accompanying the Allied advance to Paris. He later escaped and fought alongside the Maquis French resistance forces. He went on to witness the Potsdam Conference (1945) and the first United Nations meetings in London (1946). Later that year he was promoted to European manager of the *New York Sun*. His last years in journalism were spent with the magazine *European Living* as editor and publisher.
REFERENCE: Jack Stenbuck, ed. *Typewriter Battalion*. 1995.

MACHUGH, LIEUTENANT-COLONEL ROBERT JOSEPH (d. 1925). During his first stint as a war correspondent in the 1890s, he was an officer in the London Royal Garrison Artillery. He covered the Cuban campaign during the Spanish-American War* for the *Daily Telegraph* in 1898. The following year found MacHugh covering the Boer War* for the *Telegraph*. His book *The Siege of Ladysmith** resulted from his coverage of the war.
    In 1904 he covered the Russo-Japanese War* while attached to the Japanese army on the staff of General Baron Kuroki. He accompanied the Japanese First Army throughout the war, reporting the Battles of the Yalu, Mo-tien-ling Pass, and Liaoyang, in the process earning a campaign medal.
    He returned to his military career in England when he joined the Territorial Army in 1908. In 1912 he reported the Balkan War while accompanying the Serbian army for the *Daily Telegraph*. The following year he reported the Mexican Revolution. During World War I* he served with the Royal Field Artillery in France.
REFERENCE: Dennis Griffiths, ed. *The Encyclopedia of the British Press*. 1992.

MACKAY, CHARLES (1814–1889). Born in Scotland, he reported the American Civil War* for the *Times* beginning in February 1862, after the departure of W. H. Russell* and Bancroft Davis. MacKay exaggerated opposition to the Lincoln administration in the North and like his counterparts was denied special access to most policy makers due to the sympathetic treatment accorded the Confederacy by the British press. MacKay was already a minor poet and experienced newsman when he arrived in America. Although he witnessed little on the battlefield he reported the fall of New Orleans, political developments in the North, the New York draft riots, the Wilderness campaign, the Confederate raid on Washington, the fall of Savannah, the fall of Charleston, and Lincoln's reelection and assassination.
REFERENCE: Ian F. W. Beckett. *The War Correspondents: The American Civil War*. 1993.

MACKENZIE, FREDERICK A. (1869–1931). Born in Quebec, he arrived in London in the 1890s, where he joined the staff of the recently established *Daily Mail* in 1896. In 1900 he reported the Boer War* as correspondent for the *Daily*

Mail. After covering the Russo-Japanese War* in 1905, he wrote *From Tokyo to Tiflis: Uncensored Letters of the War.*

Mackenzie became the *Times* Berlin correspondent, a post he would hold until war broke out in 1914. He was one of the first reporters allowed to report from Russia after the Revolution. In 1921 he resigned from the *Mail* and became special correspondent for the *Chicago Daily News* in Russia and northern Europe for the next five years. Upon his return to England at the end of the decade he wrote several nonfiction books.

REFERENCES: Robert W. Desmond. *Windows on the World.* 1980; Dennis Griffiths, ed. *The Encyclopedia of the British Press.* 1992.

MACMILLAN, THOMAS C. (b. 1851?). Born in Scotland, he came to America with his family at the age of seven. MacMillan left the University of Chicago without graduating to enter journalism with the *Chicago Inter-Ocean* in 1873. He was one of five correspondents covering General George C. Crook's 1876 Black Hills expedition against the Sioux. This was MacMillan's second trip to the West, having covered the Jenny-Newton expedition to the Black Hills the previous summer.

MacMillan participated in the Battle of the Rosebud along with his fellow newspaper colleagues. He suffered from a hacking cough throughout his tenure with Crook's troops, necessitating his departure from the column. Following the 1876 campaign he remained in Chicago with the *Inter-Ocean* until 1895. He left the paper to serve as clerk for the federal district court and served in the Illinois House of Representatives from 1885 to 1889. The civic-minded Mac-Millan would go on to serve his community in a variety of capacities, as chairman of the Senate Committee on the World's Fair and author of the first woman's suffrage act in Illinois, while remaining active in the Chicago Council of Congregational Churches through 1910.

REFERENCE: Oliver Knight. *Following the Indian Wars.* 1960.

MAFEKING, SIEGE OF. Following the outbreak of the Boer War* in October 1899, Boer forces besieged the cities of Mafeking and Kimberley in the British Cape Colony. Mafeking was finally relieved by British forces on May 17, almost one month after the relief of Kimberley. The first reports of the relief of Mafeking were provided by Reuters* correspondent William Hay Mackay on May 18, 1900, seven months after the siege began. The news was greeted with such excitement in London that the word "mafficking," a derivation from "Mafeking" meaning "to celebrate hilariously," was added to the English language. Mackay would be one of the only two Reuters correspondents to perish in the Boer War.

Also reporting from Mafeking during the siege was Colonel Robert Stephenson Smyth Baden-Powell, who commanded British troops within the city and acted as a part-time correspondent for Reuters. Charles E. Hands* of the *Daily Mail* was wounded in the relief campaign for Mafeking, and two of the paper's

stringers,* Lady Sarah Wilson and the enigmatic Mr. Hellawell, were able to smuggle out dispatches on a regular basis.
REFERENCES: Robert W. Desmond. *The Information Process.* 1978; Byron Farwell. *The Great Anglo-Boer War.* 1976.

MALAPARTE, CURZIO. *See* SUCKERT, KURT

MATTHEWS, HERBERT LIONEL (1900–1977). Matthews was born in New York City and educated at Columbia University. Following service in the U.S. Army in World War I,* he joined the staff of the *New York Times* in 1922, beginning an affiliation that would endure for forty-five years. Matthews covered the Ethiopian War* of 1935–1936 from both sides and was awarded the Italian War Cross (Croce de Guerra) in 1936 for "valor in the East African campaign." That same year he reported the Spanish Civil War.* From 1939 to 1942 he headed the Rome bureau and was briefly imprisoned in Siena.

Following the outbreak of World War II* he reported from India in 1942 and the next year covered the last weeks of the Sicilian campaign. In 1944 he witnessed the landing at Salerno and the advance toward Naples. He was one of seven correspondents permitted to fly as observers on the first bombing raid over Rome and was among the first correspondents to enter the city following its capitulation. In August he accompanied the Allied push to Germany.

Among his reporting coups was the earliest interview with Castro, at the head of an army of less than twenty men in 1957, which made the revolutionary into an international figure. Matthews has won many awards for his reporting, including the George Polk Memorial Award and the Chevalier of the French Legion of Honor. His books include *Eyewitness in Abyssinia, Two Wars and More to Come, The Cuban Story, Cuba,* and *A World in Revolution* (1971).
REFERENCES: John Hohenberg. *Foreign Correspondence: The Great Reporters and Their Times.* 1964; Herbert L. Matthews. *A World in Revolution.* 1971.

MAUD, W. T. (1865–1903). Described as the best war illustrator for the *Daily Graphic*, Maud was trained at the Royal Academy. Prior to joining the *Graphic* some of his sketches appeared in *Punch.* His first assignment as artist-correspondent* was to cover the Armenian massacres in 1895. The next year he reported the rebel insurrection in Cuba, and in 1897 he accompanied the Greek army in Thessaly during the Greco-Turkish War* and witnessed the Greek retreat from Velestino.

Later in 1897 he was in the Sudan covering the advance on Abu Hamed. After a brief stay on the North West Frontier of India Maud returned to Africa in May 1898 to participate in the advance on Omdurman. Although Kitchener attempted to bar the press from accompanying his expedition, the intercession of the prime minister resulted in sixteen members of the press corps joining the column. Maud covered the Battle of Omdurman and the reconquest of the Sudan through 1898. Unwilling to wait for mail boats or conventional modes of transportation, he hired local tribesmen to carry his sketches in waterproof packets in their turbans while they swam down the Nile to the nearest steamer. The only criticism of his work suggests that his expertise was in showing scenes of camp life or anecdotal episodes rather than in sketches encompassing larger-than-life studies such as epic battles like Omdurman.

In September 1899 Maud was sent to cover the Boer War.* He shared a house with correspondent G. W. Steevens* during the siege of Ladysmith,* although Steevens would die from enteric fever before it ended. Maud sent a steady stream of sketches back to London, but many did not make it through until the siege was lifted. Following Steevens' death Maud joined the army as an aide to General Ian Hamilton, after he assured his paper it would not interfere with his sketching. As British troops entered Ladysmith, Maud too was stricken with enteric fever from the tainted water supply. Although he survived and returned to the battlefront, his health was shattered and he died in Aden in 1903 while on his journey back to England.

REFERENCES: Pat Hodgson. *The War Illustrators.* 1977; Robert Wilkinson-Latham. *From Our Special Correspondent.* 1979.

MAULDIN, BILL (b. 1921). Born in New Mexico, Mauldin demonstrated an early interest in the cartooning profession. After abruptly leaving the Chicago Academy of Fine Arts he returned to the Southwest but found no outlet for his pictorial satire. In 1940, with no prospects in sight, he enlisted in the army, where his talents for cartoon commentaries depicting army life led to a part-time position with the Forty-fifth Division news. By 1943 his position had become full-time as his division was shipped off to the Mediterranean to take part in the invasion of Sicily and Italy.

During the Italian campaign Mauldin's talents came to the attention of the European edition of the army's daily *Stars and Stripes,** and in 1944 he joined its staff. Following a laudatory story on Mauldin by war correspondent Ernie Pyle,* his cartoons were picked up by the United Feature Syndicate, and by the summer of 1944 his work was carried in dozens of American newspapers.

Mauldin's most recognizable work as the cartoon chronicler of the war featured the exploits of two prototypical GIs, Willie and Joe. The two characters were imbued with a darker side, untypical for cartoons, but a side that reflected the pathos and capriciousness of the war front as they journeyed together through war-torn Europe. Mauldin spoke through these two characters, taking regular trips to the front searching for new material. In one of his most ironic commentaries he recounts being slightly nicked by shrapnel and his subsequent attempts to reject a Purple Heart foisted on him by medics, which military regulations required that he accept.

His work was not without its critics. While General Mark Clark on one occasion requested his presence in his jeep so he could get an original drawing, General George Patton wrote a letter to the editors of *Stars and Stripes* threatening to ban the paper from the entire Third Army if it did not stop what he characterized as Mauldin's attempts to undermine military discipline. But, Mauldin was too popular among the rank and file, and Allied commander General Dwight Eisenhower knew that banning his work would harm morale. In 1945 Mauldin won the Pulitzer Prize for Editorial Cartooning for his "Up Front with Mauldin" series in *Stars and Stripes*.

Numerous collections of his cartoons have been published, including *Star Spangled Banter* (1941), *Sicily Sketch Book* (1943), *Mud, Mules and Mountains* (1943), and *This Damned Tree Leaks* (1945). His annotated collection *Up Front* was a best-seller in 1945. In 1959 he won a second Pulitzer Prize, and in 1962 he joined the staff of the *St. Louis Dispatch*. In 1971 his autobiography *The Brass Ring* was published.

REFERENCE: Frederick S. Voss. *Reporting the War*. 1994.

MAXWELL, SIR WILLIAM (d. 1928). Maxwell was assigned by the *Standard* to replace John Cameron* in the Sudan when the latter perished with the Hicks relief expedition in 1885. As war correspondent, he covered Kitchener's army on its advance on Khartoum in 1898 and witnessed the defeat of the Mahdi's forces at the Battle of Omdurman.

He covered the Boer War* after traveling in the Middle East, as well as the first peace conference at the Hague. He was with British forces besieged at Ladysmith* and following the relief of the garrison accompanied Lord Roberts' forces in each of its actions, from the capture of Bloemfontein to the Battles of Lydenburg and Komati Port. In 1905 he resigned from the *Standard* and joined the *Daily Mail* as correspondent to cover the Russo-Japanese War.* He was with General Kuroki's army from the Yalu to Port Arthur and received the Order of the Rising Sun.

Prior to World War I* he covered the Balkan War (1912) while accompanying Bulgarian forces. During World War I he reported for the *Daily Telegraph* and was attached to the Belgian army until its defeat by German forces. Maxwell went on to witness the Battles of the Marne and Aisne, following which he entered the army as a captain assigned to the general staff. He later rose to head of section in the Secret Service and was knighted in 1919. He wrote *From Yalu to Port Arthur* (1906).

REFERENCES: Robert W. Desmond. *Windows on the World*, 1980; Dennis Griffiths, ed. *The Encyclopedia of the British Press*. 1992.

MCCLANAHAN, JOHN R. (d. 1865). Colonel John McClanahan, a Mexican War* veteran, was coeditor of the *Memphis Appeal*, the most important Memphis paper during the American Civil War.* Along with coeditor Benjamin F. Dill, the two editors were models of the indomitable Southern spirit as they continually moved the paper one step ahead of federal troops, publishing at various times from Mississippi, Georgia, and Alabama. The peripatetic editors were able to keep the *Appeal* afloat by offering half-price subscriptions to sol-

diers in the field. Following Appomattox McClanahan returned to Memphis, where he died in a fall from a hotel window.
REFERENCES: J. Cutler Andrews. *The South Reports the Civil War*. 1970; Stewart Sifakis. *Who Was Who in the Civil War*. 1988.

MCCOAN, JAMES CARLILE (1829–1904). Born in Dunlow in Tyrone County, Ireland, McCoan attended various London schools before graduating from London University in 1848. He left the practice of law to cover the Crimean War* as war correspondent for the *Daily News*. Following the war he traveled extensively in Georgia and Circassia before arriving in Constantinople, where he returned to the practice of law until 1864. McCoan established the *Levant Herald*, the first English-language newspaper in Turkey. After selling the paper in 1870 he returned to England. He continued to travel widely, publishing several books on Egypt, *Egypt As It Is* (1877) and *Egypt Under Ismail: A Romance of History* (1889). He was accused of disloyalty over his support for Gladstone's land bill while representing Wicklow County in Parliament in the 1880s.
REFERENCE: *DNB*, 1901–1911.

MCCORMICK, FREDERICK (1870–1951). McCormick was born in Brookfield, Missouri, and got his start in journalism with *Harper's Weekly* and the *London Graphic* covering the Boxer Rebellion* in 1900. He next worked as a special correspondent in the Far East for the *New York Sun* and Laffan's Bureau before representing Reuters* and the Associated Press during the Russo-Japanese War.* He spent almost two years as the only foreign correspondent covering the Russian side of the war in Manchuria. He accompanied General Danieloff on a mission to evacuate prisoners and later witnessed the first official Russian visit to Japan following the war. He covered the Bolshevik uprising and reported from Russia and China into the late 1920s.
REFERENCES: Robert W. Desmond. *The Information Process*. 1978; *Who Was Who*. 1951.

MCCULLAGH, JOSEPH BURBRIDGE (1842–1896). Born in Dublin, Ireland, McCullagh went to sea before his teens, arriving in New York in 1853, where he became an apprentice printer for the *New York Freeman's Journal*. Soon after, he left for St. Louis and positions on the *Christian Advocate* and the *St. Louis Democrat*.

At the outset of the American Civil War* he was commissioned in the Union Army. Shortly after, he left the army to serve as war correspondent for the *Cincinnati Gazette*. In one of his early dispatches he criticized the bad conduct and drunkenness of Grant's officers during the Tennessee campaign. However, his paper refused to print the critical article. Disappointed by the rejection, he joined the *Cincinnati Commercial* in 1862. He was given free rein with this newspaper, and his articles on the Civil War appeared regularly under his pen name "Mack."

With the growing popularity of his war reports he was promoted to Washington correspondent in 1863 and became the first newspaper reporter to interview a president of the United States when he was given a meeting with Andrew Johnson. He covered the siege of Vicksburg and Sherman's march though Georgia. Apparently McCullagh was too good at his job. He was so successful because of his ability to anticipate events; however, in the fall of 1863 when he too accurately predicted Union troop movements he was reassigned to cover Washington, D.C., as capital correspondent.

Following the Civil War McCullagh experienced a checkered career, serving as editor, major shareholder, and managing editor in a succession of newspapers. While he never regained the popularity he enjoyed during the war years he is credited with being one of the founders of the new journalism. He served as managing editor of the *St. Louis Globe-Democrat* from the early 1870s until his death on December 31, 1896.

REFERENCES: Charles C. Clayton. *Little Mack: Joseph B. McCullagh of the St. Louis Globe-Democrat.* 1969; Stewart Sifakis. *Who Was Who in the Civil War.* 1988.

MCCULLIN, DONALD (b. 1935). Born in England, he was a freelance photojournalist, with his pictures first appearing in the *Observer* in 1958, before becoming a war correspondent for the *Sunday Times* for eighteen years. For thirty years he recorded the horrors of the combat zone and in the process was wounded in Cambodia, gassed in Northern Ireland, and severely wounded in El Salvador. He has covered wars in Vietnam,* Cyprus, the Congo, and Biafra. Among his books are *Homecoming, Hearts of Darkness, The Destruction Business, Beirut: A City in Crisis, Is Anyone Taking Notice?*, and *Open Skies.*

REFERENCE: Don McCullin. *Unreasonable Behaviour.* 1992.

MCCUTCHEON, JOHN TINNEY (1870–1949). Born near South Raub, Indiana, McCutcheon attended Purdue, Notre Dame, and Northwestern Universities. The well-known cartoonist and writer covered the Spanish-American* and Boer Wars* for the *Chicago Daily Tribune* and witnessed the 1898 Battle of Manila Bay in the Philippines, which he chronicled in his book *Stories of Filipino Warfare* (1900). In 1914 he accompanied the U.S. Navy in the assault on Veracruz. However, after a telegram informed him of developments in Europe he took the first train back to Chicago.

Assigned to cover World War I,* he missed the *Lusitania* by three days. Before departing he was given over five thousand dollars in gold weighing over nineteen pounds, to be used for the assistance of associates and prominent Chicagoans stranded in London and Paris. As American reporters arrived at the Belgian front despite restrictions hampering free movement of the press, it became a common practice among the Germans to detain the interlopers as spies. McCutcheon was arrested as a spy along with Will Irwin* and Harry Hansen during the German push through Belgium in 1914. In the winter of 1914–1915 many correspondents returned to the United States during a period described by one source as the "Dark Age of war correspondence." His autobiography *Drawn from Memory* was published in 1950.

REFERENCE: Emmet Crozier. *American Reporters on the Western Front 1914–1918.* 1959.

MCGURN, WILLIAM BARRETT (b. 1914). McGurn covered the Central Pacific theater of operations for *Yank** magazine during World War II.* Prior to the war he was on the staff of the *New York Herald Tribune*. Teamed with artist Bob Greenhalgh, McGurn was wounded by mortar fire during the Second Battle of Bougainville. He returned to action in time to cover the Battle of Peleliu. Following the war he returned to the *Herald Tribune* as chief of the Rome bureau, and then the Paris and Morocco bureaus. He continued to cover the battlefront, reporting conflict in Tunisia, the Algerian and Moroccan Wars, and the Hungarian revolution. He was expelled from Egypt by Nasser.

REFERENCE: Art Weithas. *Close to Glory.* 1991.

MCINTOSH, BURR WILLIAM (1862–1942). McIntosh was born in Wells-ville, Ohio, and attended Princeton and Lafayette College. He entered journalism with the *Philadelphia News* in 1884. He was a war photographer* for *Frank Leslie's Illustrated Weekly* during the Spanish-American War,* where he was stricken with yellow fever and forced to leave the conflict prior to its conclusion. Among his most noted photographs is the unusual shot of the deceased Sergeant Hamilton Fish, Jr., late of the Rough Riders, killed in the Riders' first action at Las Guasimas. Fish became one of the most recognized heroes of the conflict, his family well known and his photograph published throughout the land. Mc-Intosh lost sixty-five of the eighty-four pictures he had risked his life taking when they were ruined by quarantine officers who insisted on disinfecting the container they were in. His Cuban adventures are recounted in *The Little I Saw of Cuba* (1898).

REFERENCES: Charles H. Brown. *The Correspondents' War.* 1967; Susan D. Moeller. *Shooting War.* 1989.

MCKAY, ALEX (b. 1837). Born in Rhode Island, McKay came to California in 1871. He was working in Yreka, California, as a surveyor in 1872 when he acted as special correspondent for the *San Francisco Evening Bulletin* and the *Yreka Union* during the 1872–1873 Modoc Indian War. He was among the reporters granted interviews by Captain Jack in his stronghold and was nearby when the members of the peace commission were murdered by the Modocs in April 1873.

During the Three Days Fight he was among the retinue of reporters pooling their reports. Generally one of the correspondents would remain in camp with access to headquarters information and troop movements. The others would

accompany various forces in the field and could telegraph stories from the front to their colleagues' newspapers. As the only nonprofessional newsman to report the conflict, McKay has been credited for a workmanlike performance. He was one of only three to see the conflict to its conclusion. His career following the Modoc War is unknown.
REFERENCE: Oliver Knight. *Following the Indian Wars.* 1960.

MCMILLAN, RICHARD D. (?). Prior to the outbreak of World War II,* McMillan had spent sixteen years as a United Press correspondent in Europe. He was the first war correspondent to be licensed by the British Expeditionary Forces (BEF), and accompanied British forces in most of their campaigns in the European and African theaters of the war. Following the fall of France he was stationed in London before covering the Greek army in Albania. Over the next two years he reported the conflict in Egypt, Libya, the Middle East, and Tunisia. His exploits reporting the African theater are chronicled in *Mediterranean Assignment.*

While covering the Sicilian campaign in July 1943 he was among the seven correspondents permitted to fly as observers on the first bombing raid over Rome. During the Normandy invasion he landed with British troops in France. Later, while covering the assault on Cherbourg he was wounded in the back by shrapnel but continued to stay at his post. After a short respite in England for recovery he returned to France and was on hand for the liberation of Paris. McMillan remained with Allied troops as they advanced on the Rhine and Germany.
REFERENCE: Robert W. Desmond. *Tides of War.* 1984.

MEMORIALS TO WAR CORRESPONDENTS. One of the earliest memorials to journalists killed in action commemorates seven British correspondents killed during the 1883–1885 Sudan campaigns. A tablet in St. Paul's Cathedral remembers "the Gallant Men who in the discharge of their duty as Special Correspondents fell in the Campaigns in the Soudan 1883–1884–1885." Listed on the tablet are Edmund O'Donovan,* Frank Vizetelly,* Frank Power,* John Alexander Cameron,* St. Leger Algernon Herbert,* William Henry Gordon, and Frank J. L. Roberts.*

In 1896 a War Correspondents Arch was built in Meyersville, Maryland, by former American Civil War* correspondent George Alfred Townsend,* to honor the artists, writers, and photographers who covered the Civil War. World War II* correspondents who lost their lives while serving with the U.S. military are remembered by a memorial placed in the Pentagon by Secretary of the Defense James Forrestal in 1948. Twenty-four years later the War Correspondents Corridor in the Pentagon was dedicated to the Americans killed while reporting World War II, Korea, and Southeast Asia.

War correspondents killed during the Korean War* are memorialized by a plaque dedicated in 1976 and on permanent display at the Foreign Correspondents Press Club of Japan and by a memorial unveiled the following year in Munson, Korea, by the International Cultural Society of Korea. In 1981, on the thirty-seventh anniversary of D-Day, former World War II correspondents dedicated Normandy Park in Athens, Ohio, to war correspondents killed while covering the European theater of World War II.

In 1985 a memorial was dedicated honoring journalists killed by terrorists. The Committee to Protect Journalists, the National Press Club, and No Greater Love unveiled the plaque at the National Press Club in Washington, D.C. The next year a memorial tree and stone was dedicated in Arlington National Cemetery by the Society of Professional Journalists, the Overseas Press Club of America, Inc., the National Press Club, and No Greater Love to honor all journalists killed in the line of duty. On the stone are the words "This tree grows in memory of journalists, who died while covering wars and conflicts, for the American people. One who finds a truth lights a torch."

REFERENCES: Charles C. Arnot. *Don't Kill the Messenger*. 1994; Robert Wilkinson-Latham. *From Our Special Correspondent*. 1979.

MERTON, ARTHUR (d. 1942). Born in England, Merton embarked for Egypt in 1903 to enter the banking and shipping business. In 1912 he was employed by the Ministry of Agriculture when he became the Cairo correspondent for the *Times*. During World War I* he was employed in Allenby's Palestine intelligence service and in 1922 was the first journalist permitted access to the recently opened tomb of Tutankhamen. His reports of the discovery were widely read. He later went to work for the *Daily Telegraph* and by World War II* was one of the most recognized journalists in the Middle East. Despite his advanced age by the time war broke out, he still covered a number of campaigns before he was killed in a car crash near Cairo on May 28, 1942. One of his surviving traveling companions was Winston Churchill's son, Randolph, who was only injured.

REFERENCES: Robert W. Desmond. *Tides of War*. 1984; Dennis Griffiths, ed. *The Encyclopedia of the British Press*. 1992.

MEXICAN WAR. A new era in reporting national and world affairs was inaugurated with the birth of the modern war correspondent during the Mexican War of 1846–1848. There were numerous correspondents involved in the coverage of the war. Besides approximately ten full-time reporters, most representing New Orleans papers, there were many freelance writers. Some reporters had made arrangements to send dispatches to their hometown papers prior to enlisting. Editors as well as their subordinates joined the army, with sixteen from Massachusetts alone. Representatives of the press were often referred to as "printers" during this era, and virtually no company was without one.

War reporters were in such abundance in part due to the fact that so many had enlisted to fight the Mexican army. At least twenty New Orleans printers were found in a single company of volunteers. Among them were three correspondents for the *New Orleans Delta*, including James Freaner,* J.G.H. Tobin,* and John H. Peoples.* None was more celebrated than George Wilkins Kendall,* cofounder of the *New Orleans Picayune* in 1837. Often referred to as the first modern war correspondent, Kendall was so anxious to witness warfare himself he temporarily left General Zachary Taylor's command to join the Texas Rangers under Captain Ben McCulloch. Kendall covered most of the battles of Generals Taylor and Scott, including Chapultepec, Monterrey, Cerro Gordo, and Churubusco.

Kendall's partner, Francis Lumsden,* attempted to raise his own New Orleans regiment, but ended his recruiting drive abruptly when a better-equipped mounted company from Georgia on its way to the Mexican border elected Lumsden as its leader. Also representing the *Picayune* was West Point graduate Christopher Mason Haile,* who joined Scott's staff during the siege of Veracruz.

One of Kendall's chief rivals was James L. Freaner of the *Delta*, whose dispatches appeared under his sobriquet "Mustang." Although most newspapers outside the Deep South did not send correspondents, others were present. In 1846 the *New York Herald* claimed five correspondents, and one Lucian J. Eastin reported for the *Jefferson Inquirer* under the initial "E." In addition there were numerous correspondents and printers who founded newspapers collectively referred to as the Anglo-Saxon Press* in Mexico's occupied cities.

The only woman reporter to cover the front lines was Jane McManus Storms* whose dispatches appeared under the pseudonyms "Cora Montgomery" or "Montgomery" in the *New York Sun*. She became the only member of the press to report from behind Mexican lines and was one of the few to criticize American military efforts as well as her fellow reporters.

Following the invention of the daguerreotype* process in 1839, the Mexican War became the first war to be covered by war photographers,* although the identity of those who took the photographs of the Mexican War remains a mystery.

REFERENCES: Fayette Copeland. *Kendall of the Picayune*. 1943; Robert W. Johanssen. *From the Halls of the Montezumas: The Mexican War in the American Imagination*. 1985; Tom Reilly. "Jane McManus Storms: Letters from the Mexican War, 1846–1848," *Southwestern Historical Quarterly*. July 1981.

MIDDLETON, DREW (1913–1989). Born in New York City and educated at Syracuse University, Middleton worked for several small papers before joining the Associated Press. Shortly after being assigned to London as a sportswriter he moved into war reporting. He was reportedly the youngest correspondent with the British Expeditionary Forces in France during World War II.* He garnered his first scoop in June 1941, when after a briefing with Anthony Eden he learned that Germany was about to invade Russia.

In 1942 he moved over to the *New York Times*. Based in London, he witnessed the tragic raids on Dieppe and St. Nazaire. After joining the *Daily Telegraph* later that year he reported from the front lines in North Africa and on

Omaha Beach during D-Day. Later in the war he covered the second front in Germany and Belgium and after the war was stationed in Moscow. Following the war he reported the conflict of the Cold War for six years, including the 1949 Berlin airlift. He continued with the *New York Times* in various capacities in Europe until his appointment as military correspondent* in 1970. He retired in 1984 and died five years later. The staunch Anglophile was awarded an honorary Order of the British Empire (1947) and Commander of the British Empire (1985). Among his books were *The Struggle for Germany* (1949), *The British* (1957), *The Sky Suspended* (1960), and *Crossroads of War* (1983).
REFERENCES: Robert W. Desmond. *Tides of War*. 1984; Dennis Griffiths, ed. *The Encyclopedia of the British Press*. 1992.

MILITARY CORRESPONDENTS. The *London Times* began employing specialists on military affairs beginning in the late nineteenth century. The most notable and influential correspondent to hold this position was Colonel Charles a Court Repington* beginning in 1904. His articles appeared under the heading ''From Our Special Correspondent,'' as was the newspaper practice. Unlike war correspondents, who covered the battlefront, their military counterparts were more inclined to hold court on issues shaping defense policy at the highest level or discoursing on military strategy and related subjects. In a sense the introduction of the military correspondent created a new field of British journalism, one that would be popularized by future writers such as Basil Liddell Hart.
REFERENCES: Office of the *Times. The History of the ''Times'': The Twentieth Century Test, 1884–1912*. 1947; Oliver Woods and James Bishop. *The Story of THE TIMES*. 1983.

MILLARD, THOMAS FRANKLIN FAIRFAX (1868–1942). Born in Missouri, Millard attended the University of Missouri before embarking on a newspaper career that would earn him recognition as the dean of China hand journalists. He began his journalism career as a drama critic for the *New York Herald* in the 1890s. His lifelong interest in China and Japan was stimulated when he covered the Boxer Rebellion* in 1900 for the *New York Herald*. He came to prominence as a war correspondent in the early twentieth century, earning a disfiguring facial scar in the process. Covering the Boer War* in South Africa he developed a lifelong case of Anglophobia, and his writings on the Afrikaner struggle so enraged the British commander, Lord Kitchener, that Millard was expelled from the country before the cessation of hostilities.

In 1904 he was in Manchuria reporting the Russo-Japanese War.* He remained in the Far East following the war active in both journalism and business, and in 1911 combined the two avocations when he cofounded the *China Express* with Dr. Wu Ting-fang, former Chinese envoy to the United States. This Shanghai daily became the first U.S.-owned newspaper in China, excluding missionary publications. Millard edited the paper for six years before establishing *Millard's Review of the Far East*, a weekly Shanghai publication. In 1922 the experienced

correspondent was named advisor to Li Yuan-hung, president of the Chinese Republic. He left this post in 1925 to become Shanghai correspondent for the *New York Times,* an affiliation he would maintain for the next sixteen years.
REFERENCES: Robert W. Desmond. *Windows on the World.* 1980; Peter Rand. *China Hands.* 1995.

MILLER, LEE (1907–1977). Born Elizabeth Miller in Poughkeepsie, New York, she studied theater and art in Paris before becoming a model for *Vogue* in 1927. In 1929 Miller established her own photography studio while living with the artist and photographer Man Ray and in 1932 opened a studio in New York. With the outbreak of World War II* she joined the London staff of *Vogue* in 1940. She photographed the London blitz and British war efforts. Her pictures were published in *Grim Glory: Pictures of Britain Under Fire* (1940) and *Wrens in Camera* (1942). Although she was employed primarily as a fashion photographer, Miller convinced her magazine to run more war-related pieces. She was more identified for her fashion photography during the war, in which she demonstrated women coping with wartime conditions.

In June 1944 Miller represented *Vogue* during the Normandy invasion and also witnessed the siege of St. Malo, the liberation of Paris, fighting in Luxembourg and Alsace, and the Allied advance into Germany. While covering the front Miller wore a helmet of her own devising, with a movable front that would allow her to take pictures without taking it off. After photographing the historic linking of Russian and American forces at the Elbe she chronicled the liberation of the Dachau and Buchenwald concentration camps.
REFERENCE: Frederick S. Voss. *Reporting the War.* 1994.

MILLER, ROBERT C. (?). The United Press war correspondent landed with the first assault by U.S. Marines on Guadalcanal on August 7, 1942, and was the only member of the press to cover both the first and last battles of the Guadalcanal campaign. While he was traveling with the U.S. invasion fleet during the Normandy invasion in 1944, Miller's ship was sunk by a torpedo during the landings, and he spent two hours in the Channel before being rescued. He was taken back to England but shortly after returned to the beaches of Normandy and accompanied Allied troops in the liberation of Paris.
REFERENCE: Robert W. Desmond. *Tides of War.* 1984.

MILLER, WEBB (1892–1940). Born in Dowagiac, Michigan, Miller joined the United Press in 1916 and on his first assignment covered the punitive expedition into Mexico led by General John J. Pershing. His service to the UP took him through the Mexico City, Chicago, Washington, and New York bureaus before he landed in Europe to cover World War I* on both the American and British fronts in 1918. He witnessed the carnage at the Battles of Chateau-Thierry, the Vesle, and the Argonne. After the armistice he covered the Spanish front in Morocco during the war against the Riffs. Serving as director of a large staff of correspondents, he preferred to cover events personally. He was present at the explosive events leading to World War II,* including the Spanish Civil War* and the Ethiopian War,* which he reported from the Italian front lines. During the Ethiopian War he was nominated for the Pulitzer Prize for a forty-four-minute scoop on the announcement of the beginning of the war there.

In 1939 he served as correspondent with the British army in France and with the Finnish army, and the next year became the first U.S. correspondent to be killed covering World War II, albeit in rather unheroic fashion. As the general manager for the United Press in Europe, he had departed France to report the Russo-Finnish War. Forced to lay over in London while awaiting the proper paperwork to allow his entry into Norway, he was killed in a freak railway mishap. Since there were no witnesses to record his death, a reconstruction suggested that during the wartime blackout he must have fallen onto the railroad tracks expecting a station platform as he stepped out in the pitch darkness while changing trains. When it was announced in 1943 that each Liberty Ship would bear the name of a war correspondent killed in action, the first to be recognized was Webb Miller. The *Webb Miller* was christened by his wife and the following year carried U.S. forces onto Normandy beaches during the D-Day invasion.
REFERENCES: Robert W. Desmond. *Tides of War.* 1984; Webb Miller. *I Found No Peace.* 1936.

MILLET, FRANCIS DAVIS (1846–1912). Millet was born in Mattapoisett, Massachusetts, and educated at Harvard. He got his baptism in warfare as a drummer during the American Civil War.* Following graduation from Harvard in 1869, he studied lithography and painting in Europe. As artist-correspondent* for the *New York Herald*, Millet covered the Russo-Turkish War* in 1877–1878. He was awarded the Cross of St. Stanislaus and the Cross of St. Anne by the Russian Czar for his service during the war. In 1893 he was master of ceremonies at the World's Columbian Exposition.

In 1899 he returned to the battlefield as artist-correspondent for the *London Times, Harper's Weekly*, and the *New York Sun* during the Spanish-American War* and the Philippine insurrection. In 1912 he was killed on the fateful voyage of the *Titanic* when it sank on its way to America.
REFERENCE: Rupert Furneaux. *News of War.* 1964.

MOHR, CHARLES (1929–1989). Mohr was a White House correspondent at the age of twenty-seven, chief of the New Delhi bureau, and then chief of Southeast Asia coverage, all for *Time* magazine. Initially based in Hong Kong, by 1963 he was *Time* magazine's regular correspondent in Vietnam* at the outset of the conflict. He was often teamed with freelancer Mert Perry.* Mohr was in the habit of always being armed, usually with a customized Beretta handgun and a standard issue M-16 rifle. In 1965 he became the first American war correspondent to be wounded in the conflict. In 1967 he covered the Six Day War in the Middle East. Mohr was back in Vietnam covering the Battle of

Hue during the Tet offensive when he found himself pinned down with marines under heavy fire. Along with two other correspondents, Mohr risked his life to pull an injured soldier to safety. In 1980, five years after the end of the war, the three correspondents were awarded the Bronze Star for bravery, the only reporters so decorated during the Vietnam conflict.
REFERENCES: Michael Emery. *On the Front Lines.* 1995; William Prochnau. *Once upon a Distant War.* 1995.

MONKS, NOEL (b. 1907). Born in Tasmania, Monks reported the Ethiopian War* in 1936 as a freelancer before returning to London and employment with the *Daily Express.* Shortly thereafter, he departed to cover the Spanish Civil War* for two and a half years for the *Express.* He was captured by insurgents and threatened with execution before being expelled on Franco's orders. He returned to report from the side of the Republic. After joining the staff of the *Daily Mail* to report World War II* he was sent to France as one of the first correspondents to cover the war. His book *Squadrons Up* recounted his excursions with the RAF in 1939 and was the first best-selling book about the war. Monks was present on virtually every Allied front during the European theater, witnessing such pivotal events as the D-Day invasion, Dunkirk, and the attack on Berlin. After 1945 he continued his reporting for the *Daily Mail*, covering the Korean War,* the Malaysian insurgency, and other flash points throughout the world.
REFERENCES: Robert W. Desmond. *Tides of War.* 1984; Noel Monks. *Eyewitness.* 1955.

MONTAGU, IRVING (b. 1843). A childhood friend of the artist-correspondent* Robert Landells,* Montagu was determined to emulate him. He was hired as an artist by the *Illustrated London News* when the Franco-Prussian War* began. He found that the quickest way to get to the front from Switzerland was to accompany the ambulance corps. He covered the siege of Paris and in 1874 the Carlist War in Spain.

During the 1877–1878 Russo-Turkish War* Montagu and *Times* correspondent R. Coningsby disguised themselves as merchants to avoid the Russian prohibition on news correspondents. They survived a Turkish shell attack on their carriage and an attack on their camp by wolves on the outskirts of Plevna. Coningsby reported that they fended off the animals with one of Montagu's sketches. When the wolves returned, Montagu responded in kind, chasing them off by reading one of Coningsby's columns from the *Times.* Following the war Montagu wrote his recollections of his wartime exploits, *Wanderings of a War Artist* (1889), no doubt embellished with events both real and imaginary. He also published *Camp and Studio* (1890).
REFERENCE: Pat Hodgson. *The War Illustrators.* 1977.

MONTAGUE, EVELYN A. (d. 1948). An Oxford graduate and medalist at the 1924 Paris Olympic Games, Montague was a third-generation journalist with the *Manchester Guardian*. He began his affiliation first as a business reporter in 1928 and then as sportswriter in 1931. With the outbreak of World War II* he turned to war reporting, covering the London blitz and the fall of France. When the war began the *Guardian* was undercapitalized, leading to the practice of using war reportage provided by other papers such as the *Times*. In one major exception Montague accompanied the British First Army in the Allied landing in North Africa. He followed the campaign until the fall of Tunis and then covered the British Eighth Army during the conquest of Sicily and the campaign in Italy.

Military commentators such as Captain B. H. Liddell Hart praised his battle-field accounts for their dependability, and the *Times* often requested reprints of his dispatches. In 1944 he returned to England when his wife fell ill. He arrived home the day after the funeral. Tuberculosis prevented him from returning to the front later that year and would kill him three years after the end of the war.
REFERENCE: David Ayerst. *The Manchester Guardian: Biography of a Newspaper.* 1971.

MOORE, WILLIAM ARTHUR (1880–1962). Born in County Down, Ireland, and educated at Campbell College, Belfast, and Oxford, he was elected president of the University debating society and general club in 1904. In 1908 he joined the *Times* as special correspondent, covering the Young Turk rebellion. The following year he witnessed the hundred-day siege of Tabriz in Persia. He covered the Middle East for three years and then reported from India, Egypt, Russia, Spain, and Portugal before covering an insurrection in Albania in 1914. Also that year his book *The Orient Express* was published.

During World War I,* he was one of the first war correspondents to arrive in France. His coverage of the retreat from Mons in 1914 was his most famous scoop. Initially his dispatch was heavily censored, but before it was printed the head of the London bureau, F. E. Smith, replaced the excised passages, printing the original report. Later that year he was captured by a German cavalry patrol and then released.

In 1915 he joined the Rifle Brigade and saw action in the Dardanelles. Two years later he traded a rifle for wings, when he transferred to the Royal Flying Corps, in which he rose to squadron leader. Following the war he resumed his affiliation with the *Times*, stationed in the Middle East. In 1924 he joined the *Calcutta Statesman* as an assistant editor and two years later was elected to the Legislative Assembly at Delhi.

His account of a round-the-world air voyage in 1941 was published as *This Our War*, and the following year he retired from journalism. Subsequently he became an advisor to Lord Mountbatten and established his own weekly journal in Delhi. He continued to publish articles in various periodicals.
REFERENCES: Dennis Griffiths, ed. *The Encyclopedia of the British Press.* 1992; Times Publishing Company. *History of the ''Times,''* Vol. IV, Part 1. 1952.

MOOREHEAD, ALAN MCRAE (1910–1983). Born in Melbourne, Australia, and educated at Melbourne University, Moorehead began working for the *Melbourne Herald* while still a student. After receiving his law degree he became a full-time journalist with the *Herald* for six years before joining the *Daily Express* in England and becoming its top war correspondent during World War II.* Before the outbreak of the war he covered the Spanish Civil War* as a stringer* and courier for the *Daily Express*.

He gained wide recognition for his war reporting from North Africa through the campaigns in Europe. With the outbreak of war he left Rome in 1939 to report from Athens and then Cairo. Beginning in 1940 he covered the campaign of the British Eighth Army in Africa. Moorehead next reported from Persia, where he investigated German espionage activities, and in 1942 accompanied the Allied invasion of Africa. The following year he reported the Casablanca Conference and the campaign in Italy. His books on the African campaign, *The March to Tunis* and *Eclipse*, were popular successes. In 1944 he was an early arrival on the beaches of Normandy after the D-Day invasion and at one point was arrested by a British unit on suspicion of being a spy. He was quickly identified and released. He accompanied Allied forces through the liberation of Paris and was with the British Second Army on its advance into northern Belgium and Holland.

After resigning from the *Daily Express* immediately following the war he embarked on an unsuccessful fiction-writing career and returned to England four years later to work as a press officer at the Ministry of Defence. In 1952 he began a successful nonfiction-writing career. Among his works were *The Traitors* (1952), *Gallipoli* (1956), *The Russian Revolution* (1958), *The White Nile* (1960), and *The Blue Nile* (1962). In 1966 his writing career was cut short when he suffered a debilitating stroke, which kept him from writing or speaking coherently for the remainder of his life. He died on September 29, 1983.

REFERENCES: Richard Collier. *Fighting Words.* 1989; Robert W. Desmond. *Tides of War.* 1984; Alan Moorehead. *A Late Education: Episodes in a Life.* 1976.

MORIN, RELMAN "PAT" (b. 1907). Following graduation from Pomona College he worked for the *Shanghai Evening Post*. After returning to the United States he was called back to China when Japan invaded in 1931. By August 1941 he was the AP Tokyo bureau chief and on assignment in Indochina when he witnessed the invasion of Japanese forces. He was subsequently captured and incarcerated in Saigon before being returned to Tokyo. Following his repatriation he covered the Sicilian campaign, the landing at Salerno, Italy, and the advance on Naples. A two-time winner of the Pulitzer Prize, Pat Morin received his 1951 Pulitzer for his on-the-spot coverage during the Korean War* for the Associated Press. Six years later he received his other Pulitzer for his domestic reporting of the desegregation of Arkansas schools.

REFERENCES: John Hohenberg. *Foreign Correspondence: The Great Reporters and*

Their Times. 1964; John Hohenberg. *The Pulitzer Prizes.* 1974; M. L. Stein. *Under Fire: The Story of American War Correspondents.* 1968.

MORRISON, CHESTER (1899–1966). The Philadelphia native was educated at Rutgers and served in the navy in World War I.* Following the war he worked for the Associated Press, the *Boston Transcript*, and the *Boston Herald* before joining the staff of the *Chicago Sun.* During World War II* he served as war correspondent in the North African campaign for both the *Sun* and CBS. Beginning in October 1942 he was attached to the British Eighth Army under the command of Field Marshal Montgomery. In 1944 he was among the seventeen correspondents covering naval and ground operations resulting in the capture of the island of Elba off the Tuscany shore.
REFERENCE: Robert W. Desmond. *Tides of War.* 1984.

MORRISON, GEORGE ERNEST (1862–1920). Born in Geelong, Victoria, Australia, and educated at Melbourne and Edinburgh Universities, he was certified as a surgeon and doctor. In 1882 he walked 2,043 miles alone across Australia in 123 days. That same year he sailed to the New Hebrides to recruit farm laborers for Australia. His reports of this expedition created quite a stir. After mounting a poorly planned expedition to New Guinea, he was attacked by natives, suffering two spear wounds.

He arrived in Edinburgh to practice medicine in 1884, still carrying in his thigh part of a spear, which was then promptly removed by his tutor. Three years later he served for a short time as court physician in Morocco before traveling from Shanghai to Burma. His 1895 book, *An Australian in China*, is an account of this 3,000-mile adventure. Following this exploit he was hired as Peking correspondent for the *Times.* He was in Peking during the Boxer Rebellion* and siege from June to July 1900. His reports were the first eyewitness accounts of this conflict.

He next covered the Russo-Japanese War,* which according to the historian Trevor-Roper he openly promoted, leading some to call the war at its outset "Morrison's War." He accompanied victorious Japanese troops into Port Arthur and covered the signing of the armistice at the Portsmouth Peace Conference. Returning to China he continued his peripatetic existence, traveling to every province of China except for Tibet. His attachment to the country led him to resign from the *Times* in 1912 to become political advisor to the newly elected first president, Sun Yat-sen.
REFERENCES: Office of the *Times, The History of the "Times": The Twentieth Century Test, 1884–1912.* 1947; Cyril Pearl. *Morrison of Peking.* 1967.

MORRISON, IAN F. M. (1913–1950). The son of war correspondent Dr. George Ernest Morrison* was educated at Trinity College, Cambridge. From 1935 to 1937 Morrison was an English Professor at Hokkaido University, Japan, and then private secretary to the British ambassador in Tokyo. In 1941, follow-

ing employment with the Far Eastern Bureau of Information, Singapore, he turned to war journalism with the *Times*. Morrison covered the British retreat in Malaya, was wounded during the New Guinea campaign in 1942, and covered the Burma campaign in 1945. During the war in the Far East he was stricken with dengue fever, tropical ulcers, amoebic dysentery, and malaria, and survived two plane crashes. His accounts of the war were published in *This War Against Japan* (1943) and *Malayan Postscript* (1943). On August 12, 1950, shortly after the outbreak of the Korean War* he was killed when his vehicle struck a land mine.
REFERENCES: Richard Collier. *Fighting Words*. 1989; Dennis Griffiths, ed. *The Encyclopedia of the British Press*, 1992.

MORRISS, MACK (1919–1976). Born in Baltimore, Maryland, Morriss became one of the top writers for *Yank* magazine during World War II.* He served as staff writer from 1942 to 1945, covering campaigns on Guadalcanal and New Georgia in the Solomon Islands and on the Siegfried Line and in the Huertgen Forest in the European theater. In May 1945 he was one of the first correspondents to enter the defeated city of Berlin. During much of the war he was teamed with artist Howard Brodie.* However he lost his SHAEF (Supreme Headquarters Allied European Forces) credentials by defying the Allied ban on entering the fallen capital. He received the Legion of Merit for his stellar career with *Yank*. Following the war Morriss worked for *Life* and as a freelance writer. He wrote the war novel *The Proving Ground* in 1951. After a newspaper career in Elizabethton, Tennessee, he became its mayor in 1966.
REFERENCE: Art Weithas. *Close to Glory*. 1991.

MOSLER, HENRY (1841–1920). Born in New York City, the son of a lithographer, Mosler moved to Cincinnati on the 1850s and taught himself the art of wood engraving and painting. He joined *Harper's Weekly* as special artist in 1861, covering the western theater of the American Civil War* in Kentucky and Tennessee from 1861 to 1863, including the second day of the Battle of Shiloh. In 1863 he continued his studies in painting in Europe, settling in Paris, where he remained until 1894, when he returned to New York to open his own studio.
REFERENCE: W. Fletcher Thompson, Jr. *The Image of War*. 1959.

MOSLEY, LEONARD OSWALD (1913–1992). Born in Manchester, England, after a short journalism career at home he moved to Hollywood to write motion picture screenplays. In 1939, as a reporter for the *Daily Sketch*, he made the acquaintance of Hitler in Bayreuth. During World War II* he reported from the Middle East, Asia, Italy, Germany, and France. In 1941 he was accredited to the British Middle East Command in Egypt but left in October 1942 prior to the Battle of El Alamein. The following year he covered the Italian front and in 1944 represented the *Daily Telegraph* when he jumped with paratroopers near Cherbourg during the D-Day landings. In the latter stages of the war he was

with the British Second Army as it pushed into Holland and Belgium. Following the war he returned to the *Daily Press* as a foreign correspondent, film critic, and feature story writer.
REFERENCES: Richard Collier. *Fighting Words*. 1989; Robert W. Desmond. *Tides of War*. 1984.

MOWRER, EDGAR ANSEL (1892–1977). The younger brother of war correspondent Paul Scott Mowrer* was born in Bloomington, Illinois, and educated at the Sorbonne and the University of Michigan. Following graduation in 1913 he returned to Paris to embark on a literary career. At the outset of World War I* he was on the staff of the *Chicago Daily News* Paris bureau. In 1915 he was assigned to Rome, where he met Benito Mussolini and observed the Italian Fascists take over the country. During the conflict he acted as war correspondent, reporting battles in Belgium at Louvain and at the Marne in France, except for a brief interlude when he was expelled and deported to England. He later toured occupied Belgium with Herbert Hoover's relief commission and was reassigned to Berlin in 1923.

Mowrer was stationed in Germany in 1933 when the Reichstag mysteriously burned on February 27, leading to Adolph Hitler's rise to dictator. Mowrer, an outspoken critic of the Nazis, suggested in a dispatch to the *Daily News* that the Nazis set the fire themselves as a ploy to solidify their grip on Nazi Germany. In 1933 Mowrer received the Pulitzer Prize for his German correspondence collected in *Germany Puts the Clock Back*. Between 1933 and the outbreak of World War II* he served as president of the Foreign Press Association, reported from Paris, covered the beginning of the Spanish Civil War,* and visited the Soviet Union. He continued his career in journalism as editor, columnist, and feature writer until retirement in 1969.
REFERENCES: Robert W. Desmond. *Windows on the World*. 1980; Robert W. Desmond. *Crisis and Conflict*. 1982; Robert W. Desmond. *Tides of War*. 1984; Michael Emery. *On the Front Lines*. 1995.

MOWRER, PAUL SCOTT (1887–1971). The older brother of Edgar Ansel Mowrer* was born in Bloomington, Illinois, and attended the University of Michigan. He left school early to join the *Chicago Daily News* as its Paris correspondent in 1907. He covered the conflict in the Balkans in 1911–1913 and then World War I* beginning in 1914. He was assigned to French General Headquarters until the end of the war in 1918. Although he was not present, he put together a comprehensive account of the British defeat at Mons. Because of British censorship he was able to get the story to Chicago days before it was known in England. Mowrer covered the arrival of American force in July 1917 and reported the Chateau-Thierry campaign.

Following the war he became a well-known diplomatic correspondent. He wrote several prescient books on European affairs, including *Balkanized Europe* (1921) and *Our Foreign Affairs* (1924). In 1928 he was recognized with a

Pulitzer Prize for his work as a foreign correspondent. He married Hadley Richardson, the former wife of Ernest Hemingway,* in 1933 and wrote eleven books of poetry beginning in 1918. After leaving the *Chicago Daily News* in 1944 he joined the *New York Post* as its European editor until 1949.

REFERENCES: Emmet Crozier. *American Reporters on the Western Front 1914–1918.* 1959; Michael Emery. *On the Front Lines.* 1995.

MUNDAY, WILLIAM (1910–1943). Born in Sydney, where he started his career in journalism, he moved to London in the 1930s. In 1940 he returned to his homeland and the *Sydney Morning Herald.* With the outbreak of World War II* he covered Australian troops in the Middle East. His columns also appeared in the *News Chronicle.* In late 1941 he was transferred to Burma, where he filed his most significant reports, including "On the Road to Mandalay," and "Why We Were Beaten in Burma." He was among the last reporters to pull out of Burma.

After his escape along an almost impassable 1,200-mile road in a small car he was next assigned to the Mediterranean theater, where he covered the British amphibious landing at Salerno. Never far from the front lines, he was killed during the advance on Naples in October 1943.

REFERENCE: Dennis Griffiths, ed. *The Encyclopedia of the British Press.* 1992.

MUNRO, ROSS (1913–1990). Munro was born in Ottawa, Canada, and educated at the University of Toronto. After serving in the Canadian militia in 1940 he became the third generation of his family to enter journalism, working for the Canadian press. During World War II* he covered the Spitzbergen operation in 1941 and the ill-fated raid on Dieppe the following year. His coverage of the destruction of Canadian forces in this operation appeared in the *Daily Telegraph.* He returned to Canada after this debacle and went on the lecture tour describing the failed attack.

He returned to the battlefront, covering the landing at Sicily, and accompanied the first troops on to the shores of Normandy during D-Day. Following the war he reported the Nuremberg trials before returning to Canada, where he signed on with the Southam News Services. He went on to cover the Korean War* in 1950 and continued his career in journalism with various Canadian papers. He was awarded the Order of the British Empire in 1946 and was made officer of the Order of Canada in 1975.

REFERENCES: Richard Collier. *Fighting Words: The War Correspondents of World War II.* 1989; Dennis Griffiths, ed. *The Encyclopedia of the British Press.* 1992.

MURPHY, CARLYLE (?). Murphy survived one of the most harrowing feats of war reporting during the Gulf War.* On assignment for the *Washington Post,* she hid in Kuwait for almost a month after the Iraqi invasion while continuing to send out reports by telephone. She ultimately escaped and was awarded the Pulitzer Prize.

REFERENCE: Michael Emery. *On the Front Lines*. 1995.

MURROW, EDWARD (EGBERT) ROSCOE (1908–1965). Born Egbert R. Murrow near Greensboro, North Carolina, he became Edward while attending Washington State College from 1926 to 1930. Murrow began his career with CBS in 1935 and rapidly rose to prominence as one of the best-known radio and television personalities of his era.

In 1938 he was assigned to cover Adolph Hitler's arrival in Vienna following the annexation of Austria. Murrow is most identified with his coverage of the bombing of London in 1940. He often risked his life reporting from rooftops as bombs, antiaircraft guns and sirens blared in the background, giving listeners the ultimate sensory experience. Later Murrow accompanied American bombers on twenty-five missions over Germany.

Following the war he returned to the States as CBS vice president. In the 1950s he made the transition to television with his program *See It Now*. His most famous broadcast was in 1954 when he exposed Joseph McCarthy's bogus crusade against Communism. He left television in the 1960s disenchanted with commercial broadcasting. Forever identified with his omnipresent cigarette, he died of lung cancer on April 27, 1965.

REFERENCES: Joseph E. Persico. *Edward R. Murrow: An American Original*. 1988; R. Franklin Smith. *Edward R. Murrow: The War Years*. 1978.

MUSGROVE, HELEN "PATCHES" (b. 1918). Born in Nebraska, Musgrove joined the Coast Guard as a registered nurse during World War II* and was the first woman to be sworn into the Women's Auxiliary of the Coast Guard. She was stationed in Alaska, where she conducted radio broadcasts for soldiers in the Pacific theater of the war as "GI Jill."

Following the sudden death of her husband she established a dressmaking business in Hong Kong. Musgrove became a war correspondent in a rather serendipitous fashion. On a stopover in Saigon in 1964 she witnessed a firefight in the distance and was intrigued with the brightly hued skies. For two years these images remained with her until 1966, when she successfully sought accreditation as a correspondent with the Joint United States Public Affairs Office (JUSPAO). She witnessed bloodshed for the first time at Chu Lai several days later.

Musgrove was based in Saigon, where she contributed to seventy different newspapers, but most often for the *Jacksonville Journal*. Each month she spent twenty days in the field, traveling whenever possible with the military, eschewing the company of journalists. She earned the nickname "Patches" for her collection of patches from various units and in 1969 legally changed her name from Helen to Patches. By late 1967 she was the only woman correspondent who spoke out in favor of American involvement in the conflict.

Patches Musgrove covered the 1968 Tet offensive from Saigon, where she was cut off from communication with her newspaper editors for two weeks. In August 1969 she was the lone correspondent to participate on a "Shadow operation," when she flew in an AC 119 gunship on a combat mission. The following year she was made an "Honorary Shadow" for her "Outstanding service to Shadow operations in the Republics of Vietnam and Cambodia." In 1971, the fifty-three-year-old Musgrove collapsed in the field. Diagnosed with heart disease, she returned to the States for successful surgery. Following the war she remained an implacable supporter of the war in Vietnam.
REFERENCE: Virginia Elwood-Akers. *Women War Correspondents in the Vietnam War, 1961–1975.* 1988.

MUYBRIDGE, EADWEARD (1830–1904). Born in Kingston-on-Thames, England, he emigrated to the United States in 1852. He was a San Francisco photographer and bookseller and friend of Leland Stanford. He began taking landscape photographs in the Yosemite region in the mid-1860s and conducted several government photographic surveys along the California coast.

After a jury acquitted him of killing his wife's lover he worked for the railroad magnate Stanford, photographing American railroads and then Indian ruins in Central America. He documented the small-scale Modoc Indian War of 1872–1873 in northern California and southern Oregon. He achieved his greatest fame with his studies in time-lapse photography and animal locomotion. In 1893 he devised a photographic machine that projected pictures on the screen in a rapid, sequential order, a precursor of motion pictures.
REFERENCES: Jorge Lewinski. *The Camera at War.* 1978; Keith A. Murray. *The Modocs and Their War.* 1959.

MYDANS, CARL (b. 1907). Born in Boston and educated at the Boston University School of Journalism, this peripatetic photographer joined the staff of *Life* magazine in 1936. In 1939 he covered Great Britain's wartime preparations and the following year was on hand to chronicle the ill-fated attempts of the Finnish army to stop the invasion by the Russian army. Later that year he was sent to Italy to report on the public posturings of Mussolini despite almost constant harassment by the Fascist Blackshirts. After witnessing the fall of France in 1940, Mydans headed for the Far Eastern theater of the war, where he reported the Japanese invasion of China.

Mydans was in the Philippines when the Japanese in quick succession attacked Pearl Harbor and then Manila the following day. Unable to escape the onslaught of the imperial army Mydans and his wife Shelley,* a writer for *Life* magazine, along with many other American citizens became prisoners of war. They would ultimately spend twenty-one months as prisoners in the Santo Tomas camp just outside of Manila. They were released in a prisoner exchange in late 1943. Mydans returned to the battlefront in 1944, covering both the European and Pacific campaigns. Among his most celebrated photographs were the triumphant return of MacArthur to the Philippines, wading onto the beach at Luzon in 1944; the unconditional surrender of the Japanese on board the battleship *Missouri*; and the execution of a French collaborator. After the war he became a Tokyo bureau chief for *Time-Life International*. Mydan's resumé as war photographer would later include the Chinese Civil War, the defeat of the French in Vietnam, and the Korean War.*

REFERENCES: Carl Mydans. *More Than Meets the Eye*. 1959; Frederick S. Voss. *Reporting the War*. 1994.

MYDANS, SHELLEY (b. 1915). Born Shelly Smith in Palo Alto, California, daughter of a Stanford University English professor, she was first employed as a journalist by the *Literary Digest*, which folded in the mid-1930s. In 1936, she was hired by the new *Life* magazine, where she met the photographer Carl Mydans,* whom she married in June 1938. The Mydanses were sent to Europe, as the first *Life* correspondents to cover the outbreak of war in 1939 as a photo-reporter team. While Carl was sent to Finland and other battlefronts, Shelley was faced with assignments unrelated to combat reportage such as background stories.

As Europe became embroiled in conflict the Mydanses were called back to the States. In 1940 they were sent to cover the war between Japan and China. They were in the Philippines when Pearl Harbor was attacked and were eventually interned by the Japanese after the fall of Manila. In December 1943 they were freed and returned home. Returning to the Pacific theater of the war, Shelley became the first woman assigned to CINCPac (Commander in Chief of the Pacific), headquarters of MacArthur, and was probably the first woman correspondent to enter Manila. Following the war she worked as a *Time* broadcaster and correspondent in Tokyo. Her novel *The Open City* (1945) is based on her internment experience in Manila. She wrote several other historical novels and coauthored with her husband Carl *The Violent Peace* (1968).

REFERENCE: Lilya Wagner. *Women War Correspondents of World War II*. 1989.

N

NACHTWEY, JAMES (b. 1948). The American war photographer James Nachtwey has covered conflicts in Northern Ireland, the Middle East, and Central America. Affiliated with the *Albuquerque Journal* until 1980, he later joined the Black Star photo agency.
REFERENCE: Frances Fralin, ed. *The Indelible Image*. 1985.

NASMYTH, CHARLES (1825–1861). Nasmyth was born in Edinburgh, Scotland, and was a commissioned officer with the Bombay Artillery in the East India Company. At home on sick leave at the outset of the Crimean War,* he was hired as a stringer* by the *Times*. His first assignment was to cover the Turkish forces on the Danube River. He went beyond the call of duty while stationed at Omar Pasha's camp, when he led Turkish sorties against the Russians besieging Silistri. Although he neglected to file his dispatches, his newspaper commended him for the credit his exploits brought to the *Times*. He went on to cover the Battle of Alma and the siege of Sebastopol. Following the war he continued his army service in Ireland and Australia. He died in France on June 2, 1860.
REFERENCE: Dennis Griffiths, ed. *The Encyclopedia of the British Press*. 1992.

NAST, THOMAS (1840–1902). Born in Landau, Germany, Nast was brought at the age of six to New York City, where he would become the preeminent American cartoonist and first American caricaturist. He was virtually self-taught and was providing sketches to *Leslie's Illustrated Weekly* while still in his early teens. He covered Garibaldi's campaigns in Europe as artist-correspondent* for the *New York Illustrated News*, the *Illustrated London News*, and the Parisian *Monde Illustré* in 1860. He returned to America in 1861 and the next year began his twenty-five-year affiliation with *Harper's* as sketch artist covering the American Civil War.* Like fellow artist Winslow Homer,* Nast contributed little to the contemporary pictorial coverage of the war, directing his efforts instead toward more symbolic images such as "The Press on the Field," and supporting the weekly's various patriotic campaigns. Lincoln testified to Nast's effectiveness as a political cartoonist, noting in 1864, "Thomas Nast has been our best recruiting sergeant."

In 1863 Nast witnessed several skirmishes in the aftermath of the Battle of Gettysburg and then the New York draft riots. Following the war Nast established his reputation as a political cartoonist. Among his most enduring creations as a wood engraver were the Democratic donkey, Republican elephant, and the Indian symbol of Tammany Hall.

REFERENCES: Philip Van Doren Stern. *They Were There.* 1959; W. Fletcher Thompson, Jr. *The Image of War.* 1959.

NEILLY, EMERSON (?). He was one of a number of correspondents holed up in besieged Mafeking* during the Boer War.* Neilly represented the *Pall Mall Gazette* throughout the siege. He chronicled the siege in *Besieged with Baden-Powell* (1900).

REFERENCE: Robert Wilkinson-Latham. *From Our Special Correspondent.* 1979.

NEVINSON, CHRISTOPHER RICHARD WYNNE (1889–1946). Born in Hampstead, England, Nevinson studied painting at several art schools before being advised to pursue another profession. Following service with an ambulance unit during World War I* and a subsequent bout with rheumatic fever he returned to painting. A 1916 exhibit of his war pictures opened to great acclaim. Influenced by the Cubists, his paintings portrayed the participants in war as robotic pieces in a war machine. His work, which deglamorized war, was so influential it led to the appointment of several artists as official war artists. Nevinson would be the first in 1917. During World War II* he continued to capture the senselessness of war. His subjects included the London blitz and the ill-fated raid at Dieppe in 1942, which he witnessed while accompanying the British commandos. The next year he suffered a stroke, which ended his career.

REFERENCE: *DNB*, 1941–1950.

NEVINSON, HENRY WOOD (1856–1941). Born in Leicester and educated at Oxford, he joined the *Daily Chronicle* as a correspondent in 1897 covering the Greco-Turkish War,* including the decisive Battle of Grinboro. In 1900 he reported the Boer War,* including the 118-day siege of Ladysmith.* In 1905 he was assigned to Russia to cover the abortive revolution.

After a brief stint with the *Manchester Guardian* in 1907 he moved over to the *Daily News*, but resigned to protest the paper's position against women's suffrage in 1909. Returning to the *Manchester Guardian*, he covered the Balkan War in 1912 from the Bulgarian side. After the outbreak of World War I,*

Nevinson covered the war in France and then the Dardanelles, where he was wounded. He chronicles his exploits there in his *Dardanelles Campaign* (1918). He also covered the organized relief for the Macedonians (1903), and investigated slavery in Portuguese Angola, resulting in *A Modern Slavery* (1906). He wrote several other books and was a regular contributor to the *Nation*. He died on November 9, 1941.

REFERENCES: David Ayerst. *The Manchester Guardian: Biography of a Newspaper.* 1971; Robert W. Desmond. *Windows on the World.* 1978; *DNB*, 1941–1950; Rupert Furneaux. *News of War.* 1964.

NEWSREEL COMPANIES. The Spanish-American War* was the first war photographed by American motion picture producers. The Edison Company made some of the earliest films with its coverage of the funeral procession for victims of the *Maine* sinking. In recent years questions have arisen concerning the authenticity of early war footage, although much of the film stock has been proven genuine, including the embarkation of Teddy Roosevelt's Rough Riders for Santiago and U.S. troops landing at Baiquiri in Cuba. Obvious fakes include most action footage taken in Cuba and the Philippines. However, the Vitagraph Company followed Roosevelt to Cuba and photographed scenes of the Rough Rider assault on San Juan Hill.*

The Boer War* was one of the first military conflicts to be recorded on film. It was more thoroughly covered by British cameramen than any others; the most prominent was W.K.L. Dickson of the British Mutoscope and Biograph Company, who traveled in a horse-drawn cart with a gigantic camera, summoning up images of the late Mathew Brady* during the American Civil War.* Dickson spent more than a year with the British army as motion picture correspondent. He filmed armored trains with troops, the siege of Ladysmith,* various sorties, and campsites. He was given remarkable freedom compared to photographic restrictions of subsequent wars. There is evidence to suggest that military officials confided secret plans of future military operations so that he could set up his equipment to record the action.

The Mexican Revolution, beginning in 1911, received some of the best newsreel coverage of any war prior to World War II.* All of the major newsreel companies, as well as many of the smaller ones, sent correspondents to the border. In one of the most controversial uses of newsreel motion pictures, Pancho Villa made arrangements to fight battles during the daylight hours and waited until cameras were in place before launching attacks. In the winter of 1913–1914 Villa had let it be known that he was offering motion picture rights to his war to any entrepreneurial producer with enough money to pay for exclusive coverage of his campaign. In 1914 Mutual Film Corporation secured the rights to cover the campaign. Under the contract Villa was to receive $25,000 and fifty percent of the motion picture royalties. In return he guaranteed to bar any other cameramen from recording the conflict. Apparently, Villa made good on his promise and even delayed his attack on the city of Ojinaga until Mutual had its cameras in place.

During World War I* military officials were reluctant to allow civilian cameramen to record near the battlefront, instead using military cameramen to man the cameras. Newsreel coverage of World War I, grainy, superficial, and inadequate, paled in comparison with that of World War II,* and much of it has been proven to be faked. Cameramen during the conflict found the efforts of frontline censors to be more taxing than the battlefield dangers. Wartime cameramen resorted to various techniques to secure footage, including climbing up trees and telephone poles to obtain panoramic shots of the battlefront or hiding in second-story rooms secretly photographing enemy troops passing below.

The Chinese-Japanese war of the 1930s provided some of the most graphic motion picture images of the period. Before American entry into the war, American newsreel cameramen were granted access to both sides of the conflict. The Japanese bombing of Shanghai was recorded by American cameramen Harrison Forman of the *March of Time* and Hearst representative Wong Hai-sheng, better known as "Newsreel" Wong. The most unforgettable image to emerge from the conflict was of a solitary baby crying in the rubble of a bombed-out Shanghai train station. The scene was captured by "Newsreel" Wong and the photo was reproduced throughout the world. The footage has been alleged to have been staged, but this has never been proven. More than one hundred million people are estimated to have seen either the newsreel or the print. One of the most publicized uses of newsreel footage during this period came in December 1937, when the United States gunboat *Panay* was bombed by Japanese planes on the Yangtze River. Fortunately, two cameramen were on board and took valuable footage of the incident. When the footage was returned to the States it was promoted at movie theaters like a Hollywood premiere.

American censors went to work as soon as Pearl Harbor was bombed. Military photographers took excellent shots of the bombing, but these were suppressed immediately by military censors. Most still pictures and motion pictures of the attack were not released for more than a year. During World War II civilian war photographers and cameramen were given the same rating as war correspondents once their accreditation was approved in Washington, D.C. They would then be assigned to a particular combat unit, where they were subject to the orders of the military or naval command to which they were attached, and were required to accompany it into battle unless otherwise ordered.

During World War II most of the combat that played on American theater screens was filmed by the U.S. Signal Corps and navy photographers as combat photography passed from civilian hands to the armed forces. While civilian cameramen were still present on the front lines, their footage was pooled with the service cameramen and heavily censored before it was released to the newsreel companies. Initially many movie theater chains were reluctant to show war footage in their newsreels, and some displayed signs which read "No War News

Shown Here.'' However, according to *Look* magazine from 1942 to 1946 four fifths of all newsreel footage was war-related.

When the war ended in 1945, so did the newsreel as television came into existence. By the late 1940s the commercial television industry was well established and postwar television news coverage had improved significantly. By the next decade many newsreel theaters had closed across the country. Motion picture coverage would become virtually obsolete on the battlefield beginning in Vietnam,* when almost instantaneous coverage became available by satellite.
REFERENCE: Raymond Fielding. *The American Newsreel, 1911–1967.* 1972.

NICHOLS, FRANCIS HENRY (1868–1904). Nichols covered the Spanish-American War* for the *New York World* and was a member of the expedition sent to inform Cuban rebel leader General Gomez that the United States had declared war on Spain. Nichols followed the Ninth and Tenth Regiments up San Juan Hill.* Following the war he moved to China as a correspondent for the *Christian Herald* and wrote a book about his travels in secluded Shensi Province, where he died at the age of thirty-six.
REFERENCES: Charles H. Brown. *The Correspondents' War.* 1967; Joyce Milton. *The Yellow Kids.* 1989.

NOEL, FRANK E. "PAPPY" (1905–1966). The American photographic war correspondent covered the campaign in Malaysia following the attack on Pearl Harbor. He then reported from the India-Burma theater. He won the Pulitzer Prize in 1943 for his photograph of a seaman in a lifeboat holding his hand out for water. This took place when Noel was adrift in a lifeboat with survivors of a ship torpedoed in the Indian Ocean. After the war he was assigned to the Mediterranean, where he covered the postwar Palestinian conflict for four years. Noel was captured during the Korean War* and spent 1950 to 1953 interned in a prisoner of war camp. While imprisoned he was able to photograph captured United Nations soldiers and after an unsuccessful escape attempt spent seven weeks in solitary confinement.
REFERENCE: Robert W. Desmond. *Tides of War.* 1984.

NORRIS-NEWMAN, CHARLES L. "NOGGS" (?). A retired army captain, Norris-Newman crossed into Zululand with the British army on January 11, 1879. Reporting for the *Natal Times* and the *London Standard*, he was reportedly the first white man to cross the river into Zululand. He had somehow attached himself to the staff of the Natal Native Contingent under Commandant Lonsdale. Norris-Newman was equipped much like the native regiment, which was not issued uniforms; rather, for identification they wore a twisted piece of red cloth around the head, which "Noggs" tucked around his sun helmet.

As the British army camped at Isandhlwana on January 21, it turned out that Norris-Newman was the only English newspaper correspondent in Natal, since most papers back in England felt the campaign would be so short it would not be worth sending representatives. The next morning he left with a column to reinforce Major Dartnell's forward party, which had spotted Zulu warriors about twelve miles away. Norris-Newman was fortunate that he had the zeal to pursue the story, for the following day the British army suffered its worst military disaster of the late nineteenth century when over 1,300 soldiers were wiped out at Isandhlwana. His account of the debacle was relayed by telegraph to Cape Town, where it was put aboard a ship bound for London and the *Standard*.

REFERENCE: Robert Wilkinson-Latham. *From Our Special Correspondent*. 1979.

O

O'DONOVAN, EDMUND (1844–1883). Born in Dublin, O'Donovan studied medicine at Trinity College before beginning his career in journalism with the *Irish Times* in 1866. In 1870 he served in the French Foreign Legion during the Franco-Prussian War* before being wounded and taken prisoner.

Following the war he moved to London. As a war correspondent for various British newspapers he covered the Carlist rising in Spain (1873) for the *Times* and the *Hour* and reported from Bosnia and Herzegovina (1876) for the *Daily News*. After various travels in Asia and the Caspian region he accompanied the relief force under Hicks Pasha to the Sudan for the *Daily News*. O'Donovan was killed along with correspondent Frank Vizetelly* when Hicks' force was ambushed and massacred near Obeid sometime between November 3 and November 5, 1883. A brass tablet in the crypt at St. Paul's Cathedral commemorates the death of O'Donovan and six other journalists who perished in this expedition.

REFERENCES: Rupert Furneaux. *News of War*. 1964; *Modern English Biography*, 1214–1215. 1965.

O'KELLY, JAMES J. (1845–1916). The Irish-born O'Kelly had already lived a life of adventure before entering journalism. He left home at the age of eighteen to join the French Foreign Legion and had fought in three wars before joining the *New York Herald*. He covered the Franco-Prussian War* for the *Daily News* while serving with the French army in 1870–1871.

Upon joining the *Herald*, he was originally employed as an art critic before transfer to foreign correspondence, when he was requested to find a way through Spanish lines to interview Cuban rebel leaders in 1873. He was completing an assignment escorting a foreign dignitary on a tour of the United States when he was assigned to cover the Sioux campaign in 1876. The week following the deaths of General George A. Custer and his column, the *New York Herald Tribune* sent O'Kelly to cover General Alfred Terry's command on the Yellowstone River.

O'Kelly's main goal was to gather the true story behind the Custer story. Arriving at Custer's headquarters in Bismarck he reportedly espied the book the late general was reading prior to his fatal march. He interviewed Custer's colleagues Colonel Frederick Benteen and Major Marcus Reno. Over the next two months he continued to put together Custer's story and demanded a government investigation into what had transpired. O'Kelly was the first to report that Sitting Bull rather than Crazy Horse had commanded the Indian forces at the Battle of the Little Big Horn.

Following his coverage of the Custer defeat he returned to Ireland and a career in politics and Parliament. However, he covered one more battlefield when the *London Daily News* sent him to the Sudan in 1885, where he became lost in the desert for several months and was given up for dead before turning up along the Nile River near Khartoum.

REFERENCES: Oliver Knight. *Following the Indian Wars.* 1960; Robert Wilkinson-Latham. *From Our Special Correspondent.* 1979.

OLIPHANT, LAURENCE (1829–1888). Born in Cape Town, South Africa, he later moved with his family to Ceylon, where he served as an assistant to his father, the chief justice. In 1852, after a trip to Russia, he published *The Russian Shores of the Black Sea in the Autumn of 1852, and a Tour Through the Country of the Don Cossacks*, which received great acclaim. He was present with his father at the siege of Sebastopol during the Crimean War.*

When the Franco-Prussian War* broke out in 1870, in the scramble to recruit war reporters the *Times* hired the novice Oliphant. He was dispatched to southern France, where he was the only English correspondent to accompany the French army. Because of his political connections he remained one of the only reporters allowed to move around unimpeded. One of his most insightful stories described the impact of the German troops on France. This article contributed to a shift in British sympathy from the Germans to France. Oliphant noted the German propensity to quarter troops directly within the civilian population rather than providing their own accommodations, eschewing tents and bivouacking. Reports of Prussian depredations and the civilian backlash led to an anti-German fervor in England. He covered fighting at Orléans, Beaugency, the destruction of Chateaudun, and the siege of Paris.

Oliphant was still in Paris for the *Times* when the Germans withdrew and the city dissolved into civil war. Amidst the Paris Commune he was reportedly unpopular with Communard leaders. He was accompanying one of their demonstrations when the National Guard fired into them point-blank. Ever the mys-

tic, Oliphant took his narrow escape from this episode as a sign that he should leave. He left Paris for America that very evening.
REFERENCE: Anne Taylor. *Laurence Oliphant*. 1982.

OLIPHANT, TOM (?). He was the Washington correspondent for the *Boston Globe* during the Vietnam War.* In 1972 Oliphant uncovered figures indicating the tonnage of bombs dropped in the war in Southeast Asia. Prior to his discovery no correspondent had reported the monthly figures, although he discovered that the numbers were readily available through the South-East Asia Section of the Public Information Office of the Defense Department. Oliphant published his findings in *Ramparts* magazine in 1972.
REFERENCE: Phillip Knightley. *The First Casualty*. 1975.

O'REILLY, JOHN "TEX" (b. 1907). The son of journalist and soldier of fortune Major Edward S. "Tex" O'Reilly, John O'Reilly joined the reportorial staff of the *New York Herald Tribune* after attending Columbia University for one year. His first major assignment was the 1937 New London, Texas, school explosion, which killed hundreds of children. In 1942 he was accredited to cover the North African theater of operations during World War II.* He reported French actions near Lake Chad and Cairo and later from Iran, before being assigned to the Tunisian front, where he accompanied British desert forces throughout the entire campaign. He was present when the Afrika Corps of 250,000 German soldiers surrendered on May 9, 1943. After the African theater he covered the Italian and Sicily campaigns, landing with forces at Salerno. In late 1943 he was stricken with malaria and after hospitalization was sent back to the States for recuperation.

He returned to Europe in time to cover the Normandy invasion. In March 1945 he temporarily left the war when he went to the United States aboard a hospital plane and wrote several articles on how wounded soldiers were flown home for treatment. He later flew back to France and reported the last days of the war, including the Allied push into Germany.
REFERENCES: Robert W. Desmond. *Tides of War*. 1984; John Hohenberg. *Foreign Correspondence: The Great Reporters and Their Times*. 1964.

ORWELL, GEORGE. *See* BLAIR, ERIC ARTHUR.

OSBON, BRADLEY SILLICK (1827–1912). Known for his daredevil feats during the American Civil War,* Osbon was the preeminent Union naval war correspondent of the war, enduring twenty-seven combat actions and seven war-related wounds. Osbon was born in Rye, New York. Continually drawn to the sea since joining the crew of a sailing ship while barely into his teens, he served on whaling ships, fought pirates in the South China Sea, and enjoyed a brief stint in the Argentine navy before returning to the States and a new career.

Osbon joined the staff of the *New York World* in 1860. On April 12, 1861, he was aboard a U.S. naval vessel in Charleston Harbor in the dual capacity of signal officer and reporter when Fort Sumter was attacked. His account of the Union surrender of the fort elevated his reputation in the journalistic ranks. That same year he joined the *New York Herald* as naval editor and was awarded a roving commission which enabled him to accompany naval expeditions. Using this to his advantage, he covered the Battle of Port Royal in 1861 and the expeditions against New Orleans and Fort McAllister, Georgia.

In early 1862, Osbon was able to slip aboard the ironclad *Merrimac*, which the South was busy rebuilding. His story caused a minor sensation. In 1863 he wrote his last Civil War dispatch when he witnessed the ironclad *Monitor*'s unsuccessful assault on Fort McAllister in Georgia. He left the staff of the *Herald* in 1864 to establish his own naval news bureau, which supplied coverage to over a dozen newspapers. When one of his reports of an impending Union attack on Wilmington, North Carolina, was reprinted in a Confederate paper he was arrested and charged with violating the Articles of War. He finally was acquitted after spending six months in prison. He continued to publish his *Nautical Gazette* until he sold it in 1884. After a checkered career, which involved other newspaper endeavors as well as unsuccessful business ventures which left him destitute, Osbon died on May 6, 1912.

REFERENCE: J. Cutler Andrews. *The North Reports the Civil War*. 1955.

O'SHEA, JOHN AUGUSTUS (1839–1905). Born in Ireland and educated at the Catholic University in Dublin, he left his medical studies to join the Irish Battalion of Pope Pius IX. In 1860 he reported the siege of Ancona for an American newspaper. Following his military service he was hired by the *New York Herald* to cover the 1866 Austro-Prussian War.* He began his twenty-five-year affiliation with the *Standard* as special correspondent in 1869 and the following year reported the outbreak of the Franco-Prussian War.* While covering the Battle of Metz he was sentenced to death for spying by the French, and was only saved by the intercession of the French emperor after various appeals by fellow war correspondents. His exploits during the Franco-Prussian War are chronicled in *Iron-Bound City* (1886).

O'Shea covered the siege of Paris and the Carlist civil war in Spain in 1873 and 1875. The next few years were spent covering the great famine in India (1877–1878). After retiring from the *Standard* he continued to write for various newspapers and published several books, including *Leaves from the Life of a Special Correspondent* (1885), and *Roundabout Recollections* (1892).

REFERENCES: *DNB*, Supp., 1901–1911; Dennis Griffiths, ed. *The Encyclopedia of the British Press*. 1992.

O'SULLIVAN, TIMOTHY H. (c. 1840–1882). He was born in either New York City or Ireland; little is known about his early life. He began his apprenticeship in the craft of photography while employed at Mathew Brady's* galleries in New York and Washington, D.C. With the outbreak of the American

Civil War* in 1861, Brady and several assistants, O'Sullivan among them, went into the field to document the war. In the fall of 1861, O'Sullivan was assigned to record General Thomas W. Sherman's South Carolina campaign. He returned to Washington the following May and quit Brady to work for Alexander Gardner.* Under Gardner, O'Sullivan was appointed "superintendent of the field or copy work to the Army of the Potomac." He took some of the most outstanding images of the conflict following the Battles of Gettysburg, Fredericksburg, and Petersburg, and the surrender at Appomattox. One of his greatest scoops took place on May 21, 1864, when O'Sullivan climbed to the top of a building and photographed General Grant's council of war in the courtyard of the Massapomax church shortly before the Battle of Cold Harbor.

Though he is best known for his Civil War photographs, his western landscape work is highly regarded for its remarkable clarity and an aesthetic approach heralding the modern era. As the official photographer of the U.S. Geological Survey, he accompanied the 1867–1869 Clarence King expedition along the fortieth parallel through Nevada, Utah, and California. He also was with the Thomas O. Selfridge expedition to Panama (1870), the George Wheeler expeditions to California, Nevada and Arizona (1871–1875), and the Wheeler survey along the hundredth meridian (1870, 1873–1874). In 1880 O'Sullivan was appointed chief photographer for the Department of the Treasury. The following year he was stricken with tuberculosis. His wife died several months before he expired on January 14, 1882.

REFERENCES: Pat Hodgson. *Early War Photographs.* 1974; James D. Horan. *Timothy O'Sullivan: America's Forgotten Photographer.* 1966.

OUTLAW CORRESPONDENTS. Following the outbreak of World War I,* the British secretary of state for war, Lord Kitchener, issued orders that would bar war correspondents from obtaining credentials to cover the British Expeditionary Forces in France. Kitchener proclaimed that any British correspondent reporting the conflict in France or Belgium would be treated as an "outlaw," risking arrest and prosecution. This did little to stem the flow of correspondents to Europe, but it did interfere with the transmission of their reports to their home offices. The most effective alternative to official channels was to personally carry dispatches to London. Despite the risks, a fairly large contingent of outlaw correspondents kept the British public informed during the early months of the war. Additional news dispatches came from neutral correspondents from the United States who were in Belgium and France, unburdened by the outlaw label.

REFERENCE: Robert W. Desmond. *Windows on the World.* 1980.

P

PACIFIC WAR CORRESPONDENTS ASSOCIATION (PWCA). Established in Honolulu by twenty-two war correspondents, its goal was to maintain communications between correspondents and Admiral Nimitz' CINCPAC (Commander in Chief of the Pacific) headquarters. It was imperative to maintain a liaison which could eliminate censorship and transmission difficulties as well as attempt to improve facilities for traveling and news gathering. All accredited correspondents in the Pacific theater of World War II* were eligible for membership.
REFERENCE: Robert W. Desmond. *Tides of War.* 1984.

PACKARD, ELEANOR (1905–1972). Born in New York City, she attended the University of Washington and the Columbia University School of Journalism. The longtime Rome correspondent for the *New York Daily News* covered the Italian invasions of Ethiopia and Albania, the Spanish Civil War,* and the Sino-Japanese war of the 1930s. With the outbreak of World War II* she reported from the Sudetenland, Italy, and Germany. Following the war she left the UP for the *Daily News* in 1948. She served as its Rome correspondent until her death in 1972.
REFERENCE: Robert W. Desmond. *Tides of War.* 1984.

PACKARD, REYNOLDS (b. 1903). Born in Atlantic City, New Jersey, he attended Bucknell University before moving to Buenos Aires to study Spanish. While in Argentina he joined the United Press before moving for a brief time to the *Chicago Tribune*. He returned to the UP and reported from the capitals of Europe. Following his marriage to Eleanor Packard,* they pursued a joint career as foreign correspondents. He covered the Ethiopian War* and the Spanish Civil War.* After a transient career they settled in Rome, where he headed the Italian bureau of the UP and she was the top reporter on his staff of correspondents. In April 1941 the Packards were with Italian forces during the Axis invasion of Greece and Yugoslavia. The Packards stayed in Italy until June 1942, but the last six months following the American entry into the world war were spent in a prison camp. After a brief return to the States following their release they went back to Italy to cover the Allied invasion for the UP.

In May 1943 Reynolds and Eleanor Packard flew with other correspondents in a massive bombing raid over Palermo, Sicily. In September Reynolds covered the Allied landing at Salerno and the following January was one of fourteen correspondents to report the landings at Anzio in Operation Shingle. He was joined by his wife during the subsequent Italian campaign, and they were among the first contingent of correspondents to enter Rome. Reynolds carried with him the key to the Rome UP office, which he was forced to abandon the day following Pearl Harbor. Packard wasted no time in reopening his office and resuming his position as bureau manager three years after fleeing the German onslaught. In August 1944 he headed a four-man team covering Allied invasion forces on the French Riviera advancing toward Germany. Several months later he was sent to Greece to reopen the UP office there. He coauthored with his wife *Balcony Empire*.

REFERENCE: Robert W. Desmond. *Tides of War*. 1984.

PAGE, CHARLES ANDERSON (1838–1873). Born in Illinois, prior to the American Civil War* his only journalism experience had been editing the *Mt. Vernon News*, a small Iowa weekly newspaper. At the outbreak of the war he was a clerk in a government office in Washington. In June 1862 his offer to cover the battlefront was accepted by the *New York Tribune*, and later that month he was reporting the Peninsular and Seven Days' campaigns. Page evaded army restrictions which forbade reporters from visiting army encampments by serving as a hospital worker during the Second Bull Run campaign of 1862.

According to one source, his descriptive account of the Peninsular campaign was unsurpassed. His columns then began appearing under his own byline "C.A.P." in 1863. In that year he covered the Gettysburg campaign with the Army of the Potomac. In 1864 he again represented the *Tribune* during the Battle of the Wilderness. Following the Civil War he resigned from the paper when he was appointed consul to Switzerland. He stayed on after his diplomatic career and was involved in the evaporated milk business. He died in London.

REFERENCES: J. Cutler Andrews. *The North Reports the Civil War*. 1955; Louis M. Starr. *Bohemian Brigade*. 1954.

PAGE, TIMOTHY JOHN (b. 1944). Born in Tunbridge Wells, Kent, England, Page learned the photographic craft without formal training. He credits fellow war photographers* Horst Faas,* Larry Burrows,* and others for mentoring him in the craft. He photographed his first war in 1963–1965, covering the Laotian civil war and Hanoi-supported guerrillas in Thailand. Best known for his coverage of the Vietnam War,* he originally covered the conflict as a freelancer. From 1965 to 1969 his pictures were published by Time-Life, *Look, Life, Paris-Match*, the UPI, the AP, and many others. While covering Vietnam with Sean Flynn,* son of the noted actor, he experimented with a camera that could be attached to a rifle and would simultaneously record the death of the victim when the rifle was fired.

Page was severely wounded several times, the first time at the Battle of Chu Lai, and then more seriously in 1966 while covering the Buddhist riots. After recovering from shrapnel wounds to his head, chest, and arms he was back in action the following year. In 1967 he was the victim of friendly fire when a B-57 fired on a U.S. Coast Guard ship, killing several crew members and putting Page in a hospital for several weeks. His closest brush with death occurred in 1969 when a colleague stepped on a land mine, sending shrapnel deep into Page's brain. After eighteen months of recuperation he returned to journalism. Since 1979 Page has worked as a freelancer for *Observer Magazine, Newsweek*, the BBC, and SIPA Press in Paris.
REFERENCES: Phillip Knightley. *The First Casualty*. 1975; Jorge Lewinski. *The Camera at War*. 1978; Tim Page. *Page after Page*. 1988.

PAGET, HENRY MARRIOTT (d. 1936). Paget was a newspaper artist for the *Sphere*, covering the First Balkan War in 1912–1913. He was the only artist-correspondent* on the scene when Nazim Pasha was assassinated in Constantinople, making Paget's rendering of the event the only pictorial record of the incident.
REFERENCE: Dennis Griffiths, ed. *The Encyclopedia of the British Press*. 1992.

PAGET, WALTER STANLEY (1863–1935). Walter Paget and his brother Sydney were well-known illustrators in Victorian-era England. Walter covered his only war as sketch artist for the *Illustrated London News* with the Suakin expedition (1884–1885) to rescue general Gordon at Khartoum. Paget joined the *Sphere* when it was founded in 1900 and illustrated the classic books *Treasure Island* (1899), *Pilgrim's Progress* (1906), and *Arabian Nights* (1907).
REFERENCES: Dennis Griffiths, ed. *The Encyclopedia of the British Press*. 1992; Pat Hodgson. *The War Illustrators*. 1977.

PAINE, RALPH DELAHAYE (1871–1925). Paine was born in Lemont, Illinois. Since his father had fought in the Battle of Inkerman and the American Civil War,* it was only natural that the son would be drawn to the battlefield. In 1894, following graduation from Yale, he joined the *Philadelphia Press*. He served as war correspondent during the Spanish-American War.* William Randolph Hearst* chose Paine to transport a jeweled sword to the Cuban rebel leader General Maximo Gomez on behalf of the *New York Journal*. His quixotic mission ended when, after a journey of over five thousand miles, he was forced to send Gomez the sword through an intermediary.

Paine's coverage of the 1900 Boxer Rebellion* in China for the *New York Herald* is chronicled in his books *Dragon and the Cross* (1912) and *Roads of Adventure* (1922). In 1902, he led a successful campaign against the beef trust, and following a short interlude with the *New York Telegraph* left journalism to devote himself full-time to fiction and historical writing. Harkening back to his days at Yale, most of his nonfiction work focused on the history of Yankee shipping, including *The Ships and Sailors of Old Salem* (1909), *The Old Merchant Marine* (1919), and *The Fight for a Free Sea* (1920). He wrote numerous novels and boys' stories. During World War I* Paine was made a special observer of the Allied fleets. He died in Concord, New Hampshire.
REFERENCES: Charles H. Brown. *The Correspondents' War.* 1967; *DAB.*

PAINTER, URIAH H. (b. 1837). A Quaker from West Chester, Pennsylvania, Uriah Painter reported the American Civil War* for the *Philadelphia Inquirer.* Because of the astuteness and the proficiency of his reportage, the twenty-four-year-old war correspondent quickly became a confidant of Secretary of State Edwin Stanton, who relied heavily on Painter's dispatches, ensuring him access to military telegraph lines.

Painter covered the First Battle of Bull Run in 1861 and was the first newspaper correspondent to report the appearance of Lee's army crossing into Maryland shortly before the Battle of Antietam in 1862. Painter missed perhaps his greatest story when he left the front briefly on what a fellow correspondent termed a "Union mission," which in reality was his marriage in Ohio. The following year he made amends when he reported the Battle of Gettsysburg.
REFERENCES: J. Cutler Andrews. *The North Reports the Civil War.* 1955; Louis M. Starr. *Bohemian Brigade.* 1954.

PALMER, FREDERICK (1873–1958). Born in Pleasantville, Pennsylvania, and educated at Allegheny College, Palmer joined the *New York Press* as London correspondent in 1895. Two years later he reported the Greco-Turkish War* of 1897, beginning a long career as war correspondent. By 1897 he was affiliated with the *New York World* and *Collier's Weekly.* That year he reported a gold rush in the Klondike of northwestern Canada before moving to the Philippines to cover the Moro insurrection in the aftermath of the Spanish-American War.* In the summer of 1900 he left the Philippines to cover the Boxer Rebellion* in China. He next reported the Boer War* and then the 1904 Russo-Japanese War.*

Palmer reported the 1912 Balkans conflict for the *New York Times* and two years later was arrested in Mexico City while covering the Veracruz and Tampico incidents for *Everybody's Magazine.* Following his release he crossed the Atlantic to report the developing conflict in Europe. Palmer was the first and only American journalist accredited with the headquarters of the British Expeditionary Forces in France when tight controls were imposed shortly after the German advance westward in 1914.

While he was in Washington, D.C., for a brief respite in April 1917 the United States declared war on Germany. James Gordon Bennett, Jr.,* offered Palmer the position of chief correspondent in Europe for the *New York Herald* at an extraordinary salary of $40,000 per year. Prior to leaving the nation's capital he renewed his friendship with General John Pershing, whom he had met in the Philippines in 1899. Pershing updated him on the war situation in France.

While they sailed together on the *Baltic* to France, Pershing cajoled Palmer into accepting a commission to oversee the Press Section of G-2 at only $2,400 per year. At a fraction of what he would have received for the *New York Herald*, Palmer, ever the patriot, accepted the role with the full knowledge that he would be supervising the accreditation of war correspondents for the American Expeditionary Force (AEF) as well as directing censorship of the press. Now known as Colonel Palmer, he quickly shed his cloak as journalist for his new role as army officer and censor, becoming increasingly penurious at releasing information to his former colleagues. Palmer covered his last conflict in the early 1930s, when he reported the rebellion against the Machado government in Cuba for the *New York Herald Tribune*. He wrote numerous books, including *Going to War in Greece* (1897), *The Ways of the Service* (1901), *With Kuroki in Manchuria* (1904), *My Year of the War* (1915), and *My Second Year of the War* (1917).

REFERENCES: Emmet Crozier. *American Reporters on the Western Front 1914–18.* 1959; Robert W. Desmond. *Windows on the World.* 1980; Phillip Knightley. *The First Casualty.* 1975.

PANAMA INVASION. In 1989 U.S. forces invaded Panama to remove dictator Manuel Noriega from office after he refused to abide by democratic elections that repudiated his regime. Following the Grenada invasion* press debacle a new system of media coverage had been approved by the Pentagon. According to the Sidle Commission directed by Major General Winant Sidle, the press had agreed to a pool system in which select journalists and photographers representing various media giants would share their coverage with other media members waiting at the Pentagon. However, the Pentagon did not fulfill its end of the agreement completely, resulting in the Washington pool arriving at the scene hours after the fighting began. It was not until the conclusion of the invasion that the Pentagon offered what one source has described as ''journalism's equivalent of a cleanup mission.''

REFERENCE: Johanna Neuman. *Lights, Camera, War.* 1996.

PARRIS, JOHN A., JR. (b. 1914). Born in Sylvia, North Carolina, Parris attended North Carolina College before joining the United Press in 1934. In 1943 he was working in the London office when he was selected as one of the five UP correspondents to accompany the Allied landings in North Africa. He

went on to cover the Italian campaign and report the D-Day landings from London. He coauthored *Springboard to Berlin* with Ned Russell,* Leo Disher,* and Phil Ault.
REFERENCE: Robert W. Desmond. *Tides of War.* 1984.

PARSLOW, E. G. (d. 1899). Parslow was a correspondent for the *Daily Mail* during the Boer War.* While in the besieged town of Mafeking* he became assistant editor of one of the Boer siege newspapers,* the *Mafeking Mail.* In November 1899 he got into an argument with an artillery officer in a hotel bar. When Parslow told the officer, "You're no gentleman," the officer drew his pistol and killed the correspondent. To save embarrassment at home Parslow's death was listed as an accident.
REFERENCE: Robert Wilkinson-Latham. *From Our Special Correspondent.* 1979.

PATERSON, ANDREW BARTON (1864–1941). Born in Australia, he is probably best known as the alleged creator of the country's national song, *Waltzing Matilda.* After leaving his solicitor's practice he covered the Boer War* for the *Sydney Morning Herald* and the *Melbourne Argus.* The popularity and precision of his dispatches led the Reuters* agency to use his reports, which appeared under his nickname "Banjo," after the racehorse.

Following the campaign in South Africa he reported the Philippines insurrection for the *Sydney Morning Herald* as well as the Boxer Rebellion* in China. During World War I* he covered the western front, and ended up enlisting in the Australian Remount Service as an ambulance driver. At the conclusion of the war he had risen to major. His personal recollections were published as *Happy Despatches* (1934).
REFERENCE: C. Semmler. *The Banjo of the Bush.* 1966.

PATTERSON, JOSEPH MEDILL (1879–1946). Born in Chicago and educated at Yale, the son of *Chicago Tribune* publisher R. W. Patterson got his first taste of war reporting when he covered the 1900 Boxer Rebellion* during his summer break from Yale University. After graduating the following year he joined the staff of the paper. He left journalism in 1903–1904 for a stint in the Illinois state legislature and then in 1905–1906 was commissioner of public works in Chicago. In 1908 he left the paper to pursue literary interests, producing a novel and cowriting a play. On the death of his father in 1910 Patterson became copublisher of the *Chicago Tribune* with his cousins, but this would not deter him from returning to the combat zone in the pursuit of news.

In 1914 Patterson covered the occupation of Veracruz by American marines before promptly setting out for the Belgian front with the outbreak of World War I* just weeks later. Before departing for Europe he started a Mexican edition of the *Tribune* for the troops. He had brought along his own photographer, Edwin F. Weigel, who was assigned to bring along a motion picture camera and the requisite film. Weigel shot footage of U.S. Marine and Naval operations in Mexico. Upon his arrival in Europe, Patterson convinced a French pilot to fly him over French positions in Flanders. In addition he was able to obtain aerial photographs of bombed-out Ypres. Patterson covered the German army early in the conflict, which was much more cooperative than the heavily censored British and French forces. Patterson's account of the war prior to American entry was published as *Notebook of a Neutral* and serialized in the *Tribune* in 1915.

In 1916 he rejected an offer of a commission in the Illinois National Guard, but with American intervention in 1917 he enlisted as a private in the artillery. He eventually rose to the rank of captain, serving in France in 1918, where he was gassed and wounded in five engagements. In 1918 Patterson cofounded the New York tabloid newspaper, the *Illustrated Daily News*. Within several years its name was changed to the *New York Daily News*.

REFERENCES: Robert W. Desmond. *Windows on the World*. 1980; Lloyd Wendt. *Chicago Tribune*. 1979.

PATTON SLAPPING INCIDENT. General George S. Patton, Jr., also known as ''Old Blood and Guts,'' was commander of the U.S. Seventh Army. In August 1943, wearing his pearl-handled revolvers, Patton visited a military-hospital evacuation tent in Sicily. When he came across a soldier whom he suspected of faking illness he slapped the soldier across the face in full view of medical staff. This incident was initially unreported. But, several days later Patton visited another hospital tent. After asking a soldier what injury he was recuperating from, Patton slapped him when he answered that it was for a nervous disorder. Calling the soldier a coward, Patton kicked him when he attempted to flee. As the general left the tent he was overheard by war correspondent Noel Monks* shouting that there was no such thing as shell shock.

It turned out that the victim had heroically served in the Tunisian and Sicilian campaigns and was only hospitalized after a doctor attempted for over a week to convince him to seek convalescence. The correspondents' pool of almost two dozen reporters decided that rather than leak the story they would send a courier to General Eisenhower in an attempt to have Patton apologize to the soldier. After receiving confirmation from other sources Eisenhower ordered Patton to apologize to both soldiers and all witnesses to the incidents, as well as to other members of the soldiers' divisions, or else lose his command. Although Patton complied, he was punished by being barred from action until after the invasion of Normandy almost a year later.

While literally thousands of servicemen were privy to what had occurred, it had still not been announced in the press. Eisenhower convinced the war correspondents not to break the story because it could provide grist for enemy propaganda and embarrass the military hierarchy. For almost three months secrecy prevailed, until Washington columnist Drew Pearson got wind of the story. Incensed that the scoop was credited to a columnist rather than a war reporter,

AP correspondent Edward Kennedy* published his account of the incident, making worldwide headlines, although it was months out of date.
REFERENCES: Robert W. Desmond. *Tides of War.* 1984; Phillip Knightley. *The First Casualty.* 1975.

PEARSE, HARRY H. S. (?). The accomplished artist-correspondent* accompanied the 1884–1885 Gordon relief expedition for the *London Daily News* and the *Illustrated London News*, reporting and taking part in the Battle of Abu Klea. He witnessed and reported the Battle of Abu Kru during the reconquest of the Sudan in 1898. When not engaged by the *Graphic* in times of conflict, he wrote on hunting for the *Morning Post*. While besieged in Ladysmith* during the Boer War* he coproduced the free illustrated newspaper the *Ladysmith Bombshell*.
REFERENCES: Byron Farwell. *The Great Anglo-Boer War.* 1976; Pat Hodgson. *The War Illustrators.* 1977; Robert Wilkinson-Latham. *From Our Special Correspondent.* 1979.

PELCOQ, JULES (?). Jules Pelcoq was a Parisian book illustrator who covered the French side for the *Illustrated London News* during the Franco-Prussian War.* While covering the 1870 siege of Paris, Pelcoq dispatched his work by balloon to London. Wood engravings were then made from his sketches once they arrived in England. His work captures the attempt by Parisian troops to break through the surrounding Prussian army and the plight of citizens on the edge of starvation forced to eat animals from the Parisian zoo.
REFERENCE: Pat Hodgson. *The War Illustrators.* 1977.

PEOPLES, JOHN H. "CHAPARRAL" (?). A New Orleans printer, he had originally volunteered for a three-month enlistment during the Mexican War.* Following his discharge he continued to follow American forces as a war correspondent for the *New Orleans Delta* and then the *New Orleans Crescent*. Peoples, whose dispatches appeared under the byline "Chaparral," was among the veteran newspaper printers who published their own army newspapers for the invading troops. While running the *American Flag* from Matamoros he established the *Vera Cruz Eagle* after the American occupation of the coastal city. One of the most enterprising publishers during this conflict, he later established the *American Star No. 2* in Puebla, Mexico, shortly before General Winfield Scott's march on Mexico City. All of these camp newspapers were partially supported by printing contracts with the American army. Peoples joined Scott's forces as they left for the Mexican capital, where he would soon bring out the *American Star, Mexico*. He was later hired by the *New Orleans Picayune* to cover the California gold rush.
REFERENCES: Fayette Copeland. *Kendall of the Picayune.* 1943; Robert W. Johannsen. *To the Halls of the Montezumas.* 1985.

PERKINS, WILLIAM T. (d. 1967). Marine corporal Perkins was serving as an American military correspondent and combat photographer in South Vietnam when he threw himself on a grenade and saved the lives of several soldiers on October 12, 1967. He was posthumously awarded the Congressional Medal of Honor.
REFERENCE: Charles P. Arnot. *Don't Kill the Messenger.* 1994.

PERLIN, BERNARD (b. 1918). War artist Bernard Perlin was hired by the Office of War Information to create posters for the Domestic Section in 1942. The following year he was discharged because of a budget shortfall. In 1943 he joined *Life* as its artist-correspondent* in the Sudan and Eritrea. When he arrived in Cairo he came to the realization that there was no war-related activity in progress at his destination and made other plans without consent from *Life*. His magazine meanwhile forgot all about him and he spent several months of rest and recuperation in Cairo.

Perlin was soon restless and feeling a little guilty, so he created his own assignment without the authorization of his employers. In May 1944 he made his way by boat to the German-occupied island of Samos in the Aegean Sea. His traveling companions included a British military observer and some Greek soldiers on a mission to create a bit of havoc and plant disinformation among the Germans concerning the looming Allied invasion of Europe. The mission was only moderately successful from a military perspective, but Perlin reaped his greatest journalistic scoop with his sketches of Greek resistance fighters.
REFERENCE: Frederick S. Voss. *Reporting the War: The Journalistic Coverage of World War II.* 1994.

PERRY, HENRY (?). At the outset of the American Civil War* Perry came to Richmond to cover the Confederacy for the *New Orleans Picayune*. He covered Confederate operations at Manassas and Norfolk in Virginia before moving to Memphis in March 1862 to cover the western theater of operations. He reported the Corinth campaign and a Memphis gunboat battle. When New Orleans fell in April 1862 the *New Orleans Picayune* came under federal control, forcing Perry to transfer to the pro-Confederate *Memphis Appeal*.
REFERENCE: J. Cutler Andrews. *The South Reports the Civil War.* 1970.

PERRY, MERT (1929–1970). He was the freelance partner of Charles Mohr,* Vietnam War* correspondent for *Time* magazine. Perry had been initially sent to Vietnam by UPI, but resigned to work for *Time*. In 1962 he reported what was then the largest assault in the history of helicopter warfare as fifty H-21 helicopters loaded with two hundred American advisors and six hundred ARVN (Army of the Republic of Vietnam) troops lifted off for the war zone just north of Saigon. By 1963 he was in his second year covering the conflict and had already developed an excellent reputation for his work. According to fellow journalist David Halberstam,* Perry was the most favored correspondent among military officers. In 1963 Perry and Mohr had come under fire from both the Diem regime and American censors, leading both to resign from the magazine. Vietnam was the high point of Perry's journalistic career. After resigning from *Time* in 1963, he was never able to recapture the controversial success he enjoyed when he worked with Mohr for *Time*. He died of a massive heart attack at the age of forty-one.

REFERENCES: Michael Emery. *On the Front Lines*. 1995; William Prochnau. *Once upon a Distant War*. 1995.

PHILBY, HAROLD ADRIAN RUSSELL "KIM" (1912–1988). Best known as a Soviet spy, the Cambridge-educated Philby journeyed to Spain to report the Spanish Civil War* for the *Times* from the Nationalist side. After graduating from college in 1933 Philby worked as a freelance journalist in Vienna and then for the *Review of Reviews* in London. He was in Spain in 1936 when war broke out. The following year he replaced George Steer,* who had left the *Times* for the *Daily Telegraph*. Philby remained in Spain for the duration of the conflict. He was awarded the Cross of the Order of Military Merit for bravery on the battlefield by General Franco. Philby later became the head of the anti-Soviet section of the British Secret Intelligence Service until it was revealed he was a longstanding member of the Soviet KGB.

During the Spanish Civil War Philby was a secret agent for the Comintern and continued to act in this capacity while representing the *Times* in Berlin in 1939. The following year he became a double agent in the British Secret Service while reporting from France as a war correspondent. Philby continued as a journalist after the war, working for the *Sunday Observer* in Beirut and covering the Middle East. It was during this period in the 1950s that Philby became a triple agent, adding the American Central Intelligence Agency to his list of employers. In 1963 he fled to the Soviet Union.

REFERENCES: Robert W. Desmond. *Tides of War*. 1984; Phillip Knightley. *The Master Spy*. 1989; Phillip Knightley, with Bruce Page and David Leitch. *The Philby Conspiracy*. 1975.

PHILLIPS, PERCIVAL (1877–1937). The American-born correspondent began his newspaper career in Pittsburgh before becoming a foreign correspondent in 1897 covering the Greco-Turkish War* for the *Chicago Inter-Ocean*. The next year he reported the Spanish-American War* for the *New York World*. Joining the *Daily Express* in 1901, Phillips covered the Russo-Japanese War,* several natural disasters, the Italo-Turkish War, the Balkan Wars of 1912–1913, and World War I.* During World War I he became a British citizen and was knighted for his reportage of the conflict. Phillips remained with the British Expeditionary Forces headquarters throughout the war. He was with the Belgian army in 1914 and in 1918 accompanied the occupation forces into Germany.

In 1922, now known as Sir Percival Phillips, he joined the *Daily Telegraph* for the remaining fifteen years of his life. In the early 1930s he traveled through

China as a roving correspondent before covering the Ethiopian War* of 1935–1936. He became ill while reporting from Tangier at the outset of the Spanish Civil War* in 1936. He returned to London, where he died the following year.
REFERENCES: Robert W. Desmond. *Windows on the World.* 1980; Robert W. Desmond. *Tides of War.* 1984; John Hohenberg. *Foreign Correspondence.* 1964.

PICKERELL, JAMES (b. 1936). The photojournalist James Pickerell covered the Vietnam War* from 1963 to 1967. His pictures have appeared on the cover of *Newsweek* magazine and in other periodicals. His book *Vietnam in the Mud* (1967) chronicles the conflict from the level of the foot soldier. Beginning in 1967 he covered the White House and Congress and has gone on assignment to dozens of countries. Presently he reports the corporate scene.
REFERENCE: Frances Fralin, ed. *The Indelible Image.* 1985.

PICTURE POSTCARDS. In 1869 the Austro-Hungarian Empire issued the first postal card. By 1873 the U.S. Post Office Department had begun issuing these cards to postmasters as a method for streamlining short communications between businesses. However, it was not until 1901 that the phrase "post cards" became legal in the United States, when postal regulations against the moniker were relaxed.

The golden age of picture postcards coincided with the 1910 Mexican Revolution and the subsequent American war preparedness efforts along the border. During this era entrepreneurial photographers captured the exploits of Pancho Villa, General "Black Jack" Pershing, the U.S. naval invasion of Veracruz, and the Mexican attack on Columbus, New Mexico. Thousands of inexperienced American troops were mobilized along the Rio Grande River. All of these events were depicted on postcards, many of them graphically violent in nature, which were bought by the participants as proof of their proximity to the action and mailed by the millions throughout the world. These picture postcards remain an underappreciated component of war photojournalism during this era.

The picture postcard boom was facilitated by the invention of a postcard printer in 1910 by the Rochester Optical Company, a subsidiary of Eastman Kodak. It was inexpensive at only $7.50, with a forty percent discount to professionals, since George Eastman realized the windfall he would reap through the sale of postcard-backed paper and processing chemicals. Among the most successful practitioners of this process were such giants as the International Film Service and the Max Stein Company. Smaller enterprises included the Mexican War Photo Postcard Company and Kavanaugh's War Postals. There were numerous one-man operations as well, including that of Walter H. Horne* of El Paso, who reported during 1916 producing five thousand cards a day.
REFERENCE: Paul J. Vanderwood and Frank N. Samponaro. *Border Fury.* 1988.

PIGOTT, JOHN (?). Pigott was the Reuters* correspondent with the Gordon relief expedition who broke the news of the death of the Victorian war hero.

Pigott had a long career as a war correspondent prior to the Sudan expedition, having covered the Zulu, Afghan, Egyptian, and Burmese campaigns.
REFERENCE: Donald Read. *The Power of News*. 1992.

POLK, GEORGE (d. 1948). Polk was a CBS correspondent who was assassinated in 1948 while attempting to reach insurgent leaders for an interview during the civil war in Greece. Beginning in 1949, the George Polk Award has been conferred annually to foreign correspondents in memory of the late Polk. The award is sponsored by Long Island University's Brooklyn Center and its Department of Journalism.
REFERENCE: Kati Marton. *The Polk Conspiracy*. 1990.

POND, ELIZABETH (?). Pond studied international relations at Harvard before entering journalism. More interested in the political ramifications of the Vietnam conflict than the military aspects, Pond began covering the war for the *Christian Science Monitor* beginning in August 1967. Initially assigned to report on South Vietnamese politics, by 1968 she was writing about the rampant corruption in South Vietnamese government and the rise to power of Nguyen Van Thieu.

Following the 1970 American invasion of Cambodia, Pond decided to get a firsthand perspective of conditions in Cambodia herself. Driving with several correspondents on Highway 1 between Saigon and Phnom Penh they were taken prisoner. After five and a half weeks of being moved from village to village and rounds of interrogation they were released unharmed. Pond chronicled her experience in captivity in a five-part series for the *Monitor*. The journalists considered themselves exceedingly fortunate to have survived since twenty-nine journalists had been captured or were missing in Cambodia. She returned to the United States soon after this harrowing incident. Pond continued to cover world politics for the *Monitor*, reporting from South Korea and then Europe.
REFERENCE: Virginia Elwood-Akers. *Women War Correspondents in the Vietnam War, 1961–1975*. 1988.

POTTER, KENT (1947–1971). Born in Philadelphia, he began working as a photographer for United Press International in 1963. Five years later he was in Saigon reporting the Vietnam War.* In May 1969 he was promoted to UPI Newspictures manager for Vietnam. Potter is believed to be the youngest American war journalist killed in the Vietnam War, perishing in a Vietnamese helicopter crash over Laos.
REFERENCE: Charles P. Arnot. *Don't Kill the Messenger*. 1994.

POWER, FRANK LE POER (1858–1884). Born in Ireland, the son of a bank manager, Power was educated at Clongowes. He witnessed warfare for the first time when he served in the Austro-Hungarian army and was besieged with Russian forces in Plevna. His first position as war correspondent was on the

Bulgarian frontier during the Russo-Turkish War.* When he returned home he joined the staff of *Saunders's* in Dublin.

In 1883 he agreed to go the Sudan with Edmund O'Donovan* of the *Daily News*, with the idea of collaborating on a book on the Sudan. Power was also commissioned to make sketches for the *Pictorial World*. They accompanied the Hicks Pasha expedition into the Sudan along with British correspondent Frank Vizetelly.* Power had the good fortune to fall ill at the start of the journey and was returned to Khartoum for recuperation, thus saving his life. However, the Hicks expedition of almost ten thousand Egyptian soldiers and two British war correspondents was wiped out near El Obeid on November 5, 1883. When news reached Cairo of the disaster a month later Power provided the *Times* with the only firsthand account of events leading to the debacle.

In 1884 he would not be as fortunate. He was one of the two Britons cut off with British general Gordon in the besieged town of Khartoum. Power was entrusted by Gordon to drum up support in London for men and money to defeat the Mahdi. On April 1, a letter from special correspondent and now acting British consul Power appeared in the *Times* noting the dire straits of the garrison—the first authentic news of the critical situation in Khartoum. By the 16th telegraph lines had been cut and messages could only be smuggled out at great risk. Power's dispatches from Khartoum were instrumental in compelling the British government to launch a relief force up the Nile. After pressure from both the public and the press a relief effort was finally mounted led by General Garnet Wolseley. Unaware of the relief force, Power left Khartoum with a British officer attempting to run the Nile blockade and send out a message to Cairo, but both men were murdered on the way. Power and six other correspondents who died in the Sudan campaigns are commemorated by a tablet in St. Paul's Cathedral which bears their names. Power's letters from the Sudan were collected and published in 1885 as *Letters from Khartoum*.

REFERENCES: Office of the *Times. The History of the "Times": The Twentieth Century Test, 1884–1912.* 1947; Robert Wilkinson-Latham. *From Our Special Correspondent.* 1979; Oliver Woods and James Bishop. *The Story of the "Times."* 1983.

PRESS ASSOCIATION OF THE CONFEDERATE STATES. *See* CONFEDERATE PRESS ASSOCIATION.

PRICE, BYRON (1891–1981). Born in Topeka, Indiana, Price turned to journalism while still in college. Upon graduation from Wabash College in 1912 he went to work first for the United Press and then began his twenty-nine-year career with the Associated Press. He served in the army during World War I* and received several commendations for bravery.

Following the bombing of Pearl Harbor, Price was requested by President Roosevelt to organize and direct the government's Office of Censorship, with the goal of balancing wartime security with freedom of the press. In early 1942 he described press censorship as a "necessary evil" in wartime. Price agreed that some censorship was necessary, but as a professional journalist and advocate of press freedom he insisted that he should be responsible only to the president and that he should have a free hand in developing his agency's policies. In addition, he wanted the system of censorship to be for the most part voluntary, which meant convincing the nation's newspapers, magazines, and other media to police their own news sources. Roosevelt acceded to these requests and in 1942 the Office of Censorship was formally established with Price as its director.

Price's staff totaled over fourteen thousand employees, who were responsible for censoring all communications between the United States and Europe. The censorship office issued pamphlets setting guidelines for what war-related stories were fit to print. Emphasis was placed on the question "Is this information I would like to have if I were the enemy?" The censorship code worked well enough to keep secret the 1942 Allied invasion of Africa, the D-Day invasion, and the building of the atomic bomb. Its obvious targets included news leaks concerning troop movements and locations of important military installations.

When the war ended Price wasted no time in closing down the censorship office. Following word that the Japanese had surrendered on August 14, 1945, he received permission to close down the agency the next afternoon. After the war President Truman appointed him to investigate relations between the American occupation forces and the German populace. He later served as vice president of the motion picture censorship board and held other offices connected with the movie industry. He was also an important figure in the moving of the United Nations headquarters to its current site.

REFERENCE: Frederick S. Voss. *Reporting the War*. 1994.

PRICE, GEORGE WARD (1895–1961). Educated at Cambridge, Price was hired as a reporter for the *Daily Mail* while still a student. After covering the Balkan War he was stationed in Paris. During World War I* he covered the disastrous Dardanelles campaign and the Italian front, where he witnessed the Battle of Caporetto. After attending the Paris Peace Conference and subsequent meetings in Cannes and Genoa in 1922, he traveled widely for the paper. In 1933 he was with the French Foreign Legion during the Moroccan conflict. In the years leading up to World War II* he interviewed Hitler and Mussolini and covered the invasion of the Sudetenland. He was one of the earliest war reporters in France and covered the southeastern theater of the war in Europe. He went on to report the North African campaign and the Korean War.* He wrote *Extra-Special Correspondent* in 1957.

REFERENCES: Robert W. Desmond. *Tides of War*. 1984; Dennis Griffiths, ed. *The Encyclopedia of the British Press*. 1992.

PRICE, MORGAN PHILIPS (b. 1885). The great-grandson of a cofounder of the *Manchester Guardian*, Price covered the Russian front for the newspaper during World War I.* He was the only British correspondent with the Russian army on the eastern front when Czar Nicholas abdicated. By the time he arrived in Petrograd in 1917 he had become one of the best-informed correspondents covering events in Russia prior to the October Revolution. Price was not a newcomer to Russian affairs. His family had been importing lumber from there since the 1850s and Price had even learned the Russian language by 1910, when he joined a scientific expedition to Siberia.

In 1914 he was assigned to follow events in Russia for the *Guardian*. He subsequently reported much of the war and the Russian Revolution. Next to John Reed,* he was probably the foremost Russian correspondent of his era. Price and Reed were the only correspondents to witness the Bolshevik seizure of power, resulting in a news scoop for Price and the *Guardian*. But his greatest scoop came when he convinced Trotsky to allow him to print the secret treaties between the deposed Czar and the Allies. Price translated the document through the night. Among the most provocative plans was the Sykes-Picot agreement, which would have divided the Arab world among the Allies after World War I. This treaty caused great embarrassment in England when it was published by the *Guardian* in November 1917.

Following the Russian withdrawal from the war effort in February 1918, Britain, Japan, France, and the United States organized an Allied expeditionary force to intervene in the Russian Revolution on the side of the Whites. Price was the only Western correspondent to report the intervention from the Russian side in a bid to counteract anti-Bolshevik reporting. In an attempt to win the propaganda war, the Soviet Foreign Office printed fifty thousand copies of Price's pamphlet *The Truth About the Allied Intervention in Russia*, criticizing the British censor for blocking the publication of almost all of his dispatches since the Allied intervention. Price later reported from the Middle East, won a seat in Parliament, and continued to travel widely through the Balkans and the Soviet Union for the *Guardian*.

REFERENCES: David Ayerst. *The Manchester Guardian: Biography of a Newspaper.* 1971; Phillip Knightley. *The First Casualty.* 1975.

PRIOR, MELTON (1845–1910). Prior was born in London and attended various art schools before breaking into journalism as a print artist with the *Penny Miscellany* while still in his teens. He began his affiliation with the *Illustrated London News* in 1873 and served his first stint as war artist and correspondent covering Sir Garnet Wolseley's forces during the Ashanti War. For thirty years he covered the major wars and conflict between the Ashanti War and the 1904 Russo-Japanese War.*

In 1874 he recorded the events surrounding the Carlist uprising in Spain. Two years later he covered the Balkan conflicts, including the war between Serbia and Bulgaria, and the Russo-Turkish War,* and also accompanied Austrian forces during the Bosnian conflict. He witnessed many of the South African campaigns between 1877 and 1881, including the Kaffir, Basuto, and Zulu Wars. During the 1879 Zulu War Prior had a premonition of impending death, so he enlisted the services of another artist, who was killed on the march to Eshowe.

Prior accompanied the burial detachment assigned to the field of Isandhlwana following the destruction of the British force there by Zulu forces. He covered the First Boer War through its conclusion at Majuba Hill on February 21, 1881.

In 1882 Prior accompanied English forces as they entered Cairo during the Arabi Revolt and two years later was with Baker Pasha's forces at the Battle of El Teb. In 1884–1885 Prior followed Lord Wolseley's relief expedition up the Nile. He witnessed the Battle of Abu Klea while ensconced within the British square. After accompanying Sir Gerald Graham's forces in his 1885 Sudan campaign he was with Sir Frederick Roberts during the 1886–1887 Burma expedition. Between 1889 and 1892 he sketched revolutionary conflicts in Brazil, Argentina, and Venezuela. During the next eight years he covered frontline action in South Africa (1896), the Greco-Turkish War,* war on the North West Frontier of India, and the 1898 Cretan uprising. He was among the first correspondents to reach South Africa in 1899 during the resumption of hostilities and was with British force besieged at Ladysmith* between November 2, 1899, and February 28, 1900.

Following the Somaliland expedition in 1903 he covered his last war as war broke out between Russia and Japan in 1904. He accompanied Japanese forces under General Oku during the Liaotung Peninsula campaign. Prior reportedly spent only one year at home during his remarkable thirty-year career as war artist for the *Illustrated London News*. His life is commemorated by a tablet bearing his name in the crypt at St. Paul's Cathedral. He wrote *The Campaigns of a War Correspondent* (1912).
REFERENCES: *DNB*, 1901–1911; Robert Wilkinson-Latham. *From Our Special Correspondent.* 1979.

PYLE, ERNEST "ERNIE" TAYLOR (1900–1945). The most popular reporter of World War II,* Pyle was born near Dana, Indiana. In 1923 he dropped out of Indiana University just short of graduation to begin his journalism career at the *La Porte Herald.* Shortly thereafter he became reporter for the Scripps-Howard–owned *Washington Daily News.*

Pyle witnessed war for the first time in 1940, when he arrived in London to report the Battle of Britain. His columns, characterized by an understated humor, developed a following in the States. He quickly developed an affinity for the English and their culture as he reported the devastating raids by the Luftwaffe. From 1941 to 1942 he remained in the United States sorting out an increasingly troubled personal life just as his popularity was on the rise. Returning to wartime assignments he covered the training and minutiae of everyday life in the military. His meteoric rise to a household name in the States began in 1942 when he landed with American troops in North Africa. He covered the Tunisian front and was on hand for Field Marshal Erwin Rommel's rout of American troops at Kasserine Pass. In 1944 Pyle accompanied Allied forces to Normandy beach and then on to the liberation of Paris. That same year he won the Pulitzer Prize for his war reports.

He returned to the States briefly before being persuaded by the navy to cover the Pacific war. Despite premonitions of his death he landed with marines on Okinawa. On April 17 he arrived on the tiny island of Ie Shima and the following day accompanied a patrol which came under sniper fire. Pyle was fatally wounded by three gunshots that went under his helmet, striking him in the left temple. Among his books were *Ernie Pyle in England*, a collection of his columns on the Battle of Britain, and *Here Is Your War*, an account of his experiences in the Tunisian campaign. Pyle's writings were unique in the annals of war reportage in that they focused more on the individual combatants than on the leaders and their battle strategies. The 1945 movie *The Story of G.I. Joe* recounted his exploits in World War II. Pyle is buried at the National Memorial Cemetery near Honolulu.

REFERENCES: Lee G. Miller. *The Story of Ernie Pyle*, 1950; David Nichols, ed., *Ernie's War.* 1986.

Q

QUIET AMERICAN, THE. Graham Greene's 1955 novel *The Quiet American* offers one of the most discerning portraits of a war reporter. Fowler, the narrator of the story, is in the tradition of British expatriates who go native in exotic locales, this time in Saigon as the United States looks to inherit France's colonial war against the Viet Minh. The "quiet American" referred to in the title is an intelligence agent named Pyle who leads a misguided campaign to establish a democratic alternative to Communism and colonialism. Fowler's dilemma is whether to expose the clandestine agitator who is supplying explosives to a terrorist group or to finger him for Communists who would undoubtedly kill him. The book was adapted to the big screen in the 1958 film of the same title.
REFERENCES: Howard Good. *Images of the War Correspondent in Anglo-American Fiction.* 1985; Graham Greene. *The Quiet American.* 1955.

QUIN, WINDHAM THOMAS WYNDHAM (1841–1926). Quin was born in Adare, Limerick County, Ireland, and educated in Rome and at Oxford University. He entered the military service in 1862, joining the First Life Guards as cornet. During his career in the military he exhibited a tendency toward wanderlust, taking several leaves of absence to report foreign wars, participate in steeplechase competition, and exercise his passion for sailing.

In 1867, he joined Sir Robert Napier's military expedition against Abyssinia as war correspondent for the *Daily Telegraph*. He witnessed the capitulation of Magdala. His dispatches appeared under "Mr. Adare." During the final advance on Magdala he showed Henry Stanley* of the *New York Herald* where hundreds of murdered prisoners were dumped. Quin also represented the *Telegraph* during the 1870 Franco-Prussian War*. In 1871 he won a seat in the House of Lords and traveled to the American West to hunt buffalo with frontiersmen Buffalo

Bill and Texas Jack. Three years later he explored the Yellowstone region with Dr. George Henry Kingsley. Quin chronicled his exploits with Kingsley in *The Great Divide*, published in 1876. Over the next quarter century Quin, better known as the earl of Dunraven, pursued sports and politics in equal measures. He is best remembered as a yachtsman and as a mediator in land reform legislation in Ireland.

REFERENCES: *DNB*, 1922–1930; Windham Thomas Quin, *Past Times and Pastimes*, 1922.

R

RALPH, JULIAN (1853–1903). Born to English parents in New York City, Ralph left school early to serve an apprenticeship with a small New Jersey newspaper, where he learned most facets of the newspaper business. After a failed attempt at launching his own paper he moved on to several others before finding employment with the newly created *New York Daily Graphic* in 1873. In 1875 his work came to the attention of Charles A. Dana of the *New York Sun*, where Ralph would be employed for the next two decades. During his career with the *Sun* he became one of the most highly respected reporters in the country, covering politics and major events including the end of the Molly Maguires, the funeral of Ulysses S. Grant (1885), the New York blizzard of 1888, and the trial of Lizzie Borden (1893).

Since the *Sun* did not give its writers a byline, not until 1890, when Ralph's articles began appearing in *Harper's Weekly* and *Harper's Monthly*, did he win a wider following and name recognition. During the 1890s several collections of his works were published, including *Our Great West* (1893) and *Dixie; or Southern Scenes and Sketches* (1895). He also wrote numerous works of fiction, short stories, and poetry.

In 1895 he left *Sun* for Hearst's *Journal*, for which he reported his first wars. In 1897 he covered the Greco-Turkish War,* and in 1899 he went to South Africa to cover the Boer War* for the *London Daily Mail* and *Collier's* magazine. Along with his son Lester, who was an accomplished illustrator and journalist, he covered the major campaigns of Field Marshal Lord Roberts. He joined other British correspondents at Bloemfontein in editing the *Friend*, a daily newspaper for the army in the field. He saw his health decline during the war after he was wounded, thrown from a horse, and stricken with enteric fever. He returned to the States in 1902 and died after a long illness the following year.

REFERENCES: *DAB* 8; "Julian Ralph," *Outlook*. 240. January 31, 1903. Frank O'Brien. *The Story of the "Sun."* 1918.

RANTHOM, JOHN REVELSTOKE (d. 1923). The Australian-born Ranthom accompanied British forces in the reconquest of the Sudan in 1898, the youngest journalist with the expedition. Following the Egyptian and Sudan campaigns he moved to the United States. He reported the Spanish-American War* for the *Chicago Herald* and then expeditions to New Guinea and Alaska. In 1910 he moved to Rhode Island as editor of the *Providence Journal*. His career as war correspondent effectively finished, Ranthom served stints with the Associated Press, the *Daily Telegraph*, and other periodicals during the last decade of his life.

REFERENCE: Robert W. Desmond. *The Information Process*. 1978.

RATHER, DAN (b. 1931). Born in Wharton, Texas, following graduation from Sam Houston State Teachers College Rather worked for the UPI and the *Houston Chronicle*. In the mid-1950s he entered the field of broadcast journalism with a CBS affiliate in Houston before rising to chief of CBS' southwestern bureau in Dallas in 1961. He was posted to London by CBS news in 1964, where he began a stint as foreign correspondent covering stories in Greece and India. In the fall of 1965 and early 1966 he requested reassignment to Saigon, spending the next several months covering the Vietnam War.* According to former Vietnam war correspondent William Prochnau, Rather's adoption of safari jackets for his field reports made them "de rigeur for television," and in the process made the Saigon tailor who manufactured them wealthy overnight.

In 1966 Rather returned to Washington, D.C., and was designated to replace Harry Reasoner at the White House. In 1974 he was named anchorman-correspondent for *CBS Reports* and seven years later replaced Walter Cronkite* on the *CBS Evening News*.

REFERENCES: Gary Paul Gates. *Air Time: The Inside Story of CBS News*. 1978; William Prochnau. *Once upon a Distant War*. 1995.

RAY, MICHELE (b. 1938). Born in Nice, France, Ray seemed an unlikely candidate for war reporter. A fashion model for the House of Chanel, Ray had a predisposition for adventure and risk taking. She had tried amateur racing and organized an all-woman motor vehicle expedition from Alaska to Tierra del Fuego. Her account of the expedition was published in the French magazine *Elle*.

In 1966 Ray arrived in Vietnam without accreditation or a visa, but in no time became affiliated with the Agence France-Presse. She accompanied Green Berets on her first combat mission, which they dubbed "Operation Michele." In 1967 she became the news story when she was captured by the Viet Cong on the central coast. She was released after three weeks of Communist indoc-

trination. In high spirits and good health following her release, Ray was accused
of staging her capture. She left the country not long after this incident.
REFERENCE: Virginia Elwood-Akers. *Women War Correspondents in the Vietnam War,
1961–1975*. 1988.

RAYMOND, HENRY JARVIS (1820–1869). Born near Lima, New York,
Raymond is probably best remembered as the founder and editor of the *New
York Times*. Reportedly able to read by the age of three, he graduated from the
Genesee Wesleyan Seminary, later to be known as Syracuse University, and the
University of Vermont.
   In the early 1840s he entered journalism, working for Greeley's *New Yorker*
and then the *New York Tribune*. He left for an editorship position with the
Morning Courier and New York Enquirer in late 1843. After a short political
career he became managing editor of the recently established *Harper's New
Monthly Magazine* in 1850. In 1851, Raymond and two partners cofounded the
New York Daily Times.
   In 1857 he moved his family to Europe. Two years later Raymond, accompanied by *Times* correspondent William Johnston, traveled to Solferino in preparation for the looming battle during the Austro-Italian War.* They would be
the only Americans to report the battle. Raymond wrote most of the dispatch,
which was taken by courier to Paris, where Mrs. Raymond was to send it by
steamer to New York. Although it was published over two weeks after the battle,
well after other accounts had been published, his was the first eyewitness account printed in America.
   During the American Civil War* Raymond again acted as war correspondent
for his own paper. He was often at the front supervising the activities of his
reporters while contributing coverage of his own. He has often been credited
with inventing the display headline in 1865. Raymond was among the reporters
at Bull Run who incorrectly reported a Union victory prior to the eventual
outcome. He reported the Peninsular campaign and the Battle of Roanoke.
REFERENCE: J. Cutler Andrews. *The North Reports the Civil War*. 1955.

REA, GEORGE BRONSON (1869–1936). Born in Brooklyn, New York, and
educated in private schools, he worked in Cuba as an engineer for five years
prior to the Cuban War for Independence. He disagreed with the portrait drawn
by the yellow press* of Spanish treatment of the Cubans. From 1895 on he
blasted American press coverage of conditions in Cuba and wrote *Facts and
Fakes About Cuba*, in an attempt to tell his side of the story. Rea had traveled
widely through Cuba and reportedly found little evidence of Spanish atrocities.
   In 1896 he was hired by the *Herald* to report rebel activity on the island. He
spent the better part of nine months covering the insurrection with Generals
Gomez and Maceo. However, in 1897 he became embroiled in an argument
with the rebel leader General Gomez over an article critical of the Cuban cause.

After Gomez threatened to have him shot Rea left the island and returned to New York.

Rea returned to Cuba shortly before the Spanish-American War.* Unlike most of his colleagues, Rea was sympathetic to the Spanish side and not content to simply remain in Havana, basing his stories merely on interviews with rebel spokesmen. He was seated in a Havana café with Sylvester Scovel* of the *World* the night the *Maine* exploded. Rea was later assigned to study San Juan Harbor and its fortifications. He was with Cuban forces during the battle of El Caney.

Following the Spanish-American War, he settled in the Philippines, where he held several posts in the occupation government. In 1904 Rea founded the *Far Eastern Review* and during World War I* he was military attaché to Spain. In 1918 he moved to Peking as advisor to the Chinese government. After a falling out over economic policy matters Rea left for a post in the Japanese puppet state of Manchukuo, a position which he admitted was "the kind of job I have always wanted. The whole world is agin [sic] me."

REFERENCES: Charles H. Brown. *The Correspondents' War*. 1967; Joyce Milton. *The Yellow Kids*. 1989; G.J.A. O'Toole. *The Spanish War*. 1984.

READE, WILLIAM WINWOOD (1838–1875). Born in Oxfordshire and educated at Oxford, he first made his name as an explorer in West Africa in 1856. Reade returned to West Africa in 1871, and two years later covered the Ashanti War for the *Times*. He ended up participating in the action as well, fighting with the Forty-second Highlanders at the Battle of Amoaful and distinguishing himself at the Battle of Abakrampa, where he fought beside the Royal Navy and Marines, fending off hundreds of Ashanti warriors at a besieged church. Following his third expedition to Africa his health began to deteriorate. He died soon after returning to England. He wrote a number of books based on his experiences as an explorer and war correspondent in West Africa, including *Savage Africa, a Tour* (1863); *The African Sketch-book*, two volumes (1873); and *The Story of the Ashantee Campaign* (1874).

REFERENCES: *DNB*; Robert Wilkinson-Latham. *From Our Special Correspondent*. 1979.

REDFERN, JOHN (1903–1990). Born in Chesterfield, England, he began his journalism career with the *Derbyshire Times*, and worked for several other small papers before signing on with the *Daily Express* in 1934. As a war correspondent during World War II,* he covered the campaigns of the First and Eighth British armies in North Africa, Sicily, Italy, and northwestern Europe. Following the war he continued in his role as foreign correspondent for the *Express*. Based in Africa much of the time, he covered many of the independence movements there. He retired in 1968.

REFERENCES: Robert W. Desmond. *Tides of War*. 1984; Dennis Griffiths, ed. *The Encyclopedia of the British Press*. 1992.

REDKIN, MARK (b. 1908). Redkin was schooled in war journalism while working for the Russian army newspaper *Krasnaya Zvezda* prior to World War II.* During the Russian war he worked as a photojournalist for TASS and *Frontovaya Illustracia.* He covered most of the significant events of the war, including the fall of Berlin. Following the surrender of Germany he reported the war against Japan. After the war he worked for the Planeta publishing house in Moscow.
REFERENCE: Daniela Mrazkova and Vladimir Remes, eds. *The Russian War: 1941– 1945.* 1975.

REDPATH, JAMES (1833–1891). The Scottish-born Redpath moved to America at a young age. He developed an early affinity for newspaper writing, having published letters in the *New York Tribune* from the South before the outbreak of the American Civil War.* On one occasion he interviewed John Brown in Kansas. Some sources have described this as the first real newspaper "interview," or possibly the first use of the term "interview" to describe this method of news gathering. Redpath continued his affiliation with the *Tribune* throughout the war. He covered General Sherman's march through Georgia to the Atlantic coast in 1864 and the evacuation of Charleston in 1865. Following the war he established the Redpath Lyceum Bureau in Boston in 1868, supervising this organization for seven years. It is considered the first lecture bureau in the United States. He returned to the *Tribune* in 1879 and covered the controversial land question measures in Ireland for several years. He wrote several books, including *Echoes of Harpers Ferry* (1860), *The John Brown Invasion* (1860), *Life of John Brown* (1860), and *John Brown the Hero* (1862).
REFERENCES: J. Cutler Andrews. *The North Reports the Civil War.* 1955; Robert W. Desmond. *The Information Process.* 1978.

REED, DAVID (?). Reed covered conflicts in Africa beginning in 1953. He reported the Mau Mau uprising in Kenya and in 1960 the independence movement in the Congo as a staff correspondent for *U.S. News and World Report.* His fluency in Swahili has led to interviews with important African statesmen, including Patrice Lumumba. He traveled widely throughout the continent in the 1960s before becoming foreign affairs editor for *Reader's Digest.* In the late 1960s he began covering the Vietnam War.*
REFERENCE: David Reed. *111 Days in Stanleyville.* 1965.

REED, JOHN SILAS (1887–1920). Reed was born in Portland, Oregon, and educated at Harvard College. He entered journalism with the *New York Globe* and then the *American* magazine. In 1913 he published a book of poetry about life in the artistic enclave of Greenwich Village and began to gravitate toward radical politics. That same year he briefly left mainstream journalism and joined the radical *Masses.* Soon after this he was hired by *Metropolitan* magazine and the *New York World* to cover the Mexican Revolution.

After making contact with the rebel forces of Pancho Villa, he accompanied them through four months of battles. His portrait of Villa softened the latter's image in the minds of the American public. His war reports and several essays written for the *Masses* were collected and published as *Insurgent Mexico* in 1914. He was promoted as "America's Kipling" by his employers, and his columns became a forum for his radical politics as he wrote sympathetically of the peon cause. He spent two tours covering World War I* beginning in 1914 for the *Metropolitan*, focusing on the daily life of the common soldier in the trenches and later writing *The War in Eastern Europe* (1916). During his second trip to cover the war he traveled from the Aegean coast through Serbia to Russia, and then back to Constantinople, Rumania, and Bulgaria. He was nearly executed by czarist soldiers in 1915 who thought he was a spy.

After he married the ersatz journalist Louise Bryant in 1916, they went to Russia to cover the Bolshevik Revolution for the *Masses* and other socialist journals. Returning to the United States to successfully fight a sedition charge, he went on the lecture circuit, describing the revolution and arguing against American participation in World War I.* His involvement in radical politics led to several arrests and the publication of his most noted work and the best eyewitness account of the revolution, *Ten Days That Shook the World* (1919). He fled the United States for Russia to avoid facing federal charges for subversion, and immersed himself in the revolution. He died in Moscow of typhus, and was buried in the Kremlin on October 19, 1920, the first American so honored. Reed was the greatest radical journalist of his time. A 1981 movie, the Warren Beatty vehicle *Reds*, was based on Reed's Russian experiences.

REFERENCES: *DAB* 15, 450–451; Granville Hicks. *John Reed: The Making of a Revolutionary*. 1930; Tamara Hovey. *John Reed: Witness to Revolution*. 1975.

REID, SAMUEL CHESTER, JR. (?). The son of a prominent sea captain, Reid went to sea as a merchant sailor while still in his teens. He studied law in Mississippi, spent a term as U.S. Marshal, and served with the Texas Rangers during the Mexican War.*

Reid became one of the best-known and best-paid special correspondents covering the Confederacy during the American Civil War.* His weekly pay as a war correspondent for the *New Orleans Picayune* in 1862 began at twenty-five dollars per week. By the end of the following year he was receiving four times that amount from the *Mobile Tribune*. In addition he was given a feed allowance for his horse. According to one source, over a thirty-month period he earned almost twelve thousand dollars from various newspapers. Reid counted the *Memphis Appeal*, the *Mobile Register*, the *Montgomery Advertiser*, and the *Atlanta Intelligencer* as employers during the war.

Reid accompanied Albert Sidney Johnston's army on its march to Pittsburg Landing and reported the Battle of Shiloh in April 1862. When Union forces captured New Orleans Reid joined fellow reporter Henry Perry* and joined the staff of the *Memphis Appeal*. Soon afterward Reid became the special correspondent for the *Mobile Register* when Peter Alexander* resigned. Reid was vilified by his fellow correspondents when he was accused of breaching security with a dispatch that led to a crackdown on press coverage during the evacuation of Corinth.

In 1862 he interviewed President Jefferson Davis and covered the Richmond scene. He arrived in Chattanooga just as federal troops began their bombardment of the city. In November he covered the Battle of Perryville and the following January the Battle of Murfreesboro for the *Richmond Examiner*. When he attempted to telegraph his account of the battle to the *Mobile Register*, General Braxton Bragg refused permission, sensitive about critical press reports concerning his decisions. In retaliation Reid omitted Bragg's name from his battle account when he mailed it to the paper the next day. However, Reid provided the best account of the battle from the Southern point of view.

Reid was in Charleston, South Carolina, during the 1863 siege. In June he reported the Battle of Chancellorsville from Virginia and then traveled to Chattanooga to accompany the Army of Tennessee. He resigned from the *Mobile Register* in April over disagreements with the editors over military policy and joined the competing *Mobile Daily Tribune*. Although he did not personally witness the Battle of Chickamauga, his elaborate recounting of the battle was reportedly the most complete Confederate newspaper account. He worked for two weeks on his ten-thousand-word account, and it was published in pamphlet form as *Great Battle of Chickamauga* at Mobile in November 1863.

By October Reid was also representing the *Atlanta Intelligencer* at the Battle of Lookout Mountain and during the Battles of Chattanooga. Reid followed Joseph Johnston's army at the beginning of the Atlanta campaign but missed most of the fighting. Reid faced increasing restrictions as military censorship became more intense with each Confederate loss. Having fallen ill the day before the Battle of Kennesaw Mountain, Reid was disabled back in Atlanta; however, he did manage to return shortly after its denouement to gather enough information to file a report. By late 1864, Reid was confined to bed in Charleston with rheumatism and his career as a Civil War special correspondent had come to a close.

REFERENCE: J. Cutler Andrews. *The South Reports the Civil War*. 1970.

REID, WHITELAW (1837–1912). Reid reported the American Civil War* for the *Cincinnati Gazette* beginning in 1861 when he was assigned to follow Ohio's troops under the command of George B. McClellan. In a series of dispatches under the pseudonym ''Agate,'' Reid detailed the camp life of the fledgling Union Army in all its monotony and squalor.

During his tenure with the Union forces, Reid, as aide-de-camp to McClellan, was permitted full access to the generals or any other staff members he wished to accompany. He reported his first battle in July at Rich Mountain, Virginia, where Confederates under the command of General Robert Seldon Garnett were routed by federal troops. Later, at Carricks' Ford, Reid witnessed soldiers dying in battle for the first time as Union forces caught up with Garnett's fleeing troops. Despite Garnett's death in the battle, most of the Confederate forces were allowed to slip away. In his reportage of the battle Reid blamed McClellan for failing to destroy the enemy when they were within his grasp. Reid's accounts of McClellan's ineptitude foreshadowed the general's reputation for hesitancy and caution that would cost him his command of the Army of the Potomac.

After a brief respite back in Ohio he resumed his position as war correspondent, this time joining William Rosecrans' staff at Clarksburg, Virginia. In 1862 Reid honed his skills while covering the bloodshed at Carnifex' Ferry. Again his reportage was laced with scathing criticism of the federal leadership. His penchant for critiquing the Union war effort, from its leadership to the inadequacy of medical care and defective ammunition, led to his banishment from Camp Nevin, where he was stationed between battles.

Shortly after returning to Cincinnati, Reid was dispatched to the western theater, where he witnessed the Battles of Fort Donelson and Fort Henry, both successful actions led by Brigadier General Ulysses S. Grant. Reid resumed his letters to the *Gazette* under his pen name Agate. His trenchant coverage of every aspect of the army's activities portrayed a much more positive appraisal of federal efforts than the year before. In April 1862 he produced what became the classic newspaper account of the Battle of Shiloh. With his reputation made by his nineteen-thousand-word account of this Union debacle, Reid had earned a national reputation as his war reporting was reprinted throughout America.

After Shiloh the *Gazette* sent him to cover the tumult of Washington, D.C. In 1863 Reid witnessed bloodshed for the last time at the Battle of Gettysburg before embarking on the next stage of his journalistic career reporting military affairs from his headquarters in the nation's capital. Besides his war reports, Whitelaw Reid wrote many books, including *Ohio in the War: Her Statesmen, Her Generals, and Soldiers*, two volumes (1868). He died in London after a successful career in journalism which included owning the *New York Tribune* from 1872 to 1912.

REFERENCES: Royal Cortissoz. *The Life of Whitelaw Reid*, 2 vols. 1921; Bingham Duncan. *Whitelaw Reid: Journalist, Politician, Diplomat*. 1975.

REISNER, GEORG (1911–1940). Born in Breslau, Germany, he graduated from the *Gymnasium* in Breslau before studying law and medicine at universities in Breslau and Freiburg. Because of his affiliation with the Socialist Party, he had to cut short his studies and flee to France when Hitler came to power. He took up photography in Paris and began freelancing in 1934. He reported the Spanish Civil War* from 1936 to 1937. *Life* published some of his work in the early phases of the developing war in Europe. In 1939 he was arrested and jailed by the French, but managed to escape. He fled to Marseille, where he committed suicide rather than face internment in a French concentration camp.

REFERENCE: Turner Browne and Elaine Partnow. *Photographic Artists and Innovators*. 1983.

REMINGTON, FREDERIC SACKRIDER (1861–1909). Born in Canton, New York, Remington had a career as a writer, illustrator, and painter of the American West that overshadowed his short career as a war correspondent. Son of an American Civil War* cavalry officer and newspaper publisher, he fared poorly at school, necessitating a three-year stint at various military schools. In 1878 he entered the Yale School for Fine Arts in preparation for a painting career. He dropped out the following year, but not before selling his first illustration. He toiled unsuccessfully at a succession of jobs before taking his first trip West in 1881. As a result *Harper's Weekly* published one of his cowboy sketches that same year. He tried his hand at various western livelihoods only to find that he disliked ranching and that he could make a good income as an investor in a saloon. In 1886, he was hired by *Harper's Weekly* and assigned to the Southwest. The 1880s saw increasing artistic success as his illustrations appeared for two years in *Harper's* as well as in Theodore Roosevelt's *Ranch Life and the Hunting Trail*.

Remington was never merely an artist, for he possessed considerable literary ability as well. During the late 1880s and into the 1890s he followed the last days of the Indian-fighting cavalry in the West. He covered the developing Indian problems at the Sioux reservation at Pine Ridge, South Dakota, in 1890 for *Harper's*, which published one of his drawings of the ghost dance ceremony. When the bloodshed at Wounded Knee occurred on October 29, 1890, Remington was fifty miles away, although he filed his story of the event as if he had witnessed the actual story. Known for his attention to detail, Remington the artist and painter spent parts of two decades covering the military in the Southwest, and like most reporters he developed a close camaraderie with the soldiers. However, this did not keep him from castigating the Indian management system under the Department of the Interior in his columns for *Harper's*.

Remington had always wanted to test his mettle as a war correspondent. Although he hoped to cover some monumental campaign in Europe, his opportunity came instead in 1896 when Hearst sent him and Richard Harding Davis* to Cuba for the *New York Journal*. Remington was assigned to illustrate the reports of Davis, but the two correspondents proved ill suited for working together as they searched fruitlessly for the Cuban resistance leader General Gomez. When their search for the colonial rebellion and the elusive Gomez proved futile, Hearst supposedly responded, "You furnish the pictures and I'll furnish the war." Remington resolved to return home to the States. When the battleship *Maine* was sunk mysteriously in Havana Harbor Hearst and Remington had their war. Once in Cuba, the rotund reporter quickly became unpopular with the rank and file as he ate more than his share of the limited rations. One account reported that Remington had "a jovial way of going up and joining messes," after which he ate messmates "out of house and home." Officers, on the other hand, were put off by his consumption of more than his share of the dwindling liquor supply. He finally managed to witness actual combat at the Battle of San Juan Hill,* although his view of the fight was from a thousand yards in the rear, where he hid from snipers' bullets in a brush-covered hollow. As the American flag was raised on top of the hill, Remington finally left his sanctuary in the thick brush to join them. In the end Remington was disappointed in his "great war," a precursor of the jungle wars of the twentieth century. Hoping to record the frontline spectacle like Richard Harding Davis, Remington instead became the "chronicler of the battle's rear." Ill suited physically and temperamentally for on-the-spot war reportage, Remington was a dismal failure as a war correspondent, and the Spanish-American War* would be his last to cover.

REFERENCES: Douglas Allen. *Frederic Remington and the Spanish American War.* 1971; Douglas C. Jones. "Remington Reports from Badlands: The Artist as War Correspondent," *Journalism Quarterly.* Winter 1970; Peggy and Harold Samuels. *Frederic Remington: A Biography.* 1982.

REPINGTON, COLONEL CHARLES a COURT (1858–1925). Repington was appointed the military correspondent* of the *Times* on January 1, 1905. Educated at Eton and Sandhurst, by the age of forty-six he had established a reputation as a serious student of military literature. He served as an officer in the Omdurman campaign and in the Boer War* before resigning from the army in 1902 due to an indiscretion. His first posting as a war reporter was with the *Morning Post* before joining the *Times* in time for the Russo-Japanese War.* Under the customary heading "From Our Military Correspondent" his articles became an instant success. His classic reporting of this conflict was revised and republished as *The War in the Far East: 1904–1905* (1905).

No attempt was made to define his capacity as war correspondent for the *Times* until the conclusion of the Russo-Japanese War. He was assigned the role of critic of the British military establishment and became an ardent advocate of continental intervention and an end to British isolation in the years preceding World War I.* Repington concluded that if Britain intended to hang on to India it would be necessary to become a continental power and maintain a continental army. Most of his theorizing on military reform was meant to thwart Russian expansion. His views underwent revision in 1906 as he concentrated his editorializing on the Franco-German military situation and sending British forces to France in the event of war with Germany. His other works included *The First World War* (1920) and *After the War* (1922).

REFERENCES: Office of the *Times. The History of the "Times": The Twentieth Century Test, 1884–1912.* 1947; Charles a Court Repington. *The War in the Far East.* 1905.

REUTERS. This London-based international news agency was created in 1851 by Julius Reuter. Its heyday was the late nineteenth century, as Britain's imperial power was fading. Reuters correspondents based in Cairo accompanied the British relief column to rescue General Charles Gordon at Khartoum. While the fall of Khartoum was reported by official news sources, the fate of Gordon was unknown. On February 9, 1885, Reuters correspondent John Pigott* telegraphed the news scoop that Gordon had been killed.

During the African campaigns Reuters served the dual function of not only providing news from the British army but also relaying news to the army. In 1885 the Cairo office contributed to the morale of the desert-bound troops by providing daily telegraphic news summaries free of charge addressed to the "Army up the Nile." This tradition was continued until after World War II.*

Typically, whenever a war broke out, Reuters would appoint several correspondents who were given detailed instructions. William Wallace, who covered the 1896 Niger-Sudan campaign, was to follow a protocol in which he was required to file daily reports of fifty words.

During the Greco-Turkish War* of 1897 Reuters correspondents reported from both sides of the battlefields. Among the reporters in action were Howell Arthur Gwynne,* who covered the Turkish army, and Kinnaird Rose, who was with the Greeks. Gwynne was in charge of Reuters correspondents during the Boer War.* Censorship restrictions required reporters to write all messages in English, eschewing codes, ciphers, and other languages. The agency's greatest coup during the conflict was its scoop of the relief of Mafeking.*

Reuters' next scoop occured during the 1904 war in Tibet. It was a traditional method for Reuters representatives to establish a good working relationship with high officials. So when correspondent Henry Newman arrived at Lhasa, he did just that. While normal protocol required that war correspondents wait until two hours after the official dispatches had been communicated to deliver their own telegraphic accounts, Newman was permitted to send his account of the Battle of Guru Younghusband prior to the official communiqué, giving Reuters a two-hour beat on the story.

With the outbreak of World War I,* Reuters correspondents were dispatched to every front in which British or German forces were in action. The first correspondents attached to British forces in Flanders were assigned to headquarters and except for infrequent visits to the battlefront were generally barred from witnessing the action. Five correspondents were eventually allowed to report from the British front in France. Most newspapers were not represented at the front and relied heavily on the dispatches from Reuters.

During World War I Reuters correspondents were required to pay their way with the British army, supplying their own food, transport, and accommodations. If they were offered a military rank or position, correspondents generally refused, afraid it could compromise their integrity. Reporters were expected to file separate reports each day for both editions of the news.

Prior to World War II, war correspondents from Reuters covered the Ethiopian War* of 1935 and the Spanish Civil War.* Eight full-time reporters plus assorted stringers* covered both sides of the African conflict, while only four reported from Spain. Dick Sheepshanks reported both conflicts and was killed with three other correspondents when a shell shattered a car in which they were sitting on the last day of 1937. The only survivor was the future Soviet spy Harold Philby,* then reporting for the *Times*.

During World War II five Reuters war correspondents were killed while reporting and another eight staff members died as members of the armed forces. Some of Reuters' best coverage of the war came from the European war at sea. Arthur Oakeshott participated in numerous convoys to Russia, and John Nixon covered the pursuit of the German battleship *Bismarck* and the sinking of the British battle cruiser *Hood*. Often scooped by the better-represented and better-capitalized UP and AP, Reuters was unsurpassed in its coverage of the eastern front between Germany and Russia. Harold King was the outstanding Reuters reporter in this theater.

In preparation for D-Day, the news agency began recruiting more journalists beginning in 1943. Among the most notable was Doon Campbell,* who had been rejected from military service because he wore a prosthetic device due to a birth defect. Campbell would be the youngest war correspondent at Normandy beach. In September 1944, Jack Smyth landed with paratroopers in the ill-fated Arnhem landings. He was eventually wounded, captured, and brutally interrogated by the Gestapo. Among Reuters' scoops during the war was Gestapo chief Heinrich Himmler's offer to surrender to the Allies and the suicide of Goebbels. REFERENCE: Donald Read. *The Power of News*. 1992.

REYNOLDS, QUENTIN (1902–1965). He was born in the Bronx, New York, and educated at Brown University. After studying law at Brooklyn Law School he opted for a career in journalism, joining the *New York World-Telegram* in 1928. Due to cost cutting he lost his job in 1932 but was hired by the International News Service. He left the news service to report World War II* for *Collier's*, an affiliation that would last until 1949. He rose to the top of the profession in England with his reporting of the Battle of Britain. In 1942 he accompanied Allied forces during Operation Jubilee, which was an attempt to test German defenses along the French coast and to destroy strategic installations. That same year he reported the North African desert campaign. In 1943 he reported the Sicilian campaign and later the Dieppe raid, the fall of France, and the Russian war.

In 1949 he was embroiled in a libel suit with columnist Westbrook Pegler. Following a Reynolds book review in which he implied that Heywood Broun* died as a result of his stressful relationship with Pegler, the columnist wrote a series of columns charging Reynolds with having been an absentee war correspondent, a war profiteer, and a scoundrel. In the resulting fray *Collier's* fired Reynolds. His career in shambles, having in quick order lost his television and radio jobs and any lecture opportunities, he sued Pegler, and in 1954 a jury awarded the former war correspondent $175,000 in punitive damages, a record at that time for a libel judgement.

Reynolds was a prolific writer of books and news articles. His admitted lack of research led to his involvement in a hoax that was a minor literary sensation in 1952. His book on George DuPre, who claimed to have worked as a British agent during the war, and a subsequent article based on his exploits for *Reader's Digest* damaged his credibility when it emerged that DuPre was a poseur. In response, his supportive editor at Random House, Bennett Cerf, simply promoted his book as a work of fiction instead.

He wrote numerous books, including *Convoy, London Diary, Dieppe: The Story of a Raid, The Curtain Rises*, and the best-selling *The Wounded Don't Cry* (1941). In 1965 he died after a short bout with abdominal cancer.

REFERENCES: Robert W. Desmond. *Tides of War*. 1984; *DAB* 7; Quentin Reynolds. *By Quentin Reynolds*. 1963.

RIBOUD, MARC (b. 1923). Born in Lyons, France, he studied engineering in college and was self-taught in photography. During World War II* he served in the French resistance and the Free French army. Since 1953 he has been a freelance photographer and photojournalist and a member of Magnum Photos, Inc. In 1971 he was present when a Bangladeshi official publicly bayonetted four Bengali prisoners to death, probably for the benefit of Western journalists who were present. Riboud was among the few cameramen who refused to photograph the executions. He covered the Vietnam War* and in 1968 went to Hanoi, where he took the pictures for his book *Face of North Vietnam* (1970).

REFERENCE: Jorge Lewinski. *The Camera at War*. 1978.

RICHARDSON, ALBERT DEANE (1833–1869). Born in Massachusetts, Richardson worked for several newspapers in Pittsburgh and Cincinnati before joining the *Boston Journal* to cover the sectional conflict in Kansas. During the American Civil War* Deane became the chief correspondent in the West for the *New York Tribune*. Adventurous and self-assured, he risked being hanged as a spy to travel through the South as a secret correspondent for the *Tribune* in 1861.

Richardson accompanied Hooker's forces at the Battle of Antietam and at the Battle of Vicksburg he attempted to run the Confederate batteries aboard a hay barge with fellow *Tribune* correspondent Junius Henri Browne* when the barge was hit by enemy gunfire, killing the captain and three crew members. Richardson and Browne survived but were captured and imprisoned in the military prison at Salisbury, North Carolina. The following year the intrepid correspondents escaped. After a daring four-hundred-mile, four-week journey through the Blue Ridge Mountains they reached Knoxville, Tennessee.

He wrote several successful books about his Civil War exploits, including *Secret Service: The Field, the Dungeon and the Escape* (1865), *Beyond the Mississippi* (1866), and *Personal History of U.S. Grant* (1868). Richardson met a tragic end shortly after his engagement to the recently divorced Abby Sage McFarland on November 25, 1869, when her ex-husband fatally shot him at his desk in the *Tribune* office. Richardson and McFarland were wed in a deathbed ceremony by Henry Ward Beecher.

REFERENCES: J. Cutler Andrews. *The North Reports the Civil War.* 1955; Stewart Sifakis. *Who Was Who in the Civil War.* 1988.

RICHARDSON, DAVID (b. 1916). In 1940, shortly after receiving his journalism degree from Indiana University, Richardson joined the *New York Herald Tribune.* With the outbreak of war in 1941 he was inducted into the army. In 1942 he began covering World War II* for *Yank,* a weekly news magazine the army published for its enlisted soldiers, notable for its lack of editorial restraints.

During the war he accompanied General Douglas MacArthur's Southwest Pacific forces and participated in or witnessed almost every phase of jungle warfare. He reported the Battle of Buna on New Guinea in 1942, and unhappy with his position as a passive observer, he volunteered as waist gunner on a B-24 and participated in combat against Japanese Zero fighters over the Solomon Islands. Later he transferred to a PT boat, where he learned to handle a Browning automatic rifle. Richardson would also parachute behind Japanese lines in Burma with an Office of Strategic Service team and spent five months attached to the elite force Merrill's Marauders. He covered the siege of the Burmese city of Bahmo. As a homage to American fighting forces none of his dispatches were written in the first person. Richardson was one of the most decorated soldier correspondents of the war, receiving seven battle stars, the Legion of Merit, the Bronze Star, Combat Infantryman's Badge, and several others. Following the war he went on to a distinguished half-century career in journalism.

REFERENCES: Bob Tutt. "Combat Reporter with True Grit," *Houston Chronicle.* August 15, 1993; Art Weithas. *Close to Glory.* 1991.

RIDER-RIDER, WILLIAM (b. 1891). As of 1978 he was reportedly the only World War I* photographer still alive. He went to work for the *Daily Mirror* in 1910. Due to poor vision he was drafted relatively late in the war. After serving a stint as a bayonet instructor he was transferred to the Canadian army and accredited as their only official photographer in the French theater of the war. Promoted to lieutenant, he was given freedom along the entire Canadian sector near Vimy Ridge. He photographed the attack on Hill 70, the Passchendaele debacle, and the final stages of the conflict.

Rider-Rider took almost four thousand pictures during the war, which were printed and developed in a field darkroom and then sent to censorship headquarters and forwarded to London for distribution by the Central Agency. Following the war he somehow managed to find most of his plates and return them to Canada, where they reside in the Public Archives.

REFERENCE: Jorge Lewinski. *The Camera at War.* 1978.

RINEHART, MARY ROBERTS (1876–1958). The best-selling American mystery novelist was born in Allegheny, Pennsylvania. In 1914 she volunteered

to assist the Allied field hospitals for the Red Cross during World War I.* Reporting from the Belgian front, she was unable to corroborate stories of German atrocities. The *Saturday Evening Post* refused to run her cabled report that the Germans used poison gas against Allied troops for fear of its impact on public opinion and the possibility of drawing America into the war.
REFERENCE: Charlotte McLeod. *Had She But Known*. 1994.

ROBERTS, FRANK J. (d. 1885). Roberts was a Reuters* war correspondent attached to General Graham's forces in the Sudan when he died at Suakin of enteric fever on May 15, 1885. His name is inscribed on a tablet in St. Paul's Cathedral which commemorates the deaths of seven special correspondents during the Sudan campaigns of 1883–1885.
REFERENCE: Robert Wilkinson-Latham. *From Our Special Correspondent*. 1979.

ROBERTSON, JAMES (1813–1881). Robertson was a gifted and pioneering photographer who arrived in the Crimea shortly after the photographer Roger Fenton* left the Crimean War* and returned to England. Until about 1850, he was the chief engraver of the Imperial Mint at Constantinople. Prior to arriving in the Crimea he began his partnership with Felice Beato,* which lasted from 1852 to 1856. Some of his early pictures captured the arrival of allied troops at Constantinople en route to the Crimea in 1854. Many of his prints were used by the *Illustrated London News* as a basis for engravings.

Perhaps inspired by Fenton, Robertson arrived in the Crimea in March 1855 and stayed until the summer of the next year. Most of his photographs capture camp life and sites of battles. He was at liberty to shoot what he chose and he sent home many of his prints to the *Illustrated London News*. Robertson's work during this war was overshadowed by the more famous Fenton's. Neither took pictures showing corpses, although both were afforded many opportunities to. In 1857 Robertson was appointed official photographer of the British military in India. His photographs of the siege of Lucknow in 1857 while associated with Beato are considered among the greatest war photographs ever taken. With his partner Beato, Robertson covered the Indian Mutiny and photographed a variety of scenes which included battle casualties.
REFERENCES: Pat Hodgson. *Early War Photographs*. 1974; Lawrence James. *Crimea, 1854–56*. 1981.

ROBINSON, G. T. (?). Robinson was an architect in St. Peter's Square and the art critic for the *Manchester Guardian* when he arrived in Paris shortly before the siege of Metz during the Franco-Prussian War.* When informed that all English correspondents had been chased out of the city, the intrepid Robinson departed for Metz, where he would be the only English correspondent to record the siege. At one point he was arrested as a spy by the French and later made several unsuccessful attempts to cross Prussian lines. Together with a French engineer he set up a field post replete with balloons in order to deliver messages to his parent newspaper. However, the French commander soon put a stop to it, and for the remainder of the siege the *Guardian* was cut off from its correspondent.

When victorious German troops entered the city after it capitulated following the seventy-day siege, a *Times* correspondent, noting Robinson's straw hat, mentioned that his hat had been singled out by Prussian marksmen. Shortly after the end of the siege Robinson left Metz when he was notified that his name had been handed over to the Prussians by the French commander on a list of dangerous persons. His account of the siege was carried in the *Guardian* and was republished as *The Fall of Metz* in 1871.

REFERENCE: David Ayerst. *The Manchester Guardian: Biography of a Newspaper.* 1971.

ROBINSON, SIR HARRY PERRY (1859–1930). The Oxford-educated Robinson led a peripatetic existence in America following graduation. He tried his hand at gold mining and various journalistic endeavors before joining the *Times* in 1910, reporting from the West Indies. With the outbreak of World War I* he covered the German invasion of Belgium, barely escaping the fall of Antwerp in 1914. He went on to report from the Balkans and the western front, where he was stationed when the war ended. For his wartime service, he was rewarded by the French government with the Chevalier Legion of Honor in 1919. His recounting of his wartime activities and the Battle of the Somme were published in *The Turning Point* (1917).

REFERENCE: Robert W. Desmond. *Tides of War.* 1984.

ROBINSON, HENRY CRABB (1775–1867). Born in Bury St. Edmunds, Crabb Robinson was one of the earliest war correspondents. Educated to be a lawyer, he had his first dispatch published by the *Times* in 1807, when he recorded the fall of Danzig and then the French victory over the Russians at the Battle of Friedland. Upon his return to England in late 1807, he was promoted to editor. The following year he was posted to Spain, where he covered the Peninsular campaign between Britain and France. Robinson witnessed the final battles of the Spanish campaign, the death of the British commander, Sir John Moore, and the departure of the British troops from the Peninsula. Soon after his return to England in 1809, he left journalism to continue his legal career. He would count Lamb, Coleridge, and Wordsworth as friends, as well as continue an association with his old employer the *Times*. His memoirs, *Diary Reminiscences and Correspondence of Henry Crabb Robinson*, were published in 1869.

REFERENCE: Robert W. Desmond. *The Information Process.* 1978.

RODGER, GEORGE (b. 1908). Rodger was born in Hale, Cheshire, England, and educated at St. Bees College, Cumbria. Following service in the British merchant navy from 1926 to 1929, he joined *Life* as a war correspondent during

World War II.* He was awarded eighteen campaign medals between 1939 and 1945. His photographs were some of the most outstanding pictures to appear in *Life* during the war. One of the most memorable photo essays was his sequence capturing the bombing raid on Coventry, England, and its aftermath. He covered the London blitz and was the only British photographer to cover the North African campaign. His coverage of the North African campaign was published as *Desert Journey* in 1944. Rodger accompanied the second diversionary expedition to Ethiopia and then covered the conflict with the Free French and the war in Libya before leaving to photograph the campaigns in Burma and on the North West Frontier of India.

He covered the rearguard actions by British and Chinese forces from the fall of Rangoon in 1942 until the conclusion of the campaign during the battles for Lashio in northern Burma. In order to escape Japanese forces he had to walk across Pungsao Pass into India. His book *Red Moon Rising* chronicles his exploits in Burma. He returned from the Burma theater to capture the Allied landings in Italy and Sicily. He covered the successful Allied campaign in Italy, including the carnage during the Battle of Monte Cassino. He landed with the first wave on Gold sector during the Normandy invasion and was with Allied forces in the drive across France and Germany. However, after witnessing the liberation of the German death camps Rodger resolved to end his career as war correspondent. Following the war he was one of the four cofounders of the Magnum Agency in 1947. He concentrated the remainder of his photographic career in Africa.

REFERENCES: *Contemporary Photographers.* 1982; Jorge Lewinski. *The Camera at War.* 1978.

ROMULO, CARLOS PENA (b. 1901). A graduate of the University of the Philippines in 1918 and holder of a master's degree from Columbia in 1921, Romulo was a member of the Philippines Independence Commission and an officer in the Philippines Army Reserve in 1941. As editor for the *Manila Bulletin*, he undertook the assignment to alert the United States that Japan was about to unleash an aggressive campaign in the Pacific and that the United States would surely be drawn into the hostilities. In a series of articles distributed by the King Features Syndicate in the United States, Romulo predicted that the Western powers would lose most of their colonies during the conflict and that America would in the end prevail. Less than a month after Romulo's series the Japanese attacked Pearl Harbor and the Philippines. After Manila fell Romulo, as colonel on the staff of General Douglas MacArthur, helped lead the ill-fated defense of Bataan and Corregidor. Romulo was one of the last men to escape to Australia following the Japanese victory. In 1942 he won the Pulitzer Prize in journalism, the first Asian to win the award. In June 1945 he returned to the Philippines with General MacArthur, wading ashore at Leyte. He wrote *I Saw the Fall of the Philippines* and *Mother America*.

REFERENCES: Robert W. Desmond. *Tides of War*. 1984; John Hohenberg. *The Pulitzer Prizes*. 1974.

ROOFTOP JOURNALISM. With the introduction of satellite television, the era of rooftop journalism was inaugurated during the Gulf War.* "Rooftop journalism" refers to the new generation of war coverage in which cable news viewers can watch late-breaking events as they unfold. In the words of one authority, it is a "real-time clock on war." Disaster reporters rather than bona fide war correspondents familiar with local language and customs are now sent to cover international incidents. Trained in crisis, rather than countries and culture, their mission is to search out stories and colorful anecdotes that will draw television ratings. CNN was a prime source for this form of journalism during the Gulf War as correspondents such as Charles Jaco, Peter Arnett,* Arthur Kent, and others reported from the tops of Middle Eastern buildings as Scud missiles landed nearby, giving audiences the vicarious experience of being in a war zone.

REFERENCE: Johanna Neuman. *Lights, Camera, War*. 1996.

ROOS, TIELMAN JOHANNES DE VILLIERS (1875–1935). Roos covered the Boer side of the Boer War* for Reuters,* which fielded correspondents for both sides of the conflict. He reported the Battle of Colenso and described General Botha's headquarters and the conditions in which his staff and officer corps worked. Following the war he became auditor general in the government of the Union of South Africa

REFERENCE: Byron Farwell. *The Great Anglo-Boer War*. 1976.

ROSENTHAL, JOE (b. 1911). The World War II* photographer took probably the most famous photograph of the war during the Battle of Iwo Jima. He received the Pulitzer Prize for his often reproduced shot of six soldiers straining to raise the American flag over Mount Suribachi on February 23, 1945. Perfectly composed, this image has been described as possessing "a dramatic sense of action, sculptural clarity, and heroic patriotism." This picture would become the inspiration for wartime posters and a three-cent stamp, and was the model for the Iwo Jima Memorial near Arlington National Cemetery.

   The flag raisings that day, four days after the marines landed at Iwo Jima, marked the first time the American flag had flown over Japanese territory. Ironically, Rosenthal missed the first raising of a flag that turned out to be too small. Hearing of plans to raise a second, larger flag, he was in time to capture a much larger stars and stripes at noon. Rosenthal never received any royalties for the photo.

REFERENCE: Frederick S. Voss. *Reporting the War*. 1994.

RUE, LARRY (1893–1965). Born in Fosston, Minnesota, Rue entered journalism with the *Duluth News Tribune* in 1913. During World War I* he gained experience as an air corps pilot, and later as a correspondent he piloted his own plane while on assignment. Rue joined the *Chicago Tribune* in 1919 and early on covered the Middle East, North Africa, and southern Europe. He witnessed the Fascist takeover of Rome in 1922 and Hitler's "beer hall putsch" the following year. In 1931 he began working for the *New York Daily News* and in 1939 covered the opening events of World War II* for both the *Tribune* and the *News*. He was in Holland when the Nazis invaded and had no way to relay his story to his home office. He designed a phony document which identified him as a VIP and successfully used it to drive through almost half of Europe and back to his London office.

REFERENCES: Robert W. Desmond. *Crisis and Conflict.* 1982; M. L. Stein. *Under Fire.* 1968.

RUHL, ARTHUR (1876–1935). Born in Rockford, Illinois, prior to World War I* Ruhl was the music critic for the *New York Tribune*. He became the most active correspondent for *Collier's Weekly* during the war beginning in 1914, when he covered the fronts in Belgium and France. The following year he reported from Germany and Austria, before shifting to Russia for 1916 and 1917 to chronicle the war from both sides. He returned to France in 1918 and then reported from the Baltic states following the end of hostilities. He returned to the *New York Tribune* in the 1920s.

REFERENCE: Robert W. Desmond. *Windows on the World.* 1980.

RUNYON, DAMON (1884–1946). Born in Manhattan, Kansas, the well-known chronicler of Broadway and author of the musical *Guys and Dolls* first entered journalism while still in his teens for the *Pueblo Evening Press*. During the Spanish-American War* he spent eighteen months in the Philippines. Following the war he worked for several papers in the West before landing with the Denver-based *Rocky Mountain News* in 1906.

In 1910 he moved to New York City and the sports department of Hearst's *New York American*. He would remain with the paper in various capacities until its demise in 1937. In 1912 he covered the Madero revolution in Mexico and four years later accompanied General John J. Pershing's pursuit of Pancho Villa in Mexico for bandit depredations in America. In 1918 Runyon was in France with the American Expeditionary Force in the waning days of World War I.* After the war his reputation was soaring and his articles were widely syndicated. By the 1930s he was identified not only as one of the preeminent sportswriters but also as the chronicler of Broadway life. Among his many works are *Guys and Dolls* (1931), *Blue Plate Special* (1934), and *Take It Easy* (1938). Hollywood would buy many of his stories, making Runyon a wealthy man by the 1940s. He died of throat cancer in December 1946.

REFERENCES: Tom Clark. *The World of Damon Runyon.* 1978; *DAB* Supp. 4; Patricia Ward D'Itri. *Damon Runyon.* 1982.

RUSSELL, ANDREW J. (b. 1838). Born in Vermont, he reportedly worked in Mathew Brady's* New York studios prior to the outbreak of the American Civil War.* Russell is little known in the annals of the Civil War because many of his photographs have been credited to others. He was the only official army photographer to record the war.

Previously commissioned as a captain in a New York company, in 1863 he was reassigned to the Union military railroad chief in the capacity of official photographer. Russell was supposed to document railroad installations and personnel, but in his free time he often deviated from this task, taking pictures of various fortifications and battle sites. When not assigned to the railroad he was with the Army of the Potomac. He photographed dead horses and rebels at Chancellorsville in the aftermath of the fighting. These widely reprinted images were among his most enduring exposures. In the last months of the war Russell was fired over a salary dispute and questions over ownership of the negatives. Following the conflict he was employed by Union Pacific.
REFERENCE: Stewart Sifakis. *Who Was Who in the Civil War*. 1988.

RUSSELL, EDMUND "NED" ALLEN (b. 1916). Russell was born in Baltimore, Maryland, and began his newspaper career while still in his teens as sportswriter for the *Los Angeles Examiner*. He joined the United Press in 1936 and in 1940 covered the Battle of Britain. Beginning in 1942 Russell reported the desert war and Allied landings in North Africa, as well as the 1943 winter campaign in Tunisia while attached with the U.S. First Army. He was among the contingent of seasoned North African correspondents covering the Sicily invasion and the Italian campaign. In 1944 Russell joined the *New York Herald Tribune* in preparation for the D-Day landings, which he ended up covering from the safety of England. He coauthored the book *Springboard To Berlin* with Leo Disher,* John Parris, and Phil Ault.
REFERENCE: Robert W. Desmond. *Tides of War*. 1984.

RUSSELL, SIR HERBERT (1869–1944). Born in Northumbria, England, he entered journalism with the *Newcastle Chronicle* in 1893. Russell joined Reuters* in time to cover World War I,* reporting the Gallipoli debacle and the western front from June 1915 to November 1918. As one of the first five Reuters members to win assignment to the British front in France, he became the best-known war correspondent for the agency during the conflict in Europe. Russell covered the first day of the Battle of the Somme on July 1, 1916, when sixty thousand British troops were killed or wounded. Following the war he was made a Chevalier of the Legion of Honor by the French government and in 1918 was knighted for his coverage of the war.
REFERENCE: Donald Read. *The Power of News*. 1992.

RUSSELL, SIR WILLIAM HOWARD (1820–1907). Often referred to as the "father of modern war reporting," Russell was born in Dublin and attended

Trinity College without graduating, before joining the *Times* in 1841. Originally assigned to report on political affairs, he covered his first war in 1850 when he covered the Danish conflict over Schleswig-Holstein. He received a slight flesh wound covering the Battle of Idstedt.

When the Crimean War* broke out in 1854 Russell's career as a war correspondent began. Soon after debarking at Gallipoli his critical reports of the British army began appearing in the *Times*. The British suffered more from a shortage of weapons, medicine, fuel, and clothing than from their Russian opposition. It has been claimed that his dispatches reflecting the gross negligence of the War Office led to the resignation of Lord Aberdeen's cabinet. On October 25, 1854, he used the phrase "the thin red line" for the first time, as he described the Battle of Balaklava. Later that day he produced his account of the charge of the Light Brigade. Both reports are considered classic examples of war journalism. Rudyard Kipling* admitted borrowing Russell's words "thin red line of heroes" for his poem "Tommy." Russell's story is also often credited with inspiring Tennyson's poem "The Charge of the Light Brigade." Russell continued to publicize the deprivations of the British army. Although he was criticized by the British brass, at least one officer, Sir Evelyn Wood, believed that Russell's muckraking saved what was left of the army.

The *Times* considered his coverage of the Indian Mutiny in 1857 the best work he had done. In 1859 friends convinced him that there would be great interest in a magazine devoted exclusively to issues dealing with national security, the defense, and the various armed forces. These conversations led him in 1860 to found the *Army and Navy Gazette*. For the rest of his life he remained its major shareholder and editor. In April 1861 Russell was sent to America on the eve of the American Civil War* to investigate the growing sectional crisis. With the outbreak of war, the pro-Union Russell was entrusted by the Confederate-sympathizing *Times* to cover the war. His account of the Southern rout of Union forces at Bull Run so displeased Lincoln that he was barred from accompanying Northern forces, whereupon he returned to England.

In 1864 he witnessed Denmark's defeat by Prussia and Austria and in 1866 the Austro-Prussian War.* He followed Prussian forces while reporting the 1870 Franco-Prussian War,* but apparently was being scooped by other papers whose reporters had gravitated quickly to the new technology of the electric telegraph.

His last war was the South African Zulu War (1879), which he reported for the *Daily Telegraph* while accompanying the forces of Sir Garnet Wolseley. His journalism career was not over, for he would report the rebellion of Arabi Pasha in Egypt (1882) and travel to South America (1889) before being knighted in 1895. Upon his death on February 10, 1907, he was buried in the crypt of London's St. Paul's Cathedral. The legend on his grave notes for posterity "The First and Greatest of War Correspondents."

REFERENCES: Alan Hankinson. *Man of Wars: William Howard Russell of the "Times."* 1982; W. H. Russell. *My Diary North and South*, 2nd ed. Edited by Fletcher

Pratt. 1954; W. H. Russell. *Russell's Despatches from the Crimea, 1854–1856.* Edited by Nicholas Bentley. 1967.

RUSSO-JAPANESE WAR. The Russo-Japanese War began on February 8, 1904, when Japanese forces attacked the Russians at Port Arthur. The attack followed five months of fruitless negotiations as the Japanese attempted to get Russia to remove its troops from Korea. The subsequent war was fought at sea and in Manchuria, resulting in a final Japanese victory in May 1905.

Correspondents headed for Japan prior to the outbreak of hostilities. Almost two hundred members of the press covered the conflict. Many of the reporters were veterans of recent conflicts such as the 1900 Boxer Rebellion,* the Boer War,* the 1898 Spanish-American War,* and the Philippine insurrection.

Most correspondents covered the war from the Japanese side, while a contingent arrived in Russia bound for the Asian mainland by means of the Trans-Siberian Railroad. Correspondents arriving in Tokyo were confronted with restrictions that prevented most groups from covering the battlefront until after June 1904. Once permitted to get closer to the action the reporter pools were strictly controlled and never permitted to get within three miles of the front lines. Many chafed under the censorship and departed for home.

The Russo-Japanese War was the first conflict in which a wireless was used for transmitting dispatches from observers near the battlefield directly to their home offices. It was also the most expensive war to cover up to that time, in part due to the high cost of transmitting reports to London, New York, and other news centers. Several correspondents died covering the conflict. Lewis Etzel of the *Daily Telegraph* was killed in Manchuria and Henry J. Middleton of the Associated Press died from an illness.

Among the more recognizable names covering the conflict were Francis McCullagh of the *New York Herald* and *Manchester Guardian*, Melton Prior* for the *Illustrated London News*, Frederic Villiers* for the *Graphic*, Bennet Burleigh* of the *Daily Telegraph*, Edward Frederick Knight* of the *Morning Post*, Richard Harding Davis* for *Collier's Weekly*, Jack London* for the *New York Journal*, George Denny and Frederick McCormick* for the AP, Stephen Bonsal,* William Dinwiddie,* Thomas F. Millard,* and Wilmott Harsant Lewis* for the *New York Herald*, Luigi Barzini* of the *Corriere della Sera*, John T. McCutcheon* of the *Chicago Tribune*, Percival Phillips* for the *Daily Express*, William Maxwell* for the *Standard*, Ellis Ashmead-Bartlett* for the *Daily Telegraph*, and Charles E. Hands* of the *Daily Mail*.

The Russo-Japanese War established Japan as a world power. It was the first modern war in which a Western nation was beaten by an Asian power. In the end Japanese censorship prevented the hordes of correspondents from witnessing most of the decisive battles. Censorship was strict because the Japanese suspected that many of foreign journalists were spies. On the other hand the Japanese allowed their own correspondents more freedom than their Western counterparts. Any complete study of the Russo-Japanese War must consider the dispatches in the *Asahi, Mainichi,* and *Jiji,* whose correspondents were allowed to witness most of the pivotal battles.

REFERENCE: Robert W. Desmond. *The Information Process.* 1978.

RUSSO-TURKISH WAR. Following reports of Turkish atrocities against Bulgarian Christians, Russia declared war on Turkey in April 1877. In its declaration of war Russia made no mention of the strategic value of Turkish access to the Mediterranean.

During the war close to eighty correspondents would visit the front lines. While some accompanied Turkish forces or were based in Constantinople, the majority were with the Russians. Each correspondent was equipped with a wagon outfitted with necessities, horses, and servants or couriers for assistance. Correspondents usually carried gold specie to pay for telegraph tolls. Cabling facilities were located in Bucharest, Rumania, and were moderately censored by Russian officials. Unlike previous wars, correspondents were assigned numbers by Russian officials. Initially they wore accreditation badges before these were changed to simple armbands. In addition all reporters were required to take an oath that they would not compromise Russian security and were to pass all copies of their newspapers through Russian censors. Among those accused of violating wars and expelled was Frederick Boyle* of the *Standard.* Turkish restrictions were no less strict, as Antonio Gallenga* of the *Times* found out when he was expelled.

The *Daily News* was the best-represented newspaper during the war, just as it had been during the late Franco-Prussian War.* Among its most prominent correspondents were Januarius MacGahan* and Archibald Forbes.* Along with Frederic Villiers* of the *Graphic,* these three journalists witnessed some of the most crucial engagements of the war, including the Battles of Plevna and Schipka Pass. On one occasion *Daily News* war correspondents managed to bypass Russian censors through the implementation of a pony express service, using eight men and horses to deliver dispatches over the Carpathian Mountains to neutral Austria. *Daily News* correspondents on the Turkish side included Edmund O'Donovan* and Frank A. Scudamore.* At the outset of the conflict the newspaper exchanged dispatches with the *New York Herald,* which was represented by John P. Jackson and Francis D. Millet.*

Other notable reporters on the scene were Melton Prior* of the *Illustrated London News,* Frank le Poer Power* for a Dublin paper, three representatives of the *Daily Telegraph,* William Beattie Kingston* with the Russians, and Drew Gay and Campbell Clarke with the Turks. The war came to an end in January 1878 after Turkey appealed to Russia for an armistice. The peace process was formalized by the Treaty of San Stefano several months later.

REFERENCE: Robert W. Desmond. *The Information Process.* 1978.

RYAN, CORNELIUS JOHN (1920–1974). The Dublin-born Ryan joined Reuters* in 1941 and two years later left for the *Daily Telegraph.* He covered both theaters of World War II* and then the first Arab-Israeli War (1946–1947). He continued his career as a journalist for various American publications in the 1950s and 1960s, including *Time, Life*, and *Reader's Digest*. Ryan established a career as a best-selling writer of military history. Among his books were *The Longest Day* (1959), *The Last Battle* (1966), and *A Bridge Too Far* (1974), all of which became best-sellers.

REFERENCE: Dennis Griffiths, ed. *The Encyclopedia of the British Press.* 1992.

S

SAFER, MORLEY (b. 1931). Best known as an anchor on the popular *60 Minutes* television newsmagazine show, the Canadian-born Safer first came to prominence while covering the Vietnam War* for CBS. In 1966 he was the recipient of the Overseas Press Club Award for best television reporting with a controversial film story showing American troops burning the Vietnamese village of Cam Le, near Danang, as villagers pleaded to be allowed to remove their possessions. Safer was soundly criticized by U.S. officials in Vietnam for what was taken to be reporting detrimental to the war effort. Safer had several close brushes with death while reporting from battlefronts. Prior to Vietnam he reported the Congo and Cyprus conflicts, the 1967 Arab-Israeli War, the Soviet invasion of Czechoslovakia, the religious strife in Northern Ireland, the Nigerian civil war, and the American withdrawal from Cambodia.

REFERENCES: M. L. Stein. *Under Fire: the Story of American War Correspondents.* 1968; Clarence R. Wyatt. *Paper Soldiers: The American Press and the Vietnam War.* 1993.

ST. JOHN, ROBERT (b. 1902). He served in World War I* at the age of sixteen. Following the war he became a reporter for the *Hartford Courant* and then the *Chicago Daily News*, before briefly editing his own newspaper in Cicero, Illinois, the stronghold of the Capone mob. He left Cicero after being savagely beaten by gangsters for his attempts at exposing the activities of Al Capone's younger brother Ralph. St. John moved to Vermont and then joined the *Philadelphia Record*. In 1931 he moved to the Associated Press, but gave that up for rural life in New Hampshire.

With the war years approaching he rejoined the Associated Press in 1939. He arrived in Paris just as the Nazis were invading Poland and covered the conflict in the Balkans, including campaigns in Yugoslavia, Greece, and Crete. His best-selling book *From the Land of Silent People* (1942) chronicled the various resistance groups who opposed the German invaders.

At the outset of the European war St. John was headquartered in Budapest, Hungary, which gave him an edge over his competition in covering the Central Europe and the Balkans. After the fall of Rumania and Bulgaria St. John reported from Yugoslavia. As the German onslaught continued and ultimate capitulation of Yugoslavia seemed a foregone conclusion, he attempted to escape the country. Along with three other reporters, St. John debarked by boat from the Dalmatian coast for Greece, narrowly escaping the German forces. Upon reaching Greece he was faced with a situation similar to the one he just escaped from. Although wounded during a German air attack, St. John made it to safety in Egypt with the help of the British navy. He returned to America in 1941 to a job as news commentator with NBC and spent the remainder of the war broadcasting from England.
REFERENCE: Frederick S. Voss. *Reporting the War*. 1994.

SALA, GEORGE AUGUSTUS HENRY (1828–1896). Sala was educated in Paris and studied drawing in London. After a succession of jobs as clerk, scene painter, and illustrator he began contributing articles to *Household Words* and in 1856 was assigned to cover the Crimean War.* Sala wrote regularly for the *Daily Telegraph* from 1855 to 1893. He was one of the few British correspondents to cover the American Civil War.* He also reported parts of the Italian unification campaigns in 1858–1861, the Austro-Prussian War,* the Franco-Prussian War,* and the Carlist war of 1873–1876 in Spain. Sala was not specifically a war correspondent. Although he was more content to chronicle "areas to the rear" in wartime, his dispatches were some of the most frequently reprinted from the wars he reported. In 1881 he was assigned to St. Petersburg, Russia, to report the funeral of Alexander II and did not return to England for two years.
REFERENCE: Joseph J. Mathews. *Reporting the Wars*. 1957.

SALE, STEWART (1905–1943). A protégé of Edgar Wallace*, Sale reported for the *Buckingham Mail*, the *Sunday News*, and the *Daily Telegraph* before joining Reuters.* During World War II* he flew as an observer in a bombing raid over Berlin, covered the Salerno landing, and reported other parts of the Italian campaign. In August 1943 he was posted to Allied headquarters and the Fifth Army in North Africa, where he wrote his dispatch on the landing at Salerno. The following month he was killed along with two other correspondents when a German half-track fired on their jeep in the push to Naples. Also killed were veteran war correspondents Alexander Berry Austin* and William J. Munday.*
REFERENCES: Robert W. Desmond. *Tides of War*. 1984; Donald Read. *The Power of News: The History of Reuters*. 1992.

SALISBURY, HARRISON EVANS (b. 1908). Salisbury was born in Minneapolis, Minnesota, and educated at the University of Minnesota. He began reporting for the *Minneapolis Journal* while still a college student. He joined the United Press in 1930 and during the New Deal was assigned to the Washington bureau, where he began freelancing under a variety of pseudonyms. He got his first foreign posting in 1943 when he was transferred to London as bureau manager in 1943. He reported World War II* from the Middle East, North Africa, and Great Britain. In 1944 he was assigned to the Soviet Union for six weeks and ended up staying for eight months. He returned to New York and completed *Russia on the Way* (1944).

After a bout with depression and a stint in a psychiatric clinic he joined the *New York Times* as a correspondent in its Moscow bureau. He stayed on for six years and developed a growing affinity for the country. Upon his return to the States he wrote a series of articles on Communist Russia and its leaders, winning the Pulitzer Prize for international reporting in 1955.

In 1966 he became the first American reporter allowed into North Vietnam when he spent a month reporting from Hanoi and in 1967 he won his second George K. Polk Award. He retired from the *Times* in 1973. He eventually wrote over twenty books and became a recognized specialist in Russian affairs.

REFERENCE: Harrison Salisbury. *A Journey for Our Times.* 1983.

SALTER, CEDRIC (b. 1907). Born in Oxford, England, Salter covered the Spanish Civil War* for three years, first with the *London Daily Telegraph* in 1937, and then the *News Chronicle* and the *Daily Mail.* Attached to neither the Loyalists nor the Franco forces during the conflict, he was able to cover various battlefronts. He was in Spain from the outbreak of the war and witnessed the bombing of Barcelona and Granollérs. In his book *Try-Out in Spain* he recounts helping two nuns escape to a destroyer and interviewing General Durutti after he condemned eight hundred women to be executed.

Salter developed a reputation as "the most chased about of British correspondents" during the late 1930s and early 1940s. He continued his work for the *Daily Mail* during World War II,* covering the Polish campaign until the Germans captured Warsaw, before reporting various phases of the developing Eastern European theater of the war. With the Gestapo in hot pursuit Salter recorded events in Rumania, Bulgaria, and Turkey until 1941, when he accompanied British forces into the Far East, where he witnessed the fall of Singapore. Barely escaping Japanese forces, he returned to Burma and was the last correspondent to leave Rangoon before it fell to the Japanese. He continued to cover the war in China, India, and Tibet before returning to Ankara as the Turkish correspondent for the *Daily Mail.*

REFERENCES: Cedric Salter. *Flight from Poland.* 1940; Cedric Salter. *Try-Out in Spain.* 1943.

SANDBURG, CARL AUGUST (1878–1967). Best known as a poet and biographer of Lincoln, Sandburg was born in Galesburg, Illinois. He worked in

journalism for over two decades in Milwaukee and Chicago. In 1898 he served with the army in the Spanish-American War.* His first effort in journalism appeared in the *Galesburg Daily Mail*, when it published his letters sent from Puerto Rico recounting his wartime experiences. In 1918 he was stationed in Stockholm, Sweden, where he reported the final months of World War I* and the Russian Revolution for the *Chicago Daily News*.
REFERENCES: Harry Golden. *Carl Sandburg*. 1961; *New York Times*. July 23, 1967.

SAN JUAN HILL, BATTLE OF. The most famous battle of the Spanish-American War* was the Battle of San Juan Hill on July 1, 1898. The famous charge up the hill by the Rough Riders, led by Colonel Theodore Roosevelt, would catapult Roosevelt into the presidency three years later. The charge was witnessed by correspondents Stephen Crane,* James Hare,* Richard Harding Davis,* and other less well known reporters. This charge has been immortalized by the press, artists, and editorial writers who embellished the event to such an extent as to obscure the fact that the soldiers were not mounted and the charge was unnecessary, leading to at least one critic of Roosevelt to describe the event as the "myth of San Juan Hill."
REFERENCE: Joyce Milton. *The Yellow Kids*. 1989.

SANKOVA, GALINA (b. 1904). Galina Sankova was the most outstanding woman photojournalist covering the Russian front during World War II.* She honed her craft in the 1930s before overcoming enormous obstacles to record the war. Professionally trained as a nurse at the outset of the war, and then as a driver and mechanic, Sankova took a circuitous route to her career as photojournalist. She photographed the fighting on the western front, the Briansk and Don campaigns near Stalingrad, and the northern offensive of 1944 in the beleaguered city of Leningrad. Throughout the war she was affiliated with *Frontovaya Illustracia*.

Sankova was one of only five Russian women to photograph the war. In addition to her wartime coverage she recorded the construction projects of the Five- and Seven-Year Plans as well as events in Siberia. She was twice wounded during the war and often volunteered as a nurse at the front. After the war she remained in journalism as staff writer for *Ogonyok* magazine.
REFERENCE: Daniela Mrazkova and Vladimir Remes, eds. *The Russian War: 1941–1945*. 1975.

SAVIN, MIKHAIL (b. 1915). Prior to the outbreak of the Russian war in 1941, Savin had been a correspondent based in Byelorussia for the TASS News Agency. He covered the war as a photojournalist for the *Krasnoarmeyskaya Pravda* or *Red Army Pravda*, the army newspaper for the western front. After the war he remained active in the field as photographer for *Ogonyok* magazine.
REFERENCE: Daniela Mrazkova and Vladimir Remes, eds. *The Russian War: 1941–1945*. 1975.

SAWADA, KYOICHI (d. 1970). Born in Japan, Sawada was killed while covering the Cambodia conflict. While covering the Vietnam War* as a photojournalist for United Press International he had several close brushes with death and was captured once. In 1966 Sawada won the Pulitzer Prize.
REFERENCE: John Hohenberg. *The Pulitzer Prizes.* 1973.

SAYRE, JOEL GROVER (1900–1979). Sayre was born in Marion, Indiana, and served with the Canadian Expeditionary Forces in Siberia in 1917. Following stints as a crime reporter and screenwriter, he joined the *New Yorker* as a war correspondent covering the Persian Gulf Command during World War II.* His accounts of this conflict were published as *Persian Gulf Command: Some Marvels on the Road to Kazvin* in 1945.
REFERENCES: *New York Times.* September 14, 1979; David Shavit. *The United States in the Mideast.* 1988.

SCHANBERG, SYDNEY H. (b. 1934). Born in Clinton, Massachusetts, and educated at Harvard, he joined the *Times* as a copyboy in 1959. In 1960 Schanberg filed his first story as a reporter. In rapid succession he headed news bureaus for the paper in Albany, New York; New Delhi, India; and Singapore. In April 1975 he covered the invasion of Cambodia by Communist forces and was present at Phnom Penh when the country capitulated to the invaders. Schanberg stayed behind with several other correspondents and was able to escape to Thailand, where he filed some of the best dispatches of the conflict. He received the Pulitzer Prize for his work in 1976. He later became metropolitan editor for his paper in 1977.
REFERENCE: Haing Ngor, with Roger Warner. *Haing Ngor: A Cambodian Odyssey.* 1987.

SCHELL, FRANCIS H. (c. 1834–1909). Born in Germantown, Pennsylvania, and raised in Philadelphia, he was trained in lithography at age sixteen. During the American Civil War* he became one of the foremost artist-correspondents* for *Frank Leslie's Illustrated.* He covered the siege of Vicksburg and other action in the west. Following the war he joined a coterie of Civil War artists including the Waud* brothers, Edwin Forbes,* and Henri Lovie* as illustrators for *Beyond the Mississippi,* which was composed of historical views of America from the Mississippi River to the Pacific Coast after 1857. Schell headed the *Leslie's* art department after the war and then became partners with fellow illustrator Thomas Hogan for thirty years.
REFERENCES: Peggy and Harold Samuels. *Samuels' Encyclopedia of Artists of the American West.* 1985; W. Fletcher Thompson, Jr. *The Image of War.* 1959.

SCHONBERG, JOHANN NEPOMUK (b. 1844). The son of a noted engraver and lithographer, Johann Schonberg was born in Austria and educated at the Academy of Vienna before embarking on a career as a sketch artist with various

French illustrated newspapers. In 1866 he began an affiliation with the *Illustrated London News* when he reported the Austro-Prussian War* from the Austrian side. Nine years later he was back in the field for the *Illustrated* covering the Serbo-Turkish War of 1875–1876, and then the Russo-Turkish War* of 1877–1878.

After military service in Egypt he fought with Serbian forces against Bulgaria in 1885, while continuing to hone his war artist skills. Schonberg joined the *Sphere* as artist-correspondent* during the Boer War.* Masquerading as a German press representative, he was given preferential treatment by the Boers. However, his ruse fell short of success when the *Sphere* blew his cover with an ill-timed telegram identifying him as its London correspondent, and he was expelled from the Boer camp. Later, Schonberg was assigned to cover the 1900 Boxer Rebellion* for the *Illustrated London News*, but did not reach Peking until well after the fighting had ended.
REFERENCE: Pat Hodgson. *The War Illustrators.* 1977.

SCHULTZ, SIGRID (1893–1980). Born in Chicago, she was a daughter of the renowned European portrait artist Herman Schultz. Fluent in five languages, the Sorbonne-educated Sigrid Schultz was hired by the *Chicago Tribune* to work as an interpreter at its Berlin bureau in 1919. Stationed in Germany, she interviewed many Nazi leaders, including Hitler, and warned of the coming conflict. The war reporter Quentin Reynolds* called her "Hitler's greatest enemy." Although allowed to stay in Germany at the outbreak of World War II,* she was prevented by German officials from covering the battlefronts. In 1941 she suffered a shrapnel injury while covering the bombing of Berlin.

Working for *McCall's* and *Liberty* magazines in 1944, she covered the Battle of the Ruhr and the American advance on Berlin, and was one of the first reporters to witness the liberation of Buchenwald. After covering the Nuremberg war trials she retired from war reporting. She wrote *Germany Will Try It Again* (1944) and was at work on a history of German anti-Semitism at her death.
REFERENCES: Julia Edwards. *Women of the World.* 1989; Lilya Wagner. *Women War Correspondents of World War II.* 1989.

SCHUYLER, PHILIPPA (1932–1967). Schuyler first saw Vietnam as a guest of Ambassador Henry Cabot Lodge in 1966. Because she was an accomplished pianist, Lodge had invited her to entertain wounded soldiers at a Saigon hospital. A former child prodigy who made her concert debut at age four and could read at two, in her early teens she accompanied the New York Philharmonic Symphony Orchestra. Prior to the trip, Schuyler had already formulated plans for a career in journalism. She had previously reported from the battlefront in 1960 while covering the civil war in the Belgian Congo. Her articles from this first campaign were collected and published as *Who Killed the Congo?* in 1962.

During the Vietnam War* she contributed articles to William Loeb's *Manchester Union-Leader* and became increasingly unpopular with American officials for her reports on American racism and how American policy was flawed because of a lack of understanding of the Vietnamese. On May 9, 1967, she was killed in a helicopter crash as she attempted to evacuate children from the besieged city of Hue.

REFERENCE: Virginia Elwood-Akers. *Women War Correspondents in the Vietnam War, 1961–1975.* 1988.

SCOOP. Evelyn Waugh* wrote the satirical novel on war reporting in 1937. Waugh had covered the Ethiopian War* in 1935 for the *London Daily Mail* and was struck by the competitiveness and moral dissolution of his colleagues fighting to get news scoops. In the book, the correspondents are issued identity cards that were originally used to register prostitutes. Waugh himself was a dismal failure at this trade, sending back little news and eventually being fired. This novel foreshadows future incarnations of war correspondents as unscrupulous and shiftless creatures trading on the misfortunes of others. In *Scoop*, the protagonist William Boot is assigned to cover a war in the East African country of Ishmaelia for the *Beast*, an appropriately named newspaper. In Waugh's words, the newspaper stood for ''strong mutually antagonistic governments everywhere.''

REFERENCES: Howard Good. *The Image of War Correspondents in Anglo-American Fiction.* 1985; Evelyn Waugh. *Scoop.* 1937.

SCOTT, SIR JAMES GEORGE (1851–1935). Scott was born in Dairsie, Fife, and left Oxford short of graduation because of a lack of finances. He accompanied the 1875–1876 punitive expedition to Perak, Malaya, as special correspondent for the *London Standard*. Following the campaign he moved to Burma as headmaster for an Anglican mission school, where he introduced association football. He later returned to England and attempted to land a law scholarship. Narrowly missing the selection process, he returned to his beloved Burma and in 1882 published the two-volume *The Burman: His Life and Notions*. His reputation as an authority on Burma led him again to the attention of newspaper editors in search of a war correspondent in Asia. In 1884 the *Standard* hired Scott to cover the French armies in pursuit of the conquest of Tonkin. He chronicled this experience in *France and Tongking: A Narrative of the Campaign of 1884, and the Occupation of Further India* (1885).

In 1885 he was appointed to the Indian civil service, where he performed the service of peacemaker as British forces attempted to establish rule in the Shan states and quell a civil war among Burmese tribes. In 1891 he was appointed resident for the northern Shan states at Lashio and in 1902 was given a similar position for the southern Shan states. He retired from the civil service in 1910 and returned to London shortly after. He also wrote the five-volume *Gazeteer of Upper Burma and the Shan States* (1900–1901).

REFERENCE: *DNB*.

SCOVEL, HENRY SYLVESTER (1869–1905). Better known by his middle name Sylvester, or simply Harry, Scovel was born at Denny Station, Allegheny County, Pennsylvania. He left college early to work at a variety of occupations before landing in the newspaper profession. Since he had carved out a reputation for aggressiveness, both the *Pittsburgh Dispatch* and the *New York Herald* felt he had the makings of a correspondent and sent him to cover the conflict in Cuba in 1895. Spanish authorities quickly wearied of his persistence and had him arrested the following year. He escaped shortly after, and was next hired by the *New York World* to report the events leading up to the Spanish-American War.* He became one of the most prominent personalities of the conflict. Scovel's columns for the *World* promoted the cause of Cuban independence and elicited American support and sympathy. He lived with Cuban insurgents for almost a year, covering the guerrilla campaign and hardships until he was captured for a second time in early 1897. However, the intervention of the American government gained Scovel a quick release.

Following his escapades in Cuba, he covered the Greco-Turkish War* in 1897, returning to the States only after the sinking of the *Maine*. Scovel served as war correspondent throughout the subsequent Spanish-American War. One of his most publicized exploits was his attempt to find rebel leader General Gomez to apprise him that America had declared war on Spain. Scovel undertook several other dangerous fact-finding missions for American authorities during the hostilities. He reported the formal capitulation of Spanish forces in Havana on New Year's Day, 1899, which ended the Spanish presence on Cuba. Consistently at odds with American authorities, Scovel attempted to punch General William Shafter in the nose at ceremonies marking the end of the conflict because the general refused to allow him to be included in the official victory photograph.

Following the war, Scovel remained in Cuba as a consulting engineer to the customs service of the U.S. military government. He left this post to pursue commercial development opportunities in Havana. When he was confined to his bed by malaria in late 1904, physicians detected an abscess on his liver. In February 1905 they operated to remove it, but the wound became infected and Scovel died when doctors operated a second time.

REFERENCES: Charles H. Brown. *The Correspondents' War*. 1967; *DAB*; Joyce Milton. *The Yellow Kids*. 1989.

SCUDAMORE, FRANK (1859–1939). Scudamore covered his first war while still in his teens, reporting the Russo-Turkish War* in 1877 with Archibald Forbes* for the *Daily News*. In 1883 he covered the British campaign in the Sudan. He accompanied Baker Pasha's forces in the relief of Sinkat and Tokar after the Mahdi's massacre of Hicks' ten-thousand-man force. He later reported the Armenian massacres in 1894–99 and three years later returned to the Sudan with Kitchener's forces to defeat the Mahdi. According to one of his fellow correspondents, among his baggage, carried by two camels, was "his drink

camel," which carried his supply of alcohol and soda. He was said to have concocted the "Abu Hamed," a drink consisting of gin, lime juice, vermouth, Angostura, and soda, a remedy for what G. W. Steevens* described as the unquenchable "Sudan thirst."
REFERENCE: Robert Wilkinson-Latham. *From Our Special Correspondent.* 1979.

SEDGWICK, ALEXANDER CAMERON "A. C." (1902–1996). Born in Sedgewick, Massachusetts, he graduated from Harvard in 1924 before joining the *New York Times* in 1925. Three years later he left the paper to write a novel, supporting himself as a sherry salesman. He returned to the paper in 1937 as its Athens correspondent. When Greece was threatened by German invasion at the onset of the war he took a post in the Middle East, where he covered military matters. Sedgwick covered the British Eighth Army's desert campaign in North Africa during World War II* for the *New York Times*. He is best remembered for his coverage of the defeat of Rommel's Afrika Corps at the Battle of El Alamein in 1942. He was wounded by shrapnel fire during the battle but made no mention of it in his report. In 1945 he published his second novel and was made a member of the Order of the British Empire.
REFERENCE: *New York Times.* January 21, 1996.

SELDES, GEORGE (b. 1890). Born in Alliance, New Jersey, he was hired for his first newspaper job with the *Pittsburgh Leader* in 1909. After briefly attending Harvard he returned to journalism and in 1916 was hired as managing editor of *Pulitzer's Review* in New York City. He covered the American Expeditionary Force as a member of the press section in 1917. As the first American to enter St. Mihiel on September 13, 1918, he was received as both war hero and liberator hours before the anticlimatic arrival of Pershing and his staff. He covered the Irish uprisings in 1919 and the war in Damascus in 1926 as well as the capture of the capital city, Soueida, from the Druses. As war correspondent for the *New York Post* from 1936 to 1937 he reported the Spanish Civil War.*

A vocal critic of press censorship since being expelled from Russia while reporting the Bolshevik purges in 1923, and from Italy for his reportage of Mussolini's rise to power in 1925, he published *You Can't Print That: The Truth Behind the News* in 1929. Seldes is probably best remembered for his attacks on the American Newspaper Publishers Association in his books *Freedom of the Press* (1935) and *Lords of the Press* (1938), which became best-sellers. In 1982 he was awarded the George Polk Award in Journalism.
REFERENCES: Eugene Lyons. *We Cover the World.* 1937; George Seldes. *Witness to a Century.* 1987.

SEVAREID, ERIC (1912–1992). Born in Velma, South Dakota, he entered journalism with the *Minneapolis Journal* when he was eighteen years old. He graduated from the University of Minnesota in 1935 and continued to work for the paper until he left for Europe to study political science at the London School of Economics. While in France he reported for the *New York Herald Tribune*'s Paris edition and was employed as night editor for the United Press.

Shortly before the outbreak of World War II* he joined a stellar cast of newsmen assembled by Edward R. Murrow* to report the coming war. From 1939 to 1940 he covered the French army and air force in France and Belgium. He moved to London following the capitulation of France to Germany in 1940. In 1943 Sevareid left to report the battlefront in the China-Burma-India theater of the war. When his plane went down over the Assam jungle, Sevareid was forced to bail out with nineteen others and for a brief time lived among local headhunters. He returned to Europe and covered the Italian campaign and the advance of the first American troops into southern France. Sevareid went on to cover a wide assortment of stories in Yugoslavia, France, Germany, and Britain before returning to the States after the war.

It would be over two decades before he would witness the battlefront again, when he reported from Vietnam in 1966 for CBS news. He went on to become one of the most respected television journalists and worked for CBS until forced retirement in 1977. Among his awards were two Overseas Press Club Awards and the George Polk Memorial Award.

REFERENCE: Library of America. *Reporting World War Two: Part Two, American Journalism 1944–1946.* 1995.

SEYMOUR, DAVID "CHIM" (1911–1956). Born David Szymin in Warsaw, Poland, to the world of photography he was known simply as "Chim." He fled with his family to the Ukraine in 1914 when the German army invaded. By the age of eight he was fluent in two of the eight languages he would eventually master. Son of an early publisher of Hebrew and Yiddish authors, Seymour was drawn early to the arts. While studying graphic arts at the Leipzig Academy he began to develop his photographic skills as a hobby. With anti-Semitism sweeping through Eastern Europe he fled to Paris, where he studied at the Sorbonne and established lifelong friendships with the photographers Henri Cartier-Bresson* and Robert Capa.* All three would cover the Spanish Civil War.* Chim chose noncombatants for his subject material to demonstrate the impact of war on the refugees and floating populations.

He went on to cover World War II* in Europe and find out that most of his family and friends had been murdered by the Nazis. His pictures of the uprooted survivors of Europe following the war appeared in *Life* in 1948. As always Chim concentrated on the survivors of wars, especially the children. In 1954, when his friend Capa was killed in Vietnam, Seymour became president of Magnum Photos. In 1956 he left an assignment in Greece to cover the Arab-Israeli War in the Suez. Four days before the end of hostilities, on November 10, 1956, he was killed with photographer Jean Roy, when nervous Egyptian

soldiers sprayed their jeep with machine-gun fire as they passed Anglo-French forces only six hundred feet away.
REFERENCE: Robert E. Hood. *12 at War: Great Photographers Under Fire.* 1967.

SHANKS, WILLIAM F. G. (1837–1905). The Kentucky-born Shanks became one of the most outstanding war correspondents covering the western theater of the American Civil War* while still in his twenties. Reporting for the *New York Herald*, Shanks began his battlefield coverage in the Kentucky-Tennessee war theater in the summer of 1862. He was with General Lovell H. Rousseau's division as it left Nashville in September of that year. Shanks would serve the dual role of volunteer aide to Rousseau and reporter for the *Herald* during the Battle of Perryville, and the next January he witnessed the Battle of Murfreesboro.

Shanks reported the Battle of Chickamauga from the front lines and after leaving Chattanooga narrowly escaped death in a train accident between Nashville and Bowling Green. He was traveling with fellow correspondent William S. Furay, and both leaped from the train just before the train's engineer, a Southern sympathizer, deliberately caused a collision with another train. After he telegraphed his account of the Battle of Chickamauga to the *Herald*, the paper claimed it was "the best account of that battle" and "the best account written of any battle ever fought." However, Shanks was later castigated for portraying this battle as a federal defeat.

Shanks subsequently covered the Battles of Chattanooga, Wauhatchie, and Lookout Mountain, and the charge up Missionary Ridge. He published his *Personal Recollections of Distinguished Generals* shortly after the war and in 1871 covered the Franco-Prussian War.*
REFERENCES: J. Cutler Andrews. *The North Reports the Civil War.* 1955; Louis M. Starr. *The Bohemian Brigade.* 1954.

SHAPLEN, ROBERT MODELL (1917–1988). During World War II* Shaplen covered one of the first major advances along the northern coast of New Guinea for *Time* magazine. He filed the first eyewitness account of the atomic bombing of Nagasaki for *Newsweek* magazine and later reported the early days of the Vietnam War* for the *New Yorker* magazine beginning in 1962. Based in Hong Kong, he was one of the few correspondents to cover the war from start to finish. A seasoned chronicler of the Asian scene, he was regarded as one of the most knowledgeable correspondents of the Vietnam press pool.
REFERENCE: Clarence R. Wyatt. *Paper Soldiers.* 1993.

SHAYKHET, ARKADI (1898–1959). Shaykhet came to prominence with his photographic account of the Russian Revolution. He was a leading pioneer Soviet photojournalist in the 1920s and 1930s, and his antiwar photograph "Thank You, Sons," is considered one of the most evocative images to come out of the Russian war with Germany.

REFERENCE: Daniela Mrazkova and Vladimir Remes, eds. *The Russian War: 1941–1945*. 1975.

SHEEAN, JAMES VINCENT (1899–1975). Sheean was born in Pana, Illinois, and educated at the University of Chicago. He reported for the *Chicago Daily News* and the *New York Daily News*, before moving to Italy as foreign correspondent for the *Chicago Tribune* in the early 1920s. On his first day as a foreign correspondent he reported Benito Mussolini's march on Rome in 1922. In 1925 he evaded French and Spanish forces to become one of the few reporters to see the Riffs during the Moroccan Riff War. He interviewed both brothers Abd el-Krim and the Raisuli after his capture by the Riffs. The movie *The Wind and the Lion* is thinly based on the exploits of the Raisuli in 1904 when he kidnapped a wealthy Greek-American citizen named Ion Pedicaris. Sheean traveled widely through the rebel countryside, where he witnessed evidence of the rebel rout of the Spanish army several months earlier. His reports indicated he was convinced of the intelligence of the Abd el-Krims as well as the sincerity of their patriotic cause. Sheean found that contrary to reports of mistreatment, European prisoners were treated no better or worse than the Arab and Berber captives. He chronicled his exploits among the Riffs in *An American Among the Riffi* (1926).

Following the Moroccan campaign he turned to freelancing and reported the 1929 riots in Jerusalem, the Ethiopian War,* the early days of the revolution in China, and the Spanish Civil War.* During World War II* he served in army intelligence in North Africa and Italy. On assignment to interview Mahatma Gandhi in 1948 he witnessed his assassination. Sheean published numerous works of nonfiction, including studies of Gandhi, Nehru, Verdi, and King Faisal, as well as memoirs of Dorothy Thompson, Sinclair Lewis, and Edna St. Vincent Millay. His best-selling autobiography *Personal History* (1953) is one of the most powerful reminiscences of a foreign correspondent.

REFERENCES: Raymond Strock. "The Works of Vincent Sheean: The Dust of an Honest Man," *Journalism History*. Autumn/Winter 1984; David S. Woolman. *Rebels in the Rif*. 1968.

SHEEHAN, NEIL (b. 1936). Sheehan was born in Holyoke, Massachusetts, and following graduation from Harvard in 1958 joined the army. He became a member of the United Press International's Tokyo bureau in 1962 and began covering the developing Vietnam conflict from Saigon. In January 1963 he reported the Ap Bac disaster, where Viet Cong guerrillas shot down at least five helicopters, killing several American crew members. The Saigon press corps drew heavy criticism for its critique of the U.S.-advised Vietnamese troops.

In 1964 Sheehan moved to the *New York Times*, and after a stint in New York he returned to the Far East, reporting from Indonesia and then reporting the Vietnam War* in 1965. While on assignment at the Pentagon in 1966, he was posted to the USS *America* in the eastern Mediterranean during the Arab-Israeli Six Day War in 1967. From 1968 on he covered the White House beat.

Perhaps his greatest scoop was his obtaining the Pentagon Papers in 1971. He is the author of *The Arnheiter Affair, After the War Was Over*, and his Pulitzer Prize–winning *A Bright Shining Lie* (1988).
REFERENCES: Michael Emery. *On the Front Lines*. 1995; William Prochnau. *Once upon a Distant War*. 1995.

SHELDON, CHARLES M. (b. 1866). Charles Sheldon was born in Indiana and gained his first experience in journalism working for his publisher father. In the 1880s he traveled throughout the South as a correspondent for the American Press Association and then opened an engraving business in Kansas. In 1890 he moved to Paris and began submitting sketches to various European publications before covering the Sudan campaign as an artist-correspondent* six years later. In 1898 he chronicled the Spanish-American War* in Cuba before moving on to South Africa and the Boer War* the following year. His sketches appeared sporadically in *Frank Leslie's Weekly* and the *Black and White* in England.
REFERENCES: Charles H. Brown. *The Correspondents' War*. 1967; Pat Hodgson. *The War Illustrators*. 1977.

SHELDON-WILLIAMS, INGLIS (1870–1940). Born in England, he moved with his family moved to Canada in 1886. He joined the *Sphere* as an illustrator and covered the Boer War* and the Russo-Japanese War.* During the Russo-Japanese War the *Sphere* made an arrangement with *Collier's Weekly* which allowed both journals to publish each other's pictures and battle reports. Although both periodicals gave readers the illusion that the reproduced sketches were reprints from the actual battlefront they were usually redrawn from sketches by artist-correspondents.* Following the war Sheldon-Williams accompanied the Canadian Expeditionary Forces as their official war artist during World War I.*
REFERENCE: Pat Hodgson. *The War Illustrators*. 1977.

SHEPARD, ELAINE (b. 1923). Born in Olney, Illinois, she moved to Hollywood, California, in her teens in an attempt to break into motion pictures. After starring in several serials she left films for marriage. Following a divorce she pursued a career in journalism. In 1959 she covered her first foreign assignment when she was assigned to follow Vice President Nixon's visit to Moscow. Over the following years she traveled widely as a foreign correspondent and was the only woman reporter to accompany President Eisenhower's eleven-nation tour. Later she received an exclusive interview with Indian prime minister Nehru and in 1961 covered the civil war in the Belgian Congo.

Shepard arrived in Saigon in 1965 and began covering Operation Rolling Thunder that March. Her account of the night-bombing missions is chronicled in her book *Doom Pussy* (1967). The title of the book is drawn from a Vietnamese translation which refers to an emblem worn by the pilots of the bombers consisting of a large yellow cat with a patch over its right eye and an airplane clenched between its teeth. During the war she eschewed Saigon for frequent forays into the field to record the real war. On a visit to a Montagnard village she removed her shirt to gain the trust of the bare-breasted women who were the subjects of some of her photographs.

Vehemently anti-Communist, she became a critic of the peace movement in the States as well. During the war she was awarded two citations for her coverage of helicopter assault missions, and in 1966 she returned to the United States to complete her book and marshal support for American servicemen overseas. She continued to publish pieces on the conflict and remained to the end a staunch advocate of American intervention.

REFERENCE: Virginia Elwood-Akers. *Women War Correspondents in the Vietnam War, 1961–1975.* 1988.

SHEPARDSON, DR. WILLIAM G. (?). Shepardson was one of the most outstanding reporters for the Confederate press during the American Civil War.* He began the conflict representing the *Mobile Register* and the *Columbus Times* of Georgia, for whom he reported the First Battle of Bull Run. In September he tranferred to the *Richmond Dispatch*. During his first six months with the paper his dispatches regularly appeared over his pseudonym "Bohemian" and were reprinted in numerous Southern newspapers.

In January 1862 Shepardson wrote his last dispatch for the Richmond paper. His resignation was in part due to General Joseph E. Johnston's General Order No. 98, which prohibited all war correspondents from covering his Army of the Potomac. Johnston's action was partly in response to a security breach committed by Shepardson, who had identified the location of various brigades in a report to the *Dispatch*.

Shepardson arrived in Norfolk in time to catch a steamer for Albemarle Sound, where he reported the successful Union assault on Roanoke Island in February 1862, before being captured by federal troops. Following his parole he was back with the *Mobile Register* reporting the Richmond news scene in May 1862. In the last years of the war Shepardson attempted to relieve the monotony of city reporting by occasionally working as a naval surgeon. He sporadically sent dispatches on life in the fledgling Confederate Navy to his old Richmond paper.

REFERENCE: J. Cutler Andrews. *The South Reports the Civil War.* 1970.

SHEPHERD, WILLIAM G. (1878–1933). An early member of the United Press staff in New York City, Shepherd personally detected the outbreak of the Triangle Shirt Waist Company fire that killed 145 people in 1911. Three years later he was in Veracruz, Mexico, reporting the landing of the U.S. Marines. When World War I* broke out prior to the withdrawal of troops from Mexico, Shepherd headed for Europe. He left London for Belgium after being granted an incredible interview with the first lord of the Admiralty, Winston Churchill.

Shepherd was the first American reporter permitted to cover the British front in France. He reported the fall of Antwerp and was the only journalist to the witness the Battle of Ypres. Along with war correspondent Will Irwin,* Shepherd was credited with being the first correspondent to report the German use of poison gas in warfare at the Battle of Ypres in the fall of 1914. He reportedly saw more of the battle than any other American reporter and during the Second Battle of Ypres was the only correspondent on the British front. Shepherd was also the first to report zeppelin raids over London in September 1914.

Although he returned to the States for a respite in the winter of 1914–1915, he remained active on the war fronts between 1914 and 1916 before joining General Pershing's staff in 1917. Following the war he covered the 1919 Paris Peace Conference for the *New York Evening Post*. His exploits were chronicled in his book *Confessions of a War Correspondent* (1917).
REFERENCES: Emmet Crozier. *American Reporters on the Western Front, 1914–18.* 1959; Robert W. Desmond. *Windows on the World.* 1980.

SHERROD, ROBERT (1909–1994). Born in Thomas County, Georgia, and educated at the University of Georgia, Sherrod entered journalism in 1929 working for the *Atlanta Constitution* and a succession of other southern newspapers. During World War II* he served as correspondent for *Time* and *Life*. He was the first of *Time*'s correspondents to go overseas with American forces. In 1942 he covered the first convoys for Australia. He spent six months reporting from New Guinea and in May 1943 was assigned to Attu. He was present during the Japanese attack and witnessed the invasion of Kiska. He would later report the marine landings on Tarawa, Saipan, and Iwo Jima. Sherrod was twice decorated by the navy for bravery. Following the war he served as Far East editor for the *Saturday Evening Post*. During the Vietnam War* he reported for *Life* magazine, flying his first combat mission since 1945, and his first in a jet. Among his works on war are *Tarawa: The Story of a Battle* (1944), *On to Westward: War in the Central Pacific* (1945), and *History of Marine Corps Aviation in World War II* (1952).
REFERENCE: Library of America. *Reporting World War Two: Part Two, American Journalism 1944–1946.* 1995.

SHIMAMOTO, KEISABURO (d. 1971). He was a Tokyo-based photographer for the Asia Newspaper Alliance from 1963 to 1967. He was covering the war in South Vietnam as a freelancer for *Newsweek* and other journals when he died in a helicopter crash over Laos. Also perishing on the flight were Larry Burrows,* Henri Huet, and Kent Potter.*
REFERENCE: Charles Arnot. *Don't Kill the Messenger.* 1994.

SHIRER, WILLIAM LAWRENCE (1904–1993). Born in Chicago, Illinois, he was educated at Coe College in Cedar Rapids, Iowa, where he first entered the world of journalism with a local paper. In 1927, his coverage of Lindbergh's landing in France won him a job as a foreign correspondent for the *Chicago Tribune*. He covered the League of Nations and the rise of Mussolini before being assigned to report Gandhi's resistance movement in India. After being fired in 1932 he was hired by the *New York Herald* Paris office. By 1937 he was in Berlin as chief correspondent for the Universal News Service covering the Third Reich. As one of the correspondents who would sound the alarm in Hitler's Germany in the 1930s, he would later call his years there "the nightmare years."

In 1938 he covered the *Anschluss* and the Sudeten crisis for CBS. Faced with having to fly to London to use the cable, he was instructed to coordinate the transmission of shortwave news broadcasts in Europe to cover the approaching conflict, setting a pattern which would be relied on throughout the war. At the outset of the war Shirer reported from the German side and was in Berlin when Germany invaded Poland in 1939. He continued his broadcasts from there until faced with increasing censorship restrictions the following year. Shirer was injured during a British bombing, losing his sight in one eye, and in 1941 he published the best-selling *Berlin Diary: The Journal of a Foreign Correspondent, 1931 to 1941*.

He covered the Allied war effort and following the war covered the Nuremberg trials and the establishment of the United Nations. He was blacklisted for five years when he refused to denounce the Hollywood 10 and made his living on the college lecture circuit. His most enduring work was the highly acclaimed best-seller *The Rise and Fall of the Third Reich*, which won the National Book Award.

REFERENCES: William Shirer. *Midcentury Journey*. 1952; William Shirer. *Twentieth Century Journey*. 1976.

SIDEBOTHAM, HERBERT (1872–1940). Sidebotham was born in Manchester, England, and educated at Oxford. Upon graduation he joined the *Manchester Guardian* as a lead writer, a position he would hold for almost a quarter century. A keen student of military history, he was the paper's military critic during the Boer War,* with his columns appearing under the pseudonym "Student of War." He filled the role again during World War I* and in 1918 left the paper to become the military critic for the *Times*. He remained with the *Times* until 1921. An avid Zionist, he wrote numerous articles and several books on the subject between 1918 and 1937.

REFERENCES: David Ayerst. *The Manchester Guardian: Biography of a Newspaper*. 1971; *DNB*, 1931–1940.

SIGNAL. *Signal* was the best-selling magazine in German-occupied Europe. It was published by the *Wehrmacht* and supervised by Joseph Goebbels and his Ministry of Propaganda. Its sales peaked in 1943 when it enjoyed a readership of two and a half million in twenty different languages. It was initially created with the intention of convincing Europeans that any resistance was futile and

that the Nazi war machine was invincible. Its earliest issues reflect the heady days of German success on the battlefield. One of the first periodicals to publish color photographs by its war photographers at the front, in its heyday the magazine was unmatched in color photography and military reportage. However, by the end of 1943 *Signal* began to decline in both its quality and its readership. Due to wartime exigencies supplies of good quality paper stock were limited, and the quality of the magazine began to deteriorate. In addition, with its headquarters in Berlin coming under attack from Allied air raids it became increasingly difficult to sell an optimistic vision of the outcome of the war to German readers. By 1944 the magazine had stopped publishing regularly, but would continue to operate intermittently until March 1945, when the editor moved its archives and staff to the west in order to avoid being captured by the Soviets.
REFERENCE: S. L. Mayer, ed. *"Signal": Years of Retreat, 1943–44.* 1979.

SIMMONS, WALTER (b. 1908). Prior to World War II* Simmons had been the city editor for the *Sioux Falls Argus-Leader.* In 1944 he joined the *Chicago Tribune* and was assigned to report the war in the Pacific theater. In January 1945 he accompanied General MacArthur's troops back to Luzon, Philippines. Following the war he was chief of the *Tribune's* North Pacific bureau when the Korean War* broke out. He was in Seoul, South Korea, covering the opening of the new government under President Syngman Rhee in June 1950 when the city came under attack and war erupted. Since he was the only American correspondent on the entire front, his dispatches turned into his greatest news scoop. He would spend three months at the front before returning to Tokyo for a brief recuperation. Simmons returned in time to cover the first American troops cutting off the Communist advance, the Inchon landing, the drive to the Yalu River, and the subsequent retreat.
REFERENCE: Lloyd Wendt. *Chicago Tribune.* 1979.

SIMPLOT, ALEXANDER (b. 1837). Descended from a prominent Dubuque, Iowa, family, at the outset of the American Civil War* Simplot won a commission as special artist for the trans-Mississippi West on the strength of a sketch he submitted to *Harper's Weekly.* He was educated at Rock River Seminary and then Union College in New York. Following graduation he taught school briefly before whimsically sending his sketch of hometown troops marching off to war to *Harper's.* During the war he would submit sketches rejected by *Harper's* to the *New York Illustrated News* under the pseuodnym "A. S. Leclerc."

Simplot initially covered army encampments and war preparations before his magazine convinced him to go into the field with the armies. He attached himself first to the forces under General John C. Frémont, commander of the armies in the West at the start of the war, before covering the outbreak of the western naval war during the winter of 1861–1862. He accompanied Ulysses Grant's Mississippi squadron on the land-river assault against Confederate forts along the Tennessee and Cumberland Rivers. Simplot sketched the Battle of Fort

Henry, the aftermath of the victory at Fort Donelson, and the surrender of Island Number 10. However, it soon became apparent that Simplot did not possess the fortitude to be a successful war artist. One source described him as the unluckiest artist of the war. While Simplot sketched the relatively insignificant taking of Island Number 10, he missed the Battle of Shiloh, one of the most important battles of the war, and following the Battle of Fort Henry he dallied long enough to miss the more pivotal Battle of Fort Donelson.

General Henry Halleck ordered all war correspondents with the Army of the Tennessee to vacate the front lines in the summer of 1862. Simplot managed to circumvent the prohibition by returning to the field posing as a sutler. Following the Battle of Shiloh, Simplot covered the Corinth campaign with Halleck's forces. He left the field briefly to recuperate back home in Dubuque but by November 1862 was campaigning with Grant's army in Tennessee. Simplot resigned from *Harper's* in early 1863, unable to find a cure for the chronic diarrhea that had plagued him since the Shiloh campaign. Simplot hung up his sketch artist's pen and entered business in Dubuque, while *Harper's* replaced him with the vastly superior combat artist Theodore R. Davis.*

REFERENCES: Philip Van Doren Stern. *They Were There.* 1959; W. Fletcher Thompson, Jr. *The Image of War.* 1959.

SIMPSON, WILLIAM (1823–1899). Born in Glasgow, Scotland, with little formal education he was apprenticed to a lithographer at the age of fourteen. In 1851 he became a lithographic artist in London and rose to prominence with his plates of the Crimean War.* Although he served as a frontline artist during the conflict he was not affiliated with any newspaper or illustrated press. Rather, he was there on behalf of the London print seller, Colnaghi, for whom he was to supply paintings for a proposed series of lithographs, *The Seat of the War in the East.* In his autobiography Simpson noted that war artists were less suspect than correspondents because they were less critical in their portrayals, hence soldiers and staff treated them better.

Simpson traveled once again for Colnaghi in 1859, when he went to India to record the aftermath of the Indian Mutiny. In 1865 he joined the *Illustrated London News.* During the 1868 Abyssinia campaign he missed the action, reaching Napier's forces soon after the fall of Magdala and the death of King Theodore. But his sketches were still valuable in giving the English public an idea what conditions were like.

Following Abyssinia, he traveled widely, covering the opening of the Suez Canal, the Middle East, and the Crimea once again. With war between Germany and France looming, he reached Paris shortly after war was declared. Joining the assemblage of correspondents near Metz, he was attacked by an angry crowd who suspected his sketching of the emperor's carriage was a front for some espionage mission. France was afflicted with spy paranoia and self-doubt after two costly defeats, and any artist with a sketch pad was suspicious. Simpson thought about sketching on cigarette papers, which in the event of apprehension could be made into a cigarette, eliminating any evidence. He drew the Battle of Sedan on the back of a piece of wallpaper and witnessed the siege of Strasbourg, after which he accompanied the defeated French army back to Paris. Simpson returned to France in April 1871 to cover the Paris Commune before going back to London in June.

In 1873 he arrived in California in time to report the outbreak of the Modoc Indian War. He made a series of sketches of the Lava Beds, Captain Jack's hideout, and the assassination of General Canby. Simpson reported Schliemann's archeological discoveries at Troy and Mycenae before embarking for his last battlefront during the Afghan War (1878–1880). He quit the *Illustrated London News* in 1885.

REFERENCES: Pat Hodgson. *The War Illustrators*. 1977; William Simpson. *Autobiography of William Simpson*. 1903.

SINGER, JACK (1917–1944). A former New York sportswriter, Singer was killed aboard the aircraft carrier *Wasp* during the Battle of the Solomon Islands. Reporting for the International News Service (INS), he was the first correspondent to accompany a Navy torpedo plane mission. Following the torpedo attack that killed Singer, navy officers on board the vessel completed his last dispatch and sent it to the INS. He was awarded the Purple Heart, posthumously.

REFERENCES: Robert W. Desmond. *Tides of War*. 1984; M. L. Stein. *Under Fire*. 1968.

SINO-JAPANESE WAR. On August 1, 1894, Japanese forces attacked Seoul, Korea, seized the king, and declared war on China. The war ended by February 1895 after Chinese forces were destroyed on land and sea. This was the first war in Asia to receive Western press coverage. Most reporters covering the conflict were either stringers* or special correspondents. Barred from accompanying Chinese forces, they found Japanese press restrictions not much better, setting a standard which would be repeated in 1904–1905 during the Russo-Japanese War.*

Correspondents generally languished in Tokyo and Peking, although they were present at the Port Arthur massacre committed by the Japanese in December. The most prominent correspondents included Frederic Villiers* of the *Graphic*, James Creelman* of the *New York World*, Stephen Bonsal* for the *New York Herald*, and Julian Ralph* of the *New York Sun*.

REFERENCE: Robert W. Desmond. *The Information Process*. 1978.

SKINNER, JOHN EDWIN HILARY (1839–1894). Skinner was born in London and graduated from the University of London in 1861 with a law degree. He joined the *Daily News* in 1864 as a special with the Danish army during the war with Prussia. His book *Tale of Danish Heroism* was one of the more insightful accounts of the Schleswig-Holstein controversy. For his service during the war he was awarded the Order of Dannerbrog by King Christian IX.

He covered the Austro-Prussian War* in 1866 and then the Franco-Prussian War* in 1870, during which he was attached to the staff of the Prussian crown prince. He reported most battles from Wörth to Sedan. Following the Battle of Sedan he attempted to outmaneuver W. H. Russell* in an attempt to get his account into print in England. To their dismay, both correspondents were out-scooped by Archibald Forbes,* whose telegraph dispatch preceded theirs by two days. In 1882 he covered the invasion of Egypt.

REFERENCE: Robert Wilkinson-Latham. *From Our Special Correspondent*. 1979.

SMALLEY, GEORGE WASHBURN (1833–1916). Born in Franklin, Massachusetts, the Yale- and Harvard-educated Smalley was barred from American Civil War* military service because of poor vision. Hired by the *New York Tribune* because of his abolitionist leanings, he was assigned to Port Royal, South Carolina, from November 1861 to April 1862. His first report was an eyewitness account of the capture of Fort Pulaski. However, when the *Tribune*'s Greeley was notified that he had neglected to cover other skirmishes nearby he was sharply criticized.

Attached to Major General John C. Frémont's Union command in spring 1861 Smalley witnessed the Battles of Fort Republic and Cross Keys. After a brief respite in Washington, D.C., the next phase of his journalistic career found Smalley as a volunteer aide to Major General Joseph Hooker at the Battle of Antietam, where he wrote what has been described as one of the ''best single pieces of reporting done during the Civil War.'' On September 17, 1862, Smalley traversed the battlefield delivering orders for the wounded Hooker, and in the process gained the perspective not only to write a complete account of the battle but to scoop the other war reporters as well. His account was reprinted in over a thousand American newspapers, and he was rewarded by the *Tribune* with an editorship in New York, where he spent the duration of the war.

In 1866 he continued his career as a war reporter when he covered the Austro-Prussian War.* The following year he opened the *Tribune*'s London bureau and directed its European bureau for twenty-eight years. During the Franco-Prussian War* of 1870–1871, one of Smalley's reporters assigned to cover the Prussian army scooped the world on the French defeat at the Battle of Sedan. Smalley was one of the first journalists to make extensive use of the telegraph and cable. From 1895 to 1905 he served as American correspondent for the *London Times*. Among his published works was a two-volume autobiography, *Anglo-American Memories* (1911 and 1912).

REFERENCES: J. Cutler Andrews. *The North Reports the Civil War*. 1955; Joseph Mathews. *George W. Smalley, Forty Years a Foreign Correspondent*. 1973.

SMEDLEY, AGNES (1894–1950). Born in rural Missouri, Smedley grew up in the mining town of Trinidad, Colorado. At the age of sixteen, following the death of her mother, Agnes left the family for the Southwest. She taught school in New Mexico and studied for brief periods at the Tempe Normal School in

Arizona and the University of California at Berkeley. In San Diego she made the acquaintance of the anarchist Emma Goldman and became involved in the free speech movement. Increasingly drawn to political affairs, she moved to New York City and protested America's participation in World War I.* She was arrested and charged with violating the Espionage Act in 1918, but was released after several months in prison. She left America the following year and would spend most of the remainder of her life abroad.

She lived in Berlin until 1928 with Indian nationalist leader Virendranath Chattopadyaya. Ever the political activist, Smedley helped organize Germany's first public birth control clinic and actively worked in behalf of Indian nationalism. In 1929 she published her first book, *Daughter of Earth*, a thinly veiled critique and fictionalization of her life in America.

In 1928, Smedley arrived in China as correspondent for the *Frankfurt Zeitung* and became an advocate and supporter of Communist forces in rebellion against the government of Chiang Kai-shek. In 1930 Smedley joined the *Manchester Guardian* as its foreign correspondent, although she was not allowed into Communist-held areas until 1937.

After Edgar Snow* evaded nationalist forces in July 1936 and made his way to Mao Tse-tung's stronghold, scoring a great journalistic coup with the first Western interview with the Communist leader, Smedley attempted to replicate the feat. That December Smedley scored her own reporting coup when she was the only Western journalist present in Sian when Chiang Kai-shek was kidnapped and held captive temporarily by rebellious Manchurian troops. She continued to work on behalf of Communist forces from 1937 to 1940.

After Japan invaded China in 1937 she traveled with the Eighth Route Army following the wartime conciliation of the Red Army and Chiang's forces, as they formed a united front against the Japanese. Her book *China Fights Back: An American Woman with the Eighth Route Army* (1938) chronicles her exploits with the Red Army. During the late 1930s she periodically filed reports with the *Manchester Guardian*. In 1941, critically ill from malnutrition and malaria, she was forced to return to the States for medical treatment. She remained in America until 1949. That year General Douglas MacArthur's intelligence staff singled Smedley out as a Communist spy, and after she threatened libel actions the charges were withdrawn. But, her connections to her Communist past made it increasingly difficult for her to make a living in a postwar America living in fear of the Red menace. In November 1949 she moved to England, hoping to eventually return to China. She died in an Oxford nursing home of pneumonia on May 6, 1950. Ultimately, she returned to China when her deathbed request to be buried there was granted. She is one of only two foreigners buried in Communist China's equivalent of Arlington Cemetery.

REFERENCES: *DAB*; Peter Rand. *China Hands*. 1995.

SMITH, COLIN (b. 1944). British foreign correspondent Colin Smith worked as a roving reporter for the *Observer*, reporting twenty wars in the Middle East,

Africa, and Asia. He covered the terrorist Black September aircraft hijackings in 1970 and the Arab-Israeli War of 1973. He was captured by Katanga rebels during their invasion of Zaire in 1977 and was ambushed several times during the invasion of Cyprus by Turkey. In 1974 and 1984 he was recognized as International Reporter of the Year.
REFERENCE: Dennis Griffiths, ed. *The Encyclopedia of the British Press*. 1992.

SMITH, DAN (1865–1934). Born in Ivugtut, Greenland, and raised in New York City, he went to Copenhagen at fourteen to study art. In 1890 he joined the staff of *Leslie's* as a sketch artist. He covered the 1890–1891 Indian troubles on the Pine Ridge Reservation and Wounded Knee. Until 1897, he traveled the West sketching Native American and outdoor scenes. He left for Hearst's newspapers in 1897 and worked as artist-correspondent* during the Spanish-American War.* For the next twenty years his illustrations appeared in the *Sunday World* magazine section and were syndicated nationally.
REFERENCE: Peggy and Harold Samuels. *Samuels' Encyclopedia of Artists of the American West*. 1985.

SMITH, ELIAS (?). In July 1862 Smith scooped the competition with his account of the Peninsular campaign during the American Civil War* for the *New York Times*. On February 7, Smith witnessed the Battle of Roanoke Island when he accompanied General Ambrose E. Burnside's expedition to seize the island in order to stop Confederate blockade running. In late 1863 Smith again was with Burnside during the siege of Knoxville for the *New York Tribune*. His dispatches on the fall of Atlanta in 1864 are considered among the best accounts of the campaign. Later that year he covered the Battle of Cedar Creek.
REFERENCES: J. Cutler Andrews. *The North Reports the Civil War*. 1955; Louis M. Starr. *Bohemian Brigade*. 1954.

SMITH, ERNEST (c. 1865–1935). Smith was born in Hampshire, England, and worked for several smaller papers before moving to the *Daily News* in 1890s. In 1900 he joined the *Morning Leader* and the *Star* as a special correspondent covering the Boer War.* Employed as both photographer and writer, he covered the siege of Ladysmith.*
REFERENCE: Robert W. Desmond. *The Information Process*. 1978.

SMITH, HOWARD KINGSBURY (b. 1914). Born in Ferriday, Louisiana, Smith graduated from Tulane University in 1936 and the following year won a Rhodes scholarship to Oxford. During World War II* he joined the staff of CBS and reported from Berlin until America entered the war in December 1941. Like many of his fellow journalists he quickly fell into disfavor with the Nazis and was forced to flee Germany after the attack on Pearl Harbor. He managed to escape to Switzerland on the last train from Berlin for Americans. Smith spent the remainder of the war broadcasting for CBS from Berne, Switzerland. The following years saw the publication of his book *Last Train from Berlin*. He covered the battlefront as the Ninth Army correspondent in France, Holland, and Germany, ultimately winning much critical claim and four consecutive Overseas Club Awards. He returned to the United States and a career in radio and television, winning the George Polk Award in 1960. In 1966 he reported the expanding war in Southeast Asia for ABC.

REFERENCE: Robert B. Downs and Jane B. Downs. *Journalists of the United States.* 1991.

SMITH, W. EUGENE (1918–1978). He was born in Wichita, Kansas, and educated at the University of Notre Dame on a special photography scholarship. He entered journalism with various Wichita newspapers while still in his teens and in 1937 joined the staff of *Newsweek* magazine. He was fired from his job for using a miniature camera against company policy. He freelanced for a variety of publications during a period which he described as his "creative immaturity." His career as a photojournalist took off when *Life* magazine published some of his work, leading to an on-and-off position on the staff from 1939 to 1955.

He injured himself accidentally in 1942 while making a photograph of simulated battle conditions for *Parade* magazine. Unable to serve in the armed forces due to defective hearing as a result of the explosion, he served as a war correspondent for the Ziff-Davis Publishing Company. In 1943 he became a war correspondent for *Flying* magazine and flew sixteen combat missions in the Pacific. His photographs are memorable for his employment of dramatic techniques using aerial angles and harsh contrasts. He was known in the press corps as "Wonderful Smith" to differentiate him from other Smiths by using his first initial. Originally he covered the Atlantic theater before switching to the Pacific. He was aboard the aircraft carrier *Independence* covering the second raid on Wake Island and then the *Bunker Hill* during the attack on Rabaul. He reported the Battles of Tarawa and Naru Island, and had flown over sixteen air strikes before taking respite in San Francisco in March 1944. Much to his dismay he found, as most combat photographers during World War II* would, that censors had blocked the release of almost half of his photos. He resigned from Ziff-Davis and joined the ranks of *Life*.

He covered the invasion of Saipan in June 1944 and the invasion of Guam the following month. After bouts with dengue fever he was forced to recuperate at Pearl Harbor, where he soon rejoined the *Bunker Hill* and became the only combat photographer to accompany air raids over Tokyo in February 1945. Smith was with the marines for the assault on Iwo Jima. He covered virtually every phase of the Pacific theater as the war moved toward conclusion. He covered the invasions of Guam and then Okinawa, where he was severely injured by shell fire, requiring evacuation to Guam. Due to his injuries he was not in Japan to cover the treaty signing and spent the next two years undergoing treatment for his wounds.

His postwar career saw Smith return to freelancing after *Life* refused to give him control over his photo essay on Albert Schweitzer. During the 1960s and 1970s he photographed the industrial landscape of Japan and the devastating impact of mercury poisoning at Minimata, Japan, receiving worldwide accolades. He was severely beaten by thugs for his exposure of the Minimata poisoning in 1972, leading to a temporary loss of sight.

REFERENCES: Jim Hughes. *W. Eugene Smith: The Life and Work of an American Photographer.* 1989; W. Eugene Smith. *W. Eugene Smith: His Photographs and Notes.* 1969.

SNOW, EDGAR (1905–1972). Born in Kansas City, Missouri, Snow attended the University of Missouri and the Columbia University School of Journalism. In 1928 he joined the Hong Kong staff of the *China Weekly Review* and then the *Chicago Tribune.* Within two years he became a correspondent for the Consolidated Press Association. He traveled widely throughout Asia on assignment, and in 1933 he published his first book, *The Far Eastern Front*, while teaching at Yenching University in Peking. Shortly after leaving the university he set out to cover the Chinese Communists. Snow claimed to be the first person to penetrate the 1936 civil war blockade and interview Mao Tse-tung, Chou En-lai, and other leaders of the Chinese Red Army in his book *The Other Side of the River: Red China Today* (1962). His coverage of the civil war for the *New York Sun* and the *London Daily Herald* proved to be his greatest reporting coup, resulting in the international best-seller *Red Star over China* (1937). He covered the Chinese Civil War until 1940, when he returned home to a post as world correspondent and associate editor for the *Saturday Evening Post.*

REFERENCE: John Hohenberg. *Foreign Correspondence: The Great Reporters and Their Times.* 1964.

SOUTH AFRICAN WAR. *See* BOER WAR.

SOUTHWORTH, ALVAN S. (1846–1901). Born in Lockport, New York, Southworth attended the U.S. Naval Academy before joining the *New York Herald.* Prior to 1871 he covered the Fenian uprising in Canada and the Franco-Prussian War,* including the Paris Commune. In 1871 he was assigned to investigate the disappearance of Sir Samuel Baker, who was in the Sudan on a military mission to suppress the slave trade and annex the upper Nile for Egypt. His travels to Khartoum, the Red Sea, and Egypt are detailed in *Four Thousand Miles of African Travel: A Personal Record of a Journey up the Nile and Through the Soudan to Central Africa* (1875). Following his African adventure he returned to the United States and a career in the railroad business.

REFERENCE: *New York Times.* January 8, 1901.

SPANISH-AMERICAN WAR. In the 1890s reports of Spanish brutality against the Cubans began to attract American interest and stimulate sympathy for the Cuban independence movement. With the outbreak of the Cuban insurrection in 1896 and the subsequent declaration of independence from Spain, American newspapers provided their readership with lurid, sensationalist accounts of the growing Cuban conflict. When the U.S. battleship *Maine* exploded mysteriously in Havana Harbor on February 15, 1898, Congress recognized Cuba's independence and demanded that Spain give up the island. In response Spain broke off diplomatic relations with the United States, and on April 25 Congress declared war on Spain.

Most of the action took place in Cuba and Puerto Rico between June and July 1898. Although it was of short duration, the Spanish-American War was covered by more reporters than any previous event in history. Estimates of the number of war correspondents covering the conflict range as high as five hundred. However, Charles H. Brown, an authority on the conflict, believes the numbers were much lower. He found reference to approximately three hundred members of the press, including seventeen British journalists and three from Canada. Charles Sanford Diehl,* who represented the Associated Press during the war, placed the number as low as two hundred.

Many members of the press had noted the winds of war as early as April and were already in Cuba when hostilities broke out between America and Spain. Early arrivals included neutral British observers such as Edward Frederick Knight* for the *Times*, John B. Atkins* for the *Manchester Guardian*, George Lynch* of the *Daily Chronicle*, Charles E. Hands* for the *Daily Mail*, Seppings Wright* of the *Illustrated London News*, and H. A. Gwynne of Reuters.*

The Spanish-American War was one of the most expensive wars to cover, with the main expense involving communications. Cables connecting the island were cut at the outset of the war, forcing correspondents to rely on dispatch boats to get their reports to the nearest telegraph or cable office. The most popular transmission stations were located in Key West, Florida; Kingston or Port Antonio, Jamaica; St. Thomas in the Virgin Islands, and other West Indies ports. Companies chartering boats to the newspapers reaped a windfall profit, with fees of five to six thousand dollars a month not atypical. Telegraph dispatches from Key West to New York averaged five cents a word, with payment required in gold specie.

New York papers were the best represented of the American papers. William Randolph Hearst's* *New York Journal* provided sixty to seventy correspondents, including Hearst himself. Some of the more noteworthy journalists for the paper included James Creelman,* Frederic Remington,* and Stephen Crane,* late of the *New York World*. Present for the *New York Herald* were Richard Harding Davis,* Francis Millet,* and Stephen Bonsal.* Other notable correspondents included Charles Sanford Diehl, John P. Dunning,* and Reuben Briggs Davenport* of the AP, W.A.M. Goode,* George Bronson Rea,* Ralph D. Paine,* and Percival Phillips.* In addition to the hundreds of male reporters three women recorded the conflict at various times. Katherine White reported for the *Chicago Record* while engaged as a Red Cross nurse, and Josephine Miles Woodward and Katherine Blake Watkins* provided sporadic service.

Although the war did not produce a photographer on par with Mathew Brady,* there were several war photographers on hand who managed to obtain excellent pictures. Among them were James Burton,* William Dinwiddie,* A. D. Brittingham, and others. Physical conditions presented formidable barriers to the intrepid photographers including tropical heat, an abundance of light, and frequent rain. Film stock and plates were often ruined by the extreme moisture. Inside their darkrooms photographers turned to innovation by using alcohol to hasten the drying of negatives in order to prevent the gelatin from congealing in the tropical heat. By the time they had adapted to the new climate the war was over. Some photographers took their skills to the Philippines, where their techniques were well suited.

Few professional photographers bothered to cover the war. Among the most prominent were James Hare* of *Collier's Weekly* and John C. Hemment,* working for William Randolph Hearst. As Hearst's personal photographer, Hemment was afforded a well-equipped floating darkroom on Hearst's boat the *Sylvia*. However, his images paled in comparison to Hare's, taken in the heat of battle with a small box camera, heralding the future use of light cameras such as the Leicas in the twentieth century. Several war correspondents brought along cameras as well. Richard Harding Davis* and Burr McIntosh* supplemented their print journalism with photographic images.

War artists supplemented the photographic record and their work was often considered superior. Among the most noted artists were Frederic Remington,* John T. McCutcheon* of the *Chicago Tribune*, Howard Chandler Christy,* and William J. Glackens, a future member of the "ashcan school" of art.

The Spanish-American War was a watershed of sorts in the history of war journalism. No previous war had been so heavily covered, as American newspapers introduced true mass circulation. In addition the war brought advances in news photography and introduced motion picture photography as a supplement to news reporting.

REFERENCES: Charles H. Brown. *The Correspondents' War*. 1967; Frank Friedel. *The Splendid Little War*. 1958; Joyce Milton. *The Yellow Kids*. 1989.

SPANISH CIVIL WAR. On July 18, 1936, army generals Francisco Franco, Emilio Mola, and José Sanjuro began a revolt against the Popular Front government of the Spanish Republic formed by Manuel Azaña the previous February. The revolt was secretly sponsored by Nazi Germany and Fascist Italy. Within two days the entire country was embroiled in civil war. The war ended in March 1939 with Republican forces defeated and a new government headed by General Franco. Franco's forces were identified as insurgents, Nationalists, or Falangists, while government troops were referred to as Republicans or simply "government" forces.

In July 1936 foreign intevention on behalf of Franco's forces began with Fascist Italy and Nazi Germany sending men and equipment to the insurgents. This story was first reported by *New York Times* correspondent Frank Kluckholn,* who was with Franco's troops. Once it was revealed who broke the story Kluckholn was forced to flee for his life.

The war would prove both confusing and dangerous for the legion of correspondents descending on Spain. Journalists faced every manner of barrier in covering the war. Difficulties included problems of housing, transportation, food, news gathering, censorship, health, and language. Four journalists were ultimately killed, many wounded, and several were jailed and expelled. On New Year's Eve 1937 Harvard graduate Brad Johnson, representing *Newsweek*, and Edward J. Neil, Jr., became the only two American correspondent war deaths of the conflict. They were killed when artillery fire hit the car they were traveling in.

Since the Spanish press could not be depended on for accurate coverage of the war, and those of the Axis countries were controlled by the government, coverage was best provided by the neutrals, many of whom came to the conflict with prior experience in the recent Ethiopian War.* The scoop announcing the outbreak of the war was delivered by Lester Ziffren of the United Press, who was soon joined by Kluckholn and his *Times* colleague Lawrence A. Fernsworth. Veteran correspondents of the Ethiopian War included Vincent Sheean* for the *Chicago Tribune*, Webb Miller* and Reynolds Packard* of the UP, Herbert L. Matthews* for *New York Times*, John T. Whitaker* of the *New York Herald*, Floyd Gibbons* and Karl H. Von Wiegand for the International News Service (INS), Ladislas Farago of the *New York Times*, Ernest Richard Sheepshanks of Reuters,* George L. Steer* of the *London Times*, and Percival Phillips* of the *Daily Telegraph*.

Other experienced correspondents who arrived in Spain included Leland Stowe* of the *New York Herald Tribune*, George Seldes* of the *New York Post*, O'Dowd Gallegher* and Noel Monks* of the *Daily Express*, Henry T. Gorrell* of the UP, Arthur Koestler* of the *News Chronicle*, and Harold "Kim" Philby* of the *London Times*. Martha Gellhorn,* representing *Collier's Weekly*, was one of five women reporting the war, and her future husband Ernest Hemingway* was with Republican forces for North American Newspaper Alliance (NANA). Photographer Robert Capa* and his lover Gerda Taro,* the latter of whom would die in the conflict, were there for *Life* magazine. In addition to the dozens of other less well known journalists from Great Britain and the United States reporting the war were many representatives of the French press.

Most of the correspondents were committed ideologically to the Republicans and covered the war with a passion unmatched in previous wars. Many saw Spain as a place to stop the spread of fascism, providing a lure to prominent literary figures and the best journalists of the era. Objectivity often suffered as numerous correspondents joined the Republicans at the battlefront. At various times Hemingway, Claud Cockburn,* and Eric Blair* brandished weapons against the Nationalists. Others participated as a cover for Commintern activities, including the Soviet agent Philby and Arthur Koestler. While correspondents were quick to publicize Nationalist atrocities they generally failed to report the imperfect side of the Republicans, who were guilty of their own excesses. Among the more controversial news stories associated with the war were the bombing of Guernica* and Capa's photograph "Death of a Loyalist Soldier." REFERENCES: Robert W. Desmond. *Crisis and Conflict: World News Reporting Between Two World Wars, 1920–1940.* 1982; Robert W. Desmond. *Tides of War.* 1984; Phillip Knightley. *The First Casualty.* 1975; Trevor Royle. *War Report: The War Correspondent's View of Battle from the Crimea to the Falklands.* 1987; Peter Wyden. *The Passionate War: The Narrative History of the Spanish Civil War.* 1983.

STACKPOLE, PETER (b. 1913). Born in San Francisco, he worked with Alfred Eisenstaedt, one of the earliest staff photographers for *Life.* He worked for the magazine from 1936 to 1960. Until 1943 he mainly photographed Hollywood celebrities. However, as a photographer-correspondent during the invasion of Saipan in 1943–1944, he took some of the most memorable pictures of World War II.*
REFERENCE: Jorge Lewinski. *The Camera at War.* 1978.

STANLEY, SIR HENRY MORTON (1841–1904). Better known as an explorer, Stanley was born in North Wales as John Rowlands. Taking the name of his adoptive father, who resided in New Orleans, he became an American citizen. He returned to Louisiana from California shortly after the outbreak of the American Civil War.* He joined the Confederacy as a private but was soon taken prisoner by Union forces at the Battle of Shiloh. Switching his allegiance to the North, he was assigned to the ironclad *Ticonderoga* at the rank of ensign.

Following the Civil War he entered journalism as a special correspondent for the *Missouri Democrat* at fifteen dollars per week plus travel expenses. He supplemented his income by supplying articles for several other papers, including the *New York Herald.* In 1867 he covered the American Indian Wars* for the St. Louis–based paper, accompanying Major General Winfield Scott Hancock's force against the southern Plains Indians. While Stanley published many dispatches during the expedition, it proved uneventful.

Soon after the conclusion of the expedition Stanley resigned and headed for New York, where he was hired by the *New York Herald.* In 1867 he was assigned to cover the British expedition to Abyssinia. Stanley accompanied Sir Robert Napier's expedition on its march to Magdala, where he reported the storming of the fortress and the entry of British forces into King Theodore's stronghold. During this conflict the novice reporter firmly established his reputation as a journalist. Prior to his arrival in Abyssinia he had made arrangements for his dispatches to be given priority handling, resulting in his scoop of the fall of Magdala for the *Herald.*

In 1868 Stanley was given his most famous assignment when he was ordered to "find Livingstone." Successfully completing this mission in 1871, he returned to London the following year and was awarded the Gold Medal of the Royal Geographical Society.

The next phase of his career began in 1873, when he covered Sir Garnet Wolseley's Ashanti campaign for the *Herald*. In 1874 he was commissioned by both the *Daily Telegraph* and the *New York Herald* to find the sources of the Congo and Nile Rivers. The years 1879 to 1884 saw Stanley in the employ of King Leopold of Belgium, exploring the Congo territory. In March 1887 he was hired to rescue the German naturalist Eduard Schnitzer, better known as Emin Pasha, which he accomplished the following year. He died a year after suffering paralysis in 1903. He published numerous books on African exploration. His account of his African military exploits was released as *Coomassie and Magdala* in 1874, and in 1909 *The Autobiography of Sir Henry Morton Stanley* was posthumously published.

REFERENCES: *DNB*, 1901–1911; Robert Wilkinson-Latham. *From Our Special Correspondent*. 1979.

STARS AND STRIPES. The *Stars and Stripes* was published under the supervision of the Press Section of the Censorship and Press Division of the Intelligence Branch of the General Staff of the Allied Expeditionary Force (AEF). This newspaper was produced by the armed forces for the military beginning in World War I.* It was the premier troop newspaper of its era beginning with its first issue on February 8, 1918. An eight-page weekly, it appeared every Friday until June 13, 1919. At its peak it was produced by a staff of over three hundred. Created by order of General Quarters of the AEF, its initial goals were to keep units as well informed as possible and to function as an outlet for creative contributions by members of the AEF. It was also to provide information from home, along with general news and war reports, and to emphasize the role of the United States in the war. At first it was published at AEF Field Press headquarters in Neuchateau, but was soon relocated to larger quarters in Paris.

During World War II* the newspaper was revived as a daily in almost thirty editions and reclaimed its place as the best-known troop paper in Europe. Most sources indicate that President Roosevelt suggested resurrecting the paper. The World War II editions began in London in 1942 as the Thirty-fourth Infantry Division prepared to leave for the North African landings. A month following the Allied landings the Mediterranean edition was established in a Red Cross building in Algiers. Other editions soon followed with the opening of each new front. By January 1945 circulation exceeded 1,200,000 issues daily.

By most accounts the World War I edition was the superior of the two. Judged on its literary and technical merits it was truly first-rate. While it was faced with censorship restrictions imposed by a board of control, the content of each issue still reflected the concerns of a staff of writers drawn from the enlisted ranks who in the end exercised control over the newspaper and its operations. During World War II there were significantly more high-level officers who consistently interfered with the production of the newspaper.

Following World War II *The Stars and Stripes* continued in two editions.

With the outbreak of war in 1950, the Korean War* edition of the paper was created by a staff that eventually grew to almost seventy. One authority on armed forces newspapers noted that the World War I edition is best described as "famous" compared to the World War II incarnation, which was "professional," but that by the time of the Vietnam War* it had become simply an "organization newspaper."
REFERENCE: Alfred Emile Cornebise. *Ranks and Columns: Armed Forces Newspapers in American Wars*. 1993.

STEDMAN, EDMUND CLARENCE (1833–1908). Born in Hartford, Connecticut, Stedman joined the *New York World* in 1860. He covered the Virginia front during the first year of the American Civil War* before leaving, reporting next for the attorney general's office and then Wall Street. He wrote poetry during these years, earning the moniker "the Bard of Wall Street." He covered the Battles of Ball's Bluff and Williamsburg. His account of the First Battle of Bull Run was among the best of the campaign. During the war he wrote the poem "John Brown's Invasion" and the campaign song "Honest Abe of the West."
REFERENCES: Stewart Sifakis. *Who Was Who in the Civil War*. 1988; Louis M. Starr. *Bohemian Brigade*. 1954.

STEELE, ARCHIBALD T. (b. 1903). The Canadian-born Steele attended Stanford University before working for various Pacific Coast newspapers. In 1932 he reported from Manchuria and North China for the *New York Times* and from 1933 to 1935 covered Shanghai for the Associated Press. In 1937 he witnessed the capture of Nanking by Japanese forces. Reporting for the *Chicago Daily News*, he described the evacuation of the city and the slaying of thousands as "four days of hell."

In 1941 he was among the twelve correspondents permitted to view sanitized war zones by Soviet officials. In 1942 he escaped to India just ahead of Japanese forces that had closed the Burma road. Following the Japanese capitulation in 1945 he resumed covering China for the *New York Herald Tribune*.
REFERENCE: Robert W. Desmond. *Tides of War*. 1984.

STEER, GEORGE LOWTHER (1909–1944). Steer was a British war correspondent killed during World War II.* Born in Cambridge, South Africa, and educated at Oxford, he was hired by the *Times* in 1935 to cover the Italian invasion of Abyssinia and the subsequent Ethiopian War.* Probably the best informed of the foreign correspondents, although not always a witness, Steer reported the Battles of Tembien and Aradam. He was in Addis Ababa before its capitulation to the Italians and recorded one of the most famous descriptions of Emperor Haile Selassie as he prepared to flee the city in April 1936. Assigned to report the war from the Ethiopian victim's point of view, Steer was expelled from the country by Italian authorities.

In April 1937 he reported the Spanish Civil War,* witnessing the destruction of the Basque town of Guernica.* His report in the *Times*, which was the only paper to implicate the Germans, noted that the village was of no military significance and that Nazi Luftwaffe squadrons accompanied Spanish Nationalist forces.

In 1938 he left the *Times* for the *Daily Telegraph*, covering World War II in Africa. During the war he joined the Intelligence Corps as a lieutenant-colonel and was killed in a motor vehicle accident in Asia on Christmas Day 1944. Among his highly praised books based on his exploits are *Caesar in Abyssinia* (1936), *The Tree of Guernica* (1938), *Judgement on German Africa* (1939), *A Date in the Desert* (1940), and *Sealed and Delivered* (1942).

REFERENCES: James Dugan and Laurence Lafore. *Days of Emperor and Clown: The Italo-Ethiopian War 1935–1936.* 1973; Franklin Reid Gannon. *The British Press and Germany, 1936–1939.* 1971.

STEEVENS, GEORGE WARRINGTON (1870–1900). Born in Sydenham, England, he achieved a distinguished academic record as a classical scholar while at Oxford. In 1893 he was hired by the *Pall Mall Gazette* but left for the recently established *Daily Mail* in 1896. In 1897 he reported the Greco-Turkish War,* accompanying the Turkish army under Edhem Pasha to Thessaly. His dispatches were published under the heading ''With the Conquering Turk.'' In 1898 he accompanied Kitchener's army to the Sudan as special correspondent. His collected dispatches to the *Daily Mail* were later published in his most successful book, *With Kitchener to Khartoum.* In 1898 he covered the installation of Lord Curzon as viceroy of India and the following year the second trial of Captain Alfred Dreyfus.

With the outbreak of the Boer War* in October 1899, Steevens left for South Africa, where he joined British forces under Sir George White. The following month, the British were trapped in the siege of Ladysmith.* Three weeks later Steevens was afflicted with enteric fever. On January 15, 1900, he died holding a glass of champagne. His last words were reportedly ''This is a sideways ending to it all.'' His collected dispatches from South Africa were published posthumously as *From Cape Town to Ladysmith.* Lord Kitchener, the adversary of most war journalists, paid Steevens the highest compliment when he wrote, ''He never gave the slightest trouble. I wish all correspondents were like him.''

REFERENCES: *DNB*, 1226–1227; Rupert Furneaux. *News of War.* 1964; Robert Wilkinson-Latham. *From Our Special Correspondent.* 1979.

STEICHEN, EDWARD JEAN (1879–1973). Born in Luxembourg to peasant parents, Steichen became one of the most influential photographers of the twentieth century. His family arrived in America less than two years after his birth, settling in Michigan and then Wisconsin, where he apprenticed himself to a photographer at the age of fifteen. He made the transition from commercial photography to taking more artistic shots in the late 1890s. Moving to Paris in late 1899, he was given encouragement by the great pioneer of this art, Alfred Stieglitz, who bought several of his prints. By the age of twenty-three, Steichen was already famous, having made portraits of Rodin, Matisse, and other artists. Returning to the States he photographed Theodore Roosevelt, G. B. Shaw, and other celebrities of the era.

With the outbreak of World War I* he expressed an interest in becoming a photographic reporter like Mathew Brady.* He enlisted in the Signal Corps, commissioned as a lieutenant. Placed in charge of the photographic operations, Steichen demonstrated great managerial expertise as he fulfilled General Mitchell's request for aerial photographs before the Second Battle of the Meuse-Argonne and for a mobile photo section for the Meuse-Argonne offensive. At the battlefront his photo team worked all night developing film and printing pictures of the various battles. After the senseless trench warfare and carnage of the war Steichen apparently fell into a deep depression, a common reaction of those that survived among so many who did not.

After the war he returned to commercial photography for Condé Nast, billed as the "greatest living portrait photographer." With the outbreak of World War II,* America's most famous cameraman returned to action. Commissioned as a second lieutenant, the sixty-two-year-old Steichen organized a team of photographers to record naval activities. Serving in the Pacific theater aboard the carrier *Lexington*, he recorded the Gilbert and Marshall Islands campaign when the carrier came under air attack. He returned with the ship to the United States. He made one more visit to the battlefield, arriving at Iwo Jima the day after the battle ended. In the aftermath he made powerful images of dead Japanese soldiers partially covered by debris with hands curled and outstretched. Following the war he continued his remarkable career, organizing exhibitions such as the hugely successful *The Family of Man* exhibition at the Museum of Modern Art and taking classic photos.
REFERENCE: Robert E. Hood. *12 at War: Great Photographers Under Fire*. 1967.

STEINBECK, JOHN ERNEST, JR. (1902–1968). Better known as a Nobel Prize–winning author of socially influential novels, Steinbeck was born in Salinas, California. He attended Stanford University and worked in a variety of occupations before gaining fame with his novel *Of Mice and Men* in 1937. In 1943 he covered the war in Europe as correspondent for the *New York Herald Tribune*. He reported the campaigns in North Africa, Sicily, and Italy from June to October, including participation in naval commando raids with a special operations unit in the Mediterranean. Aligned with the hawks in the debate over the Vietnam War,* in 1966, at the age of sixty-four, he covered the conflict as correspondent for the New York newspaper *Newsday*.
REFERENCES: *DAB* 8; Warren French. *John Steinbeck*. 1975.

STEVENS, EDMUND (1911–1992). Stevens was born in Denver, Colorado, and educated at Columbia University. Following graduation he moved to Moscow to study Russian. During the 1930s he contributed articles to the *Manchester Guardian* and the *Daily Herald*. At the outset of World War II* he covered the Finnish winter campaign in 1940 and the Italo-Greek campaign for the *Christian Science Monitor*. Stevens and Leland Stowe* of the *Chicago Daily News* were in Norway during the British naval blockade of the Norwegian port of Narvik, which was a crucial link for shipping Swedish ore to Germany. They were in Oslo reporting this story on April 8, 1940, when the German invasion began. Stowe scooped the competition on the story, filing the last cable from Norway.

Stevens later reported Orde Wingate's attempt to restore Haile Selassie to the throne in Ethiopia, and beginning in 1941 he accompanied General Montgomery's forces in Africa from the march to El Alamein to Tripoli. Following the war he became the Moscow correspondent for the *Monitor* for the next forty years. He published in other papers as well and in 1950 won the Pulitzer Prize for "This is Russia—Uncensored." Among his books were *Russia Is No Riddle* (1946) and *North Africa Powderkeg* (1955).
REFERENCE: Robert W. Desmond. *Tides of War*. 1984.

STEVENS, GEORGE (1905–1975). The great American film director of such films as *Shane, A Place in the Sun, Giant*, and the *Diary of Anne Frank* was responsible for much of the black and white film coverage of Allied campaigns in Europe during 1944 and 1945. Stevens left Hollywood in 1942 to serve in the American army in North Africa and Europe, and in 1943 he assembled the Special Coverage Unit of the U.S. Army Signal Corps (SPECOU) to improve the quality of motion picture coverage. The unit was attached to the Supreme Headquarters Allied Expeditionary Force, and novelist Irwin Shaw and playwright William Saroyan wrote descriptions and captions for the footage.

According to army regulations all official footage had to be shot in black and white, reportedly because this was the standard for movie newsreels* around the world. The Technicolor process was too costly and technically cumbersome for the mobile army units of this era. Stevens apparently was never without a 16mm home movie camera, which he brandished in 1944 and 1945, sending home to the States roles of exposed films for processing. Upon his death his son found over five hours of color footage of World War II,* virtually the only color films of the war in Western Europe.
REFERENCE: Max Hastings,* *Victory in Europe*. 1985.

STEWART, BILL (1941–1978). A general assignment reporter for ABC news, the West Virginia–born Stewart had covered the Middle East and the fall of the Shah in Iran when he was assigned to war-torn Nicaragua. As he approached a National Guard post from his van, which was clearly labeled as "Foreign Press," he gripped a white flag. A soldier motioned Stewart to lie down and kicked him the side before summarily shooting him with a rifle at point-blank range. The film footage from this incident was broadcast throughout the world.

Subsequently a third of the foreign correspondents, including most of the Americans, were airlifted out of the country.
REFERENCE: Charles Arnot. *Don't Kill the Messenger*. 1994.

STILLSON, JEROME BONAPARTE (1841–1880). Born in East Aurora, New York, Stillson covered the American Civil War* for the *New York World*. He received unflattering reviews for his reporting of Grant's overland campaign in 1864, but he redeemed himself with his coverage of Sheridan's Shenandoah Valley campaign later that fall. His reportage of the Battles of Winchester and Cedar Creek are considered among the best of the war. He also reported the surrender at Appomattox.

He gave up his position as managing editor of the *New York World* in 1876 and joined the *New York Herald*. He reported the last Sioux war and was granted an interview with Sitting Bull following the defeat of Custer. In 1877, Stillson was accompanying President Hayes on a trip in the West, when he was assigned to cover the Ute war in Colorado. Stillson did not personally witness the fighting, employing a legman to report the action. By the time of the Ute war Stillson was suffering from neuritis, and he died in Denver shortly after.
REFERENCES: Oliver Knight. *Following the Indian Wars*. 1960; Louis M. Starr. *Bohemian Brigade*. 1954.

STONE, DANA (1939–1970). He was last seen riding on a motorcycle with Sean Flynn* of *Time* magazine while covering the Khmer Rouge in Cambodia. Stone was working for CBS news at the time and was reportedly traveling behind enemy lines attempting to shoot film of Communist forces in action. He was reportedly executed by the Khmer Rouge.
REFERENCE: Perry Deane Young. *Two of the Missing*. 1975.

STONEMAN, WILLIAM H. (b. 1904). Stoneman was born in Grand Rapids, Michigan, and educated at the University of Michigan. He began his long affiliation with the *Chicago Daily News* in 1925. Three years later he became a foreign correspondent, spending several years based in Scandanavia, Rome, and Moscow. He covered the Ethiopian War* while stationed in the Near East and in Ethiopia from 1935 to 1936, when he was assigned to the London bureau. He covered the North African landings and in 1943 earned a Purple Heart when he was ambushed and wounded in the Ousseltia sector of Tunisia.

After a short leave in the States he was back in action covering the landings at Salerno and then at Anzio during Operation Shingle. Stoneman was among the first correspondents to report from the beaches of Normandy following the D-Day invasion. Several weeks later he was among the correspondents who witnessed the capture of the port of Cherbourg from the Germans. In 1945 he accompanied Allied forces advancing toward Berlin.
REFERENCE: Robert W. Desmond. *Tides of War*. 1984.

STORMS, JANE MCMANUS (1807–1878). Born near Troy, New York, Storms moved to Matagorda, Texas, with her father in the mid-1830s, beginning her lifelong interest in Texas. During her stay she met many of the influential figures of the day, including Sam Houston and Mirabeau B. Lamar. In 1839 she returned to New York City and a career as lobbyist and writer. She became affiliated with the *New York Sun*, the nation's first successful penny press newspaper. Her articles found their way into other papers as well, usually under her pen names ''Montgomery'' and ''Cora Montgomery.''

During the Mexican War,* in late 1846, Storms accompanied a secret mission to sound out peace sentiments in Mexico City. On inspecting the seaport of Veracruz, she noted that it would resist American invasion and continued to criticize the U.S. Navy. As General Winfield Scott began his assault on Veracruz, Storms was requested to undertake a perilous two-hundred-mile journey from Mexico City to Veracruz to apprise the general of conditions in the Mexican capital. Arriving at Veracruz before its capitulation, she was in time to witness the bombardment and conclusion of the siege.

Storms remained a stern critic of the American military, although her sentiments were in favor of annexing all of Mexico to the United States. She continued to be one of the few critics of the American forces as well as of her fellow journalists. Her career as a war correspondent concluded in May 1847, upon her return to Washington. She continued to publish articles and books based on themes ranging from the annexation of Cuba to American Indian policy. She died when her ship went down off Cape Hatteras in December 1878.
REFERENCE: Tom Reilly. ''Jane McManus Storms: Letters from the Mexican War,'' *Southwestern Historical Quarterly.* July 1981.

STOUMAN, LOU (b. 1917). Born in Springtown, Pennsylvania, Stouman graduated from Lehigh University in 1939. During World War II* he served as photographer-correspondent on the staff of *Yank.** He also contributed photos to the New York–based *PM* magazine. Following the war he continued his career as a photojournalist and since 1966 has taught film production at UCLA. He has won two Academy Awards for documentary film work.
REFERENCE: Art Weithas. *Close to Glory.* 1991.

STOWE, LELAND (1899–1993). Stowe was born in Southbury, Connecticut, and educated at Wesleyan University, where he held his first newspaper job as campus reporter for the *Springfield Republican*. Following graduation he reported for the *Worcester Telegram* and then the *New York Herald* from 1922 to 1926. He was awarded the Pulitzer Prize in 1930 for his coverage of a 1929 conference that produced a plan for reducing and extending Germany's World War I* reparations and created the Bank for International Settlements.

Throughout the 1930s Stowe covered international developments, including events leading up to the Spanish Civil War.* In 1939 he was rebuffed by the *Herald Tribune* when he requested assignment as war correspondent. Barely an hour after being deemed too old for a foreign posting he was hired by the *Chicago Daily News*, which was then considered to have best foreign service of any American newspaper. He covered the Russian invasion of Finland in December 1939 and the subsequent Russo-Finish conflict, although usually from afar.

In 1940 Stowe barely escaped the Nazi invasion of Norway, making his way to Stockholm to transmit his scoop. Later that year he reported the Italian invasion of Greece. He also covered the war in the Balkans, Russia, and Eastern Europe. Stowe was assigned to report from China in 1941, where he uncovered evidence of massive theft and graft as Chiang Kai-shek's army attempted to hide Lend-Lease arms for later use against the Chinese Communists rather than against the Japanese. Stowe filed a series of articles exposing Chiang's subterfuge with his newspaper only to have the State Department block its publication after pressure from the Chinese ambassador. Stowe was then reassigned to the Soviet Union, where he was the first Western war correspondent to accompany Russian forces in action. He published twenty-two dispatches which appeared next to his byline "With the Russian Army." In 1942 he was one of the first correspondents to cover the Burma campaign.

Following the war he worked as a commentator for ABC radio, foreign editor of the *Reporter*, news director for Radio Free Europe, and professor of journalism at the University of Michigan. He wrote eight books, including *Nazi Means War* (1933) and *No Other Road to Freedom* (1941).

REFERENCES: Robert W. Desmond. *Tides of War*. 1984; *Who's Who in America, 1984*. 1984.

STRAHORN, ROBERT (1852–1944). Born in Center County, Pennsylvania, and educated in the printing trade, Strahorn entered the newspaper profession as a printer and writer at the age of fourteen. He joined the staff of the *Rocky Mountain News* in 1871. Strahorn accompanied the George C. Crook expedition against the Black Hills Sioux in 1876. His articles, under the pen name "Alter Ego," appeared during the campaign in the *Rocky Mountain News* and occasionally in the *Chicago Tribune, Omaha Republican, Cheyenne Sun*, and *New York Sun*.

He was the only correspondent to follow Crook until the surrender of Crazy Horse. He apparently injured his vocal cords during the winter campaign when he strained his voice in a battle during subfreezing temperatures. Sources indicate that the strain interfered with his speech for the remainder of his life and that he would lose his voice completely when sick. Maintaining good relations with Crook, he saved the latter's life by warning him of an ambush near the Red Cloud Agency.

Strahorn witnessed and took part in the Battle of the Rosebud and was among the four correspondents who followed the campaign into the Big Horn Mountains. In September 1876 he left the expedition to visit the Centennial Exposition in Philadelphia but returned in 1877 in time for the Powder River campaign and

the surrender of Crazy Horse. Following his return from the American Indian Wars* he wrote a highly acclaimed guidebook to Wyoming which came to the attention of railroad entrepreneur Jay Gould. Strahorn was hired by Gould to direct the Union Pacific publicity bureau and to travel the West promoting migration. He traveled the West for six years gathering intelligence for railroad tycoons. He went on to a successful career conducting irrigation and power projects and became the president and director of various railroad and utility ventures in the Pacific Northwest. He was the last of the Indian war correspondents when he died in 1944.
REFERENCE: Oliver Knight. *Following the Indian Wars*. 1960.

STREET, ALBERT (d. 1864). The Northern-born Street covered various phases of the American Civil War* for the Confederate *Mobile Daily Advertiser and Register* and the *Savannah Register*. Under his pen name "N'Importe" Street reported the existence of division among Confederate commanders in Mississippi and the deficiencies of the equipment provided the Quartermaster's Department in Richmond. In December 1862 he spent to weeks as a prisoner in the North. Street died from an accidental gunshot wound in May 1864.
REFERENCE: J. Cutler Andrews. *The South Reports the Civil War*. 1970.

STRINGER. The term "stringer" refers to part-time, nonstaff correspondents covering stories and locations for newspapers or news agencies operating elsewhere. Often working for one or more organizations, stringers are compensated on a fee-per-story basis. The term originated in small-town America, where local newspapers made arrangements with "country correspondents" to contribute letters and news stories from the outlying communities. Contributors were usually stalwart community members such as schoolteachers, housewives, retirees, or clerics. Compensation was determined by pasting each month's material together so that it formed a column-width "string," which was measured; the writer was then paid per column inch. The system of stringers is much more sophisticated today with professional journalists maintaining links with several papers at the same time and reporting from around the world. The string measure of compensation has been replaced by retainer fees and supplementary compensation. But nonstaff writers are still known as "stringers."

During the Vietnam War,* local Vietnamese were often ruthlessly exploited as stringers and were required to supply photographs with great personal risk and little compensation. Their pictures were then published without attribution.
REFERENCE: Robert W. Desmond. *The Information Process*. 1978.

STRINGER, ANN (b. 1918). Born in Eastland, Texas, Stringer graduated from the University of Texas with degrees in English and journalism. While in college she met her future husband Bill Stringer, whom she married in 1941. With the outbreak of World War II,* Bill went to work for Reuters,* while Ann was employed with the Associated Press. In June 1944 Bill was killed when caught in a crossfire on D-Day. Shortly afterward Ann went to Europe to report for the UP. Reputably one of the most beautiful war correspondents, she was labeled along with Iris Carpenter* and Lee Carson as one of the three "Rhine maidens." Hindered from covering the battlefront because of a rule that prevented female reporters from going beyond the perimeter where female military personnel were restricted, she ignored orders to return to Paris for violating this code. Some attributed her risk taking to a death wish after the tragic death of her husband.

Stringer covered the American assault on the Rhine, witnessing the battle of Remagen bridge and the convergence of the Russian and American armies near the Elbe River. She also reported the liberation of the concentration camps at Buchenwald and Dachau and the Nuremberg trials.

REFERENCES: Julia Edwards. *Women of the World.* 1989. Lilya Wagner. *Women War Correspondents of the World.* 1989.

SUCKERT, KURT (d. 1957). Better known as Curzio Malaparte and the author of the war novel *Kaputt*, Suckert covered the Russian theater of World War II* for the Italian newspaper *Corriere della Sera.* Born in Prato, Italy, Suckert was the son of a German master dyer. He had fought in World War I* and was the recipient of decorations from both Italy and France. Following the war he turned to journalism, reporting on the darker sides of the rise of fascism and Communism. In 1933 he was arrested in his home country for his anti-Fascist activities and imprisoned for three years off the coast of Sicily.

Prior to reporting from the eastern front, Suckert had covered the German occupation of Poland and the tragedy of the Warsaw Ghetto. He is credited with providing the best war reporting from this theater of operations. Suckert followed German forces eastward beginning in 1941. He correctly predicted the effectiveness of the Russian resistance to the German *Blitzkrieg* and was the first correspondent to demonstrate an interest in the developing siege of Leningrad.

REFERENCE: Phillip Knightley. *The First Casualty.* 1975.

SULLY, FRANCOIS (1928–1971). Sully was one of the earliest journalists to cover the Vietnam War.* He was no stranger to the battlefield, having been wounded in Paris as a member of the underground resistance to the Nazis. Following his release from the French army in Saigon in 1947 he stayed on to cover the last years of the war in Indochina and the fall of Dien Bien Phu. In 1961 he began his affiliation with *Newsweek* magazine, covering American involvement in Vietnam. The following year he was expelled from Vietnam for the first time for critical pieces on the Diem regime. Following Diem's assassination in 1963, Sully returned to Vietnam. He continued to send dispatches to *Newsweek* chronicling negative aspects of the American war effort. He was finally silenced in May 1971 when he was killed in a Vietnamese helicopter crash over Laos. He left his insurance policy of eighteen million piasters to Vietnamese orphans.

REFERENCES: Michael Emery. *On the Front Lines*. 1995; William Prochnau. *Once upon a Distant War*. 1995.

SULZBERGER, CYRUS LEO (1912–1993). C. L. Sulzberger was born in New York City and educated at Harvard. He joined the United Press after a stint with the *Pittsburgh Press*. As correspondent for the *London Evening Standard* in 1938 he reported the events leading up World War II* from Austria, Czechoslovakia, and the Balkans. He began a thirty-nine-year affiliation with the *New York Times* in 1939. Sulzberger was among the last journalists to flee Yugoslavia during the 1941 German invasion, escaping aboard a small fishing boat. He reported the 1940 Italian invasion of Greece and was in Istanbul when the Germans attacked Russia. He received the Overseas Press Club Award in 1941 for his reportage of the Russian war.

   Moving to Moscow to cover the conflict, he was faced by Soviet press restrictions which allowed correspondents to make eight trips to the front lines, but only after the fighting and only after victories. In 1943 he covered the Allied invasion of North Africa and for the next two years would be stationed in Cairo. During the winter of 1943–1944 he reported from the Italian front and in early 1944 won acclaim for his coverage of Marshal Tito's Yugoslav partisans.
REFERENCES: Robert W. Desmond. *The Tides of War*. 1984; Library of America. *Reporting World War II*. 1995.

SUTHERLAND, THOMAS A. (1850–1891). Born in California and educated at Harvard, he was the only accredited war correspondent to cover the Nez Perce Indian war of 1877. Affiliated with the *Portland Standard*, he also filed stories for the *New York Herald* and the *San Francisco Chronicle*. Sutherland characterized the conflict as one continuous chase, although he reported three inconclusive battles. Accompanying General O. O. Howard's troops, he later wrote *Howard's Campaign Against the Nez Perce Indians*. He stayed with the *Standard* for the remainder of his life, except for a brief interval in Washington, D.C., as clerk of the House Committee on Manufacturers.
REFERENCE: Oliver Knight. *Following the Indian Wars*. 1960.

SWING, RAYMOND EDWARDS (1887–1968). Swing was born in Cortland, New York. An indifferent student, Swing attended Oberlin College briefly before being suspended for poor academic progress. He began his newspaper career in 1906 with the *Cleveland Press* as a cub reporter. During his six years on various Ohio and Indiana newspapers his reporting took on an increasingly liberal complexion as he dabbled in social work and investigated political corruption. Shortly after marriage in 1912 he joined the *Chicago Daily News* as a foreign correspondent in Berlin. As the war years approached he covered developments in the Balkans and Turkey. During World War I* he witnessed the naval battles in the Dardanelles and made inspections of the trench warfare at

Gallipoli. When America joined the war effort Swing returned home and worked for the War Labor Board.

Following the war he returned to Berlin as a reporter for the *New York Herald*. In 1921 he covered the revolutionary activity in the Soviet Union, but his paper refused to print many of his columns since America refused to recognize the Communist state. He left the *Herald* for the *Philadelphia Public Ledger* and the *New York Post* in 1924. During the 1920s he reported the complex political developments in Europe as a second European conflict loomed on the horizon. He returned to Washington, D.C., in 1933 and was one of the earliest correspondents to make the transition to broadcast journalism. He filled the American end in weekly broadcasts between British and American journalists which were transmitted by shortwave. He was later teamed with fellow American Edward R. Murrow* during World War II.* As one of the most respected commentators during the war years he worked as nightly commentator for the Mutual Broadcasting Company before transferring to the National Broadcasting Company and then the American Broadcasting Company. He later became a political commentator and worked for the State Department before retiring in 1963. His broadcasts are collected in *How War Came* (1939), *Preview of History* (1943), and *In the Name of Sanity* (1946).

REFERENCES: Robert W. Desmond. *Windows on the World*. 1980; *DAB* 8.

SWINTON, WILLIAM (1833–1892). Born near Edinburgh, Scotland, Swinton emigrated to Canada with his family at the age of ten. After preparation for the ministry at Knox College and a stint teaching languages at a seminary he joined the *New York Times* in 1858. He covered the Army of the Potomac from 1861 until 1864, when he was expelled from the front lines. He reported the Battle of Fredericksburg, the naval attack on Charleston, and the Battle of Chancellorsville.

Swinton was constantly at odds with Union commanders, defying their instructions not to discuss military matters or criticize generals. In several instances Generals Grant and Burnside threatened to have him shot. In one incident Swinton was caught eavesdropping on Grant and Meade, lying outside Grant's tent while the two generals discussed the Battle of the Wilderness. Finally Grant stripped Swinton of his credentials, permanently barring him from covering the Army of the Potomac. Shortly afterward he wrote *The Times Review of McClellan; His Military Career Reviewed and Exposed*. He also wrote *Campaigns of the Army of the Republic* (1866), *The Twelve Decisive Battles of the War* (1867), and *History of the New York Seventh Regiment During the War of the Rebellion* (1870). Following the war he moved to California, becoming a professor of English at the recently established University of California in Oakland. He left the university five years later to pursue a successful career writing grade school textbooks. He died in Brooklyn, New York, on October 24, 1892.

REFERENCES: *DAB*; Stewart Sifakis. *Who Was Who in the Civil War*. 1988; Louis M. Starr. *Bohemian Brigade*. 1954.

SWOPE, HERBERT BAYARD (1882–1958). Swope entered the newspaper business while still in his teens with the *St. Louis Post-Dispatch* and in 1909 joined the staff of the *New York World*. As World War I* erupted in 1914 Swope delivered his greatest wartime scoop when he reported the sinking of three British warships by German submarines. He also was among the first journalists to report the entrance of German military forces into Belgium. He reported the war from the Berlin bureau from 1914 to 1917. Swope wrote a series of articles for the *World* in 1917 following American intervention. These pieces were collected and published as *Inside the German Empire in the Third Year of the War* that same year. He was awarded the Pulitzer Prize in 1918 for "a distinguished example of a reporter's work" for his coverage of wartime Germany. Swope was the first reporter to receive this distinction. In 1918 he reported the war from both France and Russia, one of the few war correspondents to actually witness combat from both sides.

In 1919 he covered the Paris Peace Conference at Versailles and from 1920 to 1929 served as executive editor of the *World*. In 1929 he left the newspaper to become director of the National Radio Press Association.
REFERENCE: Robert W. Desmond. *Windows on the World*. 1980.

SYMONDS, GENE (d. 1955). Symonds covered the Korean War* for the United Press and in 1955 was beaten to death by a mob while covering a Communist demonstration in Singapore.
REFERENCE: M. L. Stein. *Under Fire: The Story of American War Correspondents*. 1968.

SZATHMARI, KARL BAPTIST VON (CAROL POPP DE SZATHMARI) (?). Several sources consider him the "first war photographer."* Prior to the Crimean War* he was an amateur painter and photographer living in Bucharest. He first photographed military operations between Russia and Turkey at the outbreak of war in Wallachia, where his growing reputation allowed him to photograph the Russian army of occupation. When their Turkish adversaries occupied Bucharest, Szathmari was permitted to photograph the Turkish commander Omar Pasha, as well as other officers, and camp life. He covered warfare in the Danube basin with a photographic carriage much as Roger Fenton* followed troop movements during the Crimean War.

In 1854 he made his way to the Crimea to photograph the conflict. The following year he displayed two hundred of his photographs at the Universal Exhibition in Paris. Copies of his photo albums were presented to Queen Victoria, the French emperor Napoleon III, and Franz Joseph of Austria. Contemporary descriptions of his work compare it favorably to Fenton's pictures. Although only an engraving made from one of his plates survives, they were reportedly highly praised in their time. Full descriptions survive of the work shown in Paris. Among the photographs are shots of Russian staff officers watching a battle, troops deploying, and the disorganized withdrawal of Russian troops from Wallachia. These images are probably the closest to troops actually engaged in combat that would be taken before the twentieth century.

REFERENCES: Helmut and Alison Gernsheim. *Roger Fenton: Photographer of the Crimean War.* 1973; Pat Hodgson. *Early War Photographs.* 1974; Lawrence James. *Crimea, 1854–56.* 1981; Jorge Lewinski. *The Camera at War.* 1978.

SZULC, TAD (b. 1926). Born in Warsaw, Poland, Szulc became a top investigative reporter covering foreign affairs and the Department of State for the *New York Times* in the 1950s and 1960s. He reported the Argentine revolt against Perón in 1955, revolutions in Venezuela and Cuba, and guerrilla warfare in Colombia. In 1959 he was covering the Dominican crisis when he was arrested and expelled from the country on orders from Trujillo and sentenced to two years in absentia in prison. In the spring of 1965 he landed with U.S. Marines as civil war broke out on the island. He chronicled these events in *Dominican Diary* (1965). In 1961 he reported the Cuban invasion buildup in Miami and later inspected the battlefield with Castro after the Bay of Pigs fiasco. He recounts this debacle in *The Cuban Invasion: The Chronicle of a Disaster* (1962). Szulc also is the author of *Twilight of Tyrants, The Winds of Revolution,* and *Latin America.*

REFERENCE: Tad Szulc. *Dominican Diary.* 1965.

T

TARO, GERDA (1911–1937). Born Gerda Pohorylles in Stuttgart, she became the lover and partner of war photographer-correspondent Robert Capa.* Capa trained the German-born Taro in the basics of photography in two weeks. They arrived in Spain together in early 1936 to record the civil war and collaborated on the book *Death in the Making*, chronicling the Spanish Civil War.* *Life* posthumously published a series of her pictures under the heading ''The Spanish War Kills Its First Woman Photographer.'' Nicknamed ''La Pequeña Rubita,'' or ''little red head,'' Taro was crushed by a Loyalist tank in July 1937 shortly before the publication of *Death in the Making*, and Capa dedicated the book to her.
REFERENCES: Jorge Lewinski. *The Camera at War*. 1978; Peter Wyden. *The Passionate War: The Narrative History of the Spanish Civil War*. 1983.

TAYLOR, BENJAMIN FRANKLIN (1819–1887). Born in Lowville, New York, and educated at the Hamilton Literary and Theological Institute, Taylor moved to Michigan in search of employment shortly after graduation. After a stint teaching he moved to Chicago, where he joined the *Chicago Daily Journal* in 1845. He left his position as literary editor to become one of the most outstanding reporters with the western army several years into the American Civil War.* His coverage of the Chattanooga campaign, including the battles of Missionary Ridge, Lookout Mountain, and others, was widely reprinted. Taylor's accounts were later collected and published as *Mission Ridge and Lookout Mountain, with Pictures of Life in Camp and Field* in 1872.

He was among the numerous journalists targeted for censorship by General Sherman and in May 1864 was accused of revealing too much military information, resulting in his subsequent flight to evade prosecution. He fled to Virginia, where he covered the Shenandoah campaign. Following the Civil War, Taylor left the *Chicago Evening Journal* to pursue freelance writing and lecturing. He published several books of poetry and travelogues, including *The World on Wheels* (1874) and *Between the Gates* (1878).

REFERENCES: J. Cutler Andrews. *The North Reports the Civil War.* 1955; *DAB*; Louis M. Starr. *The Bohemian Brigade.* 1954.

TAYLOR, CORA (?). Correspondent and novelist Stephen Crane* was accompanied by Cora Taylor while reporting the Spanish-American War.* Taylor, posing as Crane's wife, had been with him in Greece during the 1897 war with Turkey. The former hotel and nightclub owner had no experience in journalism. While she is credited with filing several dispatches with the *New York Journal* under the pseudonym "Imogene Carter" during both the Greco-Turkish War* and the Spanish-American War, some sources claim that Crane himself was the actual author.

REFERENCE: Anne Sebba. *Battling for News: The Rise of the Woman Reporter.* 1994.

TAYLOR, HENRY, JR. (1929–1960). Taylor was the son of the U.S. ambassador to Switzerland and a correspondent for the Scripps-Howard newspaper chain. In September 1960 he was accompanying one hundred elite soldiers representing the Congo government of Premier Patrice Lumumba as they advanced on the eastern Congo when they were attacked by up to one thousand Baluba tribesmen. During heavy fighting Taylor was killed instantly by machine-gun fire.

REFERENCE: Charles P. Arnot. *Don't Kill the Messenger.* 1994.

TAYLOR, JAMES EARL (1839–1901). Born in New York City, he graduated from the University of Notre Dame at sixteen. By 1860 he was employed as sketch artist with *Frank Leslie's Weekly*. Taylor joined the Union Army in 1861 and in 1863 began covering the war as an artist-correspondent* for *Leslie's*. In 1864 he sketched the Thanksgiving celebrations of the Army of the Potomac. He reported Sheridan's campaign up the Shenandoah and was later sent to cover Sherman's army as it advanced through Savannah. He reported Sherman's scorched-earth campaign in the South, including the demolition of a cotton press and railroad station outside Columbia, South Carolina. He also witnessed and sketched the liberation of a Southern prison camp in Columbia. However, most of Taylor's war illustrations were not published by *Leslie's* until April 1865, shortly before the end of the hostilities.

Following the Civil War, Taylor was assigned to cover the Indian peace commission of 1867. His coverage of cattle ranching in Texas was one of the first national reports on the cattle trade. Throughout the 1860s and into the 1870s he sketched Native American and frontier life, leading to his identification as a chronicler of Indian life. He quit *Leslie's* in 1883 and embarked on a career as

an independent artist. He collected and published *With Sheridan up the Shenandoah Valley in 1864: Leaves from a Special Artist's Sketch Book and Diary.*
REFERENCE: W. Fletcher Thompson, Jr. *The Image of War.* 1960.

TELL SPARTA. Alexander Cameron Sedgwick's* novel *Tell Sparta* is a roman à clef that harkens back to Evelyn Waugh's* satire of war correspondents in Ethiopia in his novel *Scoop.* The novel reinforces images of war correspondents sipping drinks safely in a friendly bar and then writing eyewitness accounts of the "action." In this case, the correspondents covered the Italian invasion of Greece, a theater of operations Sedgwick was familiar with.
REFERENCES: Howard Good. *The Image of War Correspondents in Anglo-American Fiction.* 1985; A. C. Sedgwick. *Tell Sparta.* 1945.

THIELE, REINHOLD (?). Thiele was a German photographer living in London when commissioned by the *Graphic* to cover the Boer War* in late 1899. He accompanied Lord Methuen's Kimberley force, recording the bombardment of the Magersfontein hills and the retreat to the Modder River. Thiele made use of a ten-by-twelve-inch plate camera with a newly invented Dallmeyer lens. He recorded the British victory at Paardeberg, which led to the relief of Kimberley. Thiele was also present at the subsequent surrender of General Cronje's forces following the victory.
REFERENCE: Pat Hodgson. *Early War Photographs.* 1974.

THOMAS, LOWELL JACKSON (1892–1981). Best known as a world traveler, pioneer radio broadcaster, and confidant of Lawrence of Arabia, Thomas was born in Woodington, Ohio. He attended the University of Northern Indiana and the University of Denver before joining the staff of the *Chicago Journal* in 1912. In 1915 he received an M.A. from Princeton University and took his first trip to Alaska, inaugurating what would become a life of adventure.

From 1917 to 1918 Thomas made films and prepared material for lectures in support of the war effort for the U.S. government's Committee on Public Information. Teamed with cameraman Harry Chase, Thomas covered the Italian front and then Egypt and the Middle East. It was during this period that Thomas entered the American consciousness when he introduced Lawrence of Arabia to the world. While covering the Middle Eastern theater he met Colonel T. E. Lawrence, a British officer fighting the Turks in Palestine, who would become better known as Lawrence of Arabia. Lawrence had been ignored by other correspondents, but Thomas befriended him and promoted his exploits as Lawrence of Arabia in his highly romanticized book *With Lawrence in Arabia*, published in 1924.

At the conclusion of World War I,* Thomas became the first reporter to enter Germany and return with an eyewitness account of the German revolution. In 1930 he began an almost fifty-year affiliation with CBS as television and radio news broadcaster. In 1935 he became recognized as the narrator of the Fox

Movietine Newsreels (see newsreel companies*). Until his retirement in 1974 he continued to travel widely, filming travelogues and writing over fifty books.
REFERENCE: Norman R. Bowen, ed. *Lowell Thomas: The Stranger Everyone Knows.* 1968.

THOMAS, SIR WILLIAM BEACH (1868–1957). Born in Huntingdonshire and educated at Oxford, in 1892 he became a schoolmaster. In 1897 he joined the *Globe* shortly before its demise and then worked as a freelancer for over twenty-eight different papers before representing the *Daily Mail* as war correspondent during World War I.* He covered the conflict in France for four years and was knighted in 1920. He continued to travel, writing books and articles on nature and travel themes.
REFERENCE: Dennis Griffiths, ed. *The Encyclopedia of the British Press.* 1992.

THOMPSON, JOHN HALL (b. 1908). Thompson was born in Chicago and educated at Williams College. While representing the *Chicago Tribune* in 1942, he became the first war correspondent to parachute with the armed forces into a combat situation when he jumped into the fray near Tebessa, Algeria, during the North African campaign. He later repeated this feat, dropping behind enemy lines in Sicily. He was with the first troops landing on Normandy beach in 1944 and was reportedly the first Allied correspondent to meet the Soviet Army during its historic linkup with Allied troops on the Elbe River in the latter days of the war. Thompson was the first war correspondent to be awarded the Medal of Freedom and was also the recipient of a Purple Heart.
REFERENCES: Robert W. Desmond. *Tides of War.* 1984; M. L. Stein. *Under Fire: The Story of American War Correspondents.* 1968.

THORPE, THOMAS BANGS (1815–1878). Thorpe was a noted western humorist and painter prior to the Mexican War* of 1846–1848. Born in Massachusetts, Thorpe moved to Louisiana in 1836 to pursue literary and artistic fame. He scored on at least one count, developing a following for short stories of southwestern humor. He initially accompanied General Zachary Taylor's troops as war correspondent for the *New Orleans Tropic* in May and June 1846. He arrived in Matamoros following the battles along the Rio Grande. Almost immediately he began recording firsthand accounts from interviews with the participants through sketches and narrative. He quickly returned to New Orleans to turn his materials into a book for a public clamoring for war news. His book *Our Army on the Rio Grande* was published in August 1846. Not long afterward he followed with *Our Army at Monterey*, which was less successful.
REFERENCES: Milton Rickels. *Thomas Bangs Thorpe: Humorist of the Old Southwest.* 1962; Martha A. Sandweiss, Rick Stewart, and Ben W. Huseman. *Eyewitness to War: Prints and Daguerreotypes of the Mexican War, 1846–1848.* 1989.

TIMROD, HENRY (1828–1867). The poet Henry Timrod was born in Charleston, South Carolina, and educated at Franklin College. He wrote for several literary publications before joining the Confederate Army of the West as a war correspondent for the *Charleston Mercury* shortly after the Battle of Shiloh in 1862. Writing under the pen name ''Kappa,'' Timrod covered the Corinth campaign in Mississippi and the South Carolina campaign until the burning of Columbia, South Carolina. In later years he suffered from tuberculosis and various ailments that he in part associated with his miserable experience covering the western war.
REFERENCE: J. Cutler Andrews. *The South Reports the Civil War.* 1970.

TOBEY, WILLIAM C. (?). In September 1847, during the Mexican War,* Tobey was the war correspondent for the *Philadelphia North American.* As a member of what has been called the Anglo-Saxon press,* he founded *The North American, Mexico* as an extension of his paper in Mexico City. His articles appeared over the signature of ''John of York.''
REFERENCES: Fayette Copeland. *Kendall of the Picayune.* 1943; Robert W. Johanssen. *To the Halls of the Montezumas.* 1985.

TOBIN, J.G.H. (?). Tobin was a war correspondent and printer for the *New Orleans Delta* during the Mexican War.* His dispatches appeared under ''From Captain Tobin's Knapsack.'' He originally debarked from New Orleans as captain of one of the New Orleans volunteer groups for the war. He covered the Battle of Buena Vista.
REFERENCE: Fayette Copeland. *Kendall of the Picayune.* 1943.

TOLSTOY, LEO NICOLAYEVICH (1828–1910). Tolstoy was born at Yasnaya Polyana in the Tula Province of Russia and educated at the University of Kazan. In 1851 he enlisted in an artillery regiment in the Caucasus. Following the outbreak of the Crimean War* he volunteered for active service and joined the beleaguered garrison at Sebastopol in late 1854. Tolstoy attempted to publish a periodical during the conflict that would express his views on the war. He had intended that his journal, the *Military Gazette*, would bolster the morale of soldiers at the front. However, it met its demise before the first issue was completed. The Czar had refused permission to publish the journal on the grounds that the *Army and Navy Gazette*, which specialized in military literature, already existed. Tolstoy recorded the siege and after its conclusion wrote *The Sebastopol Sketches* (1856), which established his reputation as a writer. The book is divided into three phases—December, May, and August—re-creating the appalling conditions that Tolstoy witnessed in the winter of 1854. Tolstoy, like his English counterpart William Howard Russell,* has been referred to by some sources as the first modern war correspondent. Over the next several decades he wrote his masterpieces *War and Peace* (1865–1868) and *Anna Karenina* (1874–1876) and became an extreme moralist and rationalist, rejecting the state

and the church, and during the 1904 Russo-Japanese War* became an advocate of nonviolence.
REFERENCES: Leo Tolstoy. *The Sebastopol Sketches*. 1856; Henri Troyat. *Tolstoy*. 1967.

TOMALIN, NICHOLAS (1931–1973). Born in London, following graduation from Cambridge he worked for several papers before joining the *Sunday Times* in 1967. His coverage of the Vietnam War* reportedly brought home to Britons the manifest tragedy of the conflict. In October 1973 he was in Israel covering the Arab-Israeli War when, shortly after his first dispatch to the *Sunday Times*, he was killed by a Syrian missile.
REFERENCES: Dennis Griffiths, ed. *The Encyclopedia of the British Press*. 1992; Nicholas Tomalin. *Nicholas Tomalin Reporting*. 1975.

TOMARA, SONIA (1897–1982). Tomara was born in St. Petersburg, Russia, to wealthy White Russian parents. She was educated at the University of Moscow, and her fluency in several languages contributed to her success as a war correspondent. With the outbreak of the Russian Revolution Sonia fled with her mother and sisters, while her father stayed behind and was probably executed by revolutionary forces. In 1928, Sonia was hired by the *New York Herald Tribune*. In 1939 she covered the outbreak of World War II* in southeastern Europe, where she witnessed the fall of Poland. The following year Tomara was in Paris when the Germans invaded. She would go on to cover the Balkan conflict, the Chinese-Burma-India theater, and the Allied summit meetings in Cairo, Teheran, and Algiers. In 1944 she was the first woman journalist into liberated Paris, where she was also reunited with her family. She later covered the Seventh Army's advance through Alsace. In 1945 Tomara resigned from the *Herald Tribune* and married federal judge William Clark.
REFERENCES: Julia Edwards. *Women of the World*. 1988; Lilya Wagner. *Women War Correspondents of World War II*. 1989.

TORGERSON, DIAL (d. 1983). Torgerson was Mexico City bureau chief for the *Los Angeles Times*. On June 21, 1983, he was killed along with freelance photographer Richard Cross near the Honduran-Nicaraguan border when their car was hit by a rocket grenade fired from the Nicaraguan side.
REFERENCE: Michael Emery. *On the Front Lines*. 1995.

TOWNSEND, GEORGE ALFRED (1841–1914). Born in Delaware, he covered the American Civil War* for the *Philadelphia Inquirer* and the *Philadelphia Press*, two years after beginning his journalism career. He later transferred to the *New York Herald*, for which he reported the Peninsular campaign and the Battle of Cedar Mountain. He reported the 1865 spring campaign for the *New York World*, and his coverage of the Battle of Five Forks elevated him into the upper echelon of the era's reporters.

Following the Civil War he covered the Austro-Prussian War* of 1866 and went on to a long career as a feature article writer and political satirist under the pen name "Gath" for the *Chicago Tribune*, the *Cincinnati Enquirer*, and other papers. He established a fund-raising campaign to erect a monument commemorating Civil War correspondents. A sixty-foot stone arch was finally erected in 1896 near his home in South Mountain, Maryland, bearing the names of 151 artists and reporters.

REFERENCES: J. Cutler Andrews. *The North Reports the Civil War.* 1955; Louis M. Starr. *The Bohemian Brigade.* 1954.

TOYNBEE, ARNOLD J. (1889–1975). The Oxford-educated British historian Arnold Toynbee reported the Greco-Turkish war of the 1920s from Anatolia as a special correspondent for the *Manchester Guardian.* Sixty-five of his dispatches appeared in the newspaper between January 25 and October 4, 1921. It was during this experience that he began the outline of what would become his chief work, *A Study of History.*

REFERENCE: David Ayerst. *The Manchester Guardian: Biography of a Newspaper.* 1971.

TRAKHMAN, MIKHAIL ANATOL'EVICH (1918–1976). Born in Moscow, he worked as a documentary film cameraman from 1934 to 1939 before joining the Soviet Information Bureau as a photographer-reporter from 1939 to 1941. He became a war photographer-correspondent with the Red Army and TASS in 1941. His photographs capture the lives of guerrilla fighters and civilians behind the enemy lines. He covered the Battle of Leningrad. Trakhman found nothing romantic about the horrors of war and left war photography after covering World War II.* Following the war he was chief correspondent for the Moscow-based *Literaturnaja Gaseta* (Literary Gazette). Among his publications are several collaborations with poets and other photographers including *Zarevo* (1970) and *Ozvobozhdenye* (1974).

REFERENCES: *Contemporary Photographers.* 1982; Jorge Lewinski. *The Camera at War.* 1978.

TREANOR, TOM (1909–1944). In 1940 Treanor was a roving correspondent in France reporting on the developing war in Europe. At the beginning of the Sicily campaign in July 1943, he flew as an observer with six other correspondents on a five-hundred-plane bombing raid over Rome. During the Italian campaign he contributed articles to *Collier's* magazine. The *Los Angeles Times* reporter often promoted his dispatches with the phrase "The only American foreign correspondent from west of Chicago." Following D-Day he covered the fighting in France for the Central Broadcasting Service and the *Los Angeles*

Times until he was killed on August 14, 1944, when a U.S. Army tank ran over his jeep.

REFERENCE: Robert W. Desmond. *Tides of War.* 1984.

TREGASKIS, RICHARD J. (1916–1973). Born in Elizabeth, New Jersey, and educated at Harvard, he entered journalism while still in college, writing for the *Boston American.* Employed by the International News Service during World War II,* Tregaskis was with the first wave of marines landing on Guadalcanal on August 7, 1942. He remained there through most of August and September, witnessing the early stages of the first major successful Allied offensive against a strategic Pacific stronghold. He was present at the Battle of Bloody Ridge, where U.S. Marines repulsed Japanese attempts to recapture the island's airfield. He completed his best-selling *Guadalcanal Diary* (1943) while aboard a bomber on the way back to the States.

In November 1943 he was severely wounded when a German shell fragment pierced his skull while he was covering the advance of the Fifth Army into Italy, but he miraculously survived. He was unable to speak or move for several weeks. Six months after treatment at Walter Reed Hospital in Washington, D.C., and the insertion of a metal plate into his skull, he was back in the field. In June 1944 he was awarded a Purple Heart. Following his recuperation he followed the U.S. First Army from Normandy to Aachen. He later flew on five B-29 bomber missions in the Pacific theater and accompanied a torpedo squadron. His experiences in Italy are chronicled in *Invasion Diary* (1944). After the war he wrote for various periodicals. He also wrote several other books, including *Seven Leagues to Paradise* (1951), *X-15 Diary* (1961), *John F. Kennedy and PT 109* (1962), and *Vietnam Diary* (1963), which was awarded the George Polk Award. He died at the age of fifty-six, apparently by drowning in Honolulu.

REFERENCES: Library of America. *Reporting World War Two: Part One, American Journalism 1938–1944.* 1995; Frederick S. Voss. *Reporting the War.* 1994.

TRUMAN, BENJAMIN CUMMINGS (1835–1916). Born in Providence, Rhode Island, Truman joined the *New York Times* in 1859 as a compositor and proofreader. With the outbreak of the American Civil War* he moved to the *Sunday Morning Chronicle* and became a war correspondent. He became one of the leading reporters of the western theater of the war, eventually covering the Battle of Murfreesboro, the Atlanta campaign, and the capture of Atlanta. Besides his journalistic activities, on various occasions he acted as an aide to Andrew Johnson, military governor of Tennessee, and was on the staffs of Generals J. S. Negley, John H. King, and Kenner Garrard.

Following the war, President Andrew Johnson assigned Truman to act as his confidential agent, investigating conditions in the Deep South. He testified before Congress during Reconstruction and later served as a special treasury agent in South Carolina and Florida and as a special agent for the Post Office De-

partment in California. He returned to journalism in 1872 in various capacities
with various California newspapers. In addition to his newspaper work, Truman
wrote several books, including *The Field of Honor* (1883), a history of dueling;
Semi-Tropical California (1874); and *Life, Adventures, and Capture of Tiburcio
Vasquez, the Great California Bandit and Murderer* (1874).
REFERENCES: J. Cutler Andrews. *The North Reports the Civil War.* 1955; *DAB.*

TRUMBULL, ROBERT (b. 1917). Trumbull covered the war in the Pacific
during World War II* beginning in 1943. The former editor of the *Honolulu
Advertiser* reported the Battles of Tarawa and Makin for the *New York Times.*
Early in 1944 he became chairman of the Pacific War Correspondents Association.* In June and July 1944 he reported but did not witness most of the
landings in the Solomon, Gilbert, Marshall, and Caroline Islands. Toward the
end of the war in Asia and the Pacific, Trumbull left Guam and returned to
Honolulu. He would eventually return to the Pacific aboard the British battleship
King George V. In 1948 Trumbull was one of the first reporters on the scene
when Gandhi was assassinated in Delhi, India.
REFERENCE: Robert W. Desmond. *Tides of War.* 1984.

TUOHY, WILLIAM (b. 1926). Born and raised in Chicago, Tuohy entered the
newspaper business as a copyboy with the *San Francisco Chronicle.* He moved
to *Newsweek* in the 1960s and shortly after covering the 1964 presidential campaign was made Saigon bureau chief. In 1966 he joined the *Los Angeles Times*
and served as its Vietnam War* correspondent, winning a Pulitzer Prize for
international reporting in 1969. During his stints in Vietnam he accompanied
Green Berets on riverboat patrols, and reported the Battle of Hue and the siege
at Khe Sanh. During the 1970s Tuohy also covered the Jordanian civil war in
1970, the 1973 Arab-Israeli War, the Iranian Revolution, the 1978 Israeli invasion of Lebanon, and the conflict in Northern Ireland.
REFERENCE: William Tuohy. *Dangerous Company.* 1987.

TWEEDIE, PENNY (b. 1940). Born in England, she worked as a photographer-correspondent for the *Sunday Times.* Her war photographs have appeared
in *National Geographic, Time, Paris Match* and many journals. Tweedie has
also participated in charitable causes such as Shelter and Oxfam, and in organizations providing assistance for refugees in Vietnam and Cambodia, Montagnard orphans, and famine victims in India. While covering the 1971 conflict
in Bangladesh, she took some of the most graphic images of human violence
when she witnessed the bayonetting of four Bengali prisoners in a crowded
Dacca football stadium. One authority is convinced that the executions would
not have taken place if not for the presence of cameras. Tweedie covered the
1973 Arab-Israeli War and the Vietnam War.*
REFERENCES: Frances Fralin, ed. *The Indelible Image.* 1985; Jorge Lewinski. *The
Camera at War.* 1978.

TYOMIN, VIKTOR (b. 1908). The veteran Soviet photojournalist has covered assignments in almost thirty different countries for various publications, but he is most identified with his work during World War II.* As special correspondent for *Pravda*, he was one of the first correspondents to photograph the raising of the Soviet Banner of Victory over the Reichstag after the fall of Berlin and was one of the small pool of photographers selected to witness the executions of Nazi war criminals after the Nuremberg trials. Tyomin covered all of the major fronts during the war, witnessing the surrender ceremonies of both the Germans and the Japanese, and participating in combat during the war in Finland. After the war he became a special correspondent for the USSR Press Center.

REFERENCE: Daniela Mrazkova and Vladimir Remes, eds. *The Russian War: 1941–1945.* 1975.

U

UNDER FIRE. The 1983 movie *Under Fire*, starring Nick Nolte and Gene Hackman, is about war correspondents covering the 1979 Nicaraguan revolution and how they risk their professionalism by becoming personally involved in the conflict. Director Roger Spottiswoode described the film as "about the complexities of journalism, about journalists coping with the difficulties of being objective and yet having feelings and sensitivities about their subjects." In the film Nolte plays a photographer who fabricates a picture in order to help the rebels and perhaps reduce the bloodletting.

REFERENCE: Howard Good. *The Image of War Correspondents in Anglo-American Fiction.* 1985.

UNGER, FREDERIC WILLIAM (b. 1875). Born in Philadelphia and educated at the University of Pennsylvania, Unger reported the Boer War* for the the *Daily Express* of London. His experiences covering the action from both sides of the conflict are chronicled in *With Bobs and Kruger: Experiences and Observations of an American War Correspondent in the Field with Both Armies* (1901). He came to prominence after gaining an interview with the Boer leader Paul Kruger and was eventually awarded the South African War Medal for his service as an official service rider for Lord Roberts. He later represented London newspapers in Japan, Korea, and Manchuria during the Russo-Japanese War.*

REFERENCE: Robert Wilkinson-Latham. *From Our Special Correspondent.* 1979.

UPTON, GEORGE PUTNAM (1834–1919). Upton was born in Roxbury, Massachusetts, and received a master's degree from Brown University in 1854. He broke into journalism with the *Chicago Evening Journal* in 1855 before beginning a fifty-seven-year affiliation with the *Chicago Tribune* in 1860. Dur-

ing the American Civil War* Upton covered the Mississippi naval flotilla in the western theater of operations and reported the capture of Island Number 10, New Madrid, and Fort Pillow. In 1868 he became the *Tribune*'s music and drama critic and later served as editorial writer and Tribune Company director.
REFERENCE: Lloyd Wendt. *Chicago Tribune: The Rise of a Great American Newspaper.* 1979.

USTINOV, ALEXANDER (b. 1909). A longtime photojournalist for *Pravda*, Ustinov covered much of the Russian war with Germany. He recorded the last two years of the conflict with the First Ukrainian Front, where he chronicled the exploits of the First Czechoslovak Army Corps in late 1944 and later the liberation of Czechoslovakia by the Red Army. One of his most memorable pictures was of the linkup of Soviet and American forces on the Elbe River near Berlin in 1945.
REFERENCE: Daniela Mrazkova and Vladimir Remes, eds. *The Russian War: 1941– 1945.* 1975.

UZLYAN, ALEXANDER (b. 1908). Uzlyan has worked as a photographer for various Russian news organizations, including *Izvestiya, Pravda*, and *Ogonyok*. During World War II* he accompanied the Black Sea Fleet, better known as the ''Black Death'' to the Germans, for the Soviet Information Bureau. His photographic record of Soviet naval exploits during the war have been described as giving ''an impression of movement that is almost like a motion picture.''
REFERENCE: Daniela Mrazkova and Vladimir Remes, eds. *The Russian War 1941– 1945.* 1975.

V

VANDAM, ALBERT DRESDEN (1843–1903). The London-born special correspondent was educated in France before embarking on his career with various English newspapers covering the Austro-Prussian War* in 1866. In 1870 he reported the Franco-Prussian War* for the American press. He returned to London the following year to continue his career as a reporter for various newspapers.
REFERENCE: *DNB*, 1901–1911.

VERMILLION, ROBERT (d. 1987). Vermillion covered fighting in Italy, Sicily, and Africa during World War II* as war correspondent for the United Press. In London in August 1943 he miraculously escaped injury when a German two-ton "blockbuster" bomb, dropped during a previous air raid, exploded less than three hundred yards from where he stood. He was saved only when the irregular terrain deflected the blast. Following the war he headed the UP bureau until the outbreak of the Korean War.* He cofounded the *Okinawa Morning Sun* in Japan in 1954 before returning to the United States three years later. He worked for *Newsweek* from 1957 to 1977.
REFERENCES: Robert W. Desmond. *Tides of War.* 1984; Jack Stenbuck. *Typewriter Battalion.* 1995.

VIAUD, LOUIS MARIE JULIEN (1850–1923). Best known as the novelist Pierre Loti later in life, Viaud was a lieutenant with the French navy in Indochina in the 1880s when he began war reporting for the French newspaper *Le Figaro.* He covered campaigns in 1883 near Tonkin and Hue, and in 1900 the Boxer Rebellion* in China.
REFERENCE: Robert W. Desmond. *The Information Process.* 1978.

VIETNAM WAR. The Vietnam War was probably the most thoroughly covered war in history. Hundreds of war correspondents covered the Vietnam War between 1961 and 1975. The typical Vietnam war correspondent was between twenty-five and thirty-five years old. Representatives for the major news organizations usually brought years of foreign reporting experience but had little if any experience reporting unconventional or guerrilla warfare. Correspondents for the print media were usually limited to terms of twelve to eighteen months, with six months the norm for broadcast representatives.

Almost seventy women reported the war for such media giants as the *New York Times, Newsweek,* and the *Christian Science Monitor.* Of the forty-five correspondents and photographers killed in action, two were women. Three women were wounded in action and another four taken prisoner. Numerous photographers were killed while covering the war, including Kyoichi Sawada,* Larry Burrows,* and Henri Huet. United Press International lost Charles Eggleston, Hiromichi Mine, and Kent Potter.* Other casualties included Dickey Chapelle* of the *National Observer*, Robert J. Ellison of Empire/Black Star, Bernard Kolenberg of the AP, and noted Indochina war historian Bernard Fall.* Most journalists were killed either in helicopter crashes or by mines and snipers. The most hazardous field of operations for war correspondents was Cambodia following the 1970 invasion, with eleven journalists disappearing in the first week of April 1970 alone.

By the early 1960s several correspondents had already risen to prominence, including Malcolm Browne* of the United Press, Neil Sheehan* for United Press International, David Halberstam* for the *New York Times*, and Francois Sully* for *Newsweek*, who had been in Vietnam since Dien Bien Phu in 1954. Other early correspondents of note were photojournalist Horst Faas* and Peter Arnett* of the Associated Press, Homer Bigart* for the *New York Times*, Peter Kalischer* for CBS, Charles Mohr* for *Time*, and freelance journalist Beverly Deepe.*

Coverage of the early war years was marked by deep dissension between different generations of correspondents. Old-line war correspondents who were veterans of Korea* and World War II* tended to support American intervention. Marguerite Higgins* of the *New York Tribune*, Keyes Beech* of the *Chicago Daily News*, and Jim Lucas,* representing Scripps-Howard, were frequent critics of the interpretations and reporting of Browne, Sheehan, Halberstam, and Kalischer.

Four correspondents won Pulitzer Prizes during the conflict. Horst Faas won in 1965, Kyoichi Sawada of the UPI was a recipient the following year, Toshio Sakai won for UPI in 1968, and in 1969 Eddie Adams* of the AP won for his disturbing photo of the Saigon police chief executing a Viet Cong captive during the Tet offensive. In June 1964, Jim Lucas won the Ernie Pyle Award, and in 1967 David Douglas Duncan* of *Life* won the Robert Capa Award. However, the most controversial episode of the war escaped the attention of the vaunted Saigon press corps. It took Washington freelance writer Seymour Hersh* to uncover the story of the My Lai massacre. A former AP Pentagon correspondent, Hersh won the 1970 Pulitzer Prize for international reporting for a story he had to market through the relatively unknown Dispatch News Service.

The main focus of the American press in Vietnam was combat coverage. Pacification, South Vietnamese affairs, and other stories were generally not a priority. The fact that at its peak the press corps consisted of six hundred accredited members is somewhat misleading. Their numbers were usually lower than the number accredited. According to security regulations anyone involved in news gathering who required access to military facilities had to be accredited. So the figure of six hundred would include any employee, from the bureau chief down to the secretary, who was assigned to pick up press releases from public-affairs offices. Press corps numbers were also exaggerated because most journalists were accredited for at least six months, regardless whether they were just staying days or hours. Journalists' names would remain on the roster of accredited correspondents in the country even after they left for home.

Vietnam was the first war in which journalists were routinely accredited to the armed forces but not subject to strict censorship. Unlike World War II* there was no formal censorship. Compared to subsequent wars accreditation was relatively easy to secure in Vietnam, but correspondents were required to accept certain limitations. The process involved first acquiring accreditation from the South Vietnamese government by presenting a valid passport and entrance visa, a letter from a publishing or broadcasting group, and a record of immunization. Finally, journalists obtained accreditation from the Military Assistance Command—Vietnam (MACV) by presenting a letter from an employer in the realm of news reporting stating that the employer took full responsibility for the actions of the press representative.

One of the major changes associated with war reporting in Vietnam was the omnipresence of television coverage. Technical innovations such as lightweight sound equipment, satellites, and faster transportation facilitated the transmission of images back to the United States. Vietnam was the first television war, heralding the era of rooftop journalism* in the 1990s.

REFERENCES: Virginia Elwood-Akers. *Women War Correspondents in the Vietnam War, 1961–1975.* 1988; Daniel C. Hallin. *The "Uncensored War": The Media and Vietnam.* 1986; William Prochnau. *Once upon a Distant War: Young War Correspondents and the Early Vietnam Battles.* 1995; Clarence R. Wyatt. *Paper Soldiers: The American Press and the Vietnam War.* 1993.

VILLARD, HENRY (1835–1900). Born in Bavaria and educated at universities in Munich and Würzburg, Ferdinand Heinrich Gustav Hilgard arrived in America in 1853, where he became Henry Villard and one of the leading journalists of his era. After working for a German-language paper he joined the *Cincinnati Commercial* in 1859. He covered mining camps in the West and the 1860 Republican convention in Chicago. Shortly after the convention he was hired by the *New York Herald*.

With the outbreak of the American Civil War,* Villard covered the First Battle of Bull Run throughout the day and evening while other correspondents rushed off the field to telegraph premature reports of a Union victory. He returned to the nation's capital the next day with the first news of the Confederate victory. He joined the *New York Tribune* in time to report the Union defeat at Fredericksburg. His paper refused at first to publish the story without confirmation from another source. Villard was nonplussed, having risked capture and imprisonment for violating the Union commander's prohibition of correspondents heading north with news of the defeat.

He made it to the Battle of Shiloh but found no telegraph facilities. After only two hours of fact-finding he departed on the first mail boat in an attempt to scoop his competitors. However, upon his arrival at Cairo, he found out that *Herald* correspondent Frank Chapman* had already scooped him. In 1863 Villard was the only reporter to accompany Admiral DuPont's fleet in its unsuccessful attack on Charleston.

Following the war he served a short stint as an American correspondent in Europe. Returning home he became a railroad promoter and financier of newspapers. Villard would ultimately gain control of the Northern Pacific Railroad and buy the *New York Evening Post*. He married the only daughter of William Lloyd Garrison. Villard died in Dobbs Ferry, New York, at the age of sixty-five.

REFERENCES: J. Cutler Andrews. *The North Reports the Civil War.* 1955; Stewart Sifakis. *Who Was Who in the Civil War.* 1988; Henry Villard. *Memoirs of Henry Villard*, 2 vols. 1904.

VILLIERS, FREDERIC (1852–1922). One of the preeminent war artist-correspondents* of the Victorian era, he was born in London and educated in France. Villiers was hired by the *Graphic* in 1876 to cover the Serbian War, where he was teamed with Archibald Forbes* for the first time. The following year he covered the Russo-Turkish War,* where he witnessed the siege at Plevna, which ended when the Turks were starved into submission.

In 1878 he accompanied General Frederick Roberts' command in the Afghan War. After an around-the-world assignment for the *Graphic* he covered the battlefront again in Egypt in 1882, witnessing Lord Beresford's attack in Alexandria Harbor and Sir Garnet Wolseley's victory at the Battle of Tel-el-Kebir. Villiers barely escaped drowning in the Nile shortly before covering the battles of Abu Krea and Abu Kru in January 1885. However, he suffered the death of his fellow reporter and good friend John Cameron* of the *Standard* at Abu Kru.

He covered the Serbian invasion of Bulgaria in 1886 and the following year reported conflict in Burma. With relative peace in the world for the next seven years he went on the lecture tour in the United States and Canada. In 1894 he reported the Japanese invasion of Korea from the invader's vantage point.

In 1897, while covering the Greek army in the short Greco-Turkish War,* Villiers became the first person to use a bicycle* as transportation while on a military campaign. During this conflict he also introduced the use of the cine-matograph camera to the coverage of warfare for the first time. The next year he was with British forces in the Sudan, where he witnessed the pivotal battle of Omdurman, accompanied by his trusty bicycle and moving picture camera. For the rest of the nineteenth century and into the first two decades of the next, Villiers was occupied by the seemingly inexhaustible little wars of the Victorian era. He covered the Boer War* and the Russo-Japanese War,* where he was the only war artist with Japanese forces at the siege of Port Arthur. In 1911 he reported the Italian invasion of Tripoli, then the 1912 Balkan War, and World War I.* Villiers earned his place in the pantheon of war correspondents, covering twelve major conflicts as well as many lesser ones. Rudyard Kipling* reportedly based the character of one of his war artists in *The Light That Failed* on Villiers. Among his published works were *Pictures of Many Wars* (1903), *Port Arthur* (1905), *Peaceful Personalities and Warriors Bold* (1907), and *Villiers: His Five Decades of Adventure* (1921).

REFERENCES: Pat Hodgson. *The War Illustrators.* 1977; Robert Wilkinson-Latham. *From Our Special Correspondent.* 1979.

VIZETELLY, EDWARD HENRY (1847–1903). Born into a family tradition of war reporting, Vizetelly was educated in France before entering journalism in time to report the Franco-Prussian War* for the *Daily News* and the *New York Times*. He next reported the 1876 Turko-Serbian War and then the Russo-Turkish War* for the *London Standard*. He traveled widely over the next decade and contributed to a variety of newspapers. In 1881 he witnessed the British bombardment of Alexandria for the *Daily News* prior to the Battle of Tel-el-Kebir. In 1889, James Gordon Bennett* hired him to go to Zanzibar to wait for Henry Stanley's* return from the African interior. He delivered his scoop of the return of Stanley in a 1,400-word dispatch to the *New York Herald* in December 1889 and was rewarded with a large bonus. Following his last adventure he retired to Paris and then London.

REFERENCES: F. Lauriston Bullard. *Famous War Correspondents.* 1914; Robert W. Desmond. *The Information Process.* 1978.

VIZETELLY, ERNEST ALFRED (1853–1897). Together with his father, the war correspondent Henry Richard Vizetelly,* Ernest Vizetelly covered the Franco-Prussian War* (1870–1871) and witnessed the siege of Paris at the end of the war. His dispatches appeared in the *Illustrated London News*, the *Pall Mall Gazette*, and the *Daily News*.

REFERENCES: Dennis Griffiths, ed. *The Encyclopedia of the British Press.* 1992; Henry Vizetelly. *Paris in Peril.* 1888.

VIZETELLY, FRANK (1830–1883). Born in London and educated in Bou-logne, the brother of war correspondent Henry Richard Vizetelly* was hired as special correspondent and artist for the *Illustrated Times*, which was established by his brother in 1855. His first assignment was to cover the Austro-Italian War.* In 1860 he was with Garibaldi's Red Shirts during the invasion of Sicily. His account of the action at Palermo took three weeks to reach London. Upon his return from Italy, Vizetelly represented the *Illustrated London News* in America when the American Civil War* broke out. He covered Union troops at Bull Run in 1861 and the following year accompanied General Burnside's forces during its victorious Roanoke Island expedition. When Secretary of War Edwin Stanton withdrew the correspondents' permits, fellow reporter W. H. Russell* returned to Britain, while Vizetelly transferred to the western campaign under Halleck's command. Halleck attempted to dissuade civilians from observing his forces in action by forcing correspondents to supply their own transportation.

On one occasion, Vizetelly, who favored the South, visited Confederate general Jeb Stuart's headquarters, making several sketches in the process of camp life. He was inside Fort Fisher when it was captured by a Union amphibious assault in 1865.

After an unsuccessful stint running his own periodical with his brother James in the late 1860s he returned to the battlefield for the *Times* as a special correspondent with the forces of Don Carlos (1873–1875) in the Spanish Carlist War. In 1883 he reported the Mahdist uprising in the Sudan and was with the ill-fated Hicks Pasha column as it left Khartoum for El Obeid. Vizetelly and *Daily News* columnist Edmund O'Donovan* perished along with the poorly trained Egyptian relief force when the entire column was annihilated by dervish forces.

REFERENCES: F. Lauriston Bullard. *Famous War Correspondents*. 1914; Pat Hodgson. *The War Illustrators*. 1977; Robert Wilkinson-Latham. *From Our Special Correspondent*. 1979.

VIZETELLY, FRANK HORACE (1864–1938). A son of Henry Richard Vizetelly,* he worked as a lexicographer and writer in New York City. Unable to acquire accreditation to cover the Boer War* as a war correspondent, he was lauded for visiting Boer prisoners of war in British prison camps in Bermuda. He was the only citizen permitted to inspect and record his impressions of the captivity. He chronicled this experience for the *Illustrated London News* and several other dailies.

REFERENCE: F. Lauriston Bullard. *Famous War Correspondents*. 1914.

VIZETELLY, HENRY RICHARD (1820–1894). Born in London, he was an early innovator in illustrated press journalism. In 1855 he cofounded the *Illustrated Times*. Appointed Paris correspondent for the *Illustrated London News*, his account of the siege of Paris during the Franco-Prussian War* and the Paris Commune are remembered for his graphic coverage. His two-volume *Paris in Peril* (1888) was written with his son Ernest.* Soon after, he ended his career as foreign correspondent and returned to the publishing business.

REFERENCE: F. Lauriston Bullard. *Famous War Correspondents*. 1914.

W

WALLACE, SIR DONALD MACKENZIE (1841–1919). Born in Boghead, Dumbartonshire, England, he was a perpetual college student at various universities until he was twenty-eight years old. While studying law in Germany he was invited to Russia to study a little-known cultural group in the Caucasus. He spent the next six years studying Russia in general. Following his return to England he published the two-volume *Russia* in 1877. It is considered the standard text on pre-Revolutionary Russia.

Wallace joined the staff of the *Times* in time to cover the 1877–1878 Russo-Turkish War.* Assigned to St. Petersburg, he also covered the Berlin Congress, where he assisted Henri de Blowitz* of the *Times* and helped provide the paper one of its greatest scoops when he smuggled to Belgium the details of the Berlin Treaty sewn into the lining of his coat. From 1878 to 1884 he reported from Constantinople and demonstrated a growing interest in problems in the Balkans.

Following the Battle of Tel-el-Kebir in September 1882, he was sent on a special mission to Egypt, recounted in his 1883 book *Egypt and the Egyptian Question*. Over the next few years he traveled widely in the Middle East, before being selected to accompany the future czar Nicholas II of Russia as political officer on his Indian tour in 1890–1891. He returned to the *Times* as director of its foreign department and in 1899 was appointed to coedit the tenth edition of the *Encyclopedia Britannica*, which was then being published by the *Times*. In 1905 he covered his last major story for the paper when he attended the Portsmouth Conference in New Hampshire, which mediated an end to the Russo-Japanese War.*

REFERENCES: *DNB* Supp., 1912–1921; Dennis Griffiths. *The Encyclopedia of the British Press.* 1992.

WALLACE, EDGAR (1875–1932). Born in Greenwich, England, he covered the Boer War* for Reuters* and the *Rand Daily Mail*. His dispatches were often a blend of fact and fiction. One of his stories described Boer atrocities such as the murder of British soldiers. Lord Kitchener was called in to investigate and found that Wallace's report was unsubstantiated. Wallace's most notable accomplishment during the Boer War was scooping the peace treaty signing nearly a day before it was officially announced. He was assisted in this feat by a soldier guarding the camp who on cue was to blow his nose with a white handkerchief as a prearranged signal when the treaty was actually signed. This act earned Wallace the ire of Kitchener, who vowed to end his tenure as war correspondent.

He was known for his vivid style as a war reporter, and it served him well beginning in 1905 when he found his true calling as a writer of thrillers, detective stories, and plays. Before his untimely death in Hollywood on February 7, 1932, he had published twenty-three books, eight in 1930 alone.

REFERENCES: Byron Farwell. *The Great Anglo-Boer War.* 1976; Edgar Wallace. *Unofficial Dispatches*, reprint edition. 1975.

WARD, EDWARD, VISCOUNT BANGOR (b. 1905). The British foreign correspondent attended Harrow and the Royal Military Academy at Woolwich before joining Reuters* as its Far East correspondent. He then moved to the BBC, where he established his reputation as one of its finest reporters during World War II.* He covered the conflict in Finland (1939–1940), the fall of France (1940) and the campaign in the Middle East, where he was captured by Rommel's forces in November 1941. Following his release later in the war he covered the meeting of American and Russian forces at the Elbe River in 1945. He continued his career with the BBC until 1960. He wrote *I Lived like a Lord* (1970).

REFERENCE: Richard Collier. *The Warcos: The War Correspondents of World War II.* 1989.

WAR PHOTOGRAPHY. The first examples of war photography can be traced back to the Mexican War* (1846–1848), only seven years after the invention of the daguerreotype.* The daguerreotype process, however, was more suitable for portraiture than action because each picture needed an exposure time of five minutes. There were no negatives, so each picture was an original.

By the time of the Crimean War* in 1854 photography was still a novelty. Besides the Mexican War, several war photographs were taken during the Burma War of 1852, but the Crimean War was the first campaign systematically covered by photographers. Various photographers have been described as the "first war photographer," including Roger Fenton* and Mathew Brady,* but recent evidence suggests the title belongs to Karl Baptist von Szathmari,* an amateur photographer from Bucharest who photographed Russian generals and camp scenes during fighting in the Danube Valley between Turks and Russians in 1853.

Roger Fenton owes his reputation in part to his conversion to the calotype process in 1847. The calotype was invented by Henry Fox Talbot. Its advantage over the daguerreotype was that it produced a negative from which multiple positive images could be produced. In addition it was a simpler process and produced sharper, more detailed images when compared to the almost mirrorlike quality of daguerreotype images. Fenton's brush with war photography came about in 1855 when he accompanied the British expedition to Crimea. Fenton is the best-known war photographer of his era only because most of his images survive. Felice Beato,* James Robertson,* and Szathmari were reportedly superior war photographers but less of their work survives, and we must rely on contemporary assessments for the quality of Szathmari's work, which has been lost except for one picture.

One interesting characteristic of war imagery is that in every war from the American Civil War* to the Vietnam War* the images released to the public in the latter stages of the conflict have been more grim and graphic than in the early stages. This is true for both battle sketches and photographs. The first American war to be extensively recorded by camera was the Civil War. The most prominent name associated with this phase of war photography is Mathew Brady. It was through his efforts that Americans observed for the first time images of slaughtered countrymen on the battlefield. Brady was supremely fortunate to have fine assistants who would later earn great acclaim on their own, including Timothy O'Sullivan* and Alexander Gardner.* Brady and his staff reportedly took more than 3,500 negatives of the war, although camera speed did not yet allow cameramen to photograph motion. The Confederacy lacked a counterpart to Brady, but most towns had a photographer. Southern photographers were much less prolific because the main suppliers of photographic chemicals were in the North. Smugglers hid the chemicals in quinine containers since medical supplies were allowed South through the blockades.

Concomitant with the rise in war photography was the decline in popularity of other forms of pictorial representation. The artist's sketchbook could not compete with the sharply detailed images of the photograph. Civil War photographers were hampered in the field by cumbersome equipment and bulky cameras better suited to the portrait studio than portable studios. Most of the operatives were trained in portrait photography prior to the war. But true war photography would have to wait for quicker camera speeds. Although Civil War photographs were lifelike they retained a static quality. The shock and frenzy of battle, the cavalry charge, and hand-to-hand fighting were integral ingredients of battlefield behavior, yet only the artist-correspondents* could bring home images of men in action.

In 1855 the pioneer photographer Nadar first experimented with aerial photography. Throughout the Civil War balloon photography was used for reconnaissance. The success and popularity of war photography during the 1860s led

European armies to explore the potential of military photography. Photographers were present during the 1866–1867 Abyssinian War, the 1859 Austro-Italian War,* and the Austro-Prussian War* of 1866. The 1870–1871 Franco-Prussian War* was covered by a staff of German photographers, but their work is considered inferior. The Paris Commune of 1871 produced the majority of the images of this conflict.

The British colonial wars, referred to by Rudyard Kipling* as the "savage wars of peace," resulted in some excellent war photographs. Among the most competent photographers were John Burke,* who covered the Second Punjab War in 1878–1880 and René Bull,* who covered the 1897 Greco-Turkish War* and the Boer War.* Before the end of the century technical advances in photography would allow amateurs in the military ranks to include cameras with their campaign gear.

By the 1890s photojournalism was still a relatively new profession. Although pictorial newspapers had originated in the early 1840s, it was not until the advent of the halftone process in 1880 that newspapers could reproduce the photographic image on the page. The first halftone photograph was published in the *New York Daily Graphic* in March 1880. But most periodicals continued to rely on woodblock engravings because they provided more "character, tonal range, and detail."

The rise of general interest magazines such as *Cosmopolitan* and *McClure's* in the early 1890s signaled the emergence of the photojournalism profession. By relying on halftones over engravings publishers were able to cut the price of their publications by more than half. Mass circulation resulted, and the demand for photographic news essays heralded a new day in journalism. One of the most popular and effective photographers of this era was James Hare,* who rose to prominence covering the Spanish-American War* for *Collier's Weekly*. The Spanish-American War was the first American war photographed by amateurs and participants using Kodak cameras. Other notable photographers followed Hare to Cuba, including J. C. Hemment,* James Burton,* William Dinwiddie,* and Frances Benjamin Johnston. New photographic technology allowed cameramen to take pictures which conveyed actual battle conditions but it was still not possible to take action shots.

During World War I* the War Department made sure there would be a first-hand graphic history of the war through staff artists with the American Expeditionary Force and the staff photographers of the Army Signal Corps. One of the main barriers faced by war correspondents was that they were not permitted anywhere near the front. Matters were even worse for war photographers. In the early years civilian photographers were totally barred from frontline coverage under penalty of death. At the outset of the war two army officers were accredited to photograph the front with the goal of assembling a record of the conflict. They were prohibited from sharing their pictures with newspapers. While tens of thousands of photographs were taken during the conflict, to this day they still lack adequate documentation. Little information survives as to who was responsible for the pictures. It is perplexing that such a momentous event as World War I did not produce one outstanding photographer readily identifiable with the war on par with a Brady or a Fenton. One exception to the overwhelming anonymity of the World War I photographers during the first years of the war was William Rider-Rider,* who managed to retrieve most of his work after the war and take it to Canada, where it is now safely deposited in the Public Archives.

By 1917 more professional photographers were permitted to record the battlefront as the importance of photography as a propaganda and reporting tool began to dawn on military authorities. In the latter years of the war the threat of capital punishment was removed for taking photographs at the front. Realizing that many American correspondents were supplementing their reports with photographs taken in secret and that French official photographers were making their pictures available to various American news services, General Pershing officially removed the former prohibitions against cameramen. Beginning on Christmas Day 1917 Pershing allowed "official photographers of the Allied Armies to take photographs in our army areas" and "accredited and visiting correspondents . . . to take photographs, subject to our censorship, to illustrate our articles." For the remainder of the war close to two dozen photographers would continue to contribute to the photographic record of the war. Between May and July 1918, over 1,600 photographs would pass through the censors on the way to American publications. Among the more prolific photographer-correspondents were Arthur Ruhl* of *Collier's Weekly*, George Seldes* for the Marshall Syndicate, Junius Wood* of the *Chicago Daily News*, Frank Taylor of the UP, and Joseph Timmons for the *Los Angeles Examiner*.

Photographers were subjected to the same censorship as their print counterparts. Among the prohibited subject matter were pictures that depicted troop movements, specific war materials, and any subject deemed injurious to AEF morale. This could include photographs of soldiers improperly dressed, dead Americans, destroyed tanks or airplanes, and wounded or mutilated servicemen.

In the course of World War I none of the American civilian photographers were killed and only one military photographer perished. The American fatality was First Lieutenant Edwin Ralph Estep of the Signal Corps, hit by shell fire days before the end of the war.

In 1926 the introduction of the Leica 35mm range finder camera to the market revolutionized the war photographer's craft. Lightweight cameras that could fit in a jacket pocket allowed photojournalists to get closer to the action and the danger and create a new market in combat photography.

By the 1930s a disturbing new trend began to develop in war photography. Since the American Civil War and the Crimean War photographs have been posed and faked. This was often an alternative when technical limitations precluded using the unwieldy photographic equipment on the battlefield. However, increasingly restricted war zones led some cameramen to stage pictures for their editors. Limited by strict censorship, photographers of both the Ethiopian War* and the Spanish Civil War* of the 1930s produced numerous staged combat photographs.

World War II* was the most photographed war in history. The Imperial War Museum in London alone boasts over two million negatives from the war. With regard to the number of photographers, just taking into account the four hundred Canadian cameramen attending a reunion in 1971 testifies to the numbers involved in recording the conflict.

World War II photographers can be classified in three categories. One group consisted of those affiliated with the armed forces; another was composed of freelancers employed by various periodicals; and the final group included amateur photographers who were often either civilians or soldiers. By the end of the war in Europe most soldiers had acquired a small camera.

Government censors were intent on providing a view of the war that restricted the publication of photographs of wounded GIs, victims of Allied bombing raids or chemical warfare experiments, shell-shocked GIs, and pictures that conveyed racial strife, disunity, or confrontations between members of the Allied forces. There was a particular aversion against pictures that depicted soldiers losing control and casualties sustained in accidents. Censors also prohibited any photograph that showed American war dead being handled like inanimate objects. During the first two years of the conflict censors withheld all photographs of American casualties except for images which were deemed "comforting."

In 1943 President Roosevelt lent his voice to the chorus requesting less censorship of the photographic image. Part of the rationale behind this turn of events was of domestic origin. In part it was thought that graphic photographs could give a lift to the lagging Red Cross blood drives. In addition, *Life* magazine editors argued convincingly that pictures of wounded and dead American soldiers would help morale rather than hurt it, by bringing the war home to Americans.

The most important photographs taken during the Korean War* were taken by David Douglas Duncan,* Bert Hardy,* and Carl Mydans.* Duncan covered the conflict from the beginning for *Life* magazine and became the first photographer to accompany a jet fighter strike, taking photos of a bombing run at six hundred miles per hour. Under contract with the British *Picture Post*, Hardy made a memorable team with correspondent James Cameron.* Their stories and photographs of South Korean atrocities were the most controversial of the war. Mydans and Hardy took some of the best pictures of the landing at Inchon.

Prior to the Vietnam War,* most American wars fought in the twentieth century were photographed by government or public agencies. However, during the Vietnam War photojournalists were given unprecedented access to the battlefield, making it the freest war to cover in the modern era. Photojournalists not only were uncensored, but were also encouraged to report the conflict and were transported by the military to whatever destination they requested.

In addition to the civilian correspondents there were hundreds of military photographers sent from the Army Pictorial Center in New York City beginning in 1962. In the spring of 1962 the Pentagon created the Department of the Army Special Photo Office (DASPO) to provide worldwide coverage of military activities. However, as the American buildup began in earnest in 1965 DASPO photographers were joined by combat photographers from every branch of the armed forces. Their mandate included fully documenting activities of the U.S. military in Southeast Asia.

Photo-essays from this unpopular war led to a public backlash against the war itself, proving that photography can make a difference and sway hearts and minds. It was not unheard of during the war for television reporters to hire GIs to stage battles in the background for their broadcasts or for civilian photographers to purchase pictures from combat photographers and hire Vietnamese photographers for combat assignments. The Vietnam experience perhaps explains why the U.S. government barred photographers from covering the Grenada* and Panama invasions.*

REFERENCES: Helmut and Alison Gernsheim. *Roger Fenton: Photographer of the Crimean War.* 1973; Louis L. Gould and Richard Greffe. *Photojournalist: The Career of Jimmy Hare.* 1977; Pat Hodgson. *Early War Photographs.* 1974; Lawrence James. *Crimea, 1854–56: The War with Russia from Contemporary Photographs.* 1981; Jorge Lewinski. *The Camera at War.* 1978; Library of Congress. *An Album of American Battle Art.* 1947; Peter Maslowski. *Armed with Cameras: American Military Photographers of World War II.* 1993; Nick Mills. *The Vietnam Experience: Combat Photographer.* 1983; Susan D. Moeller. *Shooting War: Photography and the American Experience of Combat.* 1989; George H. Roeder. *The Censored War: American Visual Experience During World War Two.* 1993; Martha A. Sandweiss, Rick Stewart, and Ben W. Huseman. *Eyewitness to War: Prints and Daguerrotypes of the Mexican War, 1846–1848.* 1989; Philip Van Doren Stern. *They Were There: The Civil War in Action As Seen by Its Combat Artists.* 1959.

WASSON, JOE (1841–1883). Wasson was one of the first reporters to cover the American Indian Wars* in the West following the American Civil War.* Wasson reported General George C. Crook's expeditions in Idaho, Oregon, and northern California for the *Owyhee Avalanche* of Silver City, Idaho, a ghost town today. Wasson was nineteen years old when he came out west from Wooster, Ohio, with a company of gold seekers. He demonstrated a lifelong interest in mining. He also developed a lifelong enmity toward Indians when his wagon train was attacked by hostiles on his initial trip. In 1865 he cofounded with his brother the *Avalanche*, Silver City's first newspaper.

Beginning in the summer of 1867, Wasson would accompany Crook's Idaho campaign for four months. In addition to his own paper, his reports appeared in the *San Francisco Evening Bulletin*. He followed a set routine on each expedition of writing stories in chronological order and adding to them each day, noting whether it was Camp Number 1 or Number 2, and so on. He then sent his stories, written in the form of a letter, to his paper by army courier. Most of his dispatches are simply signed "Joe." In August he received a copy of his newspaper in the mail, which much to his chagrin indicated that he no longer

owned the *Avalanche*, his brother having sold it. Wasson remained a correspondent for the new owners nonetheless. He reported and participated in the
Battle of Infernal Caverns, the one battle of the campaign.

Following his coverage of the Crook expedition he traveled around the West.
He founded the *Winnemucca Argent* in Aurora, Nevada, and with his brother
the *Arizona Citizen* in Tucson. Nine years later in 1876, he joined Crook's Black
Hills expedition, while employed by the *New York Tribune, San Francisco Alta
Californian*, and the *Philadelphia Press*. He witnessed and took part in the Battle
of the Rosebud and later that summer was one of four correspondents accompanying Crook's forces toward the Little Big Horn Mountains.

Following his campaign with Crook, he tackled several news stories in Europe
before settling down in California. According to one account, Wasson's affinity
for mining paid off in the California mining business. After stints in the state
legislature and as a U.S. consul to Mexico he died in San Blas, Mexico, in 1883.
REFERENCE: Oliver Knight. *Following the Indian Wars*. 1960.

WATKINS, KATHLEEN "KIT" BLAKE (b. 1866). The Irish-born Catherine Ferguson Willis arrived in Canada in 1884. In order to mask her true origins
she changed her name and conveniently subtracted eight years from her age.
Five years later, following a brief marriage and divorce, she entered the journalism profession in 1889. Beginning as a columnist for the *Toronto Daily Mail*,
over the next twenty-five years Kit Watkins established an international reputation as travel writer and war reporter.

Although at least two other female correspondents were already in Cuba by
the time she arrived to cover the Spanish-American War,* the *Daily Mail* heralded Watkins as the first woman war correspondent accredited to cover a war
in June 1898. However, by June 23 most of the war correspondents were already
in Cuba while Watkins was left behind, barred by military officials and male
correspondents who considered war reporting a province of the male domain.
One other explanation has surfaced that could better explain why she was left
behind. According to one source she may have been arrested for violating censorship rules by sending coded messages that informed her editor that American
troops were poised to embark for Cuba from Florida. In one missive her editor
noted how furious he was with her for getting caught.

Kit remained undaunted in her attempts to reach the battlefields, even in the
aftermath of the conflict. After waiting three months she arrived in Cuba in late
July 1898. Noting that the war had ended in one of her dispatches, she still felt
an obligation to visit the various battle sites and record the evidence of combat.
While camping outside the city of Santiago Watkins reported sleeping "in a
boy's rubber suit," to protect herself from rape and murder. Her reports are
filled with graphic accounts of the scenes of battle and the suffering of American
forces, who lost more men to disease than in battle. Following her Cuban adventure she noted that her brief career as a war correspondent was over. As the

only accredited woman war correspondent of the Spanish-American War, Watkins won a devoted international following.

REFERENCES: Charles H. Brown. *The Correspondents' War*. 1967; Barbara M. Freeman. "An Impertinent Fly": Canadian Journalist Kathleen Blake Watkins Covers the Spanish-American War," *Journalism History*. Winter 1988.

WAUD, ALFRED "ALF" RUDOLPH (1828–1891). Born in London, after an apprenticeship as a decorator and studying art at the School of Design at Somerset House in London Waud left for the United States in 1850. He exhibited his work at the National Academy of Design, but made his living illustrating books and periodicals. He became the greatest of the American Civil War* artist-correspondents* while engaged primarily by *Harper's Weekly*. As its leading artist, he furnished the paper with detailed accounts of the Virginia theater of the war from 1861 through the Appomattox campaign. Of all the sketch artists, it was said he possessed the rarest combination of talents in that he could write as well as he could draw. Waud was one of a handful of artists to spend most of the time in the field as opposed to the studio.

He originally covered the Civil War in 1861 for Barnum and Beach's *Illustrated News*, getting his first taste of action at Bull Run. Joining *Harper's Weekly* the following year he followed McClellan's Peninsular campaign as an accredited correspondent, recording the violent clashes at Fair Oaks, Gaines' Mill, and Second Bull Run, where he was captured by rebels. As a prisoner of the Confederates, Waud relished the opportunity to make sketches of the Virginia cavalry troops, which were published in *Harper's*. He went on to cover the Wilderness, Fredericksburg, Cold Harbor, and Petersburg. The most prolific Civil War sketch artist, Waud published 344 illustrations, many of which received front-page treatment. He continued his association with *Harper's* after the war, contributing illustrations to *Picturesque America* (1872) and *Battles and Leaders of the Civil War* (1887). He later published on his own *My Diary in America in the Midst of the War*. He died in 1891 after being stricken by a heart attack while sketching Georgian battlefields.

REFERENCES: Pat Hodgson. *The War Illustrators*. 1977; Library of Congress. *American Battle Art, 1755–1918*. 1947; Philip Van Doren Stern. *They Were There*. 1959; W. Fletcher Thompson, Jr. *The Image of War*. 1960.

WAUD, WILLIAM (c. 1820s–1878). An immigrant to the United States in the late 1850s, he is not as well known as his correspondent brother Alfred.* In 1851 he served as an assistant to Sir Joseph Paxton while the latter designed the London Crystal Palace, and he spent the first two years of the American Civil War* contributing drawings to *Frank Leslie's Illustrated Newspaper* before becoming a special roving correspondent to *Harper's* in 1864.

One of his first exclusives was the coverage of the bombardment of Fort Sumter. Waud saw little action until the spring of 1862, when he covered Admiral Farragut's naval expedition against New Orleans. He later recorded the

Battle of Petersburg. After the Civil War he continued his career as artist and writer.

REFERENCES: Pat Hodgson. *The War Illustrators*. 1977; W. Fletcher Thompson, Jr. *The Image of War*. 1960.

WAUGH, EVELYN ARTHUR ST. JOHN (1903–1966). The well-known British novelist was born in Hampstead and educated at Oxford University. Following graduation he served as a schoolmaster for three years, all the while honing his writing talent. He quickly established his literary reputation with *Decline and Fall* (1928) and *Vile Bodies* (1930). He first developed his interest in foreign correspondence when he visited Abyssinia in 1930 to cover the coronation of Emperor Haile Selassie for the *Graphic*. He traveled extensively throughout Africa following this assignment, gaining experience which resulted in *Remote People* (1931) and *Black Mischief* (1932). In 1935, as war correspondent for the *Daily Mail*, he reported the Italian invasion of Abyssinia and the subsequent Ethiopian War.* He chronicled this event in *Waugh in Abyssinia* (1936), which has been criticized for its strongly pro-Italian slant. His satirical novel on war reporters, *Scoop** (1938) was thinly based on his experiences in Africa. He went on to a distinguished writing career, producing several travel books and such novels as *Brideshead Revisited* (1945), *The Loved One* (1948), and his trilogy *Men at Arms* (1952), *Officers and Gentlemen* (1958), and *Unconditional Surrender* (1961), based on his military service during World War II.* He died unexpectedly on April 10, 1966, after church services on Easter Sunday.

REFERENCES: *DNB*, 1961–1970; James Dugan and Laurence Lafore. *Days of Emperor and Clown*. 1973; Christopher Sykes. *Evelyn Waugh*. 1975.

WEBB, CATHERINE (b. 1942). The New Zealand–born Webb arrived in Vietnam as a freelance journalist in 1967, before joining the staff of the UPI. Prior to arrival in South Vietnam she had been working in Australia covering the Australian New Zealand Army Corps troops bound for the conflict for the *Sydney Daily Mirror*. While on this assignment she noted that there were no Australian or New Zealand correspondents covering the war, so she left Sydney for a five-week hiatus in South Vietnam. Webb was in Saigon as the 1968 Tet offensive broke out and recorded the battle raging within the formerly secure South Vietnamese city. Her record of the battle, which she described live on an audiotape, was a minor sensation when released in Europe. Webb left Saigon to record the offensive at Pleiku, the scene of heavy fighting.

In 1971 Webb was promoted to UPI bureau chief in Phnom Penh, Cambodia. On April 7 she was captured with five other correspondents as they were drawn to a new offensive. After three weeks they were released. One week earlier the remains of a Caucasian woman had been found with other bodies and had been identified as Webb. The remains were cremated according to Cambodian military custom and her death was reported in the American press at the same time

she was being released. Suffering from injured feet and malaria, Webb recuperated in Hong Kong, before returning to Cambodia in September. After the war Webb left journalism for public relations work.
REFERENCE: Virginia Elwood-Akers. *Women War Correspondents in the Vietnam War, 1961–1975*. 1988.

WELLARD, JAMES (b. 1909). Born in London and educated at the Universities of London and Chicago, he became a war correspondent in North Africa for the *Chicago Times* in 1942. He reported the 1943 Casablanca Conference and then the Italian campaign. Wellard reported the advance on Naples and later covered action in France shortly after the Normandy invasion. Following the war he taught at the University of Illinois and was a Fulbright scholar at the University of Teheran in Iran. He is the author of more than twenty books of fiction and nonfiction.
REFERENCE: Robert W. Desmond. *Tides of War*. 1984.

WELLER, GEORGE (b. 1907). Weller was born in Boston and educated at Harvard University. Following a student exchange fellowship to Austria he traveled extensively in Central and Mediterranean Europe. After a stint with the *Boston Journal*, he spent four years as Balkans correspondent for the *New York Times* beginning in 1932. He served in the same position for the *Chicago Daily News* starting in 1941. He was in Greece when German forces invaded and was the last American correspondent to flee Salonika, escaping aboard a small fishing boat, only to be arrested and conveyed to Berlin by the Gestapo upon reaching Athens. After a two-month detainment he escaped to Africa and landed an exclusive interview with General Charles de Gaulle.

Weller covered the Pacific theater next, witnessing the fall of Singapore, chronicled in his book *Singapore Is Silent*. He fled Singapore for Java, Batavia, and finally Australia, where he earned qualification to jump with American paratroopers. In 1943 he was awarded the Pulitzer Prize for his reporting following the fall of Singapore. He also covered the 1942–1943 New Guinea campaign. In October 1944 he covered the Allied landing in Greece. In 1945 he parachuted with U.S. and Burmese guerrillas known as the Jingpaw Raiders behind enemy lines in Burma. He was also the recipient of the George K. Polk Memorial Award and a Neiman fellowship.
REFERENCE: Robert W. Desmond. *Tides of War*. 1984.

WELSH, MARY (1908–1986). She dropped out of journalism school at Northwestern University to write for the magazine *American Florist*. After a stint with the *Chicago Daily News* and unsuccessful attempts to win a foreign posting she was hired by the *London Daily Express*. She was reportedly the only female reporter to accompany the British forces at the outbreak of World War II.*

On July 10, 1940, Welsh abruptly resigned from the London paper in order to report for an American one. During the 1940s she was regularly employed by the London bureau of *Time, Life,* and *Fortune.* Welsh covered the London blitz for the BBC and the liberation of Paris for *Life* magazine, as well as the treatment of U.S. Army casualties after the D-Day landings. Separated from her husband Noel Monks,* she met Ernest Hemingway* during her years covering the war in London and Paris. She filed her last article as a journalist on April 21, 1945, reporting the reaction of GIs to the death of President Roosevelt. Welsh became the fourth wife of Hemingway the following year. Her best-known work was her autobiography, *How It Was,* published after the death of her husband.

REFERENCES: Bernice Kert. *The Hemingway Women*; 1983; M. L. Stein. *Under Fire.* 1968; Lilya Wagner. *Women War Correspondents of World War Two.* 1989.

WHEELER, KEITH (b. 1911). Born in Carrington, North Dakota, Wheeler was a reporter for the *Chicago Times*, accredited to the navy during World War II.* In 1942 he was the first correspondent to reach the Aleutians when American forces defended the islands from Japanese incursions. He was aboard the aircraft carrier *Hornet* in the naval expedition launching bombing raids on Japan. Covering the Gilbert Islands campaign in the South Pacific, Wheeler went ashore with the marines at Tarawa Island and in 1944 he was among the twenty-two correspondents who organized the Pacific War Correspondents Association.*

Toward the end of the Pacific war he reported what came to be known as the Second Battle of Bougainville, when Japanese forces attacked American positions in Empress Augusta Bay in the Southwest Pacific. Wheeler also was present during the landings in the Marianas and the Battle of Iwo Jima, where he was seriously wounded when a bullet cut a neck artery and smashed his jaw.

He left the *Chicago Times* for *Life* and *Time* magazines in 1951. Wheeler was the author of six books and was the recipient of the Sigma Delta Chi Award in 1942, the National Headliners' Club Award in 1945, and the Overseas Press Club Award in 1956.

REFERENCE: Robert W. Desmond. *The Tides of War.* 1984.

WHITAKER, JOHN T. (1906–1946). Born in Chattanooga, Tennessee, and educated at the University of the South in Sewanee, Tennessee, Whitaker began his newspaper career as a reporter on the *Chattanooga News*. He later joined the staff of the *New York Herald Tribune* and was assigned to the Geneva office from 1931 to 1935, reporting the League of Nations. Beginning in 1936 he reported the latter part of the Ethiopian War* and then the Spanish Civil War.* During the Ethiopian War he accompanied Italian troops and in May 1936 he was awarded the Italian War Cross for "valor in the East African campaign."

In 1937 Whitaker moved to the *Chicago Daily News* as a roving correspondent. From 1937 to 1938 he covered the developing conflict in Europe and the following year was in Peru reporting the Eighth Pan American Conference from Lima. He continued to cover the South American scene, investigating Italian and German propaganda campaigns south of the American border. In mid-1939 he returned to Europe, posted to Rome until his expulsion in 1941. Whitaker was the third *Daily News* correspondent to be banished from Italy in two years, so the paper decided to close its Rome office.

REFERENCES: Robert W. Desmond. *Crisis and Conflict*. 1982; Robert W. Desmond. *Tides of War*. 1984.

WHITE, LEIGH (b. 1914). Born in Vermont, White began his career as a correspondent in 1937 writing articles on the Spanish Civil War* for the *Nation*. In 1939 he returned to the States and joined the staff of the *New York Herald Tribune*. The following year he covered the Balkans. When the Germans invaded Yugoslavia White made a desperate escape attempt on a small fishing craft with correspondents Russell Hill,* Terence Atherton, and Robert St. John.* However, his exploits as a war correspondent ended rather abruptly when his femur was shattered during a Luftwaffe attack on their boat. White ended up in an Athens hospital for five months. With Athens firmly in the grip of the German army, there was some doubt concerning White's status. However, since war had not yet been declared he was still a neutral. After he had undergone four operations and had lost fifty pounds, the Germans allowed him to return to the States. He finally recovered from his wounds by 1944 and returned to Russia for the *Daily News*.

REFERENCES: Robert W. Desmond. *Tides of War*. 1984; Leigh White. *The Long Balkan Night*. 1941.

WHITE, THEODORE HAROLD (1915–1986). Better known as a political journalist and best-selling author, ''Teddy'' White was born in Boston and educated at Harvard. Following graduation he won a fellowship that allowed him to continue his Asian studies in China, where he also began his career as a journalist, sending dispatches to the *Boston Globe* and the *Manchester Guardian*. In 1939 John Hersey* hired him for *Time* as an East Asian correspondent during World War II.* Soon after, White headed off to get a firsthand glimpse of the Chinese-Japanese war. His dispatches from Shensi solidified his standing with his editors as he journeyed to areas untouched by journalists in the province. White interviewed Communist and Nationalist Chinese soldiers, inspected damage inflicted by Japanese troops in southeastern Shansi, and witnessed the Communist guerrilla campaign to capture rural China. In 1942 he became the China-Burma-India theater war correspondent for *Time*. Stationed in Chungking, he flew as an observer on numerous bombing runs with the Eleventh Bombing Squadron.

After a falling-out with Henry Luce over the politics of China in 1945 White quit the magazine. He coauthored the best-seller *Thunder out of China* with Annalee Jacoby in 1946. He left a position with the *New Republic* to edit the World War II memoirs of General Joseph Stilwell and then moved to Paris in 1948. He chronicled postwar Europe in *Fire in the Ashes* in 1953. Returning to the United States, he began the next and most familiar stage of his career chron-

icling the American political scene with highly successful books such as *The Making of the President* (1960), *The Making of the President—1972* (1973), and *Breach of Faith: The Fall of Richard Nixon* (1975).
REFERENCE: Peter Rand. *China Hands*. 1995.

WHITEHEAD, DONALD F. (b. 1908). Born in Kentucky, Whitehead covered World War II* for the Associated Press. He accompanied General Montgomery's British Eighth Army prior to American involvement in the war and later took part in five amphibious assault landings in Italy, France, and North Africa. He was awarded two Pulitzer Prizes during the Korean War.*
REFERENCES: Robert W. Desmond. *Tides of War*. 1984; M. L. Stein. *Under Fire: The Story of American War Correspondents*. 1968.

WHITNEY, CASPAR (1861–1929). Born in Boston, Massachusetts, he is best known for having originated the "All-American Football Team" in 1889 while working as a sportswriter. He covered the Spanish-American War* in Cuba for *Harper's Weekly* beginning in 1898. He was with Chaffee's brigade during the Battle of El Caney. Whitney later served as editor of *Outing* magazine and represented the *New York Tribune* in Europe during World War I.* From 1917 to 1919 he was one of the strongest voices of opposition to wartime censorship restrictions.
REFERENCES: Charles H. Brown. *The Correspondents' War*. 1967; *DAB* 1.

WILKESON, SAMUEL (1817–1889). Born in Buffalo, New York, he was a son of one of the city's founders. He studied law at Union College before turning to journalism. He worked for several papers in Buffalo and Albany before joining the *New York Tribune*. During the American Civil War* Wilkeson wrote federal propaganda for foreign newspapers and served as Washington bureau chief and war correspondent for the *Tribune* and the *New York Times*.

Wilkeson's accounts of the 1862 Peninsular campaign were considered unsurpassed, and at the Battle of Fair Oaks he received a special mention for his bravery while serving as a volunteer aide to General Heintzelman. While reporting the Gettysburg campaign, he covered his saddest story when he learned that his nineteen-year-old son, Lieutenant Bayard Wilkeson, had been killed in the first day's fighting. He later learned that his son had been wounded in the leg and left to die in a building avoided by surgeons. He wrote his account of the battle while sitting next to the body of his dead son. Wilkeson witnessed the bombardment on Seminary Ridge, one of the most intense artillery assaults of the war, and in 1864 he reported the Petersburg mine disaster. Following the war he left the *Tribune* to work for Jay Cooke and Company selling war bonds. He then entered railroading, rising to president of the Northern Pacific Railroad.
REFERENCES: J. Cutler Andrews. *The North Reports the Civil War*. 1955; Louis M. Starr. *The Bohemian Brigade*. 1954.

WILKIE, FRANC BANGS (1832–1892). Born in West Charlton, New York, Wilkie supported himself at Union College by writing and setting type for a local newspaper. He would become one of the most outstanding correspondents covering the western theater of the American Civil War.* Wilkie was the city editor of the *Dubuque Daily Herald* at the outset of the war and in 1861 enlisted with the First Iowa. On the strength of his report of the Union defeat at Wilson's Creek, which originally appeared in his home newspaper, he was hired by the *New York Times*. Under the pen name ''Galway'' Wilkie covered the attacks on Forts Henry and Donelson and the Vicksburg campaign, and criticized the inefficiency of the army's medical department. In the fall of 1863 he left war reporting for a desk job with the *Chicago Tribune*. He continued his association with the paper for twenty-five years. His book *Pen and Powder* (1888) is considered one of the best memoirs by a member of the Union press corps.
REFERENCES: J. Cutler Andrews. *The North Reports the Civil War*. 1955; Stewart Sifakis. *Who Was Who in the Civil War*. 1988.

WILKINSON, HENRY SPENSER (1853–1937). Wilkinson was born in Manchester, England, and educated at Owens College and Oxford University. He developed an interest in military affairs and history in the 1870s before joining the bar in 1880. Wilkinson understood the complexities of warfare quite well. Already fluent in German and French, he had founded the Oxford University Kriegspiel Club, named after the military training game *Kriegspiel*, which he had brought back from Germany while still a college student. Wilkinson was also founder of the Manchester Tactical Society and a volunteer military officer.

He turned from law to journalism in 1882 when he wrote a series of columns on the Egyptian campaign for the *Manchester Guardian*. The Egyptian campaign was the first war for which the paper provided maps of the conflict, beginning a long tradition of excellent war coverage. Wilkinson prepared the maps himself, drawing from many sources, including Admiralty charts and War Office staff maps. In 1884 he represented the *Guardian* when he covered the Berlin Conference, which determined the partition of colonial Africa. He remained affiliated with the paper as special correspondent and military commentator until 1892. During his tenure with the paper he wrote several books on military topics, including his first book, *Citizen Soldiers* (1884), and translated numerous German military books. According to one source his most significant contribution to British military affairs was his appraisal of the German general staff system in *The Brain of an Army* (1890). He followed this work with *The Brain of the Navy* in 1895.

Wilkinson joined the *Morning Post* as drama critic in 1895. He remained an influential military writer, especially during the Boer War* and World War I.* He left the *Post* in 1914 to teach military history at Oxford. He wrote *The French Army Before Napoleon* (1915) and *The Rise of Napoleon Bonaparte* (1930).

REFERENCES: David Ayerst. *The Manchester Guardian: Biography of a Newspaper.* 1971; *DNB*, 1931–1940.

WILLIAMS, CHARLES (1838–1904). Born and educated in Ireland, he was sent to the American South to recover his health. Soon after, he participated in the Nicaragua filibustering expedition, which resulted in his first taste of battle. He returned to London, where he was hired by the *London Evening Herald* and then the *Standard* in 1859, beginning a twenty-five-year affiliation with the paper, most notably as war correspondent.

In 1870 he was with the French army during the second phase of the Franco-Prussian War,* and was one of the first reporters to enter Strasbourg after its capitulation. Williams was with Turkish forces under Ahmed Mukhtar Pasha in 1877 during the Russo-Turkish War,* which he chronicled in *The Armenian Campaign* (1878). Although tarnished by its pro-Turkish slant, Williams' book presents a solid account of the war through the treaty signing at San Stefano in 1878.

Williams next reported the British military campaigns in Afghanistan at the end of 1878, and the following year published *Notes on the Operations in Lower Afghanistan, 1878–9, with Special Reference to Transport*. In 1884 he accompanied the Nile expedition sent to relieve General Charles Gordon at Khartoum. His account of Gordon's death was published in the *Fortnightly Review* the following year.

He left the *Standard* in 1884 for the *Morning Advertiser* (soon to become the *Daily Chronicle*). He was reportedly the only British war correspondent to accompany the Bulgarian army in its war against Serbia in 1885. He covered the 1897 Greco-Turkish War* from the Greek side. Williams noted in the *Fortnightly* that the Greeks were vanquished because of the meddling of politicians. He would witness his last war in 1898 while in the company of Lord Kitchener's army during the 1898 Sudanese campaign. He covered the advance of General William Gatacre's forces up the Nile and was present at the Battle of Omdurman, where he suffered a minor bullet wound in the cheek. His account of this pivotal battle was published in the *Daily Chronicle*. Declining health barred his coverage of the Boer conflict and ended his career as a war correspondent, although he continued to contribute pieces on military affairs to the *Morning Leader*.

REFERENCES: *DNB*, 1901–1911; Robert Wilkinson-Latham. *From Our Special Correspondent*. 1979.

WILLIAMS, GEORGE FORRESTER (1837–1920). Born on the Rock of Gibraltar, Williams, the son of a British military officer, spent his youth in Africa. He joined the staff of the *New York Times* in 1856. Prior to the American Civil War* he had covered the 1857–1858 campaign against the Mormons and barely escaped a firing squad while accompanying William Walker's filibustering expedition to Nicaragua. He was a veteran reporter by the outbreak of the

Civil War. In 1860, the *Times* called on Williams to undertake a tour of the South disguised as an naive English tourist. It was thought that Williams, a gifted mimic and aided by his British background, could best pull off this fact-finding expedition into the heart of secessionist territory. On several occasions he fell under suspicion, but his mission was a success as the *Times* used his dispatches for editorials or printed his letters using fictitious names and dates.

Williams covered the Shenandoah campaign for the *Times* and just missed the Battle of Frederick. But this did not keep him from filing a report. Upon reaching the town Williams met a farmer who had witnessed the entire battle and was able to give Williams a rambling but descriptive account, including the colors of the different generals. After paying the farmer for his trouble Williams telegraphed his account, replete with casualty figures, to his home office. The following day the *New York Times* printed one of the best accounts of the battle, leading one general to comment on its accuracy, remarking that he had not noticed the correspondent on the field of battle that day.

Williams later delivered the first account of the Battle of Winchester to Washington and was invited to give the details in person to President Lincoln. He was provided a red-letter pass which enabled him to pass through all army checkpoints without any special credentials. He was rewarded for his scoop by being made chief correspondent for the *New York Times* with the Army of the Potomac. He also reported the Battles of Cold Harbor, Yorktown, Chancellorsville, and Gettysburg, and other important engagements, and survived serious wounds at Malvern Hill and during the Wilderness campaign. Following the Civil War, Williams covered the Franco-Prussian War,* witnessed the execution of Emperor Maximilian at Queretaro, Mexico, and campaigned in South America.

REFERENCES: J. Cutler Andrews. *The North Reports the Civil War.* 1955; Louis M. Starr. *Bohemian Brigade.* 1954.

WILLIAMS, WYTHE (1881–1956). Williams joined the *New York Evening World* in 1910. Four years later he left the paper for the *New York Times* and was in the London bureau when World War I* began. Soon afterward he transferred to the Paris office, where he worked with Walter Duranty.* He inaugurated a clever system for sending dispatches back to London through a series of innocuous-seeming telegrams. In May 1915 he was briefly jailed in Paris for covering German military action in France. Soon after, French military authorities dropped the prohibition against war correspondents. He wrote several excellent accounts from the battlefronts in France and Italy. In 1917 he began his affiliation with *Collier's Weekly* and became one of the first war correspondents accredited to the Allied Expeditionary Force headquarters, but he had his accreditation suspended in February 1918 for violating censorship regulations.

REFERENCES: Emmet Crozier. *American Reporters on the Western Front, 1914–18.* 1959; Robert W. Desmond. *Windows on the World.* 1980.

WILLS, STANLEY (1906–1944). Educated in Northhampton, he worked for several papers before joining the *Daily Herald* as an editor in 1934. In 1943 he finally fulfilled his ambition to report from the battlefront. After covering the Allied headquarters in Algiers he was assigned to Burma, and in 1944 he was the only war correspondent to witness the relief of the Seventh Indian Division after its long siege by the Japanese. His coverage of this story received many accolades. On March 24, 1944, he was with correspondent Stuart Emeny* accompanying General Orde Wingate on a flight over Burma when the plane went down, killing all on board.

REFERENCE: Dennis Griffiths, ed. *The Encyclopedia of the British Press*. 1992.

WILMOT, REGINALD WILLIAM WINCHESTER "CHESTER" (1911–1954). Wilmot was born in Melbourne, Australia, and educated at the University of Melbourne. The son of a journalist, Wilmot joined the Australia Broadcasting Commission (ABC) as a radio war correspondent in August 1940. He covered Australian forces in the Middle East and Greece campaigns.

Wilmot then reported the North African campaign. He covered the first Libyan campaign from Bardia to Beda Fromm, where he was the sole correspondent to witness the defeat of an Italian armored division in the great tank battle there. Rather than bask in the glory of such a scoop, he shared the news with fellow correspondents. He also was present at the siege of Tobruk, and his dispatches from within the fortress were broadcast around the world, adding to his growing reputation and coming to the attention of the BBC. His book *Tobruk, 1941* (1945) chronicled the siege. Following the attack on Pearl Harbor that December, Wilmot was recalled to Australia. He lost his accreditation to cover Australian forces after he was accused by the Australian commander of Allied land forces of making critical statements concerning the Australian war effort.

In 1944, Wilmot had his accreditation restored by the BBC, and he left for London to cover the Normandy invasion. The BBC had assembled a team of forty-eight correspondents to report the D-Day landings. All were given special training by the army, issued uniforms, and assigned to specific units. By June 1944, the BBC had developed new broadcasting and recording equipment, more durable and compact than anything previously available, revolutionizing war reporting, eliminating the need for radio trucks and cumbersome technical gear. For the invasion Wilmot was assigned to the Sixth Airborne Division, made up of two paratroop brigades and an airborne glider force. Its hazardous mission was to protect the Orne River bridges against an expected German counterattack. His bravery and coverage of the fighting following D-Day only enhanced his standing with the BBC as Wilmot became one of its most popular voices. Perhaps his greatest skill was an ability to interpret complex events to listeners in simple terms.

Wilmot generally eschewed "color" pieces on daily military life, the mainstay of the reporting profession, concentrating instead on analysis. He continued to report from the front lines as the war in Europe came to a close. He recorded

the last fighting in Germany and delivered the scoop of the German surrender on May 4, 1945. Following the war he remained in Europe covering the Nuremberg trials for the BBC. In 1952, after six years of work, his account of the war, *The Struggle for Europe*, was published to high acclaim. He continued in radio during the 1950s and seemed ready to make the transfer to television when he was killed in a plane crash on assignment in Asia for the BBC.
REFERENCE: Trevor Royle. *War Report*. 1987.

WING, HENRY EBENEZER (1840–1925). Born in Connecticut, following law school Wing enlisted in the Twenty-seventh Connecticut in September 1862. He covered the early stages of the American Civil War* for the *New Haven Palladium*. At the Battle of Fredericksburg he was severely wounded, losing several fingers and the full use of one of his legs, and was discharged from the army. He then reported the conflict for the *Norwich Bulletin*.

In 1864 a long-standing dispute between the War Department and the press came to a head when a proclamation was issued specifying that no civilians other than those already there would be allowed at the war front. Since every accredited *New York Tribune* correspondent was at that time stationed in the nation's capital, the proclamation would leave the paper without a war reporter. However, Wing managed to elude Union pickets and make his way sixty miles to the safe confines of a Union army encampment. He was rewarded with accreditation and a job as war correspondent by the *Tribune*.

Wing covered the first day of the Wilderness campaign and volunteered to deliver the pooled reports for his colleagues through Confederate territory. In a bizarre series of events he was escorted by the Confederate Mosby's irregulars, then chased by them, fed by New York cavalry, arrested by rebel cavalry, and finally ordered arrested as a spy by Secretary of War Stanton. When he at last reached a telegraph reserved for official military use Stanton asked him for his report. Wing replied, not until he could first send his scoop to the *Tribune*. The secretary ordered his arrest, but not before Lincoln interceded, agreeing to allow him to send in his reports. The president sent a train for Wing so he could give a more complete report in person. Arriving at the White House at 2 A.M., he was kissed by the president for the encouraging news he brought from Grant concerning the high morale of the army. Wing's greatest story was the only information received from the front that day.

Lincoln provided Wing an escort back to the front the following day, where he would remain through the completion of the war. Following the war he joined the *Litchfield Enquirer* as copublisher. Later he worked in advertising, practiced law, and then joined the ministry.
REFERENCE: J. Cutler Andrews. *The North Reports the Civil War*. 1955.

WIRGMAN, CHARLES (1832–1891). Born in London, the war artist and editor of *Japan Punch* was hired by the *Illustrated London News* in 1857 and was assigned to cover the conflict in Asia between China and Great Britain. He

witnessed the assault on Canton as well as the march on Peking. He barely escaped the British legation by crawling under his quarters to safety when the compound was overrun by Chinese forces on July 5, 1861. Following the conflict he moved to Japan, where he remained for the rest of his life. He continued his career in journalism, establishing the *Japan Punch* and becoming well known as an artist. He died on February 8, 1891.
REFERENCE: Dennis Griffiths, ed. *The Encyclopedia of the British Press.* 1992.

WOLFERT, IRA (b. 1908). Born in New York City, he attended the Columbia University School of Journalism. He joined the North American Newspaper Alliance in 1929. In 1941, he was the only newspaperman to accompany the Free French expedition which captured the French islands of St. Pierre and Miquelon off the coast of Newfoundland without incident, one of the first acts to touch North American shores directly.

In 1942 he switched to the Pacific theater, witnessing one of the greatest sea battles of the war near the Solomon Islands, with the Japanese losing nineteen ships to American forces. Wolfert was flying over the *President Coolidge*, which had been converted into a troop transport, when it hit a mine and sank. His coverage for the North American Newspaper Alliance was awarded a Pulitzer Prize in 1943. That same year he published *Battle of the Solomons* and *Torpedo 8: The Story of Swede Larsen's Bomber Squadron.*

He was with the invasion fleet during the Normandy invasion and covered the subsequent French campaign and the liberation of Paris. Wolfert continued to follow the action into Germany, but by the end of October he had returned to the States for rest and recuperation. He claimed that he had become ''bored with being afraid.'' Following the war he turned to screenwriting and fiction. His screenplay *An American Guerrilla in the Philippines* was based on actual events in the Pacific during World War II.*
REFERENCE: Robert W. Desmond. *Tides of War.* 1984; Jack Stenbuck. *Typewriter Battalion.* 1995.

WOOD, JUNIUS (1877–1957). Wood covered the Veracruz expedition in 1914 for the *Chicago Daily News* as well as the Pershing punitive expedition against Pancho Villa. During World War I* he was an accredited correspondent with the American Expeditionary Force until 1919 and one of the first to report the German breakthrough at Chateau-Thierry.
REFERENCE: Emmet Crozier. *American Reporters on the Western Front, 1914–18.* 1959.

WOODS, HENRY CHARLES (1881–1939). As special correspondent for the *Times*, he covered the Italo-Turkish War and in 1912–1913 reported the Balkan Wars for the *Evening News*. At the outset of World War I* he was made military and diplomatic correspondent for the *Evening News* and the *Weekly Dispatch*.
REFERENCE: Dennis Griffiths, ed. *The Encyclopedia of the British Press.* 1992.

WOODVILLE, RICHARD CATON (1856–1927). The ex-officer of the Royal North Devon Hussars was an artist for the *Illustrated London News* during the Russo-Turkish War* and the 1882 Egyptian campaign. In 1891 he visited the United States to cover the Sioux uprising, although it was already over and he never witnessed any actual fighting. His art worked more as heroic propaganda during the late Victorian era than as realistic renderings.
REFERENCE: Pat Hodgson. *The War Illustrators*. 1977.

WOODWARD, DAVID (?). A member of the staff of the *News Chronicle* between 1936 and 1943, Woodward served as its war correspondent in the Middle East before joining the *Manchester Guardian* to cover General Montgomery's forces. On June 9, 1944, he was one of the three reporters to land in France with a glider and parachute unit. In the process he was wounded and returned briefly to England for recuperation. He returned to France in July and followed the campaign to its conclusion and the liberation of Paris.
REFERENCE: David Ayerst. *The Manchester Guardian: Biography of a Newspaper*. 1971.

WORLD WAR I. The United States sent more correspondents and photographers to cover World War I than any other country. In 1914, the first year of the conflict, there were from fifty to seventy-five staff and stringers* on the scene. By the last year of the war several hundred American press representatives were on the western front or prowling the streets of the capital cities of Europe. Prior to American intervention reporters from the States could move freely through the cities of Berlin and Vienna. However, the U.S. Army refused to accredit women to action on the western front, even though they had been active before America formally entered the conflict. As an alternative three women did cover the war on the Russian front.

By comparison, Great Britain applied the Official Secrets Act of 1911 to the British press contingent. Conditions looked particularly bleak for correspondents at the outset of the war with Lord Kitchener, a veteran of the Sudan campaigns and an inveterate enemy of war reporters, as secretary of state for war. Kitchener ordered that no credentials were to be granted to journalists applying to accompany the British Expeditionary Forces to France. The official view was that the British public could not handle bad news. He ruled that any British correspondent reporting the war in France and Belgium would be labeled an outlaw* and would be arrested and summarily prosecuted. In order to give the appearance that the British people were being kept informed of the conflict Kitchener appointed an officer known as the ''Eye-Witness''* to prepare daily reports about the progress of the war which would bear his stamp of approval. After the first ten months of the war British correspondents were given accreditation but were still tightly controlled.

Prior to the American intervention, correspondents accredited to the British Expeditionary Forces (BEF) headquarters were classified as either British,

French, or neutral, with limited numbers of each. They were required to wear identifying armbands and uniforms, to view the battlefront only in the company of British officers, and to present their reports to official censors. In return they were fed and billeted, with access to communication and transportation facilities. By May 1915 the outlaw classification was ended as well.

During the war freedom of the press all but vanished in France as the military insisted on strict censorship. Besides the five French representatives at BEF headquarters there was very little initiative demonstrated by the French press, indicating that they were more willing to accept the war news provided by the French government.

In the early years of the war Germany and Austria were more forthcoming and lenient with foreign members of the press than their Allied counterparts. In the later years, however, this would reverse as the Allied forces gained the upper hand in the conflict. While foreign correspondents were afforded unaccustomed luxury, their own correspondents worked under strict supervision. Austria provided complimentary assistance to accredited correspondents ranging from motor vehicles and servants to haute cuisine, wine, and tobacco. Over one hundred reporters from around the world would accept Austrian hospitality in the first year of the war.

In 1915 German military news and censorship activities were placed under the Kriegpresseamt (War Press Office), which was controlled by the general staff. It encouraged the development of trench newspapers, sponsored conferences of journalists, and prepared and distributed periodicals such as the *German War Weekly Review*, as well as propaganda publications.

With American intervention in 1917, it was only natural that there would be a heightened interest in the conflict in the United States. That July a press base was established in Paris for the American Expeditionary Force (AEF). Soon after, another base was established two hundred miles away at Neufchateau in association with the Army Intelligence Section. Prior to the summer of 1918 fifty journalists were accredited to the AEF. Twenty-one of them were print correspondents and the remaining twenty-nine were either photographers or artists. Accredited correspondents were given more perks than the "visiting" correspondents and representatives of small-town papers who continued to arrive throughout the latter stages of the war. One accredited correspondent was assigned to each division and was provided transportation and cable facilities. The rest of the press corps were not afforded cars, cable facilities, or allowed to travel outside the zone of the division they were with.

Photographers were distinguished from print correspondents by a blue armband with a white letter "P" on it, while their counterparts were identified by a green brassard with a red letter "C." Accredited correspondents held the status of officer and wore uniforms without identifying insignias or emblems. To prepare for Europe, American correspondents were advised to bring telegraph credit cards, a typewriter, copy paper, topographical maps, and a small rubber bathtub. Perhaps war correspondent and World War I censor Frederick Palmer* described the changing rules for war correspondents best when he said, "There was not the freedom of the old days, but there can never be again for the correspondent."

World War I turned out to be one of the safest conflicts for American journalists. Although a number of correspondents were wounded, none of the civilian correspondents were killed during the war. Reuters,* by comparison, lost at least 15 out of 115 correspondents, with several unaccounted for. The best-covered campaigns of the war were on the western front in France and Belgium; coverage was relatively sparse on the eastern front.

REFERENCES: Emmet Crozier. *American Reporters on the Western Front, 1914–18.* 1959; Robert W. Desmond. *The Information Process.* 1978; Joseph J. Mathews. *Reporting the Wars.* 1957.

WORLD WAR II. Of the approximately 3,000 correspondents that covered the war, the United States had the largest number with 1,646 accredited around the world, including at least 100 women correspondents. Countless others were accredited by Allied and neutral countries. Thirty-seven American reporters and photojournalists would perish in the conflict, with 112 wounded. The Associated Press and the United Press each lost 5 journalists and the *New York Times* and *Time-Life* lost 3 each.

During World War II, combination or "pool" reporters were selected by American military officials in consultation with news executives for special access to battlefields and important events, providing that reporters agreed to sharing their news with nonmembers of the pool and submitted to military censorship, ground rules, and other constraints. The pool system was continually criticized for its abuse of military censorship to support political positions and public relations rather than merely to protect military secrets.

By the time war broke out in 1939, correspondents had access to many new technical innovations for news transmission. Worldwide radio broadcasts had been introduced in 1930, and Western Union had instituted a process for sending high-quality news photos by cable across the Atlantic. However, censorship initially negated some of the advances. Delays in dispatches from London rose from one to five hours shortly after war was declared.

World War II has been referred to as "the censored war" for the pervasiveness of news censorship. The news censorship process appeared in a variety of incarnations. The U.S. government took its hesitant first step toward news control when it formerly established the Office of Censorship, headed by Byron Price,* in January 1942. This agency was solely a civilian enterprise, assigned to monitor war-related news coming from the United States.

Military censorship, on the other hand, was controlled by various branches of the armed forces, which supervised the release of combat news. In addition there was the Office of War Information, which served as a clearinghouse for war news and determined what news should be released to the public.

Each theater of operations offered varying degrees of press freedom. During the North African desert campaign in 1942 war correspondents were given unprecedented freedom. This was in part due to the immense tracts of desert terrain, which encouraged freedom of movement. Under these conditions correspondents accompanied particular units and developed attachments to the unit. During the war British correspondents were distinguished by the gold letter ''C,'' worn usually as a cap badge. On their left shoulder they were required to wear a green felt strip with ''Foreign War Correspondent'' emblazoned in gold letters. Military authorities regarded the war correspondents as vital elements of the war effort and often provided them current information with the unspoken agreement that they would produce favorable reports. Prior to the invasion of Tunisia, General Eisenhower went as far as to comment publicly that he considered the press part of the military organization and believed it should be treated as such. But this was true only as long as reporters produced favorable copy. Journalists for the most part were inclined to maintain their partnership with the military, since the war would be virtually impossible to follow without the assistance of the armed forces.

World War II was a much more difficult war to cover than previous wars. During World War I* and the Spanish-American War* there might have been different fronts, but usually there was only one major battle or campaign in progress. Whereas in previous wars there was a certain esprit de corps and camaraderie among the pool of correspondents, reporters during World War II were so scattered around the world that correspondents met few of their colleagues.
REFERENCES: Richard Collier. *Fighting Words.* 1989; Robert Desmond. *Tides of War.* 1984; M. L. Stein. *Under Fire.* 1968.

WOUNDS IN THE RAIN. *Wounds in the Rain* (1900) is Stephen Crane's* collection of short stories and recollections of the Spanish-American War.* Among the stories is ''The Lone Charge of William B. Perkins,'' which satirizes the war correspondent through the character of William B. Perkins, a whiskey-besotted reporter who arrives in Cuba ''with no information of war, and no particular rapidity of mind for acquiring it.'' Another story has a contingent of novice war correspondents coming face-to-face with the romantic myths of the profession during the Greco-Turkish War.*
REFERENCES: Stephen Crane. *Wounds in the Rain.* 1900; Howard Good. *The Image of War Correspondents in Anglo-American Fiction.* 1985.

WRIGHT, HENRY CHARLES SEPPINGS (c. 1849–1937). Born in England, the son of a minister turned to art following a short naval career. He joined the *Illustrated London News* as an artist-correspondent* in the 1870s. He covered the discovery of Kimberley diamond fields in South Africa, the 1893 Ashanti expedition, and Kitchener's advance on Dongola in 1896. The next year Wright covered the conflict in Greece. He also sketched battles in the Spanish-American War* and the Russo-Japanese War.* He wrote several books chronicling his wartime experiences. During World War I* he witnessed the Russian and French fronts.

REFERENCES: Pat Hodgson. *The War Illustrators*. 1977; Robert Wilkinson-Latham. *From Our Special Correspondent*. 1979.

X

XIMENES, EDOARDO (1852–1932). Born in Sicily, he studied art in Naples before moving to Milan, where he cofounded the *Illustrazione Italiana*, which became the most widely circulated illustrated magazine in Italy. Ximenes often worked as a special correspondent for the magazine and in 1896 he directed the illustrated gazette *La Guerra Italo-Abissinia*, or *The War Between Italy and Abyssinia*. He witnessed the war himself, and his sketches and photographs of the war are reportedly the most memorable images of the conflict. Ximenes left the magazine in the 1920s but continued his career as a journalist.

REFERENCE: Nicolas Monit, ed. *Africa Then*. 1987.

Y

YANK MAGAZINE. In the tradition of army newspapers such as the *Stars and Stripes** begun during World War I,* *Yank* was created during World War II.* Unlike the *Stars and Stripes*, for which officers supervised and controlled editorial commentary, *Yank* was edited and written by noncommissioned personnel. Officers were only involved in administrative capacities. These officers were often called on to act as a buffer between the enlisted soldiers and the brass who objected to this new kind of journalism, exemplified by its motto, ''By and for the enlisted man.''

By the end of the war the magazine had established twenty-one separate editions in virtually every theater of operations. Its peak circulation was as high as two million paid subscribers, with a readership estimated at five times that number. The magazine opened its New York headquarters in May 1942 under the direction of the Army Information and Education Division of the War Department's Army Service Forces. The first issue of *Yank* was published on June 17, 1942, at five cents an issue and with no advertising allowed.

Originally only published in the United States, as the war progressed overseas editions were requested, with the first one being published in London on November 8, 1942. The usual protocol for setting up overseas publication was to send several representatives to the new location to set up new facilities and make arrangements with local printers. The members of the magazine staff filled the dual role of enlisted soldier and journalist, with many seeing action in both the European and Pacific theaters. The magazine suffered the deaths of four correspondents in action. Eight reporters received Purple Hearts in the European theater and an equal number in the Pacific. *Yank* is credited with being the first enlisted man's magazine and the first publication to carry George Baker's* popular cartoon character ''Sad Sack.''

REFERENCES: Alfred Emile Cornebise. *Ranks and Columns: Armed Forces Newspapers in American Wars*. 1993; Art Weithas. *Close to Glory*. 1991.

YEAR OF LIVING DANGEROUSLY, THE. This 1983 film, starring Mel Gibson and Sigourney Weaver, revolves around a young Australian reporter on his first foreign assignment. With violent unrest surrounding the fall of the Sukarno regime in 1965 Indonesia as the backdrop, the film conveys the dangers and culture clashes faced by Western correspondents reporting conflicts in Third World countries.

REFERENCE: Howard Good. *The Image of War Correspondents in Anglo-American Fiction*. 1985.

YELLOW JOURNALISM. "Yellow journalism" became synonymous with sensationalist reporting in the late nineteenth century. It has been persuasively argued that the press war between Hearst's *Journal* and Joseph Pulitzer's *World* promoted war fever with sensationalistic accounts of Spanish outrages in Cuba. Many sources lay the blame for the Spanish-American War* on the shrill hysteria created by the Hearst* papers and yellow journalism.

The term "yellow journalism" refers to the *New York World*'s use of a yellow-ink cartoon strip on its front page. William Randolph Hearst liked the cartoon so much that an incarnation of the "Yellow Kid" soon appeared in the pages of the *World*'s main competitor, the *New York Journal*. With both papers featuring this yellow cartoon they became identified as purveyors of yellow journalism and prime examples of the yellow press.

REFERENCE: Joyce Milton. *The Yellow Kids*. 1989.

YEVZERIKHIN, EMMANUEL (b. 1911). Yevzerikhin covered World War II* as a photographer-correspondent for the TASS News Agency. His photographs have an aesthetic appeal absent from most war photographs. After the war he worked as a freelance journalist and professor at the Peoples' University of Photography in Moscow.

REFERENCE: Daniela Mrazkova and Vladimir Remes, eds. *The Russian War: 1941–1945*. 1975.

YOUNG, ALEXANDER BELL FILSON (1867–1938). Born and educated in Manchester, England, Young went directly from grammar school into business. He began working for the *Manchester Guardian* on a part-time basis in 1896. He was engaged as war correspondent for the paper in 1899 to cover the Boer War,* but was notified that due to prohibitive telegraph costs he should mail in his longer dispatches and only send telegrams of short news stories. Young returned to England after reporting the relief of Mafeking.* During World War I* he accompanied the British Expeditionary Forces as a correspondent for the *Times*. He continued his career with various other periodicals and the BBC. He wrote *The Relief of Mafeking* (1900).

REFERENCE: David Ayerst. *The Manchester Guardian: Biography of a Newspaper.* 1971.

YOUNG, JOHN RUSSELL (1840–1899). Born in Tyrone County, Ireland, Young immigrated with his family to America, where he entered the newspaper business as a copyboy for the *Philadelphia Press* at the age of seventeen. In 1861 he was made war correspondent and wrote one of the earliest accounts of the Union defeat at Bull Run. He was probably the first to report the actual facts concerning the defeat and the retreat. In 1862, partly due to his reporting abilities, he was made managing editor of the *Philadelphia Press*, and two years later he covered the Red River expedition to northern Louisiana.

Following the war he joined Greeley's *Tribune*, becoming editor in June 1866. He was discharged in 1869 for allowing AP news to be published by a non-subscribing paper. Young executed several secret missions to Europe for various cabinet officials and in 1872 became foreign correspondent and editor for the *New York Herald*. In 1877, Young was in London when ex-president Grant asked him to be his guest on his around-the-world tour. He chronicled this voyage and the close friendship that developed between the two in *Around the World with General Grant* (1879). In 1882 he was made minister to China, thanks to his relationship with the former president. He would eventually return to the *Herald* and serve as librarian of Congress.

REFERENCES: J. Cutler Andrews. *The North Reports the Civil War.* 1955; *DAB*; Stewart Sifakis. *Who Was Who in the Civil War.* 1988; Louis M. Starr. *Bohemian Brigade.* 1954.

YOUNG, PERRY DEANE (b. 1941). Born in Asheville, North Carolina, and educated at the University of North Carolina at Chapel Hill, Young covered the Vietnam War* for the UPI beginning in 1968. He arrived in the country just prior to the Tet offensive. Young reported the Battles of Hue and Khe Sanh. He chronicled the lives and deaths of fellow war correspondents Dana Stone* and Sean Flynn* in the book *Two of the Missing: A Reminiscence of Some Friends in the War* (1975).

REFERENCE: Perry Deane Young. *Two of the Missing.* 1975.

Z

ZELMA, GEORGI ANATOLYEVICH (b. 1906). A pioneer in Soviet photojournalism, Zelma was born in Tashkent, Uzbekistan, Russia, studied photography in Moscow, and was apprenticed with the Russfoto agency in Moscow from 1923 to 1924. During World War II* he served as war correspondent and photographer with the Red Army and for the newspaper *Isvestiya*. Zelma covered the nine-hundred-day siege and Battle of Stalingrad, the conflict in Odessa, and the front against Germany from 1941 to 1945. His war reportage is collected in *Stalingrad: July 1942–February 1943* (1966) and *Living Legend* (1967).

REFERENCES: *Contemporary Photographers*. 1982; Jorge Lewinski. *The Camera at War*. 1978; Daniela Mrazkova and Vladimir Remes, eds. *The Russian Front: 1941–1945*. 1975.

Appendix A: Mexican War Correspondents

Freaner, James L.,* *New Orleans Delta*

Haile, Christopher Mason,* *New Orleans Picayune*

Kendall, George Wilkins,* *New Orleans Picayune*

Lumsden, Frances Asbury,* *New Orleans Picayune*

Peoples, John H. "Chaparral,"* *New Orleans Delta*

Storms, Jane McManus,* *New York Sun*

Thorpe, Thomas Bangs, *New Orleans Tropic*

Tobey, William C.,* *Philadelphia North American*

Tobin, J.G.H.,* *New Orleans Delta*

Sources: Fayette Copeland. *Kendall of the Picayune*. 1970; Robert W. Johanssen. *To the Halls of the Montezumas*. 1985.

Appendix B: Crimean War Correspondents

Barkley, John, the *Times*

Beato, Felice A.,* photographer

Carmichael, J. W., *Illustrated London News*

Chenery, Thomas,* the *Times*

Crowe, Joseph Archer,* *Illustrated London News*

Eber, Ferdinand, the *Times*

Fenton, Roger,* photographer

Godkin, Edwin Lawrence,* *Daily News*

Hardman, Frederick,* the *Times*

Henty, George Alfred,* *Morning Post*

Kanouy, Alfred, *Le Moniteur*

Nasmyth, Charles,* the *Times*

Paton, Andrew Archibald, the *Times*

Robertson, James,* photographer

Russell, Sir William Howard,* the *Times*

Sandwith, Humphrey, the *Times*

Simpson, William,* *Illustrated London News*

Stowe, Henry, the *Times*

Szathmari, Karl Baptist von (Carol Popp de Szathmari),* photographer

Twopenny, Captain, the *Times*

Wood, Nicholas A., *Morning Herald*

Source: Robert W. Desmond. *The Information Process*. 1978.

Appendix C:
American Indian War
Correspondents

"Albert," *St. Louis Globe-Democrat*

Allen, Charles W., *New York Herald*

Atwell, H. Wallace,* *San Francisco Chronicle; Sacramento Recorder; Chicago Inter-Ocean*

Bailey, Gilbert, *Chicago Inter-Ocean; Rocky Mountain News*

Bogart, Robert D.,* *San Francisco Chronicle*

Boyland, R. J., Jr., *St. Paul Pioneer Press*

Brown, George Center, *Cincinnati Commercial*

Budd, H. J., *Cincinnati Daily Gazette*

Bulkeley, ?, *New York Herald*

Burkholder, Alfred H., *New York Herald*

Burns, "Judge," *Chicago Times*

Butler, Guy, *Duluth Tribune*

Clark, Edward B., *Chicago Tribune*

Clover, Sam T., *Chicago Herald*

Copenharve, Charles H., *Omaha Bee*

Corbin, Captain H. C., *Washington Post; Columbus Dispatch*

Crawford, John Wallace, *New York Herald*

Cressey, Charles H., *Omaha Bee*

Curtis, William E., *Chicago Inter-Ocean*

Davenport, Reuben Briggs,* *New York Herald*

Davis, Theodore Russell,* *Harper's Weekly*

Dean, Teresa Howard,* *Chicago Herald*

Diehl, Charles Sanford,* *Chicago Times*

Fayel, William, *St. Louis Republican*

Finerty, John F.,* *Chicago Times*

Fox, Edward,* *New York Herald*

Glover, Ridgeway,* *Frank Leslie's Illustrated Newspaper*

Hall, S. F., *Chicago Tribune*

Harries, George H., *Washington Star; New York Herald*

Hawkins, Irving, *Chicago Tribune*

Howard, James William "Phocion,"* *Chicago Tribune*

Howland, John Dare,* *Harper's Weekly*

Keim, Randolph DeBenneville,* *New York Herald*

Kelley, William F., *Nebraska State Journal*

Kellogg, Marcus Henry,* *Bismarck Tribune; New York Herald*

Knox, Thomas Wallace,* *New York Herald*

Lathrop, Barbour,* *San Francisco Bulletin*

MacMillan, Thomas C.,* *Chicago Inter-Ocean*

McDonough, John A., *New York World*

McFarland, W. J., *Omaha World-Herald*

McKay, Alex,* *San Francisco Evening Bulletin; Yreka Union*

McKay, William, *San Francisco Bulletin*

Medary, Edgar F., *New York Herald*

Moorehead, Warren K., *Illustrated American*

O'Brian, Edward A., Associated Press

O'Kelly, James J.,* *New York Herald*

Remington, Frederic Sackrider,* *Harper's Weekly*

Reynolds, Milton W., *New York World; Kansas State Journal; Chicago Times*

Robert, Dent H., *St. Louis Post-Dispatch*

Seymour, Charles G., *Chicago Herald*

Stanley, Sir Henry Morton,* *New York Tribune; St. Louis Weekly Democrat*

Smith, Carl, *Omaha World-Herald*

Stillson, Jerome Bonaparte,* *New York Herald*

Strahorn, Robert,* *Chicago Tribune; Rocky Mountain News; Omaha Republican*

Taylor, James Earl,* *Frank Leslie's Weekly*

Tibbles, Suzette "Bright Eyes," *Omaha World-Herald; Chicago Express*

Tibbles, Thomas H., *Omaha World-Herald; Chicago Herald*

Wasson, Joe,* *Philadelphia Press; New York Tribune; Alta California*

Sources: Oliver Knight. *Following the Indian Wars*. 1960; George Kolbenschlag. *A Whirlwind Passes: Newspaper Correspondents and the Sioux Indian Disturbances of 1890–1891*. 1990; Elmo Scott Watson. ''A Check-List of Indian War Correspondents, 1866–1891,'' *Journalism Quarterly*. December 1940; Elmo Scott Watson. ''The Indian Wars and the Press,'' *Journalism Quarterly*. December 1940.

Appendix D:
American Civil War
Correspondents

NORTHERN CORRESPONDENTS

Adams, George W., *New York World*

Aldrich, Thomas Bailey,* *New York Tribune*

Ames, Mary Clemmer, *New York Evening Post*

Anderson, Finley,* *New York Herald*

Anderson, William, *Philadelphia Inquirer*

Armstrong, J., *New York Times*

Ashbrook, Sam C., *Philadelphia Inquirer*

Ashley, James Nye, *New York Herald*

Atcheson, Thomas, *New York Tribune*

Austen, J. A., *Chicago Tribune*

Avery, R. B., *Chicago Times*

Babcock, Charles T., *New York Associated Press*

Babcock, William A., *Philadelphia Inquirer*

Badeau, Adam, *New York Times*

Baker, William, *New York Tribune*

Barnard, Theodore, *New York Associated Press*

Barnes, Lucien J., *New York Tribune; St. Louis Missouri Democrat*

Barrett, Edwin Shepard, *Boston Traveller*

Barlett, David V. G., *New York Evening Post; Springfield (Massachusetts) Republican*

Beaman, George W., *St. Louis Missouri Democrat*

Bearrie, W. L., *Cincinnati Times*

Bellew, Frank H., *New York Tribune*

Bentley, Henry,* *Philadelphia Inquirer*

Berford, ?, *New York Times*

Betty, Edward, *Cincinnati Gazette*

Bickham, William Denison,* *Cincinnati Commercial*

Bingham, ?, *New York Herald*

Bodman, Albert,* *Chicago Tribune; New York Herald*

Bowern, George C., Jr., *Philadelphia Inquirer*

Boweryem, George, *New York Tribune; Philadelphia Press*

Brace, Charles L., *New York Times*

Bradford, Joseph, *New York Tribune*

Brady, John A., *New York Herald*

Brigham, Charles D.,* *New York Tribune*

Brittingham, J. W., *St. Louis Missouri Republican*

Brooks, Noah, *Sacramento (California) Union*

Brown, George W., *New York Herald*

Browne, Junius Henri,* *Cincinnati Gazette; New York Tribune; St. Louis Missouri Republican*

Buckingham, Lynde Walter, *New York Herald*

Buell, George P., *Cincinnati Times*

Bulkley, Solomon T., *New York Herald*

Burnett, Alfred, *Cincinnati Commercial, Times*

Burritt, Ira N., *Cincinnati Gazette*

Buxton, Frank Lacy, *New York Tribune*

Byington, Aaron Homer,* *New York Tribune*

Cadwallader, Sylvanus,* *Chicago Times; New York Herald*

Carpenter, S. M., *New York Herald*

Carroll, William, *New York Times*

Carson, Irving, *Chicago Tribune*

Carson, John Miller, *New York Times*

Cash, Thomas M., *New York Herald*

Cazaran, Augustus, *Boston Traveller*

Chadwick, James B., *New York Tribune*

Chamberlin, W. H., *Cincinnati Gazette*

Chapman, Frank C.,* *New York Herald*

Chester, Thomas Morris,* *Philadelphia Press*

Chounce, ?, *Cincinnati Commercial*

Church, Francis Pharcellus, *New York Times*

Church, William Conant "Pierrepont,"* *New York Evening Post Times*

Clark, G. C., *Chicago Tribune*

Clark, Thomas H., *Philadelphia Inquirer*

Clarke, George W., *New York Herald*

Coffin, Charles Carleton,* *Boston Journal*

Colburn, C. C., *New York Times*

Colburn, Richard T., *New York World*

Colston, ?, *New York Tribune*

Conyngham, David Power, *New York Herald*

Cook, Joel, *Philadelphia Press*

Cook, Thomas M., *New York Herald*

Cooney, Myron A., *New York Herald*

Coscorran, ?, *Chicago Post*

Crapsey, Edward, *Cincinnati Commercial, Gazette; Philadelphia Inquirer*

Creighton, F., *New York World*

Crippen, William G., *Cincinnati Times*

Croffut, William Augustus, *New York Tribune*

Crounse, Lilas Hilston, *New York Times*

Crounse, Lorenzo L.,* *New York Times, World*

Cummins, Thomas J., *New York Herald*

Cunnington, William H., *Philadelphia Inquirer*

Cureau, ?, *New York Associated Press*

Curry, Lewellan, *Chicago Tribune*

Davenport, John I., *New York Tribune*

Davidson, A., *New York Herald*

Davidson, Nathaniel, *New York Herald*

Davis, R. Stewart, *Philadelphia Inquirer*

Davis, William E., *Cincinnati Gazette*

Dawson, J. J., *New York Herald*

Deming, Sid, *New York Associated Press*

Denyse, Edwin F., *New York Herald*

Doyle, John Edward Parker, *New York Herald*

Driscoll, F., *New York Tribune*

Dugan, James, *Cincinnati Commercial*

Dunglison, Robly, Jr., *Philadelphia Inquirer*

Dunn, John P., *New York Herald*

Eaton, D.B.M., *New York Herald*

Elliott, James, *Cincinnati Gazette*

Elliott, Thomas H., *Philadelphia Inquirer*

Evans, John, *New York Tribune*

Everett, ?, *New York Herald*

Farrell, Charles H., *New York Herald*

Fawcette, ?, *New York Times*

Fayel, William A., *St. Louis Missouri Democrat*

Fiske, Samuel Wheelock, *Springfield (Massachusetts) Republican*

Fiske, Stephen Ryder,* *New York Herald*

Fitzpatrick, James C., *New York Herald*

Flint, Henry Martyn, *New York World*

Forrest, Joseph K. C., *Chicago Tribune*

Foss, G. W., *Philadelphia Inquirer*

Foster, F. E., *Chicago Tribune*

Francis, R. D., *New York Herald, Tribune, World*

Fuller, Artur B., *Boston Journal*

Fulton, Albert, *Baltimore American*

Fulton, Charles Carroll, *Baltimore American*

Fulton, Edington, *Baltimore American*

Furay, William S., *Cincinnati Gazette*

Gatchell, William, *New York Herald*

George, William, *New York Times*

Gilbert, Curtis F., *Cincinnati Gazette; New York Tribune*

Gilden, G. P. van, *New York Times; Philadelphia Press*

Gilden, Ira van, *New York Times*

Gilmore, James Roberts, *New York Tribune*

Glen, Samuel R., *New York Herald*

Glenn, Joseph, *Cincinnati Gazette*

Glenn, W., *New York Herald*

Glover, Thaddeus B., *New York Herald*

Gobright, Lawrence Augustus, *New York Associated Press*

Grafffan, Charles H., *New York Herald*

Green, John H., *Cincinnati Enquirer*

Grey, T. C., *New York Tribune*

Groves, ?, *St Louis Missouri Republican*

Gunn, Thomas Butler, *New York Tribune*

Hall, E. H., *New York Tribune*

Halpin, Charles Graham, *New York Herald*

Halstead, Murat,* *Cincinnati Commercial*

Hamilton, John R., *New York Times*

Hammond, James Bartlett, *New York Tribune, World*

Hannarm, Charles, *New York Herald*

Hanscorm, Simon P., *New York Herald*

Hardenbrook, John A., *New York Herald*

Hart, Charles H., *New York Times*

Hart, George H., *New York Herald*

Harwood, J. H., *New York Times*

Hasson, John, *New York Associated Press*

Hayes, John E., *Boston Traveller; New York Tribune*

Henderson, Thomas J., *New York Tribune*

Hendricks, Leonard A., *New York Herald*

Henry, Arthur, *New York Tribune*

Henry, Frank, *New York Times, Herald*

Hickox, Volney, *Chicago Tribune; Cincinnati Commercial*

Hill, Adams S., *New York Tribune*

Hills, Alfred Clark, *New York Herald*

Hills, William H., *Boston Journal*

Hinton, Richard Josiah, *Chicago Tribune*

Homans, Phineas, *New York Herald*

Hosmer, George Washington, *New York Herald*

House, Edward Howard,* *New York Tribune*

Houston, Alexander, *New York Herald*

Howard, Joseph, Jr., *New York Times*

Howe, O. P., *New York Herald*

Hudson, Henry Norman, *New York Evening Post*

Ives, Malcolm, *New York Herald*

Jacobs, John T., *New York Herald*

Johnson, ?, *Philadelphia Inquirer*

Johnston, George W., *New York Herald*

Judd, David Wright, *New York Times*

Kaw, Ralph, *Chicago Tribune*

Keim, Randolph DeBenneville,* *New York Herald*

Kelly, Henry C., *St. Louis Missouri Democrat*

Kennedy, ?, *Philadelphia Inquirer*

Kent, William H., *New York Tribune*

Kinney, D. J., *New York Tribune*

Knox, Thomas Wallace,* *New York Herald*

Landon, Melville D., *New York Tribune*

Latham, James, *New York Herald*

Law, W.B.S., *New York Herald*

Lippincott, Sara, *New York Tribune*

Long, Francis C., *New York Herald, Tribune*

MacDuff, J., *Philadelphia Inquirer*

MacGahan, Januarius Aloysius,* *St. Louis Missouri Democrat*

Mason, Samuel W., *New York Herald*

Matteson, Andre, *Chicago Post*

Maverick, Augustus, *New York Evening Post*

Maybard, E. L., *New York Herald*

McAran, C. S., *Philadelphia Inquirer*

McBride, R. H., *Philadelphia Press*

McCormick, Richard Cunningham, *New York Evening Post; Commercial Advertiser*

McCracken, W. B., *New York Herald*

McCullagh, Joseph Burbridge,* *Cincinnati Commercial, Enquirer, Gazette*

McDevitt, J. F., *Philadelphia Press*

McElrath, Thompson P., *New York Times*

McGregor, William D., *New York Associated Press, Herald, Times, Tribune*

McKee, Henry, *St. Louis Missouri Democrat*

McKenna, John L., *New York Tribune*

McQuillan, Milton P., *Cincinnati Gazette*

Meader, William H., *Philadelphia Press*

Medberry, W. H., *Cincinnati Gazette*

Merriam, William H., *New York Herald*

Millar, Constantine D., *Cincinnati Commercial*

Miller, John C., *Chicago Journal*

Miller, Joseph W., *Cincinnati Commercial*

Miller, Wilson, *New York Tribune*

Misener, M. C., *Chicago Times*

Mitchell, Abram S., *New York Times*

Moore, William D., *Columbus Ohio State Journal*

Murdock, D., *Philadelphia Inquirer*

Murrell, Hower, *New York Herald*

Myers, ?, *New York Associated Press*

Newbould, Thomas M., *New York Tribune*

Newcomb, J. Warren, *New York Herald*

Newell, Robert Henry, *New York Herald*

Nichols, George Ward, *New York Evening Post*

Norcross, John, *Philadelphia Press*

Noyes, James Oscar, *New York Associated Press*

Nunevile, ?, *Philadelphia Inquirer*

O'Donnell, Kane, *Philadelphia Press*

Olcott, Henry S., *New York Tribune*

Osbon, Bradley Sillick,* *New York Herald, World*

Osborne, Galen H., *New York Herald*

Page, ?, *St. Louis Missouri Democrat*

Page, Charles Anderson,* *New York Tribune*

Paige, Nathaniel, *New York Tribune*

Painter, Uriah H.,* *Philadelphia Inquirer*

Paul, Edward Alexander, *New York Times*

Pedrick, A. K., *Philadelphia Inquirer*

Peters, E. T., *Philadelphia Inquirer*

Plymption, Florus B., *Cincinnati Commercial*

Pollock, ?, *New York Tribune*

Poore, Benjamin Perley, *Boston Journal*

Post, Truman A., *New York Tribune; St Louis Missouri Democrat*

Puleston, J. H., *Philadelphia North American*

Quigg, John Travis, *New York World*

Rathbone, John F., *New York World*

Ray, Charles H., *Chicago Tribune*

Raymond, ?, *New York Herald*

Raymond, Henry Jarvis,* *New York Times*

Rea, Samuel J., *New York Associated Press; Philadelphia Inquirer*

Reden, Laura C., *St. Louis Missouri Republican*

Redfield, W. R., *Chicago Journal*

Redpath, James,* *Boston Journal; New York Tribune*

Reid, Whitelaw,* *Cincinnati Gazette*

Reilly, Frank W., *Chicago Tribune; Cincinnati Times*

Rhoads, J. S., *Philadelphia Inquirer*

Richardson, Albert Deane,* *New York Tribune*

Ricks, ?, *Cincinnati Commercial*

Ripley, Phillip, *New York World, Evening Post*

Robinson, Joseph, *Philadelphia Inquirer*

Rogers, George M., *New York Times*

Runkle, ?, *New York Herald*

Rust, George W., *Chicago Times*

Salter, George H. C., *New York Times*

Sawyer, Oscar G., *New York Herald*

Schenk, ?, *New York Herald*

School, Charles E., *Philadelphia Press*

Schrick, Julius, *St. Louis Missouri Republican*

Seward, ?, *Philadelphia Inquirer*

Seybold, Thaddeus S., *New York Tribune*

Shanahan, Charles S., *New York Herald*

Shanks, William F. G.,* *New York Herald*

Shelly, R. L., *New York Associated Press*

Shepherd, Nathaniel Graham, *New York Tribune, World*

Shoaff, James, *Chicago Times*

Shore, W. W., *New York Tribune, World*

Shrick, Ernest, *St. Louis Missouri Republican*

Silsby, ?, *Cincinnati Gazette*

Simonton, James, *New York Times*

Slack, ?, *New York Herald*

Slocum, J. D., *New York Herald*

Smalley, George Washburn,* *New York Tribune*

Smith, Elias,* *New York Times, Tribune*

Smith, Henry M., *Chicago Tribune*

Snell, James, *New York Herald*

Sparks, William J., *New York Herald*

Spenser, E. M., *Cincinnati Times*

Spofford, Ainsworth, *Cincinnati Commercial*

Stafford, ?, *St. Louis Missouri Democrat*

Stark, William J., *New York Herald*

Stedman, Edmund Clarence,* *New York World*

Stillson, Jerome Bonaparte,* *New York World*

Stiner, William H., *New York Herald*

Surface, D., *Cincinnati Gazette; Philadelphia Inquirer*

Swain, James Barrett, *New York Times*

Swinton, William,* *New York Times*

Swisshelm, Jane Grey, *New York Tribune*

Sypher, Josiah Rhinehart, *New York Tribune*

Taggartt, John H., *Philadelphia Inquirer*

Talcott, Alfred B., *New York Herald*

Tallman, Pelegg, *Chicago Times; New York Herald*

Taylor, Bayard, *New York Tribune*

Taylor, Benjamin Franklin,* *Chicago Journal*

Thompson, Henry, *New York Herald*

Thompson, Mortimer, *New York Tribune*

Townsend, George Alfred,* *New York Herald, World*

Tracey, ?, *St Louis Missouri Republican*

Trembly, J. R., *New York Herald*

Truman, Benjamin Cummings,* *New York Times; Philadelphia Inquirer, Press*

Tyler, George W., *New York Associated Press*

Upton, George Putman,* *Chicago Tribune*

Vaughn, W. W., *New York World*

Villard, Henry,* *New York Herald, Tribune*

Vosburg, J. H., *New York Herald*

Wallz, Lawrence W., *New York Herald; Philadelphia Press*

Wallington, William M., *Philadelphia Inquirer*

Ward, Ulysses B., *New York Herald*

Wardell, James, *New York Herald*

Warden, W. W., *Cincinnati Enquirer*

Ware, Joseph A., *Philadelphia Press; Washington Chronicle*

Warner, James C., *Philadelphia Press*

Warren, Fitz-Henry, *New York Tribune*

Wayland, H. L., *New York World*

Webb, Charles Henry, *New York Times*

Webb, William E., *St. Louis Missouri Republican*

Weed, ?, *New York Herald*

Weik, John, *Philadelphia Press*

Wells, William H., *New York Herald, Tribune*

Westfall, E. D., *New York Associated Press, Herald*

Wheeler, Charles L., *St. Louis Missouri Republican*

Whipple, T. Herber, *New York Herald*

White, Horace, *Chicago Tribune*

Whitely, L. A., *New York Herald*

Whittenmore, W. H., *New York Times*

Wikoff, Henry, *New York Herald*

Wilkes, George, *New York Tribune*

Wilkeson, Samuel,* *New York Times, Tribune*

Wilkie, Franc Bangs,* *New York Times*

Williams, George Forrester,* *New York Times*

Williams, Walter F., *New York Evening Post*

Williamson, D. B., *Philadelphia Inquirer*

Wilson, John R., *Chicago Journal*

Wilson, Theodore C., *New York Herald*

Winchell, James M., *New York Times*

Wing, Henry Ebenezer,* *New York Tribune*

Wisner, Henry Jacob, *New York Times*

Woodal, A. T., *Cincinnati Gazette*

Woods, George Z., *Boston Daily Advertiser*

Woodwell, Charles H., *Boston Post*

Young, Harry H., *New York Times, World*

Young, John Russell,* *Philadelphia Press*

Young, William, *Boston Herald; New York Herald*

Source: J. Cutler Andrews. *The North Reports the Civil War.* 1955.

SOUTHERN CORRESPONDENTS

Abrams, Alexander St. Clair,* *Atlanta Daily, Intelligencer*

Adams, Warren, *Mobile Daily Advertiser and Register*

Albertson, Jonathan White, Confederate Press Association

Alexander, Peter Wellington,* *Savannah Republican; Mobile Daily Advertiser and Register; Richmond Daily Dispatch*

Bagby, George W.,* *Charleston Mercury, Mobile Daily Advertiser and Register; New Orleans Daily Crescent; Columbus Daily Sun*

Barr, W. W., *Memphis Daily Appeal*

Barr, William D., *Memphis Daily Appeal*

Bass, J. N., *Atlanta Daily Southern Confederacy*

Bell, James Pinkney, *Richmond Daily Dispatch*

Britton, E. H., *Charlotte Bulletin*

Bruns, Dr. John Dickson, *Charleston Mercury*

Bunting, Robert Franklin, *Houston Telegraph; San Antonio Herald*

Carter, Captain Theodoric, *Chattanooga Daily Rebel; Montgomery Daily Mail*

Cooke, John Esten,* *Richmond Whig; Richmond Southern Illustrated News*

Courtenay, William A., *Charleston Mercury*

Cox, T. J., *Columbus Daily Sun*

Da Ponte, Durant,* *New Orleans Daily Delta*

Davis, Captain Richard T., *Savannah Republican*

Dawson, Andrew H., *Mobile Daily Advertiser and Register*

De Fontaine, Felix Gregory,* *Charleston Daily Courier; Daily Richmond Enquirer; Columbia Daily South Carolinian; Richmond Whig; Savannah Republican; Memphis Daily Appeal; Mobile Daily Advertiser and Register*

De Gournay, Captain Francis F., *New Orleans Daily Picayune*

Dill, Benjamin F., *Memphis Daily Appeal*

Duncan, David Grieve, *Charleston Mercury; New Orleans Daily Delta; Savannah Morning News; Richmond Daily Dispatch*

Dupré, Colonel Louis J., *Knoxville Daily Register*

Dutcher, Salem, *Augusta Daily Constitutionalist*

Ette, Robert, *Memphis Daily Appeal*

Farris, Captain, *Atlanta Daily Register*

Flournoy, J. G., *Memphis Daily Appeal*

Foard, N. E., *Charleston Daily Courier*

Forbes, ?, Confederate Press Association

Forsyth, John, *Mobile Daily Advertiser and Register; Atlanta Daily Southern Confederacy; Augusta Daily Contitutionalist; Charleston Daily Courier*

Fowler, W. B., *Mobile Daily Tribune*

Galbreath, W. B., *Memphis Daily Appeal*

Gibbons, Israel,* *New Orleans Daily Crescent; Mobile Daily Advertiser and Register*

Graeme, John, Jr., *Southern Associated Press*; Confederate Press Association

Gray, Alexander, *Southern Associated Press*

Hatcher, John E., Confederate Press Association; *Mobile Daily Advertiser and Register*

Hotsze, Henry, *Mobile Daily Advertiser and Register*

Hutchen, Virginius, *Columbus Daily Sun*

Jenkins, Donelson Caffery, *New Orleans Daily Delta*

Jeter, Oliver, *Mobile Daily Advertiser and Register*

Kennedy, Captain John, *Southern Associated Press*

Kirk, Charles D., *Louisville Daily Courier; Chattanooga Daily Rebel; Memphis Daily Appeal; Augusta Daily Constitutionalist*

Lane, J. J., *New Orleans Daily Delta*

Linebaugh, John H.,* *Memphis Daily Appeal*

Loommis, ?, *Southern Associated Press*

Marx, Bonhomme, *New Orleans Daily Picayune*

Mathews, L. H., *Pensacola Observer*

Matthews, Captain ?, *Memphis Daily Appeal*

Meyer, Gustave, *Richmond Daily Dispatch; New Orleans Daily Delta*

Parks, Virgil A. S., *Savannah Republican*

Perry, Major Henry H., *New Orleans Daily Picayune; Memphis Daily*

Pleasants, Hugh, *Richmond Daily Dispatch*

Posey, Ben Lane, *Mobile Daily Advertiser and Register*

Pryor, J. P., *Memphis Daily Appeal*

Purvis, Captain George E., *Atlanta Daily Southern Confederacy*

Reid, Samuel Chester, Jr.,* *Chattanooga Daily Rebel; Memphis Daily Appeal; New Orleans Daily Picayune; Montgomery Daily Advertiser; Mobile Daily Advertiser and Register; Mobile Daily Tribune; Atlanta Daily Intelligencer*

Reyburn, W. P., *New Orleans Daily Crescent*

Riordan, Bartholomew R., *Charleston Mercury*; Confederate Press Association

Roberts, Albert, *Nashville Republican Banner*

Rowe, George Henry Clay, *Daily Richmond Examiner*

Ryan, Lipscomb, *New Orleans Daily Crescent*

Sanderson, ?, Confederate Press Association

Screws, William Wallace, *Montgomery Daily Advertiser*

Semple, William M., *Mobile Daily Advertiser and Register*

Sener, James Beverley, *Richmond Daily Dispatch; Daily Richmond Enquirer*

Shepardson, Dr. William G.,* *Mobile Daily Advertiser and Register; Columbus Times; Montgomery Daily Advertiser; Richmond Daily Dispatch*

Sledge, James, *Athens Southern Banner*

Smith, J. Henly, Confederate Press Association

Smoot, ?, Confederate Press Association

Smyth, Frank, *Petersburg Daily Express*

Sneed, James Roddy, *Savannah Republican*

Sossman, ?, *Mobile Daily Tribune*

Sparnick, Henry, *Charleston Daily Courier*

Spratt, Leonidas W., *Charleston Mercury*

Stedman, George Clinton, *Daily Richmond Enquirer*

Stoddard, George W., *New Orleans Daily Crescent*

Street, Albert J., *Mobile Daily Advertiser and Register; Savannah Republican*

Thompson, J. H., *Jackson Daily Mississippian*

Thompson, John R., *Memphis Daily Appeal*

Thompson, William Tappan, *Savannah Morning News*

Timrod, Henry,* *Charleston Mercury*

Timsley, H. C., *Richmond Daily Dispatch*

Wagner, A. J., Confederate Press Association

Walker, Alexander, *New Orleans Daily Delta*

Ward, John S., *Atlanta Daily Register*

Watterson, Henry, *Atlanta Daily Southern Confederacy; Augusta Daily Constitution; Mobile Daily Advertiser and Register*

West, John M., *New Orleans True Delta*

Woodson, Will O., Confederate Press Association

Wright, Lieutenant T. D., *Atlanta Daily Southern Confederacy*

Wright, ?, *New Orleans Bee*

Yarington, Richard J., *Richmond Associated Press; Richmond Daily Whig; Columbus Daily Sun*

Youngblood, Captain J. W., *Memphis Daily Appeal*

Source: J. Cutler Andrews. *The South Reports the Civil War*. 1970.

BRITISH CORRESPONDENTS

Day, Samuel Phillips,* *Morning Herald*

Dicey, Edward James Stephen,* *Daily Telegraph*

Gallenga, Antonio,* the *Times*

Godkin, Edwin Lawrence *Daily News*

Lawley, Francis Charles the *Times*

MacKay, Charles,* the *Times*

Sala, George Augustus Henry,* *Daily Telegraph*

Vizetelly, Frank,* *Daily News*

Sources: J. Cutler Andrews. *The North Reports the Civil War*. 1955; J. Cutler Andrews. *The South Reports the Civil War*. 1970; Robert W. Desmond. *The Information Process*. 1978.

Appendix E:
Franco-Prussian War
Correspondents

Austin, Charles, the *Times*

Cardon, Emile, *Le Gaulois*

Chabrillat, Henri, *Le Figaro*

Claretie, Jules, *Opinion Nationale*

Conway, Moncure D., *Daily Telegraph*

De Blowitz, Henri Stepan Opper,* the *Times*

Forbes, Archibald,* *Daily News*

Freytag, Gustav, *Die Grenzboten*

Hance, Joseph, *New York Tribune*

Hardman, Frederick,* the *Times*

Henty, George Alfred,* *London Standard*

Holtof, Ludwig, *Frankfurter Zeitung*

Jennerod, G., *Le Temps*

Kingston, William Beattie,* *Daily Telegraph*

Labouchere, Henry ''Labby'' Du Pre,* *Daily News*

Lawley, Francis Charles,* *Daily Telegraph*

Lesage, Sir John Merry,* *Daily Telegraph*

MacGahan, Januarius Aloysius,* *New York Herald*

Muller, Gustav, *New York Tribune*

Oliphant, Laurence,* the *Times*

Russell, Sir William Howard,* the *Times*

Sala, George Augustus Henry,* *Daily Telegraph*

Shea, John Augustus, *London Standard*
Skinner, John Edwin Hilary,* *Daily News*
Texier, Edmund, *Le Siècle*
Vizetelly, Edward Henry,* *Daily News*
Vizetelly, Ernest Alfred,* *Daily News*
Vizetelly, Henry Richard,* *Illustrated London News*
Voget, Hermann, *Frankfurter Zeitung*
Wachenhusen, Hans, *Kölnische Zeitung*
Wellmer, Arnold, *Neue Freie Presse*
Whitehurst, Felix, *Daily Telegraph*
Whyte, Holt, *New York Tribune*
Williams, George Douglas, Reuters

Source: Robert Desmond. *The Information Process*. 1978.

Appendix F:
Russo-Turkish War
Correspondents

Clarke, Campbell, *Daily Telegraph*

Cockerill, John A., *Cincinnati Enquirer*

Forbes, Archibald,* *Daily News*

Gallenga, Antonio,* the *Times*

Gay, Drew, *Daily Telegraph*

Jackson, John P., *New York Herald*

Kingston, William Beattie,* *Daily Telegraph*

MacGahan, Januarius Aloysius,* *Daily News*

Millet, Francis Davis,* *Daily News*

O'Donovan, Edmund,* *Daily News*

Power, Frank Le Poer,* stringer

Prior, Melton,* *Illustrated London News*

Scudamore, Frank,* *Daily News*

Stickney, Joseph L., *Chicago Tribune*

Stillman, William J., the *Times*

Villiers, Frederic,* *Graphic*

Source: Robert W. Desmond. *The Information Process*. 1978.

Appendix G:
Correspondents Covering the Sudan and Egyptian Campaigns, 1882–1899

Bass, John Foster,* *Chicago Record*

Bell, Charles Frederick Moberly, the *Times*

Bennett, Ernest W., *Westminster Gazette*

Burleigh, Bennet,* *Daily Telegraph*

Cameron, John Alexander,* *London Standard*

Chapman, J. C., *Daily News*

Churchill, Sir Winston Leonard Spencer,* *Morning Post*

Ferguson, Fergus, Reuters*

Gay, Drew, *Daily Telegraph*

Gwynne, Howell Arthur,* Reuters

Herbert, St. Leger Algernon,* *Morning Post*

Howard, Hubert,* *New York Herald*

James, Lionel,* Reuters

O'Donovan, Edmund,* *Daily News*

O'Kelly, James J., *Daily News*

Pearse, Harry H. S.,* *Daily News*

Power, Frank Le Poer,* the *Times*

Prior, Melton,* *Illustrated London News*

Rathom, John Revelstoke,* *Melbourbe Argus*

Robinson, Philip, *Daily Chronicle*

Steevens, George Warrington,* *Daily Mail*

Vayssie, Georges, Agence Havas

Vizetelly, Frank Horace,* *Daily News*

Wilkinson, Henry Spenser,* *Manchester Guardian*

Sources: Robert W. Desmond. *The Information Process*. 1978; Robert Wilkinson-Latham. *From Our Special Correspondent*. 1979.

Appendix H:
Greco-Turkish War
Correspondents

Atkins, John Black,* *Manchester Guardian*

Bourchier, James David,* the *Times*

Burleigh, Bennet,* *Daily Telegraph*

Chadourne, Gaston, Agence Havas

Crane, Stephen,* *New York Journal*

Creelman, James,* *New York Journal*

Davis, Richard Harding,* *New York Journal*

Dillon, Emile Joseph,* *Daily Telegraph*

Ferguson, Fergus, Reuters*

Gwynne, Howell Arthur,* Reuters

Knight, Edward Frederick,* the *Times*

Maud, W. T.,* *Graphic*

Miller, William, *Morning Post*

Nevinson, Henry Woodd,* *Daily Chronicle*

Palmer, Frederick,* *New York World*

Phillips, Percival,* *Chicago Inter-Ocean*

Prior, Melton,* *Illustrated London News*

Ralph, Julian,* *New York Journal*

Rose, W. Kinnaird, Reuters

Scovel, Henry Sylvester,* *New York World*

Scudamore, Frank, *Daily News*

Steevens, George Warrington,* *Daily Mail*

Taylor, Cora,* *New York Journal*
Villiers, Frederic,* *London Standard*
Werndel, W. H. G., Reuters
Williams, Charles,* *Daily Chronicle*

Source: Robert Desmond. *The Information Process*. 1978.

Appendix I: Spanish-American War Correspondents

Addington, Oscar, *New York Journal*

Akers, C. E., *London Times*

Alvarez, Ramon, *New York Herald*

Alvord, Thomas G., *New York World*

Archibald, James Francis Jewell,* *San Francisco Post*

Atkins, John Black,* *Manchester Guardian*

Barrett, John, *New York Journal*

Barry, David S., freelancer based in Washington, D.C.

Bass, John Foster,* *Harper's Weekly*

Beach, Harry L., Associated Press

Bengough, William, artist, *New York Journal*

Benjamin, Anna Northend,* *Leslie's Illustrated*

Bennett, James O'Donnell, *Chicago Journal*

Betancourt, Alcides, *New York Herald*

Biddle, Nicholas, ?

Bigelow, Poultney,* *New York Herald; London Times*

Billman, Howbert,* *Chicago Record*

Bonsal, Stephen, *New York Herald; McClure's Magazine*

Bowen, William Shaw, *New York World*

Brandenberg, Earl B., *New York World*

Brown, Harry, *New York World*

Browne, Herbert J., *New York Journal*

Bryson, George Eugene,* *New York Journal*

Burgin, Fred, *New York Herald*

Burton, James,* photographer, *Harper's Weekly*

Caldwell, John R., *New York Herald*

Campbell, Floyd, artist, *New York Herald*

Cary, Henry, *New York World*

Casey, Daniel, *Chicago Record*

Chamberlain, Joseph Edgar, *New York Evening Post*

Chamberlin, Henry Barrett, *Chicago Record*

Chambers, Julius, *New York Journal*

Chapman, Carlton T., artist, *Harper's Weekly*

Charles, Cecil, *New York World*

Christy, Howard Chandler,* artist, *Leslie's Illustrated*

Coffin, George, *New York Journal*

Collins, Frank, *Boston Journal*

Cramer, Robert B., *Atlanta Constitution*

Crane, Stephen,* *New York World*

Creelman, James,* *New York World*

Crosby, Charles E., *Chicago Record*

Davenport, Reuben Briggs,* ?

Davenport, Walter, cartoonist, *New York Journal*

Davies, Acton, *New York Sun*

Davis, Oscar K., *New York Sun*

Davis, Richard Harding,* *New York Journal*

Dawley, Thomas R., Jr., *Harper's Weekly*

Decker, Karl, *New York Journal*

Delorme, Thomas, *New York Journal*

Denton, Hal, *New York Journal*

Diehl, Charles Sanford,* Associated Press

Dieuaide, T.M., *New York Sun*

Dinwiddie, William,* *New York Herald*

Dunning, John P.,* Associated Press

Emerson, Edwin, *Leslie's Illustrated*

Farman, T. F., *London Standard*

Fay, John, *Chicago Tribune; New York World*

Ferguson, David, *Chicago Tribune*

Flint, Grover, *New York Journal*

Follansbee, John G., *New York Journal*

Fox, John, Jr., *Harper's Weekly*

Francis, Charles R., *Minneapolis Times*

Fuentes, Manuel, *New York World*

Fulton, Harry S., *New York Journal*

Garcia, Eduardo, *New York Sun*

Gay, W. W., *New York World*

Glackens, William, artist, *McClure's Magazine*

Goode, Sir William Athelstane Meredith,* Associated Press

Goudie, Alfred C., Associated Press

Govin, Charles,* *Key West Equator-Democrat*

Graham, George Edward,* Associated Press

Halstead, Freeman, *New York Herald*

Halstead, Murat,* *New York Journal*

Hancock, H. Irving, *Golden Hours* of New York

Hands, Charles E.,* *London Daily Mail*

Harden, Edwin W.,* *New York World*

Hare, James H.,* photographer, *Collier's*

Harris, Julian, *Atlanta Constitution*

Harris, Kennett, *Chicago Record*

Hawthorne, Julian, *New York Journal*

Hemment, John C.,* photographer, *Harper's Weekly*

Herrings, J., *New York Staats-Zeitung*

Hilgert, F. J., Associated Press

Hillegas, Howard Clemens, ?

Howard, Walter, *New York Journal*

Hunt, D. V., photographer, *Harper's Weekly*

Johnson, General Bradley T., *New York World*

Johnstone, E.R., Associated Press

Jones, Hayden, artist, *New York World*

Keen, Edward L., Keen–Scripps-McRae Press

Kendrick, Marion, *New York Journal*

Kenealy, Alexander C., *New York World*

Kennan, George,* *Outlook* Magazine

Knight, Edward Frederick,* *London Times*

Koelbe, Adolph, *New York World*

Laine, Honore, *New York Journal*

Langland, James, *Chicago News*

Lawrence, Frederick W., *New York Journal*

Leary, William, New York freelancer

Leighton, Sir Bryan, ?

Lewis, Alfred H., *New York Journal*

Lewis, William E., *New York Journal*

Low, A. Maurice, *London Daily Chronicle*

Luks, George B., artist, *New York World*

Lyman, A. W., Associated Press

Lynch, George,* *London Chronicle*

Mannix, William, *Army and Navy Journal*

Marcotte, Henry, *Army and Navy Journal*

Marriott, J. Crittenden, Associated Press

Marshall, Edward, *New York Journal*

Martin, Harold, Associated Press

Masterson, Kate, *New York Journal*

Maxwell, John M., *Chicago Tribune*

McCutcheon, John T.,* artist, *Chicago Record*

McDowell, Malcolm, *Chicago Record*

McIntosh, Burr William,* photographer, *Leslie's Illustrated*

McMillan, Samuel, freelancer, Lowell, Massachusetts

McNichol, H. E., *New York Journal*

McPherson, Douglas, ?

McQueen, Peter, freelancer, Boston

McReady, Ernest W., ?

Melton, Ona, *Jacksonville Times-Union*

Michelson, Charles, *New York Journal*

Millard, Thomas Franklin Fairfax,* *New York Herald*

Millet, Francis Davis,* *Harper's Weekly; London Times*

Mumford, John K., *New York Journal*

Musgrave, George Clarke, *London Chronicle*

Nichols, Francis Henry,* *New York World*

Norris, Frank, *McClure's Magazine*

Nuttall, Frank, *London Daily Telegraph*

O'Donohue, Dennis, *Detroit News*

Ohl, Joseph, *Atlanta Constitution*

O'Shaughnessy, James, Jr., *Chicago Chronicle*

Paine, Ralph Delahaye,* *New York World; Philadelphia Press*

Peltz, Hamilton, *New York Herald*

Pendleton, C. B., *Key West Equator-Democrat*

Pepper, Charles M., *Washington Star*

Peters, G. W., artist, *Harper's Weekly*

Phillips, Percival,* *New York World*

Price, G. Ewing, *New Orleans Times-Democrat*

Quail, J.N., *New York Journal*

Quigley, W.S., *New York Mail and Express*

Ranthom, John Revelstoke,* *San Francisco Chronicle*

Rea, George Bronson,* *New York Herald*

Redding, Leo L., *New York Herald*

Remington, Frederic Sackrider,* artist, *New York Journal*

Roberts, Elmer E., Associated Press

Robinson, Philip, *London Pall Mall Gazette*

Romaine, Major, *National Tribune*

Root, Walstein, *New York Sun*

Russell, Walter, artist, *New York Herald*

Schell, Frank C., artist, *Leslie's Illustrated*

Schemedtzen, William, ?

Scovel, Henry Sylvester,* *New York World*

Seibold, Louis, *New York World*

Sheldon, Charles M.,* artist, *London Black and White*

Smith, Morton, *Atlanta Journal*

Somerford, Fred O., *New York Herald*

Steep, Thomas W., Scripps-McRae League

Stickney, Joseph L., *New York Herald*

Thompson, Howard N., Associated Press

Thrall, Charles H., *New York World*

Valesch, Eva McDonald, *New York Journal*

Walker, T. Dart, artist, *Harper's Weekly*

Watkins, Kathleen "Kit" Blake,* *Toronto Mail and Express*

Watson, Oscar, ?

Whigham, H. J., *Chicago Tribune*

White, Douglas, ?

White, Mrs. Katherine, Red Cross; *Chicago Record*

White, Trumbull, *Chicago Record*

Whitney, Caspar,* *Harper's Weekly*

Willets, Gilson, *Leslie's Illustrated*

Wilson, W. O., artist, *New York Herald*

Wright, Henry Charles Seppings,* *London Illustrated News*

Zogbaum, Rufus, artist, *Harper's Weekly*

Sources: Charles H. Brown. *The Correspondents' War*. 1967; Robert W. Desmond. *The Information Process*. 1978; Joyce Milton. *The Yellow Kids: Foreign Correspondents in the Heyday of Yellow Journalism*. 1989.

Appendix J: Boer War Correspondents

Amery, Leopold Charles Maurice Stennett,* the *Times*

Atkins, John Black,* *Manchester Guardian*

Baillie, F. D., *Morning Post*

Barnes, *Daily Mail*

Battersby, Prevost, *Morning Post*

Beresford, Robert, Central News

Bleloch, *Standard*

Booth, R. C., *Pearson's War News*

Bray, Charles, Central News

Bullen, Percy *Daily Telegraph*

Burleigh, Bennet,* *Daily Telegraph*

Buxton, *Cape Argus*

Cameron, J., *Daily Chronicle*

Campbell, Alister, Laffan's Agency

Carrere, Jean, *Matin*

Churchill, Winston,* *Morning Post*

Collett, Albert, *Daily Mail*

Davies, *Sphere*

Delaware, Lord, *Globe*

Dinwiddie, William,* *Harper's*

Donohoe, Martin Henry,* *Daily Chronicle*

Dunn, Joseph S., Central News

Ewan, *Toronto Globe*

Ferrand, Alfred, *Morning Post*

Finlason, C. E., *Black and White*

Fripp, Charles Edwin,* *Graphic*

Giles, D., *Black and White*

Goldman, Charles Sydney, *Outlook*

Goldmann, S., *Daily Telegraph*

Gotto, Basil,* *Daily Express*

Graham, A., Central News

Graham, George Edward,* Central News

Gwynne, Howell Arthur,* Reuters*

Hales, A. G., *Daily News; Sydney Morning Herald*

Hamilton, Frederick, *Toronto Globe*

Hamilton, J. Angus, the *Times, Black and White*

Hands, Charles E.,* *Daily Mail*

Hartland, Hardtford, *Navy and Army Illustrated*

Hellawell, Mr., *Daily Mail*

Hodgetts, E. A. Brayley, *Daily Express*

Hoskier, Colonel, *Sphere*

Hutton, Reuters

Hyman, *Cinematograph*

James, Lionel,* the *Times*

Jenkins, *Daily Mail*

Kingsley, Mary,* *Morning Post*

Kinnear, Alfred,* Central News

Knight, Edward Frederick,* *Morning Post*

Lambie, Mr., *Melbourne Age*

Lynch, George,* *Morning Herald; Echo*

Lyons, H., *Daily Mail*

MacDonell, the *Times*

MacHugh, Lieutenant-Colonel Robert Joseph,* *Daily Telegraph*

Mackem, *Scribner*

Mann, Harrington, *Black and White*

Manners, Lord Cecil, *Morning Post*

Martindale, W., Central News

Maud, W. T.,* *Daily Graphic*

Maxwell, Sir William,* *Standard*

Mempes, Mortimer, *Black and White*

Milne, James, Reuters*

Mitchell, Robert, *Standard*

Musgrave, George Clark, *Black and White*

Neilly, Emerson,* *Pall Mall Gazette*

Nevinson, Henry Woodd,* *Daily Chronicle*

Nissen, R.C.E., *Daily Mail*

Nissen, *Cape Times*

Owen-Scott, *Illustrated London News*

Parslow, E. G.,* *Daily Chronicle*

Paterson, Andrew Barton, *Sydney Morning Herald; Melbourne Argus*; Reuters

Paxton, R.M.B., *Sphere*

Pearse, Harry H. S.,* *Daily News*

Pollock, Major A.W.A., the *Times*

Prater, Ernest, *Sphere*

Prior, Melton,* *Illustrated London News*

Ralph, Julian,* *Daily Mail*

Ralph, Lester, *Daily Mail*

Reiss, *Manchester Guardian*

Rennett, *Laffan's*

Rhodes, Colonel F., the *Times*

Rosenthal, *Cinematograph*

Rosslyn, Lord, *Daily Mail, Sphere*

Scott, *Manchester Courier*

Scull, E. D., *Chicago Record*

Seull, G. H., *New York Commercial Advertiser*

Shelley, *King*

Smith, *Canadian*

Smith, Ernest,* *Morning Leader*

Spooner, H. H., Reuters

Steevens, George Warrington,* *Daily Mail*

Stent, Vere, Reuters

Stewart, F. A., *Illustrated London News*

Story, Douglas, *Daily Mail*

Stuart, John, *Morning Post*

Swallow, W. S., Central News

Sykes, A. A., *Black and White*

Thackery, Lance, *Sphere*

Unger, Frederic William,* *Philadelphia Press*

Villiers, Frederic,* *Graphic*

Walker, F. W., *Daily Mail*

Wallace, Edgar,* Reuters, *Daily Mail*

Wester, Captain, *Midland News*

White, *Montreal Star*

Wigham, H. J., *Daily Mail*

Wilson, Lady Sarah, *Daily Mail*

Wollen, W. B., *Sphere*

Wright, Henry Charles Seppings,* *Daily News*

Young, Alexander Bell Filson,* *Manchester Guardian*

Sources: Robert W. Desmond. *The Information Process*. 1978; Frederic William Unger. *With Bobs and Kruger: Experiences and Observations of an American War Correspondent in the Field with Both Armies*. 1901; Robert Wilkinson-Latham. *From Our Special Correspondent*. 1979.

Appendix K:
World War I Correspondents

CORRESPONDENTS ACCREDITED TO THE U.S. ARMY ON THE WESTERN FRONT DURING WORLD WAR I

NAME	ACCREDITATION	ORGANIZATION
Heywood Broun*	July 1, 1917	*New York Tribune*
Raymond G. Carroll	July 9, 1917	*Philadelphia Public Ledger*
Junius Wood*	July 9, 1917	*Chicago Daily News*
Wythe Williams*	July 10, 1917	*New York Times* and *Collier's*
Herbert Corey	July 24, 1917	Associated Newspapers
Reginald W. Kaufman	September 17, 1917	*Philadelphia North American*
Floyd Gibbons*	October 9, 1917	*Chicago Tribune*
Thomas M. Johnson*	October 9, 1917	*New York Sun*
Lincoln Eyre	October 14, 1917	*New York World*
C. C. Lyon	October 15, 1917	Newspaper Enterprise Association
Norman Draper	October 28, 1917	Associated Press
Naboth Hedin	March 1918	*Brooklyn Eagle*
Edwin "Jimmy" L. James*	March 11, 1918	*New York Times*
Wilbur S. Forrest	March 22, 1918	*New York Tribune*
John T. Parkerson	March 30, 1918	Associated Press

NAME	ACCREDITATION	ORGANIZATION
Dennis S. Ford	March 31, 1918	International News Service (INS)
Fred S. Ferguson	April 8, 1918	United Press
Newton C. Parke	April 8, 1918	INS
James Hopper	April 11, 1918	*Collier's Weekly*
Don Martin	May 1918	*New York Herald*
George Seldes*	May 12, 1918	Marshall Syndicate
Frank G. Taylor	May 12, 1918	United Press
Charles S. Kloeber	July 27, 1918	Associated Press
Bernard O'Donnell	August 23, 1918	*Cincinnati Inquirer*
Guy C. Hickok	September 1918	*Brooklyn Eagle*
Charles J. Doyle	October 1918	*Pittsburgh Gazette Times*
Damon Runyon*	October 1918	Universal Service
George Applegarth	October 14, 1918	*Pittsburgh Post*
Burr Price	October 19, 1918	*New York Herald*
Maximilian Foster	November 1918	Committee on Public Information
Edwin A. Roberts	November 11, 1918	*Cleveland Plain Dealer*
John Tinney McCutcheon*	November 19, 1918	*Chicago Tribune*
Webb Miller*	November 19, 1918	United Press
Cyril Brown	December 1918	*New York World*
Parke Brown	December 1918	*Chicago Tribune*
Ward Greene	December 1918	*Atlanta Journal*

CORRESPONDENTS SERVING AS ACCREDITED CORRESPONDENTS

H. Warner Allen, *London Morning Post*
Herbert R. Bailey, *London Daily Mail*
H. Prevost Battersby, Reuters
H. Noble Hall, *London Times*
James P. Howe, Associated Press
Clair Kenamore, *St. Louis Post-Dispatch*
Cameron MacKenzie, *London Chronicle*
Burge McFall, Associated Press
Lowell Mellett, United Press
Philip M. Powers, Associated Press

Fred A. Smith, *Chicago Tribune*

Henry G. Wales, INS

VISITING CORRESPONDENTS OF LONGEST SERVICE

Walter S. Ball, *Providence Journal*

Adam Breede, *Hastings Daily Tribune*

Cecile Dorian, *Newark Evening News*

Elizabeth Frazier, *Saturday Evening Post*

Charles H. Grasty, *New York Times*

David W. Hazen, *Portland Oregonian*

Otto P. Higgins, *Kansas City Star*

Frazier ''Spike'' Hunt,* *Chicago Tribune*

W. S. McNutt, *Collier's Weekly*

George Pattullo, *Saturday Evening Post*

Arthur Ruhl,* *Collier's Weekly*

Frank P. Sibley, *Boston Globe*

Joseph Timmons, *Los Angeles Examiner*

Raymond S. Tompkins, *Baltimore Sun*

Caspar Whitney,* *New York Tribune*

Harry A. Williams, *Los Angeles Times*

Source: Emmet Crozier. *American Reporters on the Western Front, 1914–18.* 1959.

Appendix L:
Accredited U.S. War Correspondents for World War II

Ackerman, Michael J., Acme News-Pictures

Ackerman, Robert, AP

Ackermann, Carl, Columbia School of Journalism

Adams, Benjamin P., Funk & Wagnalls

Adams, John B., CBS

Adams, Noel B., Group 2, Australian Papers

Adams, Phelps H., *New York Sun Times*

Agronsky, Martin, INS

Albayalde, Abe, *Filipino News*

Albright, Sydney, NBC

Alcine, Billy L., *Yank*

Aldridge, F. G., Group 2, Australian Papers

Alexander, Eben R., *Time*

Alexander, Jack, *Saturday Evening Post*

Alexander, William H., Oklahoma Publishing Company

Alexanderson, George, Ministry of Information (G.B.)

Allen, Lawrence Edmund,* AP

Allen, William C., AP

Allen, W. R., AP

Alley, Norman, *News of the Day*

Amato, Victor, War Dept., Bureau of Public Relations

Anderson, Alan F., Australian Dept. of Information

Anderson, Earl H., *Yank*

Anderson, F. David, *New York Times*

Anderson, Jack, *Desert News*

Andrew, John J., UP

Andrew, Philip, Philip Andrew Publishing Company

Andrews, Bert, *New York Herald Tribune*

Andrews, Steffan, *Cleveland Plain Dealer*

Andrica, Theodore, *Cleveland Press*

Angel, D. M., Australian Dept. of Information

Angelopoulous, A., INS

Angley, Joseph, *Chicago Sun*

Annabel, Russell F., UP

Antrobus, Edmund, *Yank*

Archinard, Paul J., NBC

Armstrong, John P., *Yank*

Armstrong, R. B., *St. Louis Globe-Democrat*

Armstrong, Richard, INS

Arnot, Charles P.,* UP

Arter, Theodore, *Altoona (Pa.) Tribune*

Atkins, Oliver F., American Red Cross

Atkinson, Brooks, *New York Times*

Atkinson, C. P., Civil & Military Gazette, Ltd.

Atkinson, Oriana T., *New York Times*

Ault, Philip, UP

Avery, Marjorie, *Detroit Free-Press*

Azrael, Louis, *Baltimore News-Post*

Babcock, Franklin L., *Time*

Babcock, Lawrence, *Fortune*

Bader, Jesse M., *Christian Evangelist*

Baer, Howard, Abbott Laboratories

Bagley, Henry W., AP

Bailey, Wesley L., *Time*

Baillie, Hugh,* UP

Bain, Leslie B., WIOD

Baird, Joseph H., Overseas News Agency

Baker, Richard, Religious News Service

Baker, Warren, *Chicago Tribune*

Baldwin, Hanson W.,* *New York Times*

Ball, Edward, AP

Band, John, Australian Dept. of Information

Banker, Franklin F., AP

Barber, Charles P., *Parade*

Barber, F., AP

Barcella, Ernest L., UP

Barden, Judy, *New York Sun*

Barker, Fowler W., *Air Transport*

Barkham, John, *Time*

Barnes, Howard, *New York Herald Tribune*

Barnes, John P., *Yank*

Barnes, Joseph, *New York Herald Tribune*

Barnett, Jack S., Fox Movietone News

Barnett, Lincoln, *Time*

Barnett, Martin, Paramount News

Barr, Richard M., CIAA

Barrett, Frank B., *Lowell Sun*

Barrett, George A., *Yank*

Barretto, Lawrence B., *Liberty*

Barrows, Nat A., *Chicago Daily News*

Barry, Joseph A., *Newsweek*

Bartholomew, Frank Harmon,* UP

Bartholomew, John B., ABC

Barton, Frederick B., *Plane Talk*

Baukhage, H. R., ABC

Baum, Arthur W., *Saturday Evening Post*

Bauman, Frank M., *Look*

Baxter, George E., UP

Baylor, David M., WGAR

Beall, Cecil C., *Collier's*

Bealmear, Henry A., AP

Beam, Oscar P., AP

Beattie, Edward W., Jr.,* UP

Beatty, Morgan, NBC

Beaufort, John D., *Christian Science Monitor*

Beeby, Nellie B., *American Journal of Nursing*

Befeler, Murray, AP

Belair, Felix, *Time*

Belden, Jack,* *Harper's*

Bell, Don, MBS

Bell, John A., *Miami Herald*

Bell, Borman, AP

Benedetti, Abraham, Reuters

Bennett, Lowell,* INS

Benny, Robert L., Abbott Laboratories

Berger, Meyer, *New York Times*

Bergholz, Richard C., AP

Bernard, Charles, UP

Bernstein, Victor H., *PM*

Bernstein, Walter,* *Yank*

Berrigan, Darrell, UP

Bess, Demaree, *Saturday Evening Post*

Bess, Dorothy, *Saturday Evening Post*

Best, Cort, AC/Photo Division

Bettencourt, Sylvia de, *Correio de Manha*

Biben, Joseph H., Biben Publishing Company

Biddle, George,* *Life*

Bienstock, Victor, Overseas News Agency

Bigart, Homer,* *New York Herald Tribune*

Billotte, William C., Jr., *Omaha World-Herald*

Binder, Carroll, *Chicago Daily News*

Bjornson, Bjorn, NBC

Black, John C., Gillett Publishing Company

Blackburn, Casper K., *Seapower*

Blair, Robert H., Fox Movietone News

Blakeslee, Howard W., Fox Movietone News

Blay, John S., *Yank*

Boatner, Charles K., *Fort Worth Star-Telegram*

Bockhurst, John A., *News of the Day*

Boggs, William, Abbott Laboratories

Boguslav, David, *Chicago Sun*

Bohrod, Aaron,* *Time*

Bolden, Frank E., *Pittsburgh Courier*

Bolling, Landrum, *Beloit Daily News*

Bongard, Nicholas, *March of Time*

Boni, William F., AP

Bonney, Teresa, Duell, Sloance & Pear

Booth, W., *Philadelphia Record*

Bordaam, William, INS

Bordas, Walter, International News Photos

Boren, Wallace R., *This Week*

Borgstedt, Douglas H., *Yank*

Bostwick, Albert L., Veterans of Foreign Wars

Bottomley, C., Australian Dept. of Information

Bourchet, Rene, *Ospecre Algerese*

Bourges, Fernand A., *Life*

Bourke-White, Margaret,* *Time*

Bovill, Oscar, *Pathe-Gazette*

Bow, Frank, Brush Moor Newspapers

Bowen, Lewis, American Red Cross

Bowerman, Waldo G., *Engineering-News Record*

Boyce, Ralph L., *Yank*

Boyle, Harold, *AP*

Boyle, John W., *Time*

Bracker, Milton, *New York Times*

Bracker, Virginia L., *New York Times*

Bradley, Holbrook, *Baltimore Sun*

Brady, Lloyd C., AP

Brag, Rubin, *Diario Carioca*

Braidwood, Nelson, *London Telegraph*

Bramley, George E., *American Aviation*

Brandao, Paul, *Correio de Manha*

Brandt, Bertram G., Acme Newspictures

Brandt, Frank M., *Yank*

Brandt, Raymond P., *St. Louis Post-Dispatch*

Branham, Leo, AP

Breese, Howard F., AP

Bregon, John, INS

Breimhurst, Donald W., *Yank*

Brennan, John C., *Sydney Bulletin*

Brennan, Peter, NBC

Brewer, Sam, *New York Times*

Bria, George C., AP

Bridgman, Julie, *Liberty*

Briggs, Walter L., UP

Brigham, Daniel P., *New York Times*

Brines, Russell, AP

Broch, Nathan, Aneta News Agency (Dutch)

Brock, Ray, *New York Times*

Broderick, Hugh, International News Photos

Brodie, Howard,* *Yank*

Brook, Alexander, *Life*

Brooks, Deton J., *Chicago Defender*

Brooks, Olive, INS

Brooks, William F., NBC

Brown, Arthur E., *Chicago Herald American*

Brown, David, Reuters

Brown, Dickson, *London News Chronicle*

Brown, Harold P., Reuters

Brown, Harry, *Yanks*

Brown, James E., INS

Brown, Norman E., Australian Dept. of Information

Brown, Robert E., UP

Browne, Barbara, *Christian Science Monitor*

Browne, Mallory, *New York Times*

Brumby, Robert M., MES

Bruto, Frank, *AP*

Bryan, W. Wright, *Atlanta Journal*

Bryant, Robert, International News Photos

Bryant, Vaughn M., AP

Buckley, Christopher,* Reuters

Buddy, Edward C., *Path News*

Bullard, Arthur E., American Red Cross

Bullitt, William C., *Time*

Buntin, William, INS

Burchett, Wilfred,* *London Daily Express*

Burdette, Winston, CBS

Burke, James C., *Liberty*

Burke, James W., *Esquire-Coroney*

Burnham, L. B., UP

Burns, Douglas R., Australian Dept. of Information

Burns, Eugene, AP

Burns, George,* *Yank*

Burns, John T., AP

Burroughs, Edgar Rice, UP

Burroughs, Henry J., AP

Burrows, Ted, *Yank*

Burton, L. V., McGraw-Hill

Busch, Noel F., *Time*

Buschemi, John,* *Yank*

Bush, Asahel, AP

Butler, Eldon K., AP

Buttrose, C.O.G., *Sydney Morning Herald*

Byfield, Ernest L., *Chicago Herald American*

Cafaliere, Nicholas, *March of Time*

Calabria, Frank J., *March of Time*

Calhoun, C. H., *New York Times*

Calhoun, Millard F., *Time*

Callender, Harold, *New York Times*

Calmer, Edgar M., CBS

Calvosa, Ulrich, *Collier's*

Camp, Helen, AP

Campbell, Archibald Doon,* Reuters

Campbell, Edward L., AP

Cancellare, Frank, Acme Newspictures

Capa, Robert,* *Life*

Caparelle, Peter L., *Ring*

Carley, John O., *Memphis Commercial-Appeal*

Carlisle, John M., *Detroit News*

Carnes, Disney C., *Saturday Evening Post*

Carpenter, Iris,* *London Daily Herald*

Carr, Milton L., UP

Carroll, Loren, *Newsweek*

Carroll, Peter J., AP

Carroll, Sidney, *Esquire-Coronet*

Carson, Lee, INS

Carter, Amon G., *Fort Worth Star Telegram*

Carter, Archer N., McGraw-Hill

Carter, Arthur M., *Afro-American Newspaper*

Carty, William, Australian Dept. of Information

Case, Lewis S., Paramount News

Casey, Robert Joseph,* *Chicago Daily News*

Cashman, John, INS

Cassidy, Henry C.,* NBC

Cassidy, James F., WLW

Cassidy, Morley, *Philadelphia Bulletin*

Caswell, Donald F., UP

Catledge, William T., *New York Times*

Cellario, Alberto, *La Prensa*

Chafin, Glenn M., Bell Syndicate

Chakales, Lawrence S., *AP*

Chamberlain, Charles W., *AP*

Chandra, P. T., *India-Burma*

Chang, C. B., Central News Agency

Chao, Sam, Reuters

Chapelle, Georgette "Dickey,"* *Look*

Chappelle, Minafox, *American Home*

Chaplin, William W., NBC

Chapman, Frank M., Acme Newspictures

Chapman, John F., McGraw-Hill

Chase, Milton, WLW

Chase, William T., AP

Cheng, Hawthorne, Chinese Ministry of Information

Chernoff, Howard L., West Virginia Network

Chester, John F., AP

Chickering, William H., *Time*

Childs, Marquis, *St. Louis Post-Dispatch*

Chinigo, Michael, INS

Chipping, Chu, *TaKanpPao*

Chorlian, Edward, CBS

Clapper, Raymond Lewis,* Scripps-Howard

Clark, Edgar, UP

Clark, Edward T., *Cleveland Press*

Clark, Herbert, *New York Herald Tribune*

Clark, Katherine L., WCAU

Clark, Michael, the *Nation*

Clark, Richard, UP

Clark, William E., *Life*

Clarke, Philip C., AP

Clausen, John A., War Dept., Special Services

Clausen, Walter B., AP

Clayton, Bernard, *Life*

Clayton, Frederick, American Red Cross

Cleary, Ed J., McGraw-Hill

Clements, Olen W., AP

Clover, Robert, AP

Clurman, Robert O., AP

Cobbledick, Gordon, *Cleveland Plain Dealer*

Cochrane, Jacqueline, *Liberty*

Cochrane, Robert B., *Baltimore Sun*

Codel, Martin, American Red Cross

Coe, Donald G., ABC

Coffy, Patrick V., *Yank*

Coggins, Jack B., *Yank*

Cohen, Haskell P., *Pittsburgh Courier*

Cohn, Arthur E., INS

Cohn, David L., Houghton-Mifflin

Colburn, John H., AP

Colby, Carroll B., *Popular Science*

Coll, Ray, *Honolulu Advertiser*

Collingwood, Charles Cummings,* CBS

Collins, Walter, UP

Combas, Guerra E., *El Mundo*

Combs, George H., WHN

Conefry, Walter, Scripps-Howard

Conger, Clinton B., UP

Coniston, Ralph A., Aneta News Agency (Dutch)

Conniff, Frank,* INS

Considine, Robert B., INS

Coogan, James A., UP

Cook, Donald P., *New York Herald Tribune*

Cook, George J., *Yank*

Cook, Howard N., *Life*

Cook, Max B., Scripps-Howard

Cook, Zenas D., *Newsweek*

Cooke, David C., McBride Publishing Company

Cooke, Donald E., *Yank*

Cookman, Mary C., *Ladies Home Journal*

Cool, Robert N., AP

Cooper, Edward H., *Christian Science Monitor*

Corbellini, George, *Yank*

Cornell, Douglas, AP

Corsinia, Aralbo R., *Petroleum Magazine*

Cort, Horance W., AP

Corte, Charles, Acme Newspictures

Corum, Bill, King Features

Corwin, Norman L., CBS

Costa, Joseph C., *New York Daily News*

Courtenay, William, *London Daily Sketch*

Courtney, W. B., *Collier's*

Cowan, Howard S., AP

Cowan, Ruth,* AP

Cowles, Virginia,* NANA

Coxe, George, Alfred Knopf

Coyne, Catherine, *Boston Herald*

Craig, Elizabeth M., Gannett Publishing Company

Craig, Thomas T., *Life*

Cranston, Paul F., *Philadelphia Bulletin*

Cravens, Kathryn, MBS

Crawford, Kenneth Gale,* *Newsweek*

Crider, John H., *New York Times*

Crocker, A. J., *St. Paul Dispatch*

Crockett, E. Harry, AP

Cromie, Robert A., *Chicago Tribune*

Cronkite, Walter Leland, Jr.,* UP

Crost, Lyn,* *Honolulu Star-Bulletin*

Crotchett, Earl, Universal Newsreel

Crowther, Francis B., *New York Times*

Crozier, Thomas E., *New York Herald Tribune*

Crumpler, Hugh, UP

Cuddy, John M., UP

Cuhel, Frank J., MBS

Cumming, C., *Christian Science Monitor*

Cummings, Ray, *Honolulu Star-Bulletin*

Cunha, Albelardo, *Imprensa Propoganda*

Cunningham, Bill, *Boston Herald-Traveller*

Cunningham, Chris, UP

Cunningham, Ed,* *Yank*

Cunningham, Joseph, *Yank*

Cunningham, Owen, MBS

Curran, Thomas R., UP

Currivan, Eugene A., *New York Times*

Cushing, Richard G., AP

Custer, Joseph, AP

DaFonseca, Silvio S., *Imprensa Propoganda*

Dallaire, Victor J., UP

Daly, John C., CBS

Danenberg, Elsie, NANA

Daniel, Elbert C., AP

Daniel, F. Raymond, *New York Times*

Daniel, Hawthorne, *Asia Magazine*

Daniel, James M., *New York Post*

Daniel, Tatiana, *New York Times*

Daniell, F.H.W., MacQuarie Broadcasting Company

Darnton, Byron, *New York Times*

Darrah, David H., *Chicago Tribune*

Dash, Hugh, Group 2, Australian Papers

Dashiell, Samuel, NANA

Davenport, John A., *Time*

Davenport, Russell W., *American Mercury*

Davenport, Walter A., *Collier's*

David, David R., Acme Newspictures

David, Steven A., UP

Davidson, William J., *Yank*

Davis, Gladys, *Life*

Davis, Jerome, INS

Davis, Kenneth S., Doubleday Doran

Davis, Lloyd, *Life*

Davis, Maxine, Macmillan

Davis, Myron H., *Life*

Davis, Spencer, AP

Dawes, Allen W., Group 3, Australian Papers

Day, Price, *Baltimore Sun*

Day, Richard M., American Red Cross

DeAbranches, Carlos, *Jornel de Brazil*

Dearing, Joseph A., *Collier's*

Debnam, Waldemar E., WPTF

Decormis, Anne McCormick, *Fortune*

Dees, Joseph, UP

DeGusmao, Rubin, *Coeiho Sobrinho*

Delalande, Francois, Pathé News

Delaphale, Stanto, *San Francisco Chronicle*

De Luce, Daniel,* AP

Dennehy, Edward, AP

Dennis, Gene, KMBC

Denny, Harold Norman,* *New York Times*

Denton, Nixsoin, *Cincinnati Times Star*

DeRochement, Richard G., *March of Time*

Derry, Steven, *Yank*

DeSantillana, George D., *Atlantic Monthly*

Desfor, Maxd, AP

DeSoria, Charles J., AP

Despouey, Rene, NBC

Deter, Arthur S., CBS

DeVoto, Bernard A., War Dept., Bureau of Public Relations

Dexter, Frank H., Group 1, Australian Papers

Dharma, Ernest, UP

Dick, Harold G., *Australian Depatment of Information*

Dickinson, William B., UP

Dickson, Cecil B., Gannett Newspapers

Diehl, Chandler, AP

Diggins, Mary M., INS

Disbrow, Leslie D., American Red Cross

Disher, Leo S.,* UP

Disney, Dorothy, *Saturday Evening Post*

Dixon, George H., *New York Daily News*

Dixon, Kenneth L., AP

Dixon, William R., *Pittsburgh Courier*

Dmitri, Ivan, *Saturday Evening Post*

Doan, Donald P., AP

Dodd, Howel E., AP

Dolan, Leo V., INS

Donaghey, Donald, *Philadelphia Bulletin*

Donahue, Robert F., Pathé News

Donghi, Frank, Acme Newspictures

Dopking, Al, AP

Dored, John, Paramount News

Dorsey, George, Pathé News

Dorvillier, William, UP

Dos Passos, John Roderigo,* *Life*

Douglas, Wes, *Chicago Sun*

Douglass, Richard W., *Yank*

Dowling, John G., *Chicago Sun*

Downes, Donald C., Overseas News Agency

Downs, William R., CBS

Doyle, Robert J., *Milwaukee Journal*

Drake, Catherine, *Reader's Digest*

Drake, Francis, *Reader's Digest*

Dreier, Alexander, NBC

Driscoll, David E., MBS

Driscoll, Joseph, *New York Herald Tribune*

Driver, Roy A., Australian Dept. of Information

Drummond, J. Roscoe, *Christian Science Monitor*

Duga, Dennis L., *Melbourne Age*

Dunbar, Rudolph, Associated Negro Press

Duncan, Raymond E., *Yank*

Dunn, Francis W., Bell Aircraft

Dunn, William J., CBS

Durdin, F. Tillman, *New York Times*

Durdin, Margaret L., *Time*

Duret, Fernando L., *El Universal*

Durrance, Thomas D., *Time*

Durston, John H., *New York Herald Tribune*

Dynan, Joseph E., AP

Eager, Clifton C., *Australian Press*

Ebener, Charlotte, INS

Ecker, Allan B., *Yank*

Edmonds, James E., WLW

Edmundson, Charles F., *Time*

Edson, Peter, NEA

Edwards, Clyde D., CBS

Edwards, Herman F., *Portland Oregonian*

Edwards, Leonard, Australian Broadcasting Commission

Edwards, Reginald J., Australian Department of Information

Edwards, Webley, CBS

Eitington, Lee, *Time*

Ek, Carl, Passaic *Herald-News*

Ekins, Herbert R., WSYR

Elisofon, Eliot, *Life*

Elliott, John, Australian Broadcasting Commission

Ellison, Earl J., *Look*

Emeny, Stuart,* *London News Chronicle*

Enell, George, American Red Cross

Engelke, Charles B., UP

Epstein, Clifford, *Detroit News*

Erickson, Wendell S., AP

Eunson, Robert C., AP

Evans, Druscilla, *New York Post*

Evans, Edward A., Scripps-Howard

Evans, Joe, *New York Herald Tribune*

Eyerman, J. R., *Life*

Fabinani, Henry, Paramount News

Fagans, Allen T., *Newsweek*

Falvey, William, *New York Mirror*

Faris, E. Barry, INS

Farnsworth, Clyde A., AP

Faron, Ward H., AP

Farr, Walter G., *London Daily Mail*

Fast, Howard, *Esquire-Coroney*

Faust, Frederick,* *Harper's*

Faust, Hal, *Chicago Tribune*

Feder, Sydney A., AP

Feldman, Arthur S., Blue Network

Fendell, Jack D., CBS

Feng, Paul, Central News Agency

Fenger, Austin B., Associated Broadcasters

Fenwick, Robert W., *Denver Post*

Ferber, Edna, NANA

Ferris, Dillon J., *Yank*

Ferris, Jack, *Newsweek*

Fielder, Blaine P., Group 3, Australian Papers

Filan, Frank, AP

Finan, Elizabeth S., *Harper's Bazaar*

Finch, A. Percy, Reuters

Finch, Barbara M., Reuters

Finch, Edward, *Time*

Finnegan, Herbert A., *Boston American*

Fischer, Ernest G., AP

Fisher, Alan, *PM*

Fisher, William, *Time*

Fisk, James B., *National Geographic*

Fitchett, Ian G., *London Daily Express*

Fitzhenry, L. J., *Brisbane Courier Mail*

Fitzpatrick, S. H., Australian Department of Information

Fitzsimmons, Thomas J., AP

Flaherty, Pat, NBC

Flaherty, Vincent X., *Washington Times-Herald*

Flanner, Janet, *New Yorker*

Fleeson, Doris,* *Woman's Home Companion*

Fleischer, Jack,* *Time*

Fleming, Dewey L., *Baltimore Sun*

Fleming, James, CBS

Fleming, Thomas E., *Yank*

Florea, John T., *Life*

Fodor, Marcel W., *Chicago Sun*

Folkard, F. B., Group 3, Australian Papers

Folliard, Edward T., *Washington Post*

Folsom, Charles E., *Boston Post*

Folster, George T., *Chicago Sun*

Fonda, Dow H., AP

Foote, Mark, Booth Newspapers

Forbes, Ernest D., WFBM

Ford, Corey, *Collier's*

Forrest, Wilbur, *New York Herald Tribune*

Forsberg, Franklin S., *Yank*

Fort, Randolph L., AP

Forte, Aldo, UP

Foss, Kendall, *New York Post*

Foster, Cedric, Yankee Network

Foster, John, *Aviation Magazine*

Foster, Wilson K., NBC

Fowle, Farnsworth, CBS

Fowler, Homer Wick, *Dallas Morning News*

Frank, Gerold, Palcor News Agency

Frank, H. H., Overseas News Agency

Frank, June M., *This Month*

Frank, Stanley B., *New York Post*

Frankel, Lazarus, *Billboard*

Frankish, John F., UP

Frano, John J., *Yank*

Fraser, John G., Blue Network

Frawley, Harry J., AP

Frazer, William L., *Yank*

Frazier, Benjamin W., *Yank; Look*

Fredenthal, David,* *Life*

Frederick, Pauline, Western Newspaper Union

Freeman, Beatrice, *Magazine Digest*

Freeman, Edward, *Baltimore News Post*

Freidin, Seymour, *New York Herald Tribune*

Frey, Robert L., UP

Friedman, Seymour T., *Yank*

Frisby, Herbert M., Afro-American Newspapers

Frissell, Toni, *Free Lance*

Froendt, Antonio, Religious News Service

Frutchey, Fred, NBC

Frye, William F., AP

Fulton, William J., *Chicago Tribune*

Gaeth, Arthur, MBS

Gaige, Richard T., *Yank*

Gale, Jack F., UP

Gallagher, James Wesley "Wes,"* AP

Gallico, Paul, *Cosmopolitan*

Gammack, Gordon, *Des Moines Register-Tribune*

Gannett, Lewis, *New York Herald Tribune*

Garland, Robin, *Saturday Evening Post*

Garrison, Omar, Reuters

Gask, Roland, *Newsweek*

Gaskill, Betty, *Liberty*

Gaskill, Gordon, *American*

Gaston, Carl D., War Dept., Bureau of Public Relations

Geiger, Richard, AP

Geis, Bernard J., *Esquire-Coronet*

Gelder, Stuart, London Daily Express

Gellhorn, Martha,* *Collier's*

George, Carl, WGAR

George, Collins, *Pittsburgh Courier*

Gercke, George, *March of Time*

Gercke, William F., Paramount News

Gervasi, Frank H., *Collier's*

Ghali, Paul, *Chicago Daily News*

Ghio, Robert A., *Yank*

Gilman, LaSelle, *Honolulu Advertiser*

Gilman, William, *Baltimore Sun*

Gilmore, Eddy L., AP

Gingrich, Arnold, *Esquire-Coronet*

Gingrich, Helen, *Esquire-Coronet*

Glosker, Anita, NANA

Glynn, Paul T., CBS

Goble, James B., *Yank*

Goldberg, Abraham I., AP

Goldstein, Sam, International News Photos

Goodwin, Joseph C., AP

Gopalan, J., Associated Press of India

Gorrel, Henry T.,* UP

Gorry, Charles P., AP

Goss, Frank B., CBS

Gottfried, Carl M., *Time*

Gottlieb, Sol S., International News Photos

Gould, Beatrice B., *Ladies Home Journal*

Gould, Randall, *Shanghai Evening Post*

Gowran, Clayton, *Chicago Tribune*

Graebner, Walter A., *Time*

Graffis, Herbert, *Chicago Daily News*

Graham, Frederick, *New York Times*

Graham-Barrow, C. R., Reuters

Grandin, Thomas B., Blue Network

Grant, Donald S., *Look*

Grant, Gordon N., *Tampa Tribune*

Grant, Herbert B., *Chicago Times*

Gratke, Charles E., *Christian Science Monitor*

Grauer, Benjamin F., NBC

Graves, Lemuel E., *Christian Science Monitor*; *Norfolk Journal and Guide*

Gray, Peyton, Afro-American Newspapers

Gray, William P., *Time*

Green, Allen, Scripps-Howard

Green, Clinton H., *New York Times*

Green, Janet, *Trans-Radio Press*

Greene, Hamilton, *American Legion Magazine*

Greene, Roger D., AP

Greenhalgh, Robert F., *Yank*

Greenwald, Edwin B., AP

Greenwald, Sanford, *News of the Day*

Greer, Allen J., *Buffalo Evening News*

Gridley, Charles O., *Chicago Sun*

Griffin, Bulkley, *Hartford Times*

Griffin, Henry, AP

Griffin, John, AP

Grigg, Joseph, UP

Grim, George H., *Minneapolis Star Journal*

Grossi, Daniel, AP

Groth, John A., *Parade*

Grover, Allen, *Time*

Grover, James A., *Time*

Grover, John, AP

Grover, Preston, AP

Grueson, Sidney, *New York Times*

Grumich, Charles A., AP

Grupp, George, *Boating*

Guard, Harold, UP

Gudebrod, Morton P., AP

Gunderson, Arthur R., UP

Gunn, Stanley E., *Fort Worth Star Telegram*

Gunnison, Royal A., *Collier's*

Gunther, John, NANA

Guptill, Charles H., AP

Guth, Oscar A., UP

Gwinn, John W., AP

Haacker, Charles, Acme Newspictures

Haaker, Edwin, NBC

Haas, Saul, *Portland Oregonian*

Hackler, Victor, AP

Haden, Allen, *Chicago Daily News*

Haeger, Robert A., UP

Hager, Alice R., *Skyways*

Hahn, Willard C., *St. Louis Post-Dispatch*

Hailey, Foster B., *New York Times*

Hairland, Patrick, *London News Chronicle*

Hales, Samuel D., UP

Haley, Pope A., AP

Hall, Charles H., *Springfield Republican*

Hall, Clarence, *Link & Chaplain Magazine*

Hall, Flem R., *Fort Worth Star-Telegram*

Halton, Matthew, *Toronto Star*

Hamburger, Edith I., *Cleveland Press*

Hamburger, Philip P., *New Yorker*

Hamm, Clarence L., AP

Hammond, Gilbert T., *Boston Herald-Traveller*

Hampson, Frederick E., AP

Handleman, Howard M., INS

Handler, Myer, UP

Hanley, Richard S., *Yank*

Hansen, Robert H., *Look*

Hanson, Ernest, *Saturday Evening Post*

Hardesty, Harriet C., UP

Hardy, Eugene J., Chilton Company

Hargest, William J., *American Machinist*

Hargrove, Charles R., *Wall Street Journal*

Harkness, Richard L., NBC

Harkrader, Charleton, *Newsweek*

Harmatz, Herbert J., Reuters

Harmon, Dudley Anne,* UP

Harper, Robert S., *Ohio State Journal*

Harrington, Oliver W., *Pittsburgh Courier*

Harris, Harry L., AP

Harris, Reginald S., *Australian Consolidated Press*

Harris, Richard, UP

Harrison, A. Paul, UP

Harrison, Joseph G., *Christian Science Monitor*

Harrison, Paul L., NEA

Harrity, Richard, *Yank*

Harsch, Joseph C.,* *Christian Science Monitor*

Hartrich, Eugene, *Chicago Sun*

Hartt, Julian, INS

Hartzog, Hazel, UP

Hatch, Willard A., Acme Newspictures

Haugland, Vernon A., AP

Hauser, Ernest O., *Saturday Evening Post*

Haverstick, John M., *Yank*

Hawkes, George H., Group 4, Australian Papers

Hawkins, Eric E., *New York Herald Tribune*

Hawkins, Henry E., Reuters

Hawkins, Lewis, AP

Hawkslet, G.G.M., Group 4, Australian Papers

Haworth, William F., *Yank*

Hay, John, *Yank*

Haynes, Weston, American Red Cross

Healy, Thomas, *New York Post*

Hearst, Dorris L., *New York Journal American*

Hearst, Joseph, *Chicago Tribune*

Hearst, William Randolph,* INS

Heath, S. Burton, NEA

Heinz, Wilfred C., *New York Sun*

Heinzerling, Lynn L., AP

Heisler, Philip S., *Baltimore Sun*

Hellinger, Mark J., Hearst Newspapers

Hemery, Clement, INS

Hemingway, Ernest,* *Collier's*

Henderson, Ralph E., *Reader's Digest*

Henle, Raymond Z., *Pittsburgh Post Gazette*

Henry, Henry T., AP

Henry, James E., Reuters

Henry, John R., INS

Henry, Thomas R., *Washington Star*

Henry, William M., *Los Angeles Times*

Henshaw, Fred W., *United States News*

Hensley, Malcolm S., UP

Herald, George W., INS

Heran, Arthur F., INS

Hercher, Wilmot W., AP

Herfort, Norman V., *Pix Pictorial*

Herlihy, Martin, Reuters

Hermann, Leopold, AP

Hersey, John,* *Time*

Hershey, Burnet, *Liberty*

Hewlett, Frank, UP

Hicks, George, Blue Network

Hiett, Helen,* Religious News Service

Higginbotham, W. R., UP

Higgins, Marguerite,* *New York Herald Tribune*

High, Stanley, *Reader's Digest*

Hightower, John M., AP

Hill, Carol, *Collier's; Redbook*

Hill, Ernie, *Miami Herald*

Hill, Gladwin A., *New York Times*

Hill, Max, NBC

Hill, Russell,* *New York Herald Tribune*

Hills, Lee O., *Miami Herald*

Himmelsbach, Gerard R., INS

Hinde, John, Australian Broadcasting Commission

Hindson, Curtis, Reuters

Hine, Alfred B., *Yank*

Hipple, William, *Newsweek*

Hirsch, Joseph, Abbott Laboratories

Hlavack, John M., UP

Hoffman, Bernard, *Time*

Holburn, James, *London Times*

Holland, Gordon P., Group 5, Australian Papers

Hollenbeck, Don, NBC

Holles, Everett R., CBS

Hollingworth, Claire,* *Time*

Holt, Carlyle H., *Boston Globe*

Hooley, John A., NBC, CBS, MBS, ABC

Horan, James D., G. P. Putnam's Sons

Hornaday, Mary, *Christian Science Monitor*

Horne, George F., *New York Times*

Horner, Durbin L., *Yank*

Hoskins, Francis T., MBS

Hostick, King V., *Chicago Sun*

Hottelet, Richard, CBS

Houle, Harry J., American Red Cross

Hovey, Graham,* AP

Howard, Ralph, NBC

Howard, Rosemary, *Newsweek*

Howe, Quincy, CBS

Howland, William S., Simon & Schuster

Hoyt, Palmer, UP

Hubbard, Lucien, Simon & Schuster

Hughes, John B., the *Oregonian*

Huie, William B., *American Mercury*

Hull, Harwood, NBC

Hull, Peggy,* *Cleveland Plain Dealer*

Hulls, Alan, Group 2, Australian Papers

Hume, Rita, INS

Humphreys, William J., *New York Herald Tribune*

Hunt, Frazier "Spike,"* *Reader's Digest*

Hunt, John R., War Dept., Special Services

Hunter, Kent, INS

Hurd, Peter, *Time*

Hurd, Volney, *Christian Science Monitor*

Hurwitz, Hyman, *Boston Globe*

Huss, Pierre, INS

Hutch, Donald E., AP

Hutcheson, James M., AP

Hutton, Geoffrey, *Melbourne Argus*

Ichac, Pierre, *Vainere*

Ingraham, Herbert, *Time*

Irvin, George B., AP

Irwin, Theodore, *Look*

Isaacs, Harold, *Newsweek*

Isley, Charles C., Stauffer Publishing Company

Israels, Josef II, *This Week*

Jackson, William A., International News Photos

Jacobs, Ann L., *Young America*

Jacoby, Annalee, *Time*

Jacoby, Melville,* *Time*

Jackett, S. T., Reuters

Jameson, Henry B., AP

Jandoli, Jerome B., INS

Janssen, Guthrie E., NBC

Jarrell, John W., INS

Jencks, Hugh I., UP

Jenkins, Burris A., *New York Journal American*

John, Elizabeth B., *Cleveland News*

Johnson, Albin E., INS

Johnson, Carol L., NEA

Johnson, Edd,* *Chicago Sun*

Johnson, Hugo C., Paramount News

Johnson, John R., *National Geographic*

Johnson, Mac R., *New York Herald Tribune*

Johnson, Malcolm, *New York Sun*

Johnson, Vincent, *Pittsburgh Post Gazette*

Johnson, William M., Afro-American Newspapers

Johnson, William W., *Time*

Johnston, George H., Group 1, Australian Papers

Johnston, Paul A., *Yank*

Johnston, Richard J., *New York Times*

Jones, Alexander, *Washington Post*

Jones, Edgar L., *Atlantic Monthly*

Jones, Edward F., *Time*

Jones, Edward V., AP

Jones, George, *New York Times*

Jones, George E., UP

Jones, Joe, *U.S. Engineers*

Jones, John E., *Pittsburgh Post Gazette*

Jones, Joseph M., *Time*

Jones, Victor O., *Boston Globe*

Jones, William W., International News Photos

Jordan, John Q., *Norfolk Journal & Guide*

Jordan, Lewis E., *Yank*

Jordan, Max, NBC

Jurgens, Victor J., *March of Time*

Kadish, Reuben, *Life*

Kadison, William, American Red Cross

Kaltenborn, Hans V.,* NBC

Kammerman, Eugene L., Pics, Inc.

Kantor, MacKinlay, *Enquire*

Karant, Max, *Flying*

Kasischke, Richard, AP

Kaufman, Isador, *Brooklyn Eagle*

Kay, Leon L., UP

Keene, K. C., Group 3, Australian Papers

Kehoe, Thomas, *VFW Magazine*

Keighley, Larry, *Saturday Evening Post*

Kelley, Frank R., *New York Herald Tribune*

Kelley, Hubert W., *American Magazine*

Kelly, George M., AP

Kelly, Phillip R., *Time*

Kelty, William R., *NBC*

Kempner, Mary Jane, *Condé-Nast*

Kendrick, Alexander, *Philadelphia Inquirer*

Kennedy, Edward,* AP

Kennedy, Robert E., *Chicago Times*

Kennet, Warren H., *Newark Evening News*

Kenny, Reginald, Acme Newspictures

Kent, Carleton V., *Chicago Times*

Kent, George, *Reader's Digest*

Kern, Harry F., *Newsweek*

Kessell, Dmitri,* *Life*

Keys, Henry, *London Daily Express*

Kiek, Robert H., Netherlands Press Agency

Kilgallin, James Lawrence,* INS

Kimball, Neil W., *Foreign Service*

Kinch, Samuel, *Fort Worth Star Telegram*

King, Ernest H., AP

King, Herbert G., UP

King, James F., AP

King, William B., AP

Kintzley, Russell, *New Orleans-Times Picayune*

Kirkland, Wallace W., *Life*

Kirkpatrick, Helen,* *Chicago Daily News*

Klein, Julius, *Yank*

Klerr, Edward, INS

Kluckhohn, Frank,* *New York Times*

Knauth, Percival, *Time*

Knickerbocker, Agnes G., *Nashville Tennesseean*

Knickerbocker, Herbert Renfre,* *Chicago Sun*

Knight, Clayton, AP

Knopf, Hans, *Collier's*

Kolodin, Irving, *AAF*

Konzelman, Frederic, *Yank*

Kopf, Dorothy Thompson, Bell Syndicate

Kopf, Maximillian, *Ladies Home Journal*

Korman, Seymour M., *Chicago Tribune*

Kornfeld, Alfred H., *Time*

Kreutzberg, Edgar C., Penton Publishing Co.

Krieg, Frederick P., AP

Krueger, Jess, *Chicago Herald-American*

Krygier, Henry R., Polish News Agency

Kuh, Frederick, *Chicago Sun*

Kuhn, Irene, NBC

Kulick, Harold W., *Popular Science*

Labaudt, Lucien A., *Life*

Labez, Ricardo, *Honolulu Star-Bulletin*

LaFarge, Christopher G., *Harper's*

Laird, Stephen, *Time*

Lait, George, INS

Laitin, Joseph, *Time*

Lake, Austen R., *Boston American*

Lamport, Sara M., *New York Post*

Lancaster, Herbert, *March of Time*

Landaum, Ida B., Overseas News Agency

Landry, Robert, *Life*

Landsberg, Morris, AP

Lane, Charles G., AP

Lang, Daniel, *New Yorker*

Lang, Will, *Time*

Laning, Edward, *Life*

Lanius, Charles, Trans-Radio Press

Lardner, John, NANA

Lauterbach, Richard E., *Time*

Lavelle, Elise, National Catholic News Service

Lawrence, William H.,* *New York Times*

Lawton, Fleetwood, NBC

Lea, Tom,* *Time*

Leach, Paul R., *Chicago Daily News*

Leader, Anton, CBS

Lear, John W., *Saturday Evening Post*

Learned, Albe L., American Red Cross

Leavell, David, *Fort Worth Press*

Leavelle, Richard C., *Chicago Tribune*

Lecardeur, Maurice, Acme Newspictures

Lecoutre, Martha, *Tri-Color*

Lee, Clark,* INS

Lee, J. Edgerton, INS

Lee, Paul K., AP

Legg, Frank G., Australian Broadcasting Commission

Leggett, Dudley, Australian Broadcasting Commission

Lehrman, Harold A., *Argosy*

Leimert, Walter H., CBS

Lennard, Wallace W., Australian Broadcasting Commission

Leonard, John, Reuters

Leonard, Reginald B., Group 3, Australian Papers

Lerner, Max, *PH*

Lesever, Lawrence Edward, CBS News

Levin, Meyer, Overseas News Agency

Lewis, Boyd, NEA

Lewis, Ervin G., WLS

Lewis, Flora, AP

Lewis, Fulton, Jr., MBS

Lewis, Harley C., Acme Newspictures

Lewis, Morris, War Dept., Special Services

Lewis, Robert E., American Red Cross

Leyson, Burr W., *Skyways*

Lieb, Jack, *News of the Day*

Lieberman, Henry, *New York Times*

Liebling, Abbott Joseph "A. J.,"* *New Yorker*

Limpus, Lowell, *New York Daily News*

Lindley, Ernest K., *Newsweek*

Lindsley, James S., AP

Lippmann, Walter, *New York Herald Tribune*

Littell, Robert, *Reader's Digest*

Litz, Leo M., *Indianapolis News*

Lloyd, Rhona, *Philadelphia Evening News*

Lochner, Louis Paul,* AP

Lochridge, Mary P., *Women's Home Companion*

Lockett, Edward B., *Time*

Loeb, Charles H., Negro Newspaper Publishing Association

Loehwing, David A., UP

Logan, Walter F., UP

Long, James M., AP

Longmire, Carey, *New York Post*

Lopez, Andrew, Acme Newspictures

Lopez, Carlos F., *Life*

Loring, Paul S., *Providence Journal*

Loughlin, John, Group 1, Australian Papers

Loundagin, Nicholas F., *Newsweek*

Loveland, Reelif, *Cleveland Plain Dealer*

Lower, Elmer, *Life*

Lowry, Cynthia, AP

Lubell, Samuel, *Saturday Evening Post*

Lucas, Lenore V., Overseas News Agency

Lucas, W. E., *London Daily Express*

Luce, Henry R., *Time*

Luter, George W., *Hawaii Magazine*

Luter, John T., *Time*

MaCauley, Thurston B., INS

MacBain, Alastair, *Collier's*

MacCartney, Robert R., Group 1, Australian Papers

MacCormac, Isabel, *New York Times*

MacCormac, John P., *New York Times*

MacDonald, Grant G., AP

MacDonald, James, *New York Times*

MacKenzie, DeWitt, AP

MacKenzie, Donald, *New York Daily News*

MacKenzie, Fred M., *Buffalo Evening News*

MacLean, James A., UP

MacVeane, John, NBC

Maddox, William, J., *Worked Petroleum*

Madru, Gaston, *News of the Day*

Mahon, Jack, MBS

Maisel, Albert Q., *Cosmopolitan*

Maitland, Patrick, *London News Chronicle*

Mangan, J. J. Sherry, *Time*

Mann, Arthur, MBS

Mann, Erika, *Liberty*

Manning, Bruce, War Dept., Special Services

Manning, Paul, MBS

Marden, Luis, *National Geographic*

Margulies, Leo, *Standard*

Marien, William, *Sydney Morning Herald*

Markey, Lawrence M., *Liberty*

Marsh, Reginald, *Life*

Marshall, George, *Collier's*

Marshall, James, *Collier's*

Marshall, Joseph, *Saturday Evening Post*

Martellierre, Paul, *March of Time*

Martin, Cecelia (Jackie), *Ladies Home Journal*

Martin, David S., *U.S. Engineers*

Martin, Fletcher, *Life*

Martin, Fletcher P., Negro Newspaper Publishing Association

Martin, Frank L., AP

Martin, Robert P., UP

Martin, Robert W., *Time*

Martinez, Albert W., Reuters

Mason, Frank E., NANA

Massell, Robert, Blue Network

Massock, Richard G., AP

Mathews, Ronald, *London Daily Herald*

Mathews, William R., *Arizona Daily Star*

Matthews, Herbert Lionel,* *New York Times*

Matthews, Thomas S., *Time*

May, Ernest R., *Trans-Radio Press*

May, Foster, *WOW*

McAvoy, Thomas D., *Life*

McBride, William M., *Herald News*

McBrine, Robert J., *Yank*

McCabe, Charles R., *Time*

McCabe, Gibson, *Newsweek*

McCaleb, Kenneth, INS

McCall, Frances, NBC

McCallum, Walter R., *Washington Evening Star*

McCardell, Lee A., *Baltimore Sun*

McCardle, Carl W., *Philadelphia Bulletin*

McCarthy, Francis, UP

McCarthy, Ira B., *Kansas City Star*

McCarthy, Joseph W., *Yank*

McClure, William K., Pathé News

McConaughy, John, *Ohio State Journal*

McConnell, Raymond, *Nebraska State Journal*

McConnell, Roscoe, *KOMO*

McCormick, Anne O'Hare, *New York Times*

McCormick, Robert K., NBC

McDaniel, Yates, AP

McDermott, John B., UP

McDermott, William F., *Cleveland Plain Dealer*

McDonald, John F., *London Daily Mail*

McDowell, Jack S., INS

McEvoy, Joseph P., *Reader's Digest*

McFadden, Louis, *Yank*

McGee, Mary V. P., *Toronto Globe & Mail*

McGeorge, John R., *Toledo Blade*

McGill, Ralph, *Atlanta Constitution*

McGlincy, James, UP

McGovern, Raymond T., *Yank*

McGowan, Gault,* *New York Sun*

McGraffin, William, *Chicago Daily News*

McGraw, Alvin, *Yank*

McGurn, William Barrett,* *Yank*

McIlhenny, Eleanor, *Pan-American*

McKnight, Colbert A., AP

McKnight, John P., AP

McLaughlin, Kathleen, *New York Times*

McMahon, Henry O., *Washington Times-Herald*

McManus, James L., *Yank*

McManus, Robert, *Farm Journal*

McMillen, Richard P., UP

McMurtry, Charles H., AP

McNeil, Marshall, *Scripps-Howard*

McNulty, Henry P., UP

McQuaid, Bernard J., *Chicago Daily News*

McWilliams, George, INS

Mechau, Frank A., *Life*

Mecklin, John M., *Chicago Sun*

Meier, G. Lawrence, MBS

Mejat, Francois, Pathé News

Mejat, Raymond, Pathé News

Melendez, Dorothy, *Star Herald*

Meltzer, Theodore, INS

Meyer, Ben F., AP

Meyer, Jane, *Chicago Herald American*

Meyer, Robert L., UP

Meyers, Debs, *Yank*

Meyers, George N., *Yank*

Michaelis, Ralph, *Air News*

Michie, Alan, *Reader's Digest*

Middleton, Drew,* *New York Times*

Miles, Frank F., *American Legion*

Miller, Graham, *New York Daily News*

Miller, Lee,* Scripps-Howard

Miller, Merle D., *Yank*

Miller, Robert C.,* UP

Miller, William J., *Cleveland Press*

Miller, William M., *Look*

Mills, Raymond, International News Photos

Miner, Charles S., *New York Post*

Mintzer, Leonidias, *California State Guard*

Misabe, C. R., UP

Mishael, Herbert, *Melbourne Age*

Mitchell, Bruce H., *Life*

Moats, Alice L. B., *Collier's*

Moe, M. Lorimer, *Time*

Moler, Murray, UP

Montrose, Sherman, Acme Newspictures

Moody, Blair, *Detroit Free Press*

Moorad, George L., CBS

Moore, Charles M., *London Daily Telegraph*

Moore, Pugh, AP

Moore, Robert E. L., *Trans-Radio Press*

Moore, William T., *Chicago Tribune*

Moosa, Spencer, AP

Moran, Maurice, AP

Morde, Theodore A., *Reader's Digest*

Morehouse, Ward, *New York Sun*

Morgan, Edward P., *Chicago Daily News*

Morgan, Ralph F., *AAF*

Morgan, Wilfred R., War Dept., Bureau of Public Relations

Morin, Relman "Pat,"* AP

Moroso, John A., AP

Morphopoulos, Panos, *Newsweek*

Morris, Frank D., *Collier's*

Morris, Joe Alex, *Collier's*

Morris, John G., *Life*

Morris, John R., UP

Morrison, Chester,* NBC

Morriss, Mack* *Yank*

Morrow, Thomas, *Chicago Tribune*

Morse, Ralph, *Life*

Morton, Joseph, AP

Morton, Ralph S., AP

Most, Mel, AP

Mowrer, Edgar Ansel,* *Chicago Daily News*

Mowrer, Paul Scott,* *New York Post*

Mowrer, Richard, *Chicago Daily News*

Muchmore, Gareth B., AP

Mueller, Merrill, NBC

Mueller, William A., *Chicago Times*

Muir, John, Whaley-Eaton Service

Muir, Malcolm, UP

Muller, Edwin, *Reader's Digest*

Muller, Mary T., *Reader's Digest*

Munn, Bruce, UP

Murdock, Barbara, *Philadelphia Bulletin*

Murphy, Charles J., *Fortune*

Murphy, William, *Philadelphia Inquirer*

Murray, James E., UP

Murray, William, *Pathé News*

Murray, William R., *Yank*

Murrow, Edward (Egbert) Roscoe,* CBS

Musel, Robert, UP

Muth, Russell A., Fox Movietone News

Muto, Frank, War Dept., Bureau of Public Relations

Mydans, Carl,* *Life*

Mydans, Shelley,* *Life*

Naintre, Yves, Paramount News

Navarro, Robert, *March of Time*

Neill, Franklin F., INS

Nesensohn, Carl D., Acme Newspictures

Nevin, Jack E., *San Francisco Call Bulletin*

Newhall, Scott, *San Francisco Chronicle*

Newman, Albert, *Newsweek*

Newman, Larry, INS

Newton, William, Scripps-Howard

Nichols, David M., *Chicago Daily News*

Nixon, Robert G., INS

Noderer, Elvedore R., *Chicago Tribune*

Noel, Frank E. "Pappy,"* AP

Noli, Louis, AP

Norall, Frank V., *CIAA*

Nordness, Nedville, AP

Norgaard, Noland, AP

Norris, Frank C., *Time*

Norton, Howard M., *Baltimore Sun*

Norton, Taylor E., *Time*

Norwood, William R., *Christian Science Monitor*

Noyes, Newbold, *Washington Evening Star*

Nurenberger, Meyer J., *Jewish Morning Journal*

Nutter, Charles P., AP

O'Beirne, D. P., Reuters

O'Brien, Frank, AP

O'Brien, Mary H., Fawcett Publications

O'Connell, John, *Bangor Daily News*

O'Connell, John P., *New York Daily News*

O'Conner, James A., Group 1, Australian Papers

O'Connor, Eugene, American Red Cross

O'Donnell, James, *Newsweek*

Oechsner, Frederick, UP

Oeth, Alfred J., Paramount News

Offner, Philippa G., *Life*

O'Flaherty, Hal, *Chicago Daily News*

Oggel, Dean M., *Yank*

O'Keefe, Richard J., *Philadelphia Inquirer*

O'Kelly, Raymond, Reuters

O'Laughlin, John C., *Army & Navy Journal*

Olde, George, Springfield Newspapers

Oliphant, Homer N., *Yank*

Oliver, David R., Pathé News

Oliver, Frank, Reuters

Olsen, Alphonsus G., *Melbourne Age-Sydney Sun*

Olsen, R., *Sydney Sun*

Olson, Sidney, *Time*

Omelian, L. J., WLEU

O'Neill, James P., *Yank*

Opper, Frederick B., Blue Network

O'Quinn, Judson C., AP

O'Regan, Richard A., AP

O'Reilly, John "Tex,"* *New York Herald Tribune*

O'Reilly, Martin L., Pathé News

Orro, David H., *Chicago Defender*

Osbiston, Francis, Group 4, Australian Papers

Osborne, John F., *Time*

O'Sullivan, J. Reilly, AP

Oswald, George, Universal Newsreel

Ottley, Roi V., *PM*

Ottoway, N., Group 3, Australian Papers

Oursler, William C., Fawcett Publications

Pacine, H. J., Group 2, Australian Papers

Packard, Eleanor,* UP

Packard, Nathaniel, UP

Packard, Reynolds,* UP

Paine, Ralph D., *Fortune*

Painton, Frederick C., *Reader's Digest*

Palmer, Frederick, NANA

Palmer, George J., AP

Palmer, Gretta Clark, *Liberty*

Palmer, Kyle, *Los Angeles Times*

Palmer, Mary B., *Newsweek*

Palyi, Melchoir, Booth Newspapers

Parier, Damien, Paramount News

Paris, Peter M., *Yank*

Parker, Fred, International News Photos

Parker, Jack D., WJIM

Parker, Pegge, *American Weekly*

Parker, Robert, WLW

Parr, William G., NBC

Parris, John A., AP

Parrott, L., *New York Times*

Parsons, Geoffrey, *New York Herald Tribune*

Pasley, Fred, *New York Daily News*

Patterson, Harry E., *Daily Oklahoman*

Paul, Herbert, Cowles Papers

Paul, Raymond A., Australian Broadcasting Commission

Paul, Richard H., *Yank*

Pawlak, Mason H., *Yank*

Peague, Harry H., American Red Cross

Pearson, Leon M., INS

Pepperburg, Ray L., *American Illustrator*

Percival, Jack, Group 5, Australian Papers

Perkins, Alice K., Fairchild Publications

Perlin, Bernard,* *Life*

Perlman, David A., *New York Herald Tribune*

Perry, George S., *Saturday Evening Post*

Perryman, Charles R., *News of the Day*

Person, Kriston, *Free Norwegian Press*

Peterman, Ivan H., *Philadelphia Inquirer*

Peters, Harold A., Blue Network

Peters, Walter F., *Yank*

Peterson, Elmer, NBC

Peterson, Frederick, Group 3, Australian Papers

Peterson, George L., *Minneapolis Star-Journal*

Peterson, Ralph E., NBC

Pflaum, Irving, *Chicago Times*

Phelps, Winston, *Providence Journal*

Phillips, Cecil A. C., *New York Times*

Phillips, John, *Time*

Phillips, Martha E., Afro-American Newspapers

Phillips, William L., AP

Phipps, William E., AP

Pickens, William, *Trans-Radio Press*

Pignault, Charles, *TAM*

Pimper, John A., *Yank*

Pinkley, Virgil M., UP

Pinney, Roy, *Liberty*

Pitkin, Dwight L., AP

Pitman, Frank W., AP

Plachy, Frank, *New York Journal of Commerce*

Plambeck, Herbert, *WOW*

Platt, Warren C., *National Petroleum News*

Pleissner, Ogden M., *Life*

Polier, Dan A., *Yank*

Poling, Daniel, *Philadelphia Record*

Polk, Catherine, *Los Angeles News*

Polk, George,* *Los Angeles News*

Poor, Henry V., *U.S. Engineers*

Poor, Peggy, *New York Post*

Poorbaugh, Earl R., INS

Pope, James S., *Louisville Courier-Journal*

Porter, K. R., Ziff-Davis Publishing Company

Porter, Leroy P., NBC

Potter, Henry O., Group 3, Australian Papers

Potter, John P., *Baltimore Sun*

Poulos, Constantine, Overseas News Agency

Powell, Hickman, *Popular Science*

Powers, John H., *Town & Country*

Pratt, Fletcher, *Harper's*

Pratt, Melbourne, Group 5, Australian Papers

Preston, Hartwell L., *Life*

Prevost, Clifford A., *Detroit Free Press*

Prewett, Virginia, *Chicago Sun*

Pribichevich, Stoyan, *Time*

Price, Wesley, *Saturday Evening Post*

Priestly, Thomas A., Universal Newsreel

Primm, Arthur, MBS

Prince, E., International News Photos

Pringle, Helena, *Women's Home Companion*

Pringle, Nelson G., CBS

Prist, Frank, Acme Newspictures

Pryer, Donald J., CBS

Purcell, John F., *Life*

Purdue, Marcus, AP

Purtell, Joseph P., *Time*

Putnam, Eva B., *Trans-Radio Press*

Pyle, Ernest "Ernie,"* Scripps-Howard

Pyle, Howard, NBC

Pyle, John, KTAR

Queen, Harold, UP

Quigg, Horace D., UP

Quigley, Karl, INS

Quinn, Stanley, MBS

Rae, William B., *New York Times*

Rae, William E., *Liberty*

Ragsdale, Warner R., *United States News*

Ragsdale, Wilmott, *Time*

Raleigh, John M., CBS

Ramage, Frederick J., Keystone-International

Ramsay, Paul, *Philadelphia Inquirer*

Ranft, Joseph, UP

Raper, Stoddard, *Columbus Dispatch*

Rappoport, Joan (Ann Hunter), WAIT

Raridan, Leo, INS

Ravenholt, Albert, UP

Rawlings, Charles A., *Saturday Evening Post*

Ray, Charles C., War Dept., Bureau of Public Relations

Raymond, Allen, *New York Herald Tribune*

Rayner, Pendil, Group 3, Australian Papers

Rea, Gene, Il Progresso

Reading, Geoffrey, *Sydney Mirror*

Rebiere, Marcel H., *Time*

Redger, George, *Time*

Redmond, Dick A., WHP

Reed, Philip G., INS

Reed, William K., *Yank*

Reichmann, John A., UP

Reinhart, Hans, International News Photos

Reiter, John H., *Philadelphia Record*

Reston, Sarah J., *New York Times*

Reuben, Robert E., Reuters

Reusswig, Martha S., *Collier's*

Reusswig, William, King Features

Reynolds, Emil G., Acme Newspictures

Reynolds, Quentin,* *Collier's*

Rhodenbaugh, Harold, *Look*

Rice, Jack, AP

Rich, Stanley, UP

Richards, Guy, *New York Daily News*

Richards, Robert W., UP

Richardson, David,* *Yank*

Richardson, Harold W., *Engineering News Record*

Richardson, Stanley P., NBC

Richardson, William H., *Yank*

Rickman, Theodore Z., *News of the Day*

Ridder, Walter, *St. Paul Dispatch*

Riemer, Harry, *Daily Trade Record*

Riess, Curt, *Trans-Radio Press*

Riggs, Robert L., *Louisville Courier Journal*

Roark, Eldon E., Scripps-Howard

Robb, Inez, INS

Robbins, Charles H., *American Weekly*

Roberts, Cletus, Blue Network

Roberts, David, *Cincinnati Inquirer*

Roberts, Edward V., UP

Roberts, Harrison B., Associated Press Photos

Roberts, Kenneth, Group 4, Australian Papers

Robertson, Ben, *New York Herald Tribune*

Robertson, Frank, INS

Robertson, Ruth A., Press Syndicate

Robinson, Iona, *Saturday Review of Literature*

Robinson, Pat, INS

Robinson, William E., *New York Herald Tribune*

Robson, William, CBS

Rocho, Ethel P., *Collier's*

Rollins, Byron H., AP

Rolo, Charles J., *Atlantic Monthly*

Roos, Leonard H., Pathé News

Root, Gordon, Southam Newspapers (Canada)

Roper, James E., UP

Rosen, Fred, *Yank*

Rosenthal, Joe,* AP

Ross, Nancy W., *free lance*

Rouzeau, Edgar T., *Pittsburgh Courier*

Rowe, William L., *Pittsburgh Courier*

Rucker, Joseph T., Paramount News

Rue, Larry,* *Chicago Tribune*

Ruge, John A., *Yank*

Rundle, Walter G., UP

Russell, E. A., UP

Russell, Edmund ''Ned'' Allen,* *New York Herald Tribune*

Russell, Frank (Ted Malone), Blue Network

Russell, H. T., UP

Ryan, Cornelius John,* *London Daily Telegraph*

Ryan, Robert G., *Yank*

Sabin, Jesse, *News of the Day*

Saerchinger, Caesar, *American Historical*

Salisbury, Harrison Evans,* UP

Sample, Paul, *Time*

Sanders, Branan I., AP

Sann, Paul, *New York Post*

Santin, Miguel A., *El Mundo*

Sargint, H. J., NANA

Sasso, Arthur H., International News Photos

Satonomy, Edward, UP

Sayre, Joel Grover,* *New Yorker*

Schalben, Orville, *Milwaukee Journal*

Schedler, Dean, AP

Scheer, Sam, International News Photos

Scherman, David, *Life*

Scherschel, Frank, *Life*

Schmidt, Dana A., UP

Schneider, Lieutenant Philip, *Leatherneck*

Schuck, Hugh, *New York Daily News*

Schulman, Sammy, International News Photos

Schwartz, Robert, *Yank*

Scott, Burgess H., *Yank*

Scott, David W., Pathé News

Scott, John, *Time*

Seacrest, Joseph W., *Nebraska State Journal*

Seawood, Charles P., Acme Newspictures

Sebring, Lewis, *New York Herald Tribune*

Sedgwick, Alexander Cameron "A. C.,"* *New York Times*

Selle, Earl A., *Honolulu Advertiser*

Senick, Langdon, Fox Movietone News

Sevareid, Eric,* CBS

Severyns, Marjorie, *Time*

Shadel, W. F., *Rifleman & Infantry Journal*

Shafer, Thomas, Acme Newspictures

Shapiro, Henry, UP

Shapiro, Lionel S., NANA

Shaplen, Robert M.,* *Newsweek*

Sharp, Roland H., *Christian Science Monitor*

Shaw, Albert E., *Westminster Press*

Shaw, Charles, CBS

Shaw, Jack, MBS

Shaw, John W., American Red Cross

Shaw, William, *March of Time*

Shaw, William D., *Yank*

Shayon, Robert, CBS

Sheahan, Joseph G., *Chicago Tribune*

Shean, Vincent, *Newsweek*

Sheean, James Vincent,* *Redbook*

Sheets, Millard O., *Life*

Shehan, Thomas F., *Yank*

Shelley, John D., WHO

Shenkel, William, *Newsweek*

Shepley, James R., *Time*

Shere, Samuel, *Life*

Sheridan, Martin, *Boston Globe*

Sherman, Dean F., *Alaska Life*

Sherman, Eugene, *Los Angeles Times*

Sherrod, Robert,* *Time*

Shippen, William H., *Washington Evening Star*

Shirer, William Lawrence,* CBS

Shoemaker, Leslie, UP

Shoenbrun, David, Overseas News Agency

Shoop, Duke, *Kansas City Star*

Short, Gordon H., Australian Dept. of Information

Showers, Paul, *Yank*

Shrout, William C., *Life*

Shultz, Sigrid, *Chicago Tribune*

Siegman, Harold, Acme Newspictures

Siler, Bert, NBC

Silk, A., Australian Dept. of Information

Silk, Arthur G., *Time*

Silk, George, *Life*

Simmonds, Charles J., Group 3, Australian Papers

Simmons, Walter,* *Chicago Tribune*

Simms, William P., Scripps-Howard

Simpson, Kirke L., AP

Sinclair, Frederic M., *Buffalo Evening News*

Singer, Jack,* INS

Singleton, Alexander, AUP

Sions, Harry A., *Yank*

Skadding, George R., *Life*

Skariatina, Irina, *New York Times*

Slocum, William, CBS

Slosberg, Marvin, NBC

Small, Alex, *Chicago Tribune*

Small, W. C., *Saturday Evening Post*

Smalley, Alton D., *St. Paul Dispatch-Pioneer*

Smith, A. Merriman, UP

Smith, Ardis, Pathé News

Smith, Beverly, *Collier's*

Smith, Eugene, *Life*

Smith, Frank P., *Chicago Times*

Smith, Harold P., *Chicago Tribune*

Smith, Howard Kingsbury,* CBS

Smith, Irving I., *Universal Newsreel*

Smith, Jack, AP

Smith, John C., *New York Herald Tribune*

Smith, Joseph K., INS

Smith, Lawrence, Abbott Laboratories

Smith, William E., Ziff-Davis

Smyth, James F., *Truth & Daily Mirror*

Snow, Edgar,* *Saturday Evening Post*

Soderholm, Wallace, *Buffalo Evening News*

Solon, Samuel L., *New Leader*

Sommers, Martin, *Saturday Evening Post*

Sondern, Frederick E., *Reader's Digest*

Soong, Norman, Central News Agency

Sosin, Milton R., *Miami Daily News*

Souder, Edmund L., Blue Network

Southerland, Henry J., American Red Cross

Southwell-Keely, Terence, Group 5, Australian Papers

Spencer, Murlin, AP

Spilman, Charles, *Providence Journal*

Stanfield, Lawrence, *Los Angeles Times*

Stanford, Graham, *London Daily Mail*

Stanford, Theodore, *Pittsburgh Courier*

Starr, Donald, *Chicago Tribune*

Stead, Ronald, *Christian Science Monitor*

Stebbins, Robert G., *Contractor & Engineer*

Steel, Johannes, WHN

Steele, Archibald T.,* *Chicago Daily News*

Steele, Earl B., UP

Stein, Gunther, *Christian Science Monitor*

Steinbeck, John Ernest, Jr.,* *New York Herald Tribune*

Steinkopf, Alvin, AP

Stephenson, Malcolm L., AP

Stern, Michael, Fawcett Publications

Stevens, Edmund,* *Christian Science Monitor*

Stevenson, Kenneth, *Yank*

Stewart, Benjamin A., *National Geographic*

Stewart, Ollie, Afro-American Newspapers

Stewart, William, *Canadian Press*

Stirling, Monica, *Atlantic Monthly*

Stoecker, Leo J., Acme Newspictures

Stokes, Richard L., *St. Louis Post-Dispatch*

Stone, I. F., *PM*

Stone, John L., WRVA

Stonehouse, Kenneth, Reuters

Stonehouse, Merlin, *Trans-Radio Press*

Stoneman, William H.,* *Chicago Daily News*

Stoody, Ralph W., Religious News Service

Stout, Rex, *freelance*

Stout, Wesley, *Saturday Evening Post*

Stowe, Leland,* Blue Network

Strand, William, *Chicago Tribune*

Stratton, Lloyd, AP

Strickler, Homer, *New York Sun*

Stringer, Elizabeth, UP

Stringer, William, *Christian Science Monitor*

Strock, George A., *Life*

Stromme, George L., *Occidental Publishing Company*

Strout, Richard L., *Christian Science Monitor*

Strozier, Fred L., AP

Struthers, I. O. Paramount News

Stumm, Loraine, *London Daily Mirror*

Sturdevant, Robert N., AP

Sturdy, Frank, *Chicago Tribune*

Stutler, Boyd B., *American Legion*

Sullivan, John V., *Yank*

Sullivan, Neil, Pathé News

Sulzberger, Cyrus Leo,* *New York Times*

Summers, Harold J., Group 5, Australian Papers

Sunde, Tenold R., *New York Daily News*

Sutton, Donn, NEA

Suydam, Henry, *Newark News*

Sweeney, Don G., UP

Symontowne, Russ, *New York Daily News*

Tait, Jack M., *New York Herald Tribune*

Talbott, Sprague, *Look*

Taves, Brydon, UP

Taylor, Alexander, *New York Post*

Taylor, Henry, Scripps-Howard

Taylor, Robert, *Newark Evening News*

Teatsorth, Ralph C., UP

Telegian, Manual, Abbott Laboratories

Telford, Frank, Young & Rubicam

Tepling, Lloyd, UP

Terrell, John U., *Newsweek*

Terrell, Maurice E., *Look*

Terry, John B., *Chicago Daily News*

Tewkesbury, Richard, NBC

Thale, Jack A., *Miami Herald*

Thayer, Mary V., INS

Thomas, Bryon, *Life*

Thomas, Ed, UP

Thomas, Igor, *Saturday Evening Post*

Thomas, Lowell Jackson,* NBC

Thompson, Charles H., UP

Thompson, Craig F., *Time*

Thompson, Fred, *Reader's Digest*

Thompson, George F., Fox Movietone News

Thompson, J. Flynn, *Time*

Thompson, John Hall,* *Chicago Tribune*

Thorndike, Joseph J., *Life*

Thorp, Gerald R., *Chicago Daily News*

Thusgaard, Carl, Acme Newspictures

Tighe, Dixie, INS

Tobin, Richard, *New York Herald Tribune*

Toles, Edward B., *Chicago Defender*

Tomara, Sonia,* *New York Herald Tribune*

Tomlinson, Edward, Blue Network

Tondra, John A., Fox Movietone News

Travis, Roderick, Group 3, Australian Papers

Treanor, Tom,* *Los Angeles Times*

Treat, Roger L., *Washington Daily News*

Tregaskis, Richard J.,* INS

Tremaine, Frank, UP

Troutman, Stanley, Acme Newspictures

Trumbull, Robert,* *New York Times*

Tubbs, Vincent, Afro-American Newspapers

Tucker, George, AP

Tully, Andrew, *Boston Traveller*

Tupling, William L., UP

Turcott, Jack, *New York Daily News*

Turk, Raymond J., *Cleveland News*

Turnbull, James, *Life*

Turner, Ewart (Dr.), Religious News Service

Twitty, Tom, *New York Herald Tribune*

Tyree, William, UP

Uhl, Alexander H., *PM*

Ullman, Frederick, Pathé News

Vadeboncoeur, E. R., NBC

Van Atta, Lee, INS

Valnes, Evans G., UP

Vanderbilt, Sanderson, *Yank*

Vandercook, John W., NBC

Vanderlip, Candace, INS

Vandivert, Margrethe, *Time*

Vandivert, William, *Time*

Van Sluys, C. J., Aneta

Vas Dias, Arnold, Aneta

Vaughn, Miles W., UP

Ventres, Fisko, *Hartford Courant*

Vermillion, Robert,* UP

Vern, Ike, *Quick*

Veysey, Arthur, *Chicago Tribune*

Vidner, Richard, *New York Herald Tribune*

Villanova, Anthony, *Miami Herald*

Vivian, Robert E., Reuters

Von Bovene, G. A., Aneta

Von Schmidt, Harold, *Saturday Evening Post*

Waagenaar, Samuel, INS

Wade, William W., INS

Wadsworth, Horace A., *Newsweek*

Wagg, Alfred, *Chicago Tribune*

Wagner, Theodore, *St. Louis Post-Dispatch*

Wahl, Jim M., NBC

Waite, Elmont, AP

Waldrop, Frank C., *Washington Times-Herald*

Wales, Henry G., *Chicago Tribune*

Walker, Charles L., *Harper's*

Walker, Gordon, *Christian Science Monitor*

Walker, Harrison H., *National Geographic*

Walker, John H., *Time*

Walker, Milton E., *New York Herald Tribune*

Walker, Samuel, *New York Post*

Wall, Carl B., *Reader's Digest*

Wallace, Ed R., NBC

Wallenstein, Marcel H., *Kansas City Star*

Walsh, Burke, *Saturday Evening Post*

Walsh, John B., *National Catholic WC*

Walters, John B., *London Daily Mirror*

Walton, William E., *Time*

Wang, George K., UP

Ward, Henry, *Pittsburgh Press*

Warden, William, AP

Waring, Gerald H., British United Press

Warner, Dennis, *Melbourne Herald*

Warner, Eugene P., American Red Cross

Warren, Mervyn, Group 3, Australian Papers

Waters, Enoc P., *Chicago Defender*

Watson, James B., BBC

Watson, Mark, *Baltimore Sun*

Watson, Paul R., *Our Navy*

Waugh, Irving C., WSM

Wear, Joseph R., *Fort Worth Star Telegram*

Weber, Thomas, *Look*

Wecksler, Abraham N., Conover Mast

Weil, Joseph, American Red Cross

Weisblatt, Franz, UP

Weisman, Al, *Yank*

Wellard, James,* *Chicago Times*

Weller, George,* *Chicago Daily News*

Werner, Merle M., UP

Werner, Oscar L., AP

Wertenbaker, Charles, *Time*

Weston, Joe, *Time*

Weston, Mervyn C., *Argus*

Wheeler, Elliot R., AP

Wheeler, George, NBC

Wheeler, Herbert K., *Chicago Times*

Whipple, Sidney, Scripps-Howard

Whitcomb, Philip, *Baltimore Sun*

White, Elmont, AP

White, Frank, *Indianapolis Star*

White, Herbert K., AP

White, Leigh,* *Chicago Daily News*

White, O.E.D., Group 2, Australian Papers

White, Theodore Harold,* *Time*

White, Walter, *New York Post*

White, William, *New York Herald Tribune*

White, William L., *Reader's Digest*

White, William S., *Time*

Whitehead, Donald F.,* AP

Whitehouse, Arthur G., Fawcett Publications

Whiteleather, Melvin K., *Philadelphia Evening Bulletin*

Whitman, Howard J., *New York Daily News*

Whitney, Betsey C., *Washington Times-Herald*

Whitney, Peter D., *San Francisco Chronicle*

Wiant, Thoburn H., AP

Widis, Edward C., AP

Wilcher, Lester, Cowles Newspapers

Wilcox, Richard L., *Time*

Wiley, Bonnie, AP

Wilhelm, Donald, *Reader's Digest*

Wilhelm, John R., Reuters

Wilkes, Jack, *Time*

Wilkins, Ford, *New York Times*

Williams, Donald, *Stars & Stripes*

Williams, Emlyn J., *Christian Science Monitor*

Williams, Garth M., *PM*

Williams, Glenn A., AP

Williams, Gurney, *Collier's*

Williams, Henry L., Group 5, Australian Papers

Williams, Joseph F., INS

Williams, Larry W., War Dept., Bureau of Public Relations

Williams, Leonard W., *Newark Evening News*

Williams, Maynard O., *National Geographic*

Williams, Oswald M., Australian Broadcasting Commission

Williams, Thomas V., AP

Willicombe, Joseph, INS

Willis, Douglas, BBC

Wilson, Edmund, *New Yorker*

Wilson, Gill Robb, *New York Herald Tribune*

Wilson, Lon H., *Yank*

Wilson, Lyle, UP

Wilson, Richard L., *Minneapolis Star-Journal*

Wilson, Robert C., AP

Wilson, William C., UP

Winkler, Betty, Press Alliance

Winkler, Paul, INS

Winn, Mary Day, *This Week*

Winner, Howard, Pathé News

Winter, William, Overseas News Agency

Wittels, David G., *Philadelphia Record*

Wohl, Harry, *St. Louis Star-Times*

Wolfe, Henry C., *This Week*

Wolfe, Thomas, NEA

Wolfert, Ira,* NANA

Wolff, Werner, *Yank*

Wong, N.H.S., *News of the Day*

Wood, Percy S., *Chicago Tribune*

Woodbury, Clarence M., *American*

Woodward, Stanley, *New York Herald Tribune*

Woolf, S. J., NEA

Worth, Edward S., AP

Wright, James, Paramount News

Wright, McQuown, UP

Yancey, Luther F., Afro-American Newspapers

Yap, Dioadado M., *Bataan*

Yarbrough, W. T., AP

Yates, Thom, *Yank*

Young, B. J., Group 4, Australian Papers

Young, Murray G., WHK

Young, Stanley, *Cosmopolitan*

Young, Thomas W., Guide Publishing Company

Youngman, Lawrence, *Omaha World Herald*

Zaimes, Charles J., American Red Cross

Zaimes, Margaret K., American Red Cross

Zayas, George, *Collier's*

Zegri, Amando, NBC

Zinder, Harry, *Time*

Source: Barney Oldfield. *Never a Shot in Anger*. 1989 reprint.

Appendix M:
BBC War Correspondents with the Allied Expeditionary Force, June 6, 1944–May 5, 1945

Barr, Robert

Bernard, David

Byam, Guy

Dimbleby, Richard*

Downing, Rupert

Duff, Robin

Dunnett, Robert

Fletcher, Alfred

Gillard, Frank

Johnston, Denis

Lefevre, Pierre

MacPherson, Stewart

Marshall, Howard

Maxted, Stanley

Melville, Alan

North, Richard

Ray, Cyril

Reid, Robert

Shepherd, E. Colston

Standing, Michael

Stevenson, Kent

Vaughn-Thomas, Wynford

Ward, Edward, Viscount Bangor*

Willis, Douglas

Wills, Colin

Wilmot, Reginald William Winchester ''Chester''*

Wilson, Ian

Sources: Desmond Hawkins, ed. *War Report, D-Day to VE-Day: Dispatches by the BBC's War Correspondents with the Allied Expeditionary Force, 6 June 1944–5 May 1945*. 1985.

Appendix N:
Korean War Correspondents

Baillie, Hugh,* United Press

Beech, Keyes,* *Chicago Daily News*

Bigart, Homer,* *New York Herald Tribune*

Bourke-White, Margaret,* *Life*

Boyle, Hal, *New York Herald Tribune*

Brodie, Howard,* Associated Press; CBS News

Browne, Malcolm W.,* *Stars and Stripes*

Buckley, Christopher,* *Daily Telegraph*

Burchett, Wilfred,* *London Daily Express*

Cameron, James,* *Picture Post*

Conniff, Frank,* International News Service

Considine, Bob, Hearst Newspapers

Cutforth, Rene, BBC

Duncan, David Douglas,* *Life*

Hardy, Albert "Bert,"* *Picture Post*

Higgins, Marguerite,* *New York Herald Tribune*

Hinton, Albert, *Norfolk Journal and Guide*

Jones, Charles, NBC

Jones, Eugene, NBC

Kahn, Ely Jacques "E. J.,"* *New Yorker*

Kalischer, Peter,* United Press

Lambert, Tom,* Associated Press

Levine, Hal, *Newsweek*

Lucas, James Griffing,* Scripps-Howard

Mauldin, Bill,* *Collier's*

Morin, Relman "Pat,"* Associated Press

Morrison, Ian F. M.,* *Times*

Murrow, Edward (Egbert) Roscoe,* CBS

Mydans, Carl,* *Life*

Peeler, Ernie, *Stars and Stripes*

Poats, Rutherford, United Press

Potter, Philip, *Baltimore Sun*

Price, George Ward,* *Daily Mail*

Richards, Ray, INS

Shinn, Bill, Associated Press

Simmons, Walter,* *Chicago Tribune*

Swinton, Stan, Associated Press

Symonds, Gene,* United Press

Thompson, Reginald, *Daily Telegraph*

Webb, Peter, United Press

Whitehead, Donald F.,* Associated Press

Sources: Michael Emery. *On the Front Lines*. 1995; John Hohenberg. *Foreign Correspondence*. 1965; Trevor Royle. *War Report*. 1987; M. L. Stein. *Under Fire*. 1968.

Appendix O:
Vietnam War
Correspondents

Adams, Edward "Eddie" T.,* Associated Press

Apple, R.W. "Johnny," *Time*

Arnett, Peter,* Associated Press

Arnot, Charles P.,* Associated Press

Bigart, Homer,* *New York Times*

Brodie, Howard,* Associated Press

Browne, Malcolm W.,* Associated Press; ABC; *New York Times*

Burrows, Larry,* *Life*

Cagnoni, Romano,* freelancer

Caputo, Philip,* *Chicago Tribune*

Chapelle, Georgette "Dickey,"* freelancer

Clurman, Richard, *Time*

Collingwood, Charles Cummings,* CBS News

Cronkite, Walter Leland, Jr.,* CBS News

Deepe, Beverly,* freelancer

Downing, John,* *London Daily Express*

Dudman, Richard, *St. Louis Post-Dispatch*

Duncan, David Douglas,* *Life*; ABC; *Collier's*

Eggleston, Charles, ?

Ellison, Robert J., Empire/Black Star

Emerson, Gloria,* *New York Times*

Faas, Horst,* Associated Press; *Life*

Fall, Bernard,* freelancer

Fallaci, Oriana,* freelancer

Fitzgerald, Frances,* freelancer

Flynn, Sean,* freelancer; *Time*

Gellhorn, Martha,* *Manchester Guardian*

Geyer, Georgie Anne,* *Chicago Daily News*

Griffiths, Philip Jones,* freelancer

Halberstam, David,* *New York Times*

Halstead, Dirck, *Time*

Hangen, Welles,* *New York Times*

Herndon, Ray, UP

Hersh, Seymour,* freelancer

Hoberecht, Ernest, UPI

Hollingworth, Claire,* *Daily Telegraph*

Huet, Henri, ?

Huynh, Ut Cong,* Associated Press

Kalischer, Peter,* CBS

Kamm, Henry, *New York Times*

Kazickas, Jurate,* freelancer

Kennerly, David Hume, UPI

Kilgore, Margaret,* United Press International

Kolenberg, Bernard, Associated Press

Langguth, Jack, *New York Times*

Laurent, Michel,* Associated Press

Lederer, Edith M.,* Associated Press

Leroy, Catherine,* freelancer

Lucas, James Griffing,* Scripps-Howard

McCullin, Donald,* *Sunday Times*

Mine, Hiromichi, ?

Mohr, Charles,* *Time*

Mulligan, Hugh, Associated Press

Musgrove, Helen ''Patches,''* *Jacksonville Journal*

Nivolon, François, *Le Figaro*

Oliphant, Tom,* *Boston Globe*

Page, Timothy John,* freelancer

Perry, Mert,* freelancer

Pond, Elizabeth,* *Christian Science Monitor*

Potter, Kent,* United Press International

Prochnau, William, *Washington Post*

Raffaelli, Jean, Agence France Presse

Rather, Dan,* CBS

Ray, Michele,* Agence France-Presse

Raymond, Jack, *New York Times*

Riboud, Marc,* Magnum Photos

Robinson, Jack, NBC

Russell, Jack, NBC

Safer, Morley,* CBS

Salisbury, Harrison Evans,* *New York Times*

Sargent, Tony, CBS

Sawada, Kyoichi,* United Press

Schanberg, Sydney H.,* *New York Times*

Schuyler, Philippa,* *Manchester Union-Leader*

Sevareid, Eric,* CBS

Shaplen, Robert Modell,* *New Yorker*

Sheehan, Neil,* *New York Times*

Shepard, Elaine,* freelancer

Sherrod, Robert,* *Life*

Shimamoto, Keisaburo,* *Newsweek*

Smith, Terence, *New York Times*

Steinbeck, John Ernest, Jr.,* *Newsday*

Stone, Dana,* CBS

Sully, François,* *Newsweek*

Syversten, George, CBS

Tomalin, Nicholas,* *Sunday Times*

Tuckner, Howard, NBC

Tuohy, William,* *Los Angeles Times*

Turner, Nick, Reuters

Webb, Catherine,* UPI

Webster, Dan, CBS

Young, Perry Deane,* UPI

Sources: Virginia Elwood-Akers. *Women War Correspondents in the Vietnam War, 1961–1975*. 1988; William Prochnau. *Once upon a Distant War*. 1995; Clarence R. Wyatt. *Paper Soldiers*. 1993.

Appendix P:
Pulitzer Prizes for War
Reporting, 1917–1974

WORLD WAR I

1917   Herbert Bayard Swope,* *New York World*

ETHIOPIAN WAR

1936   Wilfred C. Barber,* *Chicago Tribune*

WORLD WAR II

1939   Louis P. Lochner, Associated Press

1940   Otto D. Tolischus, *New York Times*

1941   Group award to American war correspondents

1942   Lawrence Edmund Allen,* Associated Press

1942   Carlos Pena Romulo,* *Philippines Herald*

1943   Hanson W. Baldwin,* *New York Times*

1943   George Weller, *Chicago Daily News*

1943   Ira Wolfert,* North American Newspaper Alliance

1944   Daniel De Luce,* Associated Press

1944   Ernest ''Ernie'' Taylor Pyle,* Scripps-Howard

1945   Mark Watson, *Baltimore Sun*

1945   Joe Rosenthal,* Associated Press

1945   Hal Boyle, Associated Press

1945   Bill Mauldin,* *Stars and Stripes**

1946   Homer Bigart,* *New York Herald Tribune*

1946   William Leonard Laurence, *New York Times*

KOREAN WAR

1951   Keyes Beech,* *Chicago Daily News*

1951   Homer Bigart,* *New York Herald Tribune*

1951   Marguerite Higgins,* *New York Herald Tribune*

1951   Relman "Pat" Morin,* Associated Press

1951   Fred Sparks, *Chicago Daily News*

1951   Donald F. Whitehead,* Associated Press

1952   John Hightower, Associated Press

1953   Donald F. Whitehead,* Associated Press

1954   James Griffing Lucas,* Scripps-Howard

VIETNAM WAR

1964   Davis Halberstam,* *New York Times*

1964   Malcolm W. Browne,* Associated Press

1965   Horst Faas,* Associated Press

1966   Peter Arnett,* Associated Press

1966   Kyoichi Sawada,* UPI

1968   Toshio Sakai, UPI

1969   Edward Adams,* Associated Press

1969   William Tuohy,* *Los Angeles Times*

1973   Ut Cong Huynh,* Associated Press

MIDDLE EAST WARS

1968   Alfred Friendly, *Washington Post*

INDO-PAKISTAN WAR OF 1971

1972   Peter R. Kann, *Wall Street Journal*

1972   Horst Faas,* Associated Press

1972   Michel Laurent,* Associated Press

Appendix Q: Correspondents and Photographers Who Died Covering War Zones, 1935–1994

Phillip A. Adler

James H. Alley

Gregory L. Anderson

John J. Andrew

Claude Arpin

Joe Arrequi

Lee F. C. Baggett II

Francis Bailly

John E. Bannister

Wilfred C. Barber*

John Barberio

Ralph W. Barnes*

Nat A. Barrows

Richard Beirn

Don Bell

Robert Bellaire

Dieter Bellendorf

Michael Birch

Werner Bischof

Nicholas Blake

Solomon I. Blechman

Ellsworth Smith Bradford

James Branyan

Robert Brown

William L. Brown

Philip W. Browning

Larry Buchman

Thomas Frederick Buhr

Lea Burdett

James Burke

Larry Burrows*

John Buschemi*

Asahel Bush

John L. Cantwell

Robert Capa*

John Cashman

Sam Castan

Joe Castro

Note: This list is comprised of print- and photojournalists who were killed en route to or returning from combat zones as well as those killed in combat. Also included are journalists, such as Marguerite Higgins,* who died as the result of diseases contracted while on assignment.

Richard Valentine Cecil

Georgette "Dickey" Chapelle*

William H. Chickering

Camille Cianfarra

Raymond Lewis Clapper*

George Clay

Roger Colne

Fred Colvig

Daniel J. Coughlin

E. Harry Crockett

Richard Cross

Frank J. Cuhel

Byron Darnton

Griffin Davis

Neil Davis

Philip F. DeFazio

Harold Norman Denny*

Elsie Dick

James Graham Dowling*

Robert Doyle

Gregor Duncan

Lionel Durand

Charles R. Eggleston

John Elliott

Robert J. Ellison

Dan Elson

Frank Emery

George "Bede" Ervin

Randy Fairbairn

Thomas A. Falco

Bernard Fall*

Frederick Faust*

Wilson Fielder

Sean Flynn*

John F. (Jack) Frankish

Linda Frazier

Klaus Frings

Frank Frosch

Russell Riceland Fyan

Ian H. Fyfe

"Pappy" Gallagher

Ronald D. Gallagher

Larry A. Garrison

Alan S. Gelb

William Homer Genaust

Tafki Ghazawi

William H. Graham

Charles Gratke

Gad Schuster Gross*

Paul Guihard

Stanley Gunn

Royal Arch Gunnison

Dewitt Hancock

Welles Hangen*

Don Harris

S. Burton Heath

Gerard Herbert

Marguerite Higgins*

Byron F. Highland

Albert L. Hinton

Alan Hirons

John Hoagland

Carl W. Hudgins

Henri Huet

Bertram D. Hulen

Ken Inouye

Tomoharu Ishii

Melville Jacoby*

René Jauniaux

David Jayne

Brandish Johnson

Dam Kai-Faye

David Kaplan*

Eugene M. Key

Terry Khoo

Hubert Renfre Knickerbocker*

Alfred M. Kohn

Bernard Kolenberg

Alfred Kornfeld

Edward Koterba

Hansi Krauss

Robert Krell

Wesley L. Kroenung, Jr.

Chester B. Kronfeld

Harold W. Kulick

Lucian A. Labaudt

Ronald B. Laramy

David Lardner*

Bill Latch

Michel Laurent*

Ramnik Lekhi

Rihvard Arthur Little

William B. Louri

Gaston Madru

Vincent Mahoney

W. J. Makin

Ernest A. Matthews, Jr.

Doug Maxwell

Howard McCue

James J. McElroy

William F. McHale

Shannon L. Meany

Larry Meier

Bahij Metni

Bill Middlebrooks

Ben Miller

Gerald Miller

Webb Miller*

Hiromichi Mine

George L. Moorad

Lyford Moore

William R. Moore

Joe Alex Morris, Jr.

Joseph Morton

Richard J. Murphy, Jr.

Huynh Thanh My

Kenneth E. Nance

Frederick Richard Neef

Edward J. Neil, Jr.

William H. Newton

Oliver E. Noonan, Jr.

Daniel Jerome O'Connor

Ben Oyserman

Victor L. Paine

Fred C. Painton

Keith Palmer

Damien Parer

Peter Paris

Clark E. Peden

Ernie Peeler

John C. Pennington

Harry L. Percy

William T. Perkins*

Eugen Petrov

Bruce Pigott

George Polk*

Robert P. Post

Kent Potter*

Bruce Powell

William Price

Frank Prist

Ernest "Ernie" Taylor Pyle*

Donovon R. Raddatz

Richard C. Ramsey

Pendil Rayner

Oliver Rebbot

Terry Reynolds

Ray Richards

Ben Robertson, Jr.

Greg Robinson

Jerry Rose

Charles D. Rosecrans, Jr.

Dennis Lee Royal

Harold W. Rulick

Kojiro Sakai

Robert Arthur Saucier

Paul David Savanuck

Kyoichi Sawada*

Paul Schutzere

Philippa Schuyler*

Davis Seymour*

Richard Sheepshanks

William Shenkel

Keisaburo Shimamoto*

Alexander Shimkin

Jack Singer*

Gregory Alex Sloat

John Bradford Stevens

Bill Stewart*

Richard J. Stewart

Robert W. S. Stinson

Dana Stone*

Robert G. Stricklin

William Stringer

Nicholas Stroh

Edward M. Sullivan

Francois Sully*

James O. Supple

Gene Symonds*

George Syvertsen

Brydon Taves

Henry Taylor, Jr.*

John B. Terry

Pieter Ronald van Thirl

Charles Thornton

Arthur A. Thorpe

Carl Thusgaard

Dixie Tighe

Clark Todd

Dial Torgerson*

Tom Treanor*

Ned M. Trimble

William T. Vesey

Willy Vicoy

Yoshihiko Waku

George W. Walbridge

Ralph Walz

Lester Arthur Weisghan

John Werkley

Theodore G. White, Jr.

William R. Wilson

Darryl Gordon Winters

Ted Yates

Douglas A. Young

Thomas F. Young

Jesse Zousmer

Source: Charles P. Arnot. *Don't Kill the Messenger: The Tragic Story of Welles Hangen and Other Journalistic Combat Victims*. 1994. Arnot was provided this list by the Overseas Press Club of America, Inc., and the Public Affairs Office of the Department of Defense.

Selected Bibliography

Alldritt, Keith. *Churchill, the Writer: His Life as a Man of Letters*. London: Hutchinson, 1992.

Andrews, J. Cutler. *The North Reports the Civil War*. Pittsburgh: University of Pittsburgh Press, 1955.

———. *The South Reports the Civil War*. Princeton: Princeton University Press, 1970.

Arnot, Charles P. *Don't Kill the Messenger: The Tragic Story of Welles Hangen and Other Journalistic Combat Victims*. New York: Vantage Press, 1994.

Ayerst, David. *The Manchester Guardian: Biography of a Newspaper*. Ithaca, N.Y.: Cornell University Press, 1971.

Beckett, Ian F. W. *The War Correspondents: The American Civil War*. Dover, N.H.: Alan Sutton Publishing, 1993.

Bentley, Nicolas, ed. *Russell's Despatches from the Crimea, 1854–1856*. New York: Hill and Wang, 1967.

Brown, Charles H. *The Correspondents' War: Journalists in the Spanish-American War*. New York: Charles Scribner's Sons, 1967.

Browne, Malcolm W. *Muddy Boots and Red Socks: A War Reporter's Life*. New York: Random House, 1993.

Bullard, F. Lauriston. *Famous War Correspondents*. Boston: Little, Brown and Co., 1914.

Carlebach, Michael L. *The Origins of Photojournalism in America*. Washington, D.C.: Smithsonian Institution, 1992.

Churchill, Winston. *The Boer War: London to Ladysmith via Pretoria* and *Ian Hamilton's March*. First American ed. New York: W. W. Norton and Co., 1990.

Collier, Richard. *Fighting Words: The War Correspondents of World War Two*. New York: St. Martin's Press, 1989.

Copeland, Fayette. *Kendall of the Picayune*. Norman: University of Oklahoma Press, 1943.

Crozier, Emmet. *American Reporters on the Western Front, 1914–18*. New York: Oxford University Press, 1959.

————. *Yankee Reporters, 1861–65*. New York: Oxford University Press, 1956.

Desmond, Robert W. *Crisis and Conflict: World News Reporting Between Two Wars, 1920–1940*. Iowa City: University of Iowa Press, 1982.

————. *The Information Process: World News Reporting to the Twentieth Century*. Iowa City: University of Iowa Press, 1978.

————. *Tides of War: World News Reporting, 1931–1945*. Iowa City: University of Iowa Press, 1984.

————. *Windows on the World: World News Reporting, 1900–1920*. Iowa City: University of Iowa Press, 1980.

Downs, Robert B., and Jane B. Downs. *Journalists of the United States*. Jefferson, N.C.: McFarland and Co., 1991.

Downton, Eric. *Wars Without End*. Toronto: Stoddart Publishing Co., 1987.

Edwards, Julia. *Women of the World: The Great Foreign Correspondents*. New York: Ballantine Books, 1989.

Elwood-Akers, Virginia. *Women War Correspondents in the Vietnam War, 1961–1975*. Metuchen, N.J.: Scarecrow Press, 1988.

Emery, Michael. *On the Front Lines: Following America's Foreign Correspondents Across the Twentieth Century*. Washington, D.C.: American University Press, 1995.

Farwell, Byron. *The Great Anglo-Boer War*. New York: Harper and Row, 1976.

Fewster, Kevin, ed. *Gallipoli Correspondent: The Frontline Diary of C. E. W. Bean*. Sydney: George Allen and Unwin, 1983.

Fialka, John J. *Hotel Warriors: Covering the Gulf War*. Baltimore: Johns Hopkins University Press, 1991.

Furneaux, Rupert. *News of War: Stories and Adventures of the Great War Correspondents*. London: Max Parrish, 1964.

Gernsheim, Helmut, and Alison. *Roger Fenton: Photographer of the Crimean War*. New York: Arno Press, 1973.

Gould, Louis L., and Greffe, Richard. *Photojournalist: The Career of Jimmy Hare*. Austin: University of Texas Press, 1977.

Grey, Elizabeth. *The Noise of Drums and Trumpets: W. H. Russell Reports from the Crimea*. New York: Henry Z. Walck, 1971.

Griffiths, Dennis, ed. *The Encyclopedia of the British Press*. New York: St. Martin's Press, 1992.

Hallin, Daniel C. *The "Uncensored War": The Media and Vietnam*. New York: Oxford University Press, 1986.

Hankinson, Alan. *Man of Wars: William Howard Russell of the "Times."* London: Heinemann Educational Books, 1982.

Hendricks, King, and Irving Shepard, eds. *Jack London Reports*. Garden City, N.Y.: Doubleday and Co., 1970.

Hodgson, Pat. *Early War Photographs*. Boston: New York Graphic Society, 1974.

————. *The War Illustrators*. New York: Macmillan Publishing Co., 1977.

Hohenberg, John. *Foreign Correspondence: The Great Foreign Correspondents and Their Times*. New York: Columbia University Press, 1964.

Hood, Robert E. *12 at War: Great Photographers Under Fire*. New York: G. P. Putnam's Sons, 1967.

Hooper, Jim. *Beneath the Visiting Moon: Images of Combat in Southern Africa*. Lexington, Mass.: Lexington Books, 1990.

Hughes, Jim. *W. Eugene Smith, Shadow and Substance: The Life and Work of an American Photographer*. New York: McGraw-Hill Publishing Co., 1989.

James, Lawrence. *Crimea, 1854–56: The War with Russia from Contemporary Photographs*. New York: Van Nostrand Reinhold Co., 1981.

Johannsen, Robert W. *To the Halls of the Montezumas: The Mexican War in the American Imagination*. New York: Oxford University Press, 1985.

Kapuscinki, Ryszard. *The Soccer War*. New York: Knopf, 1991.

Keim, de, B. Randolph. *Sheridan's Troopers on the Borders: A Winter Campaign on the Plains*. Lincoln: University of Nebraska Press, 1985.

Knight, Oliver. *Following the Indian Wars: The Story of the Newspaper Correspondents Among the Indian Campaigners*. Norman: University of Oklahoma Press, 1960.

Knightley, Phillip. *The First Casualty: From the Crimea to Vietnam: The War Correspondent as Hero, Propagandist, and Myth Maker*. New York: Harcourt Brace Jovanovich, 1975.

Lambert, Andrew, and Stephen Badsey. *The War Correspondents: The Crimean War*. Dover, N. H.: Alan Sutton Publishing, 1994.

Lewinski, Jorge. *The Camera at War: A History of War Photography from 1848*. New York: Simon and Schuster, 1978.

Lubow, Arthur. *The Reporter Who Would Be King: A Biography of Richard Harding Davis*. New York: Charles Scribner's Sons, 1992.

Maslowski, Peter. *Armed with Cameras: The American Military Photographers of World War II*. New York: Free Press, 1993.

Mathews, Joseph J. *Reporting the Wars*. Minneapolis: University of Minnesota Press, 1957.

May, Antoinette. *Witness to War: A Biography of Marguerite Higgins*. New York: Beaufort Books, 1983.

McCullin, Don. *Unreasonable Behaviour: An Autobiography*. New York: Knopf, 1992.

McNamara, John. *EXTRA! U.S. War Correspondents in Action*. Boston: Houghton Mifflin Co., 1945.

Mercer, Derrik, Geoff Mungham, and Kevin Williams. *The Fog of War: The Media on the Battlefield*. London: William Heinemann Limited, 1987.

Mills, Nick. *The Vietnam Experience: Combat Photographer*. Boston: Boston Publishing Co., 1983.

Milton, Joyce. *The Yellow Kids: Foreign Correspondents in the Heyday of Yellow Journalism*. New York: Harper and Row, 1989.

Moeller, Susan D. *Shooting War: Photography and the American Experience of Combat*. New York: Basic Books, 1989.

Monti, Nicolas, ed. *Africa Then: Photographs. 1840–1918*. New York: Knopf, 1987.

Mrazkova, Daniela, and Vladimir Remes, eds. *The Russian War: 1941–1945*. New York: E. P. Dutton, 1975.

Mydans, Carl, and Shelley Mydans. *The Violent Peace*. New York: Atheneum Press, 1968.

Neuman, Johanna. *Lights, Camera, War: Is Media Technology Driving International Politics?* New York: St. Martin's Press, 1996.

O'Connor, Richard. *The Spirit Soldiers: A Historical Narrative of the Boxer Rebellion*. New York: G. P. Putnam's Sons, 1973.

Oldfield, Colonel Barney. *Never a Shot in Anger*. 2d ed. Santa Barbara, Calif.: Capra Press, 1989.

Ostroff, Roberta. *Fire in the Wind: The Life of Dickey Chapelle*. New York: Ballantine Books, 1992.

O'Toole, G. J. A. *The Spanish War: An American Epic, 1898*. New York: W. W. Norton and Co., 1984.

Persico, Joseph E. *Edward R. Murrow: An American Original*. New York: McGraw-Hill Publishing Co. 1988.

Prochnau, William. *Once upon a Distant War*. New York: Random House, 1995.

Rand, Peter. *China Hands: The Adventures and Ordeals of the American Journalists Who Joined Forces with the Great Chinese Revolution*. New York: Simon and Schuster, 1995.

Ray, Frederic E. *"Our Special Artist": Alfred R. Waud's Civil War*. 2d ed. Mechanicsburg, Pa.: Stackpole Books, 1994.

Read, Donald. *The Power of News: The History of Reuters*. New York: Oxford University Press, 1992.

Reed, John. *Insurgent Mexico*. New York: Simon and Schuster, 1969.

Roeder, George H. *The Censored War: American Visual Experience During World War Two*. New Haven, Conn.: Yale University Press, 1993.

Royle, Trevor. *War Report: The War Correspondent's View of Battle from the Crimea to the Falklands*. London: Mainstream Publishing, 1987.

Russell, William Howard. *My Diary North and South*. 2d ed. New York: Harper and Brothers, 1954.

Samuels, Peggy, and Harold Samuels. *Frederic Remington: A Biography*. Garden City, N.Y.: Doubleday and Co., 1982.

Sandweiss, Martha A., Rick Stewart, and Ben W. Huseman. *Eyewitness to War: Prints and Daguerreotypes of the Mexican War, 1846–1848*. Fort Worth, Tex.: Amon Carter Museum, 1989.

Sebba, Anne. *Battling for News: The Rise of the Woman Reporter*. London: Hodder and Stoughton, 1994.

Sibbald, Raymond. *The War Correspondents: The Boer War*. Dover, N. H.: Alan Sutton Publishing, 1993.

Sifakis, Stewart. *Who Was Who in the Civil War*. New York: Facts on File, 1988.

Smart, James G. *A Radical View: The "Agate" Dispatches of Whitelaw Reid, 1861–1865*. Memphis, Tenn.: Memphis State University Press, 1976.

Starr, Louis M. *Bohemian Brigade: Civil War Newsmen in Action*. New York: Knopf, 1954.

Stein, M. L. *Under Fire: The Story of American War Correspondents*. New York: Julian Messner, 1968.

Stern, Philip Van Doren. *They Were There: The Civil War As Seen by Its Combat Artists*. New York: Crown Publishers, 1959.

Sunday Times of London Insight Team. *War in the Falklands: The Full Story*. New York: Harper and Row, 1982.

Thompson, W. Fletcher, Jr. *The Image of War: The Pictorial Reporting of the American Civil War*. New York: A. S. Barnes Co., 1959.

Tolstoy, Leo. *Sebastopol*. Ann Arbor: University of Michigan Press, 1961.

Tuohy, William. *Dangerous Company: Inside the World's Hottest Trouble Spots with a Pulitzer Prize–Winning War Correspondent*. New York: William Morrow and Co., 1987.

Vanderwood, Paul J., and Frank N. Samponara. *Border Fury: A Picture Postcard Record of Mexico's Revolution and U.S. War Preparedness, 1900–1917.* Albuquerque: University of New Mexico Press, 1988.

Voss, Frederick S. *Reporting the War: The Journalistic Coverage of World War II.* Washington, D.C.: Smithsonian Institution, 1994.

Wade, Betsy, ed. *Forward Positions: The War Correspondence of Homer Bigart.* Fayetteville: University of Arkansas Press, 1992.

Wagner, Lilya. *Women War Correspondents of World War Two.* Westport, Conn.: Greenwood Press, 1989.

Walker, Dale L. *Januarius MacGahan: The Life and Campaigns of an American War Correspondent.* Athens: Ohio University Press, 1988.

Weisberger, Bernard A. *Reporters for the Union.* Boston: Little, Brown, and Co., 1953.

Weithas, Art. *Close to Glory.* Austin, Tex.: Eakin Press, 1991.

Whelan, Richard. *Robert Capa: A Biography.* New York: Random House, 1985.

White, William, ed. *By Line: Ernest Hemingway.* New York: Charles Scribner's Sons, 1967.

Wilkinson-Latham, Robert. *From Our Special Correspondent: Victorian War Correspondents and Their Campaigns.* London: Hodder and Stoughton, 1979.

Woods, Oliver, and James Bishop. *The Story of THE TIMES.* London: Michael Joseph Limited, 1983.

Wyatt, Clarence R. *Paper Soldiers: The American Press and the Vietnam War.* New York: W. W. Norton and Co., 1993.

Wyden, Peter. *The Passionate War: The Narrative History of the Spanish Civil War.* New York: Simon and Schuster, 1983.

Index

Boldface page numbers indicate location of main entries.

Austin, Alexander Berry, **17**
Austro-Hungarian Empire, and first postal card, 237
Austro-Italian War, **17–18**
Austro-Piedmont War. *See* Austro-Italian War
Austro-Prussian War, **18**
Axelsson, George, **18**

Bagby, George W., **19**
''Baghdad Pete,'' 19
Baillie, Hugh, **19–20**
Baker, George, **20**, 356
Balaklava, Battle of. *See* Charge of the Light Brigade
Baldwin, Hanson W., **20**
Baldwin, Herbert, **20–21**
Balkan Affairs, 36–37, 44–45
Balkan War of 1912, 20, 22, 70, 118, 121, 157, 196, 230, 236
balloon service: in siege of Metz, 260; in siege of Paris, 174
Baltermans, Dmitri, **21**
''Banjo.'' *See* Paterson, Andrew Barton
Barber, Noel, **21**
Barber, Wilfred C., **21**
Baring, Maurice, **21–22**
Barnard, George N., **22**
Barnes, Ralph W., **22**
Bartholomew, Frank Harmon, **22–23**
Barzini, Luigi, **23**
Bass, John Foster, **24**
''Battle fog'' policy, 24
Bean, Charles Edwin Woodrow, **24–25**
Beato, Felice A., **25**, 260
Beattie, Edward W., Jr., **25–26**
Beech, Keyes, **26**; and Georgie Anne Geyer, 116; and Marguerite Higgins, 143, 175
Belden, Jack, **26–27**
Bengali prisoners, execution of, 258, 320
Benjamin, Anna Northend, **27**
Bennett, James Gordon, **28**, 149, 162, 328
Bennett, James Gordon, Jr., **28**
Bennett, Lowell, **28–29**
Benson, Eugene, **29**
Bentley, Henry, **29**

Berlin, fall of, 123, 321
Berlin Congress of 1878, 83, 330, 344
Bernstein, Walter, **29**
Berry, Ian, **30**
Bewley, Cyril, **30**
Biafran War, 51, 86, 108
Bickham, William Denison, **30**
bicycles, **30–31**, 327–28
Biddle, George, **31**
Bigart, Homer, **31–32**; and Marguerite Higgins, 143
Bigelow, Poultney, **32**
''Bill Dadd the Scribe.'' *See* Atwell, H. Wallace
Billman, Howbert, **32**
Biograph Company, 34, 218
Black and White, 34, 35
Black war correspondents, 60, 172
Blair, Eric Arthur, **32–33**
Blitz. *See* London Blitz
Bloemfontein Friend. See Friend, The
Blundey, David, **33**
Bodman, Albert, **33**
Boer War, 9, **33–34**, 45, 46, 111, 193–94, 156, 174–75, 189, 321, 357
Boer War siege newspapers, **34**, 232
Bogart, Robert D., **34–35**
Bohemian Brigade, **35**, 148, 283
Bohrod, Aaron, **35–36**
Bonsal, Stephen, **36**
Bourchier, James David, **36–37**
Bourke-White, Margaret, **37**
Boxer Rebellion, **38**
Boyle, Frederick, **38**
Brackenbury, Charles Booth, **38–39**
Brady, Mathew B., **39–40**; and Timothy O'Sullivan, 265, 332
Bragg, General Braxton, 6, 184, 252
Brand, Max. *See* Faust, Frederick
Brigham, Charles D., **40–41**
Bristish Mutoscope, 218
British Broadcasting Company (BBC), 3, 88
Brodie, Howard, **41**, 210
Broun, Heywood, **41–42**, 257
Brown, Cecil, **42**

About the Author

MITCHEL P. ROTH is Assistant Professor of History and Criminal Justice at Sam Houston State University. His history on the Texas Rangers and the Texas Department of Public Safety was published in *Courtesy, Service, and Protection*: *The Texas Department of Public Safety*, and his research on epidemic disease on the nineteenth-century West has appeared in *Gateway Heritage* and *Pacific Historical Review*.

ISBN 0-313-29171-3

HARDCOVER BAR CODE